Music and Society in Early Modern En

Music and Society in Early Modern England is the first comprehensive survey of English popular music during the early modern period to be published in over 150 years. Christopher Marsh offers a fascinating and broad-ranging account of musicians, the power of music, broadside ballads, dancing, psalm-singing and bell-ringing. Drawing on sources ranging from ballads, plays, musical manuscripts and diaries to wills, inventories, speeches and court records, he investigates the part played by music in the negotiation of social relations, revealing its capacity both to unify and to divide. The book is lavishly illustrated and is accompanied by a website featuring forty-eight specially commissioned recordings by the critically acclaimed Dufay Collective. These include the first ever attempts to reconstruct the distinctive early modern sounds of 'rough music' and unaccompanied congregational psalm-singing.

CHRISTOPHER MARSH is a Reader in Early Modern History at the Queen's University of Belfast. His previous publications include *The Family of Love in English Society* (Cambridge, 1994) and *Popular Religion in Sixteenth-century England* (1998). He is also the author of the satirical novel *A Year in the Province* (2009).

Music and Society in Early Modern England

CHRISTOPHER MARSH

CAMBRIDGE
UNIVERSITY PRESS

CAMBRIDGE
UNIVERSITY PRESS

University Printing House, Cambridge CB2 8BS, United Kingdom

Cambridge University Press is part of the University of Cambridge.

It furthers the University's mission by disseminating knowledge in the pursuit of education, learning and research at the highest international levels of excellence.

www.cambridge.org
Information on this title: www.cambridge.org/9781107610248

First published 2010
First paperback edition 2013

A catalogue record for this publication is available from the British Library

Library of Congress Cataloguing in Publication data

Marsh, Christopher W.
Music and society in early modern England / Christopher Marsh.
p. cm.
Includes bibliographical references.
ISBN 978-0-521-89832-4 (hardback)
1. Music–Social aspects–England–History–17th century.
2. Music–Social aspects–England–History–16th century. I. Title.

ML3917.G7M27 2010
780.942′09032–dc22
2010014312

ISBN 978-0-521-89832-4 Hardback
ISBN 978-1-107-61024-8 Paperback

Additional resources for this publication at www.cambridge.org/9781107610248

Contents

Illustrations

Tables

Music examples

Music tracks

Please see the Appendix for a full list of the 48 music tracks available at www.cambridge.org/musicandsociety

Acknowledgements

Somehow, it has taken me almost two decades to write this book. When the idea first came to me, I was young and foolish and the Research Assessment Exercise was just a twinkle in some bureaucrat's eye. The notion of devoting an extended period of time to a wide-ranging survey seemed an exciting one. Since then, English historiography has tended – with significant exceptions – to become more and more specialised as scholars have been forced to devise targets that are amusingly described as SMART (Specific, Measurable, Attainable, Realistic, Time-Bound). For reasons that now escape me, I decided to struggle on with a project that sometimes felt rather DIM (Doubtful, Ill-Judged, Monstrous). So, for better or worse, this book covers a wide range of musical practices and forms, several of which are now being tackled separately by other scholars. *Music and Society* aims to draw much of this work together, but it is also based on too many years of my own research and thus is not primarily a synthesis. Instead, it is first and foremost an attempt to extend and advance the debate while mapping out some new territory for future research. I have concentrated particularly on the decades between 1540 and 1670 but have also drawn regularly on material from beyond these limits.

One former colleague, on hearing of my intentions, said, 'So you're going to produce a hearing aid for historians?' It was a succinct description. I hope, of course, that this book will also stimulate musicologists, practising musicians, literary specialists, folklorists and general readers, but I have indeed written it with social and cultural historians at the forefront of my mind. Many of them are a little wary of music for reasons that are discussed in the introduction, but I hope that a combination of written words and recorded sounds will persuade them to overcome their anxieties (the recordings appear on the website).

I have been very fortunate in receiving grants from the Arts and Humanities Research Council, the Nuffield Foundation, the Leverhulme Trust, the British Academy and the Queen's University of Belfast. I have also enjoyed several research-packed visits to Clare Hall, Cambridge. I am immensely grateful to all of these institutions for their assistance and I apologise if I ever deployed an idiosyncratic definition of the term 'fruition'.

For various forms of academic sustenance and stimulation, my thanks also go to Ian Archer, Alastair Bellany, Peter Boardman, Roger Bowers, Mark Burnett, Bernard Capp, Marie Coleman, Trevor Cooper, John Craig, James Davis, Scott Dixon, Eamon Duffy, Andrew Elkerton, Richard English, Adam Fox, Malcolm Gaskill, Ian Green, David Hayton, Steve Hindle, Andrew Holmes, Martin Ingram, Fiona Kisby, Beat Kümin, Diarmaid MacCulloch, Dolly MacKinnon, Judith Maltby, David Mateer, John Milsom, Rosemary O'Day, Celia Parker, Bill Sheils, Bill Sherman, Roz Southey, Peter Spufford, John Walter, Helen Weinstein, Helen Wilcox, Jonathan Willis, Thomas Woodcock and Robert Yorke. I would like to make particular mention of Margaret Aston, Patrick Collinson, Margaret Spufford and Keith Wrightson, all of whom have kindly written references for me at one time or another.

I have tried out some of what follows in seminars and conferences held in Belfast, Durham, Exeter, Warwick and York. I am grateful to all who have invited me to speak and to all who have been prepared to listen. A more comprehensive review of the manuscript was provided by the publisher's anonymous reader and I wish to thank him or her for a positive response and a wealth of helpful comments and suggestions.

The entire text was also studied heroically by two other scholars, both of whom made a number of extremely shrewd remarks. It accompanied Peter Marshall on holiday, and I feel fairly sure that he could have had at least as much fun without it. My other counsellor was the musicologist Ian Woodfield, who – by a minor miracle – happens to live next door to me in south Belfast. Over the years, I have appeared on the doorstep of number 26 at all times of the day and night with technical questions about clefs, viols and rebecs, and Ian has hardly flinched.

Here at Queen's, I have also relied upon the advice and assistance of Frances Mercer and Angela Anderson, both of whom understand the financial workings of the university far better than I. The team at Cambridge University Press has been exemplary in all regards, and I have been especially grateful for the blend of cool professionalism and warm humanity that has been displayed by Michael Watson, Helen Waterhouse Joanna Garbutt, Liz Davey and Liz Friend-Smith. I am particularly indebted to Fiona Little for the extraordinary patience with which she has guided me through the copy-editing process.

Over the years, I have also worked in dozens of record offices and libraries, some of which are listed in the bibliography. I have always found the staff of these institutions friendly, helpful and efficient, and it would have taken me even longer to write the book if they had been any less so. Searching for references to music in manuscript sources requires a good deal of patience, and I thank those who have helped me to find one or two of the needles in their haystacks. I would also like to pay tribute to all who have been involved in the publication of the *Records of Early English Drama* series. These volumes – haystacks with indexes – are an exceptionally valuable resource.

The musical recordings that accompany this book were made by members of the Dufay Collective and invited guests. The website is an integral component of the publication and should be studied in conjunction with the text. The musicians have extended their normal repertoire by producing perhaps the first ever recordings of early modern 'rough music' and congregational psalm-singing, and I thank them all for rising so splendidly to the challenge: Romee Day, Vivien Ellis, Simon Grant, Jacob Heringman, Christine Stratford, Pauline Dingley, James Ingham, Glenn Keiles, Bill Lyons, Paul Norman, Nicholas Perry, John Potter, Fernando Rosende, Clare Salaman, Clara Sanabras, Peter Skuce and Pilar Subirà. I have found the process of research and collaboration extremely rewarding, and would like to make special mention of Bill Lyons and Peter Skuce for all their creative and technical assistance.

On a more personal note, I wish to acknowledge the extracurricular support I have received from an assortment of friends and relatives: Janice Carruthers, John Curran, the Goedkoops (Gail, Pippa and both Pieters), Jonathan and Lucy Kelly, the Marshes (Judith, Simon and Jonathan, the last of whom kindly took several photographs for me), Linda and Michael Montgomery, Mícheál Ó Mainnín, Nini Rodgers and, of course, Jesús Sánchez Ventura. Most importantly of all, I am grateful for the love and laughter of my daughters, Amanda, Emily and Caitriona, and my wife, Katie. Without them, I would have had to rely exclusively on Usain Bolt and Freddie Flintoff to keep my spirits up during the so-called summer of 2009.

Abbreviations

BL	British Library
CSPD	*Calendar of State Papers Domestic* (see listing of volumes in bibliography)
ChRO	Cheshire Record Office
CUL	Cambridge University Library
DRO	Derbyshire Record Office
ERO	Essex Record Office
HL	Hallward Library (University of Nottingham)
HRO	Hampshire Record Office
LA	Lincolnshire Archives
NA	National Archives
NRO	Norfolk Record Office
REED	*Records of Early English Drama* (see listing of volumes in bibliography)
SHC	Surrey History Centre
WSRO	West Sussex Record Office

Introduction: the ringing island

The ubiquity of music

'England is celebrated abroad as the ringing island', wrote Edward Leigh in 1656. Thomas Fuller agreed that foreign visitors were in the habit of applying the description to England because of its abundance of church bells. Both writers knew in their hearts that this abundance signalled God's favour and thus they accepted the label with grace. The English had pleased their maker by receiving and proclaiming the gospel, a project to which the metallic music of the bells had contributed in no small measure. Fuller went on, 'we have (God increase their number) many and melodious bels, tuneable amongst themselves, and loud-sounding the Word of God to others'. In his ears, this was a fundamentally religious sound, but visitors also noted the development and popularity of recreational ringing. Drunken Englishmen, it was reported, sometimes took to the church tower in order to demonstrate the vigour with which they could pull the ropes and clang the bells. Godly or worldly, the loud-sounding church bells of the ringing island caught the attention of continental tourists two centuries before their descendants came to know England by a rather different term, 'the land without music'.[1]

Early modern England also rang with music of many other sorts. Indeed, the sheer vibrancy of its musical culture will be the first major theme of this book. The term 'ringing' was applied not only to bells but also to singing, trumpet blasts and the calls of birds (it also described any sound that seemed to linger in the ears). These varieties of music took their place among many others, and with only a little licence we can imagine the ringing island as home to them all. When Ned Ward walked the streets of London in the very last years of the seventeenth century, he was profoundly dubious about the musical tastes of the people but he did not doubt their appetite. The satirist heard and hated the piercing outdoor

[1] Edward Leigh, *A Treatise of Religion* (London, 1656), epistle to the reader; Thomas Fuller, *Joseph's Partie-colored Coat* (London, 1640), p. 66; Dave Russell, *Popular Music in England 1840–1914* (1987; Manchester: Manchester University Press, 1997), p. 1. For further discussion of bell-ringing, see below, ch. 9 (also website tracks 47 and 48).

music of the city waits. He scorned the 'melancholy multitude' that gathered to hear a blind ballad-singer perform a song by ear. She sang her words to a sober psalm tune and 'put the people a-trembling' with her account of the pains of hell. In Bartholomew Fair, Ward encountered a particularly vile concentration of untutored music-makers. He heard the rumbling of drums and 'the intolerable squeakings of catcalls and penny trumpets'. In one booth, 'a parcel of country scrapers were sawing a tune'. At the north-west side of the fair, 'music-houses stood as thick one by another as bawdy-houses in Chick-lane'. The boom of kettledrums and the blare of trumpets signalled the commencement of appalling dance-shows. A consort of fiddlers set Ward's own teeth dancing unsympathetically in his head, and the singing of another ballad provoked him to declare that he would rather hear 'an old barber ring "Whittington's Bells" on his cittern' (many musical compositions imitated the sound of bells in this period). The 'disproportioned notes and imperfect cadences' of a group of hautboy-players 'boxed our ears into a deafness'. To his regret, Ward recovered sufficiently to hear the bawdy songs of a female fiddler whose 'hiccuping voice' and 'intolerable scrapes on her cracked instrument' were almost enough to put him off both music and women forever.[2]

As this scornful survey indicates, musical instruments existed in considerable variety. Labels were often somewhat vague and there was little standardisation in design, but a count of several thousand contemporary references suggests that the most commonly encountered instruments were drums, trumpets, fiddles and bagpipes. Between them, these four instruments and their close relations account for just over half of the references. There were, however, many other instruments too, each contributing its distinctive sound to the music of the ringing island. Some were plucked or strummed: lutes, harps, citterns, bandoras, orpharions, gitterns and guitars. Many were blown: flutes and fifes, pipes (often played with the percussive tabor by a single performer), horns, cornetts (curved wooden instruments), whistles, sackbuts (early trombones), shawms (precursors of the oboe), flageolets and recorders. Then there were the keyboard instruments: virginals, organs, regals and the occasional clavichord. Many of these music-making devices were lovingly depicted by the artist who decorated the Cavendish family's 'Heaven Room' at Bolsover Castle (Derbyshire) in 1619 (see Figures 0.1 and 0.2). In addition, there were peculiarities such as the trumpet marine, an enormous instrument on

[2] Edward Ward, *The London Spy: Ned Ward's Classic Account of Underworld Life in Eighteenth-century London*, ed. Paul Hyland (East Lansing: Colleagues, 1993), pp. 22, 180, 194, 195, 199.

Figure 0.1. Cherubic musicians adorn the painted ceiling of the Heaven Room (1619) at Bolsover Castle, where they accompany Christ as he ascends into the firmament. This one plays the cornett, a curved wooden instrument with a mouthpiece and a beautiful voice-like tone. Bolsover Castle, Derbyshire, English Heritage, Heaven Room painting, detail.

which a single gut string was delicately touched with the fingers of one hand while those of the other drew the bow or plucked the string in order to sound the resultant harmonics. Trumpet marines were a novelty and rarely heard. The jew's harp or trump, in contrast, was so common that its existence, paradoxically, was very rarely documented. Trumps are difficult to count, but when a thief stole the goods of a Kentish tradeswoman in 1658 his loot included eighteen of them (worth a mere nine pence in total).[3] The metallic twang of the jew's harp, produced by plucking the 'tongue' while the body of the instrument is held between the teeth, may well have been one of England's most familiar musical sounds.

Scholars have sometimes sounded almost as dismissive as Ned Ward in commenting upon the musical capacities of the early modern population.[4]

[3] *Calendar of Assize Records: Kent Indictments, 1649–59*, ed. J. S. Cockburn (London: Her Majesty's Stationery Office, 1989), p. 286. Many of the instruments listed here can be heard on the website that accompanies this book (a jew's harp sounds on track 35) at www.cambridge.org/musicandsociety.

[4] See below, pp. 173, 419–20.

Figure 0.2. A violinist, a harper and a sackbut-player each contribute their distinctive sounds to the Bolsover ensemble. For further discussion of this painting, see below, pp. 364–5. Bolsover Castle, Derbyshire, English Heritage, Heaven Room painting, detail.

It is an attitude in need of revision. If we abandon the tendency to conflate musicality and musical literacy (two very different entities) then we must conclude that levels of aptitude and accomplishment in early modern England were impressively high. The entire broadside ballad industry depended partly upon the ability of sellers and consumers to memorise a remarkable number of frequently recycled tunes. Metrical psalmody and change-ringing, likewise, were both founded on the musical memories of ordinary parishioners and upon their willingness to participate. Chapbooks of the period presented a society – admittedly somewhat satirised – in which men and women were likely to break into song at any moment, whether they were at work or at play. The music of the majority was primarily melodic: 'rude people', remarked Dr Wallis in 1698, preferred basic tunes to elaborate consort music because they found it easier to comprehend. Other sources suggest, however, that craftsmen were often capable not only of playing instruments but of singing in parts, adding improvised harmonies to adorn the main melody. Charles Butler lacked the scorn of many educated observers for popular music and noted how groups of artisans sometimes made 'good Harmoni . . ., of 2, 3 or 4 voices: which surely is pleasant enough to the hearers'. According to John Case, human life on all social levels was seasoned with musical pleasure from cradle to grave, and he voiced a common suspicion of those who claimed not to feel it.[5]

Musical terminology frequently migrated into other categories of expression. To early modern people, the primary associations of terms such as 'harmony', 'concord' and 'discord' were clearly musical, but these potent labels were also applied with great regularity to social and political relations. In most cases, the relations in question were among humans, but when two enormous flocks of starlings confronted one another in a strange aerial battle over the city of Cork in 1621, Londoners soon heard of it and marvelled 'that Birds should thus at discord fall'. Many other expressions did similar service. Admirers of William III promised that he would teach his continental enemies 'a new Jigg to dance'. A plague-ridden city could be described as 'all out of tune' while a woman who died a virgin was, according to one distinctively masculine viewpoint, 'Like a Song without a foot'.[6] To share in the misery of others was to 'bear a part' with them, and the individual who said too much about a personal obsession might need to apologise for having 'strucke too long on this string'. In contrast, the woman who decided wisely to fall silent in order to avoid trouble was said to have 'put up her pipes', while a person who merely prepared the way for somebody else could say deferentially, 'I am but the shawmer to your motion' or 'I am the trumpeter to your show' (in other words, the loud instrument that announces your coming). John Taylor expected his readers to understand when he said of the archetypal prostitute that 'her chiefest instrument is the Sackbut' (associated here with sex because of its sliding mechanism).[7] The language of bell-ringing was fruitful too. Even today, a football manager who dismisses half of his team after a shocking defeat is said to be 'ringing the changes', an expression that first came into use during the early seventeenth century.

[5] *Memoirs of the Royal Society; or A New Abridgement of the Philosophical Transactions ... [from] 1665 to 1740*, 2nd edn., 10 vols. (London, 1745), vol. III, p. 292; Charles Butler, *The Principles of Musik, in Singing and Setting* (London, 1636), p. 123; John Case, *The Praise of Musicke* (Oxford, 1586; facsimile edn., New York, 1980), pp. 42, 74. There is some controversy over the authorship of this work but I am assuming – as did several contemporaries – that Case was indeed the author. For the counter-case see J. W. Binns, 'John Case and "The Praise of Musicke"', *Music and Letters* 55 (1974), 444–53.

[6] *The Pepys Ballads*, ed. W. G. Day, 5 vols. (Woodbridge: D. S. Brewer, 1987), vol. I, p. 71, vol. II, p. 291; John Taylor, *All the Workes of John Taylor the Water Poet*, 3 vols. (London: Spenser Society, 1869), vol. I, p. 69; *The Delectable History of Poor Robin the Merry Sadler of Walden* (London, *c.* 1680), ch. 18.

[7] *Pepys Ballads*, vol. I, p. 146; Richard Brathwaite, *The English Gentleman* (London, 1630), p. 133; untitled manuscript play, *c.* 1642, D/DW Z5, p. 17, ERO; satirical music lecture given at Oxford, *c.* 1642, Add. MS 37999, fo. 66, BL; Taylor, *All the Workes*, vol. II, p. 258.

Most people could not, however, read music, and the vast majority of what they played and heard was performed from memory rather than from the written page. It was possible for musicians to make their livings and achieve considerable success without musical literacy, and in 1588 Anthony Munday even managed to publish a book of songs with instrumental accompaniment, despite having 'no jote of knowledge in musique'. He apologised to his readers for this shortcoming, adding 'but what I have doone and doo, is onely by the eare'.[8] Despite such evidence, it seems possible that levels of musical literacy were rising more rapidly than we might have assumed. This is not something that permits statistical measurement, but the burgeoning market for instrumental instruction manuals, part-songs, catches and dance tunes clearly suggests that the publisher John Playford, active between the 1650s and 1680s, was not selling his wares only to the gentry and the most sophisticated of professional musicians. Lower down the musical hierarchy, the early modern period evidently witnessed a steady increase in the numbers who could play by book as well as by ear. Two probate documents from Hampshire hint at this development. As early as 1577, a Winchester musician, whose goods were worth only £6 9s 8d in total, bequeathed to his son two violins, three shawms and 'suche bookes as belongs to the said Instruments'. Another poor musician, Thomas Smithe of Basingstoke, died in 1628 with goods worth £13 11s 4d (less £5 1s 6d in debts). Nearly half of his wealth was contained in his twelve musical instruments (viols, bandoras, violins, a cittern and unspecified wind instruments), but he also had twelve pence worth of 'Musick books'.[9] If such lowly practitioners were able to read 'pricksong', then it seems reasonable to assume that the skill was already widely dispersed among those who made their primary livings from music. In all likelihood, such men still performed from memory most of the time, but a slowly increasing proportion of their repertoire may initially have been learned from the printed page.

Musical knowledge and awareness were, for the most part, acquired informally as the consequence of regular exposure to the singing and playing of others. In the lower levels of society, this was how most instrumentalists developed their talents, and one searches the written record in vain for any reference to bagpipe lessons. Scholars have not in general been impressed by the extent of more formal musical education,

[8] Anthony Munday, *A Banquet of Daintie Conceits* (London, 1588), A3v.

[9] Will and inventory of Thomas Saunders *alias* Wheler, 1577 B 70/1–2, and inventory of Thomas Smithe, 1628 AD 98, HRO.

whether practical or theoretical, but there clearly were ways and means by which to develop musical competence.[10] Members of the gentry and aristocracy regularly hired private tutors. Talented boys from less privileged backgrounds sometimes found their way into one of the cathedral or collegiate schools, where music of various sorts was taught as a specialism. At Newark, a song school was founded in 1532 with places for six main choristers and an equal group of potential replacements. The school was therefore small, but it was well equipped and the regime was intensive.[11] Similar institutions survived the Reformation at Chichester, Gloucester, Winchester, Salisbury, Lincoln and many other cathedral cities. Not all of the boys who attended these schools emerged as professional cathedral musicians in adulthood, but those who chose other paths nevertheless carried the knowledge they had acquired out into wider society.[12]

The foundation charters of non-specialist grammar schools did not often mention tuition in music, but these documents may not necessarily be a reliable guide to the actual extent of such tuition. They tell us conclusively that there was music at Merchant Taylors', Westminster, Burford, Dulwich and Grimsby, though provision at all these establishments must have fluctuated with the aptitudes of successive masters.[13] We should not, however, assume that this is an exhaustive list. Other schools may have provided some musical instruction, even if it had not been specified in their charters. The boys from some schools were responsible during the seventeenth century for leading the singing of psalms in the parish church, and they presumably received preparatory instruction.[14] It is suggestive that the personal belongings of Thurstan Collinson, master of Blackburn Grammar School, included 'one lute a base violin & a Chithhorne [cittern] a recorder [and] 3 ould instruments' when he died in 1623. A quarter of a century later, the rector of Layston (Hertfordshire) bequeathed 'to the Schoole of Buntingford founded by Mistris Freeman of Aspeden my chest with five Violls & all my singinge bookes written and

[10] For pessimistic commentary, see David C. Price, *Patrons and Musicians of the English Renaissance* (Cambridge: Cambridge University Press, 1981), pp. 36–8.

[11] DC/NW/3/1/1, fo. 103v, Nottinghamshire Archives (this inventory of the school's possessions, dated 1595, listed violins and violin books, anthems, service books and madrigals). See also Brenda M. Pask, *Newark Parish Church of St. Mary Magdalene* (Newark: District Church Council, 2000), pp. 236–8, and Jane Flynn, 'The Education of Choristers in England during the Sixteenth Century' in John Morehen (ed.), *English Choral Practice 1400–1650* (Cambridge: Cambridge University Press, 1995), pp. 180–99.

[12] See below, pp. 33, 81, 112–15.

[13] Price, *Patrons and Musicians*, pp. 36–8; Ian Spink, 'Music and Society', in Spink (ed.), *Music in Britain: The Seventeenth Century* (Oxford: Blackwell, 1992), pp. 25–6.

[14] See below, p. 425.

Figure 0.3. In this Elizabethan educational scene (1592), the beating of a boy draws the viewer's attention but in the opposite corner of the schoolroom there is musical notation on a board. Was music taught more widely than we realise? Hulton Archive/ Getty Images, 51240969 (RM).

printed'.[15] Neither of these two schools has featured on previous lists of educational establishments that offered music. Similarly indicative may be the Elizabethan woodcut depicting a schoolroom scene in which musical notation can clearly be seen on a board hanging from the wall (see Figure 0.3). If this was in any sense a representative portrayal, then we must consider the possibility that there was rather more music on offer in formally founded schools than has previously been assumed. The ample provision that existed at the universities may thus have presented

[15] *REED Lancashire*, p. 5 (the invaluable *REED* volumes contain collections of primary sources, but the pressures of space prevent me from including the original documentary references in my footnotes); '"This little commonwealth": Layston Parish Memorandum Book', ed. Heather Falvey and Steve Hindle, *Hertfordshire Record Publications* 19 (2003), appendix 6 (I am grateful to Steve Hindle for drawing this piece of evidence to my attention). The musician Thomas Whythorne remarked that the general term 'schoolmaster' was often applied to teachers of music. See *The Autobiography of Thomas Whythorne: Modern Spelling Edition*, ed. James M. Osborn (London: Oxford University Press, 1962), pp. 193, 205.

students with opportunities for further development rather than an educational novelty.[16]

Our knowledge of music in the smaller 'petty' schools is even thinner. These institutions taught reading and writing to some at least of the country's poorer children, but very little can be said about their musical provision. There is one tantalising reference to a small chain of petty singing schools in Elizabethan Lincolnshire, but beyond this the sources are silent.[17] We can be sure, however, that basic musical education was sometimes offered to poor children as an act of charity, reflecting the belief that it could provide them with a means of employment (and perhaps with less tangible philosophical benefits too). Christ's Hospital in London, founded in 1553, provides the most famous example. Precise arrangements varied under the influence of new masters and successive benefactors, but during the seventeenth century a small minority of the young inmates were taught to read music and play instruments, while the majority of children learned to sing. The 'Easter psalms', performed by the children of Christ's Hospital, became an annual event.[18] Charitable tuition was offered elsewhere too. During the early years of the seventeenth century, the Collectors for the Poor in Bridgwater (Somerset) paid a musician called John Carewe (or Cary) twelve shillings per quarter 'for the teachinge of vi poore Children to singe'. They also offered Edward Edwards ten shillings 'to teache blinde Hopkins to play on the harpe for his better mayntenance'. In some places, poor children were formally bound to established musicians as apprentices. During the early seventeenth century, several examples were recorded in Southampton's 'Poor Child Register', the idea in each case being 'to dischardge the said towne of . . . and from keeping of the said childe'.[19] Clearly, the ability to make music, and in particular to sing, was understood to occupy an important position in the pauper's survival kit. Beneath this understanding lay three interrelated beliefs: that poor folk should be expected to work for their livings; that the poor person with a marketable skill had a better chance of survival than the mere beggar; and lastly, that singing was both acceptable and effective as a means of imploring charity from an audience. All three principles were set to work when, in 1574,

16 On music at university, see Price, *Patrons and Musicians*, pp. 20–6; Helen M. Jewell, *Education in Early Modern England* (Basingstoke: Macmillan, 1998), pp. 19–20; Spink, 'Music and Society', pp. 27–8; Nan Cooke Carpenter, *Music in the Medieval and Renaissance Universities* (Norman: University of Oklahoma Press, 1958), pp. 153–208.

17 See below, p. 425.

18 E. H. Pearce, *Annals of Christ's Hospital* (London: Methuen, 1901), pp. 135–44, 225.

19 *REED Somerset*, pp. 57, 58; *A Calendar of Southampton Apprenticeship Registers, 1609–1740*, ed. A. L. Merson, *Publications of the Southampton Record Society* 12 (1968), 65, 66, 73, 77.

Queen Elizabeth visited Bristol and was treated to 'a solemn song by Orphans' at the free school of St Bartholomew's.[20]

There were, therefore, many ways to learn music. Of course, these did not amount to a coherent system, but the various avenues to accomplishment can nevertheless help us to understand how it was that music was both ubiquitous and influential. Arguably, music was also the beneficiary of an age in which people felt things through their ears somewhat more acutely than we nowadays do. It is often said – with some exaggeration though not without justification – that we live in a visual age. Certainly, we tend to privilege sight over sound, and people regularly speak of having been to 'see' a concert. During the early modern period, there existed something more like parity between the two dominant senses.[21] This was reflected (or echoed) in common language and cultural practice. Where nowadays we speak of 'eye-witnesses', our ancestors spoke also of 'ear-witnesses'. Conflicting parties 'came together by the ears' and the villains of humorous ballads were sometimes 'lugg'd by the ears'. Indeed, the ears featured regularly in the contemporary culture of punishment, whether informal or formal. Out-of-tune choirboys were rung by the ears, while the ears of criminals could be burned, cut off or nailed to the pillory. To some extent, this was merely because ears stuck out and formed convenient targets, but it seems that the organs of hearing were also prominent in a deeper sense. They were a fundamental point of contact between self and society, and it was through the ears that many influences – for good and evil – made themselves felt. Cutting them off was not merely a practical mode of punishment, but a meaningful one too. The preacher Thomas Adams was even prepared to argue that ears were more powerful than eyes: 'The eare yet heares more, then ever the eye saw: and by reason of the patulous admission, derives that to the understanding, whereof the sight never had a glaunce.' He, at least, considered himself to be living in an era of the ear.[22]

Echoes, resonances and sympathies

A second important theme of this study will be music's significance within a wider culture that was characterised by richly associational thinking. Early modern people inhabited a vast and resonating universe of divine

[20] *REED Bristol*, p. 91.

[21] Jeremy Collier, *Essays upon Several Moral Subjects* (London, 1697), p. 20.

[22] *The Workes of Thomas Adams* (London, 1629), p. 148. On the ranking of the senses, see C. M. Woolgar, *The Senses in Late Medieval England* (New Haven: Yale University Press, 2006), pp. 23, 64.

design. The many parts of the cosmos were bound together by ties that were infinite in number and intimate in nature. Every object or idea echoed others and the world pulsated with correspondences. England was a ringing island in this sense too. As John Case put it, 'things that are of like natures, have mutual & easy action & passion betweene themselves'. Sometimes, the reverberations were real and physical. Acoustical echoes fascinated people for a number of reasons. Most obviously, an echo was unique in a pre-electronic age because it allowed sounds to be precisely reproduced and heard again. All others died and disappeared in an instant. At one church in Gloucester, it was reported that 'if you speak against a Wall, softly, another shall hear your Voice better a good Way off'.[23] For scientists, the challenge was to explain the echo in physical terms, though they shared with everyone else a parallel desire to understand the phenomenon as a carrier of more mysterious meanings. Echoes were other-worldly and served to remind ear-witnesses of the deeper patterns that lay behind the merely physical. In cheap printed publications of the seventeenth century, echoes sometimes signified the supernatural. When Satan and an angel both appeared in human form on an unusually exciting day in Westmorland, the superiority of the latter was expressed by the sounding of an extraordinary melody that had no apparent source. The echo affected all who heard it: 'It ravish'd the hearts of those stood by, / So sweet the Musick did abound.' In Restoration Wiltshire, the drumbeats of local players were echoed uncannily by an unseen respondent, and many felt that it was the devil himself who wielded the invisible stick. One popular chapbook story described the adventures of a boy with a pipe so magical that its music caused 'strange echoes' to rebound, 'even from sky to ground'.[24] In other printed tales, the supernatural element was less obvious, though it was perhaps implicit in the role of echoes as indicators of the exceptional. When a desperately sad man wails in anguish, 'The bordering hills and dales resound / the Ecchoes of his pittious cry.' And when an ecstatically happy ballad-writer calls on his compatriots to welcome King William III to England, he sings, 'Let loud acclamations resound, / and make the high Elements ring.'[25] These were physical effects

[23] Case, *Praise of Musicke*, p. 41; Penelope Gouk, *Music, Science and Natural Magic in Seventeenth-century England* (New Haven: Yale University Press, 1999), p. 162.

[24] *Pepys Ballads*, vol. II, p. 155; *The Diary of Samuel Pepys*, ed. R. C. Latham and W. Matthews, 11 vols. (London: HarperCollins, 1995), vol. IV, p. 186; *The Fryear and the Boy* (London, 1680), pt. 2, unpaginated.

[25] *Pepys Ballads*, vol. I, p. 65, vol. II, p. 270.

but they were also something more. When the cosmos rang back, it did so in sympathy.

Ringing and echoing often went together, and in the literary imagination birdsong achieved both effects. There were strange correspondences to be discerned here too. The song of the wren and the cry of the raven were echoed in listeners by sensations of mirth and misery respectively. Case told his readers that the singing of larks, invariably delivered on the rise, was a kind of divine teaching aid: 'learn by their example, what thy duty is & ought to be in grateful singing of psalms and songs to him that made thee'. Similarly instructive was the robin who became 'Famous for singing every day on the Top of QUEEN MARY's Mausoleum' in Westminster Abbey, following her funeral in 1695. The bird's song echoed the nation's grief but also reassured listeners, in their moments of sadness, 'That Potent France shall nere destroy the Church' (see Figure 0.4). Cosmological cross-currents were politically useful.[26]

The universe was full of such phenomena. Orderly dancing brought participants into contact with the planets, themselves moving in preordained patterns through the skies.[27] The music of humans was, at its best, an echo of heavenly harmony and thus a foretaste of eternal bliss. Four-part singing had one of its correspondences in the earthly operations of the four elements, each maintaining its allotted place in the order of things. Music also enjoyed a profound affinity with the internal workings of human beings. Bodies and souls responded sympathetically to it, and music was thus useful in the varied fields of medicine, religion, warfare, recreation and exploration. Fools were fools, said Samuel Person, because of the 'bad harmony' that proceeded from their internal organs to their thoughts, words and actions. There was indeed a dark side, for the correspondences that characterised the role of music within the cosmos could all too easily mutate into twisted and dangerous forms. Discord was diabolical in its resonances, and a vocal minority of early modern commentators felt that a high proportion of popular

[26] William Shakespeare, *The First Part of the Contention of the Two Famous Houses of York and Lancaster* (*2 Henry VI*), in *The Complete Oxford Shakespeare*, ed. Stanley Wells and Gary Taylor, 3 vols. (Oxford: Oxford University Press, 1987), vol. I, p. 21; Case, *Praise of Musicke*, p. 50; *The Robin-red-breast Famous for Singing Every Day on the Top of Queen Mary's Mausoleum* (London, 1695); *The Westminster Wonder* (London, 1695).

[27] See below, pp. 354–6. The other ideas mentioned in this paragraph are discussed more fully in ch. 1.

Figure 0.4. In 1695, a robin attracted attention by singing mournfully from its favourite position on top of Queen Mary's tomb. Its music seemed to connect heaven and earth. *The Robin-red-breast Famous for Singing Every Day on Top of Queen Mary's Mausoleum* (London, 1695). © Trustees of the British Museum, Prints and Drawings, Y,1.70.

music-making deserved to be included in this category, however smooth and seductive it sounded to the ears. The Elizabethan minister Stephen Gosson accepted that there were interesting correspondences between musical instruments and people, but he pointed out that tuning a neglected pair of virginals was a simple operation in comparison to the task of maintaining harmony within the human spirit ('man being a creature so witty, so subtle, so proude, so surlie, so wedded to his own will & opinions, & rolling upon so many wheels'). Gosson's own spirits sagged at the thought, and he concluded wearily, 'It is the hardest profession in the world to be a preacher.'[28]

Connective thinking applied not only to the mysteries of philosophy and physiology but to the cultural meanings of specific forms of music. Many sounds called to mind something beyond themselves, and people were, it seems, thoroughly adept at reading (or heeding) the signals. Church bells, rung in different ways, could speak of delight, devotion, death and danger, stimulating a variety of moods in those who listened. In balladry, individual tunes were often used for the singing of many different texts and they carried potent associations with them as they travelled from one song to the next. In psalmody, melodic motifs were recycled constantly so that every rendition echoed and reinforced others. The contrasting sounds of musical instruments also called forth a range of specific associations. The penetrating music of drums, trumpets and fifes spoke, for example, of military might. Their sound was 'clamorous', 'repercussive', 'lofty', 'rattling' and 'warlike'. Indeed, such instruments were regularly spoken of as weapons.[29] This primary association generated others. In civilian life, trumpet calls also announced the approach of pre-eminent individuals, suggesting the glitz of aristocracy while alluding to the intimidating power that lay behind it. Bagpipes spoke to cultural traditionalists of holiday happiness and the idealised solidarity of rich and poor in rural England. In contrast, many puritans associated them instead with debauchery, irreligion and resistance to all their reforming efforts. Virginals and viols were different again. Their restrained tones (and high cost) suited them perfectly to aristocratic interiors, and their primary associations were therefore with sophistication and refinement. In the words of one commentator, they provided 'Fancy Musick'.[30]

Another prestigious instrument, the lute, supplied early modern people with their favourite example of the mysterious interconnectedness of the cosmos. The author of an anonymous manuscript in praise of music provided instructions for a simple experiment: tune two lutes and lay them beside one another; next, set a small piece of straw across one of the strings of the first lute; finally, pluck the corresponding string on the second lute

[28] Samuel Person, *An Anatomical Lecture of Man* (London, 1664), pp. 23–4; Thomas Mace, *Musick's Monument; or, A Remembrancer of the Best Practical Musick* (London, 1676), pp. 3–4; Stephen Gosson, *The Trumpet of Warre* (London, 1598), fo. 60v.

[29] See below, p. 159.

[30] Nicholas Le Strange, 'Merry Passages and Jeasts: A Manuscript Jestbook of Sir Nicholas Le Strange', ed. H. F. Lippincott, *Elizabethan and Renaissance Studies* 29 (1974), p. 144. 'Fancy' was also an alternative name for an instrumental fantasia (a style of piece characterised by its free form).

and watch in wonder as the straw falls from its position on the first. There was, of course, a scientific explanation for this result, but the author – along with many others – preferred to contemplate correspondence, 'the one stringe havinge a fellow feeling of the violence offered to the other'. For Bishop Robert Skinner of Bristol, addressing his clergy in 1637, there was a valuable lesson in this: 'Now what influence devoute reverence and religious ceremonies have upon weaker mindes, all know that know anie thing. Have yee not noted how strings touched in an instrument move one another? And so good Christians strongly touched with devout reverence move all that are about them.' Associational thinking clearly came naturally and must therefore be a vital component in any attempt to understand what the Elizabethan writer John Case called 'the effects and operation of musicke'.[31]

Music and social relations: culture as a lute

A third main strand considers the part that music played in mediating human relationships of various sorts. The subject under consideration is so vast that it may be useful to propose a suitably musical model as a framework for interpretation. This model, though inspired by music, is applicable to all aspects of culture (my working definition of this infuriating but indispensable term is 'the attitudes, actions and artefacts through which people engage with their environment'). Its construction has also been driven by a desire to escape the two-tier model for early modern European culture that has proved problematic ever since it was unveiled by Peter Burke in 1978.[32] For present purposes, we should note two main difficulties: Burke's model privileged a single distinction between learned culture and popular culture, thus ignoring or relegating other lines of differentiation that were often just as important; and by building what is effectively a class divide into its very structure, it also tended to overlook or undervalue cultural consensus and the manner in which those with a foot in both camps mediated between them.[33] Culture

[31] 'The Praise of Musicke', Royal MS 18 B XIX, fo. 3r, BL; *Visitation Articles and Injunctions of the Early Stuart Church*, ed. Kenneth Fincham, 2 vols. (Woodbridge: Boydell Press for the Church of England Record Society, 1994 and 1998), vol. II, p. 190; Case, *Praise of Musicke*, pp. 53–4.

[32] Peter Burke, *Popular Culture in Early Modern Europe* (Aldershot: Wildwood House, 1978), pp. 23–9.

[33] For a more detailed critique, see Tim Harris (ed.), *Popular Culture in England, c. 1500–1850* (Basingstoke: Macmillan, 1995), ch. 1.

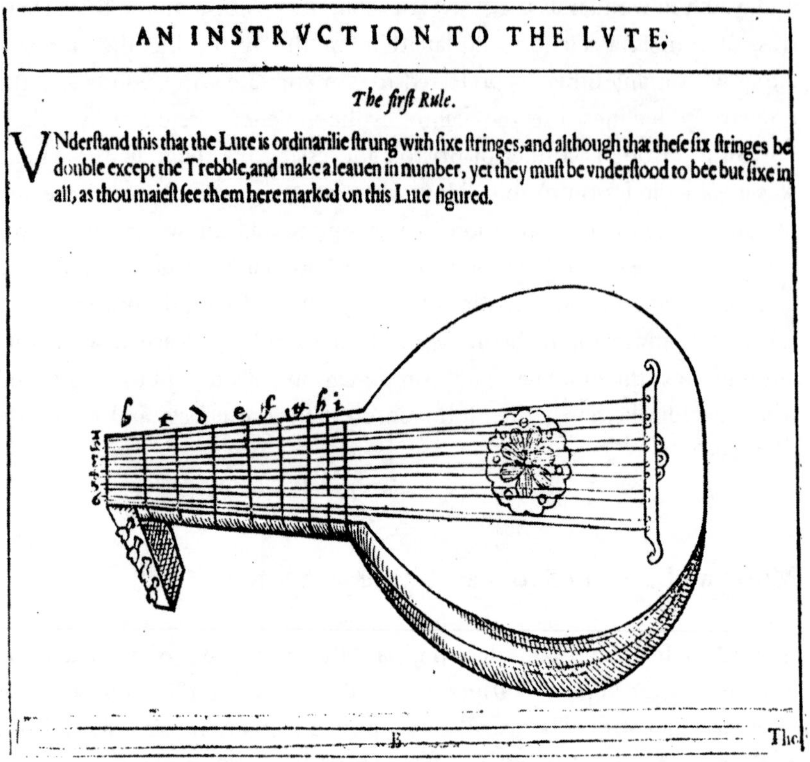
AN INSTRVCTION TO THE LVTE.

The firſt Rule.

VNderſtand this that the Lute is ordinarilie ſtrung with ſixe ſtringes, and although that theſe ſix ſtringes be double except the Trebble, and make a leauen in number, yet they muſt be vnderſtood to bee but ſixe in all, as thou maieſt ſee them here marked on this Lute figured.

Figure 0.5. The lute, with its characteristic 'rose' (sound-hole) and angled peg-box, was at its most fashionable during the Elizabethan and Jacobean periods. The British Library, William Barley, *A New Booke of Tabliture* (London, 1596), B1r.

is, of course, about dissonance as well as consonance, but perhaps we should seek a model that allows more readily for the constant interplay between these phenomena in a variety of categories.

Early modern people defined themselves not only as participants in the so-called 'great' and/or 'little' traditions but also in terms of a range of other dichotomies. Life was much more complex and contradictory than the two-tier model can easily allow, and readers are therefore invited to imagine early modern culture as an Elizabethan lute with six strings (see Figure 0.5).[34] Each string represents one of the basic socio-cultural polarities that helped individuals to understand their world and to locate themselves within it: gentle/common, male/female, old/young, clerical/

[34] Such an instrument can be heard on website tracks 6 and 7. Technically, we should speak of 'courses' (pairs of strings, tuned in unison and played as one) rather than strings. On a lute, only the highest-sounding string was typically single. I will, however, use the term 'string' as a convenient and familiar shorthand.

lay, urban/rural and native/foreign. It is well known that our ancestors tended to think in terms of oppositional polarities – 'the combat of contraries', as one preacher put it – but it should also be pointed out that each pairing, when applied to cultural life, was more like a spectrum.[35] To put it another way, poles are poles only because the rest of the world lies between them. On each string of our lute, therefore, the extremes are permanently connected and always in tension. Indeed, a lute string without tension is not doing its job (sometimes strings snap, but they can be replaced). The frets on the instrument's neck form a musical staircase that facilitates traffic in both directions. Of course, my list of social polarities is not exhaustive and some may prefer to modify them or add new ones of their own. Luckily, the metaphor is flexible: during the seventeenth century, individual lutes could be tuned in several different ways, and instruments with up to twelve strings were regularly made. 'What vast capacities the lute has', noted one excitable admirer in her notebook, 'what abundance of music, what variety both of things and manners, of fashions of playing and composing, the lute being like an ocean that cannot be emptied but is full of so much riches that the more we take from it the more remains to take.'[36]

Music, like culture more generally, performed a dual and paradoxical role. Firstly, it marked the many divisions that separated individuals or social groups from one another. Amid the ecclesiastical tensions of 1637 Humphrey Sydenham used a musical metaphor in complaining that too many people 'imploy their wit and greatnesse a contrary way, and delight altogether in the jarring of the string, as if there were no Melody but in Discords'.[37] On the other hand, musical culture also mitigated commonplace divisions by allowing the continual interplay of conflicting tendencies and even drawing them, however temporarily, towards unity. Good music, according to a range of commentators, comprehended all things. It joined contrary elements, persuading high notes to accord with low ones. Harmony was the agreement of different sounds or the combination of opposites.[38] Butler noted that harmony could even accommodate ugly clashes between notes: 'a Discord, as in Oeconomi, so in Musik, is

[35] The expression is taken from Gosson, *Trumpet of Warre*, fo. 63r.

[36] 'Miss Mary Burwell's Instruction Book for the Lute', ed. Thurston Dart, *Galpin Society Journal* 11 (May 1958), 14. On the history of the lute, see Matthew Spring, *The Lute in Britain* (Oxford: Oxford University Press, 2001).

[37] Humphrey Sydenham, *Sermons upon Solemne Occasions* (London, 1637), A2r–v.

[38] Stephen Batman, *Batman upon Bartholome, his Booke De Proprietatibus Rerum* (London, 1582), fo. 424r; William Holder, *A Treatise of the Natural Grounds and Principles of Harmony* (London, 1694), B1v; Alexander Malcolm, *A Treatise of Musik, Speculative, Practical and Historical* (Edinburgh, 1721), A3r.

soomtimes allowable, as making the Concord following the sweeter'. Naturally, these characteristics had their social and political correspondences. Thomas Rogers expressed a widely held opinion: 'For as good Musike consisteth not of one, but of divers sowndes proportionablie answering together: so doeth a Commonweale of sundrie kinds of men keping themselves within the limits of their owne callings.'[39]

Along each of our six strings, music therefore articulated both the differences and the similarities between people. Members of the gentry, for example, regarded ballads as common and coarse, yet they collected them and sang them within the safety of their own homes. Some forms of music-making were resolutely masculine (bell-ringing for example) while others were often characterised as feminine (real men did not play the virginals). And yet the gender lines were also blurred in numerous ways: many virginalists were in fact male, and female ballad-singers regularly adopted male identities in performing and selling their wares. Dancing and bell-ringing were youthful pursuits but there were regular exceptions and inversions. Many musicians passed their skills and instruments peacefully to their offspring, and in congregational psalmody the old and the young sang as one. In theory, town and country had distinctive musical traditions, yet they interacted at a number of points: the urban waits toured the countryside, and 'country dancing' was fashionable in seventeenth-century towns.[40] Members of the clergy were expected to distance themselves from the more raucous of lay musical practices, but not all of them could resist the temptation to cross the border.[41] In psalmody, the parish clerk bridged the lay–clerical divide though his presence was not invariably sufficient to defuse tension.

Lastly, an evolving sense of English nationality was explored and asserted through psalmody, bell-ringing and dancing and in numerous ballads, yet melodies flew back and forth across the sea as freely as birds. Musicians came and went too, and in 1666 John Playford complained bitterly that many fashion-conscious English people held all music in low esteem except for 'what is presented by Forreigners'. 'Not a City Dame', he went on, 'but is ambitious to have her Daughters taught by Mounseur La Novo Kickshawibus on the Gittar' (see Figure 0.6). Playford resented cross-Channel musical traffic, but others used it to their advantage. When

[39] Butler, *Principles of Musik*, p. 51; Thomas Rogers, *A Golden Chaine* (London, 1587), A3r.

[40] On urban music, see Peter Borsay, 'Sounding the Town', *Urban History* 21 (2002), 92–103; Tim Carter, 'The Sound of Silence: Models for an Urban Musicology', *Urban History* 21 (2002), 8–18; Fiona Kisby, 'Music in European Cities and Towns to *c.* 1650', *Urban History* 21 (2002), 74–83; Reinhard Strohm, *Music in Late Medieval Bruges* (Oxford: Clarendon Press, 1990).

[41] Examples can be found below on pp. 150, 207, 218–19, 274–5, 338.

Figure 0.6. The guitar, a European import, was played increasingly in England from the mid-seventeenth century. It eventually displaced older plucked instruments such as the gittern and cittern. The Pepys Library, Magdalene College, Cambridge, Pepys Ballads, *The Maids Complaint for want of a Dil Doul* (London, *c.* 1681–4), detail.

Sir John Reresby toured Europe during the 1650s, he amazed and amused his Italian hosts by bringing with him a humble musician from home: 'I had then an English boy that plaid perfectly well of the bagpipe, that I carried after with me through all my travels.' The boy, admittedly, was mentioned almost as if he were a piece of baggage rather than a companion, and Reresby – remembering that he was a gent – described the sound of the bagpipes as 'a sort of musicke more to be liked for the extraordinariness of it then the exactness'.[42] Nevertheless, he clearly appreciated his piper's ability to stimulate southern aristocrats with his strange northern

[42] John Playford, *Musick's Delight on the Cithren* (London, 1666), preface; *Memoirs of Sir John Reresby*, ed. Andrew Browning et al. (London: Royal Historical Society, 1991), pp. 8–9.

sounds. In the more exotic setting of North America, exported music of various sorts served to lure, calm and intimidate the natives.[43] This was a strange dialogue not only between civilisations but also between music as, on the one hand, a phenomenon shared by all humans and, on the other, a marker of geographical and ethnic particularity.

The lute itself was an instrument that both divided and united people along several of our metaphorical strings. It was played by musicians of all ages, but old masters and young pretenders sometimes clashed acrimoniously over questions of style and technique. Similarly, it was well known all over Europe but the sober style in which the English played it was sometimes presented as a distinguishing feature of the ringing island.[44] The lute was also 'a Womans Instrument', and some men avoided it for this reason, yet it was often found in male hands, where it not infrequently served as a tool of courtship. It thus brought men and women together and could even persuade young lovers to suspend consideration of the differences in their social status. Thomas Mace, placing his fingers on two strings at once, personified the lute as female while proposing the familiar argument that it was properly an instrument of the gentry: 'Her Matter's of such High Concern, / No Common Folks can it discern: / Twas ne'er intended for the Rude / And Boisterous-Churlish Multitude.'[45] To emphasise the point, the instruments of important individuals were a cut above the rest in decoration and design. In 1586 a Cornish gentleman, Edward Arundell, made a will in which he bequeathed to his nephew 'my best lute ... which lute is white and blacke, and the case crimson velvett imbrodered all over with golde'. Gentlefolk could not, however, keep the lute to themselves and they were generally taught to play it by expert practitioners of much lower social status. Lesser folk played the lute for recreation too. Master Arundell was proud of his instrument, but so too was the Essex yeoman Anthony Bret. On his deathbed in 1588, Bret was clearly preoccupied with the future of his instrument. He told witnesses of the money he had laid out to a Mr Jerome in London, 'For taking of the belly of a lute and for gluing her, and for new pins and strings for the said lute'. Bret was also having his lute case re-lined, covered with calf-skin and fitted with a lock. Sadly, he had tickled the strings for the last time, but he clearly intended that his own onward spiritual journey would be

[43] This subject is discussed in fascinating detail in Ian Woodfield, *English Musicians in the Age of Exploration* (Stuyvesant, NY: Pendragon Press, 1995), chs. 7–11.

[44] John Dowland, *A Pilgrimes Solace* (London, 1612), preface; Mace, *Musick's Monument*, pp. 33–4; 'Miss Mary Burwell's Instruction Book', p. 61.

[45] 'Miss Mary Burwell's Instruction Book', p. 49; Mace, *Musick's Monument*, pp. 33–4, 36.

counterbalanced by his lute's return to Essex. He told his friends that he had already paid eight pence for transporting the instrument to London 'and down again'. Lutes were not quite as aristocratic as aristocrats wished them to be, and during one ten-month period during the 1560s a remarkable 13,848 lute strings were imported into London.[46] They cannot all have been destined for the mansions of the mighty.

If we think of culture along these lines, we will perhaps come to understand its early modern history in terms of continuous dialogic tensions rather than as a series of seismic and seemingly conclusive shifts. Arguably, subjects such as secularisation and the transition from an oral culture towards a literate one invite this shift of perspective. The same can be said of that other favourite of cultural historians, namely the withdrawal of the gentry from the pastimes of the populace. In the estimation of various scholars, this occurred some time between the late sixteenth and the early eighteenth century, and was followed by an aristocratic 'rediscovery' of popular culture (bigwigs, having distanced themselves, came to take a newly dispassionate interest in the doings of the drones).[47] Remarkably, historians of the eighteenth and nineteenth centuries have claimed, in strikingly similar terms, that the withdrawal of the elite took place in their period, and not in ours.[48] Surely, it would make more sense to imagine an on-going relationship of the love-hate variety. Of course, there have been periods of particular strain and phases of comparative calm, but the notion of a grand shift from unity to disunity seems inappropriate. In all periods, members of the self-styled social elite will tend to disparage the culture of their supposed inferiors while simultaneously espousing it with some degree of disquiet. This was true of the Elizabethan gentleman who read ballads before wiping his bottom with them, and it is true of the many members of the modern intelligentsia who cannot resist the pull of reality TV.[49]

On a different note, we can perhaps imagine our instrument not only as a model for culture in its entirety but also as a metaphor for the manner in which early modern men and women communicated with the wider world, presenting self to society. In so doing, they possessed relative liberty

[46] *REED Dorset, Cornwall*, p. 530; F. G. Emmison, *Elizabethan Life: Home, Work and Land* (Chelmsford: Essex County Council, 1976), pp. 23–4; Woodfield, *English Musicians*, p. 75. It should be noted, however, that lute strings were also used in the manufacture of fine clothing.

[47] See, in particular, Burke, *Popular Culture*, pp. 270–81, and Keith Wrightson, *English Society, 1580–1680* (London: Hutchinson, 1982), pp. 220–1.

[48] See, for example, Robert W. Malcolmson, *Popular Recreations in English Society, 1700–1850* (Cambridge: Cambridge University Press, 1973), pp. 163–6.

[49] For the former example, see below, pp. 263–4.

to pluck and strum as they saw fit. This was a matter of personal choice, and Thomas Mace entitled one section of his famous book 'A Dialogue between the Author and his Lute'. Of course, players were to a degree constrained by various social conventions, but their hands were never inextricably tied. No person was immovably fixed to a single position on any of the strings, and it was therefore possible to move one's fingers into new shapes according to each particular situation. In a well-known song of the period, a jilted shepherd warns listeners not to blame the instrument he plays for the bitterness of his words since its rebounding sound is under his personal control ('My Lute and Strings do not deny, / But as I strike they must obey'). Every individual, without exception, occupied some position on every string, but not all of the strings were equally important all of the time. People of every degree constantly made choices, emphasising certain aspects of their cultural identities while temporarily neglecting others. Lute strings could sound alone, though as we already know they could also set one another vibrating. Individual choices depended on the precise nature of any situation and the aspirations with which it was approached: in what sort of company did one find oneself, and what chord did one hope to strike in the ears of listeners? The lute, said Mary Burwell, was 'a modest interpreter of our thoughts and passions to those that understand the language'. Furthermore, 'We may express upon it choler, pity, hatred, scorn, love, grief, joy; we may give hope and despair.'[50]

Ringing the changes

Our model lute perhaps tends to emphasise the ways in which individuals made continuous and immediate adjustments as they presented themselves to others, but early modern England also witnessed longer-term shifts in the nature of its music. Some of these were highly significant, generating repercussions that are still audible today. The business of publishing and selling broadside ballads, for example, expanded at an astonishing rate between the early sixteenth and later seventeenth centuries. In this development lay the origins of modern pop music (if by this term we understand a genre that was driven primarily by commercial priorities and aimed at a disproportionately youthful and urban mass audience). The period also witnessed accelerating commercialisation in

[50] Mace, *Musick's Monument*, p. 33; *The Shepherds Garland of Love, Loyalty and Delight* (London, 1682), B1r–v; 'Miss Mary Burwell's Instruction Book', pp. 48–9.

other areas: the printing of music and musical books grew into a major operation, particularly during the second half of the seventeenth century; much of this material was enthusiastically consumed by a swelling band of music-making amateurs; paradoxically, their interest in music and their desire to hire teachers also contributed to the rise of the professional. At Bartholomew Fair, for example, Ned Ward was clearly listening to the work of organised, money-making bands working the London circuit of potentially lucrative gigs. Arguably, the long-term consequences of this trend are seen in the tendency of modern people to draw a distinction between the performing professional and the paying audience.

The English hymn-singing tradition also had its roots in this period. The Reformation brought an end in all churches save the cathedrals to the rich traditions of late medieval sacred music, performed by a specialist minority (priests, parish clerks, singing men, choirboys and organists). In its place there arose the unprecedented and monumental sound of entire congregations singing metrical psalms in unaccompanied unison. This was a musical revolution that set the tone in English churches for several centuries to come (though mass congregational singing has now migrated to the football stadium). The dramatic increase in the number and uses of church bells during the seventeenth century was similarly significant in its long-term effects. Bells survived the pressures of the Reformation, and the distinctively English art of change-ringing helped to define the soundscape into the age of Handel and beyond.

If we can locate the origins of modern pop music in the early modern period, then we should perhaps also look there for signs of the controversy that it has periodically stirred. The greatest change to overcome the commoner forms of English music during this era was, arguably, the construction and dissemination of a frequently vehement critique. Of course, suspicion of music was by no means unprecedented, and medieval minstrels hardly enjoyed a spotless reputation. Nevertheless, popular music-making was not an acutely controversial topic during the late fifteenth and early sixteenth centuries. Between 1560 and 1660, however, this relative calm was disturbed by a long-running quarrel over the value of music within English society. Ballads, psalms, dances, bells and other instruments all featured in the tense debate, and the very term 'minstrel' came, in some minds, to signify debauchery and disorder.[51] Others defended music on a variety of grounds and accused its critics of listening only for discord. The controversy was partly a product of the Reformation.

[51] See below, pp. 76–7.

The shrillest voices often belonged to puritans, for whom anxiety about the most common forms of music was part of a much broader struggle for the godly transformation of English culture. For them, the high point probably occurred in the 1640s and 1650s when civil war opened the prospect of forcing this transformation through by parliamentary ordinance. The musical anxieties of puritans did not, however, distinguish them from more moderate Protestants in any simple sense because it was perfectly possible to experience concern over the dangers of music primarily as the result of the tensions thrown up by the period's unsettling economic and demographic trends. Rising population levels, escalating poverty, rapid inflation and social polarisation would probably have rendered popular music-making controversial, even without the intensifying impact of the Reformation. Trouble was further exacerbated by the rapid spread of new musical habits such as the singing of broadside ballads and recreational bell-ringing. The ears of authority are always assaulted rather than soothed by such developments, as historians of jazz and rock'n'roll know well. There were, therefore, many reasons for disquiet and, most of the time, it is impossible to separate the various motivating factors.

Controversy did not end with the Restoration of Charles II in 1660, but there is little doubt that the passions of the recent past cooled noticeably during the last decades of the seventeenth century. Or perhaps anxiety over music, now inextricably associated with the disgraced regimes of the Interregnum, was merely contained within the somewhat introverted world of the dissenting denominations. Arguably, nonconformist leaders expended more energy in disciplining their own than they did in seeking to reform society at large. The experiences of the 1640s and 1650s had tended to suggest that such ambitions were futile, and those who clung to them in any outspoken manner after the Restoration risked provoking extreme hostility. Whatever the explanation, audible tensions over music-making were far more unusual during the later seventeenth century than they had been for decades before. In a sense, a wheel had come full circle and something like the dynamic consensus of the early sixteenth century had returned to the ringing island. Of course, the tensions of the intervening decades had left many traces, some of which are still apparent today. Music had been assaulted and its lovers had accommodated themselves, sometimes painfully, to the changing times, but their art had undoubtedly survived, and in the age of Samuel Pepys it unquestionably thrived. Our over-arching narrative is, therefore, rather like a musical composition of three movements in which the last contains distinct echoes of the first. Unusually, however, the fast and furious movement is the one in the middle.

Historians and the neglect of music

The broad contours of this narrative have been mapped by recent historians engaged in the investigation of other aspects of early modern society.[52] Most scholars have, however, tended to contemplate the past with their ears partially plugged. There have, of course, been some important exceptions, and it would have been far more difficult to write this book without the lead provided by the published work of other musically minded historians. In 1981, Margaret Spufford included within her pioneering work on cheap print an intriguing section that asserted the importance of music-making in the lives of the English majority. Patrick Collinson has regularly proved himself acutely sensitive to the centrality of music within contemporary debates about religion and culture in newly Protestant England. Peter Borsay, writing of the century after 1660, acknowledged fully the significance of music-making, whether professional or amateur, in the rapidly developing urban leisure environment. Special mention must also go to Tessa Watt's acclaimed study of Elizabethan and early Stuart religion as it was presented in various forms of cheap print. The chapters on balladry were unusual in exploring the melodic dimension alongside the textual, but Watt also wrote at length of more general patterns of musical activity. Adam Fox's wonderfully rich study of oral and literate culture revealed a critical awareness of the role that music played at the interface between the two. Ian Green, finally, included within his magisterial study of print and Protestantism a chapter on psalm-singing that was more thorough and stimulating than the work of any previous historian on the subject.[53]

Despite such examples, it is undeniable that the social and cultural history of early modern England has in general been written with only fleeting attention to music. Important and influential work has tended to treat the music of the majority as merely incidental. Barry Reay's *Popular*

52 See, for example, Ronald Hutton, *The Rise and Fall of Merry England* (Oxford: Oxford University Press, 1994).

53 Margaret Spufford, *Small Books and Pleasant Histories: Popular Fiction and its Readership in Seventeenth-century England* (Cambridge: Cambridge University Press, 1981), pp. 170–82; Patrick Collinson, *The Birthpangs of Protestant England: Religious and Cultural Change in the Sixteenth and Seventeenth Centuries* (Basingstoke: Macmillan, 1988), pp. 108–12; Peter Borsay, *The English Urban Renaissance: Culture and Society in the Provincial Town, 1660–1770* (Oxford: Clarendon Press, 1989), pp. 121–7; Tessa Watt, *Cheap Print and Popular Piety, 1550–1640* (Cambridge: Cambridge University Press, 1991), pp. 11–127; Adam Fox, *Oral and Literate Culture in England, 1500–1700* (Oxford: Clarendon Press, 2000), pp. 26–30, 318–27, 383–93; Ian Green, *Print and Protestantism in Early Modern England* (Oxford: Oxford University Press, 2000), pp. 503–52.

Cultures in England, 1550–1750 is undoubtedly the best overview of its subject currently available, but its index contains no references to music (nor to bells, psalms or dance). Musicians are depicted prominently on the front cover, but within the main text they struggle to make themselves heard. Admittedly, music is not neglected entirely but the attention it receives bears no comparison to its significance within early modern culture. Surely, if any scholar were to publish an account of twentieth-century popular culture that set music to one side, eyebrows would be raised and questions would be asked. Yet this is precisely the situation that exists within the historiography of Tudor and Stuart England. Arguably, social and cultural historians know more about 'rough music', a noisy form of punishment, than they do about the many other forms of more conventional music that made this inversionary concept meaningful ('rough music' earns three references in Reay's index).[54] Indeed, there has been no major survey of English popular music since the publication in 1859 of William Chappell's quaintly titled *Popular Music of the Olden Time.* Chappell's work, though still immensely useful, was driven primarily by a desire to repel the vile allegation 'that the English have no national music' and also characterised by a fairly inventive attitude towards some of the relevant source materials.[55] It is perhaps time to think afresh.

The primacy of the visual in our own culture provides one possible explanation for the general neglect of music by historians, but there are also several others. Perhaps it has been assumed that only those with a thorough musical training should attempt the task. This attitude is understandable but regrettable. Few of us would accept the argument that only the religiously committed should write about the history of religion, or that only witches should address witchcraft, and we should not therefore be prepared to leave all consideration of music to musicians or musicologists. It will be noted that much of what follows deals with attitudes to music and with the many roles it played within English culture, rather than with the technicalities of notes, clefs and keys. To some, this may be a disappointment, but to others the untapped potential of the subject will, I hope, be an ear-opener.

Perhaps historians have also neglected music because it is famously difficult to write about. The power of music, said John Taylor in the mid-seventeenth century, could not adequately be captured in mere words. Taylor resolved to do his best but was painfully aware that he

[54] Barry Reay, *Popular Cultures in England, 1550–1750* (London: Longman, 1998). On rough music, see below, pp. 45–8.

[55] William Chappell, *Popular Music of the Olden Time*, 2 vols. (London: Cramer, Beale & Chappell, 1859), vol. I, p. vii.

would inevitably fall short, 'And run my wit on ground like ship on shelfe: / For musicks praise consisteth in it selfe.' In other words, only music could articulate its wonders, and hearing was believing. Musical history, remarked George Wither in 1619, was particularly challenging: 'For, beleeve me, I am of opinion, that among the infinite and innumerable multitudes of those things which in the world have perished or suffered any kinde of alteration, there is nothing whose losse is more irrecoverable, or whose change is lesse demonstrable, then that of Musicke: for it consisteth of inarticulate sounds.' This is not an argument that can easily be refuted, and the challenge is indeed a daunting one. Music, in another of Wither's intimidating phrases, was 'onely sounds formed of ayre, and vanishing without impression'.[56]

Fortunately, however, music does not always evaporate quite so completely. Admittedly, the phenomenon dies even as it is born (quite unlike a picture) but we are not invariably left with nothing. Wither was alleging in particular the futility of seeking to reclaim the ancient psalm tunes that had been used by the early church. These had not been written down and consequently could never be known (he was also promoting his own plans to publish newly composed melodies for ecclesiastical use). In Wither's own day, however, an increasing quantity of music was in fact being recorded on paper. Among the elaborate and original compositions traditionally studied by musicologists we also find a wealth of popular melodies drawn from balladry, psalmody and dance. Frequently, these tunes in their written forms were attired in courtly finery, and thus a degree of imagination must be applied as we seek to return them to plainer settings. This is a speculative task but not an impossible one, and written versions of hundreds of common melodies form one of the principal sources available to us. Moreover, music was widespread, marketable, powerful and controversial. This combination generated many other forms of documentation, and by exploiting the full range it is possible to counter Wither's strategically bleak assessment. In the pages that follow, information will be gleaned from ballad texts, chapbooks, plays, pamphlets, sermons, music manuals, visitation articles, woodcut pictures, paintings, court records, wills, inventories, diaries, manuscript notebooks and several forms of financial accounts (parochial, civic and domestic). It will, I hope, be demonstrated conclusively that early modern music, though formed of mere air, nevertheless made quite an impression.

The uncertain interest of historians in music means that we must look and listen elsewhere for inspiration. There is much to be learned, for

[56] Taylor, *All the Workes*, vol. II, p. 397; George Wither, *A Preparation to the Psalter* (London, 1619), p. 80.

example, from recent writing on traditional, folk and popular music as it developed in later periods.[57] Similarly stimulating are the studies of musical understanding produced by psychologists and neuro-scientists.[58] Ethnomusicologists and philosophers of music have also provided much food for thought.[59] On early modern England more specifically, the most important contributions to the understanding of music have tended to appear in disciplines other than history. In consequence, the present work also draws ideas and information from a variety of quarters: the work of literary scholars on balladry, psalmody, music in plays and poetry, the role of dance in Renaissance drama, music-making in particular localities and the acoustic environment more generally; anthropological studies of the morris dance; and the often fascinating but little-known works by antiquarians and campanologists on the history of bells and bell-ringing.[60]

Not surprisingly, however, the landmark texts have been produced by musicologists. The studies of early modern musicians published by Walter Woodfill in 1953 and David Price in 1981 have proved deservedly influential. Their findings may in some respects require revision, but the significance of their work is not in doubt.[61] Other classic studies emerged in the decades that separated these two contributions. Claude M. Simpson,

[57] See, for example, Roy Palmer, *The Sound of History: Songs and Social Comment* (London: Pimlico, 1988) and Keith Negus, *Popular Music in Theory* (Cambridge: Polity Press, 1996). Other important examples are listed in the bibliography (Boyes, Bronson, Manuel and Thomson).

[58] See, for example, Daniel Levitin, *This is Your Brain on Music: Understanding a Human Obsession* (London: Atlantic Books, 2007). Additional material can be found in the bibliography (Halpern, Dowling, Narmour, North et al., Smith).

[59] For important surveys, see Alan P. Merriam, *The Anthropology of Music* (Evanston: Northwestern University Press, 1964) and Peter Kivy, *An Introduction to the Philosophy of Music* (Oxford: Clarendon Press, 2002). Further works are listed in the bibliography under Blacking, Merriam and Wade (ethnomusicology) and under Reimer and Wright (a philosophical anthology).

[60] See, for example: Natascha Würzbach, *The Rise of the English Street Ballad, 1550–1650* (Cambridge: Cambridge University Press, 1990); Hannibal Hamlin, *Psalm Culture and Early Modern English Literature* (Cambridge: Cambridge University Press, 2004); Diane Kelsey McColley, *Poetry and Music in Seventeenth-century England* (Cambridge: Cambridge University Press, 1997); Alan Brissenden, *Shakespeare and the Dance* (London: Macmillan, 1981); Elizabeth Baldwin, *Paying the Piper: Music in Pre-1642 Cheshire, Early Drama, Art and Music Monograph Series* 29 (Kalamazoo: Medieval Institute Publications, Western Michigan University, 2002); Bruce R. Smith, *The Acoustic World of Early Modern England: Attending to the O-factor* (Chicago: University of Chicago Press, 1999); John Forrest, *The History of Morris Dancing, 1458–1750* (Cambridge: James Clarke, 1999); J. S. Sanderson (ed.), *Change Ringing: The History of an English Art*, 3 vols. (Cambridge: Central Council of Church Bell Ringers, 1987). Additional texts from each of these disciplines are included in the bibliography.

[61] Walter W. Woodfill, *Musicians in English Society from Elizabeth to Charles I* (Princeton: Princeton University Press, 1953); Price, *Patrons and Musicians.*

though employed as a literary scholar, was clearly a musicologist at heart (he held degrees both in music and in English). His astonishingly useful book *The British Broadside Ballad and its Music* first appeared in 1966. Simpson made expert use of both the strings to his academic bow in providing a systematic and exhaustive analysis of hundreds of melodies. In 1976, David Munrow published *Instruments of the Middle Ages and Renaissance*, a work that encompassed not only the lutes and viols that were well known in courtly circles but the pipes, tabors and jew's harps that rang more regularly in the ears of the poor. This book was followed shortly by Nicholas Temperley's celebrated two-volume study, *The Music of the English Parish Church*. This rich and resourceful survey has proved exceptionally valuable as a launch pad for early modern historians with an interest in psalm-singing, organs and choirs (but not bells). A little more recently, David Wulstan and Ian Spink have both published stimulating essays on the most familiar forms of music-making, including bell-ringing and the cries of market traders. Lastly, Ian Woodfield's innovative study *English Musicians in the Age of Exploration* was distinctive in paying close attention to instrumentalists of all sorts and in providing a wealth of fascinating evidence on the role of music in military encounters and international diplomacy.[62]

From the perspective of a social historian, however, musicology is not without its limitations. The discipline has traditionally concentrated on written compositions that are judged to be of high aesthetic value. Undoubtedly, the situation is beginning to change, but such traditions leave their mark. In musicology, the figure of the great composer still looms large, often casting a grey shadow over the demographic majority. Common dance music, balladry, congregational psalmody and bell-ringing have generally failed to register, either because they were primarily aural or because they have not been judged worthy of attention (beauty, we might note, is in the ear of the beholder). The focus upon written notes has also led, at times, to the neglect of the wider, deeper contexts within which early modern music wove its spell. Aristocratic patronage has been well studied, but the same cannot be said of support for music at the village level, nor of the ways in which music intersected with the other general concerns of the contemporary population (religion, gender,

[62] Claude M. Simpson, *The British Broadside Ballad and its Music* (New Brunswick: Rutgers University Press, 1966); David Munrow, *Instruments of the Middle Ages and Renaissance* (Oxford: Oxford University Press, 1976); Nicholas Temperley, *The Music of the English Parish Church*, 2 vols. (Cambridge: Cambridge University Press, 1979); David Wulstan, *Tudor Music* (London: J. M. Dent, 1985), ch. 3; Spink, 'Music and Society'; Woodfield, *English Musicians*.

morality, social relations, politics, health and happiness, for example). Typically, the articles that appear in musicological journals are very specific in their focus, concentrating tightly on particular instruments, named individuals, musical forms or privileged physical contexts. Only rarely does attention stray towards the rich and varied music of the early modern majority. Despite the signs of a shift in perspective, something still seems to dissuade most musicologists from thinking more broadly about the social history of music. Noel O'Regan noted, in a review of several general books on Renaissance music, that they all concentrated on 'a pretty restricted corner of high-level music-making, ignoring the peripheries of various sorts'. Lowly musicians, he observed, appeared on the front of Allan Atlas's *Renaissance Music* but hardly at all within the text (a familiar discrepancy, it seems). Of course, to term the music of the majority a 'periphery' is questionable in itself, but O'Regan's critical reaction to the priorities of his own discipline was compelling nonetheless. 'What we need', he went on, 'is a truly subversive history of the period to lay alongside these, one in which (for example) Atlas's piping and dancing peasants could come off the dust-cover and tell their stories too. As we enter the new century, our increased awareness of music's multi-facetedness should encourage new approaches to writing its story.'[63]

The pages that follow may not subvert the existing order but they will at least invert the established prejudice, concentrating primarily upon the musical lives of the demographic majority and upon forms of music that have not often attracted the attention merited by their ubiquity. Of course, this perspective will generate difficulties of its own. The musical worlds of artisan and aristocrat cannot, for example, be cut apart with anything resembling a clean incision. The interest lies as much in exploring the interaction between them as in delineating their differences. Moreover, we must often guess at how music sounded, relying for clues upon contemporary commentary that was highly charged or upon mediated sources that recorded aural forms of music in written form. And even if we knew exactly what most people heard we would still be left wondering about how they listened.[64] Our own relationship with music is very different from that of our forebears. Audio recording enables us to possess specific

[63] Noel O'Regan, 'Histories of Renaissance Music for a New Century', *Music and Letters* 82 (2001), 280–1.

[64] On this subject, see Smith, *Acoustic World*, pp. 287–341; John Milsom, 'Music, Politics and Society', in Robert Tittler and Norman L. Jones (eds.), *A Companion to Tudor Britain* (Oxford: Blackwell, 2004), pp. 503–4; and Shai Burstyn, 'In Quest of the Period Ear', *Early Music* 25 (1997), 692–702.

performances (or at least to feel as if we do). The world's finest practitioners, dead or alive, can be carried around in our pockets and stirred to action at our whim. Ear-pieces enable us to treat music as something deeply private and thoroughly anti-social. Historic melodies and harmonies that were designed for social consumption can now be heard inside a single head. Music, in one sense, is thus a method of withdrawal: perhaps we all need time away from the incessant bustle of modern life. Our world, indeed, is much, much noisier than that of our ancestors. In early modern England, trumpet calls ranked as one of the loudest sounds that humans produced, and it was said that even the music of a simple, solitary pipe could carry for a mile. On 28 May 1672, people in landlocked Northamptonshire reportedly heard the firing of cannons in the North Sea as the English and the Dutch did battle at Solebay, more than one hundred miles to the east. Nowadays, the drone of traffic, on land and in the air, would make this an impossibility.[65] So music can be an escape into solitude, but in the electronic age it is also inescapable. We cannot venture into society without hearing it, and some of music's most devoted advocates plead for a reduction in its use, fearing that saturation reduces its power over us. Our experience of music distinguishes us from almost all the people who have lived on earth before us. 'Live' music is sometimes considered to be under threat. How bewildering would the epoch of the iPod look and sound to an individual from the early modern era, an age in which all forms of music – echoes excepted – were, by definition, 'live'? Conversely, how challenging will it be for us to imagine what music may have meant to the people of the past?

[65] *The Figure of Nine* (London, 1662), unpaginated; *The Diary of Thomas Isham*, ed. Gyles Isham (Peterborough: Gregg International Publishers, 1971), p. 115. For a much fuller discussion of these issues, see Smith, *Acoustic World*, pp. 49–52.

1 The power of music

The idea that music holds influence over the minds, bodies and souls of those who hear it is surely one of the universal features of human culture.[1] During the sixteenth and seventeenth centuries, the power of music flowed through English society with considerable force, and was experienced in one form or another by people in all walks of life. Music bound communities, promoted good citizenship and mediated between God and humankind. For Henry Peacham, music was one of 'the fountaines of our lives good and happinesse: since it is a principall meanes of glorifying our mercifull Creator, it heightens our devotion, it gives delight and ease to our travailes, it expelleth sadnesse and heavinesse of Spirit, preserveth people in concord and amitie, allaieth fiercenesse and anger; and lastly, is the best Phisicke for many melancholy diseases'. To others, the power of music was primarily negative and extreme caution was required. Between 1560 and 1660, a succession of moralists and godly authors warned that music could all too easily become the servant of Satan, corrupting and destroying the minds of listeners. Most forms of popular music, alleged Philip Stubbes in 1583, were 'inticements to wantonness and sin'. Fiddlers, said H.S. in 1658, 'poyson the world and poor people'.[2] Such writers warned that many persons found worldly music far more appealing than church attendance, and the consequences were spiritually disastrous. It was a message that carried some weight, and official efforts to restrict the activities of itinerant minstrels in the period demonstrate that musical anxiety was not the preserve of a zealous, jealous minority. One of the early modern period's great cultural debates centred on the power of music for good and ill, and it generated many of the sources under consideration in the pages below.

This chapter presents an introduction to the web of ideas and assumptions that conditioned the experience of music for early modern men and women. Of course, remarks concerning the power of music were made

[1] For a remarkable survey, see Peter Fletcher, *World Musics in Context* (Oxford: Oxford University Press, 2001).

[2] Henry Peacham, *The Compleat Gentleman* (London, 1622), p. 104; Philip Stubbes, *The Anatomie of Abuses* (London, 1583), preface; H.S., *To the Musicioners, the Harpers, the Minstrels, the Singers, the Dancers, the Persecutors* (London, 1658), p. 8.

most clearly and frequently by those who were fully literate, highly educated and unusually committed (whether they loved or loathed the art). The cultural historian is often reliant on people who had the motive and the means to make themselves heard across the ages. It would be a mistake, however, to assume that ideas about music's influence over body and soul, and indeed its connections with cosmic harmony, were the preserve of those who had attended university. The evidence discussed in this chapter has been drawn not only from expensive printed literature, but from ballads, chapbooks, court cases, sermons, speeches, notebooks, diaries, inventories and plays. Ideas, like minstrels and their melodies, got around, and it is worth making the obvious point that William Shakespeare and John Taylor, whose writings are full of musical allusion, were both men of non-gentle origins who had not been to college. They may have been exceptionally talented, but their knowledge of musical ideas demonstrates the existence of channels of communication that were available to others too.

Formal schooling provided one of these channels, but other cultural activities were probably more significant. The theatre is a particularly good example, and provides the best evidence we have that sophisticated ideas about the power of music circulated among a substantial cross-section of the population. Such ideas were part of the common stock upon which Shakespeare and his contemporaries drew with impressive regularity. Alternative channels existed too, but the traffic that passed through them is largely inaudible to historians. Choirboys and cathedral singing men, for example, were by no means wholly isolated from the world beyond the cloisters, and the music they sang 'on the outside' included catches that spoke of music's unifying power, such as those recorded in 1580 by Thomas Lant (who probably received his education alongside the choirboys at Gloucester Cathedral).[3] The minstrels of Staffordshire and surrounding counties heard an annual address praising the power of music, and they spent the rest of the year travelling around among the general population. Many of them had probably served apprenticeships with established musicians, and this was another of the

[3] Thomas Lant's roll of catches, MS Rowe 1, King's College, Cambridge. For further discussion, see below, pp. 58, 72, 193–5. For some related comments, see James Saunders, 'Music and Moonlighting: The Cathedral Choirmen of Early Modern England 1558–1649', in Fiona Kisby (ed.), *Music and Musicians in Renaissance Cities and Towns* (Cambridge: Cambridge University Press, 2001), pp. 157–66, and Fiona Kisby, 'Courtiers in the Community: The Musicians of the Royal Household Chapel in Early Tudor Westminster', in Benjamin Thompson (ed.), *The Reign of Henry VIII: Proceedings of the 1993 Harlaxton Symposium, Harlaxton Medieval Studies* 5 (1995), pp. 229–60.

avenues along which musical ideas could travel. In London, the Gresham College music lectureship, established in 1596, was not designed purely for the benefit of an educated elite. The twice-weekly public lectures included theoretical and practical elements, and the first incumbent, John Bull, was permitted to speak in English rather than Latin.[4] And when English parishioners of all sorts and conditions sang metrical psalms in congregational unison during the seventeenth century, they learned again and again that the right sort of music was profoundly pleasing to Almighty God.

It was only towards the latter end of the early modern period that it became a little more common for writers to scoff at the power of music or to express scepticism regarding its alleged effects on earthly beings and matter. In 1698, the Royal Society asked John Wallis to investigate 'The strange effects reported of musick in former times'. His conclusions, though far from dismissive of music's power, sounded a note of doubt regarding classical claims of extraordinary harmonious influence. Many of these, argued Wallis, were 'highly Hyperbolical and next door to Fabulous'. Seventy years later, the pseudonymous Joel Collier went much further than this, and published an uproarious satire on Dr Burney's famous musical travel journal. Collier mocked his targets mercilessly, poking fun at all who followed the fashion for Italian music and talked obsessively about the musical effects achieved by the ancient Greeks. Along the way, Collier encountered many music-addicts, including a man called 'Mr. Eccho' who had forgotten how to communicate except with his fiddle, and a Signor Manselli who could fart musically and who advised Collier that a man must be castrated in order to 'fathom all the mysteries of the art'.[5]

The rise of scorn and scepticism owed something to the development during the seventeenth and eighteenth centuries of an experimental brand of science that emphasised observation, measurement and precise physical explanation, distrusting the more speculative theorising that had characterised musical philosophy since classical times. Descartes led the way, wilfully turning his back on classical, medieval and Renaissance thought concerning the place of music within the cosmos. In England, Francis Bacon urged that the science of sound be investigated empirically. As a

[4] Speech delivered at Tutbury, D4530/76/8, DRO. On the Gresham lectureship, see Price, *Patrons and Musicians*, pp. 41–2.

[5] *Memoirs of the Royal Society*, vol. III, pp. 291–3; John Bicknell *alias* Joel Collier, *Musical Travels through England* (London, 1774). In 1764–5, a famous Italian castrato named Giovanni Manzuoli performed in London (I am grateful to Ian Woodfield for this information).

consequence, many English writings about music tended to become more utilitarian, concentrating on the physics of its influence rather than on its grander, cosmological aspects. In the latter part of the seventeenth century, scholars worked on sound production, consonance and dissonance, vibrations, echoes and temperament, generally leaving the 'music of the spheres' to poets.[6] It has been argued that, even in poetry, references to cosmic harmony became increasingly superficial as the focus of attention shifted towards the purely emotional effects of music on humans. Thus, the influence of Plato retreated, and references to universal harmony became more and more rare.[7] Consequently, individuals who still made overblown remarks about 'the mysteries of the art' began to sound laughable to the more scientifically minded of their contemporaries.

On the other hand, satire and scientific scepticism represented only one strain within musical thought during the seventeenth and eighteenth centuries, and several writers remained willing to assert the power of music in extravagant terms. In 1752, for example, Charles Avison, an organist from Newcastle upon Tyne, argued that music was 'by the Constitution of Man ... of mighty efficacy in working both on his Imaginations and his Passions. The Force of Harmony, or Melody alone, is wonderful on the Imagination.'[8] Indeed, it was the continuing existence of such arguments that made Joel Collier's outrageous satire possible and, in his mind at least, necessary. Musical theorists of a scientific bent may have begun to look down their noses at Plato, but not all commentators followed their lead, as we shall hear. Throughout the period, classically rooted ideas and assumptions about the mysterious power of music were alive and throbbing.[9]

[6] These trends are discussed in John Hollander, *The Untuning of the Sky: Ideas of Music in English Poetry, 1500–1700* (Princeton: Princeton University Press, 1961), pp. 172–9; Rosamond McGuinness, 'Writings about Music', in Spink (ed.), *The Seventeenth Century*, pp. 406–20; Rebecca Herissone, *Music Theory in Seventeenth-century England* (Oxford: Oxford University Press, 2000), pp. 1–4. On the relationship between different branches of musical knowledge, see Gouk, *Music, Science and Natural Magic.*

[7] See especially Hollander, *Untuning of the Sky.*

[8] Charles Avison, *An Essay on Musical Expression* (London, 1752), p. 2.

[9] The essays of Gretchen Ludke Finney make this point in stimulating detail and are still worth careful reading: 'Ecstasy and Music in Seventeenth-century England', *Journal of the History of Ideas* 8 (1947), 153–87; '"Organical Musick" and Ecstasy', *Journal of the History of Ideas* 8 (1947), 273–93; 'Music: A Book of Knowledge in Renaissance England', *Studies in the Renaissance* 6 (1959), 36–63; 'Music, Mirth and Galenic Tradition in England', in J. A. Mazzeo (ed.), *Reason and Imagination: Studies in the History of Ideas, 1699–1800* (New York: Columbia University Press, 1962), pp. 143–54. See also Jamie James's grand survey, *The Music of the Spheres* (London: Abacus, 1995).

Even in our own age – 'eye-led', 'text-bound' and drowned in sound – music retains its power over us, and no simple narrative of an idea in decline across the centuries will suffice.[10] Nowadays, many people still achieve their deepest states of relaxation through listening to music, and some would doubtless argue that portable music machines, complete with earphones, are a means towards the intensification of our interaction with music. Many contemporary pop songs contain lyrics alleging the power of music and rhythm. An entire category of music is labelled 'soul'. Music therapy is employed increasingly in the treatment of those whose minds are disturbed or unstable. The music of Mozart, we are told, lowers the blood pressure, raises the pain threshold and strengthens the immune system. His sublime compositions render school pupils more attentive and dairy cows more productive. Modern shoppers unconsciously adjust their purchasing patterns in response to the types of music played in supermarkets, and it has been reported that vandalism on the Newcastle metro was recently reduced by the simple technique of broadcasting classical music (particularly Delius) through vulnerable portions of the system. Ancient musical theory would doubtless have attributed this effect to the soothing power of harmony over the bodies and souls of savages, but Chief Inspector Allan Curry of the North Shields police – no Platonist – proposed a different interpretation: 'They just couldn't stand it.'[11]

Explaining music's power

There exists today a substantial and complex body of literature in which scholars from various disciplines – acoustics, cognitive science and philosophy, for example – investigate the processes by which music affects us. This is not the place to attempt a thorough synthesis of this material, but a number of critical propositions clearly deserve our attention. Firstly, the susceptibility of humans to the influence of music has something to do with the ways in which rhythm, melody and harmony connect with our general experience of physical and mental life. Music may have its origins

[10] The quotations are from Walter Ong, *Orality and Literacy: The Technologizing of the Word* (1982; London: Routledge, 1990), p. 156.

[11] Don Campbell, *The Mozart Effect* (London: HarperCollins, 2001), pp. 14, 15–17, 67–9, 72–3, 224; A. C. North et al., 'In-store Music Affects Product Choice', *Nature* 390.6656 (1997), p. 132; Michael Smith, 'Metro Hooligans are Sent Packing by Delius', *Electronic Telegraph* (30 January 1998), www.telegraph.co.uk/htmlContent.jhtml?html=/archive, last accessed 20 June 2005.

in the non-verbal dialogue of mother and baby, and it reminds us at some deeply subconscious level of the natural and essential rhythms of life: hearts beating, lungs breathing, feet walking, bodies copulating. Moreover, a musical performance is built around the playing-out of changes that occur through time and involve movement, differences of pace, the raising of expectations, conflict and resolution. Music is also transient, for when a rendition is over there is nothing left but the memory. In these fundamental characteristics, music is unlike any visual art form of the pre-cinematic era. It presents to us a 'tonal analogue of emotive life'.[12] It stimulates the passions because it also simulates them.

Secondly, different musical intervals, melodic sequences and harmonic combinations of notes have demonstrable physical effects on our bodies. Musical vibrations of the air set up sound waves that are conveyed – via the auditory canal, the ear drum, the three tiny bones of the middle ear and a membrane known as the oval window – to the fluid-filled inner ear. Here the sound vibrations are sorted by frequency, converted into electrical impulses and sent along various neural pathways until, eventually, they reach the auditory cortex of the brain. Nearly all regions of the brain are hereafter involved in the processing of musical sound, and the precise locations of activity depend on the precise nature of the stimulus. Music affects the production of neurochemicals, and can thus lead to measurable changes in pulse rate, blood pressure, digestive processes, body temperature and muscle tonicity. Our responses to particular combinations of notes are influenced by a complicated mixture of innate and cultural features, but we all seem to perceive some as consonant and pleasant, others as dissonant and unsettling. Octaves and fifths are the most consonant, while the semitone, augmented fourth and major seventh are unquestionably dissonant. These perceptions are connected to the complex patterns of harmonically related frequency components – partials or overtones – that each note contains, beyond the single sound that we register consciously. Where the partials lie close together, they will set up a pulsing effect which we perceive as dissonant. Patterns of overtones may also help to explain why we hear the interval of a major third as bright and

[12] Susanne K. Langer, *Feeling and Form: A Theory of Art* (New York: Charles Schribner's Sons, 1953), p. 27; Monroe C. Beardsley, 'Understanding Music', in Kingsley Price (ed.), *On Criticizing Music: Five Philosophical Perspectives* (Baltimore: Johns Hopkins University Press, 1981), p. 70; Roger Sessions, *The Musical Experience of Composer, Performer, Listener* (Princeton: Princeton University Press, 1950), pp. 12–17. For an excellent synthesis of key texts in the philosophy of music, see Bennet Reimer and Jeffrey E. Wright (eds.), *On the Nature of Musical Experience* (Evanston: University Press of Colorado, 1992).

happy, but that of a minor third as sad and subdued.[13] In both cases, we respond via our ears, brains and bodies, for music is a physiological business.

Thirdly, nearly all of us are capable of complex automatic cognitive processing of musical stimuli, even if we consider ourselves thoroughly unmusical. The knowledge that we apply to this task is predominantly procedural rather than declarative. In other words, it is the kind of knowledge that we cannot easily articulate, but which is deeply embedded, automatically applied and absolutely vital in shaping our responses to music.[14] Some of it is innate, but much of it is built up steadily as we progress through life within a particular culture. Modern society is awash with people who insist upon their own musical ineptitude, and yet recent studies have revealed that ordinary listeners are 'remarkably adept at classifying music' and have a 'robust' sense of melody. They can identify changes made to the rhythm, mode and contour of tunes played to them in subtly different guises. With a little encouragement they can distinguish between different musical intervals. They can understand the patterns underlying a piece of music, something that helps them to develop expectations about future developments within that piece. This, in turn, allows them to feel the music emotionally. Typically, they know and can recognise hundreds of melodies. They can assess the emotional content of a tune according to a combination of musical factors (pitch, rhythm and tempo, for example). They can even infer the mode (major or minor) of a piece of music in the absence of explicit harmonic indicators, something which once again reveals the common ability of listeners to project their knowledge beyond what they are actually hearing.[15] As they get to know a

[13] John R. Pierce, *The Science of Musical Sound* (New York: W. H. Freeman, 1983), pp. 83–4, 102–6, 208–9; Reimer and Wright (eds.), *On the Nature of Musical Experience*, p. 129; Levitin, *This is Your Brain on Music*, pp. 85–7, 191–2.

[14] E. Narmour, 'Music Expectation by Cognitive Rule-mapping', *Music Perception* 17 (2000), 330–1; W. Jay Dowling, 'Procedural and Declarative Knowledge in Music Cognition and Education', in T. J. Tighe and W. Jay Dowling (eds.), *Psychology and Music: The Understanding of Melody and Rhythm* (Hillsdale, NJ: Erlbaum, 1993), p. 6.

[15] Tighe and Dowling (eds.), *Psychology and Music*, pp. 1–4; Paul von Hippel, 'Questioning a Melodic Archetype: Do Listeners Use Gap-fill to Classify Melodies?', *Music Perception* 18 (2000), 139; Lola L. Cuddy, 'Melody Comprehension and Tonal Structure', in Tighe and Dowling (eds.), *Psychology and Music*, p. 19; Andrea R. Halpern, James C. Bartlett and W. Jay Dowling, 'Perception of Mode, Rhythm and Contour in Unfamiliar Melodies: Effects of Age and Experience', *Music Perception* 15 (1998), 335–55; J. David Smith et al., 'What Child is This? What Interval was That? Familiar Tunes and Music Perception in Novice Listeners', *Cognition* 52 (1994), 23–54; Narmour, 'Music Expectation', 336; E. Glenn Schellenberg et al., 'Perceiving Emotion in Melody: Interactive Effects of Pitch and Rhythm', *Music Perception* 18 (2000), 155–71; Piel G. Vos and Paul P. Verkaart, 'Inference of Mode in Melodies', *Music Perception* 17 (1999), 223–39.

piece of music more intimately, they process it more richly and find it more aesthetically pleasing. And they do all this without thinking.

Finally, the power of music over humans can be related to the extraneous associations that individual listeners bring to a performance or a recording. These associations might be suggested by the title of a piece (for example, Vivaldi's *Four Seasons* or Elton John's 'Song for Guy') or by imitative compositional devices used within the music (bells, birdsong, thunder and so on). Alternatively, such associations may develop out of the listener's personal experience of a piece of music that is heard repeatedly. It is a modern commonplace that a familiar musical composition can transport us back in time, conjuring up a moment or phase during which it played a significant role in our lives ('they're playing our song'). Other pieces of music may remind us of a film, a nation or a brand of jeans. For most of us, such associations are extremely important in our responses to music, and many people have experienced the process by which a musical cue can generate an emotional response even before the precise association can be clearly identified. It is curious, therefore, that musical philosophers have tended to be rather dismissive of this dimension of music's power, arguing instead that emotional meaning is generated first and foremost by the music itself rather than by external associations.[16]

Writers of the sixteenth and seventeenth centuries anticipated some of these perceptions. John Case, for example, understood that music and the emotions mirrored one another in their movements. 'Surely affections dance after pipes', he remarked, '& being themselves but motions do by a naturall kind of propension apply themselves to Musick, whose efficacy stands wholy upon motions.' Descartes speculated about the power of extra-musical associations.[17] Lower on the social hierarchy, milkmaids knew by instinct and experiment that singing was good for milk yields. In many respects, however, early modern commentators adopted a tone and proposed arguments that are rarely deployed by modern scientists. Many shared the bafflement of Benedick in *Much Ado about Nothing*: 'Is it not strange that sheep's guts should hale souls out of men's bodies?' Some registered their puzzlement almost with a note of joy. In 1622, Henry Peacham was thrilled at music's capacity to 'amaze us', and asked happily 'who can shew us the reason why two Basons, Bowles, Brasse pots, or the

[16] James Mursell, *Education for Musical Growth* (Boston: Ginn and Company, 1948), pp. 35–8; Leonard B. Meyer, *Emotion and Meaning in Music* (Chicago: University of Chicago Press, 1956), p. 4; Reimer and Wright (eds.), *On the Nature of Musical Experience*, pp. 111, 122.

[17] Case, *Praise of Musicke*, p. 35; René Descartes, *Oeuvres*, ed. Adam et Tannery (Paris, 1902), p. 134, quoted by Hollander, *Untuning of the Sky*, p. 179.

like of the same bignesse; the one being full, the other empty, shall, striken, be a just Diapason in sound one to the either [sic]?'[18] Others were only too pleased to admit that music crept 'miraculously' and by 'stealth', finding its way along 'a certein secret passage into mens Soules'.[19] The primary reason for such blissful ignorance was that the mystery of musical effects was an inspiring and reassuring reminder to early modern minds that God was the author of all. The creative involvement of the Almighty was assumed by authors throughout the period, including those of a more scientific disposition. In 1694, for example, William Holder was preoccupied with the task of finding physical explanations for the properties of sound, but the necessity of resorting on occasion to speculation caused him to adore God and praise 'His Wisdom, in ordering the Nature of Harmony in so wonderfull a manner, that it surpasseth our Understanding'.[20]

There was more to this line of thought, however, than the basic assumption that God was the 'Founder and Donor' of all music.[21] Numerous commentators drew extensively upon classical thought in arguing that the creation of the universe had been in essence a musical enterprise. According to Humphrey Sydenham, 'the whole course of nature is but a Harmony; the order of superiour and inferiour things, a melodious Consort', and Sir Peter Leycester, making private notes during the 1660s, spoke approvingly of Plato's argument that 'the order & fabricke of the world, the motion of the Orbes and Starres, could not be Composed without Musicke'.[22] The 'music of the spheres' was an ancient concept, strongly associated in western philosophy with Pythagoras and Boethius. In its revised Christian form, it clearly remained something of a commonplace during the early modern period, despite Francis Bacon's scepticism concerning the 'Mysticall Subtleties' that had dominated musical theory for so long (see Figure 1.1).[23] References to cosmic music can be found in a wide range of literary and manuscript sources. When the pamphleteer John Taylor heard music in a chapel in Germany, he remarked that the

[18] William Shakespeare, *Much Ado about Nothing*, ed. A. R. Humphreys, *Arden Shakespeare* (London: Thomson Learning, 2003), p. 135; Peacham, *Compleat Gentleman*, p. 104.

[19] Thomas Naish, *A Sermon Preach'd at the Cathedral Church of Sarum, Novemb. 22. 1700* (London, 1701), pp. 14, 21; Thomas Wright, *The Passions of the Minde in Generall* (1601; London, 1604), ch. 5, section 2. The passage containing this phrase was also transcribed into an Elizabethan manuscript commonplace book now held in the Folger Library, Washington DC (MS V.a. 381).

[20] Holder, *A Treatise*, pp. 202–3. The author was both a Fellow of the Royal Society and Sub-Dean of the Chapel Royal.

[21] Ibid., p. 203.

[22] Sydenham, *Sermons upon Solemne Occasions*, p. 17; DLT/B11, fo. 25r, ChRO.

[23] Francis Bacon, *Sylva Sylvarum* (London, 1627), p. 35.

MVSICA.
MVSICK amongst the spheares first heard to sound
was heere on earth, by one TERPANDER found.
But of all kinds that heart, or eare reioyce,
none sweeter, then that Echo the from the voyce.

Figure 1.1. Apologists for music argued regularly that its origins lay in the harmonious motions of the planets. Terpander, the famous Greek musician of the seventh century BC, is here credited with the earthly discovery of music. The human voice was the purest of instruments, and fine singing continued to echo the music of the spheres. © Trustees of the British Museum, Prints and Drawings, 1870,0514.1141, George Glover, 'Musica' from *The Seven Liberal Arts* (London, 1625–35).

voices and instruments 'all strike up together, with such a glorious and delicious harmony, as if the Angellicall musicke of the Sphears were descended into that earthly Tabernacle' (the habit of treating heavenly angels and astronomical spheres as if they all belonged to a single consort was not unique to Taylor). And when the minstrels of the honour of Tutbury were addressed at their annual court, they were assured that the antiquity of music was 'noe less than that of the whole Creacon', every part of which was constructed in harmony, 'acording to the doctrine of the Ancients who observ'd and treated of the Musick of the Spheres'.[24]

Shakespeare's plays contain numerous references to cosmic harmony, evidently a concept with which he and his audiences were thoroughly familiar. In *The Merchant of Venice*, for example, Lorenzo summons the musicians outside in order to soothe Jessica's anxiety. Irresistibly, he says,

Here will we sit, and let the sounds of music
Creep in our ears. Soft stillness and the night
Become the touches of sweet harmony.
Sit, Jessica. Look how the floor of heaven
Is thick inlaid with patens of bright gold.
There's not the smallest orb which thou behold'st
But in his motion like an angel sings,
Still quiring to the young-eyed cherubims.[25]

Occasionally, writers sounded somewhat doubtful about the literal applicability of such a grand idea, but surprisingly few spoke out in clear denial. Not surprisingly, the 'new science' infiltrated deeply rooted patterns of thought only very slowly, except in the circles of its primary influence. Even at the universities, music students still learned primarily about the classical theories of music, consuming more Boethius than Bacon.[26]

Classical wisdom held that the concepts of proportion and sympathy were fundamental to an understanding of the harmonious universe. The proportionate relationships of all that existed lay at the heart of cosmic harmony, and Pythagoras and his followers argued that music was nothing but audible number. Ratios underlay all forms of harmony, whether cosmic or earthly, and the parallels between the number of known planets (with sun and moon) and the musical intervals that made up the octave were much more than coincidental. Pythagoras calculated that lyre strings tuned to consonant tones were proportionate to the distances between the planets.[27] Ideas about proportion in music and the universe were received and repeated with enthusiasm by musical scholars during the early

[24] Taylor, *All the Workes*, vol. III, p. 571; speech delivered at Tutbury, D1530/76/8 p. 4, DRO. For a fuller discussion of this institution, see below, pp. 92–4, 96–7.

[25] Shakespeare, *The Merchant of Venice*, ed. Jay L. Halio, *The Oxford Shakespeare* (Oxford: Oxford University Press, 1993), p. 215.

[26] McGuinness, 'Writings about Music', pp. 406–7; Carpenter, *Music in the Medieval and Renaissance Universities*, pp. 153–210.

[27] Bruce Pattison, *Music and Poetry of the English Renaissance* (London: Methuen, 1948), p. 1; Albert Seay, *Music in the Medieval World* (Englewood Cliffs: Prentice-Hall, 1965), p. 20; Smith,

modern period. Those with an interest in occult philosophy and mathematics were particularly devoted to this aspect of the Pythagorean tradition. When William Ingpen wrote *The Secrets of Numbers* in 1624, for example, he regarded music as an important part of his remit. Indeed, 'it is impossible the world should consist without it'. More generally, English musical commentators avoided mathematical detail, but retained an awareness that the numerical ordering of the universe was displayed in music. The music-lover who addressed the Tutbury minstrels at an unspecified date in the later seventeenth century was therefore on very familiar ground when he told his audience that all parts of creation existed in musical proportion and harmony.[28]

The proportionate nature of the created universe meant that it was also full of resonance. Heaven and earth were musically connected in many ways, and although the music of angels was generally no more accessible to human ears than that of the spheres, it nevertheless reverberated through the universe, striking up sympathetic reactions wherever it went. Earthly music, said Thomas Wright, 'resembleth in a certein manner the voyces & Harmonye of Heaven'. In 1586, Sir Philip Sidney languished on his deathbed in the Netherlands but managed to call with commendable lucidity for music 'to fashion and enfranchise his heavenly soul unto that everlasting harmony of angels, whereof these concords were a kinde of terrestriall echo'. Very occasionally, devout Christians were lucky enough to hear the real thing. One ballad, set to the tune of 'In summer time', recounted the death of an exemplary maiden in Padstow:

At her decease an harmony
Of Musick there was heard to sound.
Which ravisht all the standers by,
It did with sweetness so abound.
It pierc'd the earth and air also,
Yet no man knew from whence it came,
But each one said it came from heaven.[29]

For Thomas Browne, even the vulgar music of the tavern was touched by divinity: 'It is an Hieroglyphicall and shadowed lesson of the whole world'

Acoustic World, p. 294. In 1586, John Case discussed seven musical modes, 'answerable to the 7 planets' (*Praise of Musicke*, pp. 54–5).

28 William Ingpen, *The Secrets of Numbers* (London, 1624), p. 95; speech delivered at Tutbury, D4530/76/8, p. 4, DRO.

29 Wright, *Passions of the Minde*, ch. 5, section 2; Fulke Greville, *The Life of the Renowned Sir Philip Sidney* (London, 1651), p. 159; *Pepys Ballads*, vol. II, p. 55.

and a poignant reminder of 'the first Composer'. In John Donne's words, 'God made this whole world in such a uniformity, such a correspondency, such a concinnity of parts, as that it was an Instrument, perfectly in tune.' It was partly for this reason that so many of the metaphors used by Shakespeare in describing natural sounds were musical in conception.[30]

To many early modern minds, earthly music was audible proof of its unheard cosmic counterpart.[31] Authors were also fascinated by musical curiosities that seemed to reflect the correspondence between different created things: not only vibrating lute strings, but fishes that danced at the sound of music and buildings that 'answere to lowd & lofty musick & returne many of the sweete Notes by a grateful Eccho'.[32] In one Elizabethan satire the narrator stuffs two edible 'pillows' with the cooked ears of various animals. He applies these to his own ears, and suddenly finds himself able to hear the beautiful music of the spheres with astounding clarity (unfortunately, he can also hear every earthly sound being produced within a hundred-mile radius of London). This, of course, was not to be understood literally, yet it nevertheless echoed commonplace notions concerning resemblances and consequent influences. There were also anti-correspondences, contrasting sounds that simply could not be brought into sympathetic consonance. John Ferne recited the common argument that it was impossible to create harmony when harp strings of sheep gut were sounded in combination with those made of wolf gut: 'Be the musician never so cunning in his skil, yet can he not reconcile them to an unity and concord of sounds, so that the enmitie betweene them, seemeth not to dye with their bodies.'[33]

Sympathetic ideas also informed Sir Thomas Elyot's belief that 'the perfecte understanding of musike' was necessary 'for the better attaynynge

[30] Thomas Browne, *Religio Medici and Other Works*, ed. L. C. Martin (Oxford: Clarendon Press, 1964), p. 67; John Donne, *A Lent Sermon Preached at Whitehall, February 12, 1618* (London, 1619), quoted by V. A. Winn, 'A Bibliography of Contemporary Source Works for the Social History of English Music, 1524–1728', unpublished thesis for fellowship of the Library Association (1965), p. 266; see, for example, Shakespeare, *A Midsummer Night's Dream*, in *Complete Oxford Shakespeare*, p. 593. See also McColley, *Poetry and Music*, p. 8 (in seventeenth-century poetry, 'the "concent" between words and music reveals correspondences between cosmic design and the design of the mind'). On these and other related ideas, see Linda Phyllis Austern, 'Nature, Culture, Myth and the Musician in Early Modern England', *Journal of the American Musicological Association* 51 (1998), 1–48.

[31] Smith, *Acoustic World*, pp. 294–5. See also Finney, 'Music: A Book of Knowledge'.

[32] Speech delivered at Tutbury, D4530/76/8, pp. 12–13, DRO; Robert Burton, *The Anatomy of Melancholy* (Oxford, 1621), p. 373; Peacham, *Compleat Gentleman*, p. 104.

[33] William Baldwin, *A Marvelous Hystory Intitulede Beware the Cat* (London, 1584), C8r–D1v; John Ferne, *Blazon of Gentrie* (London, 1586), pt. 2, p. 41.

the knowledge of a publike weale'. Good music, like an ideal society, 'conteineth in it a perfect harmony'. A commonwealth, according to Robert Jones, was 'but a well tunde Song where all partes doe agree', and Andrew Marvell credited Oliver Cromwell with learning from the music of the skies how 'To tune this lower to that higher sphere'. Music was powerful indeed, and Thomas Mace believed that it could save the world. He claimed in 1676 that if children were properly taught the grounds of piety and music, then 'the vast Jarrings, and Dischording-untunablenesses, over-spreading the face of the whole Earth, might be much rectified, and put into Tune'.[34] Arguably, such ideas help to explain why some of the unfortunate children at Christ's Hospital were taught 'the Heavenly Science of Music' in an effort to 'make them worthy members both for the Church and the Commonweale' (more practically, musical proficiency might also provide them with a living).[35]

In 'rough music' or charivari – the ritual use of cacophonous sound in the punishment of moral offenders – the positive correspondence between social harmony and musical concord was deliberately flipped on its head, thereby suggesting that the ideas under discussion here had some form of currency far beyond learned London and the universities of England. Typically, angry neighbours would stage a procession or 'riding' within which their target, often in the guise of a more-or-less willing substitute, was mocked and abused (see Figure 1.2).[36] Such occasions were rich in visual symbolism and characterised by purposeful inversion (the individual who represented the target might, for example, be mounted backwards on a horse or horizontal staff). Aurally, the overturning of moral order was broadcast through the wild playing of assorted instruments, including

[34] Thomas Elyot, *The Boke Named the Governour* (London, 1531), fo. 24r (see also Case, *Praise of Musicke*, p. 67); Robert Jones, *Ultimum Vale or The Third Booke of Ayres* (1608), quoted by Winn, 'A Bibliography', p. 211; Andrew Marvell, 'The First Anniversary of the Government under O.C.', quoted in full by Hollander, *Untuning of the Sky*, p. 304; Mace, *Musick's Monument*, p. 12. See also Finney, 'Music: A Book of Knowledge'. In late sixteenth-century France, the connection between musical and political harmony was expressed with particular enthusiasm by Jean Bodin (see Hollander, *Untuning of the Sky*, p. 41).

[35] Pearce, *Annals of Christ's Hospital*, pp. 137–8.

[36] See David Underdown, *Revel, Riot and Rebellion* (Oxford: Oxford University Press, 1985), pp. 106–11; D. A. Johnson, '"Johnson is beaten!" A Case of "Rough Music" at West Bromwich in 1611', *Transactions, Lichfield and South Staffordshire Archaeological and Historical Society* 25 (1985 for 1983–4), 31–4; Martin Ingram, 'Ridings, Rough Music and Mocking Rhymes in Early Modern England', in Barry Reay (ed.), *Popular Culture in Seventeenth-century England* (London: Routledge, 1988), pp. 166–97; E. P. Thompson, *Customs in Common* (Harmondsworth: Penguin, 1991), ch. 8. In general, these works pay little analytical attention to the musical aspects of rough music (but see Ingram, 'Ridings, Rough Music and Mocking Rhymes', p. 177).

Figure 1.2. The punitive power of rough music is apparent in Hogarth's depiction of a skimmington or riding. A hen-pecked husband is humiliated by the sounds of a horn, a bagpipe, a basin being beaten and a screeching cat. © Trustees of the British Museum, Prints and Drawings, S,2.12, William Hogarth, 'Hudibras Encounters the Skimmington' from *Hudibras* (London, 1726).

not only drums and trumpets but pots, pans, basins, spades, animal horns, bells and tongs. To this, the sounds of 'whooping and hollowing' were also added, creating a din that could sometimes be heard over a mile away. One Jacobean source defined this form of charivari as 'The carting of an infamous person, graced with the harmonie of tinging kettles and frying-pan Musicke'.[37] The reference to harmony was, of course, ironic, for rough music was actually a kind of anti-harmony, designed simultaneously to expose, rebuke and humiliate those who had seriously offended a critical mass of their neighbours by sowing the seeds of 'discord'. Rough music echoed and amplified the cultural dissonance which the intended victims had themselves generated. It was a humiliating punishment, and it warned miscreants of the need to choose between orthodoxy and ostracism.

Most commonly, the resonant ritual targeted husbands whose wives had berated them verbally, beaten them physically or betrayed them sexually. At the start of the seventeenth century, the vicar of Waterbeach (Cambridgeshire) suffered physical violence at the hands of his wife, closely followed by a sonic battering from his neighbours. He later sought

[37] Randle Cotgrave, *A Dictionarie of the French and English Tongues* (London, 1611), Q2r.

revenge by bringing an ecclesiastical court case against the ringleaders, and without this retaliatory action we would know nothing of the incident. The alleged 'Lord & Capteyne of the disordered Cumpany', John Knocke, explained to the judge 'that there is a custome in theire towne that if a woman beate her husband, the next neighbour towards the Church must ride upon a cowlestaffe'. In time-honoured fashion, a procession had evidently been organised, complete with special effects, both visual and aural. The mock-vicar was carried through the village while other participants donned long black gowns and danced around him. The rough and ready rhythms were supplied by Robert Bankes junior, who found himself in court for 'playeing lustely upon the drumme, being a bruers kilderkin [a small barrel] to put beere in, whereof they all & divers others of their disordered company had taken over muche'. This vessel, relieved of its contents, was hastily redeployed as a makeshift instrument.[38]

Rough music was also applied in the management of other offences. In 1618, for example, one couple in Burton-upon-Trent stood accused of various sexual malpractices (including incest). Together, they were allegedly dragged 'along the streets of the said towne ... wth great noyce and wth ringing of Cow Bells Basons Candlestickes frying pannes and wth the sounde of a drumme'. To this cacophony was added the rhythmic chanting by a large crowd of the words 'A whore and a knave A whore a whore'. The experience was so devastating that both the 'knave' and the 'whore' left town (**Website track 1 and Appendix**). In many instances rough music was unofficial, a customary and communal response to the breach of norms, yet this was a vocabulary that, in more limited form, was also deployed in the official punishment of discordant individuals. On 22 March 1560, the diarist Henry Machyn watched as a female bawd was carted through the streets of London, 'with a basen tynglyng a-for'.[39] It was not an unusual occurrence, and the humble basin was an instrument with strong moral resonance. Unfortunately for us, those who participated in rough music were normally too busy to spell out for curious historians the musical-cosmological framework within which their activities had meaning. Such matters, one suspects, were in any case understood instinctively rather than in an intellectual format that was conducive to verbal expression. This need not put us off, however, for early modern people frequently articulated their feelings through actions rather than

[38] EDR B/2/18, fos. 174v–917r, CUL.

[39] STAC 8/104/20, NA; *The Diary of Henry Machyn*, ed. John Gough Nichols (London: Camden Society, 1848), p. 228. There are many such examples in *REED Kent*.

words. Much of what was said in this period was not said at all. In rough music, a perception that different kinds of harmony – moral, marital, social and sonic – were somehow connected was regularly and enthusiastically played out.

In more general terms, we should note the existence of a critically important sympathy between earthly music and the internal harmonies of humans. Music touched the soul, and early modern authors showed themselves, once again, eager to broadcast a Pythagorean insight. Richard Mulcaster concluded, in 1581, 'that if the constitution of man both for bodie and soule, had not some naturall, and nighe affinitie with the concordances of *Musick*, the force of the one, would not so soone stirre up, the cosen motion in the other'. Belief in the 'cosen motions' of outward and inward harmonies remained an essential component of musical commentary throughout the early modern period. Music and soul enjoyed 'soft Relations and Sympathie', and spiritual content was 'but concord of the mind'.[40] Even music's critics based their arguments on the existence of a soul–music nexus which, in their anxious perceptions, was all too easily abused. Music could form a sympathetic channel linking humans and God, but it could also operate as a sonic signpost to the devil's realm. In 1582, Stephen Batman referred critically to those who despised music, 'as if it were some odious skill ranged from hell, rather stirred up by Divells, then [than] revealed by Angels'. Either way, music demonstrated the ancient truth, articulated in typically pithy style by John Taylor, that 'Man is a little world, wherein we see, / The great worlds abstract or epitome.'[41]

The eventual decline of this interconnected and pulsating world-view lies largely beyond the chronological scope of this study. Certainly, there were those in seventeenth-century England for whom the music of the spheres, inaudible at the best of times, was no longer something to which the educated should attend. In 1632, George Sandys noted the effect of music on human affections, but denied explicitly that this occurred because 'the Soule, . . . consisting of harmony, & rapt with the sphearicall musick before it descended from Heaven to inhabit the body, affects it with the like desire'. Instead, he argued, music affected humans 'because the Spirits which agitate in the heart, receave a warbling and dancing aire

[40] Richard Mulcaster, *Positions wherin those Primitive Circumstances be Examined, which are Necessarie for the Training Up of Children* (London, 1581), p. 37; John Gamble, *Ayres and Dialogues* (London, 1657), dedicatory epistle; Katherine Phillips, quoted in John Playford, *An Introduction to the Skill of Musick*, 6th edn. (London, 1672), A5r.

[41] Batman, *Batman upon Bartholome*, fo. 424v; Taylor, *All the Workes*, vol. II, p. 294.

into the bosome, and are made one with the same where with they have an affinity; whose motions lead the rest of the Spirits dispersed through the body, raising or suppressing the instrumental parts according to the measures of the musick'.[42]

It seems doubtful, however, that a majority of musical commentators perceived the matter quite so clearly, even by the late seventeenth century. For one thing, it was perfectly possible to accommodate the first of Sandys's possibilities to the second, in other words to integrate a traditional understanding of cosmological music with an updated awareness of the precise physical mechanisms through which melody and harmony exerted their influence. Similarly, the way in which musical theorists shifted their attention from the general status of music in the cosmos to the precise nature of its influence over the affections need not necessarily be perceived as evidence that traditional ideas were already in terminal decline. As we shall hear, many authors believed that music's emotional impact was possible precisely because of its cosmological significance. Over the subsequent centuries, admittedly, the new scientific emphasis on physical explanations for musical effect clearly did undermine more classically inspired theories, but as long as people believed in a purposeful creator-God there was nothing inevitable about the collapse of the latter. Christianity had, after all, successfully incorporated musical Platonism, and, in the medium term at least, it could do the same with the discoveries of seventeenth-century science. God, though jealous, was flexible. We must therefore be careful not to exaggerate the rapidity with which the new science swept all before it.

If, for example, we return the works of highly educated musical theorists to the shelf for a moment, and attend instead to the less refined sound of balladry, then we encounter a wealth of musical references that can be comprehended in terms of the ideas considered above. Of course, balladeers rarely dwelt upon the finer points of musical cosmology, and we must therefore be ready to listen between the lines. In these cheapest of literary texts, the earth 'rings' repeatedly with good and bad news, the music of heaven exerts a conspicuous fascination, and the concord/discord antithesis is simultaneously musical and social. Music 'echoes' and 'rebounds', sometimes touching the heavens, and the songs of birds change in reaction to the turbulent spirits of human listeners. Lovers combine together in 'concordant sympathy' and the discordant conduct of anti-social scolds is

[42] G[eorge] S[andys], *Ovid's Metamorphoses Englished* (London, 1632), p. 356.

reformed and retuned by the sound of trumpets, 'sweet' and 'brave'.[43] Admittedly, the average listener probably did not spend much time in conscious contemplation of music's status in the universe, but an instinctive awareness of the interconnected harmonies that characterised existence seems to have been pervasive. This was a kind of background music but it was in no sense incidental.

Music and mood

In earthly terms, the power of music was grounded in its ability to influence, even control, human emotions. Sceptics on this point were a rare breed.[44] For those who felt suspicious of music, its hold over the moods was extremely dangerous. Even music's most ardent fans had to concede that its power could cause harm if it were not exercised with caution. Music was wonderful, said Jeremy Collier, 'Yet to have our Passions lye at the Mercy of a little Minstrelsy; to be Fiddled out of our Reason and Sobriety; to have our Courage depend on a Drum, or our Devotions on an Organ, is a Sign we are not so great as we might be.' It would be reassuring, he continued, if we could 'have the Satisfaction without the Danger . . . But such an Independency is not to be expected in this World, therefore we must manage wisely and be contented'.[45]

The ranks of the suspicious were dominated by moralists and persons of pronounced Protestant piety, and it is therefore not surprising that one common preoccupation was with the role played by music in public worship.[46] Most of these commentators, certain radicals excepted, agreed that music – in the form of unaccompanied metrical psalms – was a legitimate means of praising God. They were acutely conscious, however, of the risks of musical over-elaboration, which simultaneously insulted God and distracted the congregation by appealing to their passions. Anything that obscured the words of Scripture was to be avoided like the plague, and all but the barest of music was considered dangerous, 'bycause it carieth awaye the eare, with the sweetnesse of the melodie, and bewitcheth the minde with a *Syrenes* sounde, pulling it from that delite,

[43] *Pepys Ballads*, vol. I, pp. 30, 48, 54, 70, 154, 322, 360, 452, 454, 465, and vol. II, pp. 10, 44–5.

[44] Francis Clement, *The Petie Schole* (London, 1587), p. 45. Clement argued that Orpheus' ability to tame wild beasts should be attributed to his verbal eloquence rather than his music. After Orpheus died, Neanthius took the famous harp and sought to tame nature by playing it. The experiment did not work, and his throat was ripped out by angry dogs.

[45] Collier, *Essays*, pp. 24–5. [46] See below, pp. 392–4.

wherin of duetie it ought to dwell, unto harmonicall fantasies'. One of Thomas Becon's fictional characters, the outspoken Theophile, went so far as to anticipate the position of Quakers in the mid-seventeenth century by arguing that the only true music was within us, the work of the soul rather than the hands, mouth and ears.[47] Not surprisingly, the retention of complex polyphonic choral music with instrumental accompaniment in England's post-Reformation cathedrals and collegiate churches was anathema to the most zealous of Protestants.

The attitude of such authors towards the mood music of secular society was clearer still. Musical pleasure could lead even godly men towards an obsessional state in which they neglected their spiritual duties. During the mid-1640s, the members of a dissenting congregation in Bristol attempted to persuade their minister, Mr Ingello, that his intoxication with worldly music was endangering the church. All their efforts were in vain, however, 'For he tould them – take away his *Musick*, take away his life; which offended and Stumbled them more.' A decade later, the fiercely committed author of a tract addressed *To the Musicioners* demonstrated that the Bible could be mined not only for evidence of music's benefits, but for proof that most music drew the hearts of humans away from the Lord. In his own terms, he concluded more optimistically that 'the time is come, that the voice of Harpers and Musitioners shall be heard no more at all'.[48] With the musical exuberance of the Restoration period only two years away, he could scarcely have been more mistaken.

Non-devotional music was also condemned because it drew people away from organised worship. The sound of a minstrel on the village green could intercept the weak as they made their way to church, playing on their feelings and their bodies in an altogether regrettable manner. Preachers were all too well aware of the power of music over the heart-strings and hamstrings of their parishioners. In 1578, John Walsall told a gathering at Paul's Cross that preaching was now 'so contemned and dispised ... that every vaine fidler, and vagabound Piper in the country doth carrie away the unthankefull people, even uppon the Lorde his holy Saboth dayes'. Music's bewitching influence not only endangered souls but threatened the supposedly inclusive values associated with the parish community. Dancers and their minstrels formed alternative 'companies' that seemed to exist in opposition to orthodox Christian society, and each

[47] Mulcaster, *Positions*, p. 38 (summarising arguments of music's opponents); Thomas Becon, *The Jewel of Joy* (London, 1550), F3r–v.

[48] *The Records of a Church of Christ in Bristol, 1640–1687*, ed. Roger Hayden, *Bristol Record Society Publications* 27 (1974), p. 102; H.S., *To the Musicioners*, p. 7.

of these antithetical communities had its musical soundtrack. During the 1620s and 1630s, godly Protestants sometimes found it all but impossible to sing psalms at home, 'but with the noise of the Pipe and Taber, and Whootings in the Street, continually in our Ears'.[49]

Of course, those who gathered excitedly around the piper heard the world through different ears, and an infinitely more optimistic interpretation of music's power over the emotions was presented by a wide array of authors during the early modern period. They did not deny the risks, but insisted that their opponents had grossly distorted the truth by attending only to the abuses of music. The lovers of music drew on centuries of evidence in order to demonstrate the overwhelmingly beneficial nature of their art. Their anecdotes stretched all the way back to Pythagoras himself, who 'chanced once into a company of Drunkards, where a *Musitian* ruled their lascivious Banket: hee presently commanded him to change his harmony with a Dorion (or an heavier tone) and so with this tragicke melodie moved them to cast off their garlands, ashamed of whatsoever they had done, being brought by the accent of grave and solemne *Musicke* to sobrietie'.[50] The Dorian mode was one of the seven ancient scales, each associated by tradition with the stirring-up of a particular emotion. The medieval versions of these modes were steadily losing their importance within art music during the early modern period, as the familiar major–minor tonality of Baroque and Romantic music came to dominate.[51] There are, however, frequent references to the modes in the musical literature of the period, and while it is indisputable that their influence was declining, it is also clear that particular types of tune were still associated with the production of particular emotions. Charles Butler, for example, opened his influential book with an account of the 'moodes', and although he listed only five, he certainly did not believe that their day was over. The 'Dorik' or Dorian mode, he explained, 'mooveth to sobrieti, prudence, modesti, and godlines'. In contrast, the Ionic mode (equivalent to the modern major scale) was designed 'for honest mirth and delight, chiefly in feasting and other merriments'.[52]

[49] John Walsall, *A Sermon Preached at Pauls Crosse* (London, 1578), E3r; Richard Baxter, *The Divine Appointment of the Lords Day Proved* (London, 1671), pp. 116–17.

[50] Brathwaite, *The English Gentleman*, p. 132.

[51] A rough idea of the modes can be gained by playing scales on the white notes of a piano. Different starting points produce changes in the relative configuration of tones and semitones, giving each scale a distinctive character. The shifting keynotes produce scales in different modes: D (Dorian), E (Phrygian), F (Lydian), G (Mixolydian), A (Aeolian), B (Locrian) and C (Ionian). See also McColley, *Poetry and Music*, p. 39.

[52] Butler, *Principles of Musik*, pp. 1, 5. See also Case, *Praise of Musicke*, pp. 53–5.

The many adjectives used by authors of the period to describe the beneficial effects of music upon the passions fall into five main groups. The potent concept of 'recreation', which is rather diluted in its modern application, serves as a link between these categories. Men and women were under assault from the world around them – whether as a result of arduous work or personal troubles – and music was a vital element in the process through which they could hope to 'recreate' themselves. For William Ingpen and several others, music 'recreateth the minde of man', and when in 1641 John Evelyn heard an organ playing in Haarlem, he deduced that its purpose was 'to recreate the People, before and after their Devotions'.[53] Music could fulfil this recreational function in a number of ways. The first group of adjectives is the most basic. Music brought sensations of pleasure: it was charming, delightful, sweet and joyful. In the words of the Tutbury orator, it 'conveys to our minds a more agreeable & refined pleasure than we can possibly receive by any other our Bodily sences'.[54]

The second group of terms asserted music's power to calm the mind. It settled, moderated, composed, ordered, quieted, harmonised, mended, comforted, soothed, eased, subdued, allayed, contented, solaced, quelled and civilised the turbulent emotions. In Shakespeare's *Henry VIII*, a troubled Queen Katherine instructs her gentlewoman, 'Take thy lute, wench: my soul grows sad with troubles. / Sing and disperse 'em, if thou canst.' Appropriately enough, the servant proceeds to sing a song proclaiming Orpheus' power to calm even the elements. Elsewhere in Shakespeare's works, music kills care, whispers to weary spirits and sings the savageness out of a bear.[55] Nor was it only within the advanced literary imagination that such effects were noted. In 1553, the burgesses of Norwich ordered the waits of the city to play regular Sunday concerts on the roof of the guildhall, for the 'comforte of the herers thereof'. In Exeter, it was the duty of the waits to attend the mayor, 'for the solacynge of hym and others with theire noyses and melodies'. John Playford commended music to those who were bereaved, on the grounds that it 'gently breaths and vents the Mourners Grief', and there is a touching illustration of this particular possibility in a manuscript tune book kept by Henry Atkinson, a young coal merchant in Newcastle upon Tyne at the turn of

[53] Ingpen, *Secrets of Numbers*, p. 94 (see also Collier, *Essays*, pp. 19–20); *The Diary of John Evelyn*, ed. E. S. De Beer (London: Oxford University Press, 1959), p. 29.

[54] Speech delivered at Tutbury, D4530/76/8, p. 8, DRO.

[55] Shakespeare, *All Is True* (*Henry VIII*), in *Complete Oxford Shakespeare*, p. 432; *2 Henry IV*, ibid., p. 323; *Othello*, ibid., p. 1192.

the seventeenth century.[56] The book opens with a flourish, displaying on its first page the words 'Henry Atkinson his book 1694/5' in a confident and florid hand. Unfortunately, Atkinson's apparent optimism was to be shaken a few years later by the deaths of his only son, at the age of five, and his wife. Their names are carefully recorded, one beneath the other, on another of the opening pages. The Christian name of a surviving daughter is noted more cryptically on the same page. Atkinson turned his book sideways, and inscribed the title of a celebrated and patriotic tune of the period: 'Let Mary live long'. Did he perhaps pick up his violin and play this melody to himself in order to assuage his grief?[57]

John Case was unusual among the scholarly elite in devoting three whole pages to the musical habits of the common people. They were, he noted, well aware of music's capacity to bring 'solace'. 'And hence it is', he remarked, 'that manual labourers, and Mechanicall artificers of all sorts, keepe such a chaunting and singing in their shoppes.' How could agricultural labourers possibly endure the hardships of their work 'unlesse they quieted & even brought asleep their painfulness' by whistling and singing? Such people may have been 'base & ignoble' but they were nevertheless compelled to make music 'by the instinct of their harmonicall soules'.[58]

Music settled the turbulent passions, but it also enlivened the spirits of those who felt subdued. In the third category of adjectives, music revived, exalted, refreshed, quickened, animated, excited, cheered, roused and rejoiced the emotions. It was, in the estimation of its defenders, 'a roaring-Meg against Melancholy' and it could 'burn within us like fervent Zeal, till it eats us up, never failing to help, and nourish, and enflame our Affections'. Others were somewhat more moderate in their language, but insisted on music's power to invigorate those who felt oppressed by worldly cares, or who were involved in tedious labour. It could even stimulate dumb animals into co-operative work, and John Playford claimed to have seen a herd of deer being encouraged to travel through Hertfordshire by the sound of a violin and bagpipes. Whenever the music stopped, so did they. Above all, music generated happiness. 'No mirth without music', ran one proverb.[59] 'Mirth', indeed, is one of the terms that

[56] *REED Norwich*, p. xxxvii; *REED Devon*, p. 166; Playford, *An Introduction*, A6r; 'Henry Atkinson his Book', Northumberland Record Office (Gosforth), MS MU 207. I have pieced together the details of Atkinson's background and family history from references in a range of local sources. See below, pp. 211–14.

[57] The tune is recorded on the website, track 8.

[58] Case, *Praise of Musicke*, pp. 43–4, 76.

[59] John Banister and Thomas Low, *New Ayres and Dialogues* (London, 1678), quoted by Winn, 'A Bibliography', p. 430; Naish, *A Sermon*, p. 18; Playford, *An Introduction*, A5r; Burton, *Anatomy of Melancholy*, p. 374.

seems possessed of a distinctly aural-musical charge within early modern usage. It was a word that conjured up the sound of fiddles, clinking pots and noisy merriment.

Beyond mirth, music's uplifting influence over human moods had an important military application. It was a commonplace of the period that the martial music of 'boisterous untuned drums' and 'harsh-resounding trumpets' put courage into the hearts of one's own soldiers, and fear into the stomachs of their enemies.[60] In battle-ballads of the seventeenth century, the trumpets and drums of the English forces maintain a constant presence, working on the soldiers 'To make them all hardy, and fit for a Fight'. And in 1697, Jeremy Collier asked his readers, 'Have you not observed how a *Captain* at the Head of a Company, how much he is alter'd at the Beat of a Drum? What a vigorous Motion, what an erected Posture, what an enterprising Visage, all of a Suddain? His Blood charges in his Veins, his Spirits jump like Gunpowder, and seem impatient to attack the Enemy.' He later returned to the subject of military music, and suggested the creation of a sonic weapon of war, an instrument 'that shall have a quite contrary Effect to those Martial ones now in Use'. It would, he continued,

> sink the Spirits, and shake the Nerves, and curdle the Blood, and inspire Despair, and Cowardice, and Consternation, at a surprizing Rate. 'Tis probable the Roaring of Lions, the warbling of Cats and Schritch Owls, together with a Mixture of the howling of Dogs, judiciously imitated and compounded, might go a great way in this Invention. Whether such Anti-musick as this might not be of Service in a Camp, I shall leave to the Military Men to consider.[61]

The remaining adjectives can be dealt with more concisely. In the fourth group, music was described as diverting and transporting, an able carrier of the emotions from one place to another. Harmonious or melodic sound could distract the attention of listeners away from more troubling preoccupations. The mid-seventeenth-century song book of Archdeacon Rutter, for example, was compiled 'For the Amusement and Diversion of the Right Honourable James Earl of Derby During his Retreat to the Island of Man, in the Time of the Oliverian Usurpation'. There was nothing like music for deflecting the Earl's pensive spirit from the woes of civil war, and

[60] Shakespeare, *Richard II*, in *Complete Oxford Shakespeare*, p. 203.

[61] *Pepys Ballads*, vol. II, p. 311; Collier, *Essays*, pp. 21, 24. In the world's current conflicts, American troops are reported to intimidate their enemies by blasting them with country-and-western music at extremely high levels of volume.

one verse included the lines 'We Strike up Musick's gentle Strings, / And Understand no other Blows.'[62]

Lastly, the positive power of music was described in terms that had sexual and/or spiritual undertones. It was rapturous, alluring, irresistible, piercing, penetrating, enchanting, enflaming and elevating. Most frequently of all, it was ravishing. Many music-lovers felt ravished in this period, but none more so than Samuel Pepys after a night at the theatre in February 1668. He did not care much for the play itself,

> but that which did please me beyond anything in the whole world was the wind-musique when the Angell comes down, which is so sweet that it ravished me; and endeed, in a word, did wrap up my soul so that it made me really sick, just as I have formerly been when in love with my wife; that neither then, nor all the evening going home and at home, I was able to think of anything, but remained all night transported, so as I could not believe that ever any music hath that real command over the soul of a man as this did upon me; and makes me resolve to practise wind-music and to make my wife do the like.[63]

He evidently believed that his decaying passion for Mistress Pepys could be reinvigorated by forcing the poor woman to learn the recorder. The proverbial importance of music as 'the food of love' was, of course, a characteristic that thrilled its admirers and chilled its detractors in equal and opposite measure.

As the words of Samuel Pepys reveal, there was only a thin line separating the soulful from the sexual. Music's apologists were convinced, nevertheless, that this did not amount to a justification for curtailing too severely the place of harmony and melody within organised worship. They responded energetically to those who allowed only unaccompanied metrical psalms, and the debate continued throughout the early modern period. All would be well, the defenders of music argued, provided that the thin line were clearly drawn. Church music, they agreed, must not stimulate the passions in the wrong way. Both George Wither and Jeremy Collier therefore insisted that the music used in churches should be markedly different from that which circulated in the world beyond. In Hooker's opinion, this necessitated the avoidance of 'curiositie and ostentation of arte, wanton or light or unsuteable harmonie, such as only pleaseth the eare', but it certainly did not require the banning of choirs, organs and other instruments. John Case informed his opponents that

[62] *REED Lancashire*, pp. 270–3.

[63] *Diary of Samuel Pepys*, vol, IX, p. 94. See also Finney, 'Ecstasy and Music'.

'artificiall singing is farre better than their plain Musicke, for it striketh deeper, and worketh more effectually in the hearers'.[64]

Over the decades, the defenders of ecclesiastical music in its richer guises compiled and reiterated a forceful argument, drawing attention to the divine origins of harmony, the prominence of music in the Bible and in heaven and the historically established fact that music was the only 'science' permitted in church.[65] Their most important argument, however, was that music, properly used, could set the hearts of humans into a state that was fitting for worship. For Hooker, good church music was 'most admirable, and doth much edify if not the understanding because it teacheth not, yet surely the affection, because therin it worketh much'. 'The sweetnes of melodie', he concluded, 'might make some entrance for good things'. In 1660, Joseph Brookbank was more exuberant, claiming that the 'sweetnes of harmonical sounds, insinuates it self into the soul of man, prepares the affections for the service of God, lifts up the heart toward heaven, delights the mind, kindles Devotion, inflames desire, and ravisheth the spirit with celestial joy'.[66]

Just as music could raise the spirits of the individual, so it could strengthen and recreate communities of many sorts. Music was most commonly experienced socially, and its hearers were automatically defined as some sort of a collectivity merely through their physical positioning within a shared auditory field. The role of music as a form of social communion has been well explored by philosophers and ethnomusicologists, and this dimension of music's power can perhaps be best explained in terms of its ability to generate similar and simultaneous feelings in a range of listeners.[67] We all hear the same notes and, because we share cultural conditioning, we also tend to experience comparable (though never identical) reactions. Music unfolds through time, rising and falling in intensity, and it therefore co-ordinates our responses, binding us – however momentarily – into a unity. In the early modern age, the cosmological assumptions that surrounded music perhaps meant that its power to define groups and communities was experienced with particular intensity.

[64] Wither, *A Preparation to the Psalter*, pp. 85–6; Collier, *Essays*, p. 25; Richard Hooker, *Of the Lawes of Ecclesiastical Politie* (1594–7; Menston: Scolar Press, 1969), bk. V, ch. 38, p. 76; Case, *Praise of Musicke*, p. 143.

[65] Nicholas Brady, *Church-musick Vindicated* (London, 1697), pp. 21–2; Batman, *Batman upon Bartholome*, fos. 424v–425r; Playford, *An Introduction*, A6r (citing Bede).

[66] Hooker, *Of the Lawes of Ecclesiastical Politie*, bk. V, ch. 38, p. 76; Joseph Brookbank, *The Well-tuned Organ* (London, 1660), p. 44.

[67] Reimer, *On the Nature of Musical Experience*, p. 268; Fletcher, *World Musics*, pp. 147–50.

Examples are legion. In early modern England, no feast or group celebration was complete without music. According to one ballad, neighbours gathered together at Christmas time, 'Forgetting old wrongs, with Carrols and Songs, to drive the cold winter away'. In *A Midsummer Night's Dream*, music, in association with dance, plays its part in healing divisions within the fairy community.[68] Back in the mortal world, music could transform a hierarchical household, albeit temporarily, into something more egalitarian. Roger North remembered the household of his grandfather, in which the members of an eminent aristocratic family played and sang in the company of their musical servants, thereby making 'a society of musick'. Similarly, one Cambridge man was described in an official source as 'University "Mussission"; scholars' servant; launderer at Trinity'. Part of the genius of music, according to Renaissance wisdom, was that it 'joyneth and accordeth diverse thinges that seeme contrary, and maketh the high sound to accord with the low'.[69] This was socially useful, and experience demonstrated that music could bind groups of godly pilgrims, or the crew of a ship, or an English community on foreign soil. At the theatre, it could generate a suitably communal atmosphere prior to the commencement of a play. In the catches and rounds recorded by Thomas Lant in 1580, music's power to coalesce a group of singers (and by extension listeners) is alluded to with frequency:

Sing ye nowe after me,
& as I singe singe ye,
so shall we well agree,
five partes in unitie
dinge donge ding dong ding dong ding dong bell.[70]

The binding potential of music was therefore well known: the sound of instruments and voices, when experienced socially, could make it seem 'as if the whole audience had but one heart and one mind'.[71]

[68] Speech delivered at Tutbury, D4530/76/8, pp. 8, 10–11, DRO; *Pepys Ballads*, vol. I, pp. 186–7; Shakespeare, *A Midsummer Night's Dream*, in *Complete Oxford Shakespeare*, pp. 582, 593.

[69] *Roger North on Music*, ed. John Wilson (London: Novello, 1959), p. 10; McColley, *Poetry and Music*, p. 136; Batman, *Batman upon Bartholome*, fo. 424r.

[70] Ian Woodfield, *English Musicians*; 'Diary of the Journey of Philip Julius, Duke of Stettin-Pomerania, through England in the Year 1602', ed. Gottfried von Bülow, *Transactions of the Royal Historical Society*, n.s. 6 (1892), pp. 28–9; Thomas Lant's roll of catches, MS Rowe 1, King's College, Cambridge.

[71] T. Naish, *A Sermon Preached at the Cathedral Church of Sarum, November the 30th, 1727* (London, 1727), pp. iii–iv, quoted by Borsay, *English Urban Renaissance*, p. 268.

It should be added, however, that music also contributed to social tension, for the simple reason that not everyone felt so positive about its power over the passions. Music defined communities, but it also defined *rival* communities. In 1600, this observation was beautifully illustrated in a ferocious dispute in Yorkshire between the puritanical household of Thomas Hoby and a local Catholic family, the Eures. On one occasion, assorted members of the Eure family took up temporary residence in Hackness Hall, the Hoby house, and, according to the inhabitants, deliberately drowned out the sound of their psalm-singing with raucous renditions of ungodly songs about King Arthur and other topics. In a different court case, the claim of one party from Goodrich in Herefordshire that a social gathering 'with mirth musique and danseing' had been designed purely 'to make peace and love betweene all neighbours' was rather undermined by the fact that it led to a bitter dispute with those who considered such festivities depraved and dangerous.[72] A milder version of the same tension is suggested in Van Heemskerck's late seventeenth-century *London Tavern Scene*, the painting that appears on the cover of this book. The fiddler's music draws the dancers and customers into a unity, but a sober gentleman seems to admonish the revellers from his elevated position in the gallery. The playing cards, clay pipes and wine vessels that lie on the floor hint at the disorderly potential of the scene, and even the landlady looks a little anxious.

Music and morality

Music's role as a stimulant of the passions and an echo of heaven also endowed it with power over human morals. 'In *Harmony*', declared Sydenham, 'we may discover the misticke portraitures both of *Vice* and *Vertue*.' For enthusiasts, its capacity to sustain the moral order was crucial. Music, argued John Case, 'is a cause of breeding in us chastitie, temperance, and other morall vertues'. The harmonies and proportions of music could teach people to conduct themselves as honest members of the commonwealth. According to Charles Butler, writing in 1636, music's predominant affinity with virtue made it an important ingredient in the education of boys. For Richard Mulcaster, it was one of 'the cheife principles, for training up of youth'.[73] Many of the writers who addressed instruction

[72] STAC 5 H16/2, H22/21, H50/4, NA; *REED Herefordshire, Worcestershire*, p. 74.

[73] Sydenham, *Sermons*, p. 22; Case, *Praise of Musicke*, p. 71; Butler, *Principles of Musik*, fo. 3r; Mulcaster, *Positions*, p. 36.

books to young gentlemen also asserted the importance of music (though some were more enthusiastic than others). Henry Peacham, for example, had learned from Plato and Aristotle that nothing in the world 'better disposeth the minde to what is commendable and vertuous' than music. And Lodowick Bryskett drew on similar sources to argue that an educational combination of music and physical exercise could be expected to produce modesty, temperance and valour in the breast of the student.[74]

'A good Musician', wrote one author in 1633, 'can not choose but be an honest man'. He thus went further than most, and inverted his argument for good measure: 'nor doe I see, how an honest man can be ought els, then a good Musician; since Musick is no more then a harmonie and sweet accord of divers tones into one melodie, without any jarre or discord between them'. Charles Butler also expected his musicians to possess moral fibre, and he argued that sacred anthems were at their most powerful 'where the Sobrieti, Decenci, and Pieti of the Singers concur with the Art and sweetnes of the Song'. The early sixteenth-century scribe of the curious 'Leckingfelde Proverbs' adopted a distinctly moral tone in warning instrumentalists of their duty to play truly, cleanly and without affectation. He concluded,

The modulacion of musyke is swete and celestiall
In the speris [spheres] of the planettis makynge sownde armonicall
If we moder oure musyke as the trew tune is
In hevyn we shall synge Osanna in excelsis.

Musicians in the employ of towns and cathedrals were frequently reminded of their moral duties, and the scrutiny under which they lived may have owed something to the perception that music was supposedly an instrument of virtue. The Tutbury minstrels were warned against perverting, abusing and dishonouring the excellency of music: 'You that are the knowne Masters of concord & harmony let noe brawls quarells or discords arise amongst your selves.' In particular, they were told to avoid profane oaths, beastliness, drunkenness, 'obscene or bawdy Songs or any thing that tends to promote vice & make you like panders or Factors of the devil'.[75]

[74] Peacham, *Compleat Gentleman*, p. 103; Lodowick Bryskett, *A Discourse of Civil Life* (1606), quoted by Dennis Brailsford, *Sport and Society: Elizabeth to Anne* (London: Routledge, 1969), p. 75.

[75] H.A. [Henry Hawkins?], *Partheneias Sacra* (London, 1633), p. 140; Butler, *Principles of Music*, p. 41; Royal MS 18.D.11, BL (transcribed in full in Hollander, *Untuning of the Sky*, pp. 427–32); speech delivered at Tutbury, D4530/76/8, p. 16, DRO.

This comprehensive list suggests an awareness on the speaker's part that not all minstrels could be trusted to uphold 'the decency of good Musicke & manners'. Music's moral power had its darker side. ''Tis good', says the Duke in *Measure for Measure*, 'though music oft hath such a charm, / To make bad good, and good provoke to harm'. Indeed, even the most exuberant of musical apologists had sometimes to admit that there were dangers. Mulcaster, for example, was concerned that some otherwise admirable individuals were virtual enemies of music, convinced of its wicked role in 'opening the minde, to the entrie of lightnesse'. In response, he gently suggested that such critics, though often of 'honest and well disposed natures', were 'to[o] stearnly bent'. If they could only listen without prejudice, they would come to hear that music's power for virtue outweighed its tendency towards vice. Charles Butler also stood up in resolute defence of music, and made the common argument that its critics ignored what was good, while developing an unhealthy obsession with those who abused its power. The reprehensible conduct of 'debosht Balad-makers and Dance-makers' in 'leading their silly proselytes hedlong into hell' did not amount to a justification for the silencing of all musical sound. Instead, it argued the need for control.[76]

Those who regarded music as a primary agent of moral degradation were no more convinced by such arguments than were the more recent enemies of rock'n'roll. Indeed, the early modern conflict over the morality of music was just one battle in an age-old war, but it was a battle fought with distinctive energy. Butler's opponents would have been little reassured by his nod towards censorship, for they knew that music was notoriously difficult to monitor and control. Minstrels, instruments and tunes were all highly mobile and hard to track. In the words of Agrippa, translated into English by an Elizabethan gentleman, 'Musicke hath ever bene wandringe here and there for price and pence, and is the servaunte of bawdrie.' John Milton agreed with the first part of this statement, though he was not much exercised by the sentiment expressed in the second. In 1644, his celebrated work *Areopagitica* argued that the promotion of good morals through press censorship was a futile and ridiculous exercise. Music, he remarked, was far too slippery for such control to work: 'It will ask more then [than] the work of twenty licencers to examin all the lutes, the violines, and the ghittarrs in every house ... The villages also must

[76] Speech delivered at Tutbury, D4530/76/8, p. 16, DRO; Shakespeare, *Measure for Measure*, in *Complete Oxford Shakespeare*, p. 806; Mulcaster, *Positions*, p. 38; Butler, *Principles of Music*, p. 130.

have their visitors to enquire what lectures the bagpipe and rebbeck reads ev'n to the ballatry, and the gammuth of every municipal fiddler.'[77]

Not only was music elusive, but it was also capable of cunning disguise. Even that committed lover of music Thomas Naish was forced to concede, in 1701, that music, wrongly used, could present 'a foul thing in such a pleasing Dress, and delightful Air, that our Minds, which of themselves are too prone to Impurity, are soon captivated by its Deluding Charms'.[78] Music could not only trick the mind but throw it completely out of kilter. According to Agrippa, musicians, 'with a certaine venemous sweeteness, like to the Mermaides, with voices, gestures, and lascivious soundes, doo destroie and corrupte mens mindes'. Anxious souls attributed to music the power to foment all manner of vile immorality. Very few authors denied the positive value of music entirely, but the sorry sins that seemed inevitably to come tripping along behind it convinced them that the only justifiable music was spiritual or soberly and privately recreational. The wilder forms of popular music – particularly those connected with dancing – were associated in their writings with bawdry, lust, vanity, wantonness, whoredom, uncleanness, lewdness, immodesty, poison, debauchery and obscenity.[79] 'Virtue', needless to say, was not on the list. For the zealous puritan William Prynne, the music associated with the London playhouses was 'effeminate, delicate' and 'lust-provoking', while Francis Osborne warned his son that the modesty of women tended to decline in proportion to the progress they made in music. For incandescent rhetorical exuberance, however, the fictional moralist created by Philip Stubbes had few equals. In a neat little skit on Elizabethan educational advice literature, Philoponus warns his long-suffering neighbour,

> if you would have your sonne, softe, wommanish, uncleane, smoth mouthed, affected to bawdrie, scurrilitie, filthie rimes, and unsemely talking: brifly [sic], if you wold have him, as it were transnatured into a woman, or worse, and inclyned to all kind of whordome and abhomination, set him to dauncing school, and to learn musicke, and then shall you not faile of your purpose. And if you would have your daughter whoorish, bawdie, and uncleane, and a filthie speaker, and such like, bring her up in musick and dauncing, and my life for yours, you have wun the goale.

[77] *Henrie Cornelius Agrippa, of the Vanitie and Uncertaintie of Artes and Sciences*, trans. James Sanford (London, 1569), fo. 29r; John Milton, *Areopagitica* (London, 1644), p. 16.

[78] Naish, *A Sermon*, pp. 14–15.

[79] *Henrie Cornelius Agrippa*, fo. 29v. For further discussion, see below, pp. 356–61.

One common theme in such outbursts was the power of music to turn men into women, thus undermining at a stroke one of the fundamental principles of hierarchical order.[80]

Critics of music did not want for real-life examples of individuals who, perhaps under its influence, crossed the line separating harmony from discord and virtue from vice. The early modern period supplies a constant stream of musicians who placed themselves in trouble by defying authority, committing adultery, fighting among themselves, impregnating their pupils, singing 'filthy songs', fiddling throughout the night and so on. We will encounter many of them in the chapters that follow, but, for now, a brief meeting with John Mace will be quite sufficient. Mace was a Nottinghamshire musician who, in 1624, was described by his former employer, Mr Handolf Wastner, as 'desperately dangerous, and of notorious ill conversation for barretting, drunkennes, nightwalkinge, and haunting alehouses and suspitious places, and lewd companye continuallye'. While resident in Wastner's house, Mace had taken exception to a visiting preacher for daring to criticise his drunken ways. The musician 'thereupon flu upon him and buffeted and abused him' before retiring to the alehouse, where he boasted of his deed. Wastner informed a fellow esquire that Mace should not be released on bail, except perhaps for an enormous sum of money, 'hee being not wourth anye thing himselfe and the wourst place and companye in the gaole tooe good for him'.[81] Such musicians were not, of course, typical, but they certainly caught the eye (sometimes with a firm fist).

At the other end of the spectrum were those musicians whose deeply rooted religious scruples led them through painful crises of conscience, during which they questioned the validity of their vocation. Solomon Eccles provides a particularly fascinating example. Born into a musical family in 1618, he grew up to become a composer and a teacher of viol and virginal playing. During the Civil Wars and Interregnum, he remained a musician while experimenting with a series of new religious identities (presbyterian, Independent, Baptist and Antinomian). Around 1660, however, he joined the Quakers and soon forsook the vanity of worldly music

[80] William Prynne, *Histrio-mastix* (London, 1633), p. 273; Francis Osborne, *Advice to a Son* (London, 1656), p. 17; Stubbes, *Anatomie of Abuses*, O5r (see also N4v, O3r, O4r–v). On the relationship between music and femininity, see Linda Phyllis Austern, '"My mother musicke": Music and Early Modern Fantasies of Embodiment', in Naomi J. Miller and Naomi Yavneh (eds.), *Maternal Measures: Figuring Caregiving in the Early Modern Period* (Ashgate: Aldershot, 2000), pp. 239–81.

[81] DP 123/26 and 125/4, Nottinghamshire Archives.

for the deeper stimulation of God's inward harmony, silent and spiritual. 'O it was hard to flesh and blood to give it up', he later exclaimed. In order to bear witness to the change, Eccles took himself and his equipment to Tower Hill, where he 'burnt and broke many good Instruments of Musick'. Others were mystified at this parody of a public execution, pointing out that music was itself a gift from God, and accusing Eccles of bringing a respectable calling into disrepute. Eccles, however, would have none of it: ''tis Babylons Musick, and down it must and shall for ever'. In his reformed opinion, all music was like that of Nebuchadnezzar and brought only murder and madness in its wake. In the years following Eccles's conversion, his behaviour became increasingly eccentric – on several occasions, he walked 'naked' through parts of London urging repentance upon its citizens – and one wonders whether, ironically, he missed music's stabilising influence.[82]

The Quakers, indeed, were well known for their zealous hostility to all music, excepting only spontaneous songs that were obviously and directly inspired by the spirit within. Enemies of the Friends sometimes taunted them for the militancy of their position. George Fox recorded in his journal a spell of imprisonment in Carlisle, during which the cruel and violent under-gaoler 'fetched a fiddler, and brought him in where I was, and set him to play, thinking to vex me thereby; but while he played I was moved in the everlasting power of the Lord God to sing; and my voice drowned the noise of the fiddle, and made the fiddler sigh and give over fiddling and pass away with shame'.[83] Quite what he sang we can only guess.

Music, bodies and health

Music possessed not only a 'kindred with the soule' but 'a kinde of affinitie with the Body'.[84] Its influence therefore produced physical effects. Scientific authors of the period knew that this chain reaction was to be understood in terms of reactive vibrations. Traditional Aristotelian theory held that the pure air of the inner ear was responsible for the translation of

[82] Solomon Eccles, *A Musick-lector* (London, 1667), pp. 7, 10, 14. In seventeenth-century usage, the term 'naked' was sometimes applied to those who had merely stripped to their undergarments.

[83] *The Journal of George Fox*, ed. Norman Penney (London: J. M. Dent and Sons, 1924), p. 89.

[84] Martin Fotherby, *Atheomastic: Clearing Foure Truthes, against Atheists and Infidels* (London, 1622), pp. 338–9.

outward sounds into inward perceptions. During the early modern period, anatomists added to this by establishing the transmitting function of the ear's tiny bones, and the existence of neural connections between the ear and the brain. The pure air of the inner ear retained its role, however, and became identified with the 'animal spirits' that were believed to operate throughout the body. These spirits carried stimuli from the ear to the brain and on to the heart, and were thus responsible for the conveyance of musical pleasure. The various parts of the body worked in harmony and, under the influence of good music, the heart and arteries dilated, altering body temperature and the balance between the four humours. Music could thus prolong life.[85]

In all ages, music also affects the body in a more obvious manner. Wherever there is melody and rhythm there is physical movement, certainly among the performers and often among the listeners too. People dance, crowds sway, and, even in the more repressive setting of a modern classical recital, toes will tap. Music, in both a spiritual and a bodily sense, is one of the great animators of humankind. The authors and publishers of early modern chapbooks, one of the cheapest forms of literature available, were well aware of this fact. In *The Famous History of Friar Bacon*, the eponymous hero outwits two thieves by inviting his servant, Miles, to provide them with some music. Obligingly, Miles plays lustily on his pipe, and the thieves are swiftly undone: 'so soon as they heard him play (against their wills) they fell a dancing, and that after such a labourious manner, that they quickly wearied themselves'. Unable to resist the urge to dance, they are then led out into the countryside and along a muddy way, 'where a Horse might very well have been up to the bells'. Eventually, Miles performs a farewell song 'To the tune of, O do me no harm, good man', and leaves the hapless criminals to sleep off their ordeal.[86]

This, of course, was somewhat far-fetched, but more serious-minded authors also testified to the physical benefits of participation in musical activities. Singing, in particular, was good for the body's pipes and lungs. It could also help those who stammered or suffered from other speech defects. Beyond this, music was useful in the treatment of various ailments and illnesses. Most impressively of all, it could expel evil spirits from the body, 'and will drive away the Divell himselfe'. Because music stirred and restored the mind, it had significant soothing and healing powers within

[85] Smith, *Acoustic World*, pp. 103–5; Batman, *Batman upon Bartholome*, fo. 422r; Richard Brocklesby, *Reflections on Ancient and Modern Musick, with the Application to the Cure of Diseases* (London, 1749), pp. 1, 17–25, 31, 70–5; Peacham, *Compleat Gentleman*, pp. 97–8.

[86] *The Famous History of Friar Bacon* (London, 1679).

the body. Insomniacs everywhere knew that harmony could help, and Shakespeare's Henry IV refers jealously to those who are lulled to sleep 'with sound of sweetest melody'.[87] Music could also ease the suffering of the sick, and John Case trawled through an incredible range of historical sources to prove its efficacy in the treatment of everything from deafness to the plague. Robert Burton entitled one section of a celebrated book on melancholy 'Music a Remedy', and he was effusive in its praise. Nothing, he argued, was more effective in the treatment of melancholic illness, which sapped body and mind alike. Music, he said, was 'a soveraigne remedy', 'affecting not only the eares, but the very arteries, the vitall & animall spirits, it erects the mind, and makes it nimble'. And what was more, 'it will performe all this in an instant'.[88]

Other writers agreed, and there is evidence drawn from manuscript sources to demonstrate a common awareness of music's power against melancholic illness. In 1595, Richard Champernoun of Modbury (Devon) wrote to the powerful Sir Robert Cecil, attempting politely to resist the latter's request that he hand over his favourite singing boy. 'I must confess', Champernoun explained, 'being naturally & often oppressyed with melancholy more then I would wysh; I have in that respect (though to my charge with my purse) boght such as I have found whose voyces contentyd mee.' He therefore made his case on grounds of health, pleading that if the boy were to be relinquished, 'my whole consort of musyck; which most delytes mee, were clean overthrowen'. There was, at this time, a rumour that Champernoun's reliance on music had even led him to castrate some of his singing boys in order to preserve their unbroken voices, but he forcefully denied the charge. Some years later, a servant from Somerset sent a letter to one of his master's friends, inviting him to spend Christmas with the family at Lydeard. After signing it, he added an extra note: 'my master would farther pray you according to your promise to lay your autoryty uppon tom taberer and bring him with you to drive of[f] Melancholly'.[89]

Music's apologists also illustrated its health-giving properties with examples drawn from the past and from other countries in contemporary

87 Mulcaster, *Positions*, p. 42; Butler, *Principles of Musik*, p. 123; Playford, *An Introduction*, A5r; Burton, *Anatomie of Melancholy*, p. 373; Shakespeare, *2 Henry IV*, in *Complete Oxford Shakespeare*, p. 313.

88 Case, *Praise of Musicke*, pp. 57–64; Burton, *Anatomie of Melancholy*, p. 372. For further remarks on music's power against melancholy, see Philip Barrough, *The Methode of Phisicke* (London, 1583), p. 36.

89 *REED Devon*, pp. 288–90; *REED Somerset*, p. 421.

Europe. The ancients had reportedly used music in the treatment of sciatica, and 'Chyron the Centaure' was said to have cured many diseases by music alone. Burton had read that French physicians of his own day used music in the treatment of those 'that are troubled with St Vitus bedlam dance'. Other French doctors had successfully cured 'the phrensy' by playing patients their favourite melodies.[90] The most celebrated example, however, came from Calabria in Italy, where special 'solemn Songs and Tunes' provided the only known cure for the madness induced by a tarantula bite. Each year, as the biting season approached, the local citizens would take precautions and 'lay by a little provision for the musick'.[91] To them we owe the dance term 'tarantella'.

Nevertheless, it is difficult to determine whether English doctors of the period made systematic use of music in treating their patients. It would be rather surprising, given the currency of enthusiastic ideas on this subject, if they had not at least experimented with musical cures, but the evidence is at best suggestive. When, in 1749, Richard Brocklesby wrote his *Reflections on Ancient and Modern Musick, with the Application to the Cure of Diseases*, he urged his fellow physicians to make use of a powerful therapy. He had himself prescribed it in the treatment of madness, and had been able to 'appease the disorderly rovings of fancy, and as it were to re-establish the former union of the body and mind by the powers of musick'. He also reported that an esteemed Edinburgh physician had brought a patient back from the brink of grief-induced death by employing a harpist 'to approach him with such soft and solemn sounds, as were formerly known to give him most delight'. Brocklesby clearly felt, however, that his was a lonely voice. He spoke as one seeking to 'revive' an ancient practice, and, after quoting from an earlier and like-minded physician, he lamented 'how difficult a matter it is for a private man, even of great abilities, to establish any opinion, when the sentiments of his contemporaries do not nearly coincide with his own'.[92]

Evidence for the sixteenth and seventeenth centuries is thinner still, perhaps because so few of the surviving records contain adequate detail. We can say, however, that some physicians were clearly men of music. John Case is the most obvious example, but there were others. In 1589, a printed book of prayers included 'A spiritual song to the praise of Almightie God, for delivering ENGLAND from the Spaniards. By

[90] Brocklesby, *Reflections*, pp. 61, 66; Burton, *Anatomie of Melancholy*, p. 374.

[91] Playford, *An Introduction*, A5r; Brocklesby, *Reflections*, p. 60. See also Case, *Praise of Musicke*, p. 65, and Peacham, *Compleat Gentleman*, p. 98.

[92] Brocklesby, *Reflections*, pp. 35, 63–4.

P. Turner Doctor of Phisicke'. And when a Bristol physician, Richard Brace, died in 1642, he left behind him, among other things, 'one paire of old virginalls, two Citterns, & a Rebicke or violin'.[93] Lower down the medical hierarchy, barber-surgeons were associated with music rather more strongly. We should at least wonder whether the instruments that hung habitually on the walls of the shop were provided not only for the entertainment of those who had popped in for a trim, but also to ease the suffering of those whose teeth were being pulled. Barber-surgeons kept the teeth they extracted and displayed them publicly, hung up on lute strings. Certainly, they were a disproportionately musical group. In Elizabethan Bristol, Nicholas Holden was both a trumpeter and a 'surgeon'. In Jacobean Dorchester, George Burford had served consecutive apprenticeships with a musician and a barber-surgeon. In Restoration London, too, Samuel Pepys was familiar with a Greenwich barber-cum-fiddler named Golding, who 'plays very well and all tunes'. Other sources reveal the existence of musical barber-surgeons in Chelmsford, Norwich, Yarmouth and Cambridge.[94] Is it possible that the 'barber shop quartet' has one or two of its roots in commonplace Renaissance ideas about musical pain relief?

On the other hand, writers who were suspicious of music's power naturally lacked enthusiasm for its medical application. It is striking that most of them simply ignored the argument, rather than addressing it directly. They nevertheless found ways of arguing that music's influence over the body was a matter of grave danger. Dancing and its associated music were singled out for attention, particularly by the Elizabethan moralists. For them, the power of music to animate bodies in troubling ways evidently outweighed its capacity to ease physical pain. A similar anxiety is encountered in non-literary sources too, and the language used is sometimes distinctive. In 1577–8, for example, a group of drunken Shrewsbury men entered an alehouse and set up a mock court in which they pretended to try selected locals, whom they summoned one by

[93] O. Pygge, *Meditations Concerning Praiers to Almighty God, for the Safety of England, when the Spaniards were Come into the Narrow Seas* (London, 1589), E2r; *REED Bristol*, p. 246.

[94] *REED Bristol*, pp. 258–60; *REED Dorset, Cornwall*, p. 100 n. 154; *Diary of Samuel Pepys*, vol. VI, pp. 263, 279; Queen's Bench indictments ancient 711, pt. 1, no. 118, and Assize file 35/44/2, transcripts of both documents available in ERO; Margaret Pelling, *The Common Lot: Sickness, Medical Occupations and the Urban Poor in Early Modern England* (London: Longman, 1998), pp. 222–3; *Books in Cambridge Inventories*, ed. E. S. Leedham-Green, 2 vols. (Cambridge: Cambridge University Press, 1986), vol. II, pp. 44, 49. See also John Gurney, *Brave Community: The Digger Movement in the English Revolution* (Manchester: Manchester University Press, 2007), p. 69.

one: 'And soo at every ther Jeste struke upp with a gytterne to pleasur there bodyes with such Lewd behavurs & undecent termes that they waked neybors ther beinge faste a slepe.' Perhaps it was possible to cure illness with music, but it was also possible to 'pleasure' one's body in a thoroughly unsavoury manner.[95]

These, then, were some of the ideas and assumptions that influenced early modern listeners. Of course, there was much less music to be heard in this period than in our own electronic age, but such music as there was rebounded energetically around the place, and, for this reason, was considered both precious and perilous. In 1698, Dr Wallis suggested that 'rude people', for whom music tended to mark special occasions, were more likely than their sophisticated contemporaries to feel its full effects: 'upon such a little music will do great feats; as we find at this day [with] a fiddle or bag-pipe at a country morrice dance'.[96] In the sixteenth and seventeenth centuries, the use of musical language within general speech often seems to have signalled the strong and ancient sympathies that existed between harmonious sounds and order in the cosmos. The early modern universe was for many people alive with resonance and resemblance, and music undeniably played its part in the operation of the whole. When John Taylor reported that the arrival of the plague in London 'brings all out of tune' until 'all her Melodie is Maladie', he meant something more than that the scene was a dismal one. ''Tis Concord keeps a Realme in Stable stay', he argued in another work, 'But Discord brings all Kingdomes to decay.' More famously, Shakespeare has Ulysses say,

Take but degree away, untune that string,
And, hark, what discord follows. Each thing meets
In mere oppugnancy.[97]

Music touched everything, and one wonders about the relationship between two of the early modern meanings of the term 'composer': it referred both to a creator of new music and to anything that promoted peace or settled the turbulent spirits. Music, said Brocklesby, was 'the best composer of a fancy unsettled'.[98]

95 *REED Shropshire*, pp. 223–4. 96 *Memoirs of the Royal Society*, vol. III, p. 291.

97 John Taylor, *All the Workes*, vol. I, p. 69, and Taylor, *Works of John Taylor not Included in the Folio Volume of 1630*, 5 vols. (Manchester: Spenser Society, 1870), vol. II, pp. 19–20; Shakespeare, *Troilus and Cressida*, in *Complete Oxford Shakespeare*, p. 754.

98 Brocklesby, *Reflections*, p. 41.

Shakespeare's world was full of meaningful music. In contrast, some of his contemporaries turned their ears away from music wherever possible, either fearing its power or merely indifferent to its charms. Such individuals were sufficiently numerous that professional composers suffered regular, if rather stylised and self-serving, moments of doubt concerning the low esteem in which their art was allegedly held.[99] Music's critics, however, were surely outnumbered, for most people considered them 'too sternly bent'. According to one rather awkward proverb, imported from Italy, 'Whom God loves not, that man loves not Musicke.'[100] Those who could not appreciate music were subjected to a torrent of abuse. Richard Mulcaster, the music-loving schoolmaster, generally strove to adopt a charitable tone towards his opponents, but he nevertheless argued that any man who could not delight in music had 'a head out of proportion'. The man who addressed the Tutbury minstrels thought that those who did not savour music should 'weare hornes or Eares (I care not which) . . . soe Mankind might know and avoid 'em as Monsters'. Samuel Pepys may well have agreed, but he wisely kept his views to himself when Lord Lauderdale exclaimed 'that he had rather hear a Catt mew then [than] the best Musique in the world – and the better the music, the more sick it makes him. And that of all instruments, he hates the Lute the most; and next to that, the Bagpipe.' Pepys confided in his diary that such an opinion was 'strange'. Many musical men were thus suspicious of their untunable contemporaries, but Shakespeare's words are, as usual, the most memorable. In *The Merchant of Venice*, Lorenzo advises Jessica,

The man that hath no music in himself,
Nor is not moved with concord of sweet sounds,
Is fit for treasons, stratagems, and spoils;
The motions of his spirit are as dull as night
And his affections dark as Erebus:
Let no such man be trusted. Mark the music.[101]

[99] See, for example, John Wilbye, *The Second Set of Madrigales* (London, 1609), dedicatory epistle.

[100] Peacham, *Compleat Gentleman*, p. 96.

[101] Mulcaster, *Positions*, p. 37; DRO, speech delivered at Tutbury, D4530/76/8, DRO D4530, pp. 1–2; *Diary of Samuel Pepys*, vol. VII, p. 225; Shakespeare, *Merchant of Venice*, in *Complete Oxford Shakespeare*, p. 627.

2 Occupational musicians: denigration and defence

Fee-earning musicians came, like their instruments, in all shapes and sizes. The most fortunate were gainfully employed in noble households or, better still, at the royal court itself. At the opposite end of the scale, there were the poor beggars who hoped to stimulate generosity by playing on simple bells, trumps or fiddles. In between, there existed many more who made music to make money: city waits, itinerant minstrels, part-time pipers who played for their neighbours, cathedral singing men, military drummers and trumpeters, ballad-sellers and other street vendors (with their characteristic musical cries). With the exception of the last two categories, those who relied on music for their livelihood were overwhelmingly male (there are more women in Chapter 4). Musicians were also, by custom and necessity, a resourceful crew. They were often proficient on a variety of different instruments. The Norwich musician Robert Munde possessed the unusual combination of trumpet and virginals when he died in 1584. During the 1590s, the church organist at Wimborne Minster (Dorset) was also said to be skilful on the harp, the lute and the rebec. In 1633, Robert Strowger of Great Yarmouth owned 'three Sitterns & two treble vialles' along with 'a Tenor Hoboie & a Cornett'. He could thus supply music for a range of occasions, both indoor and outdoor.[1] This facility for variety contributed to the vagueness with which occupational labels were applied, and it helps to explain how Samuel Harsnett could write, 'the Fidler comes in with his Taber, and Pipe'. Most musicians could sing too, hence the description of a particular ballad in 1627 as 'a songe usually sunge by fidlers'.[2]

A similar flexibility was applied to the matter of making a living. Many had dual or multiple occupations and regarded music as one of several potential sources of income. Raynolde Prickett of Pensford (Somerset) was said in 1611 to make his living 'partlye by being a Minstrell and partlye by his Taylores crafte'. In Elizabethan Essex, James Linewood of Finchingfield

[1] DN/INV2A/5, NRO; *REED Dorset, Cornwall*, p. 34; DN/INV45/129, NRO.

[2] Samuel Harsnett, *A Declaration of Egregious Popish Impostures* (London, 1603), quoted by Winn, 'A Bibliography', pp. 195–6; Fox, *Oral and Literate Culture*, p. 389.

was described at his death as a 'basketmaker otherwise musician', while a weaver from Rayleigh bequeathed to his son a tabor and pipe.[3] Composite occupations were, of course, extremely common during the early modern period, and music should be understood within this wider context. We might also include here the servants in aristocratic households who combined musical performance, tuition and even composition with their other, more general, duties. In 1602, for example, Francis Mitchell, servant to a Yorkshire esquire, was supplied with information on the sexual malpractices of another gentleman from the county before being asked 'to make a songe thereof That they might bee merrie in christmas withall'.[4] Dutifully and energetically, he obliged. Further south, a servant named Thomas Lant had been resident with Lord and Lady Cheyney in Bedfordshire in the years between 1579 and 1582. He is not known to have been employed specifically as a musician, and his later career was with the College of Heralds, yet he compiled a manuscript collection of catches and rounds while in the Cheyneys' service and had a childhood background as one of the boy singers in Elizabeth I's Chapel Royal.[5] The Cheyneys are known from other sources to have been a music-loving family, and it seems certain that they must have called on Lant to sing when he was not busy with other tasks.[6]

The notion of the musical 'professional' is thus somewhat misleading as a description of most early modern performers. Admittedly, the term was occasionally used, and a profession was beginning to develop, promoted partly by self-protecting musicians and partly by anxious authorities, keen to suppress the lasciviousness that was associated with the less respectable forms of minstrelsy. Nevertheless, a high proportion of England's music continued to be made by those who had more than one string to their bows. Even the musicians employed by England's monarchs often required or desired sidelines. The violin virtuoso Davis Mell performed at many great state occasions – including the funerals of James I and Oliver

[3] *REED Somerset*, p. 205; *Essex Wills*, multiple volumes (on-going; Chelmsford: Essex Record Office, 1982–), vol. VI, nos. 139 and 1029.

[4] C. J. Sisson, *Lost Plays of Shakespeare's Age* (Cambridge: Cambridge University Press, 1936), p. 132.

[5] 'The Observations and Collections of Tho: Lant Portcullis, Concerning the Office and the Officers of Armes', College of Arms, fos. 2r–3r; Thomas Lant's roll of catches, MS Rowe 1, King's College, Cambridge; letter from Lant to Lord Burghley (1590s), transcribed in Anstis, 'Officers of Arms', vol. III, p. 156, College of Arms. I am extremely grateful to Messrs Robert Yorke and Thomas Woodcock of the College of Arms for their assistance in piecing together Lant's life story.

[6] See below, pp. 193–5.

Cromwell – but he also occupied his spare time, appropriately enough, in making clocks. This activity was perhaps an extension of his musical personality, for his timepieces were decorated with musicians and played tunes to mark the passing of the hours.[7]

This chapter and the next present an introduction to the shifting world of the occupational musician, concentrating primarily upon those whose names have scarcely registered in the musicological and historiographical literature published to date. This account is based on information regarding more than 1,000 individuals, and focuses throughout on the complex and changing status – legal, economic and cultural – of the musician within English society. It will later be argued that there are good reasons for sounding relatively positive, but we shall begin in the doleful Dorian mode by considering evidence suggestive of persecution, misery and hardship.

The case for the prosecution

Musicians have always found it difficult to establish reputations for respectability. They seem to enjoy themselves for a living, and they keep unusual hours. Their product is difficult to police and slippery in meaning, a fact compounded by the wanderlust that often seems to characterise the lives of occupational musicians. They seem evasive and they attract suspicion. This suspicion was particularly intense during the late sixteenth and early seventeenth centuries, a notoriously difficult period for the country's less privileged musicians. They were subjected to a degree of legal and moral pressure that was unprecedented in its force. The anxieties concerning order that featured prominently within Elizabethan governmental thinking tended to gather like a dark cloud over the head of the travelling minstrel, who appeared almost rootless and almost masterless. The habits and lifestyle of such performers had sometimes caused concern in medieval England, but suspicions clearly escalated during the mid-sixteenth century. In 1556, Queen Mary's Privy Council ordered the nation's judges to ban theatrical players and minstrels from touring the countryside because of their alleged success in spreading Protestant heresy and political sedition. Under Elizabeth I, minstrels came to be regarded not as agents of reform but as vagabonds, unless they could show that they were retained by aristocrats of baronial status or higher,

[7] Maria P. Fernandez and Pedro C. Fernandez, 'Davis Mell, Musician and Clockmaker', *Antiquarian Horology* 16.6 (1987), 602–17.

or that they had been licensed by two justices of the peace in any shire within which they travelled. In 1572, this requirement was set out in 'An acte for the punishment of vacabondes, and for relief of the poore and impotent', the first statute to mention minstrels by name. Under its terms, any unlicensed minstrel was to be 'grievously whipped, and burnt through the gristle of the right ear with a hot iron' for a first conviction, judged a felon for a second (unless able to find a place in service) and executed for a third.[8]

In 1597, The 'Acte for punyshment of rogues, vagabonds and sturdy beggars' was even harsher: it omitted the clause exempting the musical retainers of noblemen (unless they were the players of interludes) and made no provision for the issuing of licences to legitimate minstrels. Offenders could now expect to be whipped until bloody, returned to their home parishes or sent to a house of correction for up to twelve months. Sixty years later, parliament passed a new act against vagrants, retaining the punishments established in the earlier statutes but now extending the definition of a rogue to include all fiddlers or minstrels who made or offered music in any inn, alehouse or tavern.[9] In official terms, therefore, this was not a congenial era in which to live the life of a minstrel. The message evidently got through to the nation's judges, and was disseminated with particular vigour by those of a puritanical disposition. In Somerset, for example, judicial efforts to eradicate 'church ales' (traditional fund-raising events) during the early seventeenth century inevitably affected those who provided the festive music and thus allegedly stimulated vice. A quarter sessions order, issued in 1627, insisted that all participating minstrels were rogues 'by the Statute' and should be punished accordingly. One Somerset judge drew up a list entitled 'who be Rogues', in which he included minstrels in disorderly company with fortune-tellers, beggars, fencers, bearwards and 'Scollers'.[10]

Hundreds of musicians fell foul of these regulations, particularly in the decades between 1570 and 1660. In every county for which suitable records survive, fiddlers and pipers encountered difficulties. The significance of the Elizabethan vagrancy statutes in facilitating and encouraging

[8] *CSPD 1553–8* (London: Public Record Office, 1998), p. 421; *The Statutes of the Realm: Printed by Command of His Majesty King George the Third*, 12 vols. (1810–28; London: Dawsons, 1963), vol. IV, p. 1, pp. 590–8.

[9] *Statutes of the Realm*, vol. IV, pt. 2, pp. 899–902; *Acts and Ordinances of the Interregnum, 1642–60*, 3 vols., ed. C. H. Firth and R. S. Rait (London: His Majesty's Stationery Office, 1911), vol. II, p. 1098.

[10] *REED Somerset*, pp. 437, 749.

such prosecutions is clear. These laws were invoked, both explicitly and implicitly, on numerous occasions: by the governors of Norwich who, in 1588, ordered the visiting minstrel John Gyrlyng to depart the city with his family or face punishment as a rogue, 'according to the statute'; by the constable of Great Dunmow (Essex) when, in 1610, he presented Roger Jonson and Richard Aylett, musicians, for fiddling in the town without licence; and by the Worcestershire village constable who, in 1616, attempted to arrest a minstrel in order to 'punish him on the statute against rogues'. In Jacobean Salisbury, the authorities regularly arrested visiting minstrels, then whipped them and sent them packing. Most poignantly, George Michell, 'an idle person wandering & using a kind of play upon bones and bells', was bloodied and given thirty days to reach Edinburgh, the city of his birth.[11]

Other legislation could also be deployed in the battle against the minstrel. In 1563, the famous Statute of Artificers had banned individuals from practising crafts in which they had not served a formal apprenticeship.[12] Ten years later, certain justices in Essex drafted 'A bill ... to be made against these using the trade of musician not being apprenticed thereto'. This unique and fascinating document reveals the energy with which some were prepared to pursue the lowliest musicians, and also affords us a remarkable glimpse of the moonlighting minstrels of Essex at a single moment in time. The bill lists the names of fifty-six men, drawn from thirty-nine widely distributed parishes. It presents no information on the instruments they played, but it does record their primary occupations: there were twenty-six husbandmen, fourteen tailors and much smaller numbers of carpenters, smiths, weavers, bellows-makers, butchers, lime-burners, millers, shoemakers and wheelwrights.[13] Doubtless, these humble men saw no wrong in their customary practice of eking out their income by playing their instruments to their neighbours, but there were those at work in this period who wished the world to change.

There were musicians of this sort in all counties, but the historian can hope to meet them only occasionally. Early in 1599, three musical men travelled into Winchester for a weekend of pastime and profit. The trip did not go according to plan, and all three were arrested and locked up in the hugely solid West Gate while their case was investigated. Under

11 *REED Norwich*, p. xliii; Q/SR 189/81, ERO; Woodfill, *Musicians in English Society*, p. 206; *Poverty in Early Stuart Salisbury*, ed. Paul Slack, *Wiltshire Record Society* 31 (1975), p. 37.

12 J. A. Sharpe, *Early Modern England: A Social History, 1550–1760* (London: Edward Arnold, 1987), p. 209.

13 Q/SR 43/23, ERO.

examination, the men told their story. The first was Robert Furnesse, a tailor who 'also professeth to be a Musician, upon a harpe'. The second was a shoemaker called Thomas Monday, who came from Bishops Waltham and was blessed with 'skill to play on a base vyall'. The trio was completed by William Noble, a sailor, 'who plaieth upon the violett'. They had come to town, admitted Furnesse, with 'no other errand but to use there minstrelsy & to make merry, & to gett som watt if they could' (in other words, to earn money). They got as far as tuning their instruments while in their lodgings, but when they ventured onto the streets of the city they were apprehended before they so much as played a note. This, perhaps, was their one lucky break, for it probably saved the men from a public whipping. They were released after two days and warned not to repeat their offence. The mitigating circumstances affecting the sailor may also have been taken into account: he claimed 'that he was at Sea when the statute in this behalf was made, and being now advertized thereof he protesteth that henceforth he will not offend against the same'.[14]

The Elizabethan statutes also effected a significant shift in the occupational labels that were applied to music-makers. During the first six decades of the sixteenth century, the term 'minstrel' was very commonly deployed as a comparatively neutral designation for those who offered music and other forms of entertainment for monetary or dietary recompense. After the statute of 1572, however, habits changed. The unattached 'minstrel' had now been identified by parliament as a despicable figure, and many music-makers and employers sensibly switched to 'musician' and other closely related terms. The rapidity of the transition varied considerably: in the civic records of Nottingham, for example, payments to 'minstrels' ceased almost instantly, but in Chester the process was rather more gradual. Here, 'minstrels' were utterly dominant through the 1570s, relinquishing this position only during the early seventeenth century. Throughout this period, the substitute term was at an experimental stage and therefore occurred in several variant forms: 'musicioner', 'musysson', 'musiner' and 'musickesoner'. These were becoming the respectable labels, yet in Chester it was not until the 1630s that the city's scribes managed an entire decade without recording some payment to a 'minstrel'. Eventually, the new terminology settled down and 'musician' established itself as the dominant label.[15] A piece of legislation had rendered the 'minstrel' disreputable, and the term fell into general disuse or, alternatively, became

[14] W/K5/8, p. 8, HRO.

[15] Woodfill, *Musicians in English Society*, pp. 57–8; *REED Chester*, pp. 88–467.

primarily pejorative. Many governors, puritans and moralists continued to speak of 'minstrels' in the wake of the statutes, but never with a happy tune in their hearts. In 1615, for example, one angry Somerset gentleman prefaced his use of 'minstrel' with the tell-tale adjectives 'loose, vagrant and disordered'.[16] By this date, 'minstrel' was sometimes bandied about as an insult. In Merrott (Somerset), John Goffe and Alexander Atkins squared up to one another in the chancel of the church on a Sunday in 1615, as keen as gorillas to establish which of them was socially superior. One of Goffe's tactics was to mock the late father of his adversary, 'sayeng that he was a Minstrell, and did play upon his lute for a penny'. A few years earlier, a Colchester music-maker named Stephen Mumford had seen the writing on the wall. During the 1580s, he was still known to his neighbours as 'the minstrel', but when Mumford made his will in 1594 he took care to identify himself as a 'musician'.[17]

Music-makers also came under pressure in the ecclesiastical courts. Elizabethan and Jacobean efforts to ensure high levels of church attendance and respect for the Sabbath entangled musicians with some frequency. Again, patterns varied, depending on the cultural and religious complexions of each region. In the records relating to Sussex, Cambridgeshire and the Isle of Ely, for example, offending musicians are encountered only rarely and fleetingly. In Lancashire, on the other hand, where a squad of puritan ministers and justices did cultural battle with hordes of Catholic recusants, church papists and traditionalists, the historical record is humming with bagpipers. In puritan ears, the lowly pipers of Lancashire, like those of Ireland, achieved symbolic status in the battle for Reformation. It was alleged that they deliberately played on Sundays in order to tempt people away from church. Protestant governors perceived them as distinctly subversive, and therefore commanded in 1616 that they lay down their instruments for the entire duration of the Lord's Day, and not merely for the portions of it that were taken up by morning and evening prayer.[18] In the decades between 1588 and 1640, forty-two musicians, nearly all of them pipers, were presented to the courts for Sunday performances or, less frequently, for playing on or near church property. Controversial piping hotspots included Wigan, with four individual pipers active between 1610 and 1614, and Cockerham, with three between 1623 and 1632. Up and down the county, pipers were accused of 'prophaning the lordes day' or 'abusing

[16] *REED Somerset*, pp. 398, 576.

[17] Ibid., pp. 163–4; *Essex Wills*, vol. IV, no. 662, vol. VI, no. 857. See also William Ingram, 'Minstrels in Elizabethan London: Who were they and What did they Do?', *English Literary Renaissance* 14.1 (Winter 1984), 29–54.

[18] *REED Lancashire*, pp. 228, 231–4.

themselves by playing at service tyme' or 'drawinge the people from the Church'. One or two even dared to cross the sacred threshold with their instruments. Shortly before Christmas in 1596, a Winwick man was accused of entering the church during a service with a piper named Spode playing contemptuously before him. In order to deal with such individuals, the authorities sometimes considered it necessary to reinforce ecclesiastical injunctions against Sunday piping by issuing quarter sessions bonds. In 1574, the judges with responsibility for the Salford hundred went further still, ordering that no further licences be issued to minstrels and that all existing licences be revoked.[19] This tendency to go beyond the letter of the law in the projected imposition of godly Protestant culture was a pronounced feature of Lancashire governance, and it guaranteed a hostile reaction.

The atmosphere was similarly tense in Dorset, Shropshire, Somerset and Devon, where the future of church ales was the particular point of controversy, and in Herefordshire, another county with a reputation for religious and cultural traditionalism. Here, musicians were reported with some regularity for playing in service time, suffering phases of particular vulnerability during the 1580s (five cases) and in the years between 1610 and 1630 (seventeen cases).[20] The profile of cases in Nottinghamshire looks comparable, and musicians who dared to pick up their instruments during times of divine service risked presentment from the 1580s onwards. Most notably, the puritan parson of Cromwell, Hugh Osborne, conducted a campaign against an equally purposeful group of his parishioners in 1609. He began by presenting to the consistory court one Richard Towell *alias* Holmes, alehouse-keeper, 'for harboringe in his house the sixt of August beinge the Sabboth day Talbot the Piper a rogge, wth divers others, And there suffered them to swager, to bozell & drinke all the time of Eveninge prayer'. On 20 August, three other men had ignored 'the lords hevie judgements of immoderate rain ... , movinge us to sorow and repentaunce', and had spent the day piping and dancing in an alehouse. Mr Osborne apparently failed to catch up with Talbot the piper, but he successfully located and presented Richard Barker of Normanton, who, on Sunday 22 August, turned up in Cromwell 'and there piped in time of Catechisme, & therby withdrew the servantes & children from the same'. Barker did put in a concessionary appearance at evening prayer, but he swiftly burned the bridge he had thus begun to build by leaving church

19 Ibid., pp. 4–235 (the quotations, in order, are on pp. 25, 4, 75, 112, 218).

20 *REED Herefordshire, Worcestershire*, pp. 62–187. See also the *REED* volumes for the other counties mentioned.

halfway through the service in order to 'bezell & drinke' in the alehouse. The vicar was desperately concerned at the state of affairs, and took the unusual step of attaching a personal note to his presentment. In this, he urged the ecclesiastical judge to promote 'the advancement of gods glorie & his majesties lawes' by forcing the miscreants to attend court and receive sentence, 'for if such prophane persons be not restrained by some punishment we shall have open profession of Athisme & all impietie'.[21]

Not surprisingly, it became customary in educated circles to pour scorn on the minstrel, the fiddler and the piper. Puritans and moralists led the way during the second half of Elizabeth's reign. In 1581, Thomas Lovell portrayed minstrels as elusive, seductive agents of the devil. They lazed around all week when others worked, then spent 'the Lords holy day' making music and encouraging all and sundry to worship the 'Idole of wanton pleasure'. This, he warned, 'provoketh Gods indignation'. Lovell even went into verse, presumably hoping thereby to reach his target audience of wantons and wastrels:

Moste minstrels by ungodly meanes,
there maintenance obtain:
What evill, a penny to possesse,
To do wil they refrain?
Their instruments, if you respect,
They use them to intise
Wilde youth, olde age (which should be grave)
Oftimes to practise vice.

Minstrels were dangerous because they appealed across society's generational divides. They were, in Lovell's estimation, 'fond', 'lewd', 'idle', 'bewitching', 'devilish', 'filthy', 'ungodly' and 'lascivious'. They were not good people. Lovell also commented on the statute of 1572: minstrels deserved their identification as vagrants, but the loophole that allowed them to bypass the licensing system by wearing the liveries of barons was thoroughly disgraceful. Others joined the chorus of criticism, raging against England's minstrels for their parasitical lifestyles and their loose-mindedness. Again, they crossed boundaries that God had instituted for a purpose.[22]

[21] AN/PB 294/2/308, HL (see also AN/PB 292/9/27, 293/8/37, 339/2/56, 341/4/45).

[22] Thomas Lovell, *Dialogue between Custom and Veritie Concerning the Use and Abuse of Dauncing and Minstrelsie* (London, 1581), dedicatory epistle and D3r–5r. For similar hostility see Stubbes, *Anatomie of Abuses*; John Northbrooke, *Spiritus est Vicarius Christi in Terra* (London, 1579); Christopher Fetherston, *A Dialogue against Light, Lewde, and Lascivious Dauncing* (London, 1582).

Figure 2.1. The fiddler was a symbol of disorder during the seventeenth century. Ostensibly, this woodcut warns us not to copy him, though it also seems to suggest that no punishment will have much impact on his music-making, beer-drinking and happy disposition (he has only one foot in the stocks, after all). The Pepys Library, Magdalene College, Cambridge, Pepys Ballads, *A Statute for Swearers and Drunkards* (London, 1624), detail.

A different breed of writer soon perceived that there was humour to be found in such stereotyping, and the lousy, lowly minstrel evolved into a frequently recast figure of fun. The 'Poore Fidler', in particular, took on a satirical life of his own. Most famously, John Earle's fiddler was 'One that rubs two stickes together (as the Indians strike fire) and rubs a poore living out of it'. On the social scale, he was one notch above the beggar, and 'he sells nothing dearer then [than] to be gone'. He could smell out a feast or a Whitsun-ale at five miles' distance ('& you shall tracke him againe by the sent'). He was also drawn to the houses of the gentry and to any inn that accommodated such prosperous individuals. Here, he would learn the names of the guests from the tapster, and then torment them by playing in the morning when it was time to wake up. 'The rest of him', concluded Earle, 'is drunke, and in the Stocks' (see Figure 2.1). In 1626, Henry Parrot depicted his 'common fidler' as 'an inevitable squeaking slave of time, one that intrudes into any company under pretext of that old motto, wil't please you Gentlemen to heare any Musicke'. He earned most of his fees from lascivious drunkards, and his highest ambition was to obtain songs, clothes and 'so much money as will buy new Fidle-strings'. Three years later, R.M.'s fidler often played at taverns, positioning his boy outside in the street in order to advertise the music within. He was also a regular attendant at country weddings, for which he decorated his humble attire: 'You may perceive by the Rosemary and Ribbon in his hat where he was the last Sunday, nor can the Clarks booke better certifie you who was the Bride and Bridegroom.' His favourite kind of music was produced by 'the chinking of money'.[23]

These authors knew that they were onto a good thing, and so they created musical cousins for their fiddlers. Richard Brathwaite portrayed 'A Piper' as 'a very droane, ever soaking and sucking from others labours'. He was rarely sober, and was unable to stop his foot from tapping whenever he played. He cared more for his pipes than for his children, and he had a different tune to accompany each seasonal agrarian task (shearing, reaping and so on). The festivities of mid-winter were particularly important to him, hence his reputation as 'An ill wind that begins to blow upon Christmas eve, and so continues, very lowd and blustring all the twelve dayes'. When not in the country, he could be found in city taverns, 'where he rores like the Divell in a vault'. His pet ape, dressed in a coat, would entertain the audience as he played, 'and so foole his spectators out of their coine'. John Earle also described 'A Trumpeter' (who differed from the fiddler 'onely in this, that his impudence is dearer') and a collection of cathedral 'Singing Men'. These musical men of God were said to 'roare deepe in the Quire', but 'deeper in the Taverne'. Drinking was their primary exercise, and prayer but a pastime. They sang sacred anthems in order to warm themselves up for the performance of worldly catches, and when they turned up for divine service their gowns were laced with 'streamings of ale'.[24] This caricature was merely the descant to an existing chorus of complaint. Negative reviews had begun with Elizabethan puritans who deeply resented the fact that, despite the advance of Protestantism, England's cathedrals – in contrast to its parish churches – had managed to retain their traditions of elaborate polyphonic music. For opposite reasons, it was also in the interests of those who campaigned for a

[23] John Earle, *Micro-cosmographie or A Piece of the World Discovered*, 6th edn. (London, 1633), pp. 41–2; Henry Parrot, *Cures for the Itch* (London, 1626), A8v–B1r; R.M., *Micrologia*, C7v–D1r.

[24] Richard Brathwaite, *Whimzies: or, A New Cast of Characters* (London, 1631), pp. 26–34; Earle, *Micro-cosmographie*, pp. 96–7, 115–16.

strengthening of cathedral music to argue that it was poorly sustained and therefore struggling.

In sum, the literary stereotypes contributed to a state of affairs in which the less fortunate of musicians were imagined to present some combination of characteristics reprehensible and risible. Thomas Dekker offered his readers advice on how to avoid being 'haunted' by fiddlers when out in public, and in 1609 he also penned a rather grim satirical prophecy for those who 'scrape out a poore living' from 'dryed cats guts': they would shortly be afflicted by 'abominable noises' in their heads, and many would die as beggars. He went on:

> those that survive shall feede upon melody for want of meate, playing by two of the clock in a frostie morning under a Window, and then being mock'd with a shilling tyed (through a hole) to a string, which shall be thrown to make it Jingle in your ears, but presently be drawn up again, whilst you rake in the durt for a largesse.[25]

Ballad-writers depended heavily on minstrels to distribute their wares, but even they were not above presenting the fiddler or piper as a promoter of lewdness and debauchery. And when John Taylor sought to characterise, in typically pithy style, the welcoming committee that existed in a typical alehouse, he settled upon the description, 'A noyse of Fidlers and a brace of Whores'.[26]

Not surprisingly, early modern musicians sometimes experienced feelings of anxiety and low self-esteem. The sources will hardly allow an investigation of the psychological conditions of common pipers and fiddlers in the period, but the attitudes expressed in print or manuscript by more privileged musicians make the point forcefully enough. Such people seem to have spent precious little time in counting their comparative blessings. The autobiography of Thomas Whythorne suggests that he existed in a state of almost continual insecurity, and the scholar John Case expressed his regret that modern musicians were so poorly regarded in comparison to those who had entertained the rulers of ancient Greece.[27] Numerous published works of music commenced with dedications to members of the aristocracy in which the good taste of the music-loving patron was contrasted favourably with the apathy and ignorance of other men and women of rank. In 1657, John Gamble's *Ayres and Dialogues*

[25] Thomas Dekker, *The Guls Horn-booke* (London, 1609), p. 34, and *The Raven's Almanacke* (London, 1609), C1r–v.

[26] *Pepys Ballads*, vol. I, pp. 214–15, 288, vol. II, p. 9; Taylor, *All the Workes*, vol. III, p. 507.

[27] *Autobiography of Thomas Whythorne*; Case, *Praise of Musicke*, pp. 20–1.

included a preface addressed 'To the Noble, Few, Lovers of Musick'.[28] Musicians tended to moan, and John Playford returned again and again to the proposition that, in England, his cherished art and its followers carried little prestige (unless they were pretentious visiting Frenchmen).

In another sign of the difficult times, musicians were prone to quarrel among themselves. There were obvious tensions between those who saw themselves as a musical elite and those who could make no such claim. The reputation of minstrels, fiddlers and pipers for undesirable characteristics of all sorts clearly did nothing to unite the musical fraternity in harmony. The self-styled 'professors' of music – whether they were performers or literary apologists – were at pains to dissociate themselves from lower life-forms who, in their less than humble opinion, were incapable of producing true music at all. Occupational music was, in the unhappy words of Thomas Whythorne, 'a chaos or a confused lump of degrees and sorts heaped up in a bundle'. Lines had to be drawn. In about 1580, Thomas Lodge defended music against Stephen Gosson's charge that it was a stimulant of debauchery, 'But as I like Musik, so admit I not of thos that deprave the same: your Pipers are so odius to mee as yourselfe; nether alowe I your harpinge merye beggars.' Naturally, John Case agreed: 'Our alehouse, vagabond & beging minstrelsie I defend not, liberal sciences are for liberal men.' Even Leonard Wheatcroft, a musical yeoman from Derbyshire, clambered aboard the bandwagon, inscribing in his notebook certain rather clumsy 'Verses upon Fidlers':

Are not those fidlers rouges, That upon their backes do beare
A great fidle, with a hole I'th midle, Base lowsy Roges they are
Th'le prate, and talke, and sing, And draw their mouths aside,
Theile drinke and dance & fling, I cannot those Rouges abide.[29]

Such opinions were common enough to receive satirical treatment in a humorous lecture delivered by one 'J. Bourne' in Oxford, some time around 1642. 'Every thing that weares a fiddle is not of the list of these professors', he insisted, for an instrument 'is but the luggage of this Divine Art and noe more makes a Musitian then [than] a gowne makes a schollarr.' The sound produced by common fiddlers grated on the ears

[28] See, for example, John Hilton, *Ayres* (London, 1627), preface; Gamble, *Ayres and Dialogues*, preface.

[29] *Autobiography of Thomas Whythorne*, p. 206; Thomas Lodge, *A Reply to Stephen Gosson's Schoole of Abuse, in Defence of Poetry, Musick, and Stage Plays* (*c.* 1580; London: Shakespeare Society, 1853), p. 21; Case, *Praise of Musicke*, p. 31; Wheatcroft, 'Verses upon Fidlers', in Leonard Wheatcroft's poems, D5433/1, unpaginated, DRO.

Figure 2.2. Highly trained occupational musicians played from the written page and considered themselves a cut about the rest. Here, the sophisticated violinist – a creature of the indoors – must compete with the deafening street music of ballad-singers, shawm- and horn-players, hawkers and children with rattles and drums. © Trustees of the British Museum, Prints and Drawings, S,2.62, William Hogarth, *The Enraged Musician* (London, 1741).

of educated people, 'yet 'twould make one laugh to see how they soure their Antique faces, hanging downe their heads like one nearly turnd of from the Gallows while their haire (long enough to make a fiddle string) dances to their tunes'. Common minstrels, he claimed, were lacking in even rudimentary musical education. They played 'not by Rules but by Custome' and 'could not tell whether a Diapason were flesh or fish'. Moreover, they failed to understand that the true musician achieved a beautiful harmony that encompassed not only his notes, but his reason and his bodily gestures too. 'His hand with a posed quality must dance ore the stringes like sunbeames ore a wall, till at last [in] a swift Charriot of fire, he sends soft jewells to our ears' (see Figure 2.2).[30]

30 Add. MS 37999, fo. 66, BL.

Musical equals also squabbled, occasionally in sinister and spectacular fashion. The life of George Cally (or Kelly), a prominent performer in the city of Chester, was a case study in discord. In 1599, he was involved in a tense dispute with his similarly musical brother Robert. Their ability to make sweet harmony together was threatened by a disagreement regarding the distribution of the spoils. Arbitrators were summoned, and the two men agreed a financial scheme and promised 'to Contynue be and remayne in one Company and be lovinge and frendlie thone to thother during & to thend of their naturall lyves without separation or departure one from another'. Ten years later, however, George was once again annoyed with his brother. In a neighbour's house, several witnesses heard him complain about the way in which Robert had sought and secured the patronage of the local knight whose livery he now wore. Robert, said George, 'did Creepe unto Sir John Savages arse for his patches'. In any case, his own patron was a far better man: Cally, as Alice Leneskey recalled, clapped a hand upon his own badge and said that 'Sr John Savages Colycence was not to be compared to the Lord of Darbyes'.[31]

At the same date, George Cally was also temporarily imprisoned because of his part in a bitter and violent dispute with Clement Pemburton and Thomas Williams, both employed as musicians in the city's band of waits. Cally's feud with the official civic ensemble rumbled on for years, but the plot thickened suddenly in 1613 when he petitioned the city assembly on behalf of his own band. Cally expressed his desire 'that he and his felow Musitians may be admitted waytes of this Cittie in steede of the Waytes now absent'. The assembly members, apparently somewhat perplexed at this unexpected vacancy, voted to postpone a decision 'untill it may be understoode what are become of the ould waytes'. In the following year, Cally and his group were duly appointed as waits of the city. George Cally, father of ten, was clearly a man of great energy, and it seems that he had skilfully out-manoeuvred his opponents in this battle of the bands and won himself a position on the city payroll. Readers will be reassured to learn that he had not actually done away with his adversaries, for both Pemburton and Williams resurfaced at a later date, and both were still capable of strumming and blowing their instruments.[32]

[31] *REED Chester*, p. 195.

[32] Z QSE/9/8, ChRO; *REED Chester*, pp. 280, 285. See also Baldwin, *Paying the Piper*, pp. 67–70. Further evidence of waits in conflict can be found in Mark Brayshay, 'Waits, Musicians, Bearwards and Players: The Inter-urban Road Travel and Performances of Itinerant Entertainers in Sixteenth- and Seventeenth-century England', *Journal of Historical Geography* 31 (2005), 437.

In other cases, musicians allegedly stalked, intimidated or even killed one another.[33] Of course, it is difficult to know whether or not they were more prone to such argument than those working in other occupations, or more quarrelsome in this period than in others. Perhaps disputes such as those in which George Cally participated were products not only of the tense times but of the artistic temperament. One ballad of the later seventeenth century picked up the theme, and provided one of the earliest known examples of a band torn apart in true rock'n'roll style by sexual jealousy. *The Downfall of Dancing*, set to the tune of 'Robin Goodfellow', describes the self-destructive 'overthrow of three Fidlers, and three Bagg-Pipe-Players, Who Lately broke all their Fiddles and Bagg-pipes, and Tore their Cloaks; so that, they are utterly ruin'd. All this was done in a fearful Fray, when one of the Fidlers catch'd his Wife with his Fellow Bagg pipe player, at Uptails all.'[34]

It all flew in the face of the claims made by literary music-lovers that sonic harmony bred social harmony. In the world inhabited by George Cally and others, it appears to have done nothing of the sort. Musical apologists sometimes rebuked practitioners for bringing their art and science into disrepute by criticising one another (though this call for restraint clearly did not apply to the ranks of poor fiddlers and harpers, who were considered fair game). They had in mind instances such as that in which an ageing John Dowland spoke out against the younger generation of lutenists, who considered his style of playing old-fashioned. Friction between musicians young and old is also nicely reflected in a print depicting an elderly fiddler who criticises the bagpipe-playing and ageist attitudes of his allegedly idle son-in-law (see Figure 2.3). Robert Jones, contemplating the state of musical relations in 1600, warned that the mutual hostility of some performers was endangering music's good name. 'In their own singularitie', he alleged, 'they condemne every mans workes, as some waie faulty.' The problem had not gone away by 1752, when the organist Charles Avison argued that music as a whole would benefit if 'the Professors themselves, would cultivate a sincere and frendly Commerce with each other, and cherish that benevolent Temper, which their daily Employ, one should think, ought naturally to inspire'.[35]

[33] See, for example *Records of the Borough of Nottingham, Being a Series of Extracts from the Archives of the Corporation of Nottingham*, 9 vols. (Nottingham: Thomas Forman, 1882–1956), vol. V, pp. 171–2; QSB/1/199/7, Lancashire Record Office; *Calendar of Assize Records: Surrey Indictments, James I*, ed. J. S. Cockburn (London: Her Majesty's Stationery Office, 1982), p. 119.

[34] *Pepys Ballads*, vol. III, p. 188.

[35] Dowland, *Pilgrimes Solace*, preface; Jones, *The First Booke of Songes and Ayres* (London, 1600), dedicatory epistle; Avison, *Essay on Musical Expression*, pp. 93–4.

Figure 2.3. The potential for friction between old and young musicians is indicated by the words of this elderly violinist. The bagpipes of his lazy and scornful son-in-law can be glimpsed behind him. The British Library, C20 F7–F10, Roxburghe ballads, vol. I, opening pages ('You idle knave').

In sum, it is not difficult to portray the early modern period as one in which minstrels and musicians suffered and misbehaved. The less fortunate were targeted by zealous parliamentarians, judges, ministers, churchwardens and moralists. They were lampooned by poets, playwrights and other authors. Sometimes crime and sin became irresistible temptations. Lewdness, as John Case acknowledged, was 'an hoale in the musicians coate'.[36] The reputation of fiddlers and pipers deteriorated, and higher-ranking musicians felt tainted by association. That, at least, is the story so far.

[36] Case, *Praise of Musicke*, p. 30.

The case for the defence

It would be misleading to conclude on such a sorry note. 'Feast-finding minstrels' were, after all, famous for their capacity to seek out and enhance the good times of life. Indeed, it was precisely this talent for merriment that rendered them so suspicious in the eyes and ears of their critics. The century before 1660 was, without doubt, a controversial one in which to make a musical living, but with controversy comes excitement. While it is true that many voices were raised in criticism of minstrelsy, it is also abundantly plain that an equal and opposite number sounded in its defence. Numerous minstrels were prosecuted under the vagrancy statutes, but many others avoided trouble, either through skilful evasion or merely by adjusting their practices in order to comply with the new requirements. 'Honest minstrels' were not a breed recognised by animated Elizabethans such as Thomas Lovell or Philip Stubbes, but they nevertheless existed.

In Lancashire – that hotbed of subversive piping – it is possible to identify more than fifty lowly minstrels whose names have not been found in the records of prosecution. 'Harry the piper of Pilling', for example, is known to us only because, in 1632, his wife gave birth to a son in the parish of Cockerham. Either such people had powerful protectors, or they prudently put up their pipes on the Sabbath.[37] In 1642, a musician named William Knowstubbs journeyed to Grantham (Lincolnshire), accompanied by a humble cooper. The two men offered the chamberlain's court £10 for the privilege of becoming freemen of the town, and must have been gratified when the leading inhabitants decided to admit them for half of this standard sum, 'in regard they were poore men & like to prove good townes men, nor like to hurte anie freeman being of their trades'. Knowstubbs, despite being impecunious and musical, had clearly made a good impression.[38] Such sympathetic attitudes were perhaps more common or more dominant after the Restoration than they had been during the hundred years before it. From 1660, musicians seem, in general, to have attracted lower levels of controversy. They were still mocked, but they were less frequently feared, and vagrancy statutes ceased to mention them by name.[39] Suspicions remained, of course, but the individuals who

[37] *REED Lancashire*, p. 243. Other references to unblemished pipers can be found dotted throughout this volume.

[38] *Grantham during the Interregnum: The Hallbook of Grantham, 1641–49*, ed. Bill Couth, *Lincoln Record Society* 83 (1995), p. 13.

[39] See, for example, *Statutes of the Realm*, vol. VII, pp. 607–8.

experienced them with the greatest intensity – particularly the more zealous of Protestants – could no longer aspire with much realism to drive the mood of the nation.

Even before this, the minstrel's lot was not always quite as grim as it might seem. The parliamentary act of 1572 increased the pressure under which such performers operated, and threatened to entangle them in Tudor red tape, but it was aimed primarily at those who spent most of their time on the road, rather than at music-makers who operated largely within their own localities. In any case, the statute made allowance – to the disgust of some moralists – for minstrels with licences or liveries. In subsequent decades, an unknowable number of travelling musicians made appropriate applications and played by the rules. Only a handful of licences survive in the archives, but they nevertheless indicate that a system for granting or refusing permission to perform did develop during the late sixteenth century. In September 1572, George Writt, a tailor-cum-musician from Great Maplestead (Essex), was quick off the mark, perhaps because he knew that his name was to appear on the forthcoming list of moonlighting musicians. He asked the court of quarter sessions for a licence 'to travell the countrye with his instruments to bridhales and other places being thereunto required'. He also informed the judges that he was 'a pore man having a wyfe and fyve children and towe prentices laboring for his living with thes towe s[c]iences as an honest man ought to do'. His application was endorsed by one gentleman and nine other individuals, and the official record bears the positive instruction, 'Let licence be made by the Court.'[40] The statute of 1597 did not mention the system of licensing, and thus seemed to imply that a stricter regime was to supersede it. It appears, however, that licences could still be obtained in practice, or, to put it another way, that minstrels and musicians who travelled without licences could still be prosecuted for failing to secure them (it is always easier to find miscreants). In 1631, two minstrels, originally from Monmouth, confessed that they had come to Shropshire without a pass signed by two justices of the peace, and they promised never again to take to the road without one.[41]

County judges were not the only officers with the power to exercise control over minstrels and musicians. There were alternative authorities too, a situation that presumably created opportunities for minstrels to take advantage of loopholes, overlaps and rivalries. Licences could, for

[40] Q/SR 42/18, ERO. For a model licence, see *REED Dorset, Cornwall*, pp. 118–19.

[41] *REED Shropshire*, p. 319.

example, be issued by the Master of the Revels, who sometimes dealt with applications from travelling minstrels and musicians (often in association with companies of theatrical players). In 1623, Sir Henry Herbert issued licences 'to Barth. Cloye with 3 Assistants to make show of a Musicall Organ, with diver Motions in it', and eight years later he did the same for the musicians – specifically a drummer and a trumpeter – who served as mobile publicists and accompanists for one Sisley Peadle and her troupe of rope-dancers. Sisley's group had permission 'quietly to passe' from place to place without molestation, provided that they did not perform on the Sabbath.[42] In London, those who delivered brassy blasts in order to announce theatrical performances were, in theory, expected to obtain licences from the Sergeant Trumpeter. Many, however, seem not to have bothered. During the 1660s, both the Sergeant Trumpeter and the Master of the Revels were engaged in efforts to enforce their licensing authority against those who flouted or rejected it. The Master of the Revels claimed the right to control music throughout the country, but complained that 'many are very obstinate, and refuse to take lycenses, especially in cities and townes corporate, under the pretence of being freemen'.[43] This obstinacy probably owed something to the cultural atmosphere in Restoration England, which allowed musicians to feel increasingly confident and secure about what they did for a living.

There is also evidence to suggest that musicians, responding to criticism, sought to deploy and develop the existing mechanisms by which their medieval predecessors had, in theory at least, regulated their own affairs. Admittedly, this meant yet more scrutiny and cannot have pleased those minstrels who had no intention of working within any system, but from the viewpoint of musicians who aspired to respectability such attempts to set the musical house in order were probably welcome. In London, a company consisting of 'the master, wardens, and commonalty of the Art or Science of the Musicians of London' received a royal charter in 1604. This company had its origins in a medieval fellowship of minstrels, but the Jacobean generation was intent on enhancing previous efforts to control music-making in the capital and to protect the interests of its members. The charter endowed it with authority over all musicians

[42] *The Dramatic Records of Sir Henry Herbert, Master of the Revels, 1623–1673*, ed. Joseph Quincy Adams (New Haven: Yale University Press, 1917), p. 42; *REED Herefordshire, Worcestershire*, pp. 539–40.

[43] *The King's Musick: A Transcript of Records Relating to Music and Musicians*, ed. Henry Cart de Lafontaine (London: Novello and Company, 1909), p. 134; *The Dramatic Records of Sir Henry Herbert*, p. 134.

in the city itself and the surrounding area, to a distance of three miles. Two years later, the company's revised by-laws stated its ambitions with some clarity and force. It would punish any musician who endangered the livelihoods of its members by playing at any 'triumphs, marriages, revels, feasts, dinners, suppers, banquets, meetings, guilds or brotherhoods', unless he was a freeman of the city. No musician was to play at the windows or lodgings of wealthy Londoners without the company's express permission. Members were to refuse to perform for those who would not hire at least four of them. Aspiring members would be selected or rejected on the basis of their musical ability, and any musician working in London could at any time be summoned for an audition and, if necessary, rejected or disallowed 'for his insufficiency and want of skill'. The company would restrict the numbers of apprentices employed by its freemen, and would prevent such apprentices from playing in taverns, except when accompanied and monitored by freemen. Several of these regulations were attempts to improve the public image of the musician. Members were not to sing ribald songs, nor to walk in the streets with their instruments 'uncased or uncovered in any part' (naked violins and trumpets were apparently unseemly). All offences would incur fines or imprisonment, while the affairs of the company were to be conducted by annually elected masters, wardens, assistants and stewards.[44]

The company frequently found it difficult to enforce its discipline, particularly over musicians who did not belong (often because they were already freemen within other London companies). It tried to cajole non-members into joining by setting a fine for refusal that was double the entrance fee. In 1634, the king's musicians challenged the Jacobean charter in the Court of Chancery, successfully claiming that it infringed their own pre-existing regulatory rights. As a result, the company lost its charter and had to re-form itself as a guild within the city. Moreover, it was always one of the poorest of the London companies, and made provision in its by-laws for the relief of impoverished members. Despite these difficulties, it continued to function throughout the period and is the ancestor of the present Worshipful Company of Musicians. The royal musicians, meanwhile, obtained their own charter in 1635 and thereby acquired the theoretical right to govern occupational music-making in all but one of England's counties.[45] Once again, however, it seems clear that the

[44] Richard Crewdson, *Apollo's Swan and Lyre: Five Hundred Years of the Musicians' Company* (Woodbridge: Boydell Press, 2000). The charter and by-laws are included in ibid., appendix 4, pp. 248–66.

[45] Ibid., pp. 85–92, 255, 262.

existence of a number of somewhat contradictory jurisdictions must have allowed many minstrels to squeeze through the gaps, particularly in the newly permissive atmosphere of the Restoration.

Beyond the capital, there were other institutions with powers over musicians and minstrels. In York, there existed from 1561 a guild of musicians that was similar in most respects to its London counterpart. This fellowship does not appear to have been particularly effective, and is mentioned only rarely in seventeenth-century sources. Much the same can be said of the attempts made to form or maintain musical solidarities in Canterbury, Hull, Beverley and Shrewsbury.[46] In the last of these towns, we find occasional and intriguing references to an annual minstrels' court, but scholars have questioned the authenticity of the crucial document. This account of the court's medieval origins, written in a seventeenth-century hand, may be a fabrication based on an ill-founded local myth. Alternatively, the existence of such a court would help to explain why, in 1638–9, the churchwardens of St Julian's mentioned in their accounts 'a little Chest belonging to the company of musitians'.[47] Sadly, we cannot peer into this chest as we seek to understand how the musicians of Shrewsbury responded to the pressures of the age.

A more accessible institution was the 'Minstrells Court' held annually at Tutbury in Staffordshire. This court licensed music-makers in the royal honour of Tutbury, an area situated mainly in Staffordshire and Derbyshire, but also encompassing portions of Nottinghamshire, Leicestershire and Warwickshire. Two documents from the 1620s, motivated by the crown's desire to maximise its revenues, enable us to build up a colourful picture of the court's activities at this time.[48] All the musicians and minstrels within the jurisdiction were required to travel to Tutbury for three days every August, 'that is to saye, the vigell, the daye, and the daye after the Feast of St Mary the Assumption'. The court's activities were concentrated on the final day. The minstrels processed from the royal bailiff's house to the church. Along the way, music played before them, and the out-going stewards each carried a white wand. The remaining members of the company wore the liveries and scutcheons of their patrons. After the church service, each minstrel offered a penny to the vicar of Tutbury before they all made their way to the Moot Hall. Here,

[46] Woodfill, *Musicians in English Society*, pp. 114–16.

[47] *REED Shropshire*, pp. 319, 507–12.

[48] 'The Trew Maner, Use and Forme of the Kinges Majesties Court of Musicke Holden att Tutburie', Royal MS 18 BX, fos. 63r–67r, BL; 'Orders for Regulating the Minstrels' Court at Tutbury', Add. MS CH 42681, BL.

the names of all the musicians owing attendance were read out from a roll, and twenty-four of them were selected to form a jury. The chosen minstrels vowed to make true presentments, punish offenders and uphold the ancient liberties of their company. Next, their consciences were stirred by an address in praise of music, after which they retired to consider their business, leaving the stewards 'to make them selves merye with a bankitt, And a noise of Musicons to pleae before them'.

In seclusion, the jury identified and allotted fines to offending musicians in a number of categories: those who had not served legitimate apprenticeships; those who owed suit but had failed to appear; and those from other counties who were known to have crossed into the honour of Tutbury and stayed in one place for more than nine hours with the intention of making music for profit. It was also necessary to settle any points of controversy, and it was decided in 1630 that such minstrels as were licensed by the court should be permitted to perform on Sundays 'at weddings & such like solemne meetinges', provided that they fell silent during time of divine service. Without such allowance, it was felt that the region's musicians, 'whose poore estate this Court doth much tender', might not be able to support their wives and children. The court could not only administer fines, but could also distrain musical instruments and pass offenders, where appropriate, to the conventional authorities for punishment according to statute.

When the jurymen returned to the company, they announced the names of the 'kinge' and four stewards whom they had elected to serve for the forthcoming year. The old king then drank a toast to the new one, and presented him with a white wand. When the jury had made its presentments, the company went for dinner. Meanwhile, two of the stewards went from door to door in the town, with music playing before them, and collected a customary twopence from every household. This was referred to as a fee 'for wiche ... they are to playe musicke every Morninge and Eveninge throughe every streete in the Towne duringe the tyme of theire aboode'.

After dinner, the fun really started. Firstly, 'the Musicons Repaere theym selves to the Abbie gate in Tutburye, haveinge noe maner of weapon in theere handes, nor about them'. The minstrels dispersed in groups to the ends of nearby streets, then turned to witness the release of a bull from the abbey. This creature cannot have been in a particularly good mood, having had 'the tippe of his hornes cutte of, his eares stoved, his tayele cutt of by the strumble, All his bodye oyeled over with sope and blackinge, And his noose [nose] blowen full of pepper.' In the hours between this pivotal moment and the setting of the sun, the minstrels, at considerable risk to their precious fingers, attempted to tame or restrain the poor animal. If successful, they were required to 'cutt off some peece of his eare, and bringe yt to the markett crosse in Tutburye in token they have taken him'. The bull's day, and presumably its life, would then draw to a close in a fight with the dogs belonging to various dignitaries and officers of the court. If, however, the bull evaded capture and managed to escape across the river Dove, then it was returned to its original owner once more. At times, this detailed account sounds almost fanciful, yet the surviving documents all support one another, and the court was sufficiently well-known to receive passing mention in a printed song of the late seventeenth century. *A Proper New Ballad of Bold Robin Hood* describes, among other things, a battle fought by the merry men 'near to Titbery Town, / when the Bagpipes baited the Bull'. Robin and his companions attended the feast and savoured the dancing, the fiddling, the piping, the bare-backed riding of the bull, the mad staring and the 'strange shouting'.[49]

The Tutbury court supervised musicians within the honour, but did not exempt them from the requirements of statute law. The only region to enjoy such an exemption was Cheshire, where a minstrels' court had been in existence since around 1186. In the seventeenth century, the privilege of summoning the Midsummer court belonged to the Dutton family, who profited from the right to license every minstrel in the county. The sound of them all playing their various instruments in unison at Chester's East Gate in order to salute their lord at the opening of proceedings must have been impressive. Like that in Tutbury, the Cheshire court elected a jury and proceeded to levy fines and administer licences for fees that apparently ranged from 4½d to 2s 6d. Unfortunately, there are very few surviving records of the court's actual proceedings during the early modern period, but isolated sources indicate that it was a serious and long-running institution.[50] A case of 1610 suggests that the Duttons guarded their rights assiduously. In this year, a Chester tallowchandler named John Burton was tried at quarter sessions for his involvement in an affray. Under examination, he explained that on Midsummer Eve he and other members of the Company of Tallowchandlers had been walking through the streets in the annual procession, 'havinge before them iii musitioners upon vialles playinge'. All of a sudden, 'there Came ii or iii of Mr Duttons men of

[49] *Pepys Ballads*, vol. II, pp. 116–17.

[50] DDBL 24/22, Lancashire Record Office; MA/B/V/9, ChRO; *REED Chester*, pp. 65–6, 461–6, 486–9, 501–3; Chas F. Forshaw, 'The Minstrel Court of Cheshire', *Notes and Queries* 4 (1899), 178–9; Baldwin, *Paying the Piper*, p. 120.

Dutton unto them and tooke the instrumentes from the musike'. The tallowchandlers made an official complaint, and Burton was sent to communicate the mayor's response to Dutton's officious servants. They were determined not to return the instruments, and one of them assaulted Burton, causing his nose to bleed, before asking, 'what should wee talke with such a skervie boy as this?' Other witnesses from various city companies told the same story, but the court's verdict is unknown.[51]

The existence of such courts and companies exerted contradictory influences on the occupational music-makers as a whole. To those who did not belong, disciplinary organisations were either an irritant (in the case of musicians who refused to join because they were secure within other civic companies) or a significant threat (to those who were excluded because they were itinerant, untrained or allegedly disorderly). In the latter case, musical fraternities served to reinforce the pressures being applied by judges, constables and churchwardens. To those who did belong, however, courts and companies must have generated self-esteem and sensations of legitimacy. Musicians had never enjoyed a secure and specific place on the social hierarchy, but the fraternities in which they gathered went some way towards easing the inevitable anxiety. Under the institutional umbrella, music-makers held rights and responsibilities, just like other respectable members of society, and they experienced the beginnings of a sense of professional solidarity. Musicians sometimes quarrelled, as we have already heard, but the courts and companies seem to have managed their internal tensions well. There is little evidence to suggest that internal squabbles regularly grew serious enough to necessitate the intervention of other legal bodies. Members of the London company did battle with the royal musicians, but they seem to have esteemed their own brethren highly enough. In 1616, Henry Walker made a will in which he asked the company to administer a charitable stock of £120 on behalf of the poor and lame from the parish of his birth in Herefordshire. He also left money and a mourning cloak to each of his two apprentices, future members of the company. A year later, Robert Bateman bequeathed 'to his companye beinge the companye of Musicians tenne poundes to buy them a Cupp withall'. He also remembered the company's beadle, and shared out five viols and violins among his two servants.[52] These men, at least, were proud to belong.

[51] QSE/9/69, ChRO.

[52] Prerogative Court of Canterbury Wills, 94 Cope and 18 Meade, NA.

Presumably, the regular gatherings of musicians for court sessions and company meetings were also valuable in facilitating the exchange of melodies, instrumental innovations and information. The annual meetings at Tutbury and Chester, in particular, were reminiscent of the Lenten minstrel schools held in medieval European towns for the dissemination of new songs and skills. These continental events conveyed a certain prestige, and minstrels occasionally had their travelling expenses paid by high-ranking employers.[53] In seventeenth-century England too, there are signs that the courts and companies of musicians were not quite as ineffectual and poorly regarded as historians have sometimes suggested. Sir George Buck, Master of the Revels in 1603, described the members of the new London company as 'the best Musicians of this kingdom, and equal to any in Europe for their skill either in composing, and setting, or in singing, or for playing upon any kind of musical instruments'. Three decades later, the musical scholar Charles Butler recited Buck's words with obvious approval, and commended England's recent kings for awarding the company its coat of arms. In Cheshire, the musically minded were evidently proud of the court, and several sources drew attention to the fact that the minstrels of Cheshire were exempt from the vagrancy statutes. As Sir Peter Leycester, musician and antiquarian, commented, 'the Fidlers of Cheshire, Licensed by the Heirs of Dutton of Dutton, are no Rogues'.[54]

There survives in the papers kept by the Wright family of Eyam Hall (Derbyshire) a contemporary copy of one of the annual music speeches delivered before the minstrels at Tutbury each August. This previously unnoticed document, dating from the late seventeenth century, is particularly interesting for the efforts its author makes to bolster the local minstrels' sense of identity and worth.[55] The speaker was a 'well wisher' to music rather than an occupational minstrel, but he was clearly fully aware of the local scene and the more general issues affecting his audience of specialists. His central purpose was to stimulate in the jurymen a mood of high-mindedness for their present purpose, namely the preparation of presentments. This he did by praising music to the skies, drawing attention to its many good effects and great antiquity. The ancient Britons, he observed, 'had Musicians before they had Bookes'. He addressed his audience as 'Gentlemen Minstrells', and praised in extravagant terms their

[53] Isabelle Cazeaux, *French Music in the Fifteenth and Sixteenth Centuries* (Oxford: Blackwell, 1975), p. 98; Maricarmen Gómez, 'Minstrel Schools in the Later Middle Ages', *Early Music* 18 (1989), 213–18.

[54] Butler, *Principles of Musik*, fo. 4r; *REED Chester*, pp. 488–9.

[55] All quotations are from the speech delivered at Tutbury, pp. 1–18, D4530/76/8, DRO.

role within society. 'In a word', he asked, 'what Feast what Ball for dancing what wedding what Country wakes or entertainement soever can be well held without the helpe of some of your Society[?]' To answer his own question, he referred by name to certain members of the gathered company: 'I dare say old Will Ward of Leeke (one of the top of your kin) with his melodious Large pipes & his son James with his violin are oftner & further sent for than any doctor or Chirugeon in the place where they live.' In short, minstrels pleased men and women of all sorts, and could even stimulate a sense of well-being in the beasts of the field. When minstrels played, birds sang in harmonious response. With such power, however, came responsibility. The 'known Masters of concord & harmony' should take care not to abuse or pervert the true purpose of their occupation by arguing with one another or by wicked manners, profane oaths, beastly drunkenness or bawdy songs. It was, of course, both acceptable and necessary 'to be at fit times pleasant & jovyall pipers & Fidlers – yet remember at the same time that you are or ought to be alwayes good Christians'.

The speaker, carried away by his own eloquence, also proposed an experiment involving the 'strong & lusty Bull' who was, at that very moment, being prepared for action. For once, he suggested, the contest for the bull should be conducted according to 'a gentler method'. His horns, neck and tail, instead of being mutilated, should 'be adorned with Flowers Garlands & fine Ribbands like the Beasts of old offered to Apollo the God of Musick'. Upon his release, the bull would then be spared the 'crabbed Cudgells & cruell Blows' of the mob, and encouraged to make his decisions on alternative grounds:

> doe you Gentlemen of the Minstrelsy advance before him with your Musicall Instruments & try the power of your Fingers & Fiddlesticks upon him: I dare almost say or hope that the generous Bull would quickly & quietly determine to whome he ought to belonge by following the best & most harmonious Musicians: This either was or should be the true intent of our Tutbury Bulrunning.

Regrettably, the results of this experiment are currently unknown. Nor can we tell whether the minstrels themselves perceived it as a worthwhile innovation. We can be certain, however, that by the time this speech on the 'Usefulness, dignity & excellency' of their art drew to its conclusion, most of them felt rather positive about what they did for a living. The influence of musical courts and companies may also help to explain why, in some quarters, the term 'minstrel' survived as a relatively neutral designation. Clearly, it was not inevitably pejorative in Derbyshire, Cheshire or even London.

Another source of succour for the frequently embattled musicians of early modern England was the readiness of sympathetic men and women to stand up for them in times of crisis. Admittedly, printed defences of the less sophisticated players were not common, for musical apologists tended to disown all mere fiddlers and pipers. Occasionally, however, an author struck a different note. Samuel Person's pen-portrait of the archetypal 'musician', written in the warmer world of 1664, was far more generous than most earlier versions. This Restoration musician was an enchanter, a joiner of concord and discord and a striker of heart-ravishing harmony. He was 'a conjurer in the circle of the ear', and his music warmed grief-frozen spirits. Person went on, 'He is a merry man, a Jolly Fellow, a Boone Companion, and a Friend to Bacchus.' Just as the Tutbury orator advised, Person's musician enjoyed good fellowship but aspired to 'sing his part with those warbling Sphears . . . , to bear a part in the Quire of Heavenly Angels'.[56]

Published defences may have been rare, but it was by no means unusual for individuals of wealth, education and influence to express a measure of sympathy for those in the lower ranks of the musical hierarchy. In 1560, a minstrel in Kent was presented to the church court for failing to attend church as required under the recent Act of Uniformity, but escaped punishment by claiming economic necessity and by promising to come to services every other Sunday from that point onwards. Half a century later, Nicholas Yeomans, a musician from Hutton in Somerset, successfully asked the court of quarter sessions not to punish him as a wandering rogue. He had been reported for his allegedly itinerant lifestyle, and was 'now like to be dealt with accordinge to the statute of Roges and vagabundes which to avoyd he hath left the said parishe & his wife and children'. Yeomans explained, in his defence, that he travelled only within a three-mile radius and never stayed away from home for an extended period. Moreover, he played his instruments only to those who had specifically requested his presence. The judges, swayed by the plea of this 'poore man', decided that his case was 'not . . . within the compasse of the said Statute' and ordered that Yeomans should be 'noe farther troubled' by the local constables.[57] Music could thus be a point of sympathetic contact between society's unequal parts as well as a site of conflict.

[56] Person, *An Anatomical Lecture*, pp. 66–9.

[57] *Church Life in Kent being Church Court Records of the Cantertury Diocese, 1559–1565*, ed. Arthur J. Willis (London: Philimore, 1975), p. 29; *REED Somerset*, pp. 142–3.

The tolerance of influential individuals was one of the cultural features against which many puritans and moralists set their backs. When James I issued his so-called Book of Sports in 1617 and 1618, it seemed that the king himself had become a friend of fond fiddlers. The documents mentioned musicians only sparingly, but both had an obvious bearing upon the rights of musicians to work on Sundays and other holy days. Instrumentalists were, after all, the very heartbeat of the newly sanctioned 'May-Games, Whitson Ales, and Morris-dances'.[58] Perhaps the king omitted to draw attention to the nation's musicians more extensively for the simple and rather embarrassing reason that he was effectively giving pipers, fiddlers and drummers special permission to work on the day of rest.

Enforcement of the declaration was somewhat patchy, but it swiftly became a guidebook for those involved in the Jacobean and Caroline fight-back on behalf of traditional culture. In Gloucestershire, for example, the colourful vicar of Bisley, Christopher Windle, promoted it with great enthusiasm. Back in 1610, he had offended the scruples of some of his parishioners by asserting the legitimacy of summer ales, piping, dancing and maypoles. The Book of Sports presented Windle with an excellent opportunity for the further advancement of his views, and the fact that he was, by 1618, in prison for debt did not deter him. A summary of his opinions is contained in 'A Book, for a Buck with a Parke or, for a good Bishopricke or, for a fatt Benefice at least', a Latin manuscript addressed to the king in support of the declaration. Windle's central and most interesting argument was that many of the celebratory physical activities traditionally conducted on Sundays and holy days were, in God's eyes, an aspect of worship rather than its very antithesis: 'For we always rejoice in our bodies and there is always something to be done by them.' It was the clergy's responsibility to teach moderation and decorum, but not to deny outright the spiritual value of recreation. Windle attached to his puritan enemies various unflattering labels – 'presumptuous', 'arrogant', 'insolent', 'useless', 'contentious' – and asked them, 'Does anyone not know, is anyone ignorant either that music is one of the liberal arts, part of a liberal education, or that it is to no purpose and of no value without practice, playing, round dances, applause, rejoicing, happiness and delight?'[59]

[58] The full text of the 1618 Book of Sports can be found in *REED Cumberland, Westmorland, Gloucestershire*, pp. 365–8.

[59] Ibid., pp. 285, 403, 409, 414.

He concluded his address by recounting an occasion upon which he and other local clergymen had been invited to Cirencester to dine with the archdeacon. As the assembled company stood in the cloisters, they were approached by a band of musicians – the servants of Lords Grey and Chandos – who offered 'some of their music, harmony, and melody'. In response, a misguided minister named Alder exclaimed, 'Be off with them! Be off! What are they doing here? They are vagabonds under the Act and the head and cause of many evils among the people.' In his opinion, there was no place for worldly musicians at a gathering of clergymen. The musicians, sensing that they were not welcome, prepared to depart without a murmur. Windle, however, gathered his wits and kindly called the men back. He asked his angry colleague, 'Why should they go, pray tell? … Do they not come with affection and respect for us? Is not divine providence revealed in this as in other events? Is not music allowed us just as much as tables and dinner parties are?' On one level, the quarrel was about the status of musicians; on another, it addressed the status of the clergy and the nature of their relationship with the laity. Were ministers to stand apart or should they more properly demonstrate in their lifestyles that they understood the value of earthly pleasure? The rhetorical questions continued to flow as Windle contemplated the life histories of the musicians before him:

> Might not those men gladly have the fruits and reap happiness as well as utility from their art, skill and profession, as we do? Alas, how many days, nights, weeks, months, years, not to say their whole miserable life, have these wretches spent, passed, and used up, starving, in order to acquire some skill in singing, playing a stringed instrument, striking strings either by using the pick or touching them gracefully with the fingers so as to please, wonderfully delight, exhilarate, and gratify us the more? … Let us be silent and rather treat them with humanity.

Windle's supporting arguments won the day: 'Mr Archdeacon, Mr Sutton, and all the rest as far as I know agreed with the sweetest concord; the musicians came nearer, harped, played, sounded their instruments, made a loud noice, and jingled: they pleased and delighted us.'[60] The grateful clergymen contributed towards an informal payment of several shillings, and the musicians went gratefully away. There was, of course, something a little fantastical about Windle's victory in this argument. As he well knew, the broader battle could not be won so easily.

[60] Ibid., pp. 418–19.

Equally significant for local musicians were the many defences mounted by ordinary people, mere foot-soldiers in the battle for English culture. At times, it was necessary to do no more than apply the changing rules with moderation and flexibility. The puritan author Christopher Fetherston was concerned about churchwardens who permitted music and dancing on Sundays when, in his view, they should have been patrolling their parishes with their ears pricked and their eyes peeled.[61] Surviving church court documents reveal that this phenomenon was not restricted to Fetherston's imagination, though we generally hear of flexible churchwardens only when sterner individuals reported them for their laxity.[62] Others intervened in the legal process, encouraging judges to treat named individuals with a measure of kindness. In Somerset, six men and women spoke out on behalf of John Huishe, a fiddler from Litton, when he found himself in trouble with the bishop in 1594. His character witnesses were two vicars, a vicar's wife, two middle-aged yeomen and an elderly miller. Together, they presented a consistent account of 'a very poore man' who 'goeth from parishe to parishe to play on his fiddle upon revill daies and churchales'. They all knew him well, and the miller said that Huishe's musical merry-making was always done 'in good and honest sort for ought that this deponent ever hard or sawe'.[63] Such cases suggest that the English minstrel or musician was evolving during this turbulent period. Where once he had travelled widely and stayed away from home for weeks at a time, now his journeys took him to and fro within a more tightly concentrated cluster of neighbouring parishes.

On other occasions, people expressed their support for music-makers by refusing to assist in their apprehension. In 1641, a constable in Shrewsbury got into a fight with some unruly singers. He claimed to have been struck so hard that 'the fire burst out of his Eyes'. Despite this injury he noticed that 'the reste of the neighbors stirred not to ayde or asseste him' (some went a little further, calling him 'Base Roge, Welshe Rogue, & Buttermilke Rogue'). There were also many instances in which the instinct to support the minstrel led to direct intervention that was committed, energetic and occasionally violent. The most compelling of cases were concentrated in the counties of the south-west during the first three decades of the seventeenth century. Here, customary recreations with any connection to the church or the Sabbath were under fierce pressure, and musicians were regarded by cultural reformers as important and

[61] Fetherston, *Dialogue*, C1r. [62] See, for example, *REED Sussex*, p. 39.
[63] *REED Somerset*, pp. 157–9.

symbolic targets. In Wells, the monumental conflict of 1607 witnessed numerous attempts by the puritanical constable's men to arrest and thus silence the enemy's musicians. On several occasions, the minstrels and drummers who played for the revellers were captured but then rescued and set free. Leaders of the crowd were both possessive and defensive in their attitude to the musicians, constantly looking out for them, collecting money for their maintenance and even presenting one lame viol-player with a garter to support his instrument. When John Hole, the zealous constable, threatened to manhandle a minstrel, Mr Watkins allegedly intervened, telling him 'that the said constable should have the said Minstrells fidle or Croud if he would, but his person he should not have'. According to Hole, the minstrels were duly rescued, causing a huge company to celebrate by 'shouting, hooping, & hallowing'.[64]

Aggressive actions on behalf of musicians were relatively common in the west country. When, in 1610, Joan Etherege of Wimborne Minster (Dorset) was 'gently warned' of her fault in listening to music in the street when she should have been in church, she abused the churchwardens with delicious ambiguity, '& bad them kisse her asse twice'. A few years later, William Thomas of Langport (Somerset) reportedly warned that if any constables or other such cuckolds dared to arrest his favourite minstrel, 'he would frye them and Cut them to small peeces'.[65] In Keynsham (Somerset), the constable came to fear just such a fate in his running battle with an allegedly combative alehouse-keeper named Mansell. One Sunday in August, the constable found Mansell's establishment full of wine, beer and fiddle music, before and during evening prayer. He moved to arrest the musicians, but 'they Intreated that they might be sufered to depart quietlie' and promised to 'goe home to Bristoll & truble the towne noe further'. The constable accepted the offer, not because he thought it was a good one but because 'the companey gathered abought me with there clubes and Trunches'. When the fiddlers failed to act on their promise, the dogged law-enforcer brought reinforcements and escorted them physically out into the street. Somehow, they escaped, and returned once again to the Mansell mansion. The constable was too frightened to enter the premises again until the following evening. On this occasion, he eventually found the fiddlers making music behind a locked door, and was in the process of arresting them when Mansell himself, master of the house, burst upon the scene. The constable, more in hope than in

[64] *REED Shropshire*, p. 32; *REED Somerset*, pp. 275, 283–4, 335.

[65] *REED Dorset, Cornwall*, p. 286; *REED Somerset*, p. 156.

expectation, ordered him to assist with the arrest, but Mansell answered, 'I will be merie in mine oune house & will mayntane them here.' He then turned to his fiddlers and instructed them to play up. They obliged, 'playing more earnestly then [than] before' while their employer jumped and leapt about the place, 'as if he had ben besides hemselfe'. The rest of the company followed his lead, and the constable retreated once more in fear. On the following Thursday, the fiddlers finally left town of their own volition.[66]

There were comparable cases in counties to the east and north, but they were more isolated. In 1615, the constable of Alton (Hampshire), a yeoman named Richard Serle, brought a case in Star Chamber against nine local men. He existed in a state of continuous conflict with them, but drew particular attention to events that had occurred on the previous Whit Sunday. Certain members of the gang had 'unlawfully procured one Peter Smyth a mynstrell & vagrant person' to play while they made merry. Constable Serle made repeated attempts to arrest this musician for profaning the Sabbath, but could find no other officer to assist him. Repeatedly, he 'laid handes on the said mynstrell', and repeatedly his prisoner was freed by physical violence and intimidation. The company posted a lookout, and whenever Serle approached, cries of 'Beware the fydler' rang out. According to Serle, members of the dissolute company had already been tried in a different court, specifically for rescuing Peter Smith, the vagabond minstrel, from his clutches. On this occasion, they had pulled the wool over the jurymen's eyes by producing witnesses who were prepared to perjure themselves. Three different men argued that Smith was not a vagrant at all, but a settled resident of their town. Furthermore, they reported that he had in fact been hired by the churchwardens 'to play as a mynstrell that saboth day'. The witnesses had thus persuaded the jury that Peter Smith 'was noe vagabond within the ... statute', and the minstrel-protectors of Alton were all acquitted.[67]

These cases present several common features. It is apparent that puritans-in-power were fully aware of the importance of capturing the musicians, while their adversaries knew how vital it was to preserve their freedom. At one level, this was a practical matter, for there could be 'no mirth without music'. But the minstrels in these troubled parishes were also symbolic, and a single arrest – if it could be achieved – was so much more than a mere crime statistic. To the minstrel's friends, he stood for custom, neighbourliness and even charity, at a time when these concepts

[66] *REED Somerset*, pp. 154–5. [67] STAC 8 262/11, NA.

were all perceived as existing in a state of danger or decline. To his enemies, he was nothing less than a devilish obstacle on the highway to truth. England's godly constables clearly did not select the minstrel for attention because he was an easy target. On the contrary, he could be maddeningly elusive, and we can be certain that many more Sunday fiddlers and pipers evaded the courts than were ever successfully prosecuted. Moving within sympathetic networks, they developed a number of tricks and tactics with which to elude hostile authority. Most obviously, they tended to play away from their home parishes, though not so far away that they could be arrested as vagrants. This made escape and disappearance rather easier than it would otherwise have been, and it often prevented investigating officers from establishing the names of their suspects. On countless occasions, the ecclesiastical courts dealt with those who had procured music (for example, dancers or alehouse-keepers), but could do nothing against the minstrels. In 1634, the vicar of Yarlington (Somerset) reported a group for morris dancing during service time, 'but who the fidles weare, and drumer I cannot yet learne'.[68] The same pattern of behaviour may help to explain why, in most English counties, very few Sunday musicians were caught out more than once. Minstrels, like the ephemeral notes they played, could be here and gone.

Another useful trick was to travel in groups rather than as individuals, and to pose as the retained band of an aristocrat or gentleman. 'Since hee was enacted Rogue by Parliament', said Richard Brathwaite of his archetypal piper, 'hee ha's got hold of a shamelesse tuneless Shalme [shawm-player] to bee his consort, that the statute might take lesse hold of his single quality. And to grace it the more, he ha's shrowded himself with the incorporate reverence of a pye-colour'd livery.' In 1647, another author referred in passing to 'Fidlers who are Rogues when they goe singly, and joyned in consort, gentlemen Musitioners'.[69] This was perhaps the intention of the two men arrested as singing rogues in Shrewsbury, just after May Day in 1594. They both wore livery coats, but confessed to the bailiff that these had been purchased on the black market. Thomas Jones had paid a milliner four shillings for his, while Richard Golborne's coat had cost him seven shillings. The shady provider of the second garment had informed Golborne that 'it was a livery Coote of Mr Edward Cluddes'. Both men had abandoned their proper occupations some years earlier,

[68] *REED Somerset*, p. 400.

[69] Brathwaite, *Whimzies*, pp. 26–34; John Cleveland, *The Character of a Country Committee-man* (London, 1647), p. 4.

preferring the insecure excitement of a musical life on the local roads. During the previous three weeks, Jones explained, the two men, accompanied by Golborne's wife, had been 'synginge of may songes abrode the contrey'. In other words, they had taken themselves on tour within their locality, offering their musical services to those who planned to celebrate the coming of May.

When the bailiff asked Jones what he had been up to on the previous Saturday evening, he received an incredibly detailed answer:

> he was in the company of the persons foresaid singinge at Uckington, donington, yeaton, leighton & from thense in the next morning he went over the water to Cressege & upon sonday they dyned at harley & from thense to wiggwige, from thense to belserdyne, from thense to sheynton. & so that night back againe to Cressage upon Sonday night to Coonde & from thense to harnage & from thens backe againe to Cressage & there staide untill the eveninge on Monday, & then they went to the Iron furnaces, from thense to Mr Christapher lacons from thense to Kenley & then to Litle Langley & from thens backe againe to Cressage to the house of one Churche their accustomed lodginge & there staied upon Tuseday untill the eveninge, & then went to Coonde & there staied all night at the house of william hoggins, And upon may daye in the mornynge ... came to Shrewesbury, to thentent to by for this Examinat ... the Coote foresaid & a paire of shoes.[70]

One can well understand the need for replacement footwear. Jones's unique account provides a wonderful insight into the itinerary of some of the least prestigious of England's musicians. Paradoxically, it reveals just how active travelling musicians could be without attracting hostile attention, provided that they did not venture too far. The group made eighteen stops before encountering trouble. Clearly, the trip had been a profitable one, and Jones must have hoped that the protection afforded by his costly livery coat would stand him in even better stead for the future. Unfortunately, Shrewsbury's eagle-eyed bailiff had spotted the deception.

The case of the Shrewsbury singers provides a timely reminder that music-making was often far less controversial than the records of conflict – colourful and compelling though they are – may lead us to believe. Our ears are drawn to discord, and its extent is probably exaggerated by the nature of the surviving sources. The clamour is loudest in regions where ambitious puritans fought the forces of cultural tradition. In some areas, the sounds are more harmonious, though we must strain to hear them. Ecclesiastical court books are a good source for historians seeking

[70] *REED Shropshire*, pp. 279–80.

tunesmiths-in-trouble, but sometimes the strike-rate is poor. Bishop Redman's visitation of the Norwich diocese in 1597 discovered only one disreputable musician (Thomas Fuller of Waborne, who 'draweth resort of youth together to the hindrance of godly exercise'). There were nearly 2,000 other presentments. Similarly, a 'detection' book from the archdeaconry of Chichester, covering the years between 1601 and 1603, contains the names of some 2,000 suspects, only one of whom was a musician.[71] Alongside the truly troublesome fiddlers discussed above, with their bodyguards and their defiant attitudes, we must therefore set an indeterminate number of apparently law-abiding and generally invisible musicians. We glimpse them only occasionally. Such a man was John Tendreng of Wakering (Essex), a husbandman and musician. Admittedly, he was one of the men reported in 1573 for musical moonlighting, but his copybook is otherwise unblotted. In 1598, his pious and sternly moral brother, Thomas, lay on his deathbed and contemplated his affairs. He bequeathed to John a share in his house, and appointed him to govern, counsel and admonish a beloved kinswoman in the years ahead.[72] The testator clearly did not perceive John Tendreng as a disseminator of disorder.

[71] *Diocese of Norwich: Bishop Redman's Visitation, 1597*, ed. J. F. Williams, *Norfolk Record Society* 14 (1941), p. 79; EP1/88/41, WSRO.

[72] *Essex Wills*, vol. VII, no. 63.

3 | Occupational musicians: employment prospects

It is not surprising, given the pressures of the times, that some of the available evidence indicates a contraction in the opportunities available to musicians during the early modern period. Again, there are two sides to the argument, but musicologists have tended to emphasise hardship over happiness and it is therefore with the pessimistic evidence that we shall begin.[1] The Elizabethan vagrancy statutes struck hard at the mobility of minstrels, whose customary habit of travelling to towns in search of temporary employment suddenly became hazardous. Crucially, the success with which an ugly stereotype of the minstrel was disseminated meant that even those musicians who were lucky enough to wear the coats and badges of great households now found it rather more difficult to make money on tour. In many towns, payments to liveried minstrels collapsed under the combined weight of godly anger, governmental anxiety, satirical mockery and economic concern. It was all a far cry from the situation that had pertained during the early years of the sixteenth century. In Exeter, the leading townsmen had paid the visiting minstrels of named patrons on eighty-eight occasions between 1500 and 1550. Payments became less regular from the 1560s onwards, and only two were recorded after 1580. The pattern was similar in Shrewsbury, Dartmouth, Plymouth and Rye.[2] The presence of zealous Protestantism was a crucial factor in several of these locations, yet towns and cities of all sorts were far less likely to welcome groups of musical retainers in 1600 than they had been a century earlier. At least until the statute of 1598, such groups were legally valid, but their numbers were falling nonetheless.

The rapid decay of employment prospects in churches and cathedrals was equally telling. Choirs, song schools and organs all came under fire from the mid-sixteenth century onwards. The surviving posts were limited mainly to cathedrals, and the attendant salaries failed to keep pace with rapid inflation during the reign of Elizabeth. Moreover, the dissolution of

[1] Price, *Patrons and Musicians*, p. 206; Woodfill, *Musicians in English Society*, pp. 243–4.

[2] *REED Devon*, pp. 62–70 (Dartmouth), 114–207 (Exeter), 214–77 (Plymouth); *REED Shropshire*, pp. 163–322 (Shrewsbury); *REED Sussex*, pp. 69–167 (Rye).

the monasteries had removed many opportunities for minstrels, and the late Elizabethan assault on church ales and parochial drama only added to the pain. The decay of ecclesiastical employment forced musicians of all sorts to seek work in gentry households, but this, it has been argued, was rarely either lucrative or secure.[3]

The difficulties faced by musicians throughout the period were particularly acute during the Civil Wars and the years of parliamentary rule. Warfare disrupted social music-making, and the composer William Lawes was a famous casualty for the royalist cause. Early in the 1640s, the city of Bath's fashionable season was ruined by political uncertainty, and one facetious parliamentarian mocked the local fiddlers who were 'ready to hang themselves in their stringes for a pastime, for want of other imployments'. In many towns, the civic bands known as waits were either officially disbanded or allowed to lapse into semi-retirement.[4] The closing of London's theatres in 1642 and the disbanding of the nation's cathedral choirs within the next few years only made matters worse. In 1643, *The Actors Remonstrance, or Complaint: For the Silencing of their Profession* lamented the sad plight of theatrical musicians, suddenly left with no alternative but to 'wander with their instruments under their cloaks, I meane such as have any, into all houses of good fellowship, saluting every roome where there is company with, Will you have any Musike Gentlemen?' Out on the streets, they probably bumped into former cathedral singing men, themselves drifting around in a similar state of disillusionment. In 1656, five highly accomplished 'professors of Musicke' petitioned the promisingly named 'Committee of the Counsell for Advancement of Musicke' in order to sound an alarum. They reported that the abolition of the cathedral choirs had left good musicians destitute: many 'have during the late Warres and troubles dyed in want, and there being now noe preferment or Encouragement in the way of Musick Noe man will breed his Child in it, soe that it must needes be that the Science it selfe must dye in this Nacon . . . , or at least it will degenerate much'. The petitioners asked for the establishment of a new college of musicians that would regulate all matters pertaining to the practice of their art, but nothing came of it.[5] Clearly, it was not only the lowly fiddler who felt the mid-century pinch.

3 Woodfill, *Musicians in English Society*, ch. 3.

4 *REED Somerset*, p. 29. For the troubles faced by the waits in one city, see David Griffiths, *A Musical Place of the First Quality: A History of Institutional Music-making in York, c. 1550–1990* (York: York Settlement Trust, 1994), p. 66.

5 *The Actors Remonstrance, or Complaint: For the Silencing of their Profession* (London, 1643), p. 7; SP18, 153 (123), NA.

Even in better times, musicians of all sorts were more frequently associated with poverty than with wealth. Sophisticated composers made little money out of publishing their works, and the supposedly exalted musicians of the Chapel Royal sometimes complained of their penury.[6] The salary of a cathedral singing man or civic wait did not guarantee economic security, and many augmented their livings by working as parish clerks, alehouse-keepers, tobacco pipe makers, tailors, weavers, dyers or barbers.[7] Brathwaite's archetypal piper was destined to die in want: 'His wealth may appeare by his Inventorie which containes the over worne remains of a Motley Livery, a decayed Pipe-bagge, and halfe a shirt; all which, without his Neighbours charity, will scarce amount to the purchase of a sheete' (in which to wrap the corpse). The actual wills and inventories recorded on behalf of some of the poorest musicians indicate that this was not too dramatic an exaggeration. When Edward Hadshead of Chesterfield (Derbyshire) died in 1578, his goods were valued at £2 5s, a third of which comprised his bagpipes with their leather case and a box of reeds. Almost a century later, a naval trumpeter on a royal ship called the *Montagu* made his will while sick or injured at sea. It is not a lengthy document. Richard Colley bequeathed his unpaid wages to two fellow sailors, adding that the gift was to come in to force 'if it should please god that I should not doe well'. Sadly, he did not do well and his inventory was drawn up following the ship's return to Portsmouth. Those who recorded it seem to have felt the need to explain the apparent poverty of Colley, 'he being a simple man and having noe place of residence on shoare'. The grand total of £15 8s 6d was surprisingly high, but £14 comprised the overdue wages. Beyond this, Colley had very little: 2s 6d in cash, clothes worth 16s and 'one brasse Trumpett' valued at 10s.[8]

Music was rarely considered a suitable occupation for boys born into society's upper ranks. Fortunatas, the hero of one chapbook tale, encountered on his continental travels a group of fallen gentlemen who had turned to music in desperation, but such examples were rare and usually fictional.[9] More typical were the apprentice musicians listed in Bristol between 1540 and 1640. Two came from relatively prosperous yeoman

[6] Woodfill, *Musicians in English Society*, p. 171.

[7] *REED Norwich*, p. xxxix; Woodfill, *Musicians in English Society*, p. 139; Richard Culmer, *Cathedrall Newes from Canterbury* (London, 1644), A3v.

[8] Brathwaite, *Whimzies*, p. 34; *Chesterfield Wills and Inventories, 1521–1603*, ed. J. M. Bestall and D. V. Fowkes, *Derbyshire Record Society* 1 (1977), p. 150; 1667 B 16/1–2, HRO.

[9] *The History of the Birth, Travels, Strange Adventures, and Death of Fortunatas* (London, 1682), p. 30.

stock, but the rest were the sons of an assortment of artisans, tradesmen, husbandmen and labourers. A comparable profile can be observed wherever there are suitable records. The indenture of John Hill from Maldon (Essex) is unusually detailed but otherwise representative. In 1597, this sixteen-year-old son of a deceased 'sealer' bound himself, with his mother's consent, to John Cooke *alias* Watson of Yarmouth (Norfolk), 'with him to dwell tarie & serve as becometh an Apprentice in the Arte, trade, facultie & misterie of a mynstrell'. The boy pledged loyalty to his new employer, and agreed that 'Tavernes Tipplinge houses & other like places of Comon resorte he shall not haunte or frequent except it shalbe about the busynes of his M[aste]r'. In return, John Cooke promised to teach him all the skills of a musician, to feed him, clothe him and, when necessary, chastise him. At the successful conclusion of the seven-year term, Hill would receive double apparel (one suit for holy days and one for weekdays), twenty shillings in cash and 'one Instrument of the value of Tenne shillinges'.[10] Information on the friends and associates of musicians also locates them primarily among people from the lower and middle orders of society. When Walter Sowth, a musician from Castle Hedingham (Essex), was accused of sheep-stealing in 1608, his accomplices were two labourers. When other musical miscreants needed neighbours to guarantee their good conduct before the courts, they generally turned to shoemakers and glovers, rather than merchants and gentlemen.[11]

Occupational music was frequently regarded as one of the provinces of the poor, and charitably minded benefactors knew that it was a living appropriate to the least privileged of English children. The blind or disabled musician was a well-known figure in early modern England. In 1601, a benevolent Cornishman named Richard Clere endeavoured to enhance three vulnerable lives by bequeathing 'unto one blynde boy one harpe & unto an other blynde boye an other harpe & unto a meheamed [maimed] man a trumpett that canne use the same'. Three years later, another such life came to an end in Lancashire when the parish clerk of Eccleston recorded the burial of the otherwise unnamed 'blind harper of Charnock'. In the same year, the clerk of Standish noted the burial of a 'blind harper's man', perhaps employed previously as the disabled musician's guide and publicist. Around 1600, one of the entertainers doing the rounds in Worcestershire was 'Jacke the cleane foole' with his 'song of

[10] *REED Bristol*, pp. 256–68; D/B 3/1/33, ERO. See also P27/14/1/3, Cambridgeshire Record Office.

[11] Ass 35/50/1/39, ERO; *REED Shropshire*, pp. 619–20.

Derries fayre'. Jack's greatest asset was a severe stammer that became particularly acute when he encountered the sounds 'b' and 'p'. The gentry loved it when Jack, during the course of his song, came up against the expression 'brave beggars'. However much the audience howled, he persevered. 'It would make a man burst with laughing', said one witness.[12]

Overall, however, the melody is not so pitiful. A wealth of contrasting evidence demonstrates that musical opportunities were not all of this rather dubious sort. Throughout the period, supply and demand both remained healthy, and new prospects emerged and developed to make good the undeniable losses. Most tellingly, English musicians continued to encourage or permit their children to follow them into the occupation, and there are many examples of families whose members made money from music in successive generations. The Purcells were a famous case, but there were many more. Solomon Eccles, the Quaker who abandoned music in the 1660s, recalled that his father, grandfather and great-grandfather had all been musicians (so too were a whole string of his nephews, later in the century).[13] Lower down the musical hierarchy, the dynastic tendency was equally pronounced, and the performances of father-and-son combinations were a common occurrence. Evidence of inter-generational musical tensions is therefore balanced by sources suggesting that the passing of skills from adults to children was often a smooth and natural process. We have already encountered Spode, the disorderly Lancashire piper who sounded his instrument contemptuously in Winwick church shortly before Christmas in 1596. Seventy-eight years later, it was presumably a different Spode who made music on Edge Green, not four miles away. The diarist Roger Lowe noted that 'old Jane Whittell', shortly before she died, had asked to be placed in a chair from which she could 'heare hime play and Eles Shawe dance'. At the grand age of eighty-four, Jane Whittell was one of very few locals who may also have heard the tunes of Spode's disruptive ancestor.[14]

Ironically, the critical onslaught of the earlier reformers, by rendering the solitary minstrel disreputable, may have stimulated a taste for the music of ensembles in some quarters, and thus an expansion of local opportunities. The craft companies of Chester, for example, became more likely to hire groups than individuals as the decades passed, and later

[12] *REED Dorset, Cornwall*, p. 475; *REED Lancashire*, pp. 242–8; Robert Armin, *Foole upon Foole* (London, 1600), E2r–v.

[13] Eccles, *A Musick-lector*, p. 12.

[14] *The Diary of Roger Lowe*, ed. Ian Winstanley (Wigan: Picks Publishing, 1994), p. 74. For the earlier Spode, see above, p. 78.

editions of Playford's *Dancing Master* tended to include more references to 'the musicians' and fewer to 'the musician'.[15] In the eyes and ears of music's critics, certainly, there were far too many scrapers, puffers and pluckers in circulation. This was already true in 1566, when an author whose primary aim was to reform the statute of apparel included in his draft a bitter little comment about the swarms of young men who were training as musicians when the country needed husbandmen. It was still true in 1579, when Stephen Gosson complained implausibly that the number of pipers in England was 'infinit'. And it remained true when Ned Ward described his walk around London right at the end of the seventeenth century, though his objections were more aesthetic than those of his predecessors.[16] Of course, these men exaggerated, but the evidence accumulated in the following pages suggests that they did not distort the soundscape beyond recognition.

Cathedral employment

Not surprisingly, the most desirable employment was available in England's towns and cities. Some of this was still connected with the church, despite the generally negative impact of the Reformation upon occupational music-making. In cities with cathedrals or collegiate churches, individuals of musical aptitude could do worse than join the 'singing men'. Not all contemporary accounts were hostile, and it seems that the continuing existence of musical employment within cathedral churches was valuable to English performers in an age of change and challenge. The jobs, though hardly well paid, were often sought after. When, in 1583, Robert Barker was sacked as one of the singing men at the collegiate church of Southwell, he was desperate to regain the position. He denied an adultery charge that had been levelled at him, and brought a countercase against his employers in the Court of Requests. At Peterborough, there was pressure for places, and the dean and chapter kept a waiting list of those appointed to fill future vacancies.[17] In some choirs, admittedly,

15 *REED Chester*, pp. 64–402; *The Complete Country Dance Tunes from Playford's Dancing Master*, ed. Jeremy Barlow (London: Faber Music, 1985), p. 10.

16 *CSPD 1553–8*, p. 964; Stephen Gosson, *The Schoole of Abuse* (London, 1579), B1r; Ward, *The London Spy*, pp. 22, 180, 194, 195, 199.

17 REQ 2 181/11, NA; *The Foundation of Peterborough Cathedral AD 1541*, ed. W. T. Mellows, *Publications of the Northamptonshire Record Society* 13 (1941), pp. lii–liv; *Peterborough Local Administration: Elizabethan Peterborough. The Dean and Chapter as Lords of the City*, ed. D. H. Gifford, *Publications of the Northamptonshire Record Society* 18 (1956), pp. 46–51.

there were problems, but these did not prevent Lieutenant Hammond, a musical tourist, from declaring himself thoroughly impressed during the 1630s with the choral music he heard at Rochester, Canterbury, Winchester, Lincoln, Southwark, York, Durham, Carlisle, Lichfield, Worcester, Rochester and Exeter. In such establishments, a typical service would have included chanted renditions of the Creed, the Lord's Prayer and the Litany, as well as various sung responses, antiphonal psalms and contrapuntal anthems.[18] Hammond did not visit Salisbury Cathedral, but we know that its music was potent enough to transport no less a figure than George Herbert into what he called 'his Heaven upon Earth'. In *The Sack-ful of News*, a chapbook of 1685, one countryman experienced something similar when he crossed the rural–urban divide and heard the music in St Paul's Cathedral for the first time. He thought he had gone to heaven, and loudly lamented the fact that he had not brought his white stick and black hood with him ('Whereat all the people laughed heartily'). Clearly, cathedral music was one of the sounds that distinguished the city from the country. Even the presbyterian diarist Roger Lowe, who might have been expected to disapprove of such music, was 'exceedinglie taken with the mellodie' when he heard the choristers at Manchester's collegiate church in 1665.[19] The fortunes of cathedral musicians waxed and waned throughout the early modern period – declining during the reign of Elizabeth, rising again under Laudian influence in the 1630s, collapsing as a result of parliamentary rule, then improving once more after the Restoration – but the available posts never lost their desirability for suitably qualified musicians.

Each cathedral choir comprised vicars-choral or singing men (also known in some places as lay clerks), boy choristers and their master. In several cathedrals, the music of the choir received instrumental support, most often from an organ, but also in some places from cornetts, sackbuts and viols. Most establishments had choirs with a total of between twenty

On cathedral music, see Stanford E. Lehmberg, *The Reformation of the Cathedrals* (Princeton: Princeton University Press, 1988), ch. 8, and Ian Spink, *Restoration Cathedral Music, 1660–1714* (Oxford: Clarendon Press, 1995).

[18] *A Relation of a Short Survey of 26 Counties, Observed in a Seven Weeks Journey Begun on August 11, 1634*, ed. L. G. Wickham Legg (London: Robinson and Company, 1904); *A Relation of a Short Survey of the Western Counties: Made by a Lieutenant of the Military Company in Norwich in 1635*, ed. L. G. Wickham Legg, *Camden Miscellany* 16 (1936); Spink, 'Music and Society', p. 47.

[19] Izaak Walton, *The Lives of Dr John Donne, Sir Henry Wotton, Mr Richard Hooker, Mr George Herbert* (London, 1670), p. 60; *The Sack-ful of News* (London, 1685); *The Diary of Roger Lowe of Ashton-in-Makerfield, Lancashire, 1663–74*, ed. William L. Sachse (London: Longmans, 1938), p. 94.

and forty members, though the average number fell between 1540 and 1640. In this period, the income from old endowments did not keep pace with inflation, and some vacancies therefore went unfilled as repeated attempts were made to improve the salaries of the remaining singers. Individual singing men were paid between £6 and £10 per year, and the vicars-choral earned between £10 and £13. Such salaries were unquestionably meagre – an agricultural labourer could earn as much – and in practice it was accepted that choirmen needed to supplement their incomes by taking on other kinds of work. This was not ideal, and the situation sometimes created clashes of interest, but it has recently been pointed out that the workload of a singing man was not particularly onerous (perhaps four hours a day, on average). The Reformation had reduced the duties of cathedral choirs, leaving ample free time for the development of additional economic interests.[20] Some took on unrelated jobs, while others apparently earned extra money by singing for secular employers. In 1581–2, the chamberlain of Ludlow spent 2s 8d 'to make the syngynge men drynke that came from harford [Hereford] to St gorgys fest'. More controversially, four of the boy choristers of Wells were recruited to participate in the remarkable anti-puritan processions of 1607. According to one witness, they wore white habits (either their official vestments, or close copies) and took their place just in front of a representation of the goddess Diana. The choirboys then processed 'thoroughe the Markett place and streetes of the sayed Cittye, singinge certayne sacred Hymnes or Anthems which this deponent hathe knowen to bee used to be sounge in the sayed Cathedrall Churche of wells, the which Hymnes or Anthe[ms] he cannot nowe expresse but thinckethe they were made uppon som parte of the Psalmes of the Prophett Davyd'.[21] It was often said that choir members also supplemented their wages by singing in alehouses and inns. In Jacobean Norwich, one enterprising member of the choir even ran his own alehouse.[22]

Occasionally, cathedral establishments found it difficult to recruit choir members, but this does not seem to have been a common or continuous difficulty. Most cathedrals, even the poorer ones, were able to fill the stalls with sufficiently musical men, some of whom passed their lives in moderate wealth and comfort.[23] It should also be remembered that choir

[20] Woodfill, *Musicians in English Society*, pp. 135–6, 149–50; Saunders, 'Music and Moonlighting', pp. 157–66. See also the sources cited in n. 7 above.

[21] *REED Shropshire*, p. 86; *REED Somerset*, pp. 339–40, 341.

[22] Earle, *Micro-cosmographie*, pp. 115–16; Saunders, 'Music and Moonlighting', p. 163.

[23] Saunders, 'Music and Moonlighting', pp. 164–5.

members often had the right to free meals and subsidised housing, though many quite understandably preferred to live elsewhere with their families. It has been argued that such perquisites counted for little by 1600, but when Lieutenant Hammond was treated to a tour of Worcester Cathedral in the summer of 1634, he received a rather different impression:

> Next came wee into a brave, and ancient privildeg'd Place, through the Lady Arbour Cloyster, close by the Chapter House, called the Vicars Chorall, or Colledge Cloyster, where 12 of the Singing Men all in Orders, most of them Masters in Arts, of a gentile Garbe, have there, their convenient several dwellings, and a fayre Hall, with richly painted windowes Colledge-like, wherein they constantly dyet togeather, and have their Cooke, Butler, and other Officers, with a fayre Library to themselves, consisting all of English Books, wherein (after wee had freelie tasted of their Chorall cordiall Liquor) wee spent our time till the Bell toll'd us away to Cathedrall Prayers; There we heard a most sweet Organ, and voyces of all parts, Tenor, Counter-Tenor, Treble, and Base; and amongst that orderly snowy crew of Queristers, our Landlord-Guide, did act his part, in a deep, and sweet Diapason.[24]

The lieutenant had perhaps imbibed a little too freely of the choirmen's alcohol, and some allowance must be made for the idealised tone of his account. Even so, it is difficult to avoid the conclusion that the life of a singing man was not without its pleasant aspects. He may have been fairly poor, but he nevertheless had the opportunity to sing some of the finest music ever written for the church in England. The anthem, in particular, flowered and flourished in the century following the Reformation, and many of its greatest exponents – Orlando Gibbons and Thomas Tomkins, for example – learned and developed their craft as cathedral or college musicians.

Town waits

The most attractive posts for urban musicians were, however, within the official bands known as waits. These had evolved from medieval watchmen, stationed on battlements or town walls in order to guard against intruders. Loud musical instruments were used in order to alert residents to danger or merely to sound out the hours. By the sixteenth century, the

[24] *A Relation of a Short Survey of 26 Counties*, pp. 82–3. When Archbishop Laud examined the cathedrals in the Canterbury province during the mid-1630s, he found their musical establishments imperfect but far from disastrous (see Spink, 'Music and Society', pp. 41–3). For a more pessimistic diagnosis, see Woodfill, *Musicians in English Society*, pp. 136–46, 151–3.

policing function had receded somewhat, while the purely musical aspects of the waits' role had expanded. This was part of a broader and generally positive transition that was interrupted only by the disruption of the Civil Wars and Interregnum. In the period as a whole, the waits appear to have done fairly well. Several towns hired bands for the first time, or placed existing groups on a firmer footing.[25] In many more places, the size of the waits' bands increased, typically from two or three members during the mid-sixteenth century to four or five by the 1620s.[26] By the early seventeenth century most towns of any size seem to have employed waits, and the urban community that had not moved with the times could be portrayed as backward and barbarous. In 1635, Lieutenant Hammond spoke most rudely of the fenland town of Crowland, where the local drink reputedly put the inhabitants 'into a drowsy and dead sleep, which they hold very convenient and necessary to avoyd the divellish stinging of their humming Gnatts, which is all the Towne Musicke they have'. Hammond did not visit Crowland himself, but peered at it from the top of Peterborough Cathedral, which was quite close enough.[27]

The duties of England's waits comprised an interesting combination of the old watching functions and the newer musical responsibilities. The musicians clearly had not shed completely their role as night-time security guards and walking alarm clocks. Indeed, the duty that was specified most commonly in civic records throughout our period was that of patrolling the streets in winter, during the hours before daylight. Up and down the land, the waits, their hands presumably frozen, sounded their instruments and used their voices not only to warn of danger but also to forecast the weather and to mark the passing of the hours. In Shrewsbury, the waits described themselves in 1568 as 'comon travellers Every mornynge with theire instrumentes for that all artificers myght know the due owre for their famylye to goe to theire nessaris [necessary?] buisiness'. The Coventry waits began to play at 2 a.m. while the solitary musician in Liverpool started work two hours later (4 a.m. marked the end of the night-time curfew). He retained his alarm-raising responsibility until 1629, when

[25] *REED Cumberland, Westmorland, Gloucestershire*, p. 254; *REED Herefordshire, Worcestershire*, pp. 311–12.

[26] J. C. Brydson, 'The Minstrels and Waits of Leicester', *Musical Times* 89 (1948), 143; C. E. C. Burch, 'Minstrels and Players in Southampton 1428–1635', *Southampton Papers* 7 (1969), p. 47; *REED Bristol*, p. 211; *REED Devon*, pp. 411, 416, 425. Similar evidence exists for Gloucester, Norwich, Newcastle, Cambridge and London.

[27] *A Relation of a Short Survey of the Western Counties*, p. 90.

the bellman took it over. In Manchester and other places, however, the waits were still charged in the 1620s with discovering 'dangers and mysedeameanors which maye happen to fale out in the night'.[28] When members of parliament debated a bill against rogues in the mid-1650s, Alderman Foot said, 'I hope you intend not to include the waits of the City of London, which are a great preservative of men's houses in the night.' Typically, the waits' role as musical policemen ran from Michaelmas until Candlemas or Easter, after which the sun could be relied upon both to subdue the criminal and to arouse the more law-abiding townsfolk.[29]

Beyond this, all waits contributed regularly and extensively to the music that echoed through the streets on important occasions. They provided the civic soundtrack and distinguished town from country. In London, they played at fairs, during the Lord Mayor's procession, and whenever members of the royal family went on the move.[30] Over in Bristol, they played when James I was proclaimed king and when his queen came to visit. The waits of Elizabethan Newcastle upon Tyne provided the music at the corporation's audit dinners, at shows put on by visiting players, and at a banquet staged in honour of the Governor of the Netherlands.[31] These three cases present a typical range of duties, but others were more unusual. The Norwich waits played Sunday evening concerts on the roof of the guildhall between 1553 and 1629 (when puritan scruples brought an end to the tradition). In Ipswich, the waits staged a play at the Moot Hall in 1571–2, and in 1590 one of the musicians in Exeter put down his instrument temporarily in order to assist with the task of 'making white Crosses over the doores where the plage was'.[32] Over the years, the official duties of England's waits changed somewhat as they became, for example, less likely to combine music with drama. In some places, they suffered serious hardship during the political disturbances of the mid-seventeenth century, but their troubles eventually passed. Certainly, there was plenty of work for the waits during the swinging 1660s. In Chester, for example, they were

[28] *REED Shropshire*, p. 213; Spink, 'Music and Society', p. 7; *REED Lancashire*, pp. 52, 54, 66.

[29] *Diary of Thomas Burton*, ed. John Towill Rutt, 4 vols. (London, 1828), vol. I, p. 23; *The Boston Assembly Minutes, 1545–75*, ed. Peter and Jennifer Clark, *Lincoln Record Society* 77 (1987), no. 768; *REED Cumberland, Westmorland, Gloucestershire*, p. 111.

[30] *Chamber Accounts of the Sixteenth Century*, ed. Betty R. Masters, *London Record Society Publications* 20 (1984), p. 239; *Diary of Henry Machyn*, pp. 47, 129–30.

[31] *REED Bristol*, pp. 157, 173–5; *REED Newcastle upon Tyne*, pp. 56, 79, 100.

[32] *REED Norwich*, p. 33; *The Town Finances of Elizabethan Ipswich*, ed. John Webb, *Suffolk Records Society* 38 (1996), p. 104; *REED Devon*, p. 172.

still to be heard 'playing morneing and evening in the streets of the said Citty as was anciently used by the waytes'. And when Charles II visited Thetford (Norfolk) in 1668, he and his gentlemen compelled the musicians of Thetford 'to sing them all the bawdy songs they could think of'.[33]

Most bands clearly performed to a high standard, and negative reviews were rare. By 1600, the vast majority of those operating in the larger cities could probably play both by ear and by book, and those in Norwich had been musically literate since the 1530s. According to one poem of the late seventeenth century, the waits of a typical town, attending the lodgings of eminent visitors, would 'play them some fine Ayre / Or brisk new tune'.[34] It is difficult to be more precise than this about the actual music they offered, though a varied repertoire consisting of arrangements of dance and ballad tunes, songs, fanfares and composed ensemble music seems a certainty. When Elizabeth I visited Norwich in 1578, the waits performed, among other pieces, the consort songs 'From Slumber Soft' and 'What Vayleth Life, where Sorrowe Soakes the Harte'. They were probably some way ahead of the pack, and Roger North later reported that the less highly renowned waits of Thetford waited until the 1660s before attempting their first 'polite piece' ('The Bells', by Mr Jenkins).[35] Hitherto, they had presumably specialised in less taxing material.

Some civic bands even attracted ear-catching accolades. The composer Thomas Morley was famously impressed with the 'excellent and expert Musicians' who made up the waits of late Elizabethan London, and he commended the contents of his *First Book of Consort Lessons* to their 'careful and skilful handling'.[36] A number of other composers – Simon Ives and Robert Taylor, for example – had served among the waits themselves, as had the father of Orlando Gibbons.[37] To one character in an Elizabethan dialogue, the night-time music of the London waits had the disadvantage of preventing sleep, but the overwhelming benefit of giving those who lay abed the sensation of being 'ravished in an earthly paradise'. William Kemp was a different kind of entertainer, but this famous clowning actor was deeply impressed by the waits of Norwich. Kemp

33 ZA/B/2, fos. 157r, 175v, ChRO; *Diary of Samuel Pepys*, vol. IX, p. 336.

34 George A. Stephen, 'The Waits of the City of Norwich through Four Centuries to 1790', *Norfolk Archaeology* 25 (1935), pp. 7–8; Spink, 'Music and Society', p. 9.

35 *REED Norwich*, p. xliii; Spink, 'Music and Society', p. 8.

36 *The First Book of Consort Lessons: Collected by Thomas Morley, 1599 and 1611*, ed. Sydney Beck (New York: C. F. Peters Corp., 1959), A2r.

37 Spink, 'Music and Society', p. 12; *REED Cambridge*, pp. 249–51; Tim Healey, 'The Story of the Oxford Waits', *The Consort* 59 (2003), 76–85; John Harley, *Orlando Gibbons and the Gibbons Family of Musicians* (Aldershot: Ashgate, 1999), pp. 3–24.

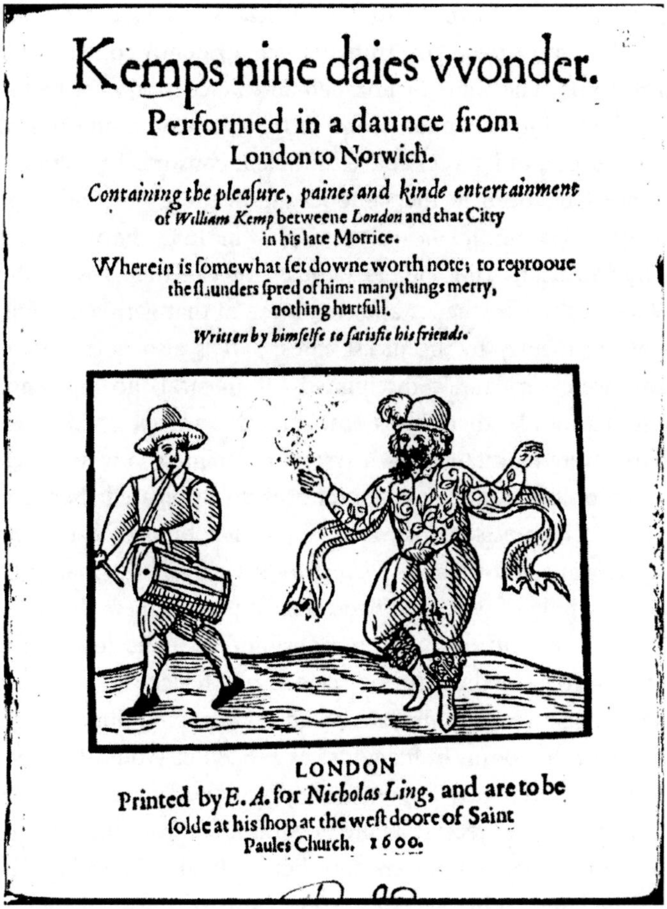

Kemps nine daies vvonder.
Performed in a daunce from
London to Norwich.
Containing the pleasure, paines and kinde entertainment of *William Kemp* betweene *London* and that Citty in his late Morrice.
Wherein is somewhat set downe worth note; to reprooue the slaunders spred of him: many things merry, nothing hurtfull.
Written by himselfe to satisfie his friends.

LONDON
Printed by *E. A.* for *Nicholas Ling*, and are to be solde at his shop at the west doore of Saint Paules Church. 1600.

Figure 3.1. In 1599, the comic actor William Kemp performed a marathon morris dance that took him from London to Norwich, accompanied by his trusty pipe and tabor man. The Bodleian Library, Oxford, *Kemp's Nine Daies Wonder* (London, 1600), title page.

staged a remarkable publicity stunt in 1599, dancing all the way from England's first city to its second (see Figure 3.1). On arrival in Norwich, the waits stood ready to refresh him with a musical welcome. It is a fair guess that they played 'Kemp's jig', a well-known tune that was named after their visitor (**Website track 2 and Appendix**). The actor was bowled over and exclaimed, 'such Waytes (under Benedicitie be it spoken) fewe Citties in our Realme have the like, none better'.[38] It must certainly have been more

[38] Claude Desainliens, *The French Schoolemaister* (London, 1573), pp. 68–70, quoted by Woodfill, *Musicians in English Society*, p. 53; William Kemp, *Kemp's Nine Daies Wonder: Performed in a Daunce from London to Norwich*, ed. Alexander Dyce (London: Camden Society, 1840), p. 17.

difficult for smaller, poorer towns to attract musicians of such exceptional calibre. Nevertheless, most town governments were evidently content with their musical servants. The waits of Elizabethan Manchester were highly commended by the leading inhabitants, and in 1630 the Common Council of Gloucester was proud of its 'very able & sufficient consort'. The waits of Lichfield may not have been in the same league as those of London or Norwich, but when Hammond heard them play in 1634, he was most impressed: 'The Musicians (for Fidlers I must not call them) were the Gentleman Waytes of the Towne ... and they were of that garb, and skill, as they were fitting to play to the nicest eares.'[39] It is also notable that individual waits were very rarely disciplined for musical incompetence (though they sometimes let themselves down in other ways).

High standards were maintained by a system of training in which each wait took on one or sometimes two apprentices and prepared them for subsequent service. The precise terms varied somewhat, but in most towns it is clear that the waits and their employers took seriously the matter of ensuring a steady supply of well-qualified musical practitioners. In 1627, the waits of Cambridge confirmed their responsibility to 'educate learne & teach' their apprentices 'in the Arte or science of Musicke to our best power and skill'. Their recently deceased leader, Stephen Wilmott, had even set aside one of the rooms in his house as a 'Scoole'. Would-be waits in Norwich served a seven-year apprenticeship, followed by a period of probation. They then had to receive a vote of confidence from the existing waits, and sometimes their employers too, before finally achieving full membership of the band (subject to vacancies). In many towns, the more advanced 'boys' performed with the waits, thus swelling the size of the available band considerably. The hierarchical nature of these bands was also reflected in the fact that most seem to have had an acknowledged leader or 'head wait' who took responsibility for organising the affairs of his underlings.[40]

The range of instruments upon which the waits performed grew steadily during the early modern period. In the first half of the sixteenth century, most waits appear to have played primarily upon the shawms, and a particular association with these instruments persisted for 200 years (indeed, shawms were also known as 'waits'). Over the decades, however, considerable diversification occurred. When Benet Pryme, a wait from

[39] *REED Lancashire*, pp. 59, 62; *REED Cumberland, Westmorland, Gloucestershire*, p. 323; *A Relation of a Short Survey of 26 Counties*, p. 59.

[40] *REED Cambridge*, pp. 610–14; *REED Norwich*, pp. xxxix–xl.

Cambridge, died in 1557, his goods included pipes, sackbuts, viols, violins, flutes and regals. He was precocious, and the other end of the spectrum was represented by the solitary Liverpool wait who appears to have played only the bagpipes during the reign of Elizabeth.[41] By the end of the century, however, the bigger towns at least were catching up with Cambridge. In 1590, the waits of Chester played not only 'how boies' (shawms) but also recorders, cornetts and violins. Sackbuts were purchased for the waits of Bristol and Gloucester during the early seventeenth century. By the 1660s, moreover, many bands could play stringed instruments as well as the more traditional wind.[42]

The information for Norwich is particularly rich, and the development of instrumental variety can be charted quite precisely. The city's waits began, like most others, with the 'loud noyse' of the shawms. By 1584, however, the city also possessed two trumpets, four sackbuts, five recorders ('beeying a Whoall noyse', or compatible set), one 'old Lysardyne' (probably a large S-shaped cornett) and four drums. In 1608, a tenor cornett was added. The waits may not have played the trumpets or drums, but they were surely the primary users of the remaining instruments. This musical arsenal remained fairly stable through to the end of the period. A list written in 1676 mentions four sackbuts, three hautboys and three cornetts (there is no mention of the recorders, nor of the lizardine). The official lists do not include stringed instruments, but the waits evidently provided these for themselves. In 1583, they requested a pay rise on the grounds that they had recently obtained several new instruments at their own cost. This cannot have referred to the expanding array of wind instruments, for which the city paid. The possibility of new expertise on stringed instruments is confirmed by Kemp's account. When he danced into town in 1599, he was impressed both by 'their excellency in wind instruments' and by 'their rare cunning on the Vyoll and Violin'. In 1612, a musician named Thomas Quashe was admitted to the waits only on condition that he came equipped with his own 'treable violin'. He died in 1638, possessed of 'two Cornets one treble viall and a flute recorder'.[43] Overall, it seems probable that only the waits of London enjoyed better resources. To the traditional shawms, they added sackbuts, viols, recorders, cornetts and curtals during the reign of Elizabeth, followed

[41] *REED Cambridge*, p. 744; *REED Lancashire*, pp. 39–40, 45, 47.

[42] *REED Cheshire*, p. 164; *REED Bristol*, p. 172; *REED Cumberland, Westmorland, Gloucestershire*, pp. 327–9.

[43] *REED Norwich*, p. xl; NCR 16a/24, fo. 359r, NRO; Kemp, *Kemp's Nine Daies Wonder*, p. 17; DN/INV44/168, NRO.

by specialist voices, violins, lutes, an orpharion and a polyfant during the next four decades.[44]

Conditions of employment varied widely from town to town, and it is difficult to generalise about the livings made by waits. At first glance, the wages they received look pitiful. Some towns paid their waits no salaries, but allowed and encouraged them to collect voluntary contributions from the citizenry. Liverpool appointed its solitary bagpipe-playing wait in the early 1580s, offering no official fee but merely permission 'to receyve the rewarde of the townespeople' (he even had to make his own badge). In Elizabethan Manchester, the contributions were compulsory, and the jury of the court leet occasionally had to rebuke those townspeople who had refused to pay their portion of the waits' customary stipend. The waits in Carlisle were unsalaried, but they received payments from time to time at the discretion of the mayor. It is impossible to establish the number of performances that were covered by each payment, but the sums handed out ranged from 18d to 6s 8d. Similar payments were made to the town's drummers and trumpeters.[45]

In other towns, musicians' annual salaries were more reliable but hardly generous. The waits of London – undoubtedly the luckiest in the land – earned £6 each in 1562 and £20 from the early seventeenth century. This was a substantial pay rise, but even an agricultural labourer could earn around £15 a year in wages (and this was barely enough for the maintenance of a family).[46] The next-best-paid waits were the men of Norwich. They each received £1 in 1536, £3 in 1583 and £6 in 1666.[47] Many were considerably poorer. In Nottingham, for example, the seventeenth-century waits received annual wages of only 10s per man, though these were augmented by compulsory, means-tested contributions from the populace (in 1628, aldermen paid 4s each, commoners 'of the better sort' paid 1s each, and those of 'the lower rank' were to contribute whatever they could manage). In other towns, the annual salaries of a typical wait ranged, by the mid-seventeenth century, from 10s in Chester to £4 in Barnstaple (Devon). For comparison, we might note that in 1631–2 a shepherd from Essex was paid around £10 per year by a single employer.[48] In most places,

[44] Woodfill, *Musicians in English Society*, appendix A, pp. 247–51.

[45] *REED Lancashire*, pp. 46, 57; *REED Cumberland, Westmorland, Gloucestershire*, pp. 65–125. See also Woodfill, *Musicians in English Society*, pp. 93–8.

[46] *Chamber Accounts of the Sixteenth Century*, p. 299; Woodfill, *Musicians in English Society*, p. 37; Sharpe, *Early Modern England*, p. 214.

[47] Woodfill, *Musicians in English Society*, p. 93; NCR case 18, shelf B, fo. 55r, NRO.

[48] Woodfill, *Musicians in English Society*, pp. 93–4; ZA/B/2, fo. 175v, ChRO; Keith Wrightson, *Earthly Necessities: Economic Lives in Early Modern Britain, 1470–1750* (2000; London: Penguin Books, 2002), p. 196.

the wages paid to waits increased from time to time between 1500 and 1700, though in real terms they were obviously worth little more at the end of this period than at the beginning.

This brief survey of waits' wages leaves one wondering why it was that independent musicians were often extremely keen to join the civic bands. In 1587, Roger Squire of Hereford implored the mayor to appoint him as head wait, following the death of the previous incumbent. He admitted that he was not a shawm player, but declared an eager willingness to learn. Thirteen years later, he petitioned again, making light of the fact that he was now over eighty years old. Once more his request was rejected. Christopher Burton of Chester had been one of the city's waits, but he committed certain unspecified misdemeanours and was dismissed during the mid-1590s. He subsequently struggled hard to rejoin the band, petitioning the city assembly on two occasions. Since losing his job, Burton had 'fallen into great want & povertie' and was unable to support 'a great nomber of smale children' following the death of his wife, herself 'an honest mans daughter'. He begged for reinstatement, 'for godes sake & in the name of charitie'.[49]

The puzzle can be solved by considering the various fringe benefits that attended employment as a wait. Indeed, the official salary itself was no more than the economic core of a civic musician's living. In most places, firstly, the waits were also paid in cloth, and in some towns this was their only official wage. The cloth was used for the manufacture of the waits' distinctive liveries, and the sums laid out by their employers could be substantial In Chester, poor Christopher Burton had, in happier times, been one of the waits when, in 1588, the city treasurer paid 'for xviii yeardes of . . . Collored broade Cloth att vii s iiii d the yearde Viz for three of the eldest waytte men x yeardes for iii gownes [and] iii yerdes for towe Coate Clothes for towe of the Yonger Wayttmen'. The Exeter waits had separate 'winter robes' and 'summer tunics'.[50] In Shrewsbury and several other towns, the gowns were 'orange tawnye' in colour, but some waits wore black, and the men of Kendal strutted the streets in red and blue broadcloth coats adorned with buttons and baize. The inhospitable Westmorland climate seems to have necessitated frequent replacements. New coats and cloaks were purchased for the waits on twenty-one occasions between 1582 and 1640.[51] The Kendal waits may not have received a

[49] *REED Herefordshire, Worcestershire*, pp. 123–4; *REED Chester*, pp. 179–80, 184.

[50] *REED Chester*, pp. 154–5; *REED Devon*, p. 411.

[51] *REED Shropshire*, p. 226; *The Assembly Books of Southampton . . . 1602–08*, ed. J. W. Horrocks (Southampton: Southampton Record Society, 1917), p. 43; *REED Cumberland, Westmorland, Gloucestershire*, pp. 170–214.

generous salary, but they cut a dash. The characteristic 'look' of a wait was completed by a badge which he wore on a chain or ribbon around his neck while on duty. In Southampton, these civic symbols were described as 'scutchins or cog'izauncs [scutcheons or cognizances] of silver impressed wth the Townes Armes; Namely, three Roses; the l[ett]re H; and the forme of a Tonne [a cask?]'. Each one weighed 4¼ ounces. As in all towns, the badges were merely on loan to the incumbent waits and had to be returned upon dismissal or departure. In 1629, however, one of the Southampton men was so attached to his badge that he had his initials engraved upon it, where they remain to this day.[52]

One Elizabethan text describes the appearance of an unnamed wait in remarkable detail. He came from Islington and was hired to play before the queen at Kenilworth Castle in 1575. Our witness, Robert Laneham, watched and listened as the wait tuned his harp and rehearsed a song about King Arthur. He wore no cap, and his hair, treated with 'a spoonge deintly dipt in a little capons greaz', was 'finely smoothed too [to] make it shine like a Mallard's wing'. His fashionable shirt had starched ruffs and he sported a side gown of 'kendall green', fastened under his chin with a white clasp. From his red girdle hung a pair of knives, and in his breast pocket he carried a napkin, edged with blue lace and decorated 'with a truloove, a hart' and the letters A.D. The resplendent musician also displayed double sleeves of black worsted cloth, a pair of red 'neatherstockes', green lace about his wrist, a red ribbon around his neck and a pair of shiny black pumps on his feet. Finally, he wore a chain from which hung a colourful metal scutcheon bearing 'the auncient armes of Islington'. He had clearly taken an age to dress, and he was equally diligent in tuning his harp, but sadly his big moment never arrived. The queen's visit to Kenilworth was packed with entertainment of many sorts, and the anonymous wait was crowded out by other performers. Somehow, his clothes failed to attract the attention of the master of ceremonies.[53]

Perhaps he should have stayed at home and relied instead upon the protection against musical competitors that many town governors offered to their waits. Once again, systems varied. The Chester waits seem to have fended for themselves in most situations, but those in Manchester were, at times, quite energetically defended by their employers. In 1588 and 1603, local residents were banned from hiring 'foreign' pipers or minstrels to

[52] *Assembly Books of Southampton*, p. 43; Burch, 'Minstrels and Players in Southampton', p. 47.

[53] Laneham, *A Letter whearin Part of the Entertainment unto the Queenz Majesty at Killingworth Castle . . . is Signified* (London, 1575), also printed in *Captain Cox, his Ballads and Books; or, Robert Laneham's Letter*, ed. Frederick J. Furnivall (London: Ballad Society, 1871), pp. 36–42.

play at weddings. Here, and in Beverley (Yorkshire), the waits themselves were given the responsibility for identifying and presenting those who breached the rules. The Norwich waits did exactly this during the 1670s when they repeatedly reported a rival band of local men who had all 'left their Trades and turn'd fiddlers'. The city council duly responded by ordering the men to resume their proper callings and to cease their musical activities forthwith.[54] Furthermore, any wait who fell ill or suffered some other unpredictable misfortune could look to his employers for a measure of charitable support. In 1631, the mayor and aldermen of Newcastle upon Tyne paid a generous 20s to Robert Mawpous, one of the waits, to cover a period of sickness. In Norwich, some of the waits lived in subsidised housing. During the mid-seventeenth century, the city chamberlain regularly received a nominal rent from Peter Sandlyn for his occupancy of one of the 'Suffragans Tenements'.[55]

The advantageous position of the waits also enabled them to make money over and above their salaries, and it seems probable that the resultant earnings formed the more substantial portion of their total incomes. In 1633, the Nottingham waits fell into dispute at a time when they each received only 10s per year in salary. In an attempt to settle the argument, the town governors dismissed two of them, Humphrey Coggs and his son, but ordered the remaining three to pay the older man a full £3 a year during the rest of his lifetime. This offers us some indication of the substantial disparity that existed between salary and overall earnings, and the fact that the ejected waits declined the deal as insufficiently generous further reinforces the point.[56] How, then, did the official town musicians boost their incomes? As we have already heard, they often played at weddings, but they also performed more regularly in local inns, alehouses and private homes. When a Shrewsbury shearman entered Richard Harris's house, one Saturday afternoon in 1612, he found a group of drinkers and revellers being entertained by John Ludman and the other town waits. Waits also received small sums from the visiting dignitaries whom they awoke on those cold winter mornings. They sang carols at Christmas and they provided the music at the regular feasts held by trade guilds and companies. In Gloucester, for instance, the waits played for the tanners and the bakers on a number of occasions in the early seventeenth century,

[54] *REED Lancashire*, pp. 58–9, 63; *Beverley Borough Records, 1575–1821*, ed. J. Dennett, *Yorkshire Archaeological Society Record Series* 84 (1933), p. 18; Stephen, 'Waits of the City of Norwich', pp. 29–31.

[55] *REED Newcastle upon Tyne*, p. 155; NCR case 18, shelf A, fos. 126r, 145v, 186r, NRO.

[56] *Records of the Borough of Nottingham*, vol. V, pp. 165, 171–2.

receiving cash and beer for their efforts.[57] From time to time, groups or individuals were recruited to join the households of aristocrats for special occasions. The Islington wait who almost played before the queen in 1575 was described by Laneham as 'a squier minstrel of Middilsex, that travaild the cuntree this soommer seazon unto fairs & worshipfull mens hoousez'. In the same year, the waits of Derby apparently spent the Christmas holiday earning extra money in Chesterfield, thirty miles to the north. We would know nothing of their trip but for the sad and slightly suspicious fact that two of them died there.[58]

Civic musicians also enjoyed and made full use of the right to travel more widely than this during the summer months, wearing their colourful tunics as signifiers of respectability. This was an important privilege at a time when other mobile musicians were having to exercise caution. In a sense, waits-on-tour were the new minstrels. As usual, it is difficult to be precise about the profits that were made by wandering waits but it seems likely that well-managed groups could return home significantly richer than they had been upon departure. In 1587, the leader of the Hereford waits complained that his stipend was too small and that he therefore had to make a substantial proportion of his living by travelling beyond the city. One of the issues in dispute among the waits of Nottingham in 1633 was the lucrative right to tour, and the town council expressly banned the Coggs duo from travelling in gowns of the same colour as those worn by the official band. Furthermore, it was ordered that they should give the town's authorised ensemble a head-start during the touring season: 'when the ... waites have a purpose to travell to London or ellswhere, as usually they have done ... , Homfrey Coggs, nor his sonne, shall nott travell that way, to forstall them, untill a forttnighte after they be gone, att the least'. Coggs and son were clearly reluctant to relinquish the profits that could be made by liveried town waits on the road.[59]

Certain destinations were well known as particularly favourable ports of call. Hardly anybody went to puritanical Rye, but many – like the men of Nottingham – headed for London. Carlisle was also an astoundingly attractive musical magnet. Between 1602 and 1643 the city recorded 114

[57] *REED Shropshire*, pp. 303–5; 'Diary of the Journey of Philip Julius', p. 63; *REED Bristol*, p. 127; *REED Cumberland, Westmorland, Gloucestershire*, pp. 314–27.

[58] Laneham, *Captain Cox, his Ballads and Books*, p. 38; *Chesterfield Parish Register, 1558–1600*, ed. Mary Walton, *Derbyshire Record Society* 12 (1986), p. 67. Godfrey Lee, 'one of the musicians of Derbie', and James Oke, 'the other of the musicians of Derbie', were both laid to rest on 17 January 1576.

[59] *REED Herefordshire, Worcestershire*, pp. 122–3; *Records of the Borough of Nottingham*, vol. V, pp. 165, 171–2.

payments to visiting waits from 35 other places. They came not only from towns in Cumberland, but from Atherton in Lancashire, Boston in Lincolnshire, Kendal in Westmorland and Darrington in Yorkshire. They even came from Bristol and from Canterbury. The sums paid to the visiting bands by the chamberlain of Carlisle ranged from 6d (to the waits of Penrith, Cumberland, in 1635) to 5s (to those of Knaresborough, Yorkshire, in 1614), but most payments were concentrated in the 2–4s range. In some months, waits from a number of different towns evidently coincided. Disbursements for the period between 19 April and 7 May 1635 included small payments to the waits of Orton (Westmorland), Cockermouth (Cumberland) and Askrigg and Bradford (Yorkshire).[60] We can be sure that, in Carlisle, tunes and musical ideas were discussed and disseminated among practitioners from many locations.

Touring waits did not, of course, restrict themselves to urban locations. The Islington musician was one of many who stopped off with receptive members of the gentry and aristocracy as he pursued his summer itinerary. In the spring of 1621, for example, we glimpse the waits of Lancaster, already over fifty miles from home, pausing for performances first at Carlisle and then a further ten miles away at Naworth Castle, the house of Lord William Howard. Fees of 18d and 12d respectively suggest that these were merely passing visits, rather than longer sojourns.[61] The combination of Carlisle and Naworth, surely part of a much more extensive tour, was a favoured one among travelling waits. Those of Ripon, Kendal, Middleham and Penrith all made the same double stop-over at some point during the 1620s. This suggests that different groups shared information regarding potentially lucrative hosts, and tended to pursue pre-arranged itineraries. Naworth Castle was close to the main route that led invitingly from Carlisle towards Northumberland.[62]

Hospitable families were, it seems, concentrated most heavily in the north and west of the country, where a traditional readiness to receive musical visitors survived more strongly than elsewhere, sometimes in association with Roman Catholicism. Thomas Walmesley of Dunkenhalgh (Lancashire) was a high-ranking church papist, and his gates seem to have opened almost automatically for visiting waits. Between 1613 and 1640, Walmesley's steward paid out rewards to the waits of Wakefield, Halifax,

[60] *REED Cumberland, Westmorland, Gloucestershire*, pp. 65–125. [61] Ibid., pp. 101, 140.
[62] Ibid., pp. 98–9, 101, 107, 139, 142 (and see map on p. 57).

Durham, Leeds, Preston, Ripon, Lancaster and Nottingham. Most visited repeatedly, and the groups from Wakefield and Leeds made the trip of over fifty miles on eight occasions each. Walmesley rewarded visiting waits with standard fees of 12d or 18d, though he probably fed them too. Occasionally, however, musical callers at Dunkenhalgh were better paid, presumably because, by arrangement, they stayed longer. Most noticeably, the waits of Preston received 10s in 1626–7. This payment was made in January, suggesting that the group had been in residence during the Christmas period.[63] Not all of those who paid touring waits were Catholics, however. During the late sixteenth and early seventeenth centuries, the Lancashire Shuttleworths welcomed the entertainment provided at various times by the waits of Pontefract, Elland, Carlisle, Manchester, Wakefield, Durham, Leeds and Chester. In Lincolnshire, the family of the Duke of Rutland received waits less regularly but did nevertheless reward those of Newark, Doncaster, Pontefract and Grantham. And in 1671, the waits of Daventry (Northamptonshire) took up residence with the Ishams of Lamport between 26 and 31 December. According to the diary of young Thomas Isham, they had been hired 'to practise their skill'.[64] All over the realm, therefore, England's waits delivered the sound of the town to the heart of the countryside.

To the governors of a civic band's home town, the right of the waits to go on tour represented a seasonal loss of control, but in most cases the benefits were sufficient to subdue any anxiety. In 1588, the leading citizens of Manchester said of their waits, 'it is a creditt to the towne to see theym well mayneteyned'. The town that could pay its waits, dress them in colourful tunics and spare them for months at a time clearly deserved its place on the map. Travelling waits were musical ambassadors, unofficially charged with promoting their home town's image across the country. Once in a while, they went further still. The only band that is known to have gone global hailed originally from Norwich. In 1589, Sir Francis Drake asked if they could accompany him on a voyage to Portugal. The city was clearly flattered, and went to the expense of paying for six new 'cloakes of Stamell cloath', replacement hautboys (as well as a recorder) and 'A wagon ... to carry them and their Instruments' to London.

63 *REED Lancashire*, pp. 184–212.

64 Ibid., pp. 166–79; *The Manuscripts of His Grace the Duke of Rutland*, 4 vols. (London: Historical Manuscripts Commission, 1888–1905), vol. IV, pp. 399, 407, 529; *Diary of Thomas Isham*, pp. 71, 75. On travelling waits, see also Mark Brayshay, 'Waits, Musicians, Bearwards and Players', pp. 426–40.

The journey to London evidently went smoothly, but the onward voyage was a disaster, and three of the musicians never returned home.[65]

England's waits may not have earned large salaries, but when the entire package of perquisites and additional opportunities is considered, it becomes easier to understand why other musicians were eager to join them. In addition to earning their salaries, they travelled around widely, apparently depositing their various extra fees into some sort of communal bag or box. Such details come to light only when arrangements went awry. In 1632, Edmund Hanny, Southampton's leading wait, grew suspicious when he unlocked the band's money box in order to divide up its contents. Finding less cash than anticipated, Hanny pointed an accusing finger at his own apprentice, Henry Combes, who had recently been observed 'spending moneys abroad in Companie'. Combes denied the charge, but was undone when a witness claimed to have heard him admit, 'with the said Boxe in his hand', that he had previously teased it open with a card. Without this information, the apprentice might successfully have defended himself by arguing that he had earned the money in teaching local gentlemen to play 'on the violl and some other Instruments'.[66] Even a wait's apprentice could plausibly argue that he made substantial cash on the side. It is not, therefore, surprising that some of those who had lived their lives as waits approached death as comparatively wealthy men. Thomas Quashe of Norwich had been not only a wait, but an ecclesiastical singing man, an innkeeper and a shopkeeper (he perhaps had too much on his plate, for he was repeatedly rebuked for neglecting his duties at the cathedral). He died at Christmas in 1638, and his probate inventory suggests a life of some comfort. There were ten rooms in Quashe's house, and they were clearly well furnished. He possessed not only several musical instruments and a wealth of more mundane items, but also 'foure turnd chayers', a glass case, two pairs of 'playinge tables', six pictures, curtains, silver plate and some 'fine turky worke Cushens'. This was no threadbare minstrel.[67]

Of course, the waits had to earn their privileges. Town governors reminded them periodically of their duty to conduct themselves in an orderly fashion, and, as Christopher Burton of Chester knew only too well, waits faced disciplinary measures if they failed so to do. Burton was by no

[65] *REED Lancashire*, p. 59; *REED Norwich*, pp. 92–3. See also Woodfield, *English Musicians*, pp. 11–12.

[66] *The Book of Examinations and Depositions . . . 1627–34*, ed. R. C. Anderson, *Publications of the Southampton Record Society* (1931), pp. 118–20.

[67] *REED Norwich*, pp. xl, xlii, 137, 144, 154, etc.; DN/INV44/168, NRO.

means the only Chester wait to earn rebuke for immoral or anti-social behaviour. In 1609, Thomas Williams was already under arrest when he allegedly said he 'woulde burne the gowne wch hee receaved of Mr Wm Gamell late maior'. He later admitted that, on one occasion, he had left prison without licence in order to visit the house of a Mr Ravenscroft in Bretton (Flint). Here, he had stayed for two days, ' played in Consorte & receaved for his musicke vs'. The authorities gave Williams every opportunity to apologise and return to the waits, but he said 'hee had formerlie made a vowe to the Contrarie never to plaie wth them throughe the streetes for this yeare'. His behaviour suggests the mind-set of the conceited virtuoso rather than the disorderly attitude of the lewd and lowly fiddler.[68]

Independent urban musicians

Waits dominated urban music-making but they rarely if ever enjoyed a monopoly. In many towns, the opportunities available to freelancing musicians remained plentiful, despite the efforts that were periodically made to restrict them. The prizes were worth the risks, and in 1672 seventeen London men were intent on ignoring all attempts to discipline them for performing without licence from the 'Marshall and Corporation of Musick'.[69] Some independent musicians were specialists, and did not compete directly with the waits. Trumpeters, for example, could always pick up fees from town councils, but they seem to have been particularly desirable at the official proclamation of a new monarch. At the accession of James I, the mayor of Bristol sent a messenger into the surrounding countryside to fetch a specific trumpeter. His subsequent performance at the high cross in Bristol was described in detail by the chronicler William Adams. Before the reading of the proclamation, the leading men of Bristol stood in their scarlet gowns and listened while 'Trigges the trumpeter sownded 4 times solemnely and mourefully [sic], turning himself 4 severall wayes uppon the Crosse, for the death of her majestie, and so for a while rested. Then began againe, sownding 4 times and 4 waies turning his face as before, but now joyfully for the entrance of King James.' The town scribe lacked Adams's ear for detail, and wrote prosaically in the account book, 'Item paid Trigge for sounding att that proclamacion vi^{s}'. Drummers were equally useful, though they generally earned only small

[68] Z QSE/9/2, ChRO. [69] *The King's Musick*, p. 249.

fees. They played at the musters, during processions and when announcements were made. Their potential to intimidate was recognised in Portsmouth, where, in 1676, the bailiffs hired two drummers when they went to arrest a miscreant named Mrs Collins (the musicians also prevented the bailiffs from apprehending Mrs Young by mistake).[70]

Drummers and trumpeters also found work with theatrical companies. From 1576, when the first public theatre opened in London, trumpet signals announced the commencement of stage plays and featured regularly within the dramatic action itself. The attention-grabbing qualities of the drum were used out on the streets in order to publicise performances, and again within the theatre for a variety of sound effects. During this period as a whole, employment opportunities for musicians in connection with the stage increased significantly. Under Elizabeth I, the development of the London theatres inaugurated this trend, though most of the music was, at this early date, fairly basic and provided by the actors themselves. Several companies owned collections of instruments, and it is evident that numerous actors were also men of music. According to Stephen Gosson – a playwright turned puritan – many of them had begun their disreputable careers as 'common minstrels'. Elizabethan actors were therefore well qualified to sing short pieces within the drama, and to provide simple music during any intervals. At the end of a play, it was customary for them to stage additional light entertainment in the form of jigs (short song-based narratives), ballads and dances.[71] The most musical companies, however, were those associated with choirboys, namely the children of the Queen's Revels and of St Paul's. In their productions, music moved closer to centre-stage and pointed the way forward for the adult companies. Choirboy plays of the late sixteenth and early seventeenth centuries featured consort songs (for voice and instrumental accompaniment), rustic part-songs and curtain-raising instrumental numbers. The boys, or their hired adult musicians, also played to audiences in between acts, and ear-witnesses referred to the use of organs, lutes, bandoras, pipes, viols, recorders and flutes.[72]

70 *REED Bristol*, pp. 157–8; *Borough Sessions Papers, 1653–88*, ed. A. J. Willis and Margaret Jean Hoad, *Portsmouth Record Series* 1 (1971), p. 56.

71 *Henslowe Papers: Being Documents Supplementary to Henslowe's Diary*, ed. W. W. Greg (London: A. H. Bullen, 1907), p. 115; Stephen Gosson, *Playes Confuted in Five Actions* (London, 1582), G6v; Woodfill, *Musicians in English Society*, p. 237.

72 Peter Holman, 'Music for the Stage I: Before the Civil War', in Spink (ed.), *Music in Britain: The Seventeenth Century*, pp. 292–5.

The early decades of the next century witnessed an intensifying demand for specialist musicians in adult theatre. This occurred partly as a result of the development of the more intimate, indoor 'hall' theatres, within which instruments less strident than the trumpet could make themselves heard. Not surprisingly, some of this new work went to London's waits, but other musicians also felt the benefit. Theatrical companies began employing independent instrumentalists more regularly, and setting aside special 'music rooms' from which they could perform. Where Elizabethan actors had typically sung mere snatches of ballads, now they also performed newly composed songs with elaborate off-stage musical accompaniment. Around 1609, the King's Men began to pay their own band of instrumentalists, and a list of 1624 contains six names, none of whom was a serving wait. The extension of theatrical music was evidently pleasing to many audience members, and when Nathaneal Tomkyns went to see and hear *The Witches of Lancashire* at the Globe in 1634, he reported to a friend that although it was a work of mediocre poetry, it was transformed into 'a merrie and excellent new play' by being 'mixed with divers songs and dances'. In this famous theatre, approximately six musicians gathered in a small space over the stage, where they played from behind a curtain.[73] William Prynne did not like any of it. In his zealous opinion, the theatres of London were far too closely associated with 'amorous, obscene lascivious lust-provoking Songs', all of them 'melodiously chanted out upon the Stage between each several Action'. Such entertainments were 'too to[o] rife', and had recently begun to spread out of the theatre and into 'private Christians Feasts, and other Tavern-meetings'. Such extra-theatrical performances were, it seems, a precursor of the short dramatic 'drolls' that would be performed in taverns and at fairs during the decades after 1660.[74] To London's musicians, of course, these were most pleasing developments.

The closing of the theatres in 1642 unquestionably damaged the prospects of a generation of musicians, though it has been argued that musical drama actually advanced during the years of turbulence. Plays continued to be staged in schools, and the first fully musical English opera, *The Siege of Rhodes*, was composed by the royalist Sir William Davenant in 1656. After the Restoration of the monarchy in 1660, theatrical opportunities for musicians accelerated markedly. During the next decades, the size

[73] Ibid., pp. 296–8; *REED Somerset*, p. 416; Spring, *The Lute in Britain*, p. 188.

[74] Prynne, *Histrio-mastix*, pp. 261–3; Peter Burke, 'Popular Culture in Seventeenth-century London', in Barry Reay (ed.), *Popular Culture in Seventeenth-century England* (London: Routledge, 1985), p. 40.

of theatrical bands increased, and the wages of individual members also grew (to 2s 6d or more per day). 'Curtain tunes' sounded at the commencement of plays, and short instrumental interludes were performed between acts. There were also songs within the action, some of them integral to the drama but many of them merely decorative. The opening-up of new opportunities for actresses in this period was a boon for musical women, enabling them to make money from public singing much more freely than they had done before (a trend that also spread beyond the theatre). The last decades of the century represented a high point for English musical theatre, with Henry Purcell and his son Daniel at the forefront of composition. The continuing evolution of dramatic opera provided work for some of the best of London's musicians, and several of Purcell's tunes spilled out onto the streets, where they were sung and sold in broadside form by balladeers. 'If love's a sweet passion', one of the top street tunes of the 1690s, began its life in the third act of Purcell's *The Fairy Queen*.[75]

When companies of players went on tour, they often took their own music with them. Edward Sutton, Baron of Dudley, issued a warrant to two of his servants in 1595, allowing them 'to travell in the quality of playinge & to use musicke in all Cittys Townes & Corporations within her majestyes dominons [sic]'. Like other Elizabethan actors, they made the music themselves. Around the same time, a story was circulating about some enterprising Spaniards who had recently attempted an invasion of Cornwall. After landing in the night, they approached the town of Penryn with aggressive intent, but abandoned their mission when they heard 'a lowd alarme' on drum and trumpets. In fact, it was merely the music of a troop of players, performing a battle scene on stage. The intruders were frightened, 'and so in a hurly-burly fled disorderly to their boats'. Half a century later, another group of players arrived in Gloucester, but by this date they were more specialised: three actors and 'one Jarvis Gennatt, a mynstrell'.[76]

Such self-sufficient bands brought little benefit to locally based musicians, and the decline of the strolling player during the early seventeenth century was perhaps a blessing in disguise. The evolution of more stable

[75] Spink, 'Music and Society', pp. 13–16; Margaret Laurie, 'Music for the Stage II: from 1650', in Spink (ed.), *Music in Britain: The Seventeenth Century*, pp. 306–40; Thomasin LaMay, 'Preliminaries', in LaMay (ed.), *Musical Voices of Early Modern Women: Many-headed Melodies* (Aldershot: Ashgate, 2005), pp. 1–13; Simpson, *British Broadside Ballad*, p. 359.

[76] *REED Chester*, pp. 177–8; *REED Dorset, Cornwall*, p. 505; *REED Cumberland, Westmorland, Gloucestershire*, pp. 319–20.

provincial theatre during the later seventeenth century may have been partly a delayed consequence, and must certainly have been a welcome development. For its disjointed origins, we must look back a century and more. Late medieval musicians had contributed to the various forms of religious drama that were staged annually in many towns, but during the reign of Elizabeth such opportunities were in decline. Fortunately, the requirements of newer, more secular, drama provided some compensation. In 1582–3, for example, the chamberlain of Bath paid two shillings to the musician William Tucker 'for playing on his Instruments' during a drama produced by one of the city's schoolmasters. In the decades following the Restoration, the music associated with provincial drama became steadily more elaborate, and theatrical groups once more went on tour. The establishment of new civic companies of players and, during the eighteenth century, the construction of purpose-built urban theatres in cities other than London were developments that benefited local musicians. Admittedly, the theatrical opportunities available to provincial musicians were neither as regular nor as reliable as the prospects in London, yet they contributed to the composite bundle of possibilities by which such performers made their livings.[77]

Unsalaried urban musicians could make money in a number of other ways too. Some of these were specific to certain towns. The colleges of Oxford and Cambridge, for example, provided many opportunities, and both towns supported a number of independent musicians throughout the period. In late Jacobean Cambridge, several of them lived on Green Street (today the location of a specialist music shop). There was work at college feasts, plays and ceremonies, and bands of musicians rivalled the city waits, sometimes earning the unofficial title of 'university waits'. In Queen's College, Oxford, even the college servants sometimes got in on the act. On New Year's Day 1640, the diarist Thomas Crosfield recorded the sight and sound of 'Morrice the gardener goeing to every fellowes chamber with musicke – 6d or 12d of each'. During the years between 1618 and 1640, Crosfield also remarked upon college 'music nights' (with specially written songs), repairs to various instruments, performers of novelty instruments in the streets and processions featuring trumpet players.[78]

Further possibilities were more generally available. The waits, particularly in larger towns and cities, could not possibly provide all the music

[77] *REED Somerset*, p. 13; Borsay, *English Urban Renaissance*, pp. 117–21.

[78] *REED Cambridge*, pp. 740, 745; *The Diary of Thomas Crosfield*, ed. Frederick S. Boas (London: Oxford University Press, 1935), pp. 8, 36, 54, 90, 96.

that was required in taverns, inns and private houses, nor at weddings, dances and company dinners. According to Stephen Gosson, writing in 1579, 'London is so full of unprofitable Pipers and Fidlers, that a man can no soner enter a taverne, but two or three caste of them hang at his heeles, to give him a daunce before he departe.'[79] In using the adjective 'unprofitable', he juxtaposed the musicians' quest for cash with his own belief that their behaviour benefited nobody. Of course, Gosson's anxious Protestantism predisposed him to exaggerate the numbers – to hear double, as it were – but other sources allow us to make the passing acquaintance of some genuine, flesh-and-blood urban musicians. In 1550, for example, an enterprising Bristol innkeeper named Thomas Rancock took on three apprentices at once. At the conclusion of their terms, the first two were each to receive a loud shawm and a still shawm (together with viols, recorders and rebecs), while the third would earn a viol and a rebec (this looks suspiciously like England's first artificially contrived boy band).[80] The century that followed produced a string of comparable examples: the young Elizabethan man who toured the common inns of London and 'shewed his skill on the Virginals, to the no little contentment of the hearers'; the Bristol musician who, in 1622, put out word that he was looking for somebody 'to joyne in Consort with him, this Christmas tyme' (a musical tailor from Frome heard the call and travelled into the city); and Thomas Maxwell of Rye (Sussex), who, in 1617, received from the mayor a passport allowing him to travel to and from the Low Countries with his 'company' and all their instruments. Maxwell had evidently been making a living in Rye, despite the anti-musical tendencies of its governors, and this was no escape bid. Instead, the musician planned to escort his nephew back to the Low Countries, where the boy's father worked as a merchant. Sure enough, Thomas returned to Rye some time later, and in 1630–1 received from the chamberlain a payment of five shillings 'for his Musicke at the Brotherhood' (a meeting of the representatives of the Cinque Ports).[81]

Independent musicians could also teach others to play, and a healthy appetite for music lessons among England's wealthier social ranks enabled Solomon Eccles to make £130 per year in London, during the period before he decided that all music was evil.[82] Furthermore, the development

[79] Stephen Gosson, *The Ephemerides of Phialo* (London, 1579), p. 87.

[80] *REED Bristol*, pp. 256–7.

[81] Robert Greene, *The Third and Last Part of Conny-catching* (London, 1592), C4v–D1v; *REED Bristol*, pp. 219–20; *REED Sussex*, pp. 152–3, 161.

[82] Eccles, *A Musick-lector*, p. 10. See above, pp. 63–4.

during the later seventeenth century of a concert culture brought impressive rewards to the country's most accomplished musicians. Public concerts evolved from the music meetings that had taken place in London and Oxford from the late 1640s onwards.[83] The development can perhaps be related to the turbulence of civil war. In the words of Roger North, sophisticated music did well in this period, 'for many chose rather to fidle at home, than to goe out, and be knockt on the head abroad'. The trend towards concert life accelerated after the Restoration. North reported that, during the early 1670s, John Banister 'procured a large room in Whitefryars ... rounded with seats and small tables alehouse fashion. 1^{s} was the price and call for what you pleased. There was very good musick, for Banister found means to procure the best hands in towne.' By the early 1700s, there were public concerts not only in the capital but in many provincial centres too. In this atmosphere, the cult of the professional virtuoso, often a fashionable foreigner, could begin. After the master violinist Thomas Baltzar performed at a music meeting in Oxford during the 1650s, a highly esteemed member of the audience was said to have lifted up his foot to search for devilish hooves. In 1703, the diarist John Evelyn estimated that a female Italian singer had 'carryed with her out of this vaine nation above 1000 pounds, every body coveting to heare her at their privat houses, especially the noble men'.[84]

All in all, there were clearly livings to be made by musicians who did not belong to cathedral choirs or bands of waits (see Figure 3.2). The parish registers of All Saints', Newcastle upon Tyne, provide numerous examples. Between 1620 and 1700, the scribes consistently recorded the occupations of adult male parishioners. During this period, at least twenty-six independent music-makers were active at one time or another in this single city parish. They included fourteen 'musicians' (also 'musicker' and 'musicianer'), eight 'pipers', one 'trumpeter', one 'drum major', one 'teacher of musicke' and one 'fiddler'.[85] Of course, the quality of the livings made by such performers varied extensively. The probate inventories of independent urban musicians during this period present lists of personal goods worth anything from £6 14s 6d (Lincoln, 1628) to £252 (Andover, 1646). Most valuations fall between £20 and £70, suggesting a level of wealth that was roughly comparable to that of individuals in the lower to middling ranks of English society (lesser yeomen, husbandmen, artisans,

[83] See below, pp. 220–1.

[84] *Roger North on Music*, p. 294; Spink, 'Music and Society', pp. 17, 19; Anthony Wood, quoted by Spring, *The Lute in Britain*, p. 327; *Diary of John Evelyn*, pp. 1094–5.

[85] Transcript of All Saints' parish register, City Library, Newcastle upon Tyne.

Figure 3.2. Occupational musicians often played several different instruments. This one practises the cittern but also possesses a kit (a portable miniature violin, often associated with dancing masters) and a viol. The third instrument on the wall is a spare cittern. © Trustees of the British Museum, Prints and Drawings, 1884,1213.48, plate from John Playford, *Musick's Delight on the Cithren* (London, 1666).

tradesmen and labourers).[86] Few of them were wealthy, but many were somehow managing, despite the pressures of the age. By the late seventeenth century, moreover, these pressures had eased somewhat and independent musicians were probably more happily situated than they had been for a century or more.

Employment opportunities also existed for those who manufactured musical instruments, though specialists in this activity were comparatively rare. The city of Bristol was a special case, being home to at least fourteen instrument-makers during this period. Elsewhere, the evidence is much thinner, though this implies not so much an absence of instrument-makers as an absence of individuals who chose to label themselves as such. It is obvious that many of the period's instruments were made by carpenters, joiners and tanners, and often by musicians themselves. One man in Elizabethan Chester made not only instruments of music, but weapons of war (particularly bows). George Styddie of York described himself in 1585 as an 'instramentmaker or joyner'. In 1633, a Southampton musician named Edmund Hanny took on an apprentice 'to learne that trade as

[86] INV 134/49, LA; 1646 A 25/1 and 25/2, HRO.

allso the making of instruments'. This combination was probably commonplace, though rarely specified.[87]

Not surprisingly, specialists are encountered a little more regularly in connection with instruments that were unusually expensive or intricate. An Elizabethan goldsmith named George Langdale was granted a monopoly of trumpet-making in 1583, and he later claimed to have been the first such maker in England (the best trumpets had previously come from Germany). Langdale, however, had trouble enforcing the monopoly, and he alleged in 1597 that his former assistant had broken their agreement by producing three or four hundred trumpets – an impressive number – on an independent basis. There were undoubtedly other makers at work, and Langdale's claim that he was the originator of English trumpet-making was undermined by another petition, dating from the mid-1580s, in which Simon Brewer asked that he be permitted to continue manufacturing trumpets and sackbuts, despite the privilege recently granted to Langdale.[88] A century later, William Bull was London's leading trumpet-maker, and one of his pictorial trade cards survives in the British Museum (see Figure 3.3). Viols and virginals enjoyed a similarly refined reputation, and we can therefore acquaint ourselves with some of the individuals who constructed and repaired them. The names of leading English makers – John Rose (viols), Thomas and James White (virginals), for example – are well known to musicologists. Beyond these exalted ranks, wood-working craftsmen often produced instruments, and they sometimes described themselves specifically as 'virginal makers'.[89] The merchants' guild in Leicester admitted one in 1579. In mid-seventeenth-century London, some of them worked 'at the Sign of the Virginal' in Threadneedle Street and placed advertisements in printed music books of the day. During the early seventeenth century, Isaac Bryan of Bristol specialised in making virginals and trained four apprentices in succession.[90] In 1642, the probate inventory of Steven Hussey, another Bristol man, included no occupational label but did record his possession of 'one unfinished harpsicall, one vyall and a dulcimer'.[91]

[87] *REED Chester*, pp. 169–70; Michael Fleming, 'Viol-making in England, *c.* 1580–1660', unpublished PhD thesis, Open University (2001), p. 167; *Calendar of Southampton Apprenticeship Registers*, p. 73.

[88] REQ2 235/17 and SP12/175 (109), NA.

[89] Fleming, 'Viol-making', pp. 126, 129–30, 170.

[90] Brydson, 'The Minstrels and Waits of Leicester', p. 143; Thomas Campion, 'The Art of Descant', printed in Playford, *An Introduction*, p. 41; *REED Bristol*, pp. 263–7.

[91] Ibid., p. 246.

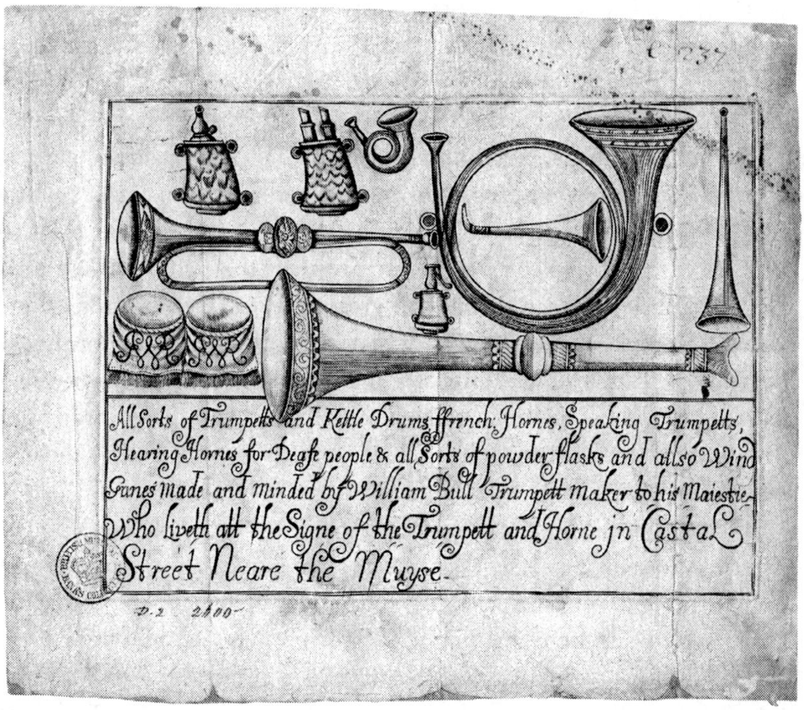

Figure 3.3. William Bull, 'Trumpett maker to his Majestie', distributed cards in order to advertise the full range of his wares to a wider audience. © Trustees of the British Museum, Prints and Drawings, D,2.2600, trade card of William Bull (*c.* 1680–1720).

Out-of-town opportunities

Towns and cities were sonic centres, distinctive primarily in terms of the concentration and variety of their musical activity, but there were also many possibilities elsewhere. The most adventurous of musicians could take to the sea, where opportunities were on the increase. As the number of voyages made by English ships escalated, so too did the need for trumpeters, drummers and even consort players. In 1595, Sir Francis Drake apparently used a recruiting agent in order to ensure that his expedition to the West Indies was well supplied with musicians (the agent presumably did not tell prospective players about what had happened to the last lot). At sea, those who played viols and other refined instruments were present primarily for the 'ornament and delight' of the gentlemen on board, while the trumpeters performed a wide range of more practical duties. They set the watch, hailed other ships, held the fleet together in fog, greeted visitors, attended the captain if he went ashore, carried messages to the enemy, delivered a variety of signals in the event of battle and sounded the knell at funerals. In 1590, trumpeters attempted to locate the lost men of the Roanoke colony in America. They rowed along the shore and 'sounded with a trumpet a Call, and afterwardes many familiar English tunes of songs', but all to no avail.[92] Some of their duties, particularly those undertaken during combat, were perilous. John Taylor told the grim tale of one musician's heroic death under Turkish fire in 1616: 'William Sweat Trumpetter, as hee sounded in the fight had one arme shot off, yet hee sounded till another great shot stroke off his other arme, with his Trumpet and all, then after that hee was kild with a shot thorow the body.'[93] This example indicates the importance, in enemy eyes, of disabling the individual whose signals were crucial to the co-ordination of military action. During battle at sea, it was a good idea to shoot the messenger.

For musicians who preferred a quieter life, there was work in the English countryside too. It was not only the civic waits, for example, who earned fees on visits to the grand estates of the gentry. Before the 1570s, such visits were comparatively uncontroversial, and the case of Richard Sheale provides us with a marvellous opportunity to hear how they were conducted. Sheale was a minstrel based at Tamworth (Staffordshire) and, like the combative George Cally of Chester, named as his principal patron the Earl of Derby. We would know little about him, but for the survival of a manuscript book of poems and songs in which five of Sheale's own compositions were recorded by an anonymous collector at some time between 1557 and 1565. They appear to have been either transcribed from or designed for oral delivery, and the author's name is recorded in one of two forms: 'Expliceth, quoth Rychard Sheale' or 'Amen, quothe Rycharde Sheale'. Sheale almost certainly played and sang mainly by ear, though his verses reveal that he was also familiar with the emerging genre of the printed broadside ballad. It is our good fortune that somebody chose to copy out a selection of his pieces for posterity, though it is regrettable that no reference is made to the melodies. Even without these, the songs or poems shed a uniquely revealing light on the lifestyle of a mid-Tudor minstrel and on the role of music in connecting the high with the low in English society.[94]

[92] Woodfield, *English Musicians*, pp. 5, 10, 14, 51–68.

[93] Taylor, *All the Workes*, vol. III, p. 516.

[94] MS Ashmole 48, Bodleian Library; printed in *Songs and Ballads, with Other Short Poems, Chiefly of the Reign of Philip and Mary*, ed. Thomas Wright (London: J. B. Nichols and Sons, 1860).

Sheale, to judge by his surviving verses, was not a lewd man. Of course, his repertoire must have contained many more pieces than are recorded in the manuscript, and we may be attending to a sample that is slanted towards the more polished and genteel of his songs. Most Tudor notebooks of this sort were kept by members of the gentry, and Sheale's songs would clearly have suited an audience of 'glittering folks' (though there is no reason why they might not also have been performed in humbler contexts). One piece has earned him a certain status among literary scholars, for it is an early version of the celebrated ballad *The Hunting of the Cheviot.* This tells the violent and heroic tale of a confrontation between the Earls of Percy and Douglas at an unspecified date during either the fourteenth or the fifteenth century. In Sheale's text, the long lines and variable metrical patterns would surely have made it difficult to sing the song to a fixed tune, and one wonders whether it was instead recited as a poem, perhaps to the accompaniment of the minstrel's harp. Another of Sheale's compositions is more obviously a metrical song. It contains traditional moral advice, and dwells in particular upon the value of wisdom, love and the fear of God in the cultivation of reputation. The accredited motives are not invariably spiritual: 'A good name dothe wynne renoune, and shall not be forgotten, / But fame shall sounde it forthe abrode when we be ded and rotten.' Sheale endeavoured to fulfil his own prophecy when he wrote a lengthy verse-eulogy for his patroness, Lady Margaret, Countess of Derby, who died in January 1559. This was a conventional outpouring of poetic praise, in which the good lady's charity, familial love, exemplary death and stately funeral were all fully documented. Its clear metre and its presentation on the page suggest that Sheale may have intended it for publication as a broadside.[95]

A fourth piece was in the form of a farewell speech that Sheale evidently delivered upon his departure from any house in which he had entertained the residents. The minstrel purposefully mentions his own name on two occasions, perhaps in an effort to implant it in the minds of his hosts, but the general utility of the verse is preserved by the avoidance of specific references to the names or homes of audience members. It opens,

Ser, for the good chear
That I have hade heare,
I gyve youe harrte thankes,
With bowyng off my shankes.

[95] *Songs and Ballads*, pp. 24–8, 54–7, 179–82.

He commends his hosts on their liberality,

For I perseve here
At all tymis is goode chear,
Both ayle, wyne and bear.

Further flattery follows. The minstrel lists some of the edible goodies available in the house, and comments, 'Both mutton and veile / Ys good for Rycarde Sheill.' His main objective, expressed repeatedly, is to obtain permission to return again at a later date:

I desyre youe allway
Marke what I do saye;
Althoughe I be a ranger,
To tayk me as no stranger.

Having made his request, Sheale takes his leave:

Now, farwell, good myn oste,
I thank you for yor coste
Untill anothar tyme.
Thus do I ende my ryme.[96]

The final song was composed as an appeal for help following a period of extreme misfortune in Sheale's life, and it provides a wealth of fascinating autobiographical detail. The syllabic patterns are rather variable, and when the text is recited aloud it is almost possible to imagine it as a form of early Elizabethan rap music. The song opens with a conventional swipe at social climbers and a joke about those who claim to be short of cash whenever a minstrel arrives upon the scene. Swiftly, however, it becomes more personal. Sheale explains in rhyming couplets that he has recently been attacked by thieves, and is now finding it difficult to pursue his calling: 'After my robbery my memory was so decayde, / That I colde neather syng nore talke, my wyttes wer so dismayde.' Some in the audience, he remarks, have known him 'myrry as a hawke' and well able to 'play the myrry knave', but the jolly minstrel now stands before them in a state of distraction, 'trublyde with phansis in my mynde'. At the time of the robbery, Sheale was in the extremely unusual position of possessing more than £60 in ready money. It appears that he and his wife – who traded in clothing at local markets – had managed to accumulate this sum from their earnings, with the intention of paying off Sheale's various debts to his friends in

[96] Ibid., pp. 162–3.

London. He was clearly a widely travelled man, and now, imprudently, he took to the road with his cash, never imagining that highway robbers would consider it worth their while to mug a minstrel:

Because my carryage shulde be lyght, I put my mony ynto golde;
And withowt company I ryde alone, thus was I folisshe bolde.
I thought beth reason off my harpe no man wolde me susspecte;
For minstre[l]s offt with mony the[y] be not moche infecte.

His four assailants, Sheale now alleged, must have heard on the grapevine about his unprecedented wealth. By now, Sheale was working his audience and eliciting their sympathy with every phrase. He explained that the episode had 'well nyghe kylde my harte', yet he was able to thank God that his suffering had not been worse still. Immediately after the robbery, he had somehow made his way home to Tamworth, where he recounted his story to his desperately disappointed wife. Sheale also informed the local bailiffs of his misfortune, but was unable to prove that he had been carrying so substantial a sum of money. Phlegmatically, he commented, 'I am not the first that hath hade an offull daye.'

In the last portion of the text, Sheale finally makes his appeal. Many former friends have deserted him in his hour of need, though notable exceptions include his 'good lord and master', whose support has never wavered, and most of his 'lovyng neabors' in Tamworth, who have attended a fund-raising ale in his benefit. Such kindness is greatly appreciated, yet Sheale is still some way from paying off his debts. He therefore ends by asking the members of his audience to reach into their pockets:

God save my good lorde, for whos sayke I fynd frenndes,
That helppes me every whar, and thus my tall enddes:
Desyryng youe all to bear this tayle in mynde,
That I among your pursis now sum frendshipe may fynde.
Every man a lyttell wold satisfye my nede,
To helpe a poor man owt off dett, it ys a gracious dede.[97]

Such was the life of a minstrel. Sheale, like all travelling tunesmiths, had to know his audience. He had to manipulate them through words, music and gesture. He had to know when to flatter, and when to adopt the sterner stance of a moral counsellor. Above all, he had to keep the proverbial wolf from the door.

[97] Ibid., pp. 156–61.

From the late sixteenth century onwards, it became more difficult to sustain the lifestyle of a musical 'ranger', but it did not become impossible. The household accounts of many high-ranking families demonstrate that visiting musicians were not all salaried civic waits. It seem unlikely that licences to operate were officiously demanded and inspected on every occasion. Catholic households, bastions of customary culture, were often particularly welcoming to travelling performers. Thomas Walmesley, as we have heard, rewarded the waits of eight towns, but he also made seventy payments to a variety of independent musicians in the years between 1613 and 1642. Christmas was consistently the busiest period, and the household accounts present an evocative impression of cultural traditionalism in the depths of the northern winter: 13s 4d 'given Thomas Lathom the piper for pipeinge all christmas' (1626–7); 2s 4d 'given vii pipers that Came in Christmas' (1628–9); 6d 'given William Bradshay for makinge songhes' (1629–30); 20d 'given fyve pypers that Came to the gaites this Christemas' (1631–2); 2s 'given mrs. Elenor which she gave the fidlers at Christenmas' (1633–4); 33s 'given ix pipers and fidleres iiii d each after ould Costome' (1637–8). Some of these musicians were summoned, while others turned up more speculatively. It is generally impossible to tell one sort from the other, though the higher fees presumably went to the performers whose presence had been actively requested. Music was obviously plentiful, and the desire to stand out sometimes led performers to develop supplementary gimmicks. Most impressively, a group of 'tomlinge fidlers' performed for the entertainment of a visiting knight in 1631–2. If these individuals combined violin playing with acrobatic 'tumbling', then we must clearly take our hats off to them.[98]

Conforming Protestants of various shapes and shades also rewarded freelance musicians of all sorts. Walmesley's fellow Lancastrians the Shuttleworths matched his generosity during the late sixteenth and early seventeenth centuries, regularly paying small sums to pipers, minstrels, fiddlers and trumpeters. In Norfolk, Lady Alice Le Strange was ready to receive visiting musicians during the mid-seventeenth century. Her household accounts record payments to numerous 'Musisians' (3s in June 1615) and to 'George the fidler' (1s in January 1632). In 1672–3, the Ishams of Lamport (Northamptonshire) accepted visits from 'A Venetian ... with his marine trumpet' and 'four soldiers ... with drums' (5s was paid on both

[98] *REED Lancashire*, pp. 184–212.

occasions). The records kept by many gentry families all over the country suggest that occasional payments of this sort were commonplace.[99]

In some instances, humble musicians were even bold enough to try their luck at the gates of the self-styled 'godly'. Of course, most puritans accepted that music, even in its more secular guises, could serve as a legitimate and beneficial personal recreation. Published sources suggest, however, that they were often acutely sensitive to the attendant dangers, which seemed most likely to materialise in the presence of lowly minstrels. Oliver Cromwell's household was musical, but it was probably not a location in which the poorer sorts of mobile musician could hope for a warm welcome when they dropped in. It is therefore interesting to consider the accounts kept by the Barringtons of Hatfield Broad Oak (Essex). The Barringtons were sympathetic to the puritan cause, but even during the 1650s – when zealous Protestantism was in the ascendant – Sir John Barrington's servants made payments to 'a bagpiper at the dore' (6d in August 1654), to 'a man, who playd on a Cymball' (1s 6d in July 1655) and to 'the men that danced in their disguise, & to the fidler, at the making an end of Christmas' (4s 6d in January 1657). Occasionally, there were hints that Barrington's scribe may not have approved of his generosity. A mere pen-pusher was of course in no position to chide his master, but he did somewhat grudgingly write out a note concerning the shilling that he paid to various 'druncken fidlers'.[100] The most regular recipient of cash was a local fiddler named Peake, who came to the house on several occasions, often accompanied by his musical sons, in order to entertain Barrington and his own children 'at his Chamber & in the Nursery'. Here was an encounter that must have warmed the relations between old and young and rich and poor simultaneously, at least within the confines of these two disparate families. Of course, we cannot know what all these hopeful visitors played when they arrived at the house, but the music is unlikely to have consisted entirely of metrical psalms and sacred songs. Similar payments made by the family during the 1660s suggest an intriguing and rather surprising degree of cultural continuity in this godly Protestant household between the decades of Interregnum and Restoration.[101]

99 Ibid., pp. 166–79; LEST/P7, fo. 15v (of second foliation), pp. 4, 48, NRO; *Diary of Thomas Isham*, entries for 27 August 1672 and 1 January 1673.

100 D/DBa A5, fos. 1r, 6v, 17v, ERO; W. A. Mepham, 'History of the Drama in Essex from the Fifteenth Century to the Present Time', unpublished PhD thesis, University of London (1937), p. 274. The 'cymbal' referred to here was probably a hurdy-gurdy (an instrument that is encountered only very rarely in the English sources).

101 D/DBa A5, fos. 5r, 6v, 11v, 12v, 14r, 17r; D/DBa A8, fos. 1r, 1v, 3r, 4r, 6r, 12v, ERO.

Not all prestigious families were eager to open their gates and their purses at the sound of visiting pipers and fiddlers, but it is difficult to find detailed household accounts that are entirely devoid of payments. Less receptive homes were, in any case, balanced at the opposite end of the spectrum by a minority of families whose members were prepared to go beyond the norm in their support of occupational musicians. Most commonly, gentlefolk or aristocrats simply granted a band of performers the right to wear their household livery while touring the countryside. During the late sixteenth century, the Earls of Derby – mighty men of music – may well have had more than one group displaying their badge at any single date, in addition to individual performers like Richard Sheale, the Derbyshire minstrel, and George Cally, the wayward wait of Chester. Until the 1630s at least, the earls' companies travelled the country from top to bottom and side to side, though the terminology employed in local records does not always enable us to distinguish between musicians and actors. In passing, we might note that the Earls of Derby also supported better-known musical figures such as the scholar John Case and the composer Francis Pilkington.[102] Liveried bands were not, however, restricted to the super-elite. Between 1580 and 1620, the groups doing the rounds in Lancashire included the musicians of Masters Tutton, Atherton, Warren and Ratcliffe, all of whom were untitled gentlemen. Sometimes, we encounter such retainers purely by chance. In 1610, for example, a piper 'which had Sir Peeter Leighes Cloath' earned his place in the historical record by participating in a fight at Wilmslow in Cheshire. Admittedly, liveried and itinerant musicians were becoming much less common from the early seventeenth century onwards, but the opportunities had not evaporated completely.[103]

As this door threatened to close, another opened. From the late sixteenth century, music-loving aristocrats became rather more likely to appoint a proportion of their resident domestic servants primarily on the basis of their instrumental or vocal abilities. For many a performer, the prospect of permanent employment in a country mansion 'where music was of the family' was enticing indeed.[104] The most famous Catholic example was Hengrave Hall in Suffolk, home of the Kytsons, where the walls resounded with sophisticated music played on dozens of different instruments by musicians who had a chamber and a parlour to

102 Price, *Patrons and Musicians*, p. 72. References to performers who were supported by the earls can be found in many of the *REED* volumes. See also above, pp. 55, 85, 140.

103 *REED Lancashire*, pp. 166–79 (see also p. 199); Baldwin, *Paying the Piper*, p. 26.

104 The quotation can be found in *Roger North on Music*, p. 344.

themselves. Several leading composers of the Elizabethan and Jacobean periods found reasonably secure employment here, and Edward Johnson's wage of £5 per year made him the Kytsons' most highly paid retainer during the 1570s. The household also employed singing boys, whose duties presumably included contributing to the celebration of musical masses in the private chapel.[105] On the Protestant side, one thinks first of Sir Robert Cecil, fellow patron of musicians and connoisseur of choristers. Cecil's possessive attitude to his domestic musicians was well known, and when the Kentish knight Percival Harte discovered in 1598 that he had inadvertently hired a young musical runaway from the great man's house, he swiftly endeavoured to make amends. The musician, Henry Phillips, had no wish to return and promptly fell ill when the idea was mooted. Harte, reluctant to proceed by force, therefore invited Cecil to send along a servant who could 'persuade' the boy.[106] On both sides of the religious divide, there were many other examples, and privileged Protestants and Catholics appear to have exchanged music and musicians without inhibition.[107]

The ability of a high-ranking family to maintain its own musicians clearly carried a certain kudos, not least because it imitated the expanding musical resources of the royal court.[108] Sir Henry Sidney must have felt suitably puffed up when, on 19 March 1583, he swept into the town of Shrewsbury 'with hys troompeter blowynge very joyfully to behold and see'. In the next century, Sir John Reresby took a boy bagpiper to Europe with him to impress the foreigners, and Sir Thomas Monson reportedly employed musicians of a quality unsurpassed in England. His servant Simon was, according to Anthony Weldon, a particularly fine performer. Simon was an all-rounder, 'a more generall Musician than ever the world had', but he also had a unique and peculiarly impressive party-piece:

He had a Catzo [presumably a penis] of an immense length and bignesse, with this, being his Tabor stick, his palme of his hand his Tabor, and his mouth his Pipe, he would so imitate a Tabor and Pipe, as if it had been so indeed: To this Musicke, would Mrs. Turner, the young Ladies, and some of that Ging [sic] dance

105 MANN MS 17/443, pp. 141–7, NRO; Price, *Patrons and Musicians*, pp. 76–8.

106 Price, *Patrons and Musicians*; pp. 173–6; *Calendar of the Manuscripts of the Most Honourable the Marquis of Salisbury*, 24 vols. (London: Historical Manuscripts Commission, 1883–1976), vol. VIII, p. 498. See also Lynn Hulse, 'Musical Apprenticeship in Noble Households', in Andrew Ashbee and Peter Holman (eds.), *John Jenkins and his Time* (Oxford: Clarendon Press, 1996), pp. 75–88.

107 Price, *Patrons and Musicians*, pp. 79–80.

108 On this subject, an excellent resource is Andrew Ashbee and David Lasocki, *A Biographical Dictionary of English Court Musicians, 1485–1714* (Aldershot: Ashgate, 1998).

ever after Supper; the old Lady, who loved that Musicke as well, as her Daughters, would sit and laugh, she could scarce sit for laughing.[109]

These were noisy novelties, but the basic sense of pride that talented musicians could instil in the breasts of their privileged employers was something that must have been felt much more widely. The fact that not all high-ranking families could manage such opulent provision must have been part of the attraction for those that could.

Overall, it is probable that the opportunities available to occupational musicians in the households of the social elite were increasing during the early modern period, though the change probably brought disproportionate benefit to the more sophisticated and highly educated practitioners, who were better equipped to resist association with the supposed evils of minstrelsy. The improving opportunities were driven to a considerable degree by Renaissance fashions and the perceived desirability of courtly refinement among the gentry. In practice, this meant that performers with aspirations to live among the aristocracy required the ability to read music, and often to write it too. Many gentlemen were still happy to hear the memorised renditions of song and dance tunes that presumably dominated the repertoire of illiterate fiddlers, but they were also developing a taste for composed consort music, played from the page by experts on viol, violin and virginal. They expected, moreover, that their musical servants would be able to pass on some at least of their skill and literacy to members of the family. The tutoring duties of England's musicians, and the results of their efforts, will be discussed more fully in the next chapter.

Most musicians, however, relied much more heavily for their income on the ordinary men and women among whom they lived, and here the opportunities were consistently plentiful throughout the period. Musicians played at rural weddings, wakes, ales, feasts and dancing sessions (see Figure 3.4). In May and June, they accompanied the summer games of the nation's youth. At Christmas, they played and sang as the old year gave way to the new. They promoted romance, and sometimes aided those with an uncontrollable urge to disseminate libellous songs about their rivals in love and life.[110] Considering the period as a whole, there is astonishingly little evidence to suggest that the campaign of puritans and moralists to reform popular tastes in music had any significant long-term impact upon the day-to-day employment prospects of musicians in villages and small

[109] *REED Shropshire*, pp. 236–7; *Memoirs of Sir John Reresby*, p. 14; Weldon, *The Court and Character of King James* (London, 1651), pp. 99–100.

[110] See below, pp. 272–6, 323–7.

Figure 3.4. The hurdy-gurdy or cymbal is only rarely encountered in English sources of the early modern period but this print suggests that its distinctive sound was not unknown. Drinkers make merry in a barn while their musician winds the wooden wheel that sounds the strings of his instrument. © Trustees of the British Museum, Prints and Drawings, 1939,0603.2, Robert Robinson, picture of barn interior (*c.* 1674–1706).

towns. Of course, the same campaign is responsible for the fact that the historian hears of musicians most frequently when they were associated with disorderly behaviour, but even this evidence seems to imply the underlying solidity of opportunity. Court cases are concentrated in the first three decades of the seventeenth century, but they provide a flavour of musical possibilities throughout the period. In 1609, for example, a man from Eastnor (Herefordshire) was reported for allowing Sunday dancing in his alehouse, and Thomas Harnatt was accused of being 'his minstrell ready at call'. Two years later, there were rumours in Harescombe (Gloucestershire) that Katherine Hasleton had committed adultery with an unnamed partner, while 'one Bond a Musitian did play at the bedes feete in the meane tyme'. On 3 July 1614, the vicar of Ribchester (Lancashire) seems to have crossed the line that should have distinguished his behaviour from that of his neighbours: he allegedly recruited no fewer than eleven fiddlers to play in his house, 'to the great Greeff of all good parishoners'.[111] Music sometimes served to distinguish men from women, or clerics from layfolk, but in these cases it worked towards the disorderly merger of opposites.

It is also within the context of prosecution that we encounter, at long last, some of the rare women who made money from instrumental music. In 1620, for example, an ecclesiastical court in Dorset heard that, on Ascension Day, 'old Bright with his boy and his daughter played at Cowgrove with their fiddells and Continued there all Evening prayer time with much companie'. Rather more conspicuous was the vagrant female fiddler who turned up alone in Merriott (Somerset) one day in 1637. She proceeded to play on her instrument during service time, and was therefore placed in the village stocks by the local tithingmen. Later that day, she was secretly released, and William Hooper was observed 'goinge through the Towne with the same woman sayenge unto her "come away for I will dischardge thee"'.[112]

There is little in either case to suggest that a female musician was commonly regarded with particular horror or fascination, unless she followed the example of Mary Frith *alias* Moll Cutpurse, who, during the 1620s, mesmerised London with her sensational gender-bending antics. She dressed as a man and sang provocative songs on stage to the accompaniment of her own lute. By her own admission, she also indulged in blasphemy, hard drinking and theft, 'to the disgrace of all womanhood'.[113] Others were less conspicuous. When the diarist Henry Prescott observed a social gathering in 1694 at which 'the young sparks were merry with a woman piper', he did not seem unduly concerned. She was clearly a novelty, but she earned no further comment. The evidence is not extensive, but what little we have makes it clear that instrumental music in particular was not perceived as a suitable occupation for most women, despite its ability to render men effeminate. The 'famous woman drummer' who featured in a ballad of the seventeenth century owed her notoriety to the

[111] *REED Herefordshire, Worcestershire*, p. 73; *REED Cumberland, Westmorland, Gloucestershire*, p. 331; EDC5, 1614.7, ChRO.

[112] *REED Dorset, Cornwall*, p. 288; *REED Somerset*, p. 164.

[113] *REED Ecclesiastical London*, pp. 208–9. See also Raphael Seligman, 'With a Sword by her Side and a Lute in her Lap: Moll Cutpurse at the Fortune', in Lamay (ed.), *Musical Voices of Early Modern Women*, pp. 187–210.

strangeness of her chosen occupation and to the fact that she dressed as a man in order to pursue it.[114] Singing was a rather different matter. Female ballad-sellers sang their wares, and it was clearly permissible for other singing women to call hopefully at the houses of the wealthy. In January 1613, Sir Richard Paulet, master of two estates in Hampshire, paid 12d 'to certeine poore women of Alton that came hether to sing thease xmas hollydes'. Similarly, the Le Stranges of Norfolk paid 1s 'to a singing woman' in 1631, though hers was a summer visit. The apparent disparity between the numbers of female instrumentalists and singers is probably related to the common cultural assumption that women expressed themselves most readily and naturally through words rather than deeds. The voice was therefore a more appropriate tool than the violin, though it could of course be misused. The Thetford woman who, in 1606, was given to composing 'libellous and lascivious ballads' about her neighbours was effectively a singing scold, the embodiment of two word-wielding female types.[115]

Evidence of embattled music-makers is far harder to come by in the latter part of the period. This was due partly to the breakdown in record-keeping during the 1640s and 1650s, and partly to the more permissive atmosphere of subsequent decades. We must therefore look to other types of source. In the world conjured up by the cheap print of the period, fiddlers and pipers are never far away. They are widely available and happy to play for dancers, drinkers and sweethearts. England's youth, in particular, are animated by the sound of rustic music and ever ready to 'follow the Bagpipes droane'. In one ballad, shepherds and their maidens chant and prance in happy harmony together (to the tune of 'Now the tyrant has stolen my dearest away'):

With Bagpipes and taber,
and Hoby sometimes
We dance and skip and sing,
and our natural Rymes;
Two Jews-trumps well play'd
on, with Violin soft,
Makes spirits to rise, and
our bloods mount aloft.

[114] *The Diary of Henry Prescott*, ed. John Addy, John Harrop and Peter McNiven, *Record Society of Lancashire and Cheshire* 133 (1997), p. 899; Roxburghe ballads, C20F7–F10, vol. III, pp. 234–5, BL.

[115] 44M69/E4/28, HRO; LEST/P7, p. 4 (of second foliation), NRO; Fox, *Oral and Literate Culture*, p. 305.

And when they are up,
and our Lasses lye down;
Each Shepheard turns Taylor,
and gives a green gown.

The hautboy, an unusual instrument in a rural context, is available only from time to time. In more normal circumstances, the music is provided by a simple combination of melodic instruments (bagpipe or violin) and percussion (the thump of the tabor and the twang of the trump). The mixture is intoxicating, and leads towards the sexual interplay that is euphemistically indicated in the final line.[116]

The ideal outcome from such interaction was a wedding, and these occasions too were alive with music. During the 1660s, the Sussex vicar Giles Moore regularly paid sixpence to the piper or fiddler when he attended local weddings. In *A Pleasant Dialogue betwixt Honest John and Loving Kate*, the betrothed partners plan their special day, and decide to hire 'old Rowly and his company' to provide the music. 'They will make a roaring noise', says Kate. 'And they will sing well too', adds John, 'to please the young people'. In their future life together, the couple plan to establish an alehouse. Kate wishes to name it 'The three fair maids', but John objects that people will take it for a bawdy house. He suggests instead 'The three Fidlers', a name designed to draw punters in by suggesting the prospect of music. In a comparable dialogue between Andrew and Joan, it is the woman who organises the music for the forthcoming nuptials: 'I'le speak to the Old Taber and Pipe man', she says, 'and our Ralph shall play upon the Tongs, that will make such sweet Musick that they must needs dance whither they will or no.' The irresistible sounds are therefore to be provided by the combined forces of an occupational musician and a family member with a sense of rhythm.[117] The autobiographical courtship narrative of Leonard Wheatcroft, a Derbyshire yeoman, adds some detail concerning the role of music on the big day itself. As the bride and groom entered the village on 20 May 1657, the musicians came out to meet them, 'and after salutation done they merrily played before them' as they proceeded to the church. The following morning, the music-makers appeared again, this time within the nuptial bedchamber, 'and saluted us with

[116] *Pepys Ballads*, vol. I, pp. 330–1, vol. III, p. 55.

[117] Spufford, *Small Books*, pp. 170–1; *A Pleasant Dialogue betwixt Honest John and Loving Kate* (London, 1685); *A Merry Dialogue between Andrew and his Sweet Heart Joan* (London, c. 1682).

pleasant lessons and choice tunes'. Others pressed into the room too, all of them anxious to know 'what rest we took'.[118]

Overall, it is thus abundantly plain that occupational music, in country and town, survived the pressures to which it was subjected, and emerged at the end of our period in a comparatively robust condition. Of course, music-making was a minor occupation within society's overall profile, even when the efforts of the uncountable part-timers are taken into account. Musicians were rarely well paid, and were often rewarded in beer and bread (sometimes called 'fiddler's wages'). On the other hand, such items were essential to life, and the poor person who had them was better off than the one who did not. Partly for this reason, the supply of musicians never threatened to dry up, and everybody in the nation surely lived within reach of a variety of possible performers.

Despite the overall continuity of opportunity, there were some significant changes to occupational music-making in this period. To some extent, the age of the professional was dawning. Highly trained and thoroughly literate instrumentalists were more prominent in 1700 than they had been a century earlier, and the most famous of them expected to be known by their own names rather than by reference to the instruments they played. Sixteenth-century musicians, in contrast, had sometimes been listed in account books and other records merely as 'pipes' or 'fiddles'. Creeping professionalism also had other effects. During the second half of our period, musicians still wandered the countryside, but those who travelled most widely and with the greatest confidence were liveried, salaried city waits rather than hopeful part-time minstrels such as the men who strolled haplessly into Winchester in 1599.[119] Such minstrels could still supplement their livings through the performance of memorised and improvised music, but as time went by they probably tended increasingly to concentrate their efforts within a ring of parishes relatively close to home. For the player who had neither badge nor licence, it was wise to be recognised. The late sixteenth century brought stricter controls to bear on the lives of occupational musicians, and from this time onward they had to be somewhat more careful about where they went and whom they approached. The atmosphere brightened considerably after 1660, but a system of licences and a mental habit of associating common musicians with disorder were permanent legacies of the previous hundred years.

118 *The Courtship Narrative of Leonard Wheatcroft*, ed. George Parfitt and Ralph Houlbrooke (Reading: Whiteknights Press, 1986), pp. 85–7.

119 See above, pp. 75–6.

Across the same period, the progress of musical literacy created the potential for a new divide between those who had acquired it and those who had not, though it is difficult to investigate the topic in any depth. The publisher John Playford urged his readers, for obvious reasons, that it was much better to play by book than by ear, and gradually musicians added literacy to the aurality of custom.[120] Finally, the role of the church in employing musicians declined markedly as a consequence of the Reformation, chiefly because England's ordinary parishes needed far fewer organists, liturgical singers and festive instrumentalists than they had once done.[121] In 1700, there was still plenty of work for musicians to do, but it tended to be more secular.

Musicians, instruments and social status

What conclusions should we draw concerning the status of occupational musicians during this period? The classic account, written half a century ago, tended towards acute and inoperable pessimism. It concentrated on the higher ranks of occupational musician – royal employees, servants of the aristocracy, waits and so forth – but even here it found little to suggest that the rewards they earned were anything other than mediocre. Talented, educated musicians were 'little more than tolerated', being generally 'regarded with suspicion'. Indeed, 'most professional musicians started and ended as menials', members of the 'lower middle class' at best.[122] This is depressing stuff, and there is some cause for revision. In the first place, these judgements were thoroughly elitist. This was hardly surprising, given the fact that the account was written during the early 1950s from a perspective within the discipline of musicology, a field of study not generally renowned for its attentiveness to the music of illiterate pipers. In assessing the status of early modern musicians, there has been a tendency to think only of those who played primarily for society's most wealthy and powerful ranks. This might have had a positive effect on our interpretations, had not the social standing of musicians been gauged primarily by absorbing and echoing the perspectives of the privileged. In other words, musicians were found to be mere menials because this was their official status in, for example, the grand houses of the aristocracy. Arguably, this was peer-assessment by the wrong sort of peer. If we open

[120] Playford, *An Introduction*, p. 102. [121] See below, ch. 8.

[122] Woodfill, *Musicians in English Society*, pp. 243–4.

our ears to other voices, a rather different verdict may emerge. Secondly, the negative assessment was perhaps informed too loudly by monetary matters. Admittedly, musicians were not in general highly paid, and very few of them ended their lives in material splendour. There is, however, rather more to status and identity than this, and once again it might be interesting to cast the evidential net more widely.

Musicians may have been poor, but they made other people feel good, and this stimulating fact generated its own kind of status. When guests made their way to a wedding, they could anticipate a 'Cup of good ale … and a lame fiddler to make them merry'. On board ship, lowly musicians had it within them to raise the spirits of an entire crew. As John Baltharpe put it in his verse-journal,

Our Fidlar did in Triumph fetch
His Fiddle from Aboard a Ketch
Call'd the Portsmouth, and did play,
Oft times to pass the time away;
Sometimes to passe sad Cares away,
On Fore-castle we dance the Hay.

Samuel Pepys was simultaneously perplexed and intoxicated by the musician whose performance he heard on board the *Assistance* on the last day of April in 1660. The captain treated Pepys and his friends well, 'and he did give us such musique upon the harp by a fellow that he keeps on board, that I never expect to hear the like again – yet he a drunken simple fellow to look on as any I ever saw'. This encapsulates the curious low-high status of the musician.[123]

Musicians, though 'not moche infecte' with money, played a central role in the social life of their communities and regions. Everybody knew that there was 'no mirth without music', and its practitioners were often welcomed and even admired by their neighbours. In *Old Meg of Herefordshire*, published in 1609, the author paid tribute to several local musicians. 'Old Hall', *alias* Harry Rudge, was not only a renowned ox-leach (or cattle-doctor) but the county's most ancient pipe and tabor player. His drum, we are told, had been a wooden water-pail until Old Hall himself converted it to its present use, way back in 1549. The writer addresses him directly as 'a most exquisite Taber-man' who brings great pleasure to his neighbours by making as much music with his simple instruments as 'the Wayts of

[123] Spufford, *Small Books*, p. 170; Baltharpe, quoted by Woodfield, *English Musicians*, p. 85; *Diary of Samuel Pepys*, vol. I, p. 119.

three Metropolitane Cities': 'The people of Hereford-shire are beholding to thee, thou givest the men light hearts by thy Pype, and the women light heeles by thy Tabor: O wonderful Pyper, O admirable Taber-man.' What is more, he has served society for sixty summers, 'And noble Hall himselfe, hath stoode (like an Oake) in all stormes, by the space of foure-score and seventeene Winters, and is not yet falling to the ground.' In the event of such a sad demise, the author asks the aged minstrel to leave his body to the science of music: 'bequeath in thy last will, thy Velom-spotted skin, to cover Tabors: at the sound of which, to set all the shires a dauncing' (there was apparently a precedent for this macabre course of action in the example of 'that Bohemian Zisea').

The pamphlet seems to hover between eulogy and satire, but before we label it a work of fantasy, it would be wise to note that another of the musicians who attracted praise definitely existed beyond the text. We last encountered Roger Squire of Hereford when, in 1600, the city authorities declined his request to become one of the waits. He was old even then, and it is therefore remarkable to find that he was still playing in 1609. The author of *Old Meg* was mildly cryptic, but spoke of a famous local musician who was 'a Squire borne and all his sons Squires in their cradles'. The tribute continued,

> The Instrument he tickled was a trebble Violim [sic], upon which he played any old lesson that could be called for: the division hee made on the strings, being more pleasing then the Diapason. In skill he out-shines blind Moone of London, and hath out-played more Fidlers, then [than] now sneake up & downe into all the Taverns there. They may all call him their father, or (if you reckon the yeares rightly which are scored upon his head) the Musitions Grandsire, for this tuneable Squire is one hundred and eight yeares old.[124]

It is interesting that in both of these tributes, the lowly musician is associated, perhaps ironically, with gentility: old Hall is 'noble', and Squire's name is allowed to speak for itself. Indeed, this was a common device among those who spoke or wrote in praise of music. Respectable players, though menial according to one register, were regularly addressed and described as 'gentleman musicians' (or something similar). The vocabulary of the gentleman–commoner hierarchy was thus appropriated and re-deployed in order to distinguish honourable musicians from the ranks of mere fiddlers.[125]

[124] *Old Meg of Herefordshire* (London, 1609). [125] See above, p. 120.

It is very unusual to receive such information on the cultural status of local musicians, but there is enough to suggest that similar individuals existed in all corners of the land. In 1641, a member of the Catholic household of the Blundells in Lancashire composed or transcribed 'A Contry song remembring the harmetless [sic] mirth of Lancashyre in peaseable tymes. To the tune of Roger o'Coveley'. The word 'harmless' probably indicates that the song was politically charged, but our present concern is with the musicians to whom it subsequently refers. The ballad-style text tells the tale of a dancing match featuring various local lads and lasses. The young men of Chowbent arrived on the scene,

And thither then they had brought Knex
to play Chowbent hornepype that Nicks
Tomms and Geffreyes shoone
weare worne quit through with the tune.

In the margin, an additional note has been added alongside the first of these lines: 'Thomas Knex: most famous pyper'. This man may well have been famous, but his name has not been found in any other source. The same can be said of two other musicians mentioned in the song: 'James Pyper of Formeby' and 'Bell' (though a piper of this name had been paid 4d by the Shuttleworth family some thirty years earlier). These references indicate not only the prestige that a piper could earn, but the vexing probability that there may have been many other musicians who were slightly less famous and whose names simply have not reached us.[126]

Occasionally, commentators spoke rather more generally about the rich reputations of poor musicians. In 1677, a godly miller from Leicestershire addressed his former friends, recalling the heady days in which dissenting preachers had been 'esteemed by some of you as them that could play well of an Instrument'. The speaker who addressed the Tutbury minstrels in the same period elaborated further on this, reminding his audience that theirs was an art that appealed to all the family: 'The innocent Boys & Girls by the very instinct of nature follow you when you strike upp in our Streets & their Fathers & Mothers Grandsires and Grannnams [sic] are all ready to bid you welcome to their houses.' The only pity was that musicians were not paid as well they should have been ('shame for them that send for you').[127]

[126] *REED Lancashire*, pp. 32–5.

[127] Spufford, *Small Books*, p. 177; D4530/76/8, pp. 9–11, DRO.

Indeed, it was the intense popularity of the musician that caused some commentators to despise him. In 1592, Robert Greene told his readers the cautionary tale of a young woman who had ruined her own life by yielding her virginity to 'a fellowe of small reputation, and of no lyving, neither had he any excellent qualities but thrumming on the gittron [gittern]: but of pleasant disposition he was, and could gawll out many quaint and ribadrous [sic] Jigges and songs, and so was favourerd of the foolish sect for his foppery'. There are informative contradictions here: the musician has no reputation yet is favoured by many; playing the gittern may just be an excellent quality, yet the tone in which the concession is made is disparaging (does an excellent man 'thrum' and 'gawll' his rude songs?). Francis Clement told a story about the Roman musician Hippomachus who once rebuked a conceited pupil for his joy at being 'highly commended of the vulgar multitude'. The master patted the scholar on the head with his staff, 'and bad him cease his magnified melodie: saying that it argued ill fingring and errour, that he was so ... praysed of the ignorant people'. Clement agreed whole-heartedly that mere popularity brought no genuine credit, and he concluded with the approving comment, 'This doubtlesse was masterly done.'[128]

It is difficult to know how musicians of the sixteenth and seventeenth centuries responded to the stimulus of their high-low status, but it would clearly be foolish to assume that their generally poor livings necessarily made them miserable. It is partly a question of aspirations. From our perspective in the comparatively egalitarian twenty-first century, it is tempting to assume that early modern musicians must have aspired to escape from their menial occupation. Many, however, were apparently happy for their sons to join them, and may even have enjoyed the round of weddings, ales, dances, feasts and fairs. The monetary rewards were often meagre, but the task was certainly not thankless. Let it be remembered that one of the defining characteristics of Henry Parrot's archetypal fiddler was his complete lack of ambition for anything except new songs and strings.[129] Early modern music-makers rarely recorded the emotional and psychological responses that performance induced in them, and we must therefore resort to some speculative questions. How did it feel to be Thomas Richards, the humble harpist with an unusual wire-strung instrument, whose attendance was urgently requested at the houses of several

[128] Greene, *A Disputation between a Hee Conny-catcher, and a Shee Conny-catcher* (London, 1592), D4v; Clement, *The Petie Schole*, p. 31.

[129] See above, pp. 80–1.

knights, including Sir Philip Sidney, in February 1584? Or the unnamed tabor and pipe man who, for a fee of just four pence, headed an elaborate procession of the Earl of Devon's tenants as they entered Exeter on the eve of Lammas Day in 1590? Or Thomas Wingood, a vagrant and masterless drummer, who was hired in 1607 by the anti-puritan faction of Wells to thump his drum before a whooping, hollering, dancing crowd of hundreds?[130] Of course, we cannot know for we were not there, but we might hazard a guess that such experiences were both gratifying and invigorating.

Drummers, from one perspective, were the most menial musicians of all and they were invariably paid in pennies rather than pounds. In another sense, however, they were individuals of conspicuous power, responsible for communicating a wide variety of important messages. Drums, along with trumpets and fifes, were most strongly associated with warfare. In the ears of Shakespeare and his contemporaries, the sound of the drum was 'thundering', 'roaring', 'rumbling' and 'churlish'. In war, it regulated the rhythms of marching, sent out signals to soldiers and, most fundamentally, stimulated bravery in their hearts. According to one ballad, 'The Martiall musickes ratling sound, / sayes Soldiers, stand & keep your ground.' Such music announced that a force was ready to fight, and threw down a challenge to the enemy. The refrain of another patriotic song mimicked the sound of drums and trumpets:

Dub, a dub dub,
thus strikes the Drums,
Tan ta-ra ta-ra-ra,
English men comes.[131]

Even in civilian life, drums were often spoken of and indeed employed as weapons, so unmistakable was their belligerent resonance. In early Jacobean Wells, the embattled and puritanical constable John Hole was in no doubt that his local opponents were using trumpets, drums, gunshot 'or some suche warrlyke munition' as weapons against him.[132] In other settings, drums aided trumpets in proclaiming the presence of great dignitaries, contributing an undertone of warlike menace to the celebration of hierarchy. When Prince Charles visited Ludlow in 1616–17 for his investiture as Prince of Wales, 'a great Volley of shot was discharged by

130 Samuel Butler, *Sidneiana, Being a Collection of Fragments Relative to Sir Philip Sidney* (London: Roxburghe Club, 1837), p. 81; *REED Devon*, pp. 167–8; *REED Somerset*, pp. 276, 350.

131 *Pepys Ballads*, vol. I, pp. 102–3; *The Garland of Good-will* (London, 1688).

132 *REED Somerset*, p. 335. See also *Diary of Henry Machyn*, p. 191.

the ... Muskettiers and Calivers, which so pierced the Ayre with the great noyse of Drummes, and sound of Trumpets, Fifes, Flutes, and other instruments, as the like in these parts hath not been seene, to the great admiration, and much rejoycing of all the Spectators'. Many towns deployed the muscular music of drums in order to impress, and perhaps repress, their citizens. In puritanical Rye there was almost no other publicly funded civic music during the early seventeenth century (the early sixteenth century had been so very, very different). Melody and harmony, it appears, were considered immoral, but the pounding sound of stick on skin was another matter. The governors did not pay for tunes but they repeatedly found cash 'for mendinge the Townes drum'.[133] All over England, the enemies of puritanism knew how to use drums too, and percussion was one of the indispensable features of summer revelling. Here too it hinted at the force behind the festivity and warned critics to stand clear.

Lastly, drummers were also called upon to administer punishment. They sounded at executions, at the expulsion of soldiers from an army (hence 'drummed out') and during the performance of rough music. One seventeenth-century ballad describes *The Cucking of a Scould* (to the tune of 'The merchant of Emden') in glorious sonic detail. The woman in question has a notoriously 'unquiet tongue', and is prone to railing, raging and thunderous fits. She is eventually brought to heel following a mighty procession, complete with archers, gunners, trumpets, fifes and drums (which, in comparison to her, sound 'sweet' and 'pleasant'), at the culmination of which she is ducked in the pond over and over again:

And every time that she
Was in the water dipt,
The drums & trumpets sounded brave,
For joy the people skipt.

The scold remains impressively defiant for some time, but eventually she agrees to mend her ways. The disorderly sounds of her tongue are silenced and reformed by the imposing harmony of military music.[134] In this example, we also witness the imposition of an intensely male musical discipline upon an errant female. Drums were played almost exclusively by men, and it can hardly be doubted that those who wielded the

[133] *REED Shropshire*, p. 97; *REED Sussex*, pp. 141–67. [134] *Pepys Ballads*, vol. I, p. 454.

Figure 3.5. The penetrating high-low combination of the fife and the drum was central to the military music of the period. It co-ordinated the marching of soldiers and stirred them to courageous deeds. The Pepys Library, Magdalene College, Cambridge, Pepys Ballads, *Jockies Lamentation* (London, 1657), detail.

sticks must have experienced feelings of potency, despite their poverty (see Figure 3.5).[135]

The short journal of Adam Wheeler, a military drummer, presents a unique and interesting account. Wheeler played his part in the defeat of Monmouth's rebellion during the summer of 1685, and he clearly did not feel that his role was an insignificant one. He expresses exuberant devotion to his superiors, yet he manages simultaneously to situate himself and his instrument at the heart of the drama (he makes hierarchy his own). In Wheeler's account, the dub-a-dub-dub of the drum reverberates far more loudly than it generally does in modern military histories of the episode (it is ironic that 'drums-and-trumpets' history is often written without much reference to either). Each new movement of troops is directed 'by Beate of Drum', and particular attention is drawn to the moment on 6 July when the Lord Lieutenant came in a hurry to Wheeler's commanding officer, bringing news of imminent battle 'and askeinge for his Drums'. The narrative continues, 'There being then noe Drum in the house but Adam Wheeler, who opened the doore and answered his Lordship that he was ready to obey his Command; Soe his Lordship immediately commanded him to beate an Alarum, which he presently performed.' Other drummers

[135] There is rich evidence in *REED Kent* relating to the role of drummers within town life.

had since attempted to claim that they had been the first to perform this vital 'peece of Service', but Wheeler knew the truth. He may not have been high of rank and heavy of purse, but he wrote like a man who enjoyed a certain status. In a sense, Wheeler's performances were not a confirmation of his menial position, but an escape from it. He experienced a buzz that money could not buy.[136]

The somewhat paradoxical status of the military musician is also suggested by several cases in which drummers and trumpeters were singled out for clemency following capture by enemy forces overseas. Commanders whose musicians fell into hostile hands were also reassuringly anxious to retrieve them. Both patterns of behaviour have been explained partly in terms of the musicians' functional importance as signallers and providers of recreational relief in faraway lands, and partly in terms of an accepted European custom of regarding them as non-combatants. Either way, it can be argued that musicians were, in practice, worth rather more than their salaries, and were treated accordingly.[137] The life of William Byrd, the celebrated Elizabethan composer, reveals a curious and partial resonance. Byrd was a well-known Catholic, yet he does not appear to have suffered for his faith as severely as we might have expected. Clearly, he was no military trumpeter, and he made a good living in royal service, but Byrd – like poorer performers – was to some degree protected by his musicality. Anthropologists have argued that, in some societies, musicians combine inferior social status with high cultural importance, a disjuncture that generates certain peculiarities in the way they are treated (for example, sexual deviance and the use of mocking or insulting language may be tolerated in musicians more readily than in others of similarly low rank).[138] We might apply a modified version of this interpretation to early modern England. It does not seem likely that the occupational musician was any more likely to escape punishment for anti-social or immoral conduct than were the rest of his contemporaries, but there are at least indications that he sometimes enjoyed a special kind of status that was not adequately represented by the pennies in his pocket.

The mixed repute of musicians was also related to their crucial role as cultural brokers in a wide variety of settings. They linked town and countryside, old and young, male and female. Cathedral singing men, sometimes scorned for their mongrel musicianship, mediated between the

[136] Adam Wheeler, 'Iter Bellicosum, or A Perfect Relation of the Heroick March of his Majesties Truly Loyall Subject and Magnanimous Souldier Colonell John Windham', ed. Henry Eliot Malden, *Camden Miscellany* 12, *Camden 3rd Series* 18 (1910), pp. 155–68.

[137] Woodfield, *English Musicians*, pp. 23, 132–4.

[138] Merriam, *Anthropology of Music*, ch. 7.

church and the alehouse in a period that has been credited with driving a wedge between the two institutions. In warfare, musicians were the messengers *par excellence*, and many a tense situation was resolved, in one way or another, following the dispatch of a trumpeter into the camp of a foreign enemy. In an age of exploration, musicians of many sorts were also of immense and subtle importance in opening channels of communication between Europeans and native peoples in east and west. In the Americas, for example, inquisitive 'savages' were enticed onto beaches and nudged into negotiation by musicians who played drums, bells, jew's harps, whistles, bagpipes, bugles, trumpets and viols. The cheaper items were often distributed as gifts, while the more expensive ones were sounded in order to tempt and impress. On the coast of Brazil in 1578, Francis Drake and his men encountered people who were 'exceedingly delighted with the sound of the trumpet and vialles'. They were readily 'ravished with mellodye', but demonstrated different responses to different types of music: 'They did admire at our still musick, but the sound of our trumpet, noise of the drum, and especially the blow of a gunn was terrible to them.' Given the exploitative intentions of most Europeans overseas, these things were useful to know. Nobody but a musician could operate quite so effectively as an agent of both war and peace, qualified to wield his trumpet simultaneously as a lure and a weapon. Such a man may not have been wealthy, but he was worth having on board.[139]

Most strikingly, the musicians who stayed at home mediated between 'high' and 'low' society more extensively and continuously than any other group. The stammering singer who wandered Worcestershire at the start of the seventeenth century was 'welcomed to all places, and bar'd of none'. In a book of 'characters' published in 1629, it was said of the typical fiddler that 'He traverses all Companies, feeds on all sorts of dyet, receives all mens gratuities.' The piper, according to another such pen-portrait, had 'no peculiar station' in society, but instead indulged in 'a roving recreation'.[140] Like all good caricatures, these were immediately recognisable. Musicians of the period often enjoyed access to the wildly different worlds of the labourer and the lord. The Tutbury orator reminded the musicians assembled before him that the greatest princes and aristocrats of the age enjoyed learning to play music for themselves. He added, ''Tis that which gaines you admittance & acceptance within their palaces & in the houses

[139] Woodfield, *English Musicians*, pp. 96–7, 101.

[140] *REED Herefordshire, Worcestershire*, p. 392; R. M., *Micrologia*, C7v–D1r; Brathwaite, *Whimzies*, p. 33.

of lords ladyes & Gentry of the highest quality & distinction whilst the inferiour persons of all sorts earnestly covet your Company & are even charm'd & raptured with your performances.'[141]

Most musicians played before extremely varied audiences, moving between alehouse and country estate with considerable ease. Richard Sheale, the Derbyshire minstrel, certainly performed in both settings. A few decades later, the poor singers who went on tour in Shropshire must have made much of their money in alehouses, but they also visited the gentleman Mr Christopher Lacon. One of their number, Richard Golborne, explained that he made part of his living by going 'from gentilmans house to gentilmans house upon their benevolence'.[142] The interplay between radically different social contexts can also be detected in the frequency with which music-loving aristocrats were immortalised in ballad stories and popular tune titles, as if music that was first performed to flatter them in their homes was then transported by its players into the wide world beyond the gates.[143]

Unfortunately, we can say little about the shifts in repertoire and performance style that musicians may have made as they moved from one social context to the next. The paucity of contemporary comments on the matter may indicate either that few such adjustments were necessary or that they came so naturally that no comment was required. The increasing numbers of musically literate players could also offer both the polish of composed pieces and the freer style of ballad and dance tunes, played with divisions (the equivalent of variations). In 1581, Thomas Lovell drew attention to the intolerable cunning of minstrels in modifying their music to suit the moral sensibilities of a range of hosts:

With modest men they modest be,
with sober they be grave:
With Lewd and naughtie companie,
they also play the knave,
For he that cannot give and jest,
ungodly scof and trump
is thought unmeet to play with pipe,
on Tabret or to thump.[144]

[141] D4530/76/8, p. 9, DRO. [142] *REED Shropshire*, pp. 279–80.

[143] See, for example, *Lord Willoughby: or, A True Relation of a Famous and Bloody Battel Fought in Flanders* (London, *c.* 1586), in *Pepys Ballads*, vol. II, p. 131.

[144] Lovell, *Dialogue between Custom and Veritie*, D5v.

There may have been a social dimension to such tactical fine-tuning, though it has to be said that the kind of gentry who welcomed visiting musicians seem to have been perfectly at home with the sound of pipes and tabors. At the courts of James I and Charles I, such 'rude musique' featured regularly within the elaborate and evolving tradition of the masque. Supposedly plebeian instruments – bagpipes, kettledrums, flutes and tabors – were played during the satirical anti-masques, which brought temporary relief from the lutes, viols and other respectable instruments that dominated the main spectacle.[145] In this rarefied setting, therefore, it was necessary to conceal a liking for common music behind a mask of humour and satire. Up in Lancashire, however, the Shuttleworths appear to have had no such scruples.

The movements of musicians clearly rendered problematic the contemporary orthodoxy that some instruments were suitable for the ears of aristocrats while others were appropriate to the common people. Musicians carried their instruments between audiences, and the curious social trajectory of the violin is a case in point. Two contrasting narratives deserve consideration. The first proposes a top-down or court-to-country process of dissemination in which the Italian violin, an acoustic revelation, arrived first at the court of Henry VIII in 1540, then spread into the homes of aristocrats by the 1560s, before finally reaching town waits, theatre musicians and humbler instrumentalists by 1600. By this date, it had largely displaced traditional box fiddles of the sort that were discovered in the wreck of the *Mary Rose*.[146] A second narrative is rather different, and was proposed by two celebrated musical commentators of the late seventeenth and early eighteenth centuries. According to Roger North, writing in 1728, the violin was 'scarce knowne' in aristocratic circles before 1640, though it already had a place in the hands of humble country musicians. Anthony Wood agreed: before 1660, English gentlemen 'esteemed a violin to be an instrument only belonging to a common fiddler'. Its social elevation occurred, he argued, as a result of Charles II's fondness for the violin.[147] It seems that the invasion of England by a new and foreign instrument created considerable confusion concerning its status. This confusion, indeed, is perhaps the most interesting aspect of the story. It suggests the complexities of cultural interchange during the

[145] Peter Walls, *Music in the English Courtly Masque* (Oxford: Clarendon Press, 1996), pp. 117–19, 148–50.

[146] Peter Holman, *Four and Twenty Fiddlers: The Violin at the English Court, 1540–1690* (Oxford: Clarendon Press, 1993), ch. 6.

[147] North and Wood, both quoted by Brian W. Harvey, *The Violin Family and its Makers in the British Isles* (Oxford: Clarendon Press, 1995), p. 14.

period: traffic between the aristocratic mansion and the common cottage was unstoppable, but there were nevertheless those who hoped to police the situation by labelling the violin either as an instrument of the vulgar or as the producer of music that was distinctively courtly.

It seems sensible to combine the two narratives rather than to regard them as contradictory alternatives. The violin certainly began at court and spread rapidly outwards in the hands of occupational musicians. Its success was such that, by the early seventeenth century, violins were in the hands of some of the lowliest practitioners. In 1609, for example, a Somerset miner named William Pickering told a court that, one Friday in July, he 'went to Stokelane, to one Claves, where he founde a vyolyn and played uppon the same, where there was daunceinge & Typpling'. The information is revealed incidentally in a court case, and has reached us only because Pickering, on the same day, also found time to steal a rabbit (allegedly).[148] The case tells us that a humble miner had learned to play the violin well enough to accompany dancing, and that a neighbour – probably an alehouse-keeper – happened to have one lying about his home. Indeed, the earliest surviving English instrument to show all the basic characteristics of a modern violin was reputedly made and played by a certain tinker named John Bunyan (whose name is inscribed upon it). It must have been built before 1650, for in that year Bunyan turned his back on popular music to follow a more pious calling, and the instrument ended up in the possession of an old woman in twentieth-century Milton Keynes. It is now in Bedford's John Bunyan Museum. In most respects, it looks like a conventional and well-designed violin. According to one modern expert, 'there is a distinctly Brescian cut to the soundholes', which seems to indicate that at least one young tinker knew what a proper Italian-style violin was supposed to look like.[149] He may, however, have known less about what it was supposed to sound like, for he constructed it of metal. Such violins were and are unusual, primarily because they lack the resonance and rich tone of wooden instruments.

Bunyan's violin is a unique and extraordinary survival, and a great deal rides on the various expert statements that have verified its authenticity. If miners and tinkers were really playing Italian-style violins in this period, then it becomes easy to understand how the instrument came to sound common and coarse. Its reputation was, however, to rise again under the

[148] *REED Somerset*, p. 225.

[149] Harvey, *The Violin Family and its Makers*, pp. 70–2. On the fascinating subject of Bunyan and his fiddle, see also Percy A. Scholes, *The Puritans and Music in England and New England* (London: Oxford University Press, 1934), pp. 384–7.

Figure 3.6. This woodcut appeared on a ballad of the seventeenth century and seems to suggest that the refined sound of the viol was sometimes heard at ordinary taverns. The depiction of the instruments is, however, confusing. Their heavily indented shape and the underhand bowing technique of the player on the right suggest that they are viols, but the other musician holds both bow and instrument as if he is a violinist. The Pepys Library, Magdalene College, Cambridge, Pepys Ballads, *A Mad Crue; or, That shall be Tryde* (London, *c.* 1625), detail.

personal encouragement of Charles II. His establishment of a royal band, the 'Twenty Four Violins', may help to explain why North and Wood perceived the instrument as upwardly mobile, arriving at the court from the country rather than vice versa.[150] Perhaps the violin was merely reclaiming its aristocratic aura.

Viols, lutes and virginals were more solidly aristocratic than were violins, but here too the 'roving recreation' of musicians undermined the association. The social penetration of such instruments was rather deeper than we might have expected. In the first place, the gentry's love for them created powerful incentives for professional musicians – most of whom had more humble social origins – to learn the necessary techniques. There was money to be made from teaching privileged persons to play, and indeed from performing before them. Many of those who made their livings from music were the owners of lutes, viols and virginals, whatever their social background (see Figure 3.6). Indeed, some of England's poorest children were taught to play in the hope that this would provide them with a means of bettering themselves in later life. The tactic worked remarkably well in the

[150] On the development of this ensemble, see Peter Holman's excellent study *Four and Twenty Fiddlers*.

case of Thomas Brewer, who was taken into Christ's Hospital at the age of three but ended up teaching members of the gentry to play the viol and composing songs that some of them copied eagerly into their personal notebooks (an example of Brewer's work can be heard on website track 4).[151] Almost inevitably, such circumstances had the secondary effect of bringing aristocratic music to the masses, and there were numerous instances in which the instruments of the 'better sort' were heard at theatres, inns, alehouses, marketplaces, churches, cathedrals and other places not associated exclusively with the gentry. We have already met Thomas Monday, the shoemaker from Bishops Waltham who walked into Winchester with his bass viol and two fellow instrumentalists one afternoon in February 1599. The incident landed him in trouble, but it apparently did not put him off music. When Monday's probate inventory was drawn up twenty-two years later, his possessions were distinctly modest. He had sold some of his clothes 'to pay for Phisicke and Apothecarie ware', but he held onto 'a paire of smale virginalls'.[152] Of course, his instrument is likely to have been considerably less ornate than those found in aristocratic mansions. There existed a hierarchy within a hierarchy, one that distinguished between good and bad viols rather than between courtly viols and common fiddles. Nevertheless, comparatively humble people not infrequently owned and played instruments of a type that was associated strongly with the gentry.

All this musical mediation mattered. In some circumstances, it bridged the gap that existed between artisan and aristocrat, helping to release some of the tensions that were the inevitable consequence of extreme inequality. Common bagpipers in the homes of the mighty at Christmas are a good example, and cheap print from the period sometimes celebrated the bagpiper's role as a unifier of rich and poor.[153] Even this was controversial, however, for puritan opinion tended to associate festive piping not only with the lower orders but with 'papistry' and the resistant socio-spiritual solidarities of traditionalism. In 1574, the presbyterian Thomas Cartwright mocked the written expression of John Whitgift (the future Archbishop of Canterbury and scourge of the puritans), alleging that he was 'disposed to make himself and his reader merry; but it is with the bagpipe or country mirth, not with the harp or lute, which the learned were wont to handle'. It was presumably a metaphorical charge, but

[151] *Elizabeth Rogers hir Virginall Booke*, ed. Charles J. F. Cofone (1975; New York: Dover Publications, 1982), pp. xvii, 104–7, 124; Julia Gasper, 'Brewer, Thomas (1611–*c.*1660)', *Oxford Dictionary of National Biography* (Oxford: Oxford University Press, 2004), http://www.oxfordndrb.com/view/article/3368 (last accessed 1 April 2010).

[152] 1620 B 27/2, HRO. See above, pp. 75–6.

[153] *Pepys Ballads*, vol. I, pp. 76–7.

Whitgift made the interesting decision to interpret it more literally. He replied, 'And I thank God, I can be merry with the bagpipe: I am neither ashamed of the instrument, nor of the country. But what divinity call you this? Alack, poor spite at the bagpipe.'[154] For the moment at least, he presented the bagpipe as an instrument that brought rich and poor together. Where lutes, viols and virginals were concerned, the mediating role of musicians was more obviously problematic for members of the social elite. They hoped to use these instruments in order to preserve social distance but, in practice, they found it difficult to do so. Musicians and their allies were well aware of the supposed gentility of these instruments and were capable of turning it to their advantage. In the dispute that rocked early Jacobean Wells, the puritan constable claimed that Edmund White, one of his enemies, had shown favour to a disorderly musician by giving him a garter to tie on his 'fiddle'. In response, White explained that the instrument had in fact been a bass 'viol', while the ribbon had helped the physically disabled musician to support it (presumably because he was standing). At a stroke, vulgar indulgence became creditable charity.[155]

The musical servants of aristocrats and monarchs generally had their roots in the middle and lower orders of society, yet within the mansions of the mighty they could find themselves in situations of some intimacy with their employers. This was yet another form of social mediation, and it distinguished musicians from other servants. It seems that the musical menial had certain advantages over his fellows. In 1556, a court violinist named Mark Anthony had stood so close to Queen Mary that he could report 'she wants her teeth' and 'her breath stinks'. He, like his mistress, should perhaps have kept his mouth shut, for it was not long before the Privy Council heard of his comments. Over a century later, Charles II regularly listened to his servant, John Wilson, playing the lute, and 'while he played, did usually lean or lay his hand on his shoulder'.[156] Such incidents were rarely recorded, but may have been commonplace.

In 1603, the young Lady Anne Clifford presumably spent time alone with a servant from whom she learned 'to sing & play on the Bass Viol'. In her diary, Clifford recorded that her teacher at North Hall in Hertfordshire was 'Jack Jenkins my Aunt's boy'.[157] This servant, better known as John

[154] *The Works of John Whitgift*, ed. J. Ayre, 3 vols. (Cambridge: Cambridge University Press, Parker Society, 1851–3), vol. III, pp. 321–2. There are further examples of the use of musical metaphor within religious polemic in Thomas Dorman, *A Prouf of Certeyne Articles in Religion* (Antwerp, 1564). I am grateful to Peter Marshall for this reference.

[155] *REED Somerset*, pp. 275, 283–4.

[156] SP11/7 (46), NA; Spink, 'Music and Society', p. 59.

[157] *The Diaries of Lady Anne Clifford*, ed. D. J. H. Clifford (Stroud: Alan Sutton, 1990), p. 27.

Jenkins, was the son of a musical carpenter from Maidstone (Kent), and at the age of eleven was just beginning a remarkable career in music. Jenkins became a virtuoso on his favoured instrument and one of the supreme composers of consort music. By the time of his death in 1678, he had built close relationships with many more members of the gentry and aristocracy. Roger North, son of Lord North of Kirtling, was another of his pupils, and tells us that on one occasion Jenkins was summoned to play before Charles I, 'which he did in his voluntary way, with wonderful agillity, and odd humours, as (for instance) touching the great strings with his thumb, while the rest were held imployed in another way. And when he had done the King sayd he did wonders upon an inconsiderable instrument.' Jenkins, in the words of North, was not only 'a most happy person', but 'a very gentile and well bred gentleman . . . , greatly valued by the familys wherever he had taught and convers't'. Among the social elite, he was 'ever courted and never slighted, but at home wherever he went; and in most of his friends houses there was a chamber called by his name'. Through music, the carpenter's boy had come a long way. Only very rarely does North offer a hint that Jenkins never quite joined the gentleman's club. One of the reasons for the musician's ready acceptance everywhere, North suggested, was that he was always so 'well behaved'. This, perhaps, was the sort of thing a gent said about a servant rather than an equal. We might also observe that Jenkins's upward mobility did not completely isolate him or his music from wider society. Of all his compositions, recalled North, 'none flew about with his name so universally as the small piece called his Bells'. This was a hit with 'country fidlers', who were always grateful to 'a master that made new tunes for them'. The piece was universally popular and 'never failed to pass in all companys'.[158]

In the homes of the gentry, even 'country fidlers' and musical part-timers sometimes enjoyed a measure of intimacy with the inhabitants, especially if they were regular visitors. Members of the fiddle-playing Peake family were, as we have heard, admitted to the nursery and to the master's own chamber at Hatfield Broad Oak in Essex. According to Henry Peacham, there had dwelt in Jacobean Cambridge 'one Godfrey Colton, who was by his Trade a Tailor, but a merry companion with his taber and pipe, and for singing all manner of Northern songs before Noble and

[158] *Roger North on Music*, pp. 295–9, 343–8. See also Andrew Ashbee, 'Jenkins, John', *Grove Music Online, Oxford Music Online*, www.oxfordmusiconline.com/subscriber/article/grove/music/142557, last accessed 1 April 2010; Ashbee and Holman (eds.), *John Jenkins and his Time*; and *Autobiography of Thomas Whythorne*, which amounts to a case study in the status-anxiety endured by an elite musical servant.

Gentlemen, who much delighted in his company'.[159] To find more detailed evidence of such interaction we must venture into the early eighteenth century. The journal of Nicholas Blundell, a Catholic squire from Little Crosby (Lancashire), suggests that he held several local musicians in warm affection. Not only did Blundell bring them into the house for music on at least twenty-three occasions between 1702 and 1711, but he also regarded some of them as friends. The piper, William Anderton, was a particular favourite. He played regularly in the house, sometimes alone and sometimes with a companion, helping the residents to celebrate Christmas, their landlady's birthday and the completion of various agricultural tasks. 'We had a Merry-Night', commented Blundell after a session on New Year's Eve 1707. When the two men put their arrangement on a more contractual basis in 1707, the deal sounded thoroughly congenial: 'I sold my Hors Buck to William Anderton for one dayes playing of the Pips [pipes] per Annum as long as he lives in Lancashire and for 25s; to be payed by Parcells as he can get it, if the Horse prove ill I promiss to bate him 5s.'

Blundell was concerned when Anderton was pressed for the army, and probably relieved when the piper somehow managed to return home within three months. On one occasion, they went 'to course a horse' together, and in January 1708 the landlord visited the musician at home after he injured his shoulder. Anderton apparently did not play for a time, but by March he was on the mend and the two men went fishing together.[160] Such a close relationship may have been unusual, but it probably was not unique. A century earlier, the accounts of Sir Richard Shuttleworth, a Protestant from the same county, lacked the warmth and detail of a diary, but we do learn that the lord and lady of Gawthorpe welcomed a Ribchester piper named Arthur Gurney into their house on several occasions. In 1617, they even bought him a New Year's gift.[161]

Early modern musicians inhabited a world of contradictions. They were loved and loathed, defamed and defended. Their employment prospects seemed to improve and deteriorate almost at the same time. They were agents of harmony, but prone to discord. They were, by instinct, itinerant 'rangers', yet under pressure many of them stayed close to home. They provided their contemporaries with something that was both a luxury and

[159] Henry Peacham, *The Worth of a Peny* (London, 1641), p. 29.

[160] *The Great Diurnall of Nicholas Blundell of Little Crosby, Lancashire, 1702–11*, ed. Frank Tyrer, *Record Society of Lancashire and Cheshire* 110 (1968), pp. 51, 59, 65, 92, 127, 129, 153, 158, 160, 164, 168, 184.

[161] *REED Lancashire*, pp. 166–79.

a necessity. On household lists, they appear among the lower servants, yet they could be regarded by their employers almost as trusted companions. They were poorly paid but richly rewarded. They were ordinary, yet they communicated distinction and trumpeted fame. In short, they were not necessarily of low social status in any simple sense of the term.

On 7 February 1667, Solomon Sebastian, one of the waits of Nottingham, lay dying. The neighbours who attended his deathbed and witnessed his will were a glover, a cordwainer's widow and two spinsters. Most of them could not write their names, and the musician's final wishes went unrecorded until a scribe was found, some time after he died. The will was therefore nuncupative, and a series of marks and poorly formed single letters accompany the witnesses' names.[162] This, then, was Sebastian's social environment, and his will gives no impression of great wealth. The status of those who stood beside him tells us something about his own. It does not, however, tell us everything, for Solomon Sebastian was a man of many milieux. He had played with the waits, on and off, for over fifty years, and had worn his coloured coat and his 'scutchion' on many occasions. During this period, Solomon's regular duties had included performing for the mayor and burgesses at civic feasts, and for the county's judges when they assembled in Nottingham during assize week. The visiting dignitaries who must have heard him included James I in 1621 and Charles I in 1642.[163] In addition, he had undertaken regular summer tours with his fellow waits, wearing the arms of his home town on the streets of several others. He had played regularly in Coventry, where he rubbed shoulders with the waits from several other cities. He had also travelled further afield, to London and to Cambridge. In the last of these locations, he had entertained the fellows at Trinity, Clare and Emmanuel colleges.[164] Finally, he was no stranger to the homes of the gentry. In 1631, for example, the waits of Nottingham were paid 12d – not much to go on – by Thomas Walmesley of Dunkenhalgh (Lancashire). It is just conceivable that our musician was also the 'Mounsieur Sebastian' hired as a dancing master by the Earl of Rutland at Belvoir (Leicestershire) for a month in 1643.[165] All in all, this friend of glovers and cordwainers had lived quite a life.

[162] PRNW Solomon Sebastian, Nottinghamshire Archives.

[163] Woodfill, *Musicians in English Society*, p. 81; *Records of the Borough of Nottingham*, vol. IV, pp. 345, 374, vol. V, pp. 167, 208.

[164] *REED Coventry*, pp. 396–445; *REED Cambridge*, pp. 549, 626–99; *Records of the Borough of Nottingham*, vol. V, pp. 171–2.

[165] *REED Lancashire*, p. 203; Woodfill, *Musicians in English Society*, p. 272.

4 | Recreational musicians

Not all musicians performed for profit. Men and women who made their livings in other ways also played music, whether in private or among friends. It is notoriously difficult to establish the extent of such informal creativity, and previous scholars have reached divergent conclusions.[1] Occasionally, the English people have been presented as almost obsessively musical. More often, however, all but the super-wealthy have been portrayed as far too busy with other matters to bother with music. Leading scholars have conceded that some of the English sang, while a few played 'primitive instruments', but hardly any, we are told, proceeded much beyond this. They could afford neither the equipment nor the tuition, and they rarely encountered the finer forms of music. If they had been fortunate enough to hear an expert virginal player in action, they would have admired 'more his technical skill than the music'. They might well have found the experience entertaining, but only 'in the same way that they found a rope-walker entertaining'. The 'mass of the people' could neither play nor appreciate such music. They therefore muddled through life with their rough and rustic folk music, their street cries and their alehouse songs. One eminent commentator has argued that England cannot possibly have been 'bathed in melodious waters' on the grounds that 'Most of the populace could not read anything, let alone music.'[2]

Underlying such commentary is the extravagant assumption that melodic or harmonic sound counts as music only if it is read from the page. It is important to dispense with this assumption, and to consider the possibility that recreational music played a far more significant part in the cultural lives of the majority than has been recognised. Admittedly, the surviving sources are slanted towards the privileged. There is no escaping the gentry, though there is clearly a case for considering their

[1] Compare Woodfill, *Musicians in English Society*, ch. 9, with Price, *Patrons and Musicians*, ch. 3 and pp. 10–18, 205.

[2] Woodfill, *Musicians in English Society*, pp. 201–3; Wulstan, *Tudor Music*, p. 39.

music-making alongside that of the population at large. There are many intriguing interrelationships and a continuous interplay between the forces of attraction and repulsion. For this reason, it seems appropriate to investigate the subject under musically inspired headings rather than according to the distinctions of rank. In social terms, we shall rise and fall repeatedly as we proceed, hoping that the interest of the material will be sufficient to distract us from the risk of motion sickness.

Music in conduct literature

Those who took it upon themselves to offer advice on recreational music-making wasted little ink on the common people. While the sterner moralists used pen and pulpit to warn everyone against over-indulgence, the majority of writers simply assumed that music was and would remain a feature of most lives. The gentry, however, attracted considerable attention. 'Conduct' literature of the period suggests that opinion was somewhat divided regarding the appropriate place of practical music in the life of a gentleman or gentlewoman. Given the controversial status of music itself during much of the period, this was hardly surprising. Enthusiasts such as Henry Peacham, John Milton and William Higford all believed that music was essential to a rounded education. 'In all ages', declared Higford, 'music has been esteemed a quality becoming a noble personage.' Music, in the estimation of such enthusiasts, was not only a wonderful recreation but a stimulator of virtue and health. They knew, however, that others disagreed, and Peacham had harsh words for the 'disproportioned spirits' who wilfully avoided music's company.[3] Such spirits used whatever influence they possessed in order to warn England's impressionable young gentlefolk against music's allegedly destructive influence. They did not, in general, use the moral argument developed by puritans and other reformers, preferring to base their case on the power of music to consume precious time. Music, they warned, could develop into an obsession. According to James Cleland, those who played instruments were all too often 'fantasticke and ful of humors, accounting more Sometimes of the tuning of their Lute, then of the entertaining and plesant Companie of their friends'. Music, said the ninth Earl of Northumberland, was 'but lost labour', no better than playing at cards or dice. It was, agreed

[3] William Higford, *Institution of a Gentleman* (London, 1660), p. 77; Peacham, *Compleat Gentleman*, p. 96.

Francis Osborne, 'so unable to refund for the time and cost required to be perfect therein, as I cannot thinke it worth any serious endeavour'.[4]

Outright hostility was, however, unusual. Most commentators stopped well short of condemnation, though most were aware of the need to balance discussion of music's benefits with warnings about the risks. Music was a valuable means of diversion and could serve as both an ornament and a delight to the aristocratic practitioner. Competence was thus a badge of status, though it had to be developed in accordance with certain guiding principles. Moderation was the key quality, and its careful cultivation was held to be vital in ensuring that aristocratic music-making was good for its practitioners. Modesty in body language was regularly urged. Thomas Elyot warned in 1531 that the noble musician should play 'without wanton countenance and dissolute gesture'. In practice, this meant that certain instruments were preferable to others. 'And amongest us', said John Case, 'every one will not blow a bagpipe, that will finger the Lute or Virginals.' Plucking, strumming and striking were permissible, but blowing was out of the question. It distorted the shape of the face, and Case reminded his readers that Minerva had thrown away her shawm for shame.[5] The need for moderation also meant that public performance of any sort was forbidden. High-ranking amateur musicians, said Elyot, were to avoid 'open profession of that craft' and must only 'use it secretely'. Peacham was a committed advocate of music-making, but he too advised the gentleman to play music 'privately to your self'. Privacy was also a means towards the avoidance of any taint of professionalism. Cleland warned noblemen against learning all instruments, 'but especiallie ... such as commonlie men get their living by'.[6]

Moderation was also required where levels of proficiency were concerned, and Peacham advised that no noble or gentleman should 'proove a Master' in musical performance. 'It is a kind of diparagement', wrote Owen Felltham, 'to be a cunning fiddler; it argues a man's neglect of better employments, and shews that he has spent much time upon a thing unneccesary. Hence it has been counted ill, for great men to sing or play like a professional musician.' Technical mediocrity was thus required, though in specific terms the bar was set surprisingly high. Peacham told

[4] Cleland, *Hero-paideia, or The Institution of a Young Noble Man* (London, 1607), p. 229; *Advice to a Son by Henry Percy*, ed. G. B. Harrison (London: Ernst Benn, 1930), p. 64; Osborne, *Advice to a Son*, p. 16.

[5] Elyot, *The Boke Named the Governour*, fo. 21v; Case, *Praise of Musicke*, p. 33.

[6] Elyot, *The Boke Named the Governour*, fos. 23v–24r; Peacham, *Compleat Gentleman*, p. 100; Cleland, *Hero-paideia*, p. 229.

his readers, 'I desire no more of you then to sing your part sure, and at first sight, withall, to play the same upon your Violl.'[7] Confident sight-reading is rather more than a rudimentary skill. Dekker mentioned the same ability, and his list of suitable instruments for the hands of a gent comprised virginals, lute and cittern. In sum, music was a legitimate source of delight to high-ranking players, provided that their delight never became, in Elyot's word, 'inordinate'.[8]

At its best, music could actually instil moderation, and Thomas Nash characterised the more lascivious of London women as those who had not been taught 'what belongs to a Needle, Violl, Virginall or Lute'. Even the tonal quality of such instruments echoed the dignified self-containment that was expected of Renaissance gentlefolk. In marked contrast to trumpets and tabors, they produced sounds that combined a sometimes exquisite beauty with an air of introversion, prudence and privacy. While trumpets 'brayed', lutes 'warbled' and 'whispered'.[9] The restrained timbre of the lute made it particularly appropriate for the education of young ladies, and the term 'virginals' probably grew out of this association. These instruments allowed a measure of self-expression to female players but also taught them to keep quiet. For one reason or an other, young Mary Burwell loved her lute. In about 1670, she recorded some of her thoughts in a notebook: 'All the actions that one does in playing of the lute are handsome'; 'The lute is a noble instrument, not made for debaucheries, ranting or playing in the streets to give serenades to Signora Isabella. 'Tis a grave and serious music for modest sober persons, and for the cabinet rather than for a public place'; 'the noise of a mouse is a hindrance to that music'.[10] Commentators argued, furthermore, that women who had dutifully acquired the requisite musical skills rendered themselves attractive to high-ranking suitors. There was thus a connection between refined music-making and refined courtship (just as there was between vulgar music and bestial sex). 'To heare a faire young gentlewoman to play upon the Virginalls, Lute, Viall, and sing to it', wrote Robert Burton in 1621, 'must needs be a great entisement.' Instrumental tuition was 'the next way their

[7] Peacham, *Compleat Gentleman*, pp. 98, 100; Owen Felltham, *Resolves, Divine, Moral, and Political* (1623; London: Temple Classics, 1904), p. 243.

[8] Dekker, quoted by Thurston Dart, 'The Cittern and its English Music', *Galpin Society Journal* 1 (1948), 49; Elyot, *The Boke Named the Governour*, fo. 23r.

[9] Thomas Nash, *Quaternio or a Fourefuld Way to a Happie Life* (London, 1633), p. 155; Shakespeare, *The Life and Death of King John*, in *Complete Oxford Shakespeare*, vol. I, p. 245; John Dryden, *A Song for St. Cecilia's Day* (London, 1687). On the website, virginals are played on tracks 3 and 4. A lute can be heard on tracks 6 and 7.

[10] 'Miss Mary Burwell's Instruction Book', pp. 43, 48, 61.

parents think to get them husbands'. The same thought may well have been in the mind of the London gentleman who, in around 1600, greeted an eminent tourist from Europe by calling upon his six daughters to perform before him. The visitor was suitably impressed, remarking that the girls 'sang and played most beautifully on various kinds of musical instruments'.[11]

Failure to play by the rules exposed musical gentlefolk to a number of dangers. They might descend into wantonness and vanity. Those who could not resist the temptation of performing 'in a commune audience' might lose the respect of their social inferiors. Elyot warned the young gentleman that ordinary people would forget their reverence if they beheld him 'in the similitude of a common servant or minstrell'. In 1656, Francis Osborne advised his son to beware of the social tightrope that any gentleman walked when others invited him to play an instrument in company. Osborne described, presumably from bitter experience, 'the trouble of calculating the difference between the morose humour of a rigid Refuser, and the cheap and prostituted levity and forwardnesse of a mercenary Fidler: Deniall being as often taken for pride, as a too ready complyance falls under the notion of ostentation'. It was not a happy choice, but Osborne believed on balance that it was better to seem rigidly resistant than ostentatiously forward.[12]

Practical music was also fraught with gender-bending risks. Its links with lady-like conduct meant that it could feminise men. In a dialogue by Roger Ascham, written in 1545, the character Philologus warns that music softens men, rendering them unfit for proper study. A century later, the brothers of Margaret, Duchess of Newcastle, shared the same misgivings: they rarely played music, 'saying it was too effeminate for masculine spirits'. Richard Brathwaite recommended music, though he listed it among the 'soft and effeminate Recreations'. It was thus a notch down from manly pursuits such as hunting and wrestling, though it had an important function in any balanced recreational regime: 'wee are sometimes to unbend the bow, or it wil lose his strength'.[13] Few writers were as animated on this point as the moralist Philip Stubbes, but the

[11] Burton, *Anatomy of Melancholy*, pp. 580, 586; *Diary of Baron Waldstein*, trans. G. W. Groos (London: Thames and Hudson, 1981), p. 171.

[12] Elyot, *The Boke Named the Governour*, fos. 2r, 23r, 24r; Osborne, *Advice to a Son*, p. 17.

[13] Roger Ascham, *Toxophilus, the Schole of Shooting* (London, 1545), fo. 10r; Margaret Cavendish, quoted by Woodfill, *Musicians in English Society*, p. 221; Brathwaite, *The English Gentleman*, pp. 167, 174.

danger was clearly one to be watched.[14] Where women were concerned, most writers appear to have accepted the value of music as an accomplishment and a kind of romantic lure, but some felt strongly that the risks outweighed the potential benefits. Francis Osborne wrote sarcastically of women, 'who do not rarely decline in modesty, proportionably to the progresse they make in Musick; such (if hansome) being Traps baited at both ends, and catch strangers as often as their Husbands'. Musical maidens were, in Robert Burton's approving phrase, 'a great entisement' to potential husbands, but Osborne's less optimistic eyes were drawn to the potential adulterers lining up behind them. The lure of the lute might extend beyond one's husband. Perhaps this was why James Kirkwood advised parents that their daughters should avoid instruments altogether, learning instead to 'repeat every day some passages out of the Word of God'.[15]

Ownership of instruments

Not everybody accepted this advice, and many members of the gentry, male and female, possessed musical instruments. Not surprisingly, viols, virginals and lutes were the front-runners, being delicate, refined and reassuringly expensive. Musical commentators drew attention to the classical origins of these instruments, and readers were assured that previous masters of the lute had included Achilles, Apollo and Orpheus. The music of such instruments, said Solomon Eccles's imaginary friend, 'delights the ears of Kings and wise men, and grave sage men'.[16] In early modern England, they were evidently perceived as objects that cultured and high-ranking individuals really ought to possess, and their traces can be found in many surviving documents. They were *de rigueur* in aristocratic homes such as Belvoir Castle, seat of the Dukes of Rutland. Here the household accounts of the period mention lutes, viols, 'harpsicalls', harps and citterns. In 1655 the Countess of Rutland was also seeking a polyfant (a rare and complicated form of lute). Gentry of much lower rank also possessed instruments, though not with the same regularity and not in the same numbers. In 1648, for example, Mrs Ursula Masters of Farewell

[14] See above, p. 62.

[15] Osborne, *Advice to a Son*, p. 17; Kirkwood, *The True Interest of Families* (London, 1693), preface.

[16] Eccles, *A Musick-lector*, p. 11.

(Staffordshire) died with a pair of virginals in her parlour and two viols in her 'lodging chamber'.[17]

Ownership was of course no guarantee of use, and inventories that record the presence of 'old' instruments in obscure corners of the house do not inspire confidence. On the other hand, many instruments clearly were played and maintained by their owners. Lady Margaret Hoby, a godly gentlewoman who wrote a diary at the beginning of the seventeenth century, evidently kept her favourite instrument in good condition and played it for relaxation. On 26 January 1600, she wrote, 'after diner I dresed up my Clositte and read and, to refreshe my selfe beinge dull, I plaied and sung to the Alpherion' (an orpharion was a wire-strung instrument tuned like a lute).[18] This was probably a common form of recreation, and we can say with confidence that, from the reign of Elizabeth onwards, a substantial and increasing proportion of the gentry lived within easy reach of a selection of instruments. In September 1666, Samuel Pepys watched the wealthy of London taking to the Thames in order to escape the fire of London, and observed 'that hardly one lighter or boat in three that had goods of a house in, but there was a pair of virginalls in it'.[19] At other times, provision for musical instruments was a matter of household routine. New instruments were purchased and old ones were tuned or mended. In Lincolnshire, the early Elizabethan accounts of the Berties recorded payments for lute strings, lute repairs and brand new instruments for the children of the house. The Le Stranges of Norfolk were particularly keen on viols, and in the first half of the seventeenth century paid regularly for 'viall Bookes', spare strings, new cases, 'Caryinge vialls' and the repair of instruments. The Barringtons of Hatfield Broad Oak, as we have heard, sometimes listened to the fiddles and bagpipes of visiting musicians, but when they played music for themselves they did so on the virginals.[20] These examples derive from fairly typical gentry households rather than from the homes of super-musical families like the Kytsons of Hengrave Hall with their live-in musical servants and their vast array of instruments.

[17] *Manuscripts of His Grace the Duke of Rutland*, vol. II, pp. 5, 99–350, vol. IV, pp. 294–552; *Probate Inventories of Lichfield and Diocese, 1568–1680*, ed. D. G. Vaisey, *Collections for a History of Staffordshire*, 4th series 5 (1969), pp. 81–5.

[18] *The Private Life of an Elizabethan Lady: The Diary of Lady Margaret Hoby, 1599–1605*, ed. Joanna Moody (Stroud: Sutton Publishing, 1998), p. 56.

[19] *Diary of Samuel Pepys*, vol. VII, p. 271.

[20] Anc VII/A/2, fos. 31r, 107v, LA. See also Woodfill, *Musicians in English Society*, p. 253; LEST/P6, P7, P10, NRO; D/DBa A5, A8, A9, ERO.

Not surprisingly, beautiful instruments could be the objects of considerable pride and devotion. During the early 1650s, Sir Peter Leycester went to considerable lengths to reunite a set of seven viols (two trebles, two tenors, two basses and one lyra-viol) that had become separated – like many human families – during the political turbulence of the previous decade. Originally, they had been the property of Sir George Ratcliffe, but they had been seized by parliamentarian officers when Chester surrendered in January 1646. The new custodians fell into an argument, during which the set was apparently broken up, the bows lost, and several of the instruments damaged. Leycester was determined to bring them back together again, and took the financial risk of buying two of the viols back from men who probably had no legitimate claim to their possession. He also ordered new bows, which were, he said, 'very hansome & well made for use'. To men like Leycester, it mattered deeply that armigerous instruments were properly respected.[21]

Occasionally, snippets of evidence suggest a casual familiarity with these instruments among some at least of the gentry. In 1662, the highly musical gent Roger L'Estrange faced the potentially damaging accusation that he had, during the Interregnum, deliberately ingratiated himself with Cromwell by visiting the famous leader with 'his Fiddle under his Cloak to facilitate his entry'. This sounded a little improbable, but L'Estrange was sufficiently perturbed to mount a defence, into which he dropped the names of two more respectable instruments. The source of the story, he claimed, was an occasion upon which he had overheard a chamber organ 'touch'd in a little Low Room' as he was passing through St James's Park. Drawn to the sound, he entered the room and was invited by the company assembled there 'to take up a Viole, and bear a Part'. After a while, 'In comes Cromwell; He found us Playing, and (as I remember) so left us.'[22]

Furthermore, groups of politically disaffected individuals sometimes seem to have used the choicest of instruments as a supposedly respectable cover for their dark dealings. In the mid-1550s, Mary's government was attempting to track the activities of those suspected of plotting on behalf of her half-sister Elizabeth. A letter was intercepted in which Sir John Mason wrote rather cryptically to the Earl of Devon regarding the attitude

[21] DLT/B11, fos. 1–7, ChRO.

[22] Roger L'Estrange, *Truth and Loyalty Vindicated* (London, 1662), p. 50. See also Andrew Ashbee, '"My fiddle is a bass viol": Music in the Life of Roger L'Estrange', in Anne Dunan-Page and Beth Lynch (eds.), *Roger L'Estrange and the Making of Restoration Culture* (Aldershot: Ashgate, 2008), pp. 149–66.

of a third party: 'If he might have help he would prove very good at the lute and the viol.' Other suspects accounted for their recent movements by explaining that they had merely been buying lute strings for Princess Elizabeth. In April 1556, a suspected conspirator in the Tower of London informed his interrogators that another prisoner, John Throckmorton, had once called to see him, 'and finding a lute on the bed or cupboard, passed the time therewith and with some trifling talk I do not remember'. Additional instruments – not quite so aristocratic but respectable nonetheless – were also part of the web. In another intercepted letter, Devon asked Thomas Gresham for money to purchase a cittern and its accompanying implements. The earl was also reported to have exchanged secret communication with Peter Carew by means of a cipher, carved into the wood of a guitar.[23] Of course, once one has been sucked into this murky world, it is tempting to see secretive significance in the most innocuous of musical exchanges. Nevertheless, the occurrence of these and other peculiarities in the state papers gathered by several Tudor and Stuart governments does suggest that some individuals trusted, not altogether wisely, in the deflective capacity of a prestigious musical instrument.[24]

Lute, viols and virginals were supposedly the instruments of the gentry, but their refined music was occasionally to be heard in the homes of lesser folk. The proud owners included several who clearly enjoyed considerable wealth – merchants, mercers and physicians – but also many whose means were more modest. Examples exist from all parts of the country but we shall focus briefly on two locations. The city of Bristol was home to an innkeeper with viols (1550), a joiner with virginals (1612) and a pinker with lutes (1613). One local clothworker had an old pair of virginals in his bedchamber when he died in 1595.[25] In the contrasting environment of rural Essex, lutes were owned by a tailor (1567) and a yeoman (1574).[26] In the same county, viols were to be found in the hands of a blacksmith's servant (1573) and a husbandman (1574), while in West Ham another husbandman bequeathed a pair of virginals to his daughter (1575).[27]

[23] *CSPD 1553–8*, pp. 150, 218, 194, 101–2 (in order cited); *Calendar of Letters, Despatches, and State Papers, Relating to the Negotiations between England and Spain*, 13 vols. (London: His Majesty's Stationery Office, 1862–1954), vol. XII, p. 139.

[24] See also *CSPD 1547–80*, p. 179: here, a letter written in Paris on 10 July 1561 includes the suspicious lines, 'Mr Thomas has no great taste for the lute, but likes the cittern. He has been presented to the Queen of Scots.'

[25] *REED Bristol*, pp. 59, 195, 199, 245.

[26] *Essex Wills*, vol. I, no. 1015, vol. III, no. 335. See also above, pp. 20–1.

[27] *Essex Wills*, vol. III, nos. 187, 310, 403.

He was by no means the only middle-ranking testator to send his refined instrument of music along the female line.

Attempts by the gentry to claim the finest instruments as their own may only have created additional, extra-musical incentives for personal possession. John Taylor advised a man with aspirations above his station that he should purchase not only valuable books, but lutes, viols and other instruments: 'And then his Musicke and his learning share, / Being both alike, with either might compare.'[28] It is one of the features of hierarchical societies that supposedly inferior individuals will sometimes imitate those above them, no matter how sternly they are warned of the dangers. People of middling and lower rank were told to respect the gentry, but not to copy their culture. The advice was problematic, for most humans instinctively mimic those whom they admire. The ineffectual sumptuary legislation of the period is the most obvious example of these issues in practice, but they were also set to music. We should not assume, however, that social emulation was the only motive behind ownership of supposedly elite instruments by individuals from the middling and lower social orders. Predominantly musical motives were almost certainly just as strong. Wherever the inspiration lay, it is clear that one did not have to be a gentleman in order to develop a recreational interest in the more highly esteemed musical instruments. Most strikingly, a painting of the mid-sixteenth century depicts the lowly born pirate Henry Strangeways holding a lute (see Figure 4.1). It is only just visible, and the eyes of the viewer are drawn more immediately to Strangeways's wild orange hair, but the lute's presence nevertheless suggests that the man had a 'gentle' side (or was it a joke?).

Lutes, viols and virginals were thus somewhat less successful than the gentry might have wished in preserving the social space between the best and the rest. Other stringed instruments – harps, citterns, gitterns and guitars – never attracted quite the same prestige and enjoyed a less complex and more universal cultural status. They were heard at court and in the homes of many aristocrats, gentry and wealthy merchants. They were sometimes listed alongside lutes and viols as instruments that privileged and prosperous persons learned to play for themselves, but it was rarely implied that the gentry claimed an exclusive right over them.[29] Citterns were perhaps most prominent in society's middle ranks. They were clearly a feature of family life for the Heyrickes, a rising family of

[28] Taylor, *All the Workes*, vol. III, p. 506.

[29] See, for example, Richard Flecknoe, *Enigmatical Characters* (London, 1658), p. 44.

Figure 4.1. Even a base-born pirate might play the lute. The artist Gerlach Flicke painted these portraits of himself (left) and the bold man of the seas Henry Strangeways (right) while both men were prisoners in London in 1554. When the painting is viewed in colour, Strangeways's wild orange hair picks up the rich brown of his lute quite pleasingly, but the two features otherwise send out contradictory messages. © The National Portrait Gallery, NPG 6353.

goldsmiths in sixteenth-century Leicester and London. On 29 August 1584, John Heyricke wrote a typically loving letter to his brother William, concluding with the request, 'I pray yow send those buttons by hary whyt, and if you can spare your sittern I pray yow send it by him allso and I will please him for the caridg.' In various counties, harps, citterns or gitterns were owned by barbers, sadlers, schoolmasters, tanners, masons and tailors. The misdemeanours for which the apprentices of Newcastle upon Tyne were rebuked in 1554 included their disorderly 'use of gitterns by nyght'.[30] The London mercer Robert Laneham played his instruments for the entertainment of 'court ladies' during the 1570s: 'noow with my

[30] MS Eng hist c.474, no. 178, Bodleian Library; *REED Newcastle upon Tyne*, p. 25.

Gittern, and els with my Cittern, then at the Virgynalz: ye know nothing cums amisse to me'.[31]

Individuals of middling rank sometimes possessed and played other instruments too, and the diary of Samuel Pepys is a particularly fine and famous source. It appears that the range of instruments considered suitable for men of rank was expanding during the second half of the seventeenth century. Between 1660 and 1670, Pepys therefore tried his hand at the flageolet, recorder, lute, theorbo, viol, violin and spinet. He also contemplated purchasing a chamber organ. Recreational music was similarly important to an anonymous and little-known diarist who moved from London to Chelmsford in the summer of 1675. Like Pepys, he chose his instrument – the violin – partly because it was newly fashionable and partly because it was therapeutic. In the case of the new man in Chelmsford, however, one senses that his instrument was, in practice, more valuable for emotional succour than for social advancement. He invariably played it alone in his lodgings, and he usually did so in the hope of cheering himself up. On 14 December 1675, he wrote: 'played 3 or 4 tunes to compose myself because my L:L: [landlord] was out of humour'.[32]

Admittedly, demonstrable instrument ownership beneath the level of the gentry was not statistically significant. The vast majority of probate inventories contain no mention whatsoever of music. There is a suspicion, however, that instruments were regularly overlooked by the untrained neighbours who drew up these documents. Confidence in probate sources as a register of musical instruments is vigorously shaken by the high incidence of dying 'musicians' who apparently possessed none. Three such men died in mid-seventeenth-century Oxford alone.[33] Furthermore, there is evidence that instruments were frequently lent and borrowed on all social levels. Around Christmas in 1592, for example, a Shrewsbury labourer named Thomas Dawes took temporary custody of 'a violett ottherwise called a fiddle with ii stringes' from a tall man in a blue coat. Dawes planned to learn to play it, and we hear of him only because he grew rather attached to the instrument and neglected to return it on time. And in 1606, John Noniley of the same town was locked up after he misused a poor musician late at night by 'takinge his harpe from him &

[31] Laneham, *Captain Cox, his Ballads and Books*, pp. 59–61.

[32] *Diary of Samuel Pepys*, vols. I–IX; MS Rawl. D. 1114 (14 December 1675), Bodleian Library.

[33] Original wills/inventories, 12/3/29 (Thomas Charles), 141/1/39 (John Michell), 77/1/12 (Thomas Burte), Oxfordshire Archives.

playenge upon the same alonge the streetes'.[34] Ownership was not necessarily essential to musical participation.

Instruments were also stolen with some regularity. Citterns appear to have been particularly vulnerable. In 1601, three men – a labourer, a mariner and a glover – were sentenced to death by an assize judge for burgling a house in Surrey and stealing items that included a cittern. Three decades later, a Somerset servant confessed that he had spotted one in his master's house, 'lyinge uppon a shelfe in a roome next adjoyninge to the kitchinn ... Which Sitterne hee ... did take & carry away unto a place called the Wall & there did hide it in the hedge.' He later made the mistake of boasting of his crime in the presence of his father-in-law (never a good idea).[35] Elsewhere, viols, violins and horns were stolen by a lowly assortment of labourers, shoemakers and servants. Historians deal only with the thieves who were caught, but their numbers were sufficient to suggest the existence of an instinct for music-making that is not fully documented in surviving inventories.

Labourers were far less likely than lords to generate such documents, and precise examples of the ownership of instruments by named individuals become harder to find as we move further down the social scale. When the evidential net is cast more widely, however, references to musical instruments among the lower orders are not in fact particularly difficult to find. The cheaper forms of print portray many characters who played instruments for recreation. The humble shepherd of English balladry is rarely without his pipe or bagpipes, making music to pass the time, to express romantic devotion and 'to drive away all cares'. Friar Bacon's boy, meanwhile, plays his pipe and tabor to keep himself awake 'With his own musick' while performing a tedious task for his master.[36] Lovers, too, are frequently driven or drawn to music. In a chapbook of 1685, 'honest John' introduces the song he has composed for 'loving Kate'. Proudly, he tells her that he devised it while working in the malt house, '& when done turning the Mault, I sat down ... and played the tune on my Flagellet'. John was apparently more honest than modest, for he added, 'It went so sweetly, it ravisht mee.' In one ballad, a young woman says of her ideal suitor, 'He'll court, he'll kiss, he'll sing or play', before adding the hasty qualification, 'but it shal be in a modest way'.[37] In other songs and

34 *REED Shropshire*, pp. 277–8, 291.

35 *Calendar of Assize Records: Surrey Indictments, Elizabeth I*, ed. J. S. Cockburn (London: Her Majesty's Stationery Office, 1980), pp. 503–4; *REED Somerset*, p. 68.

36 *Pepys Ballads*, vol. I, pp. 77, 366, vol. III, p. 59; *The Famous History of Friar Bacon.*

37 *A Pleasant Dialogue betwixt Honest John and Loving Kate*, pp. 17–18; *Pepys Ballads*, vol. III, p. 29.

tales, fictional sweethearts sing soulfully to their lutes, whether in hope or misery. Such references can, of course, be interpreted as part of an attempt to flatter potential customers by mentioning the more fashionable and courtly instruments, but we should also consider the possibility that instrumental name-dropping was effective because it signalled something familiar. In certain occupations, the ability to make recreational music was almost a badge of status. The Elizabethan writer Thomas Deloney warned that no shoemaker deserved credit unless he could 'sound the Trumpet, or play upon the Flute'.[38]

He may of course have been exaggerating this informal cultural requirement for humorous effect, though some English sailors clearly possessed trumpets even though they were not employed as musicians. Some of them may have aspired to fill any official musical vacancies that arose during a voyage, but the same cannot be said of the sailors who possessed not only whistles and weapons, but citterns, fiddles and pipes. On the wreck of the *Mary Rose*, marine archaeologists found one pipe in the vicinity of a cabin known to have been occupied by a carpenter and an archer. There were also two simple box-shaped fiddles on board, and it seems likely that these too were played by ordinary sailors rather than by occupational musicians.[39] At sea or on land, basic pipes and fiddles were objects of the sort that was probably ignored by the compilers of most probate inventories, and we simply cannot say how common such instruments were. Itinerant chapmen and chapwomen sometimes carried considerable numbers of pipes and 'jew's' trumps' in their packs.[40] Such instruments were both portable and marketable, and they were probably played more by recreational musicians than by their occupational brethren. In 1676, Thomas Mace struggled to bolster the flagging fashionability of the lute, and regretted the existence of

Pipes of Bartholomew,
Like those which Country-Wives buy, Gay and New,
To please their Little Children when they Cry.[41]

[38] *Pepys Ballads*, vol. I, pp. 354–5, 516, vol. III, p. 27; Deloney, *The Gentle Craft* (1598; London, 1637), C4r.

[39] Woodfield, *English Musicians*, pp. 81–4; Andrew Green, 'Middle Sea', *Early Music Today* 9.3 (June–July 2001), 8–9. I am grateful to Andrew Elkerton of the Mary Rose Museum for showing me the reconstructions of the two fiddles and for allowing me to try them out. I also thank the violin-maker Peter Boardman for discussing the design of these instruments with me.

[40] See above, p. 3, and *Pepys Ballads*, vol. I, p. 238.

[41] Mace, *Musick's Monument*, p. 33.

This may have been one of the most common uses for basic musical instruments as they helped to mediate between adults and infants. In Jacobean Wells, a shoemaker stood accused of beating his drum defiantly from within the walls of his master's house: he denied the charge, but recalled helpfully that 'a maiedservant of the house did with her hand or with a sticke strike & tapp the saied drumm to a little child which she carried to please & keepe the child from Crienge'. According to Mace, 'country people' who could not lay their hands on conventional instruments were adept at constructing ingenious musical devices with which to amuse themselves. He described how items of furniture were sometimes transformed into stringed instruments with considerable imagination and a basic grasp of acoustical principles: six or seven ranks of strings were nailed onto a table or cupboard, then 'lifted up a little' from its surface with stones or sticks to create tension in the strings and allow them to 'sound the wood' (meaning, apparently, to resonate through the furniture). In this way, children learned 'to play them in order like bells, & then do changes'. This was, said Mace, makeshift music, learned 'without a Rule (and yet by Habit) well enough'. It would actually have been easier, he concluded, to master the much-neglected lute.[42]

This is perhaps the only known reference to the cupboard-cum-double-bass, and it reminds us that there may have existed a murky world of resourceful music-making that is echoed only very rarely in the surviving sources. References to the percussive redeployment of household utensils and other readily available objects are rather more common, and it seems likely that 'kitchen music' was heard with some frequency. In Christopher Fetherston's Elizabethan *Dialogue agaynst Light, Lewde, and Lascivious Dancing*, a godly minister is incensed when he hears Juvenis, a fun-loving layman, describe his plans for the Lord's Day. These involve church attendance, but also dancing, football and drinking. Finally, Juvenis explains, 'I will see what melody a payre of bones will make, if I can get the company.'[43] Chapbook percussionists sometimes played tongs, and music of a similar sort also featured in courtly entertainments of the period, where it served to introduce a little low life into the high life. In 1633, the relief was provided in one masque by a procession 'of cripples and beggers on horseback' with 'their Music of keys and tongs, and the like, snapping and yet playing in consort with them'. They helped to represent 'The Wilderness', contrasting with the 'noble Musicke' of more

42 *REED Somerset*, pp. 300–2; Mace, *Musick's Monument*, p. 44.

43 Fetherston, *A Dialogue*, A7r.

refined instruments in a manner that reportedly delighted the aristocratic audience. In 1672, a grand London pageant displayed, in the midst of much else, 'severall Kitchen Musicians, that Play upon Tongs, Gridirons, Keys and other such-like confused Musick'.[44] Of course, all such portrayals must be handled with care, for they mocked and manipulated the music that they represented. Nevertheless, they do seem to indicate the existence of rough-and-ready customs of recreational music-making that have not often been noted.

Singing

Of course, 'kitchen music' was popular at the bottom end of society primarily because it was cheap. Singing possessed the same advantage and was undoubtedly the most common form of recreational music among the lower orders. It was expressive and instinctive. The country's poorer people, said John Rhodes in 1588, were 'naturally given to sing', and his opinion is confirmed by a wealth of sources.[45] At the most basic musical level, people sang ballads and other songs, sometimes solo but often in small groups. In 1595, the Sabbatarian Nicholas Bownde was alarmed at the increasing enthusiasm with which 'poore husbandmen' sang ballads for their recreation, in preference to psalms. New ballads, said Robert Burton in 1621, were soon on the lips of 'carmen, boys, and prentices' in the streets. Some time later, Izaak Walton enjoyed the sound of a milkmaid singing ballads from memory in a country alehouse.[46] Surviving collections of cheap print present many a fictional maiden whose singing voice is among her most alluring assets (an interesting lower-order version of the aristocratic lure of the lute). Indeed, for men and women alike, the ability to sing well is presented as a mark of esteem. Ballad characters also make music for relaxation and to pass the time. In one publication, three merry butchers break into song as they travel along a road ('With a high ding ding dee, and God bless all good people from evil company'), while a far sterner ballad warns the people of England to 'cease their Ale-house

[44] Bulstrode Whitlocke, *Memorials of the English Affairs*, 4 vols. (1682; London, 1853), vol. I, p. 57; Thomas Jordan, *London Triumphant* (London, 1672), p. 9.

[45] Rhodes, quoted by Fox, *Oral and Literate Culture*, p. 30.

[46] Nicholas Bownde, *The Doctrine of the Sabbath* (London, 1595), pp. 241–2; Burton, quoted by Fox, *Oral and Literate Culture*, p. 206; Izaak Walton, *The Compleat Angler* (London, 1653), p. 203.

songs, / the which their credit wrongs' (set, perhaps deliberately, to the inappropriate tune of 'Dainty come thou to me').[47]

'Alehouse songs' could, on occasion, turn into a neighbourly nuisance, and cases of anti-social singing provide our best evidence that the production of exuberant vocal music was not merely the figment of the literary imagination. In Shrewsbury, fights broke out every few years when young men received reprimand for singing in the streets at night. In 1637, a mixed group at Bridport (Dorset) drank in an alehouse through the night while three of their number sang loudly, 'wherby the neighbours could not sleepe' (to make matters worse, the next day was a Sunday). In the same decade, a group of parishioners from Staunton (Nottinghamshire) was reported for spending one Sunday afternoon in the alehouse of Edward Colethirst ('being a very disorderly & intemperat man'). They drank beer and played cards when they should have been in church, 'And hearing that Prayers were ended (as they sate at their Cups) they said each to other (ironically) "Come let us pray" & ther uppon (very prophanely) they fell a singing in ridiculous sort: neither did they void the place untill (at length) a drunken fray dispersed them.'[48]

The singing of lullabies was, in contrast, thoroughly uncontroversial, and most of our evidence is therefore literary rather than archival. Music, argued Roger Ascham, was a vital component of the maternal repertoire, 'For even the litle babes lacking the use of reason, are scarse so well stilled in suckyng theyr mothers pap, as in hearynge theyr mother syng.' Lullabies were a distinctively female genre: soothing songs through which mothers established musical connections with the wailing representatives of the next generation. A common literary device was to present the lullaby as the lament of a mother deserted by her lover and left to soothe the baby alone. A popular example was found in *The New Balow: or, A Wenches Lamentation for the Loss of her Sweetheart*, set to the tune 'Balow'. This word, sometimes rendered as 'Baloo', was clearly a staple of the calming nursery vocabulary. Admittedly, ballad lullabies were often cast in a form that was perhaps rather too long and complex for the task at hand, but they at least offer us some guidance regarding the vocabulary that seemed appropriate. Another example contains a range of suitable expressions: 'Come little Babe, come silly soul'; 'Sing lullaby and keep it warm'; 'Why dost thou weep? Why dost thou wail?'; 'my only joy'; 'Come little boy and

[47] *Pepys Ballads*, vol. II, p. 176, vol. I, p. 431.

[48] *REED Shropshire*, pp. 234, 315, 320–2; *REED Dorset*, p. 168; AN/PB 328/1/34, HL. On noise as nuisance, see Emily Cockayne, *Hubbub: Filth, Noise and Stench in England* (New Haven: Yale University Press, 2007), ch. 5.

Rock asleep'; 'God bless the babe and Lullaby'; 'Come silly wretch'.[49] These words seem to capture rather well the combination of devotion and frustration that is the timeless lot of the lone mother.

Rounds (or roundelays) and catches were a little more challenging in musical terms because they required each singer to hold his or her part against the melodic lines of others. This required practice, but lack of leisure time did not prevent songs of this sort from being associated regularly with recreational musicians of relatively low social status. In contemporary ballads, rounds were sometimes sung by groups of fictional young lovers as they celebrated the arrival of spring: 'Hand in hand they take their way, / Catching many a rundelay.' Archbishop Harsnett mentioned with distaste the catches or rounds 'sung by Tinkers, as they sit by the fire with a pot of good Ale betweene theyr legges'. Shakespeare connected the singing of catches with weavers and cobblers, though he also created characters of higher status who indulged in the practice.[50] Catch-singing cobblers appear again in chapbooks of the period, and a broadside of about 1620, entitled *A Merry New Catch of All Trades*, aimed to attract an audience wide and deep by including lines on bakers, tailors, tinkers, pewterers, bricklayers, plumbers, carpenters, hat-makers, weavers, carters, watermen and many more.[51]

Another common vocal form was the freemen's song or three-men's song. It is not entirely clear which of the two terms is the linguistic original and which the corrupted or modified form. In 1609, Ravenscroft published several 'Freemen's songs' in his *Deuteromelia*, each of them in three parts. The alternative label had been used in 1553 when the city of London sought to ban non-musicians from moonlighting by touring taverns and alehouses to 'sing songs called three men's songs'.[52] The particular targets of this restriction were small groups of musical craftsmen (particularly shoemakers and tailors), some of whom were presumably freemen of the city. It is thus easy to understand how the confusion arose. Musically, the form seems to have involved the improvisation of two harmonic parts around a well-known melody. According to Thomas Deloney, any journeyman-shoemaker who could not 'bear his part in a three-man's song' deserved to be fined for his inadequacy and 'counted for a colt'.

[49] Ascham, *Toxophilus*, fo. 11r; *The New Balow: or A Wenches Lamentation for the Loss of her Sweetheart* (London, 1670); *Pepys Ballads*, vol. I, p. 481.

[50] *Pepys Ballads*, vol. I, p. 337; Harsnett, *Declaration*, p. 49; Shakespeare, *Twelfth Night, or What You Will*, in *Complete Oxford Shakespeare*, p. 728.

[51] *The Pleasant and Delightful History of King Henry the 8th and a Cobbler* (London, *c.* 1670), B2v; *Pepys Ballads*, vol. I, pp. 164–5 (Website track 19).

[52] Thomas Ravenscroft, *Deuteromelia, or The Second Part of Musicks Melodie* (London, 1609), B1r; Watt, *Cheap Print*, p. 34.

In *The Winter's Tale*, the shearers at a feast are described by Clown as 'three-man-song men all, and very good ones'.[53] And in the courtly *Maske of Flowers*, staged by the gentlemen of Gray's Inn in 1614, two rival groups of working men participate in a musical contest involving the performances of catches and 'freemans songs' (in practice, the two musical forms may often have been conflated). Such songs were also known in the countryside, however, and Richard Carew included three-men's songs as one of the pastimes that delighted the minds of west country people in the early seventeenth century. 'Cornish three mens songs', he said, were 'cunningly contrived for the ditty, and pleasantly for the note'.[54]

Craftsmen sang while they relaxed, but they and many others also sang at work. Indeed, those who chose instead to labour in silence occasionally attracted suspicion. In Beaumont's *The Knight of the Burning Pestle*, for example, Old Merryweather advises his audience, 'Never trust a tailor that does not sing at his work: his mind is of nothing but fitching.' It was a commonplace of literary commentary that working people made music in order to alleviate or co-ordinate their toil: weavers at their looms; country people as they carted the harvest home; and sailors as they weighed anchor.[55] Music, argued John Case, was a wondrous source of solace to such people, 'And hence it is, that manual labourers, and Mechanicall artificers of all sorts, keepe such a chaunting and singing in their shoppes, the Tailor on his bulk, the Shomaker at his last, the Mason at his wal, the shipboy at his oare, the Tinker at his pan, & the Tylor on the house top.' This singing was clearly connected with the rhythms of work. When Case spoke of 'that petie & counterfait Musick which carters make with their whips, hempknockers with their beetels . . . , smithes with their hammers', he seems to have been referring both to the rhythmic sound of the tools and to the accompanying singing, as if the two were inextricably bound. The same point was made musically in *A Merry New Catch of All Trades*:

The Taylor sowes, the Smith he blowes,
The Tinker beates his pan:
The Pewterer ranke, cries tinke a tanke tanke
The Apothecary ranta tan tan.[56]

53 Deloney, *Gentle Craft*, C4r; Shakespeare, *The Winter's Tale*, in *Complete Oxford Shakespeare*, p. 901.

54 John Coperario, *The Maske of Flowers* (London, 1614), B3v–4v; *REED Dorset, Cornwall*, pp. 537–8.

55 Francis Beaumont, *The Knight of the Burning Pestle*, ed. Michael Hattaway (London: Ernest Benn, 1969), p. 54; Fox, *Oral and Literate Culture*, pp. 29–30.

56 Case, *Praise of Musicke*, pp. 44, 76; *Pepys Ballads*, vol. I, p. 164 (Website track 19).

This song seems to evoke the complex, overlapping rhythmic sounds of early modern London at work.

This was all rather masculine, but working women were just as musical. 'Who does not straitwaies imagin upon musick', asked John Case, 'when he hears his maids either at the woolhurdle or the milking pail?' Thomas Deloney's female spinners and carders, not to be outdone by his male weavers, sang while they worked. When the king visits Jack of Newbury's idealised workshop, for example, he listens happily (and patiently) as the toiling maidens chant their thirty-five-verse song, 'two of them singing the ditty, and all the rest bearing the burden [singing the refrain]'.[57] Wye Saltonstall's archetypal country dame liked to spend her winter evenings among her serving girls, 'while they sit round about her spinning, and merrily chanting some old song, that may keepe time with the drawing out of their thred'. In 1653, Dorothy Osborne wrote a letter in which she recounted her delight at hearing ballads sung on the common by 'a great many young wenches' as they sat in the shade, tending to the sheep and cows of their employers. Mistress Osborne's impressions were perhaps conditioned by the romantic ideals of the literary material, for she also noted the profound happiness of the young women (the only problem being that they did not seem to realise just how contented they were).[58]

Not all recreational singers were content to make do with songs written by others or passed down through oral tradition. The composition of musical libels demonstrates just how creative the people of the early modern age could be when the need arose to lampoon and humiliate their least favoured neighbours. In Jacobean Southwark, a large group of labouring people devised and wrote out a song before pinning it over the porch of their enemy. By way of a title, they came up with the rhyme 'Within this doore / Dwelleth a verie notorious whore.' In 1636, Richard Jenkins of Shrewsbury was prosecuted in the ecclesiastical court 'for singing of Rimes against all the men and their wifes or the most parte of them in the parish'.[59] A few years before this, a group of men and women had gathered at an alehouse in Nottingham. The town's official bellman, William Hall, was among them, but his enjoyment came to an abrupt end when a tiler named Henry Eare snatched his bell 'and began to singe a

[57] Case, *Praise of Musicke*, p. 76; Thomas Deloney, *The Pleasant History of John Winchcomb, in his Younger Years Called Jack of Newbury*, in Paul Salzman (ed.), *An Anthology of Elizabethan Prose Fiction* (Oxford: Oxford University Press, 1987), pp. 350–4.

[58] Wye Saltonstall, *Picturae Loquentes* (1631; London, 1635), no. 28; Osborne, quoted by Würzbach, *The Rise of the English Street Ballad*, p. 278.

[59] Fox, *Oral and Literate Culture*, p. 317; *REED Shropshire*, p. 323.

songe of the Bellman of Saint Peeter's and Madge of the Tylehouse, and such like ribble rabble'. The song was locally composed, but Eare, when pressed, would say only that he had learned it from a fellow tiler 'on the Lowe Pavemente'.[60] Comparable creativity existed all over the country, and there were individuals in many communities who earned reputations for libellous inventiveness. Husbandmen, wheelers, weavers, masons, barbers, maidens and children were all at it, displaying the capacities both to compose and to perform their own songs. Fortunately, we will later have cause to attend to their efforts a little more closely.[61]

Of course, the gentry sang too and they did what they could to sing differently. In 1660, Higford advised them that singing was in fact superior to the music of instruments, being a direct and natural gift of God. He added, 'But you will be most compleat, when you joyn the vocal and the instrumental both together.' To this end, Higford recommended a book of four-part psalms: 'When you are oppressed with serious and weighty business, to take your viol and sing to it, will be a singular ease and refreshment.'[62] Four-part singing from the printed page, to the accompaniment of viols, was an activity calculated to set the gentry apart from the masses, and the same was true of lute songs and madrigals. As usual, however, the necessary involvement of occupational musicians combined with the musical appetites of the upwardly mobile middle orders to endanger the distinction. Other forms of vocal music were significantly less successful as markers of social separation. Three-men's songs, though associated with lowly artisans, had been fashionable at the Henrician court and prominent within Tudor interludes. The status of ballads was similarly ambiguous. Even the alehouse song was not quite the monopoly of the menial: in the 1690s, the minor Suffolk gentleman William Coe regularly sat up late in local inns, 'takeing delight in filthy and wanton discourse and unchast songs'.[63] It is unlikely that he drank and sang alone.

Catches were equally successful in traversing the boundaries of social status, particularly among men.[64] A unique insight into the catch-singing habit of one gentry family is afforded by the manuscript roll of songs 'Collected and gathered by Thomas Lant' in 1580. This intriguing source

[60] *Records of the Borough of Nottingham*, vol. IV, pp. 379–80. [61] See below, pp. 272–6.
[62] Higford, *Institution of a Gentleman*, pp. 78–80.
[63] *Two East Anglian Diaries*, ed. Matthew Storey (Woodbridge: Boydell Press, 1994), p. 211.
[64] On catches, see Eric Ford Hart, 'The Restoration Catch', *Music and Letters* 34 (1953), 288–305, and Stacey Jocoy, 'The Role of the Catch in England's Civil Wars', in Barbara Haggh (ed.), *Essays on Music and Culture in Honor of Herbert Kellman* (Minerve: Centre d'Études Supérieures de la Renaissance, 2001), pp. 325–34.

can now be set into a precise context for the first time.[65] Lant lived an interesting and varied life: he spent part of his childhood singing in the Chapel Royal before serving as page to Richard Cheyney, Bishop of Gloucester; in adult life, he travelled to the Low Countries in the service of Sir Philip Sidney until the latter's death there in 1586, and he also spent time in the employ of Sir Francis Walsingham; Lant devised the famous engravings of Sidney's extraordinary funeral, published a book of prayers and worked for twelve years at the College of Heralds. For now, however, our primary interest is in Lant's whereabouts in 1580. The collection of catches was, it seems, a product of a three-year period in the service of Lord Cheyney of Tuddington (Bedfordshire) between about 1578 and 1581. Independent evidence suggests that the Cheyneys were a musical family with an interest in recreational participation. In 1613, H. Lichfield dedicated his *First Set of Madrigals* to Lady Cheyney, reporting that she had listened contentedly when they were 'presented by the Instruments and voyces of your owne familie'.[66] It therefore seems probable that Lant collected and recorded his catches for use within this aristocratic context.

Lant introduces his collection thus: 'Here are within this rowle divers fine Catches, otherwise called Rounds of 3, 4 and 5 parts in one, of 9 & 11 parts in one, with many songs to passe away the tyme in honest mirth & solace.' He advises prospective performers to 'Sing, tune well, Hould fast, geve eare, / And you shall finde good musicke heare'. His remarks encourage us to imagine a small group of singers clustered around the manuscript, though the narrowness of the roll and the small handwriting may imply an assumption that the performers would memorise the short songs. The catches themselves cover an interesting range of subjects: drink and good fellowship; bell-ringing and calls to divine service; singing and the sol-fa system of musical tuition; traditional carols; birdsong; allegiance to Elizabeth I; extracts from liturgical psalms; gender relations; prayers; life at sea; the advertising cries of street vendors; hunting with hounds; lullabies; an appeal to Pope Nicholas to pray for the souls of the singers; and an equally traditional call upon the living to remember the soul of a

[65] Thomas Lant's roll of catches, MS Rowe 1, King's College, Cambridge. Lant's biography has been reconstructed from the following sources: 'The Observations and Collections of Tho: Lant Portcullis, Concerning the Office and Officers of Armes', fos. 2r–3r, College of Arms, London; letter from Lant to Lord Burghley (1590s), transcribed in John Anstis, 'Officers of Arms', vol. III, p. 156, College of Arms, London; Lant, *Sequitur celebritas and Pompa funeris* (London, 1587); Lant, *Daily Exercises of a Christian, Gathered and Collected out of the Holy Scripture* (London, 1590). There were also a number of musical Lants at the University of Oxford in this period, but I have so far been unable to confirm their connection with Thomas.

[66] H. Lichfield, *First Set of Madrigals of 5 Parts* (London, 1613), dedicatory epistle.

lesser-known individual named John Cooke. Most of the texts are in English, though several are wholly or partly in Latin, French or Italian (there is also some mixing of languages within individual songs). It is notable that many of the songs were presumably drawn from Lant's childhood career at the Chapel Royal and Gloucester Cathedral.

The tutorial tone that Lant adopted for his introductory remarks may suggest that he imagined himself in the role of teacher and director, co-ordinating the efforts of assorted family members and servants to sing his catches. Many of the songs aimed clearly at fostering an intense sense of community and an atmosphere of equality, however transient, among individuals of higher and lower social rank. The fifty-first catch, for example, is a manly drinking song that opens with the mutually affectionate lines, 'Troule troule the bowle to me, / & I will troule the same agayn to thee' (**Website track 5 and Appendix**).[67] Lant's catches may thus afford us a unique opportunity to investigate the Elizabethan culture of aristocratic singing. His roll is an important source, and seems to have exerted some mysterious influence on the many printed collections of catches that appeared during the seventeenth century. It is a remarkable and mildly perplexing fact that forty-eight of Lant's fifty-seven songs also appeared in the famous catch books published by Thomas Ravenscroft between 1609 and 1611.[68] These books, and many others like them, were clearly popular among the gentry, though their commercial success also suggests the existence of a market among the wealthier middling sorts. Catches were the music of everyman.

Carols were even more clearly an instrument of social unity, though their religious content also ensured a measure of controversy. These festive songs had roots in the late medieval period, when they were sung not only at Christmas but on other feast days too. The carolling habit clearly survived the Reformation, though the term itself came increasingly to be associated primarily with Christmas (the financial accounts of one early sixteenth-century bookseller in Oxford reveal that the peak month for the purchase of single sheet carols was already December).[69] It can be assumed that many old carols simply continued to sound, despite the periodic opposition of puritans – most forceful in the years between 1645 and 1660 – to the customary celebration of Christmas. In the early 1620s,

[67] Thomas Lant's roll of catches, MS Rowe 1, no. 51, King's College, Cambridge.

[68] Thomas Ravenscroft, *Pammelia. Musicks Miscellanie* (London, 1609); *Deuteromelia*; and *Melismata. Musicall Phansies* (London, 1611).

[69] *The Day-book of John Dorne, Bookseller in Oxford, A.D. 1520*, ed. F. Madan, *Oxford Historical Society*, 1st series (1885), pp. 71–177.

somebody saw fit to transcribe one onto the opening leaf of an ecclesiastical court book in Nottingham. It was designed for Twelfth Night and began 'Farewell good Christmas / adue adue [a]due.'[70] Throughout the early modern period, authors also published collections of carols, some gathered from common use and others apparently composed afresh. From the Elizabethan period, these were regularly set to popular ballad tunes in order to promote their use. John Rhodes included some in his *Countrie Mans Comfort*, first published in 1588. In 1630, the clergyman William Slatyer published a set of metrical psalms, 'Intended for Christmas Carols, and fitted to divers of the most noted and common, but solemne tunes, every where in this Land familiarly used and knowne'. This was an interesting attempt to create carols suitable for committed Protestants, but Slatyer's decision to mix Scriptural texts and profane tunes was to prove controversial.[71]

Others wisely avoided this combustible combination, and further collections of more traditional carols were published during the mid-seventeenth century. Festive singers could find suitable material in a number of pamphlets. One collection of 1642 bore the tempting title *Good and True, Fresh and New, Christmas Carols*, and contained eleven songs that followed closely the unfolding of the festival. There were two carols for Christmas Day, two for St Stephen's Day, two for St John's Day, two for Innocents' Day, one for New Year's Day, one for Twelfth Day and finally 'A modest Carol for any of the Twelve dayes, or to be sung at any time of the yeere'. Throughout, a careful balance was achieved between the sacred and social dimensions of the festival, and the overall purpose of the collection was to join 'Modesty with mirth', 'And let each Christian merry make / For Jesus Christ our Saviours sake.' On Innocents' Day, for example, carollers could sing in gory detail of Herod's fearful massacre of infants before raising their spirits with a song that celebrated festive hospitality (**Website tracks 11 and 12 and Appendix**).[72]

It is difficult to establish whether such songs were truly 'fresh and new', or merely revised versions of existing carols. Certainly, their content sounded thoroughly traditional, often presupposing performance by

[70] 'Extracts from the Act Books of the Archdeacon of Nottingham', ed. R. B. F. Hodgkinson, *Transactions of the Thoroton Society* 30 (1926–7), 40–57. The history of carols can be explored in the following works: *Medieval Carols*, ed. John Stevens, *Musica Britannica* 4 (1958); Hutton, *Rise and Fall of Merry England*, pp. 14, 58; Watt, *Cheap Print*, pp. 14, 64–5, 113, 121.

[71] John Rhodes, *Countrie Mans Comfort, or Religious Recreations* (1588; London, 1637), D7r–E6r. On Slatyer, see below, pp. 420–1.

[72] *Good and True, Fresh and New, Christmas Carols* (London, 1642), A7r–8r.

grateful tenants or servants at a Christmas feast laid on by a benevolent master and his dame. Healths are drunk to friendly neighbours, and wassail bowls are passed around among the company. In religious terms, the emphasis is upon colourful narrative rather than advanced theological reflection, and the frontispiece carries a woodcut picture of the Madonna and child, flanked by angels. Furthermore, the first carol in the collection hints at the medieval dramatic custom of presenting Joseph as an old fool who suspects his saintly wife of adultery. The social message of the carols is equally customary, emphasising the pursuit of unity through the tried-and-tested combination of mirth, meat and music. Carol collections of the later seventeenth century maintained this solid tradition.[73]

Carol-singing was evidently a widespread seasonal recreation, and it remained so despite the reforming efforts of puritans.[74] One of the period's many Robin Hood ballads refers to the role of the carol as an essential preliminary to Christmas feasting. A squire welcomes his lesser neighbours into his house, adding, 'But not a Man here shall taste my March-Beer, / till a Christmas-Carrol be sung.' The guests listen attentively to his words, 'Then all clapt their hands, & they shouted & sung / till the Hall and the Parlor did ring.' In one chapbook, Laurence Price imagines a personified Christmas travelling from house to house, seeking hospitality and entertainment. A miser sends him away, but a tradesman promises a joyously sociable celebration during which 'my maid Margaret shall sing three melodious Carrols of several pleasant Tunes, and so we'll be higly pigly one with another'. Of course, this sounds hideously quaint to modern ears, but the final phrase suggests once again the role of music in helping to engineer a temporary and invigorating release from the normal rules of hierarchical interaction. 'Me thinks I shall fare like a Prince, and sit in gallant state', exclaims the singer in a carol of 1642, while another tells the landlord, perhaps a little presumptuously, 'I here am come as a bold Guest, / And know Ime welcome to your Feast.'[75] For these and other reasons, the English people – poor and rich – were not to be deprived of their Christmas songs.

[73] See, for example, *New Carolls for this Merry Time of Christmas* (London, 1661) and *Christmas Carolls* (London, 1674).

[74] On these efforts, see Christopher Durston, 'Puritan Rule and the Failure of Cultural Revolution, 1645–1660', in Christopher Durston and Jacqueline Eales (eds.), *The Culture of English Puritanism, 1560–1700* (Basingstoke: Macmillan, 1996), pp. 219, 223–4.

[75] *Pepys Ballads*, vol. II, p. 116; Laurence Price, *Make Room for Christmas All You that Do Love Him* (London, *c.* 1686), p. 5; *Good and True*, A4r, A8r.

Given the vibrancy of England's song culture, it is not surprising that some of the technical vocabulary associated with commonplace vocal music found its way into the general language of mirth and metaphor. The visitor who was reluctant to bid a host farewell could be said to have 'sung loth to depart' (referring to a tune title), even when literal music was not involved.[76] In 1580, an apologist for the allegedly heretical Family of Love employed an extended musical metaphor to describe the extraction of a public confession from fellow members, one of whom had said far too much shortly before dying in mysterious circumstances: 'it is thought some were constrained, to sing a song at Paul's Cross, in which one among the rest, overreached himself so high above his accustomed note, that soone after in quavering, he lost his voyce for ever'. Decades later, John Taylor attacked his rival William Fenner in print, dismissing his best rhymes as 'the highest straine / Thy borrowed stolne invention can attaine'.[77] Such vocabulary was obviously in common currency, reflecting the status of singing as the most frequently experienced of musical activities.

The music lesson

If carols and catches blurred the boundaries between rich and poor, then the formal music lesson – delivered by a visiting expert in return for a fee – should have reasserted and reinforced the distinction. In reality, however, this meeting point of unequals proved just as controversial as all the others. Household accounts indicate that teachers of music were quite generally available to the gentry, particularly if they lived within easy reach of major cities. Typically, their efforts were concentrated upon the younger and/or female members of the household. In 1636, for example, the Le Stranges of Hunstanton (Norfolk) paid £2 to Thomas Brewer 'for Teaching of Roger on the Voyall', and in 1642–3 the steward at Belvoir Castle gave £4 2s 6d to 'the gittarman that taught the Lady Francis for 2 monethes, and for her book'. Families sometimes shared information and recommended teachers to one another. In 1587, Edward Paston wrote to the Earl of Rutland in order to sing the praises of an organist from Norwich, who was ideally qualified to teach his daughter to play the virginals: 'your L. shall hardlie get the like. I have good experience of his

[76] *A Relation of a Short Survey of 26 Counties*, p. 9.

[77] *An Apology for the Service of Love* (London, 1656), p. 5; Taylor, *All the Workes*, vol. II, p. 320.

honestie and good condycion.'[78] Many examples featuring teachers at work in gentry households could be cited, and in almost all cases we can safely assume a very substantial discrepancy between the social origins of tutor and pupil. This has interesting implications for the cultural traffic in tunes and techniques that connected the constituent sections of society. Musical accomplishment helped to set the gentry apart from the lower orders, yet they relied upon individuals with roots in the lower orders to show them how. This contradiction threw up another. The gentry, in order to distinguish themselves from their teachers, generally heeded the advice that they should avoid public performance and the cultivation of unseemly expertise.

All in all, a music lesson was a complicated encounter: social superiors placed visiting inferiors in a position of artistic authority over them, then reasserted their own social superiority by preserving their technical inferiority. The situation was further complicated by the fact that, on many occasions, the socially superior pupil was a girl or young woman, and thus – according to two further hierarchies – inferior to her teacher. Music tutors had to choose their words carefully when addressing their charges, striking an appropriate balance between authority and deference. When Edward Lowe presented a female pupil with some written virginal music, he was suitably cautious:

> Most vertuous M[ist]ris Barbara.
>
> I humbly beseech you to play thes Lessons in the Order sett downe Constantly once a day, if you have health and leasure. Play not, without turninge the Lesson in your Booke before you & keep your eye (as much as you can) in your Booke. If you Chance to miss goe not from the Lesson, till you have perfected it. Above all, Play not too fast. Thes few rules observed you will gaine your selfe much Honnour & some Creditt to your master.[79]

The 'master' in this case gives every indication that he was walking a cultural tight-rope in his contact with the young 'mistress' (see Figure 4.2).

Complications of this sort clearly did not dissuade many members of the gentry and aristocracy from organising musical tuition for their daughters. In Peter Erondell's *The French Garden*, published in 1605, a young and exemplary gentlewoman describes her daily routine: 'Our

[78] Le Strange accounts, LEST/P5, p. 123, NRO (on Brewer, see above, p. 168); *Manuscripts of His Grace the Duke of Rutland*, vol. IV, p. 532; Price, *Patrons and Musicians*, p. 97.

[79] Percy Scholes, *The Puritans and Music*, p. 163. On a slightly later period, see Richard Leppert, *Music and Image: Domesticity, Ideology and Socio-cultural Formation in Eighteenth-century England* (Cambridge: Cambridge University Press, 1988), pp. 58–9.

Figure 4.2. The music teacher who visited a wealthy household was both a menial servant and a figure of authority. Here, he stoops submissively while pointing a little sharply at his demure young pupil. The sexual tensions of the encounter – unspoken and unspeakable – are also expressed through the interplay of openings and closures (the virginals and their key, the sensuous painting on the wall with its half-drawn curtain, the girl's tightly laced bodice and the door which must not be shut). © Wallace Collection, London/Bridgeman Art Library, TWC 62159, Jan Steen, *The Harpsichord Lesson* (*c.* 1660–9).

dauncing Maister commeth about nine a clocke: one singing Master, and he that teacheth us to play on the virginalles, at tenne: he that teacheth us on the Lute and the Violl de Gambo, at foure a clocke in the after noone.' This was excessive, but probably not beyond the parameters of the familiar. Music, said Burton, was 'A thing ... frequently used, and part of a Gentlewomans bringing up, to sing, and dance, and play on the Lute, or some such instrument, before she can say her Pater noster, or ten Commandements, 'tis the next way their parents thinke to get them husbands'. In 1658, Richard Flecknoe was more openly scornful of the young country gentlewomen, living in remote villages, who 'have the worst Masters can be got, for love or money; learning to quaver instead of singing, hop instead of dancing, and rake the Ghitar, rumble the Virginals, and scratch and thrumb the Lute, instead of playing neatly and handsomely'.[80] Music was also central to the curriculum of the girls' boarding schools that were established during the seventeenth century for the daughters of the gentry. It is well known that a school in Chelsea staged the first production of Purcell's opera *Dido and Aeneas* about 1689. Admittedly, this was an unusually advanced example, but music-making was common in all such schools. When Celia Fiennes visited Shrewsbury in 1698, for example, she noted the existence of 'a very good Schoole for young Gentlewomen for learning work and behaviour and music'. There was a similar establishment in Manchester, 'as good as any in London'.[81]

Music was thus one of the accomplishments that fitted young ladies for marriage, and one of the risks attending the music–courtship association was the possibility that the impressionable female pupil would fall for her accomplished, but socially inferior, male teacher. This was every aristocratic family's nightmare, and occasionally it came true. Early in 1686, for example, Lord Banbury's sister, Frances, caused him and her other relatives extreme concern by marrying 'Abell the singing master'. One-to-one music lessons combined not only melody, harmony and rhythm, but also personal intimacy and the potent cross-currents associated with contradictory relationships of authority and subordination. It is not surprising that inappropriate emotions were sometimes stimulated.[82] One technique that minimised the danger was to employ a female teacher. This does not appear to have been common, but nor was it unknown. During the mid-1650s, the Barringtons of Hatfield Broad Oak (Essex) made several payments to Rebecca Bridge for teaching the young Mistress Anna to play the virginals. She was sometimes referred to as 'Goodwife Bridge', a title that indicates non-gentle status, and it seems that she was also responsible for the schooling of the other Barrington daughters.[83]

Male tutors occasionally featured in stage plays of the period, and their efforts allow us to investigate the teacher–pupil relationship a little further. Most famously, the music lesson occupies a central place in the discourse of harmony, discord, rebelliousness and reclamation that dominates

[80] Peter Erondell, *The French Garden* (London, 1605), F3v; Burton, *Anatomy of Melancholy*, p. 586; Flecknoe, *Enigmatical Characters*, p. 44.

[81] Brailsford, *Sport and Society* p. 234; *The Journeys of Celia Fiennes*, ed. Christopher Morris (London: Cresset Press, 1947), pp. 224, 227.

[82] *The Manuscripts of His Grace the Duke of Rutland*, vol. II, pp. 100–1 (this was John Abell, the famous Scottish countertenor). See also Richard Leppert, *Music and Image*, p. 59, and *The Sight of Sound: Music, Representation and the History of the Body* (Berkeley: University of California Press, 1995), pp. 161–7.

[83] D/DBa A5, fos. 11v, 14v, 17v, ERO.

The Taming of the Shrew. Bianca's love of music is contrasted with Katherina's 'loud alarums', and their divergent temperaments are displayed in their responses to tuition.[84] Their teachers are, of course, Hortensio and Lucentio in disguise, both of whom are intent upon courting Bianca. The tutor–suitor interplay is a fruitful source of humour, and is relevant to the present discussion for two reasons. Firstly, the ability of the two gentlemen to present themselves as teachers suggests again the wide dissemination of musical competence in society's higher ranks. Secondly, the music lesson is clearly imagined as an occasion that will permit intimacy and romance, despite the feigned social inferiority of the teachers (Hortensio refers to his 'trade').[85] Both sisters are aware of their superior status, though they express this awareness in radically contrasting registers. Katherina is distinctly uncooperative, and smashes her lute over Hortensio's head. He tells her father,

I did but tell her she mistook her frets,
And bow'd her hand to teach her fingering,
When, with a most impatient devilish spirit,
'Frets, call you these?' quoth she, 'I'll fume with them.'
And with that word she struck me on the head,
And through the instrument my pate made way,
And there I stood amazed for a while,
As on a pillory, looking through the lute,
While she did call me rascal fiddler
And twangling Jack, with twenty such vile terms,
As she had studied to misuse me so.[86]

This is a delectably complex image. A gentleman, pretending to be a lowly music teacher, is made to feel like a law-breaking common fiddler by being pilloried through his own lute, a courtly instrument. The insults that Kate chooses to hurl are calculated to emphasise the comparatively low social status of the music teacher, yet Hortensio's report also captures something of the bodily intimacy between pupil and tutor that a lesson allowed. Katherina's outburst is triggered by Hortensio's attempt to 'bow . . . her hand', an expression that presumably implies tactile contact.

Bianca is different. In her lesson, she must respond to and manage the tensions between the two rival music tutors as they jockey for position, and this she does with effortless calm and a natural air of playful superiority:

[84] Shakespeare, *The Taming of the Shrew*, ed. Brian Morris (London: Routledge, 1981), pp. 176–7.
[85] Ibid., p. 221. [86] Ibid., p. 204.

And, to cut off all strife, here sit we down.
Take you your instrument, play you the whiles;
His lecture will be done ere you have tun'd.

She remains unruffled as the two men compete for her attention, and flirts only a little as first one and then the other begins his musical advance. The lesson itself never progresses as far as actual lute-playing, for Bianca is called away before the preliminaries have been completed. She therefore hears only Lucentio's philosophical lecture on the purpose of music and Hortensio's respectfully delivered instruction on the basics of musical practice:

Madam, before you touch the instrument
To learn the order of my fingering,
I must begin with the rudiments of the art,
To teach you gamut in a briefer sort,
More pleasant, pithy, and effectual,
Than hath been taught by any of my trade.

'Why, I am past my gamut long ago', Bianca objects gently, but her tutor-suitor is not to be dissuaded. Lucentio, jealously looking on, remarks, 'Our fine musician groweth amorous.'[87]

Manuscript music books were one of the fruits of such encounters.[88] Typically, a teacher would copy or compose a series of 'lessons' into the book of a pupil, perhaps adding one or two new pieces at every meeting. Sometimes, such initiatives petered out quickly, perhaps withering under the influence of elite pupil apathy. Christopher Lowther, resident in Hamburg in 1637, obviously had the best of intentions when he carefully prepared his manuscript music book to receive a wide variety of 'lessons'. He was twenty-six years old, and he noted at the front of the book that he had hired a Dutchman to teach him on the lute: 'he is to come to me dayly from 7 of the clocke till nighte (or from 3 till 4 in the after noone ...)'. Lowther divided his book into several sections, each with its own promising heading: 'English Psalmes the choyseste', 'Lutheran Dutch psalmes', 'Calvinist Duch psalmes', 'Melancolicke English Tunes', 'English merry Tunes' and 'Dutch &

[87] Ibid., pp. 219–22.

[88] Extant examples include Priscilla Bunbury's virginal book, Mf. 57, ChRO, and Jane Pickeringe's lute book, Egerton MS 2046, BL. These and other manuscripts are discussed in Price, *Patrons and Musicians*, pp. 195–204, though there is much work still to be done on the precise social contexts in which such sources were produced.

Flemmish merry tunes'. Sadly, Christopher did not see this project through, and most of his pages remained blank.[89]

In other circumstances, the results were more impressive, though many carefully recorded manuscripts are now lost. In 1645, Francis Parker, a gentlemen from Southwell (Nottinghamshire), bequeathed to his niece a book of lute lessons, adding, 'I would have her preserve them [for] her posterity, for they are worthy to be accounted of.' Seven years earlier, the will of Mathias Johnson, another Southwell gentleman, was full of musical references and bequests. Unusually, the clause in which he bequeathed his soul to God anticipated the general resurrection and the prospect of being able 'to singe praise to the sacred Trinitie world without end'. The testator knew that he would not need his instruments nor his written music in the heavenly choir, so he lovingly left these behind him: 'I will & my desire is that my Theorbo lute bee from mee humbly presented to the right honorable my good Lord the Erle of Newcastle', accompanied by 'one booke of Musicke belonging to it written with my owne hand'.[90] Johnson thus took his place in one of the many musical networks that bound together like-minded gents and aristocrats. The Earl of Newcastle was William Cavendish, whose children apparently inherited his musical interests. The name of Charles Cavendish appears on a manuscript music book preserved in the British Library, and Elizabeth Cavendish married musically, attaching herself to the Earl of Bridgewater, a well-known patron, in 1641.[91]

Manuscript tune books of all sorts were the products of an age in which members of the gentry were increasingly aware of the status-enhancing potential of moderate musical accomplishment. In the upper reaches of the social hierarchy, musical literacy was clearly rising, as indicated by the gradual accumulation of written music, both in manuscript and in print. Some families not only employed teachers but appointed agents to track down music for them, and many more recorded in their accounts and correspondence the purchase of music books.[92] Sir William More of Loseley House (Surrey) provides an early example. In 1569, Thomas Coppeley sent him, in manuscript, 'an Italian song well sett to the lute … for the gentlewoman your daughter to sing'. He added, 'I thinke

[89] MS Mu 688, Fitzwilliam Museum, Cambridge.

[90] PRSW 70/24 and 65/26, Nottinghamshire Archives.

[91] Sloane MS 3992, BL; Betty S. Travitsky, 'Egerton, Elizabeth, Countess of Bridgewater (1626–1663)', *Oxford Dictionary of National Biography* (Oxford: Oxford University Press, 2004), http://www.oxforddnb.com/view/article/68253, last accessed 1 April 2010.

[92] Price, *Patrons and Musicians*, pp. 18–19.

youe will leeke [like] it well if youe have it not allready.' In the event of such duplication, Coppeley promised that he would 'caus to be pricked foorth [written out] songes for her wch I thinke youe have not'. He flattered Sir William by commenting that 'Shee & the rest of your Children doe so well that they are woorthy to have good Muzicke putt in to their handes for they will (I see) make good delivery therof.' Coppeley was also in possession of some 'very excellent Neapolitanes of iiii partes' and promised to pass on copies of the best of them, 'if Mr Pakington cann sett them foorthe to the virginalles or lute'. More's young son would then be able to sing the treble part, with instrumental accompaniment. 'And if I have any other Muzicke, or other thing that may please youe or yours youe shall Commawnd it.' The letter reveals not only the escalating fashion for Italian music and the growing expectation that young members of the gentry should be musically educated, but also the sycophantic value of musical manuscripts within relationships of patronage and deference. Coppeley's tone is both hopeful and worshipful: he clearly intends the songs to earn him credit in the eyes and ears of a powerful acquaintance.[93]

Composers, many of whom doubled as teachers, cast additional light on the role of practical music in the lives of the gentry by dedicating numerous publications to their patrons. Typically, the musicians played their parts with expertise, crawling on their bellies in order to praise the unique musical insight of the recipient, and sometimes comparing it favourably with the ignorance of others. For such well-judged words, they could hope to earn approximately £5 from their patrons.[94] John Wilbye dedicated his *Second Set of Madrigales* to Lady Arabella Stuart in 1609, referring regretfully to 'these times when Musick sits solitary among her sister Sciences and (but for your Honour) often wants the fortune to be esteemed (for she is worthy) even among the worthyest'. Many other epistles were variations upon this theme. In 1659, for example, Christopher Simpson lamented music's persecuted status but offered profound gratitude to Sir Robert Bolles for offering 'That innocent, and now distressed Muse ... a chaste, a cheerfull Sanctuary' within his walls. Music was invariably in trouble, and each particular patron was its solitary saviour. Of course, it would not be wise to accept such testimony as reliable evidence either of a patron's prowess or of the musical apathy of his or her social equals. We can assume that most dedicatory epistles exaggerated both the former and the latter. On the other hand, it is clear that the musical leaders of high society not only heard music but played and sang

[93] LM/COR/3/106, SHC. [94] Price, *Patrons and Musicians*, p. 185.

it too. When J. Farmer dedicated his *First Set of English Madrigals* to the Earl of Oxford in 1599, he was effusive in his praise of the great man: 'for without Flatterie be it spoke ... that using this science as a recreation, your Lordship have overgone most of them that make it a profession'.[95] This was dangerous ground, for eminent aristocrats were not supposed to emulate jobbing musicians.

Of course, there must also have been families who resisted the temptation to participate in recreational music-making. The household accounts of the Revell family in Derbyshire, for example, contain no references to musical tuition or recreational participation during the early seventeenth century (though many documents are evidently missing from the original series).[96] Others learned their music, but not with any particular enthusiasm. Sir Thomas Gresham, founder of the London lectureships, was clearly a man of music, but his married daughter Anne hardly sounded keen when she wrote to him in 1572. Her surly tone will be familiar to many modern parents: 'My husbande causethe me to use my singinge, & besides to learne some songes upon the virginalles. I writ this the rather because you willed me not to forget my songes. I am driven to borowe virginalles to learne upon.' Decades later, Robert Burton would refer to the young women who gave up their music lessons once they had acquired husbands. Virginals and virginity were put aside at the same time. Before marriage, said Burton, maidens took 'such pains to sing, play and dance, with such cost and charge to their parents'. Once married, however, they would 'scarce touch an instrument'.[97]

The gentry, despite their exclusive aspirations, could no more keep formal musical tuition to themselves than they could restrict the movements of courtly instruments. Evidence of music lessons in the middling ranks of society is difficult to find, though it seems likely that this reflects the rarity of meticulously recorded account books rather than a genuine lack of provision. Other sources suggest that, by the seventeenth century, music lessons were available for those who desired them. When Playford published *A Musicall Banquet* in 1651, he attached to his mixed menu of pieces a list of twenty-seven 'excellent and able' tutors who were available

[95] Wilbye, *Second Set of Madrigals*, dedicatory epistle; Christopher Simpson, *The Division-violist* (London, 1659), dedicatory epistle; J. Farmer, *First Set of English Madrigals* (London, 1599), dedicatory epistle.

[96] D37 M/RE2, DRO.

[97] *Papers of Nathaniel Bacon of Stiffkey ... 1556–77*, ed. A. Hassell Smith, G. M. Baker and R. W. Penny, *Norfolk Record Society* 46 (1979), p. 26; Burton, quoted by Price, *Patrons and Musicians*, p. 40.

for house-calls in London. During this period, Solomon Eccles was earning £130 a year in the city, teaching its citizens to play the virginals and viol. The music lesson was an institution sufficiently familiar to take its place in the bawdy innuendo of the ballad-writers. In a song of 1675, a young London maiden resists the advances made by men 'of all sorts and trades'. To the tune of 'Traps delight' or 'I know what I know', she sings about the occasion upon which

A Master of Musick came with an intent,
To give me a Lesson on my Instrument,
I thankt him for nothing, and bid him be gone,
For my little Fiddle should not be plaid on:
My thing is my own, and I'le keep it so still,
Yet other young Lasses may do what they will.[98]

Those who lived beyond the reach of the capital city cannot have found it so easy to employ teachers, but we need not descend into pessimism. The tutors who visited the homes of the gentry must have been alert to the possibility that others in a locality – whether through musical aptitude or social aspiration – might also seek lessons. In 1631, one scornful author said of the archetypal farmer's daughter, 'if shee learne to playe on the Virginalls, 'tis thought a Courtlike breeding'. Such customers did not, in general, keep records and so we must rely for illumination on occasional shafts of light. In 1614, for example, Edward Stockley of Prescot (Lancashire) bequeathed to his son 'an old paire of virginalls & Lute to teach the Children on untill they be readie to goe to be prentisses'. He did not say who was to teach them, apparently feeling that the availability of tuition could be taken for granted. In other cases, the information is a little more precise, and it suggests that teachers could often be found within a provincial neighbourhood. In 1586, godly surveyors of the ministry in Warwickshire were unhappy with the qualifications of Henry Flatche, the curate of Snitterfield. They conceded that he was an honest man, but 'far unfit for the ministerie'. He was poorly educated and unable to preach, and, to cap it all, 'he teacheth to plaie on instrumentes'.[99] Flatche was not, however, quite as dangerous as George Hooper, the musical constable of Crewkerne (Somerset) who, in 1600, impregnated Grace Maysters of

[98] John Playford, *A Musicall Banquet* (London, 1651), unpaginated section at front of book; Eccles, *A Musick-lector*, pp. 9–10; *Pepys Ballads*, vol. III, p. 17.

[99] Saltonstall, *Picturae loquentes*, F2r; *REED Lancashire*, p. 81; *Minutes and Accounts of the Corporation of Stratford-upon-Avon and Other Records, 1553–1620*, 5 vols., *Publications of the Dugdale Society* 1, 3, 5, 10, 35 (1921–90), vol. IV, p. 3.

nearby South Petherton. In this case, both parties were presented to the church court, where the scribe noted, 'the man is cunstable of the parish, she did ... goe to Crewkerne to learn to play uppon the virginalls wheare the said Hooper was verie familiar'. Grace's father, hoping to protect the family from shame, had since 'conveyd her away'. A few years later, a schoolmaster's daughter from Wells (Somerset) was learning to play the lute under the guidance of a local man named William Tidderleigh. She did not become pregnant, and we know of the relationship only because Tidderleigh was also caught up in the extraordinary confrontation that rocked this cathedral city in the summer of 1607. Unusually, the tutor in this case was a gentleman and thus of much higher social status than his pupil.[100]

Men and women of modest wealth were also an important component of the market for printed instruction manuals. Some of these were expressly designed to bring elementary tuition to the geographically disadvantaged, and the pieces they contained were commonly termed 'lessons'. Musical publishing developed more slowly in England than on the continent, and tended to experience periods of stagnation. Nevertheless, a substantial number of books for amateurs did appear, and there is little doubt that commercially minded publishers and authors realised quickly that they did not have to rely exclusively on the aspirations of the aristocracy and gentry (though their works were almost invariably dedicated to such people). Thomas Robinson's *Schoole of Musicke*, published in 1603, aimed to spare readers the cost of hiring teachers as they took their first steps on the lute, bandora, orpharion or viola da gamba. He promised to show them 'how you may be your owne instructor ... , without any other teacher'. Robinson may have had in mind the recreational musicians for whom regular payments to visiting tutors were close to the limit of what seemed affordable. The same objective surely lay behind many of the instruction manuals for aspirant instrumentalists that were published throughout the period. Their authors set their sights on those who wished to learn 'by their own industrie'. In 1599, Richard Allison provided an easy cittern accompaniment for his psalm settings, and designed his book 'for the use of such as are of mean skill, and whose leysure least serveth to practize'. Half a century later, John Playford carried this intent to a new level, and for decades thereafter he exploited the market for music that existed in the bustling middle ranks of English society with remarkable energy and success. Playford offered printed

[100] *REED Somerset*, pp. 85, 295, 351.

tuition for amateurs keen to play viols, violins, citterns, virginals and flageolets. From the start of his career, he knew that a broad market existed. In 1652, for example, Playford's *Booke of Newe Lessons for the Cithern and Gittern* included a scatter-gun combination of bawdy songs, sacred psalms and military melodies associated with both the Roundheads and the Cavaliers.[101]

A small selection of the surviving hand-written music manuscripts from the period can probably be attributed to members of the 'better sort' in their localities, though it is generally difficult to establish whether the tutors of these obscure musicians were books or humans. Clement Matchett had been admitted to Caius College, Cambridge, in 1609, and his temporary residence in that famously musical city must have given him access to expert tuition. It may also have encouraged an interest in creating his own modest collection of music, and this son of a Norwich schoolmaster duly compiled a virginal book in about 1612. It contains eleven pieces, most of them settings of popular Elizabethan tunes such as 'The whistling carman' and 'Fortune my foe'. Four of the compositions are anonymous, but Matchett was also in a position to transcribe seven works by William Byrd, John Bull and John Wilbye. This young musician was a Catholic, and by no means the only one to reveal an interest in recording keyboard music, a significant proportion of which was composed by co-religionists.[102] Richard Mynshall's manuscript is equally intriguing. Somehow, this Elizabethan teenager from Nantwich (Cheshire) acquired a blank lute book, embossed on its cover with the queen's arms. It had apparently been designed for use at court before being mysteriously diverted some way to the north-west. Mynshall, the son of a mercer, was evidently learning to play the lute, and he transcribed into his book – untidily and with errors – some forty relatively simple pieces. The repertoire was dominated by popular ballad and dance melodies, including 'Spanish pavian [pavane]', in a setting by the local composer Francis Pilkington, and 'Fortune [my foe]', arranged by John Dowland (**Website tracks 6 and 7**

[101] Thomas Robinson, *Schoole of Musick* (London, 1603), title page; *Most Perfect and True Instruction* (London, 1593), title page, quoted by Dart, 'The Cittern and its English Music', 51–2; Richard Allison, *The Psalmes of David in Meter* (London, 1599), title page; John Playford, *Booke of Newe Lessons* (London, 1652). John Milsom argues convincingly that there was already a lively market for printed part-songs in London during the 1520s. See his 'Songs and Society in Early Tudor London', *Early Music History* 16 (1997), 235–93.

[102] *Clement Matchett's Virginal Book*, ed. Thurston Dart (London: Stainer and Bell, 1963). See also Price, *Patrons and Musicians*, pp. 195–6. The Fitzwilliam book is, of course, the most famous example of a keyboard manuscript that was strongly associated with English Catholicism.

and Appendix).[103] There were other comparable manuscripts, but in many cases we currently know little or nothing about the personal circumstances of those who compiled manuscripts. Often we are given just a name. 'Joseph Palmer of Cropready' was probably the man who transcribed several Dowland lute songs during the early seventeenth century. Dowland also featured, along with John Jenkins and others, in the manuscript compiled at some point in the mid-seventeenth century by 'Thomas and Richard Shinton of Wolverhampton'.[104]

'Elizabeth Rogers hir Virginal Book' is a particularly stimulating example, and it enables us to consider a little more closely the complexities of the music lesson. The woman who signed and dated the manuscript on 27 February 1657 has for years proved elusive but a probable identity can now be tentatively suggested. At the front of the book, she also registered her maiden name, 'Elizabeth Fayre', and many of the musical pieces that formed her repertoire were written out before her marriage to Thomas Rogers, a wealthy Londoner, in 1651. We might also speculate that her teacher was the otherwise unknown virginalist, Thomas Strengthfield, whose name appears alongside several of the compositions carefully recorded in the book (there was certainly a man of this distinctive name in Elizabeth's neighbourhood). If so, then they journeyed together through an undulating musical terrain: marches, trumpet tunes and pieces imitating the sounds of battle; numerous courtly dances, particularly courants, sarabands and almains (**Website track 3 and Appendix**); ballad tunes, vocal psalm settings and several love songs. With the exception of a solitary lullaby, the contents were generally more masculine than feminine. Even the love songs were written from the male perspective, and young Elizabeth must frequently have played the man as she performed before her teacher. One wonders if they experienced a certain frisson as she described in song the characteristics of the perfect woman: 'Yes, I could love; could I but find / a mistress fitting to my mind' (**Website track 4 and Appendix**).[105]

[103] *The Mynshall Lute Book*, ed. Robert Spencer (Leeds: Boethius Press, 1975). For music in the wider Mynshall family and in Nantwich more generally, see Baldwin, *Paying the Piper*, pp. 101–5. Another musical manuscript is discussed in David Mateer, 'Hugh Davies's Commonplace Book: A New Source of Seventeenth-century Song', *Royal Musical Association Research Chronicle* 32 (1999), 63–88.

[104] Price, *Patrons and Musicians*, pp. 196–7.

[105] Add. MS 10337, BL; published as *Elizabeth Rogers hir Virginall Booke*. This paragraph represents work in progress and must, for now, remain somewhat speculative. Elizabeth 'Farr' married Thomas Rogers at St Alphage, London, in 1651. They had two sons, and Elizabeth outlived her husband. Her manuscript is also discussed in Candace Bailey, 'Blurring the Lines: "Elizabeth Rogers hir Virginall Book" in Context', *Music and Letters* 89 (2008), 510–46.

In contrast, the tune book of Henry Atkinson may bear the hallmarks of an individual who progressed in music primarily 'by his own industrie'. His name appears in florid handwriting on the opening page of this interesting and neglected source, along with the date '1694/5'. Beyond this, Henry offers no precise information regarding his whereabouts or his social status, but a good deal can be pieced together by patient toil in the archives. He was born in 1670, the son of a yeoman from Gateshead (County Durham). When he was sixteen, he made the short journey to Newcastle upon Tyne (Northumberland), where he was apprenticed to one of the city's hostmen (middlemen in the coal trade). The mid-1690s were evidently an important period in Henry's life: he became a hostman in his own right, married and started a family. He also wrote his name into the tune book, though it is possible that he had noted his first melodies a year or two earlier. Occasionally, Henry used his book in order to record the names of his family members or to make monetary calculations. Indeed, business went well, and, during the next thirty years, Henry established himself as an important figure in Newcastle. He trained many apprentices, contributed to the founding of a charity school in 1709 and even assisted the antiquarian Henry Bourne in preparing his published history of the city. Henry Atkinson died in 1759 and was described in the *Newcastle Courant* as a man 'whose Character in publick and private Life has left his Memory an Honour to Trade, dear to Friends, and exemplary to all'.[106]

How, then, does Atkinson's home-made music book fit into this model life story? Its origins were clearly associated with the phase during which the boy from a farming background came of age in the city. He may well have learned music before 1694, but one look at the front page of his book confirms that this was a special and upward moment in his career. Henry presumably derived recreational pleasure from his melodies, but it also seems likely that he understood the acquisition of musical skills and the ability to record tunes as signals of high status. His book was an educational enterprise as well as a repository of tunes, and the music it contained was evidently designed for performance on the violin (certainly not

[106] This potted biography has been assembled from the following sources: 'Henry Atkinson his Book', MS MU 207, Northumberland Record Office (Gosforth); *Extracts from the Records of the Company of Hostmen of Newcastle upon Tyne*, ed. F. W. Dendy, *Surtees Society* 105 (1901), pp. 273–9, 288–91; parish registers for Gateshead and all the Newcastle parishes, transcripts available in Central Library, Newcastle upon Tyne; Atkinson ledgers, ZGRx, Northumberland Record Office (Gosforth); Henry Bourne, *The History of Newcastle upon Tyne* (Newcastle upon Tyne, 1736), list of subscribers and p. 102; *Newcastle Courant* (17 February 1759); DPR Henry Atkinson (will, 1759), Durham University, Archives and Special Collections.

the bagpipes, as some have supposed). By this date, the violin had become fashionable among well-heeled amateurs, losing its reputation as an instrument that belonged properly to the occupational musician. At the back of the book, Henry noted some basic information on note values, violin tunings and the musical scale, which suggests that he was in the process of learning how to read and write music. Perhaps he had previously played by ear, but now perceived the social and musical value of being able to perform from the page. Playford's advice was that the truly modern violinist should not content himself with memorising tunes, for to do so was to restrict one's repertoire and thus one's musical potential.[107]

Within Henry's book, the musical handwriting also suggests the work of a learner. In the early stages, there are frequent smudges and errors. He often confuses note values, omits or misunderstands key signatures and adds nonsensical accidentals (additional sharps and flats). In several instances, the tunes as written become incoherent if played without adjustment. Some of his pieces were clearly copied from printed sources, but even here there are occasional mistakes. He transcribes musical symbols without necessarily comprehending their significance. Other tunes were probably recorded from memory and doubtless made perfect sense to Henry, despite the errors. Perhaps he was a musician who moved between aurality and literacy, aspiring to sophistication but for many years insecure in his mastery of the written note. To Henry, it may not have mattered that some of the tunes were incorrectly written: he knew what he meant and probably tended to trust his ear before his eye. As time went on, his penmanship and musical knowledge both improved, and he sometimes wrote out his earlier tunes again in far more polished versions.[108] We know nothing of the contexts within which Atkinson played. The format of the book is ideal for practice, performance and portability: leather-bound and rectangular in shape, with sides measuring 15 cm and 10 cm respectively. It is thus similar in size and design to Playford's *Dancing Master*, a printed work that Henry almost certainly possessed. Perhaps his music-making was a private recreation, though it is also worth noting that the role of a hostman traditionally involved accommodating and entertaining visiting merchants. It is possible, therefore, that he also performed for the pleasure (and economic seduction) of his business associates.

The melodies themselves present a sort of musical diary that spans several decades. Henry wrote out his first melodies in the 1690s, and many

[107] Playford, *An Introduction*, p. 102.

[108] 'Reed House Rant', for example, appears on pp. 6–7 and p. 137.

of the tunes can be shown from other sources to have originated during the years between 1680 and 1700. Some of them, however, can only have been recorded after 1716.[109] All in all, the book contains 188 tunes of many different sorts. There are dance tunes, several of which also appeared in Playford's published collections.[110] On occasion, Henry records a Playford tune, but gives it a different title. Playford's 'Child grove', for example, was evidently known in Newcastle as 'Such a wife as Wille had'. Henry was also a connoisseur of ballad melodies, particularly those that had political (and predominantly royalist) associations. 'Let Mary live long' was such a tune (**Website track 8 and Appendix**). Some of these pieces were written out in simple form, while others were set down as numbered divisions upon the main theme. In these more sophisticated arrangements, Henry was clearly transcribing his music from printed collections such as Playford's *The Division Violin.* From this and other published sources, he also gathered some of the most sophisticated pieces in his book. Typically, the titles identified the composers: 'Minuet Mr Franks', 'Mr Thomas Tollates groundes' and 'Farinells ground' (**Website track 9 and Appendix**). In the latter case, Henry wrote out both the melody and the accompanying ground (a repetitious bass line), but he failed to notice that the second part requires a different clef from the first. Other pieces that must have originated in printed sources include 'Prince Eugins march', which requires the violinist to double-stop the strings (thus producing chords). Of a different order entirely were the numerous tunes that did not appear regularly in published music books. These included locally inspired titles like 'Mineway' and 'Gingling Geordy', and apparently Northumbrian tunes such as 'Claw her warm' and 'The farther be in the welcomer' (**Website track 10 and Appendix**). Finally, the collection displays a strong Scottish influence. Melodies with a Scottish flavour were highly fashionable in London during this period, and some of the tunes that became known as Scottish were actually written for the playhouses of London. Henry recorded one or two of these, but he must certainly have had more authentic sources for some of the 'Jock' tunes he noted.

In short, Henry Atkinson's tune book is a mine of melodies, and it demonstrates the importance attached to the acquisition of musical skills by at least one prosperous townsman. It also reveals the vital significance

[109] 'The Earle of Darwin's Farewell' on pp. 24–5 (pagination from back of book) can probably be related to the execution of the Jacobite third Earl of Derwentwater in 1716. I am grateful to David Hayton for suggesting this possibility.

[110] The tunes from all eighteen editions of Playford's *Dancing Master* are gathered in *Complete Country Dance Tunes from Playford's Dancing Master.*

of middle-ranking recreational musicians as social and cultural mediators. Henry was a broker by occupation, one of the 'fitters' who linked the mine-owners with the merchants at Newcastle's docks. In musical terms, he played a similar role, bridging the potential divides between various groups. He was clearly a man of Newcastle, and he knew the local melodies; yet he also gathered many tunes that had originated on the streets and in the playhouses of London. Presumably, the merchants who visited Newcastle from the south of England helped him to stay in touch. He recorded Northumbrian tunes that must have been played by local fiddlers and pipers; but he also transcribed sophisticated compositions by the leading musicians of his day. In addition, he helped various Scottish melodies on their journey south and perhaps sent English tunes the other way too (one of his melodies was entitled 'The new road to Berwick'). He also connected town and country, and perhaps even Jacobites and loyalists. The melodic juxtapositions are often enlightening. 'London's loyalty' and 'Cocke up thy beaver Jemme' appear on consecutive pages. Elsewhere, town and country are in close proximity with 'Gingling Geordy' and 'The lad that keeps the cattle' (a ledger book kept by Henry reveals that he maintained an economic interest in agriculture throughout his life). He and others like him were cultural cogwheels, vital in maintaining the connections between interest groups whose members might otherwise have grown further apart.[111]

Sadly, we must end this consideration of musical tuition with an inappropriate moment of silence, for there is very little to be said about the music lesson as it was experienced beneath the ranks of the moderately prosperous. No references to tuition on bagpipe or drum have so far come to light. Such tuition must have occurred, but we can only assume that it was organised informally among friends, relatives and neighbours. Parents passed their skills to their children, or called in favours from their wider acquaintances. Records were not kept and money may not even have changed hands. There survives, however, one lute manuscript that perhaps originated in the lower reaches of society during the first half of the seventeenth century. 'John Strickland his Book' was evidently the work of a servant of some sort, for he noted not only the music of John Dowland but the travel expenses of his employer.[112]

[111] For the regional context within which Atkinson lived, see Roz Southey, *Music-making in North-east England during the Eighteenth Century* (Aldershot: Ashgate, 2006).

[112] Add. MS 15, 117, BL (discussed by Price, *Patrons and Musicians*, pp. 196–7).

The music meeting

There is something intimate and private about a manuscript music book. Music has in all ages offered succour to the solitary, and never more so than nowadays. It is equally effective, however, in the expression of communality. Recreational music-making was sometimes a private affair, but in many situations it was a group activity. At the lower levels of society, informality is once again our enemy, though the sources – particularly those that related to singing – suggest the commonplace occurrence of sociable musical gatherings. Instrumental sessions are more elusive, usually coming to light only when the participants attracted suspicion for some reason. One evening in or before 1650, for example, Captain Francis Freeman was invited by one of the parliamentary soldiers under his charge to come and hear some 'excellent music'. After supper in the soldier's quarters, one of the company 'rose from the table, and went to a presse-cupboard, here he took out a fife-recorder and a Citern'. He handed the instruments to an old man and his son, and the two of them 'played half a douzen lessons, very well in consort'. Freeman was impressed and asked the players whether they could 'sing prick-song' (or read musical notation). To this, 'they answered no, but they had some delight to play on these foolish instruments (as they call'd them) and so played three or four lessons more, and lay'd them aside.' There was nothing controversial about this, and Freeman, according to his own account, maintained the momentum by leading the group in a singing session. His first choice was an old song called 'New Oysters', clearly based upon the street cries of London:

> And after I had sung it once or twice over, I set them in their parts, and showed them their time, and strook time for them with my hand, and found them very tractable, for after twice or thrice singing over, they sung their parts and kept their time very well, insomuch, as I conceived, the two men of the house who played on the musick before, were much taken with it and liked our music very well.

We would know nothing of this occasion had not Freeman proceeded to deliver solo renditions of a pair of allegedly bawdy songs entitled 'I met with Joan of Kent' and 'There Dwells a Pretty Maid, her Name is Sis'. When word of the performance later reached the ears of Freeman's colonel, an investigation was inaugurated (the colonel already had his eye on him, suspecting Freeman of holding various heterodox religious beliefs). The singing soldier denied the allegation of lewdness, and appealed to all who knew the titles in question to support him. Indignantly, he declared, 'And truly for my part, I sung mearly for the musick sake, not thinking any hurt at all. Neither had I indeed any evil thought in my heart in singing any of these songs, which my conscience will bear me witness.' Freeman made the mistake of singing suggestive songs within a military milieu which, though not hostile to music *per se*, was nevertheless influenced by radical puritanism and therefore prone to anxiety. We, unlike his colonel, can be thankful that he took the risk, demonstrating in the process that considerable musical accomplishment – practical rather then theoretic – existed in some relatively lowly social settings. The urge to participate and the lure of over-indulgence were equally apparent. When the great scholar Percy Scholes wrote about the case in 1934, he considered the words of Freeman's songs to be unprintable![113]

As we climb the social ladder once more, the sounds of the musical meeting grow louder.[114] From the late sixteenth century onwards, wealthy individuals with musical aspirations and enthusiasms participated in sociable sessions that were also attended by occupational musicians. Most famously, the first published book of madrigals with English words grew out of the meetings hosted by Nicholas Yonge in Elizabethan London. Yonge made a musical living as a lay clerk at St Paul's Cathedral, but many of those who came to his home were 'gentlemen and merchants of good account'. Similar events, precursors of the modern public concert, took place throughout the early modern period. George Herbert's soul may have been elevated most impressively by the music he heard in Salisbury Cathedral, but he was also in the habit of unwinding on the way home by stopping off at a music meeting. He is said to have justified his attendance thus: 'Religion does not banish mirth, but only moderates, and sets rules to it.' Oxford was a crucial centre for such harmonious get-togethers. In 1627, the diarist Thomas Crosfield recorded his attendance at a 'Musick night' in Queen's College, and even listed the songs that were sung.[115] Such gatherings remained a central feature of Oxford's musical life during

[113] Freeman, *Light Vanquishing Darkness* (London, 1650), pp. 18–19; Scholes, *The Puritans and Music*, pp. 146–8; one of the offending songs can be found in John Hilton, *Catch that Catch Can* (London, 1652), p. 63.

[114] On music meetings, see: Ian Spink, 'The Old Jewry "Musick-Society": a Seventeenth-century Catch Club', *Musicology* 2 (1967), 35–41; Bryan White, '"A pretty knot of musical friends": The Ferrar Brothers and a Stamford Music Club in the 1690s', in Rachel Cowgill and Peter Holman (eds.), *Music in the British Provinces, 1690–1914* (Aldershot: Ashgate, 2007), pp. 9–44; H. Diack Johnstone, 'Claver Morris: An Early Eighteenth Century English Physician and Amateur Musician *Extraordinaire*', *Journal of the Royal Musical Association* 133 (2008), 93–127.

[115] Nicholas Yonge, *Musica Transalpina* (London, 1588), dedicatory epistle (see also Woodfill, *Musicians in English Society*, p. 229); Izaak Walton, *The Lives of Dr John Donne . . .*, p. 60; *Diary of Thomas Crosfield*, p. 8.

the 1650s. William Ellis lost his job as a church organist, and subsequently devoted some of his time to the weekly music meetings held at his house. These were attended both by celebrated virtuosi and by accomplished recreational musicians of high social rank.[116] Many miles to the east, Sir Nicholas Le Strange of Hunstanton (Norfolk) was also thoroughly familiar with the concept of a music meeting. He recorded in his book of jests an occasion upon which a certain Mr Saunders had been irritated by the disruptive mumblings of assorted ladies during 'a meeting of Fancy Musick, only for the violes and Organ'. Saunders, evidently a gentleman, rose from his seat, viol in hand, and spoke sharply to the offending section of the audience: 'This Musicke is not vocall, for on my Knowledge, These Things were never made for words.' The put-down may not have been quite as witty as Le Strange believed it to be, but it had the desired effect on the ladies: 'after That they had not one word to say'. Saunders was, it seems, a recreational musician, but the individual who reported the incident to Le Strange was John Jenkins, the carpenter's son who had risen to greatness as a specialist performer, teacher and composer.[117]

By 1660, several music meetings were being held regularly in London too, and they continued to develop in subsequent decades. Some, such as those organised by John Banister, were more like concerts, featuring occupational performers and fee-paying listeners. The famous meetings co-ordinated from 1678 onwards by the entrepreneurial 'small coal-man', Thomas Britton, appear to have been similar. One regular member of the audience was Sir Roger Le Strange, a talented viol player and the younger brother of Sir Nicholas. He and other musical gents attended weekly get-togethers in Britton's cramped and dusty quarters chiefly because of 'the unexpected Genius to Books and Musick that they happen'd to find in their smutty Acquaintance'. This, at least, was the opinion of Ned Ward. The gentlemen were well aware that the coal-man was far inferior to them, but they liked the fact that Britton resisted the temptation to develop ideas above his station. He never gave up his day-job, and 'the Prudence of his Deportment' was a reassurance to his grand guests. The local housewives loved him too, and when he plied his trade in the streets they regarded him as if he had been 'a nobleman in disguise' (Ward's account was charged with playful sociological cross-currents).[118] At other meetings,

[116] Spring, *The Lute in Britain*, p. 327; *The Life and Times of Anthony Wood*, ed. Andrew Clark, 5 vols. (Oxford: Oxford Historical Society, 1891–1900), vol. I, pp. 204–5, 273–5.

[117] Le Strange, 'Merry Passages and Jeasts', p. 144.

[118] *Roger North on Music*, pp. 302–4, 352; Edward Ward, *The Secret History of Clubs* (London, 1709), pp. 349–53; Spink, 'Music and Society', pp. 18–19.

recreational and occupational musicians actually played together. In the Castle Tavern, a society of musical gentlemen came together for 'private diversion', but they also paid a number of 'hired base-violins [violinists] . . . to attend them' and reinforce their performances. Here was yet another forum in which occupational musicians of lowly origins met their social superiors in order to cultivate concord. For a time, individuals from radically divergent backgrounds met, bound fleetingly together as if they were equals in what Ward termed a 'Harmonious society of Tickle-Fiddle Gentlemen'.[119] Music meetings are clearly part of the reason for the impossibility of drawing clear lines between the musical cultures of the gentry and the majority in terms of tastes, tunes and instruments.

In most circumstances, the complex combination of occupational and recreational musicians appears to have produced a satisfactory blend. On occasion, however, the potential for social tension was realised. One fascinating musical meeting of a slightly different kind occurred on the streets of Chester in October 1594. Richard Preston, a musician from Warrington, had come into the city with his company in order to earn some money. Late on a Tuesday evening, he and his fellows were playing their instruments as they walked 'up St warburg lane out of the Eastgate street' on their way back to their lodgings. Along the way, a certain Master William Hicock emerged from a tavern, heard the music, and asked Preston to lend him his treble violin. Hicock clearly did not identify himself at this point as the rector of St Peter's parish, and the musicians appear to have taken him for an accomplished recreational musician. Preston duly handed over his violin and noted with approval that the latest addition to his band 'plaid very excellent well'. The group continued to move along the streets of the city as Preston took another instrument and added a bass part to Hicock's treble. When the musicians reached their lodgings, the vicar-cum-gentleman returned the violin to its owner.

So far so good. At this point, however, the mood of the meeting changed. Preston, having reclaimed his instrument, took his new companion by the cloak and invited him into the house 'to drink with him'. Master Hicock did not like this, clearly interpreting it as a concordant gesture too far. He not only rejected the invitation, but allegedly tripped the musician over so aggressively that his sword was broken in the fall. Hicock then stole the damaged weapon and hurried off towards his own house. Preston followed him, hoping to retrieve his sword but also, it seems, to apologise for his social gaffe. In the musician's own words,

[119] *Roger North on Music*, p. 304; Ward, *Secret History of Clubs*, p. 349.

he 'spake him faier in that he knew not whoe he was'. Hicock, however, was not to be mollified. On entering his home, he locked the door, lit a candle and said, rather bizarrely, 'loe now none can make me cookorlded [cuckolded]'. At the time of the resultant quarter sessions case, Preston had still not regained his weapon.[120]

This case demonstrates that music could build bridges between different social groups, but also that it could generate confusion by muddying the waters of social distinction. Hicock's initial intervention, and its reception by the musicians, revealed the harmonising power of music, but this very power produced contrary reactions once the melodies ceased. For Preston the musician, it seemed momentarily appropriate that the two men, having shared instruments, should now share a drink together in the presumably humble lodgings of the visiting band. For Hicock, however, the dangers of creative co-operation suddenly became apparent, and he lost his temper in seeking to reassert his pre-eminence. Perhaps he regretted his own spontaneous decision to join in the music. After all, eminent men – particularly clergymen – were not supposed to perform in public, nor to play 'very excellent well'. He forgot all this as he emerged from the tavern and, carried away by the mood of the moment, indulged his urge to play. Hicock came to his senses only when the musician dared to touch his cloak and make a socially improper suggestion. Preston too lost his way for a moment, perhaps intoxicated by the boundary-crossing music the two men had just made. Or did the unrestrained public musicianship of the guest performer encourage Preston to underestimate Hicock's social status? It was unfair, but predictable, that the lower-ranking man would be made to pay the price for the misjudgements of them both. The symbolism of the sword may also be significant. It was a weapon supposedly associated with the gentry, and yet here was a mere musician armed to the hilt. We can only guess at the workings of the rector's mind, but it seems possible that, in stealing the sword, he believed himself to be exacting revenge on an uppity underling and/or a disrespectful layman.

Similar underlying tensions must have existed at more formal gatherings. Indeed, it is possible that the music meeting as a coming-together of occupational musicians and gentlemen-practitioners in joint performance was inherently unstable. Both parties had an interest in exaggerating the technical gap that existed between them. For the gentry, it did not do to sound too proficient. For the money-making musicians, in contrast, proficiency was all, and the music they brought to such meetings became

[120] Quarter sessions, Z QSE/5/46, ChRO.

steadily more demanding. In the middle of the century, Nicholas Le Strange was already recording humorous anecdotes about recreational musicians who could not keep up with their occupational brethren. One gentleman noted the preponderance of fast-flowing quavers and semi-quavers on the sheet of music placed before him, and excused himself with a musical pun: 'I see the Air Growes so Blacke, as I know there is a Storme or Tempest coming, and no Shelter or Refuge left for me, but your Indulgence and Dispensation from so Perillous a Taske.' A second tension grew from the need of occupational musicians to earn money by attracting fee-paying listeners from beyond the ranks of the gentry. Occupational players had, in Roger North's words, 'found out the grand secret, that the English would follow musick and drop their pence freely', and they did not care particularly whose coins were falling into their hats.[121] Thomas Britton's concerts were, for example, open to 'any Body that is willing to take a hearty Sweat'. If the audience expanded, then the active participation of aristocrats became even more problematic. During the late seventeenth century, both of these tensions reportedly influenced the development of the Castle Tavern meeting. The music grew more challenging, the public were allowed in, and the gentlemen-musicians ceased to play.[122]

Historians have described the dramatic upsurge in public performance that took place in England between 1660 and 1770. This was an age of concerts, clubs, festivals and purpose-built music rooms.[123] Cecilia, the patron saint of music, was publicly feted as never before or since, and music became the 'principal attention, or great business of a people'. Yet it was also, arguably, the age in which the now familiar relationship between the active professional and the more or less passive audience began to develop. Roger North regretted the trend, and so he over-stated it. Nostalgically, he recalled the days when 'the Art was plain and practicable, and most sober familys in England affected it'. Nowadays, he claimed, most music-lovers had developed a taste for the 'high flights' of established

[121] 'Merry Passages and Jeasts', p. 157; *Roger North on Music*, p. 305 n. 53.

[122] Spink, 'Music and Society', p. 18; *Roger North on Music*, pp. 305, 352. For evidence of eighteenth-century tensions between professionals and amateurs, see Leppert, *Music and Image*, pp. 11–13.

[123] See, for example: 'A Calendar of References to Music in Newspapers Published in London and the Provinces 1660–1719', ed. Michael Tilmouth, *Royal Musical Association Research Chronicle*, 1 (1961), 3–107, and Michael Tilmouth, 'Some Early London Concerts and Music Clubs', *Proceedings of the Royal Musical Association* 84 (1958 for 1957–8), 13–26; Susan Wollenberg and Simon McVeigh (eds.), *Concert Life in Eighteenth-century Britain* (Aldershot: Ashgate, 2004).

professors. Consequently, 'the promiscuous and diffused practise of musick in remote parts about England is utterly confounded'. With music at such 'a pitch of perfection', he concluded sadly, 'the plain way becomes contemptible and ridiculous, [and] therefore must be laid aside'.[124] North was mistaken in implying that recreational music among the social elite was dying, for it continued to thrive throughout the eighteenth century. He was perhaps misrepresenting a perpetual set of tensions as evidence of a disastrous and progressive cultural shift. Even in a dawning age of public concerts and professional celebrities, aristocratic amateurs continued to mix quite freely – if a little uncomfortably – with the experts.

At the music meeting, tensions between occupational and recreational musicians were clearly generated in part by the underlying friction between members of the gentry and the more prosperous of their social inferiors. Where there is togetherness there is trouble, for community breeds both pleasure and pain. In 1714, a music meeting in London was described as 'a mixture of Gentlemen, Lawyers and Tradesmen'. Here, the participants still sang songs together, though the harp music they heard was presumably performed by a specialist. As usual, we can only speculate regarding the nature of the interaction between these varied groups. In a beautifully crafted sentence of two halves, our witness commented, 'Here is nothing drunk but Ale, and every Gentleman hath his separate Mug.' It was necessary to preserve distinctions in the midst of conviviality. Healths were drunk but vessels were not shared. The aristocratic Roger North noted 'an inclination of the citizens to follow musick', but it was not an inclination with which he felt entirely comfortable. He described, for example, the singing sessions held during the 1660s by Ben Wallington in 'a large room in an alehouse, where stood a chamber organ'. Here, 'with help of a dull organist and miserable-singers, folks heard musick out of the Catch-book, and drank ale together'. Wallington himself was a singing goldsmith, whose voice, in North's estimation, was 'literally base and his composition altogether rustic and inartificial'. His companions consisted mainly of 'shopkeepers and foremen'.[125] North's account was shot through with the language of social distancing. The gent scorned the commoner, associating him – despite his urban occupation and residence – with the untrained roughness of a peasant.

[124] Borsay, *English Urban Renaissance*, pp. 121–7; Brailsford, *Sport and Society*, p. 76; *Roger North on Music*, pp. 12, 314.

[125] John Macky, *A Journey through England* (London, 1714), pp. 189–90; *Roger North on Music*, pp. 304, 352.

North believed that tradition was in trouble, but private musical accomplishment nevertheless remained a badge of high status. This association had developed during the reigns of Elizabeth I and James I, when recreational music-making at the pinnacle of the social pyramid became firmly established. By 1669, Edward Chamberlayne was able to list 'Singing' and 'all sorts of Musical Instruments' among the common recreations of the English gentry.[126] During the previous hundred years, musical practice and musical literacy had spread together until it became socially perilous for a gentleman to admit that he could not bear his part in a cultivated session. Yet the advance of musicality was always triply controversial: if taken too far, it implied the practical know-how and payment-by-results mentality of the occupational musician, a mere artisan; it might also denote wantonness and a dangerous lack of temperamental restraint; lastly, musical refinement would lose some of its value as a status-signifier if it advanced too far beyond the ranks of the gentry.

Recreational music-making was common on all social levels. Admittedly, there were some constraints: among the gentry, practical music was never entirely beyond suspicion, for it could bring not only honour but disrepute; and at lower levels of society, shortage of time and money must also have placed certain restrictions upon the fulfilment of musical potential. Nevertheless, many members of the gentry clearly felt that the benefits outweighed the dangers, while those of lower rank often made the best of the opportunities that arose. Recreational music-making generated a certain amount of controversy, but it rarely reached dangerous levels of intensity. Indeed, musical activity among the general population was as likely to earn commendation for its role in relaxing those who laboured for a living as it was to attract condemnation for its power to corrupt or distract. At all levels, therefore, recreational musicians were an acceptable sub-species, provided that they did not allow their pleasure to become excessive.

Finally, it should be acknowledged that the fluidity of music bedevils any attempt to devise analytical categories based upon socio-economic status. Of course, there would be something to be said for investigating the music-making of the gentry, 'better sort' and common people as distinct entities, but the effectiveness of the enterprise would be restricted by the tendency of such boundaries to disappear before our eyes and ears. There were many connections between the musicians on different social levels.

[126] Edward Chamberlayne, *Angliae Notitia* (London, 1669), p. 46.

Courtly instruments found their way into the hands of comparatively humble musicians. Catches and carols were obviously sung throughout society. Most of the manuscript music books kept by wealthy gentlefolk and merchants include rustic dances and simple ballad tunes alongside the more sophisticated material. Melodies also passed in the opposite direction. 'Cook Laurel', for example, began life in a courtly Jacobean masque but rapidly spread into the alternative contexts of street balladry and country dance (acquiring in the process a range of other titles, including 'An old man is a bed full of bones').[127] Musical clubs and gatherings frequently brought together aristocrats and wealthier members of the middling sort. During the seventeenth century, published music books were increasingly aimed at the widest possible audience, rather than primarily at the gentry. In 1622, the part-songs published by Thomas Tomkins were, he claimed, 'sutable to the people of the world, wherein the rich and the poore, sound and lame, sad and fantasticall dwell together'.[128] All channels of communication were maintained by the occupational musicians who clambered willingly up and down the social ladder with their instruments slung over their shoulders. All in all, the musical cross-currents were so prevalent that it is often impossible to establish whether a particular piece of music began among the aristocracy and fell through society or started towards the bottom and bubbled upwards. Cultural historians have often recognised the tendency of customs, ideas or artefacts to sink or rise, but it would perhaps be more enlightening to think in terms of a never-ending process of circulation.

This process ensured that there was an on-going contrapuntal conversation between people on different social levels, and that music was continually refreshed and renewed. The fluidity of music did not, however, unite and bind society in any simple sense. Rather, it contributed simultaneously to the existence of complex interactive tensions that were always beneath the surface, and occasionally above it. When popular melodies were written out for the gentry, they were usually decorated and developed in an act of appropriation (though the act itself was often carried out by an occupational musician of lowly origins). Musical clubs may have brought people together, but temporary equality also generated disquiet. For this reason, gentlemen-musicians perhaps tended to reduce their active participation from the later seventeenth century onwards, preferring instead to attend professional concerts while restricting their own playing

[127] Simpson, *British Broadside Ballad*, p. 130.

[128] Thomas Tomkins, *Songs of 3, 4, 5 and 6 Parts* (London, 1622), dedicatory epistle.

to conditions of more reassuring privacy and segregation. When an occupational musician of humble rank taught a young gentlewoman to play the virginals, the potential for dissonance existed in the midst of harmony. Musical notes and exciting status-contradictions floated together in the air. And how might an aristocrat have felt upon purchasing a music book that was designed not only for him and his kind, but for all 'the people of the world'? Tomkins half-anticipated a problem: he dedicated his songs to the music-loving Earl of Pembroke, but apologised in advance for 'the lightnesse of some of the words'. He sought a global audience, but he was painfully aware that he risked upsetting a far more restricted one.

5 | Ballads and their audience

Ballads were everywhere. This, at least, was the perception of a succession of critical commentators in early modern England. Whenever such people cocked their ears, hoping to hear the sacred sound of psalmody, they instead heard ballads being sung. And wherever they turned their eyes, seeking out signs of piety, they instead saw printed ballads on display. 'Scarce a cat can looke out of a gutter', complained one witness, 'but out starts a halfpeny Chronicler, and presently A propper new ballet of a strange sight is endited.' If the hostile testimony is to be believed, there was no escaping them, and ballads – with their musical tales of sex and sensation – had a detrimental effect upon the spiritual and moral standards of the population. Ballads were also a potent political tool: they helped to make a hero of the Earl of Essex, executed for high treason in 1601; they humiliated the Duke of Buckingham during the mid-1620s; and two songs, *When the King Enjoys his Own Again* and *Lilliburlero*, are said to have contributed respectively to the Restoration of Charles II in 1660 and the deposition of James II in 1688. England's pre-eminent men sometimes worried that the entertaining narratives of balladry subverted the proper order of things by making kings familiar and shoemakers heroic. Others, in contrast, celebrated ballads as a unique cultural barometer, capable of revealing 'the Complexion of the Times' more accurately than other indicators.[1]

The ballad business

Broadside ballads were already an established feature of cultural life in early sixteenth-century England. Between January and December 1520, for example, a bookseller in Oxford sold a total of 201 ballads at a standard rate of a halfpenny per sheet (though he offered slight reductions to those

[1] *Martine Mar-Sixtus* (London, 1591), epistle dedicatory; Simpson, *British Broadside Ballad*, pp. 449–55, 747–8, 764–8; John Oldmixon, *The False Steps of the Ministry after the Revolution* (London, 1714), pp. 32–3; John Selden, *Table Talk* (London, 1689), E2r. *When the King Enjoys his Own Again* is recorded on the website as track 23.

who bought more than six at a time).[2] The output of the London presses clearly increased dramatically during the century after 1550, and the price of a single ballad rose to a penny. The sheer numbers of songs in circulation grew rapidly, and it has been estimated that up to 4,000,000 ballad-sheets may have been printed by 1600. In 1636, Charles Butler could not help but notice 'the infinite multitude of ballads' doing the rounds in England.[3] The expansion of the ballad business necessitated improvements in the organisation of production. The Stationers' Company had been founded in 1557, with responsibility for the registration of all books and ballads. By the early seventeenth century, when James I reorganised the company, 'Ballad Stock' was one of the five main subdivisions. During this period, a group of booksellers steadily acquired the copyright to the most successful, or 'stock', ballads, and in 1624 a syndicate that became known as the 'ballad partners' was formed. This group, and its descendants, dominated the trade for centuries to come. It was still possible for other publishers to market ballads, but the partners established a near monopoly on the most profitable titles. In theory, successive governments monitored and licensed the production of ballads through a variety of mechanisms. There were occasional prosecutions, and many surviving ballads of the later seventeenth century bear the official endorsement, 'This may be printed.' In practice, however, censorship of balladry was far less intrusive than the authorities might have wished.[4] England's governors barked loudly but bit selectively, and it has been estimated that the 3,000 registered ballads from the years between 1557 and 1709 were dwarfed by approximately 15,000 unlicensed songs.[5] Sadly, only a very small proportion of publications from either category has survived.

As ballad production grew more organised, so the format of the texts themselves settled into a mature, standard pattern. Ballads were generally printed in black-letter, the most widely recognised of early modern typefaces, and most were divided into two roughly equal parts on the page.

[2] *Day-book of John Dorne*, pp. 71–177.

[3] Watt, *Cheap Print*, p. 11; Butler, *Principles of Musik*, p. 8.

[4] On the growth of the ballad business, see Robert S. Thomson, 'The Development of the Broadside Ballad Trade and its Influence upon the Transmission of English Folksongs', unpublished PhD thesis, University of Cambridge (1974); Watt, *Cheap Print*, pp. 39–127; Würzbach, *The Rise of the English Street Ballad*, pp. 18–26; Simpson, *British Broadside Ballad*, pp. ix–xxii; Hyder E. Rollins, *An Analytical Index to the Ballad-entries (1557–1709) in the Registers of the Company of Stationers of London* (Chapel Hill: University of North Carolina Press, 1924); and Rollins, 'The Black-letter Broadside Ballad', *Publications of the Modern Language Association of America* 34 (1919), pp. 258–339.

[5] Simpson, *British Broadside Ballad*, p. xi n. 6.

From the early seventeenth century, certain features that had been occasional in previous decades came to appear on the vast majority of broadside ballads. Woodcut pictures, for example, were used much more generally and soon emerged as one of the defining components of the seventeenth-century ballad. One character in William Cavendish's play *The Triumphant Widow* interrupts the patter of a song-selling pedlar by exclaiming to his sister, 'Oh, Cicely, here's the brave Ballet you and I use to sing, I know it by the Picture.'[6] Occasionally, pictures were commissioned and cut for a specific ballad, but most were recycled from previous songs. A similar imbalance between old and new characterised the tunes, many of which were re-used over and over again. Melodies were generally identified by title only ('to the tune of Fortune my foe', for example) and only very rarely was musical notation included.

Ballad texts were written on a wide range of topics, and the many possibilities were sometimes summarised in satirical form by playwrights and other authors during the first half of the seventeenth century. Ballads, said one of Thomas Middleton's characters, dealt with 'Fashions, Fictions, Fellonies, Fooleries'. The typical ballad-writer, commented John Earle, devised hypocritical songs about executions, monstrous births and divine judgements while 'sitting in a Bawdy-house'.[7] The ten 'Heads of Assortment' under which Samuel Pepys arranged his collection of over 1700 broadsides provide a somewhat less scornful perspective, though of course the relative proportions within each category also reflected his personal preferences (particularly for sex and the sea): 'Devotion & Morality' (5 per cent); 'History – True & Fabulous' (3 per cent); 'Tragedy' (5 per cent); 'State & Times' (13 per cent); 'Love – Pleasant' (28 per cent); 'Love – Unfortunate' (22 per cent); 'Marriage, Cuckoldry &c' (5 per cent); 'Sea' (6 per cent); 'Drinking/Good Fellowship' (10 per cent); 'Humour, Frollicks &c mixt' (3 per cent). Comparison of these percentages with those pertaining to earlier ballad collections seems to indicate a number of trends.[8] Religion declined as a ballad subject after its early Elizabethan heyday (though God put in regular appearances in ballads that were not specifically religious, and song-writers always remained capable of adopting a stern and moralising tone).[9] Political ballads increased

6 William Cavendish, *The Triumphant Widow* (London, 1677), p. 7.

7 Thomas Middleton, *The World Tost at Tennis* (London, 1620), B4v; Earle, *Micro-cosmographie*, p. 78.

8 I have compared the ballads gathered by Pepys himself (*Pepys Ballads*, vols. II–V) with the early seventeenth-century collection he inherited from John Selden (essentially, vol. I of the collection) and with the Elizabethan and Jacobean collection later published as *The Shirburn Ballads*, ed. Andrew Clark (Oxford: Clarendon Press, 1907).

9 Watt, *Cheap Print*, pp. 46–9.

their share of the market during the first half of the seventeenth century, and stabilised at around 15 per cent. Courtship and marriage were, however, the dominant themes throughout the period, and their importance appears to have risen across the period (unless this is an illusion created by Pepys's inability to resist ballads with titles such as *The Swimming Lady: or, A Wanton Discovery, being a true relation of a gay lady, betrayed by her lover, as she was stripping her self stark naked, and swimming in a river near Oxford*). There were ballads about love triumphant, love thwarted and love feigned. There were happy lovers, sick lovers and suicidal lovers. There were ballads commending the married state for both sexes and ballads warning against it. There were women desperate to lose their virginity and women desperate to get it back again. This, indeed, was one of the period's most frequently recycled jokes, a fact that reflects the robustly formulaic traditionalism that characterised balladry. Paradoxically, however, balladeers were often at pains to emphasise the novelty of their material. The recycling instinct may have been strong, but it was not alone. This should remind us that in the ballad – a printed text designed for singing – the features of oral and literate cultures worked in inseparable association.

Ballad-writers were generally anonymous and usually male (this, at least, was the assumption of most commentators). They were heavily disparaged by their self-appointed literary superiors. William Webbe, writing about poetry in 1586, had no regard for the 'uncountable rabble of ryming Ballet makers' who could merely 'frame an Alehouse song of five or sixe score verses, hobbling upon some tune of a Northern Jygge, or Robyn hood, or La lubber'. Song-writers, according to John Davies, were 'Paper-spoylers' and purveyors of 'filth'. Henry Chettle was similarly dismissive of those who considered themselves poets because they could 'write a true staffe to the tune of fortune'. Other commentators considered balladeers and their creations 'ragged', 'lame', 'miserable' and 'lousey'.[10] In 1643, hard-up actors and musicians feared that their plight would leave them with no alternative but to write cheap pamphlets or, worse still, ballads. And when John Dryden felt frustrated with his lot, he compared it to that of 'some doggrel rhymer, who makes songs to tunes, and sings

[10] William Webbe, *A Discourse of English Poetrie* (London, 1586), D1r; John Davies, *A Scourge for Paper-prosecutors* (London, 1625), title page and p. 2; Henry Chettle, *Kind-Hart's Dreame* (London, 1593), B1r; Thomas Nash, *The Anatomie of Absurditie* (London, 1589), B4v; Brathwaite, *Whimzies*, p. 10; Kemp, *Kemp's Nine Daies Wonder*, p. 21; Taylor, *John Taylor Being yet Unhanged, Sends Greeting to John Booker* (London, 1644), printed in *Works of John Taylor not Included in the Folio Volume*, vol. II. Tracks 17 and 20 on the website feature songs to the 'Fortune' melody.

them for a livelihood'.[11] In the light of such evidence, it is perhaps not surprising that the author of a ballad was generally identified only if the inclusion of his name could be expected to add to the marketability of the product. Even the most famous (or infamous) of writers were not invariably credited on their published sheets.

Having said this, we do know the names of more than twenty individuals who specialised in composing ballads and attempted to make a substantial part of their living from the trade (there were many others who wrote only one or two songs). In most cases, we have no more than a name. John Wallys, for example, was a ballad-writer during the mid-sixteenth century, but scarcely anything can be said of his life history. Eleven of his songs were transcribed into the notebook that is more commonly associated with Richard Sheale, and he was presumably the John 'Wally' who, in 1557–8, licensed a ballad asking the classic rich man's question, 'who lyve so mery and make such sporte as they that be of the pooreste sorte[?]' The songs that appeared in the Sheale notebook suggest that Wallys specialised in tongue-in-cheek ballads about the virtues and vices of womankind. One typical text praises the patience of men who have married shrews, and advises all others to imitate their forbearance: 'Then mum and be dum, when she jobbars and jyves.' It is therefore interesting that he also licensed a number of ballads in some kind of partnership with one 'Mrs. Toy' (the widow of a London bookseller).[12] It would be clearly be interesting to know something more of the creative relationship between them. Of course, we cannot be certain that any of the Wallys ballads that survive in manuscript were ever printed, but their style is certainly consistent with that found in broadside songs of the period.

In a handful of cases, however, limited biographical information concerning named ballad-writers is also available, and a number of general points can be made. The majority clearly had their origins in the middling and lower orders of society, and many combined their balladeering with other occupations. According to one early seventeenth-century source, a ballad-writer could expect to receive from the publisher a fee of 40d per ballad. Without supplementary income, such a person would have had to work extremely hard in order to prosper, and it is therefore no surprise that England's ballad-writers included sailors, soldiers, vintners, stationers

[11] *Actors Remonstrance*, p. 17; John Dryden, *Albion and Albanius* (1685; London, 1691), B1r.

[12] *Songs and Ballads*, pp. 119–56, 171–4; Simpson, *British Broadside Ballad*, p. 775; I. Gadd, 'Toy, Humphrey (*b.* in or before 1537, *d.* 1577), *Oxford Dictionary of National Biography* (Oxford: Oxford University Press, 2004; online edn. 2008), http://oxforddnb.com/view/article/27643, last accessed 2 April 2010.

and shoemakers. Thomas Nash, a hostile witness, added stitchers, weavers, spendthrifts and fiddlers to the list. The famous Elizabethan author Thomas Deloney came from a family of silk-weavers in East Anglia, and, despite his prolific output, is said to have died poor.[13] Martin Parker, equally well known during the mid-seventeenth century, was both a ballad man and an alehouse-keeper. There were, however, several ballad-writers with more respectable backgrounds, particularly in the early decades of the Elizabethan period. A number of Protestant clergymen – Thomas Brice and John Cornet, for example – turned to ballad-writing in their drive to evangelise the nation. Other authors included a merchant-tailor (William Fulwood), the son of an alderman in Calais (Thomas Broke) and an aristocrat's former page who retained his courtly connections (Thomas Churchyard). William Elderton, the most celebrated of early Elizabethan song-writers, was unusual in the degree to which he specialised in balladry, but even he combined his creative endeavours with work as a legal attorney and a master of the acting children at Eton College and Westminster School. As late as 1591, the hostile author of *Martine Mar-Sixtus* could complain that ballads were being written by Cambridge graduates who deflected criticism and derision by ensuring that their names did not appear on their songs. A century later, not many ballad-writers could claim privileged backgrounds, though Thomas D'Urfey did his best by adding the pretentious apostrophe to his name.[14]

Most ballad-writers were probably motivated, first and foremost, by the need to make money. It was, after all, a job, and one surviving diary, written by a balladeer in the nineteenth century, conveys the impression of a solid and workmanlike practitioner, drafting and revising ballad after ballad before delivering them, one by one, to his publishers. Two hundred years earlier, one of Martin Parker's many critics had told him, 'Rather than lose half-a-crown, you will write against your own fathers.' This was perhaps a little harsh, for Parker, nicknamed 'the Prelates' poet', was sufficiently principled to support the royalist cause with consistency during the Civil Wars. His most famous ballad, *When the King Enjoys his Own Again*, is such a powerful composition that it can hardly have been

[13] Thomson, 'Development of the Broadside Ballad Trade', p. 177; Angela McShane Jones, '"Rime and Reason": The Political World of the English Broadside Ballad, 1640–1689', unpublished PhD thesis, University of Warwick (2004), pp. 64–8; Watt, *Cheap Print*, pp. 52–4; Nash, *Anatomie of Absurditie*, B4v; Kemp, *Kemp's Nine Daies Wonder*, p. 21.

[14] Thomson, 'Development of the Broadside Ballad Trade', pp. 171–2; Palmer, *Sound of History*, pp. 20–1; Watt, *Cheap Print*, pp. 53–4; McShane Jones, 'Rime and Reason', p. 10. Track 23 on the website is a ballad by Parker.

written for money alone.[15] In less trying times, however, the majority of ballad-writers probably did regard their creative efforts primarily as a means to put bread on the table (or ale in the pot). Elderton's pen poured forth godliness and worldliness according to need, and seventeenth-century authors willingly adopted a variety of different, and often antagonistic, subject positions in ballads. In this manner, they aimed to broaden their commercial appeal, both by singing on behalf of a range of social types and by stimulating controversy.

Authors also fed off one another, frequently composing songs that either imitated or mocked the efforts of their rivals. One commentator estimated that, in 1641, there were twenty-five ballad-writers working in London, and the evidence suggests that they kept a close ear on each other. They were competitors, but they also knew that broadside banter was good for business. The publication of ballads in interconnected pairs was a common phenomenon, and sometimes whole series of songs were churned out as the authors sought to jump on one another's bandwagons. Martin Parker and Laurence Price, in particular, were well known for their rivalry and their tendency to indulge in this kind of singsong ding-dong.[16] At other times, ballad-writers drew upon their own personal experiences and upon what they heard in the streets. They absorbed the news and the rumour that buzzed in London's air, and they sought out opportunities to turn it to their advantage. More simply, ballads were frequently lifted from pre-existing sources. Some were certainly drawn from traditional oral and aural culture, but others had their origins in more expensive forms of literature. Courtly poetry was a significant source of ballad texts, and Christopher Marlowe, Sir Walter Raleigh, Sir Edward Dyer and George Wither were among those whose works were raided for poems that could be set to common tunes. Perhaps it was partly this experience that drove Wither to denounce the 'many Muses perpetually ymployed for the composing of new Straynes'. Superficially, they served the publishers, but at a deeper and more disturbing level they were the agents of 'the Flesh and the Devill'.[17] Lastly, song-seeking ballad-writers also enjoyed rich pickings at the theatre, and numerous broadsides,

[15] Diary of Thomas Haynes Bayley, 3 DIXON/5/17, LA; *The Downfall of Temporising Poets* (London, 1641), p. 4. Parker's famous song was written in *c.* 1644, though the earliest surviving copies were printed a few years later (Simpson, *British Broadside Ballad*, pp. 764–5).

[16] *Downfall of Temporising Poets*, p. 4; Simpson, *British Broadside Ballad*, p. 688.

[17] Simpson, *British Broadside Ballad*, p. 121 (Marlowe); *Pepys Ballads*, vol. I, p. 230 (Wither), vol. II, p. 7 (Dyer), vol. IV, p. 6 (Raleigh); George Wither, *The Schollers Purgatory* (London, 1624), pp. 13, 19.

particularly in the later seventeenth century, were published with subtitles claiming that they had been 'much us'd at the Theatres' or 'lately Sung at the Curtain Holy-Well'.[18]

The physical dissemination of printed broadsides was the responsibility of the mobile and much-maligned ballad-singers. Gentlemen and scholars often presented them as the very dregs of society, a sub-species whose members deserved contempt for several reasons: they were itinerant, like beggars and minstrels; they drew crowds, a potential source of danger; and they peddled bawdry (the moral tone of many ballads and the existence of numerous godly songs was either ignored, or portrayed as evidence of rank hypocrisy). According to Nicholas Bownde, legions of ballad-singers were touring the country, leaving a trail of debauchery behind them, and he feared that godly psalm-singing was being drowned out as a result of the evil inspiration they provided. Others accused them of working in close alliance with the pick-pockets who moved among the listening crowd. Henry Chettle took ballad-singers to task for stealing the livelihoods of mere beggars, who, by tradition, were the only people permitted to sing for money in public. There was no more despicable act of theft than this, and Chettle also recommended that all 'runnagate song-singers' should be 'burned in the tongue, that they might rather be ever utterly mute'.[19]

Many of those who sold ballads were non-specialist chapmen or chapwomen who carried a small number of songs among their other wares. There were, however, also a substantial number of ballad specialists at work, and they must have grown more numerous as the trade expanded. It is difficult to count the numbers of such sellers, though an anonymous pamphlet of 1641 contained an estimate that there were then 277 ballad-singers at work in London.[20] Some ballad-singers operated independently, and publishers were keen to draw them in by advertising their willingness to supply broadsides for distribution. The system was simple: the ballad-singer bought up multiple copies of selected songs, and then took to the road in the hope of selling them at a profit. Some individuals were, it seems, loosely employed by particular publishers or shopkeepers, and could presumably expect slightly more favourable terms.

[18] *The Euing Collection of English Broadside Ballads in the Library of the University of Glasgow* (Glasgow: University of Glasgow Publications, 1971), no. 322; *Pepys Ballads*, vol. I, p. 503.

[19] Bownde, *The Doctrine of the Sabbath*, p. 242; John Gay, quoted by Thomson, 'Development of the Broadside Ballad Trade', p. 175 (see also McShane Jones, 'Rime and Reason', p. 87); Chettle, *Kind-Hart's Dreame*, C2v, C3v, G4r.

[20] *Downefall of Temporising Poets*, p. 5.

In 1593, one of Henry Chettle's characters was critical of employers who took on apprentices and, 'after a little bringing them uppe to singing brokerie', sent them out into the world 'with a dossen groates worth of ballads' to sell (12 groats = 4s). Such employment was insecure but there were modest livings to be made. The publisher Henry Gosson sold ballads to hawkers at 13s 4d per ream (480 sheets) during the early seventeenth century. If they sold for a penny each, the hawker could in theory make a maximum profit of £1 6s 8d. To break even, he or she would have needed to sell 160 ballads, exactly one third of the total. Of course, there were many slips 'twixt cup and lip, but the financial prospects cannot have been wholly unappealing to those who combined a suitable temperament with a lack of more promising alternatives.[21]

Balladry and musicality

Historians and literary scholars make regular use of ballads, but the source is not well understood in its musical dimensions. Indeed, some writers scarcely consider balladry to have been a musical form at all. An unquestionable tendency to concentrate on visible verbal texts has been apparent, and in libraries volumes of ballads are often catalogued as poetry rather than as music.[22] Nor have musicologists in general striven to advance our understanding of balladry, preferring to concentrate their efforts on, for example, the output of the celebrated Lawes brothers than on that of their beer-swilling, ballad-singing contemporary Martin Parker. To early modern people, however, ballads were undoubtedly and almost inescapably a form of music. Ben Jonson, seeking humour in this fact, told a joke about a man who once lit his pipe with the paper from an out-dated ballad and subsequently experienced 'a great singing in his head'.[23] Some loved ballads and some hated them, but nearly all agreed that they usually involved melodic sound and social performance. The silent scholar, sitting alone in the library, inhabits another world.

Most obviously, the overwhelming majority of the ballads published in the early modern period named but did not notate specific tunes. At any

[21] Chettle, *Kind-Hart's Dreame*, C2v; Thomson, 'Development of the Broadside Ballad Trade', p. 42.

[22] See, for example, McShane Jones, 'Rime and Reason', pp. 3–4 (the author questions the status of balladry as music, but many of the primary sources cited throughout her thesis clearly undermine this argument); Würzbach, *Rise of the English Street Ballad*, pp. 9, 16.

[23] Jonson, quoted by Thomson, 'Development of the Broadside Ballad Trade', p. 201.

one time, several hundred melodies were in use, and many travelled under a variety of different titles. A substantial proportion of these tunes were used again and again, though others were described as new and fashionable. We can assume that occupational musicians performed a vital function in disseminating tunes ancient and modern among the population. In 1589, Thomas Nash referred to 'our babling Ballets ... , which every rednose Fidler hath at his fingers end', and one seventeenth-century ballad was set 'To a new Tune, called, The willow green, Sung by Musitians, and in the Theator'. Somehow, the melodies got around and entered people's heads. In 1676, Thomas Mace said that there were many ballad tunes, 'very *Excellent*, and *well contriv'd Pieces, Neat*, and *Spruce*', adding that they were 'Commonly known by the *Boys*, and *Common People, Singing them in the Streets*'.[24] It was not until the eighteenth century that the system of recommending specific tunes finally broke down.

During the last decades of the seventeenth century, some ballad publishers broke with tradition by printing musical notation on their broadsides. To a degree, this presumably reflected and further stimulated an increase in musical literacy. In many cases, however, such notation served primarily as a pictorial representation of melodic sound rather than as an applicable version of the actual melody to which a ballad was set. Publishers sometimes printed completely different tunes or even random jumbles of almost meaningless notes. *The Boon Companion*, for instance, was set to the tune of 'Fond boy', but the music that was printed on the sheet was a disjointed series of symbols, way ahead of its time in 1692.[25] Its purpose was not to aid singing but to tempt potential customers by representing music to them, and perhaps to feed their vanity by allowing them to imagine or pretend that they were musically literate.

Most of the period's ballad tunes cannot, therefore, be reclaimed from the broadsides themselves, and many have been lost. Luckily, however, it was not only the boys in the early modern streets who knew these tunes, and we can be grateful that many of the period's composers chose to draw on the music of balladry for their own instrumental compositions.[26] The celebrated dance books published by John Playford during the second half of the seventeenth century are another rich source. Thanks to the

[24] Nash, *Anatomie of Absurditie*, B4r; *Pepys Ballads*, vol. III, p. 330; Mace, *Musick's Monument*, p. 129.

[25] *Pepys Ballads*, vol. V, p. 95. See also Richard Luckett, 'The Collection: Origins and History', in R. Latham (ed.), *Catalogue of the Pepys Library at Magdalene College, Cambridge*, 7 vols. (Woodbridge: D. S. Brewer, 1978–84), vol. II, pt. 2, p. xv.

[26] On the website, examples can be heard on tracks 6 and 7.

remarkable labours of Claude Simpson, a great many melodies have thus been identified.[27] Of course, it is not always easy to extract the bare tunes from their more elaborate instrumental versions, and it is clear that individual melodies must have sounded in a variety of guises depending on the purpose of the performance and the social level upon which it occurred. Nevertheless, it is possible in many cases to recover plausible core versions of the tunes, and to reunite them with their texts.

The list of the period's most popular tunes shown in Table 5.1 has been compiled by counting the number of citations in several of the major collections of ballads, though I have also added two 'hit' tunes that clearly deserve a place in the charts because of the intensity of their popularity at particular points in time. On this basis, it is possible to draw some conclusions concerning the main characteristics of the period's 'top fifty' ballad melodies (there are actually fifty-six distinct tunes, though five of them are either lost or of uncertain identity).[28] The group reveals a clear preference for melodies in some form of triple time (61 per cent) over those in duple or quadruple time (39 per cent). In other words, English balladeers and their customers particularly enjoyed melodies made up of units of three beats, though they also appreciated the alternatives. In terms of the tonality of the tunes, half of them are in what we would think of as major keys (tending to strike us as bright and happy) and half are in minor keys (sounding sadder, to our ears at least). A number of the latter tunes are clearly constructed in the Dorian mode rather than on what we would recognise as a modern minor scale. In Charles Butler's estimation, this was the mode most favoured by those who composed ballads.[29] Most of the top tunes contain either four or eight lines, with a roughly even distribution between these dominant categories (35 and 41 per cent respectively). This comes as no surprise, for four- and eight-line melodies tend to be

[27] *Complete Country Dance Tunes from Playford's Dancing Master*; Simpson, *British Broadside Ballad* (most of the tunes discussed in this chapter and the next can be further studied in this indispensable work).

[28] I have counted citations (including all variant tune titles) in the Shirburn, Selden, Roxburghe, Pepys, Euing and Bagford collections. The exercise presents a number of difficulties, most notably that of compensating for the fact that there are far fewer surviving ballads from the late sixteenth and early seventeenth centuries than from the decades after 1660. To avoid the eclipse of earlier tunes, I have adopted the crude but effective method of including the top tunes from the Shirburn and Selden collections, regardless of their place in the overall rankings. Conversely, I have included tunes from the enormous Pepys collection only if they were cited on twenty or more ballad sheets. 'When the king . . .' and 'Lilliburlero' would not have made the list on this basis, but they have been included because of their immense popularity during the 1640s–1650s and 1680s–1690s respectively.

[29] Butler, *Principles of Musik*, p. 8. On the website, examples are recorded on tracks 17 and 20.

Table 5.1. The top fifty ballad tunes (with numbers of citations)

Fortune my foe (105)	The king's delight (20)
Chevy Chase (67)	New game at cards (20)
Packington's pound (55)	Come live with me and be my love (19)
Russell's farewell (51)	Greensleeves (19)
Let Caesar live long (49)	The languishing swain (19) [identity uncertain]
The country farmer (49)	Rogero (18)
O man in desperation (48)	Why are my eyes still flowing? (16)
Cupid's courtesy (39)	Dainty come thou near me (15) [lost]
Hey boys up go we (37)	Lie lulling beyond thee (16)
Old Simon the king (37)	Amarillis (14)
Queen Dido (37)	I prithee love turn to me (14)
The pudding (34)	Crimson velvet (13)
Daniel Cooper (34)	The Duke of Norfolk (13)
Bonny sweet Robin (31)	London is a fine town (13)
Fond boy (29)	Selenger's round (13)
Jenny Gin (29)	Lord Willoughby (11)
Cupid's courtesy (28)	Hey ho my honey (12)
Dulcina (28)	Wigmore's galliard (12)
The rich merchant (28)	Cook Laurel (11)
Ladies of London (28)	Whoop do me no harm good man (11)
If love's a sweet passion (28)	The bride's good morrow (10) [identity uncertain]
In peascod time (27)	Shackley Hay (10)
Robin Hood and the stranger (27)	The Spanish pavin (10)
The spinning wheel (27)	Bragandary (9) [lost]
Franklin is fled away (24)	When the king enjoys his own again (9)
Logan water (24)	Triumph and joy (7) [identity uncertain]
I'll never love thee more (21)	Over and under (5)
Lilliburlero (22)	Welladay (4)

perceived within western music as the most natural and satisfying. We should also note, however, the popularity of more irregular tunes such as 'Robin Hood and the stranger' (five lines) and 'The king's delight' (seven lines). Three tunes are considerably longer, each comprising twelve lines ('Crimson velvet', 'Hey ho my honey' and 'Under and over').[30]

The structural patterns into which the musical lines fit within each melody are rather more surprising. We might have expected that clear and repetitive trends would emerge, but the fifty-one tunes reveal a striking

[30] The last of these can be heard on the website, track 15.

degree of variety. The most common tune structure is ABCD, in which each of a tune's four lines is different from the others (good examples include 'In peascod time' and 'Chevy Chase': see Example 5.1). Such tunes, however, account for only 24 per cent of the total. The remaining thirty-seven melodies are distributed among no fewer than twenty-two other patterns. Of these, the most frequently encountered are ABACDEFG (for example, 'I'll never love thee more'), AABC (like 'Fortune my foe': see Example 5.2) and ABABCDEB ('When the king enjoys his own again', for instance), but a remarkable seventeen tunes are constructed in patterns that are unique within the sample. Each of the three twelve-line melodies, for example, presents a different structure. It is also notable that specific musical motifs are only rarely shared by different tunes, a feature that distinguishes ballad melodies from those used in metrical psalm-singing.[31] Within many of the ballad tunes, however, the initial phrases are echoed, though not duplicated, in later motifs, suggesting that musical memorability was, as it were, internally generated.

Chevy Chase

Example 5.1. 'Chevy Chase' or 'Flying fame' (from Simpson, *British Broadside Ballad*, p. 97)

Fortune my foe

Example 5.2. 'Fortune my foe' or 'Aim not too high' (from Simpson, *British Broadside Ballad*, p. 227)

[31] The website includes recordings of the tunes 'In peascod time' (track 18), 'I'll never love thee more' (track 24), 'Fortune my foe' (tracks 7, 17 and 20) and 'When the king . . .' (track 23). On psalmody, see below, pp. 416–17.

The range of patterns was probably related to the eclectic origins of this body of tunes, though it is often impossible to trace a specific melody back to its roots. We can be certain, however, that England's hit tunes were not all from similar sources: 'Greensleeves' and 'Rogero' were both built on fashionable European chord progressions of the sixteenth century, and they probably reached the streets of London via instrumental music played at court; stately dance music familiar in the same elevated setting presumably provided the balladeers with tunes such as 'The Spanish pavin [pavane]'; the title of 'The Duke of Norfolk' may indicate that this tune was composed by musicians in honour of a favourite patron; 'Packington's pound' (see Example 5.3) and 'Wigmore's galliard', in contrast, may refer to the musicians who were originally responsible for, or strongly associated with, these tunes; 'If love's a sweet passion' was a theatre tune by Henry Purcell; he may also have had a hand in 'Lilliburlero', though the tune's distinctive opening phrases bear a close relationship to part of an earlier country dance tune called 'Hockley in the hole'; country dance music may also have provided 'Selenger's round' and 'Shackley Hay', and the comparative simplicity of 'Chevy Chase' and 'The lady's fall' (also called 'In peascod time') perhaps indicates rustic roots, though the suggestion is a speculative one; other tunes – 'Let Caesar live long', for example – were clearly composed specially for their original ballads, before spreading far and wide. Nobody knows where 'Fortune my foe' originated, though it seems possible that this mini-masterpiece in the Dorian mode may have evolved in relation to another Elizabethan melody: in 1589, Oliver Pygge's *Meditations* on England's recent deliverance from the Spanish threat included a song by a godly physician, set to a tune that bore an extremely close affinity to 'Fortune', despite being in a major key.[32]

The varied structures of these tunes suggest that the men and women who sold ballads for a living cannot have lacked musical ability. The compass of the melodies reinforces the point. Admittedly, twenty melodies (43 per cent) were contained within the span of a single octave, but twenty-seven (57 per cent) required a wider vocal range (two famous tunes, 'Shackley Hay' and the appropriately named 'Hey boys up go we', stretched the singer over a perfect twelfth). The dominance and longevity

[32] Simpson, *British Broadside Ballad* (see tune titles in index); Spink, 'Music and Society', pp. 5–6; Watt, *Cheap Print*, p. 63; *Complete Country Dance Tunes*, no. 40; Pygge, *Meditations Concerning Praiers to Almighty God*, E2r. Several of these tunes can be heard on the website: 'Greensleeves' (track 34), 'The Spanish pavan' (tracks 6 and 12), 'If love's a sweet passion' (track 22), 'Selenger's round' (track 35), 'Let Caesar live long' (track 21) and 'Fortune' (tracks 7, 17 and 20).

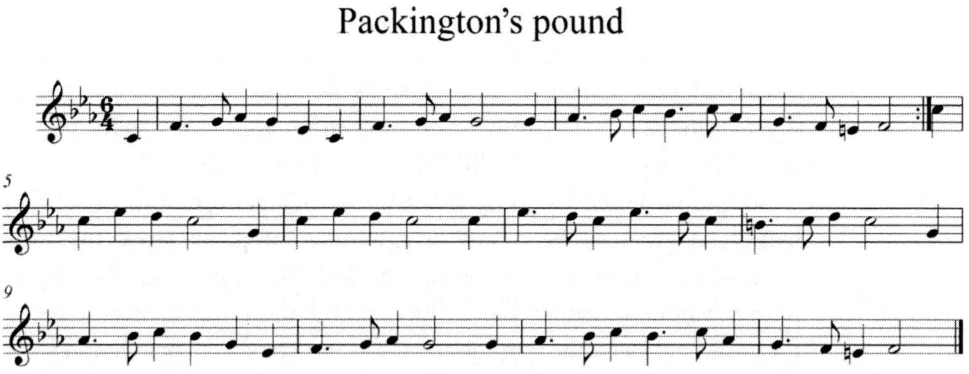

Example 5.3. 'Packington's pound' (from Simpson, *British Broadside Ballad*, p. 565)

of the occupational label 'ballad-singer' points in the same optimistic direction and warns us against any assumption that the distributors of these songs were incapable of singing. Historians, indeed, have sometimes been too ready to take their lead from hostile contemporary testimony alleging that the musical talents of the singer-sellers were almost non-existent. The evidence against ballad-singers is culturally charged and prone to endowing them, for humorous effect, with a certain cartoon quality. They produced, said William Brown in 1616, 'as harsh a noyce as ever Cart-wheele made'. According to John Earle, they sang 'to a vile tune, and a worse throat'. And in 1642, a satirical music lecture, delivered in Oxford, urged the audience of the need to distinguish 'betwixt the Ballad-singer in the market and the Chaunter in the Quier', for the two were as different 'as a Gossips prating and a Philosophers discourse'.[33]

Of course, there must indeed have been some musically incompetent ballad-sellers, particularly among the non-specialist petty traders. The counter-evidence is, however, quite persuasive. In all sorts of source, the capacity of the humble ballad-singer to attract and work the crowd – through gesture, words and music – was acknowledged. During the 1630s, religious zealots in Essex were said to flock around one of their ringleaders 'as people use where balletts ar sunge'. Indeed, it was precisely this ability that earned for the singers a measure of scorn from the country's literary snobs, and some of the alternative evidence flowed from their own pens. The same writer who drew the cartwheel analogy also referred to the 'attentive rout' that gathered around the singer. We are, of course, reading

[33] William Brown, *Britannia's Pastorals. The Second Book* (London, 1616), p. 11; Earle, *Micro-cosmographie*, p. 78; Add. MS 37999, fo. 66, BL.

such evidence against the grain, for the central point, from William Brown's perspective, was that ordinary people were stupid enough to be drawn in by the lamentable screeching of the ballad-monger. Earle's singer is much the same. He performs dreadful songs appallingly badly, yet 'the poore Country wench melts like her butter to heare them'.[34]

Additional hints regarding the musical and performative prowess of ballad-mongers can be found in a number of plays. Here, the focus of critical attention was not on the musical shortcomings of the singers, most of whom were male, but on their gleeful mastery of the art of fleecing the great English public through the captivating power of melody and verse. The behaviour of Shakespeare's Autolycus, Jonson's Nightingale and Cavendish's Footpad enables us to build up a composite picture of the stage ballad-singer at work.[35] He is a happy rogue, commercially motivated, criminally inclined and thoroughly manipulative, but the man is also musical. His performance is extremely effective, and invariably culminates in a rush of enthusiastic customers. It begins, however, with his attempts to subdue other sounds by loudly trumpeting the names of his best ballads. Nightingale must compete with the cries of rival vendors, all struggling to sell their hobby-horses, gingerbread and mousetraps. These cries – famously musical themselves – were regularly tamed and transposed in the imitative works of more refined composers.[36] Nightingale, of course, drives them all into the sonic margins with his exuberant outburst:

Ballads, ballads! fine new ballads:
Hear for your love, and buy for your money!
A delicate ballad o' The Ferret and the Coney!
A Preservative against the Punks' Evil!
Another of Goose-green Starch, and the Devil!
A Dozen of Divine Points, and The Godly Garters!
The Fairing of Good Counsel, of an ell and three quarters!
What is't you buy?
The Windmill blown down by the witch's fart!
Or Saint George, that O! did break the dragon's heart!

[34] Fox, *Oral and Literate Culture*, p. 372; Brown, *Britannia's Pastorals*, p. 11; Earle, *Micro-cosomgraphie*, p. 78.

[35] Unless otherwise indicated, all quotations in this section are from Shakespeare, *The Winter's Tale*, ed. Ernest Schanzer (London: Penguin Books, 1996), pp. 119–22, 132–40; Ben Jonson, *Bartholomew Fair*, ed. E. A. Horsman (Manchester: Manchester University Press, 1960), pp. 53–4, 84–91; Cavendish, *Triumphant Widow*, pp. 4–8, 55–7.

[36] See Wulstan, *Tudor Music*, pp. 43–8. Track 20 on the website opens with a rougher rendition of some of the hawkers' cries.

The stage ballad-singer insists not only upon the newness of his ballads but upon the truth of their contents ('Why should I carry lies abroad?' asks Autolycus), and his sales patter is rapid and compelling. He warms up the audience by singing snatches from a variety of songs, thus demonstrating that he has ballads 'for man or woman, of all sizes' and musical ability to boot. An excited servant reports that Autolycus 'sings several tunes faster than you'll tell money; he utters them as he had eaten ballads and all men's ears grew to his tunes'. Ballads are also placed on display for the attention of onlookers, and potential customers are excited by the pictures they see. Ears and eyes are stimulated simultaneously by the skilful song-seller.

The ballad-singer thus grabs and holds the attention of passers-by, luring them in as he prepares to perform one of his songs in a fuller version. This rendition is introduced with another burst of promotional patter, and Nightingale selects his song in reaction to a question from the audience regarding the threat of cutpurses. 'Sir', he replies, 'this is a spell against 'em, spick and span new; and 'tis made as 'twere in mine own person, and I sing it in mine own defence. But 'twill cost a penny alone, if you buy it.' He announces that the song is 'To the tune of *Paggington's Pound*' and prepares to sing. By this stage, a proportion of the crowd is already hooked, and attention levels do not falter as the ballad-monger begins to sing, expertly fitting the words to the specified tune. The style of singing is left to the actor, but other sources suggest the use of a range of voices. The archetypal ballad-monger in *Whimzies* is mocked for his habit of singing 'with varietie of ayres (having as you may suppose, an instrumental Polyphon in the cranie of his nose). Now he counterfeits a naturall Base, then a perpetuall Treble, and ends with a Countertenure. You shall heare him feigne an artfull straine through the Nose, purposely to insinuate into the attention of the purer brother-hood.' William Brown's imagined ballad-monger adopts another tactic: teasingly, he sings only half of the song, advising his listeners that they must buy their own copies if they wish to know how it ends.[37]

Back on stage, some of our ballad-man's listeners are clearly mesmerised by his song, and he or his agents take the opportunity to pick pockets and cut purses. There is, however, no atmosphere of rapt and reverent silence, for other members of the audience continue their conversations or call out comments, despite the efforts of the most attentive listeners to silence them. 'Peace, peace', says one of Footpad's female fans, 'let him troll it away, he sings curiously.' The singer must rise above all disruptions, and he

[37] Brathwaite, *Whimzies*, p. 13; Brown, *Britannia's Pastorals*, p. 11.

does so by working with, rather than against, his audience. The active participation of listeners is an integral feature of the encounter, and part of the ballad-singer's task is to teach them any unfamiliar tunes. Autolycus takes advantage of the mêlée of enthusiasts in order to add stolen items to his legitimate takings. The sound of the song, he gloatingly reports, 'so drew the rest of the herd to me that all their other senses stuck in ears: you might have pinched a placket, it was senseless'.

Not all stage ballad-singers were male. An incomplete play of the mid-seventeenth century, preserved in manuscript in the Essex Record Office, features a character described as 'Troulmadam, a ballad singer'. Her general approach is similar in most respects to that of her male counterparts, though her particular interest in selling religious ballads sets her apart. She stocks one about 'a huge shole of strange fish never seene before on these coasts all marked with myters, Crosyers, and triple Crownes driven in by an army of herrings, which put the beseiged in great comfort'. When she sells the whole bundle for sixpence, she thanks the buyer with the lines, 'Read and may your studyes prosper child, and make you able to cry downe Antichrist, and raise Hubbubs i' th city against discipline.' Her patter is brought to an abrupt end by the arrival of the local constable. Ballad-singers were perceived as a nuisance, and Troulmadam declares, 'I must put up my pipes then and bee gone: otherwise I shall sing in Newgate' (see Figure 5.1).[38]

Ballad-singers in the world beyond the theatre could rely upon their printed texts to offer them plenty of assistance in conjuring up a crowd-pleasing musical performance. Opening verses were often composed specifically to draw an audience, sometimes with inclusive phraseology and sometimes with an appeal to a more specific social group. 'Now listen to my song good People all', began one ballad on witchcraft, while an ABC sought out young women (or perhaps their parents) with the instruction 'All youthfull Virgins, to this Song give eare'. In many ballads, the emotional involvement of the singer was inscribed into the text ('With sobbing griefe my heart will break / Asunder in my breast'), while dialogue ballads offered the singer scope to experiment with different vocal registers and to generate mirth.[39] Catchy tunes and singalong refrains invited participation, and the final verses of numerous songs

[38] D/DW Z5, pp. 9, 15–17, ERO.

[39] Roxburghe ballads, C20F7–F10, 4 vols., vol. II, p. 531, vol. I, pp. 430–1, BL; *Pepys Ballads*, vol. I, p. 146.

Figure 5.1. Ballads were often sung and sold by women, particularly during the second half of the seventeenth century. Male and female sellers alike were often depicted as poor and uncouth, but this couple is romanticised rather than degraded by the artist. © Trustees of the British Museum, Prints and Drawings, 1972,U.370.25, 'A Merry New Song' from *The Cryes of the City of London Drawne after the Life* (London, 1688).

allowed the performer to draw matters to a close by reminding listeners of the central message while preparing the way for the transition from singing to selling. The conclusion of *A True Relation of the Great Flood* was not exactly upbeat, but it must have rounded off a rendition quite effectively:

So to conclude let us our lives amend,
Then God his blessing speedily will send
To keep this song in mind do not deny
And all ways think that one day thou must dye.

The final lines of *A New Merry Ballad* were more obviously mercenary:

A packing penny,
if you will bestow,
I will goe to Dinner,
I tell you but so.[40]

The theatrical evidence seems to undermine the assumption that most ballad-singers lacked the ability to sing ballads. Of course, career guidance was minimal, and balladry was well known as a recourse of the disadvantaged – many real singers were some combination of poor, young and female – but are we to assume that such people were necessarily unmusical? It seems more logical to suppose that a proportion of the lower orders were indeed capable of song, and that it was from this proportion that many ballad-singers were drawn. In a *Garland* of 1669, a character called Mr Lovesong is heard to boast that he can sing all the broadsides he buys 'with the very air and tune of your most exquisite ballad singers o' the streets'.[41] It is suggestive that several ballad-singers also had other musical abilities or connections. Those who sold ballads were sometimes identified as 'fiddlers', a label that – despite a certain looseness – probably implied instrumental ability. The interconnection of musicians and ballad-sellers is also suggested by a fascinating exchange that took place in a Chester alehouse, late in the summer of 1588. A former soldier from Lancashire was troubled to hear '2 fidlers ... synging of the last Triumphe of england against the spaniards'. This was presumably one of the many ballads issued shortly after the deflection of the Spanish Armada into the North Sea, but the soldier knew that the danger had not yet passed. He refused to offer the musicians any financial reward for their song, and warned them that it was dangerous 'for a man to rejoice before the victory'. Helen Aspinall, a ballad-singer who in 1651 caused a disturbance in Clerkenwell by attracting a throng of disorderly followers, was the wife of a musician. Decades earlier, Thomas Lovell's impassioned critique of England's itinerant musicians had apparently

[40] Roxburghe ballads, C20F7–F10, vol. II, p. 236, BL; *Pepys Ballads*, vol. I, p. 177.

[41] *A Garland for the New Royal Exchange*, quoted by H. E. Rollins, 'The Black-letter Broadside Ballad', p. 332. Unfortunately, I have so far been unable to locate the original pamphlet.

made no clear distinction between the 'minstrels' – his main target – and those who sang ballads. The allegation that his hypocritical enemies, like Autolycus, disseminated songs to suit the tastes of all people – the godly, the filthy, the sober, bawds, papists, Familists, 'modest men' and 'naughtie companie' – could equally well have been aimed at musical performers in either category. And in 1636, Charles Butler used the term 'minstrel' in his condemnation of those who acted as sordid distributing agents for London's ballad-authors and publishers.[42]

Perhaps the majority of ballad-mongers did not sound quite like cathedral choristers, but this may have been primarily because their task was to dominate a bustling and crowded outdoor space rather than the reverent resonance of a church interior (see Figure 5.2). Roger North was no great admirer of ballad music, but he had to admit that it was not the worst one might hear. He spoke of the women who sang in the streets 'with a loudness that downs all other noise, and yet firme and steddy. Now what a sound would that be in a theater, cultivated and practised to harmony!' Ballad-singers had to be both musical and loud if they were to achieve results, and the multiple references to the eager crowds they gathered demonstrates that many of them possessed the attributes necessary to succeed on both fronts. The ballad-singers Dick and Wat Wimbas were said to be capable of making twenty shillings in a single day (selling, in other words, something like 240 ballads). This was obviously exceptional, but competent performers may have been more widespread than has been suggested. One ballad in the Roxburghe collection introduces us to a 'proud pedlar' – not even a ballad specialist – who claims that he only has to sing a song once in order to remember it forever.[43]

Those who found themselves incapable of holding the attention of a crowd must often have withdrawn in search of alternative employment. There was probably no future in balladry for the disheartened singer who, at some point during the mid-seventeenth century, found it impossible to sell his sheets at the market in Abingdon. As luck would have it, Dr Richard Corbet, the well-known divine, was sitting in a nearby tavern. According to John Aubrey, he took pity on the despairing pedlar: 'The jolly doctor puts off his gown, and puts on the ballad singer's leather jacket, and being

[42] Z QSE/3/84, ChRO; McShane Jones, 'Rime and Reason', p. 87; Lovell, *Dialogue between Custom and Veritie*, D5r–v; Butler, *Principles of Musik*, pp. 130–1.

[43] *Roger North on Music*, p. 215; *The House and Farm Accounts of the Shuttleworths*, ed. John Harland, in *Remains Historical and Literary Connected to the Palatine Counties of Lancaster and Chester, Chetham Society* 46 (1858), p. 814; Roxburghe ballads, C20F7–F10, BL, vol. III, p. 656.

Figure 5.2. A ballad-singer's first aim was to attract and hold the attention of a crowd in the face of many distractions and rival attractions. A loud voice and an imposing personality were both essential, but a stool was also useful. © Trustees of the British Museum, Prints and Drawings, 1877,1013.929, Claude Dubosc, 'Friendly as a Ballad Singer at the Country Wake' from *The Humours of Hob at the Country Wake in the Opera of Flora* (London, *c.* 1745).

a handsome man, and had a rare full voice, he at once sold a great many, and had a great audience.' The anecdote encourages two observations: firstly, musical ability and a measure of charisma were vital to success; secondly, some ballad-singers were inadequate, but their failings were likely to lead rather rapidly towards disillusionment and pastures new. The final point may also help to explain the uniquely wayward Elizabethan career path of Thomas Spickernell, 'sometyme apprentice to a bookebynder, after a vagrant pedler, then a ballett singer & seller, and now a minister & Alehousekeeper in Maldon'.[44] The discussion ends, therefore, with a churchman who missed his vocation as a ballad-monger, and a ballad-monger who reportedly found his vocation in the church.

[44] John Aubrey, *Brief Lives*, ed. R. Barber (Woodbridge: Boydell Press, 1982), p. 80; D/B 3/3/397/18, ERO. By 'minister', we should perhaps understand 'parish clerk'.

Once a purchase had been made, it was of course possible for the customer to enjoy the ballad without a musical performance. Song-writers occasionally felt the need to warn people that their texts were 'not to be said but sung', thereby implying that some people consumed broadsides by reading them without music. In October 1640, one of Martin Parker's ballads was read out, but apparently not sung, to a group of card-players in a London house. A quarter of a century later, Pepys once read a ballad, apparently to himself, as he crossed the Thames by boat. It may be inappropriate, however, to assume that the individual who 'read' a ballad was necessarily oblivious to its melodic aspect. Pepys, in particular, was a thoroughly musical man and a connoisseur of balladry. He must have known the old tune of 'St George' to which the song was set. It seems likely, therefore, that on this occasion he would have heard the melody in his head while he perused the ballad (readers may like to try the surprisingly difficult task of recalling the words of their own national anthem while suppressing all awareness of the tune). Arguably, he did not sing aloud for three reasons: he considered the particular ballad 'ridiculous', his companion was a lowly ferryman, and it was 'wondrous cold' out on the water. It should be remembered, furthermore, that to early modern minds, the boundary between poetry and music was less obvious than it is to us. In 1589, for example, George Puttenham's famous discussion of poetry drew freely on a range of expressions – 'tunes', 'concords', 'cadences', 'symphonical', 'melodious' and 'harmonical' – that we nowadays associate primarily with music.[45]

One unique and intriguing piece of evidence suggests that England's less confident ballad-lovers may commonly have employed a chanting mode of delivery. In 1664, the Duchess of Newcastle wrote a letter to a friend in which she remarked that the best type of voice for the performance of ballads was 'vulgar' and 'plain'. She considered herself well qualified to achieve this boundary-busting effect, though she felt that her musical aptitude was inadequate to the task of singing more challenging and sophisticated music. The duchess went on, 'neither should Old Ballads be Sung so much in a Tune as in a Tone, which Tone is betwixt speaking and singing, for the Sound is more than Plain Speaking, and less than Clear Singing'.[46]

[45] Bagford ballads, C40M9, fo. 79r, BL; McShane Jones, 'Rime and Reason', pp. 76–9; *Diary of Samuel Pepys*, vol. VIII, p. 99; George Puttenham, *The Arte of English Poesie*, ed. Gladys Doidge Willcock and Alice Walker (Cambridge: Cambridge University Press, 1936).

[46] Margaret Cavendish, *CCXI Sociable Letters* (London, 1664), pp. 428–9. On the website, we have experimented with something like this style of rendition on track 33.

On the other hand, the composers of ballads generally assumed that members of the public were capable of singing their texts to the tunes that were specified. Indeed, the musical capacities of consumers were often written into the verses themselves ('Come, O come and sing with me'). Moreover, the persistence with which composers named tunes demonstrates that neither they nor their publishers perceived this custom as an obstacle to commercial success. Music was marketable. In 1668, *Poor Robin's Dream* was set 'To a compleat Tune, well known by Musicians, and many others'. The author hoped that by picking such a tune, the economic potential of his song would be enhanced. Even in subsequent centuries, it was possible for ballad-sellers to argue that a tune was the crucial feature of a saleable song.[47] By the nineteenth century, specific melodies were recommended only rarely on the published sheets, but it is apparent that ballads remained a musical form. Sellers and consumers were presumably left to choose the tunes for themselves. Back in the age of Martin Parker, tune titles were standard issue. A few of them may have been verbal inventions designed to produce satirical effect, but the vast majority clearly referred to actual melodies. It may be difficult for us to accept that many members of the target audience were sufficiently musical to recall dozens of tunes, learn new ones and fit fresh texts to them all, but it is equally difficult to explain why the system prevailed for so long if this were not the case. Artisans and husbandmen, said an angry Nicholas Bownde in 1595, bought ballads and grew 'cunning' in singing them, when they should instead have been learning the psalms (see Figure 5.3). And in *Bartholomew Fair*, one of Nightingale's listeners begins humming the melody in advance of the performance.[48]

Several literary sources present us with customers who approached with some eagerness the task of growing cunning in balladry (see Figure 5.4). When Autolycus introduces a ballad set to the tune of 'Two maids wooing a man', Dorcas and Mopsa, the shepherdesses who hang upon his every word, grow excited. They already know the tune, and now they begin accommodating it to the new text. It is in the form of a three-way conversation, and Autolycus obligingly assists them by singing the extra part. Clown, their male companion, is pleased by their rendition, and undertakes to buy a copy of the ballad for each woman.

[47] *Pepys Ballads*, vol. I, pp. 254–5; *Euing Collection of English Broadside Ballads*, no. 285; Mayhew, quoted by Reay, *Popular Cultures*, p. 59.

[48] Bownde, *The Doctrine of the Sabbath*, p. 242; Jonson, *Bartholomew Fair*, p. 86.

Who laugh to heare mee sing, lett them begone:
I mind them not, for I will still sing on.

Figure 5.3. The consumers of ballads came in many forms and could be extremely dedicated. In this picture, imported from Holland, an old woman resolves to continue her efforts despite the mockery of others. The British Library, C20F7–F10, Roxburghe ballads, vol. I, opening pages ('Who laugh to hear').

'We'll have this song out anon by ourselves', he remarks, and he promptly joins in the rehearsal. Clown's efforts to learn 'both tune and words' draw in a larger audience. Saltonstall's country wenches, like Dorcas and Mopsa, love to buy a romantic ballad, 'to get by heart at home, and

Figure 5.4. Ballad-singing, whether by day or by night, was usually a sociable activity. Here, a group of young men sing eagerly from a window, perhaps to entertain those who pass in the street. Trustees of the British Museum, Prints and Drawings, 1855,0512.96, John Smith, *Singers in a Window* (London, *c.* 1706).

after sing it over their milke payles' (another author said this served as a harmless charm to bring the milk down). In a poem of 1731, a crowd gathers around the ballad-singer in order 'to hear the tune', and the typical purchaser throws a coin to the ballad-seller, collects his copy and departs, 'Humming it as he walks along, / Endeavouring to learn the song.'[49]

[49] Shakespeare, *Winter's Tale*, pp. 121–2; Saltonstall, *Picturae Loquentes*, E10r; Brathwaite, quoted by Smith, *Acoustic World*, p. 177; *The Weekly Register*, quoted by Dianne Dugaw, *Warrior Women and Popular Balladry* (1989; Chicago: University of Chicago Press, 1996), p. 18.

The shape of the audience

The audience was, therefore, a passably musical one, but what were its other characteristics? Broadside ballads were associated with the common people but collected by the gentry, and the complex currents that circulated within the ballad community clearly deserve our attention. The audience was broad, but it cannot have been unlimited. Not everyone had equal access, and it may be instructive to proceed by identifying and assessing the various factors that conditioned opportunity. A number of questions present themselves. Could the poor afford to participate in the culture of balladry? Did those who lived in the country's more remote regions have the opportunity to do so? Did one have to be literate in order to make the most of a ballad? Could the rich ignore the voices warning them that ballads were beneath them? Could anyone overlook the insistence of moral commentators that scurrilous songs endangered their souls? The obstacles to access form quite a roadblock when lined up in this manner. No social group faced every disincentive, however, and the available evidence encourages considerable optimism regarding the social and geographical reach of balladry.

Financial constraints must obviously have prevented members of the lower orders from purchasing ballads as regularly as those whose disposable wealth was more impressive. The Coventry mason who, in 1575, possessed a collection of over one hundred ballads was presumably a man of means. It is equally obvious, however, that ownership was not an exclusive privilege of the prosperous. It is well known that the young and single, often living in service with their board provided, were ideally situated to spend a few pennies on cheap print from time to time. Thus ballads were sometimes associated particularly with the young, and love songs even more particularly with unmarried maidens. In 1631, Wye Saltonstall identified 'country wenches' as the people most likely to purchase such ballads at a rural fair.[50] As we have heard, a single song cost one penny, roughly the same as a loaf of bread. Of course, the labouring woman with a single penny and several children probably did not include ballads on her daily shopping list. If she were having an unusually good week, however, and there were extra coins in her purse, then the purchase of a ear-catching broadside from the singer at the market may not have been completely out of the question. Even if she could not afford a copy, she had nonetheless heard the song and potentially fallen under its spell.

[50] Laneham, *Captain Cox, his Ballads and Books*, pp. 28–30; Saltonstall, *Picturae Loquentes*, E10r.

Possession was merely one form of interaction with a ballad. Partly for this reason, ballads were regularly connected by commentators with lowly occupational groups such as shepherds, milkmaids and spinsters (those who spun wool).[51] According to one interpretation, they were the songs of the common people.

For various reasons, the lower orders probably had more regular contact with balladry in 1700 than they had done in 1560. This was partly because the business had expanded and because literacy levels had risen, but these trends were reinforced by general demographic and economic developments. During the middle of the seventeenth century, the rapid population growth that had characterised the previous hundred years came to an end, as did the price inflation that had attended it. The pressure on livelihoods therefore eased and the demand for consumer goods was stimulated. Of course, this was a demand expressed more obviously by the middling sort in society than by men and women of poorer rank. Nevertheless, our typical labouring woman was far more likely to possess an occasional spare penny in the later seventeenth century than her great-grandmother had been.[52] It was for this reason that the connection drawn by commentators between balladry and the lower orders grew stronger as the seventeenth century progressed. It was, as we shall hear, an association that created a dilemma for the gentry as they contemplated balladry for themselves.

One's chances of encountering broadside ballads must also have been influenced by geography. Before 1695, virtually all of them were printed in London. When ballads passed out of the capital, they tended to follow well-worn trading routes between market towns, and it is therefore not surprising that urban settings are a common feature of ballad texts. There was, however, no impassable barrier between urban and rural environments, and a high proportion of those who lived in the countryside had frequent contact with at least one market town. The economic networks were surprisingly extensive in their coverage.[53] If ballads could reach provincial markets, then rural people could reach ballads. Singer-sellers

[51] Ibid. Several other examples can be found in the primary sources gathered by Würzbach, *The Rise of the English Street Ballad*, pp. 253–84.

[52] On the economic trends outlined in this paragraph, see Wrightson, *Earthly Necessities*, pp. 316–18; Joan Thirsk, *Economic Policy and Projects* (Oxford: Clarendon Press, 1978), pp. 174–5; Margaret Spufford, *The Great Reclothing of Rural England* (London: Hambledon Press, 1984), pp. 4–6; Lorna Weatherill, *Consumer Behaviour and Material Culture in Britain, 1660–1760*, 2nd edn. (London: Routledge, 1996), pp. 168, 192–3.

[53] Spufford, *Great Reclothing*; Michael Frearson, 'The English Corantos of the 1620s', unpublished PhD thesis, University of Cambridge (1993).

travelled widely, and through their efforts ballads that had started life in the capital spread outwards 'as from a spring', being carried 'in every pedlers packe sent to publike meetings in other places'. According to Richard Brathwaite, hawkers with new ballads would work the streets of London until the marketability of their songs was exhausted ('like stale fish'), at which point they would 'ride poast for the Countrie'. Nicholas Bownde claimed that at every fair and market one or two persons were to be heard and observed 'singing and selling of ballades'.[54]

We catch snatches of their singing only when they attracted unusual attention or became embroiled in controversy, as in the case of the London man, apprehended in 1620 at Trowbridge Fair on suspicion of vagrancy, 'carrying with him a store of ballads to sing in his travels'. Even on this limited basis, however, it is possible to demonstrate the presence of visiting ballad-singers in many other places during the seventeenth century: Norwich, Ely, Salisbury, Kirkby Lonsdale (Yorkshire), Abingdon (Oxfordshire), Worcester, Ambleside (Westmorland), Devizes (Wiltshire) and Ramsbotham (Cheshire).[55] The ballad-monger who in 1626 passed through the last of these settlements would surely have eluded us had he resisted the temptation to enter the chapel pulpit and deliver a hilarious but imprudent mock-sermon. Of course, we cannot tell how often the people of Ramsbotham listened to travelling hawkers, but the experience was clearly not unknown.[56]

Furthermore, the textual content of many broadsides suggests an awareness on the part of the writers and publishers of the need to engage with their provincial audiences. The ballads listed in the Stationers' Registers describe strange happenings in all regions of the country, and a selection of entries from a modern index to these records presents a suitably sensational summary: 'Adlington, Lancashire, monstrous child born in . . ., Chelmsford, Essex, three witches executed in . . ., Orford, Suffolk, peas grow on rocks in . . ., Worcester, thrifty maid of . . ., York, houses overthrown at, by a flood'. From one perspective, the point of such publications was to carry sensational news from the provinces to London, but they also served to reassure those who lived elsewhere that ballads were for them too. A similar point can be made about the 'pleasant

[54] Chettle, *Kind-Hart's Dreame*, G4r; Brathwaite, quoted by Thomson, 'Development of the Broadside Ballad Trade', p. 177; Bownde, *The Doctrine of the Sabbath*, p. 242.

[55] Watt, *Cheap Print*, pp. 24–5; McShane Jones, 'Rime and Reason', pp. 80–1; *Poverty in Early Stuart Salisbury*, p. 58; Spufford, *Great Reclothing*, p. 85; Aubrey, *Brief Lives*, p. 80; *REED Herefordshire, Worcestershire*, p. 453; EDC5 1626.56, ChRO.

[56] See below, p. 470.

northern tunes' that were regularly added to the musical resources of balladry, and about the occasional songs that were addressed explicitly to 'West-Country men'.[57]

Ballads, though printed in London, were regularly associated by commentators with the countryside. In 1625, John Davies wrote scornfully of the popularity of ballads 'in North-Villages, where every line / Of Plumpton Parke is held a work divine'. Certainly, the Derbyshire yeoman Leonard Wheatcroft was thoroughly familiar with the broadside format in the later seventeenth century, and he imitated it in several of his own compositions. He was in no sense a man of the city, yet his handwritten songs were often set to common broadside tunes and included many lines that revealed the influence of London balladry: 'Come you galants looke and by: / Heare is mirth and melody'; 'You Batchellers all cum listen awhile / I'le singe you a songe will make you to smile'; 'You Gentellmen of Derbyshire that minding are to ring / If you'l be pleas'd to stay awhile then y[ou] shall here me sing.' The last of these examples, typically, blended local references with a verbal and musical style that was grounded in the cheapest form of print. Wheatcroft also wrote a personal and eminently singable song for use in his work as the parish clerk of Ashover. It is entitled 'My Sounge when I Gather Clerk-wages' and is set 'to the tune of gerards mistris' (a complex melody, originally from a broadside of 1656).[58] Overall, therefore, it is clear that ballads were accessible in both rural and urban locations. Indeed, they mediated between the two environments, pointing out the divide even as they crossed it. It is nonetheless difficult to deny that ballads must have enjoyed their greatest concentration in London, and that songs on one recurring theme – the idiotic countryman floundering amid the alien complexities of city life – were aimed particularly at residents of the capital.[59]

Illiteracy was another possible constraint upon access to balladry, but once again its influence must not be overestimated. England's literacy profile, measured by the ability of individuals to sign their names, is well known. By the 1650s, approximately 30 per cent of men and 10 per cent of women could manage this act. Within these figures, there were marked regional differences. East Anglia was much more literate than Northumberland, for example, and London was more literate than anywhere else. Within each region and community, a hierarchy of literacy existed which

[57] Rollins, *An Analytical Index to the Ballad-entries*, index; *Pepys Ballads*, vol. II, pp. 116–17, 291.

[58] Davies, *A Scourge for Paper-prosecutors*, p. 4; D5433/1, DRO (for the tune, see Simpson, *British Broadside Ballad*, pp. 250–2).

[59] A fine example of the genre is *The Great Boobee* (*Pepys Ballads*, vol. IV, p. 232).

coincided roughly with the gradations of the social and occupational structure. Those who had no need to write – labourers in the diocese of Norwich, for instance – generally could not do so. Only 15 per cent of this particular group were able to sign their names in the period between 1580 and 1700.[60]

For several reasons, the statistics are misleading, particularly in their application to balladry. Firstly, they underestimate the ability to read, perhaps by a very significant margin. In early modern England, children learned to read before they learned to write, and a substantial proportion of the poorer ones left school with some training in the first skill but little or none in the second.[61] Many people were probably capable of reading a ballad, but not of signing their names. Secondly, early modern people did not in general regard illiteracy as a cause for acute embarrassment, and they apparently thought nothing of asking others to help them decipher a text.[62] An inability to read was not, therefore, equivalent to an inability to engage with print. In 1595, the preacher Nicholas Bownde spoke of people who, 'though they can not reade themselves, nor any of theirs, yet will have many Ballades set up in their houses, that so they might learn them, as they shall have occasion'. Bownde's observation suggests a third point: for many people, a ballad was something to be committed to memory, and it had a life beyond the printed page. In 1613, a drunken Worcestershire man allegedly insulted his vicar and all godly preachers by saying that they 'conned a ballet without booke and thereof made a sermon'.[63] His precise intentions are a matter for debate, but the reference to memorising songs from print seems clear enough. Ballads passed from page to mouth to ear to mind to page and round and round again in a continuous cycle. In the process, individual texts and tunes were gradually modified, and successive written versions may be quite different from one another. There was no fixed or 'correct' form. Printed or manuscript texts were still comparatively novel, and they were absorbed and disseminated within a culture that remained substantially oral and aural. Memories were powerful, and Bownde also commented on the capacity of people to retain lengthy stories in their minds after a single

[60] The classic study remains David Cressy, *Literacy and the Social Order: Reading and Writing in Tudor and Stuart England* (Cambridge: Cambridge University Press, 1980). A more recent summary of the evidence can be found in Reay, *Popular Cultures*, pp. 39–42.

[61] Margaret Spufford, 'First Steps in Literacy: the Reading and Writing Experiences of the Humblest Seventeenth-century Spiritual Autobiographers', *Social History* 4 (1979), 407–36.

[62] Several examples can be found in *The Diary of Roger Lowe*, ed. Sachse.

[63] Bownde, *The Doctrine of the Sabbath*, p. 241; STAC 8 281/13, NA.

hearing (though he noted with frustration that the ability did not necessarily extend to passages from the Bible). In a country alehouse, Izaak Walton's fictional anglers were introduced to a handsome musical milkmaid by her proud mother: 'Maudlin shal sit by and sing you the good old Song of the Hunting in Chevy Chase, or some other good Ballad, for she hath good store of them.' Until this point in the description, we might be tempted to assume that the milkmaid possessed a physical collection of broadsides, especially in view of the fact that another of Walton's alehouses displayed 'twenty Ballads stuck about the wall'. The maternal tribute concludes, however, with the remark, 'Maudlin hath a notable memory.' The anglers also sing ballads to one another in the evenings, invariably 'without book'. Where their memories fail them, they simply invent additional lines to fill the gaps.[64]

Even when a printed text was present, reading was often performed aloud, as both a private and a public activity. And even silent reading was probably imagined as sound, for early modern people felt more acutely than we do that 'writing is no more than the image or character of speech'. People were much taken with 'the clinking of syllables', and in 1660, Thomas Rugg noted in his diary the publication of several 'jeering books about the Rump Parliament'. If syllables clinked and books jeered, then ballads were louder still. 'Give ear to me you youngmen whilst I write', commanded one moralising author.[65] The period provides abundant evidence of perpetual exchange between orality and literacy, and a striking number of modern folksongs – lovingly collected from ageing singers by early twentieth-century scholars who scorned anything printed – can be dated back to broadside ballads of the early modern period. It is a satisfying irony that many of these cherished folksongs may owe their longevity to the preservative power of print.[66] Through the early modern centuries, orality and literacy circled one another constantly, like partners in a country dance. We cannot assess the ability to sing by measuring the ability to sign.

Among the gentry, access was to some degree constrained by a rather different factor: ballads were cheap, common and coarse, and often presented as unsuitable for men and women of refinement. At the top of society they were apparently held in low esteem. Ballads were the songs

[64] Bownde, *The Doctrine of the Sabbath*, p. 216; Walton, *The Compleat Angler*, pp. 49, 122, 203.

[65] Puttenham, *Arte of English Poesie*, p. 264; Fox, *Oral and Literate Culture*, p. 24; *The Diurnal of Thomas Rugg, 1659–1661*, ed. William L. Sachse *Camden 3rd Series* 111 (1961), pp. 66–7; *Pepys Ballads*, vol. II, p. 36.

[66] Thomson, 'Development of the Broadside Ballad Trade'.

'that are sung in the Streets by the Vulgar' or pinned up on posts for the benefit of 'every dull mechanic'. William Webbe spoke of 'sencelesse sonets' and 'grosse devices', and Thomas Nash was no more benevolent. Ballads that were composed in praise of eminent councillors or patriots were, he alleged, merely insulting. 'A few ragged Rimes', concocted by 'some stitcher, Weaver, spendthrift, or Fidler', constituted a negative tribute to the deeds of the great and good: 'It makes the learned sort to be silent, when als they see unlearned sots so insolent.'[67] Nash, keen to humiliate Gabriel Harvey, alleged that his enemy had exhibited an extreme fondness for balladry in his younger days, obsessively buying up all the broadsheets that went on sale at the markets and fairs of Essex. Harvey, as portrayed by Nash, found one popular song 'more transporting and ravishing than Platoes Discourse of the immortalitie of the soule was to Cato'. Thus was his idiocy proven. Puttenham added depth to this derision by drawing a distinction between the learned and popular ears. The former was 'delicate' and capable of comprehending sophisticated poetry written to complex rhyme schemes; the latter was 'rude and barbarous', easily satisfied by simple couplets of the sort found in balladry. A century later, John Playford understood the difference, and was therefore at pains to defend himself against the charge that most of the songs in one of his books were 'worse than common Ballads sung about the Streets by Foot-boys and Link-boys'.[68]

This, however, was only half of the story, for there was a much brighter aspect to the relationship between gentlefolk and ballads. It was generally conducted more privately than its antagonistic counterpart, but its traces are nevertheless unmistakable. On occasion, ballad-singers or singing musicians were permitted to perform at the mansions of the mighty, and rewarded for their trouble. According to Anthony Weldon, James I himself was in the habit of hiring fiddlers to assist favoured courtiers in the task of amusing him with bawdy songs. Weldon was hostile to the king, but he is not our only informant. A ballad with the suggestive title *A Maydens Lamentation for a Bedfellow* (to the tune of 'I will give thee kisses one, two, or three') was published in about 1615 with a subtitle claiming that 'it hath beene sung at the Court'. A few decades later,

[67] Dyche-Pardon, quoted by Graham Strahle, *An Early Music Dictionary: Musical Terms from British Sources, 1500–1700* (Cambridge: Cambridge University Press, 1995), p. 25; Webbe, *Discourse of English Poetrie*, D1r; Nash, *Anatomie of Absurditie*, B4v.

[68] Nash, *Have with You to Saffron Walden, or Gabriell Harvey's Hunt is Up* (London, 1596), K3r, L1r; Puttenham, *Arte of English Poesie*, p. 87; Playford, *Choice Ayres and Songs to Sing to the Theorbo Lute and Bass-viol. The Fourth Book* (London, 1683), A2r.

the godly Barringtons of Hatfield Broad Oak (Essex) once paid four pence to 'an old ballet singer' who passed their way. Ballads may also have been in the repertoire of the 'singing woman' who received a shilling from the Le Stranges in May 1631 and the '2 singers that came from Newberye' to perform for Sir Richard Paulet at Christmas in 1613.[69]

Nor did suspicion of ballads prevent some gents from purchasing copies for munificent distribution among their employees. In Restoration Westmorland, Daniel Fleming regularly bought ballads, and some at least of them were destined for his 'young men'. In Lancashire, Nicholas Blundell gave 'Ballets and Apples' to some of his labourers after they sang for him in a field on 17 August 1705. Perhaps this was also what had motivated John Heyricke to write to his brother in about 1580, asking him to send from London 'one hundred of ballits, as many of shocking of the shits as yow cane get and as many of mannington' (the first of these is more commonly known as 'The Shaking of the Sheets').[70] Sometimes, servants not only received ballads but performed them for the pleasure of a household's more privileged members. In 1541, the Seymours rewarded Pecock and his company (probably resident musicians) 'for syngyng their ballets'. At the end of the seventeenth century, the Stukeleys had a servant with a 'collection of old songs made on Robin Hood . . . which he used to sing over to us in a winter's evening'. This was a common pastime, though some commentators considered it a dangerous one too. In 1735, a correspondent in the *Gentleman's Magazine* rebuked 'our middling Gentry' for allowing their daughters to learn ballads from mere household servants: 'By such foolish stories Miss is deluded; sighs, pities, and at last loves; and so too often undone without remedy' (clearly, the ballads in question were those in which true love triumphed in the face of oppressive convention). Ballads could thus form socially beneficial links between gents and commoners or between men and women, but they could also lead to more unseemly couplings.[71]

Other eminent men went further, singing ballads for themselves at gatherings of the supposedly genteel. As a young man, the future bishop

[69] Weldon, *Court and Character of King James*, pp. 84–5; *Pepys Ballads*, vol. I, pp. 286–7; Barrington accounts, quoted by Mepham, 'History of the Drama in Essex', p. 274; LEST P7, fo. 4v (after pagination recommences before the year 1631), NRO; 44M69/E4/28, unpaginated, HRO.

[70] Payments for ballads on 29 May 1660 and 23 February 1665/6, Fleming accounts, WD Ry box 119, Cumbria Record Office (see also McShane Jones, 'Rime and Reason', p. 81); MS Eng. Hist c.474, no. 159, Bodleian Library.

[71] Price, *Patrons and Musicians*, p. 123; Fox, *Oral and Literate Culture*, p. 42; *Gentleman's Magazine*, cited by Thomson, 'Development of the Broadside Ballad Trade', p. 179.

Richard Corbet had relished his experience of singing and hearing ballads such as *John Dory*, *Chevy Chase* and *Arthur*. He was thus amply qualified to pose as a ballad-singer on market day at Abingdon.[72] According to Robert Burton, many 'silly gentlewomen' were all too easily bowled over by finely attired 'swaggering companions' who could ride, dance, talk freely of knightly adventures 'and sing old ballet tunes'. The diary of Samuel Pepys confirms that ballads were thoroughly familiar among the gentry and aristocracy in Restoration London. On 23 April 1660, Pepys was present when his employer, the Earl of Sandwich, 'fell to singing of a song made upon the Rump, with which he pleased himself well – to the tune of *The Blacksmith*'. Samuel was more complimentary when he himself provided the entertainment: on 2 January 1665 he joined Lord Brouncker and company at Covent Garden and 'occasioned much mirth with a ballet I brought with me, made from the seamen at sea to their ladies in town – saying Sir W. Penn, Sir G Ascue, and Sir J Lawson made them'. In other words, he applied a general ballad to the specific circumstances of his acquaintances. Admittedly, Pepys does not tell us that he actually sang the ballad to the group, but it seems abundantly probable. He certainly sang on other social occasions, and his musical session with the actress Elizabeth Knepp on 2 January 1666 seems to have involved ballads. Samuel does not tell us what he himself sang, but his companion performed 'her little Scotch song of Barbary Allen' (which certainly appeared in broadside versions).[73]

When pre-eminent individuals purchased broadsides, therefore, they did not necessarily pass each and every one to their servants. Indeed, a minority built personal collections of ballads, or had them painstakingly transcribed into notebooks. Without their efforts, our knowledge of the genre would be thin indeed. During the seventeenth century, substantial numbers of ballads were gathered, pasted and copied out by a galaxy of stars (or their servants): Elias Ashmole, John Selden, John Aubrey, Anthony Wood, Samuel Pepys, Edward Lhuyd, Robert Harley (Earl of Oxford) and his caterer John Bagford. Pepys did not begin collecting ballads seriously until after he ceased keeping his diary in 1669, but even before this date he clearly kept his eyes and ears open, occasionally obtaining songs and asking his servants to transcribe some of those that he found particularly stimulating. On 16 June 1668, he dined in Newbury

[72] Richard Corbet, *Certain Elegant Poems* (London, 1647), pp. 37–8. See above, p. 245.

[73] Burton, *Anatomy of Melancholy*, p. 581; *Diary of Samuel Pepys*, vol. I, p. 114, vol. VI, p. 2, vol. VII, p. 1.

and heard a rendition of 'a song of the old Courtier of Q. Eliz'. This ballad, normally chanted on a single note with a short melodic refrain, 'did please me mightily and I did cause W H to write it out'.[74] Pepys collected with a new assiduity during the 1680s and 1690s, but by this time, sadly, he had ceased to document his activities in the journal. We might speculate that ballad-collecting was in some measure a substitute for diary-keeping, satisfying Pepys's famous urge to impose order on his world in a manner that did not consume his time and endanger his fragile eyes to quite the same degree. Many other gentlemen bought or transcribed ballads, apparently for their own private use, but without the level of devotion exhibited by those named above.[75] Overall, it seems likely that a substantial minority of the gentry at least dabbled in ballads.

It is clear that like-minded gents conferred together, assisted one another and perhaps even swapped sheets (like schoolboys of the 1950s with their stamps). In 1598, John Chamberlain wrote to Dudley Carleton in Ostend, thanking him 'for the ballads, books, and papers sent'. Lord Conway, in London during the mid-1630s, paid out 3s 6d 'For ballads and a play book' and, interestingly, a further 2s 'to Mr Selden's boy' for purposes unspecified. When John Prideaux travelled to Worcester in 1641 to become its bishop, a local gentleman offered a speech of welcome, concluding with the suggestion, 'lend me what ballads you have, and I will let you see what I have: I know you to love all such things'. Occasionally, there was subterfuge. It has been suggested, for example, that several of the Earl of Oxford's songs (the Roxburghe collection) had been surreptitiously removed from Anthony Wood's own body of ballads. There are traces of Wood's handwriting on some of the sheets, and the margins of others have suffered suspicious snipping, apparently to conceal the crime.[76] Musical collecting, as many Elvis fans know, can all too easily become an uncontrollable stop-at-nothing obsession. It can also attract scorn. In 1774, Joel Collier mocked the ballad-collecting habit when he wrote his *Musical Travels*. One country esquire, he reported, led him proudly into his hall, 'which was stuck round with various antique pieces of music, such as Chevy Chase, The children in the wood, Three children sliding on the ice, The history of St. George, &c. which he kindly permitted me to enrich my collection with'. This sounds innocuous enough, but when the ballad-loving gentleman is placed alongside other characters

[74] *Diary of Samuel Pepys*, vol. IX, p. 242.

[75] See, for example, manuscript ballads, Portland Literary Collection, Pw V 41, and notebook of Sir William Cavendish, Pw V 25, fo. 62r, HL.

[76] *CSPD 1598–1601*, p. 96; *CSPD 1634–5*, p. 590; *Shirburn Ballads*, pp. 4–5.

in the book – 'Lord Diddle-doodle' and 'Dr. Hiccup', for instance – it is clear that we are not being invited to admire his hobby.[77]

Others were not quite collectors, but they nevertheless encouraged or allowed the display of ballads within their homes. In 1595, Bownde apparently referred to the presence of ballads in 'the houses of great personages'. Bartholomew Cokes, the ballad-loving esquire created by Ben Jonson, turns to his sister and asks, 'do your remember the ballads over the nursery-chimney at home o' my own pasting up?' And when Joseph Addison visited the country residences of the gentry during the early eighteenth century, he always made a point of studying the printed sheets that were pasted on the walls. 'The last Piece that I met with', he revealed, 'gave me the most exquisite Pleasure. My Reader will think I am not serious when I acquaint him that the Piece I am going to speak of was the old Ballad of the Two Children in the Wood.'[78] This, clearly, was a song that generated both admiration and derision among the social elite.

Some members of the gentry were sufficiently familiar with the ballad style and format that they composed songs of their own. A particularly fascinating example appears in the assize records for Essex. In 1594, Thomas Hale of Walthamstow, gentleman, was accused of composing a ballad that lamented in poignant terms the demise of Roman Catholicism in England. The text is given in full, and although no tune is specified it is obvious that the verses were intended for the melody known as 'Sick, sick' or 'Weep, weep'. The Walthamstow ballad opens with the second of these repetitive pairings: 'Weep, weepe, and still I weepe, / For who can chuse but weepe' (**Website track 14 and Appendix**). The text fits the tune precisely, and it is obvious that the alleged composer was a knowledgeable consumer of balladry. The first line, indeed, is lifted directly from a broadside by William Elderton, published some years earlier. Hale, it has to be said, denied authorship and was judged merely to have transcribed the ballad. The court also noted, however, that a copy had been found in a house formerly owned by his father.[79] The circumstances were somewhat suspicious. There are rather less controversial home-made ballads, with named tunes, in the papers of several wealthy families, including the Blundells of Lancashire and the Molineuxs of Surrey.[80] Of course, we cannot be sure

77 Bicknell *alias* Collier, *Musical Travels*, p. 36.

78 Bownde, *The Doctrine of the Sabbath*, pp. 241–2; Jonson, *Bartholomew Fair*, p. 86; Addison, quoted by Dugaw, *Warrior Women*, p. 17.

79 Assize file 35/36/2, no. 34, transcript available in ERO. For information on the earlier ballad, see Simpson, *British Broadside Ballad*, pp. 660–1.

80 *REED Lancashire*, pp. 32–5; LM/1800, SHC.

whether members of these families actually composed such songs themselves, but they clearly commissioned them and ordered the making of transcriptions. Balladry was by no means an alien form of music.

Perhaps a known receptivity to song helps to account for the manner in which certain privileged families supplied heroes and heroines for the narratives of balladry. The heroism of the music-loving Berties was proclaimed through the trumpet of balladry for two centuries and more. Thomas Deloney's song of 1602 *The Dutchesse of Suffolkes Calamitie* told the story of Catherine Bertie, a Protestant heroine who, 'for the love of God alone', endured great hardship and a period of exile during the reign of Queen Mary. It began in a book, but soon became a broadside. In one verse, we learn of an heir, born in exile: 'A Son she had in Germany, / Peregrine Bertie call'd by name.'[81] This boy was to become Lord Willoughby, himself celebrated by balladeers for one of his military successes against the Spanish in the Low Countries during the later 1580s ('with 1500 English, against forty thousand *Spaniards*, where the English obtained a notable Victory'). The melody soon became known as 'Lord Willoughby' and provided the musical setting for a number of other ballads.[82] The Berties are known from other sources to have been musically inclined, and their fame among the ballad-writers may in part be a consequence of this fact. It is interesting to note, for example, that in January 1562 the Duchess of Suffolk and her husband had paid out 46s 8d 'for a lute bought of Rose for mr Peregrine'. Here, one star of future ballads was endeavouring to pass on her musical interests to another.[83]

In the light of such evidence, it becomes less surprising that ballad-composers sometimes addressed their songs specifically to the gentry. Of course, this was to some degree an affectation, designed to flatter the humble, but it also had a more direct and literal purpose, for gentlemen did buy and sing ballads. 'Come Gentlemen all, and listen a while', instructed one ballad. 'Come light and listen you Gentlemen all', suggested another. Ballads were also addressed regularly to 'brave Gallants', a term designed to draw out from the bustling crowd men with a certain swagger. In *Bartholomew Fair*, Nightingale attracts attention by calling on 'My masters and friends', and his most enthusiastic customer is an esquire.[84]

[81] *Pepys Ballads*, vol. I, p. 544. See also Simpson, *British Broadside Ballad*, pp. 587–90, and Watt, *Cheap Print*, pp. 91–4.

[82] *Pepys Ballads*, vol. II, p. 131; Simpson, *British Broadside Ballad*, pp. 467–71.

[83] Anc VII/A/2, fo. 31r, LA. The musical family of the Earls of Rutland attracted similarly devoted attention from balladeers.

[84] *Pepys Ballads*, vol. II, pp. 109, 113, vol. IV, p. 184; Jonson, *Bartholomew Fair*, pp. 84–90.

Once in a while, a gentleman might even allow his guard to slip by saying something essentially complimentary about balladry. At such moments, it was necessary to qualify one's enthusiasm with a distancing remark of some sort. Indeed, this pattern of expression was intriguingly entrenched. Most famously, Sir Philip Sidney was ashamed of his love for the ballad *Chevy Chase*:

Certainly I must confesse my own barbarousnes, I never heard the olde song of Percy and Douglas, that I found not my heart moved more then with a Trumpet: and yet it is sung by some blinde Crouder, with no rougher voice then rude stile: which being so evill apparelled in the dust and cobwebbes of that uncivill age, what would it worke trimmed in the gorgeous eloquence of Pindar?

Others framed their thoughts according to the same template. John Rous, a prominent minister in Suffolk, transcribed ballad verses into his diary, but once added the remark, 'I hate these following railing rimes, Yet keepe them for president of the times' (even his clerical disdain for the songs of the lower laity was expressed in a balladesque couplet). Charles Butler referred happily to 'the infinite multitude of Balads (set to sundry pleasant and delightfull tunes, by cunning and witti Composers)' on one page of *The Principles of Musik*, but elsewhere in the same book he described ballads as 'filthy', 'obscene' and offensive 'to modest ears and eys' (this was a circle that Butler attempted to square by arguing that balladry was in the process of cleaning up its act).[85]

A more earthy variation upon the same theme was provided by Sir William Cornwallis. He confessed to having enjoyed ballads and other forms of cheap print in his youth, but reassured his readers that he had since come to handle the works of 'two penny Poets' with greater circumspection: 'I would know them but beware of being familiar with them. My custome is to read these and presently to make use of them. For they lie in my privy.' Cornwallis even admitted to enjoying the performances of common ballad-singers, though he was careful to add that his particular fascination was threefold: 'to see earthlings satisfied with such course stuffe, to hear vice rebuked, and to see the power of vertue that pierceth the head of such a base Historian, and vile Auditory'. In other words, his interest was mainly anthropological and he had nothing in common with the rank-and-file listeners: 'The recreation to see how thoroughly the standers by are affected, what strange gestures come from them, what strained stuffe from their Poet,

[85] Philip Sidney, *An Apologie for Poetrie* (London, 1595), F4r–v; *The Diary of John Rous*, ed. Mary Anne Everett Green (London: Camden Society, 1856), p. 109; Butler, *Principles of Musik*, pp. 8, 130–1.

what shift they make to stand to heare, what extremities he is driven to for Rime, how they adventure their purses ...' Ballads were the songs that the socially pre-eminent hated to love, and Cornwallis may not have been the only gentleman who turned them into toilet paper. Cheap broadsides were a guilt-inducing pollutant of high culture, and the soiled knight was perhaps cleansing himself in more ways than one.[86]

The contradictions of the relationship were nicely illustrated by Aaron Holland, gentleman, in 1624–5. In a deposition, he told the Court of Star Chamber that he had recently had cause to rebuke a ballad-singer near Clerkenwell Cross. Noting that the pedlar was 'a lustie fellow, and fit for labour', Holland grew angry 'and much blamed and reprehended him, that being so strong and able a person hee followed so idle a course of life as ... singinge of ballets upp and downe the streets'. At this point, the hierarchical code of conduct naturally required that the ballad-singer shuffle off with his eyes down and his tail between his legs, but instead he replied 'that hee would sell & sing ballets, notwithstanding what [Holland] saied to the contrarie'. We might be tempted to conclude that this model gent despised balladry and all its agents. There is, however, more to the case than meets the eye, for it was Holland, rather than the ballad-singer, who stood accused before the court, under suspicion for the role he had allegedly played in the production of a libellous play and, ironically, an accompanying ballad. Holland owned the Red Bull theatre, where the play had been staged, and a different ballad-singer claimed that Holland had hired him to perform the offending song under the window of its intended victim, a widow named Anne Ellesden (who had allegedly been forced to drink sufficient spirits to kill a horse before being tricked into marriage while all but insensible). It thus appears that the wily old gentleman was striking a pose for the court, presenting himself publicly as the righteous enemy of balladry while, behind the scenes, promoting scurrilous songs. He played the hierarchy card, hoping thereby to stimulate the sympathy of the judge. In a delicious twist, he even claimed that the Clerkenwell singer had opened their fraught exchange by trying to sell him a copy of *Kepe the Widow Waking*, the very ballad that he and his associates had allegedly commissioned. If Holland did indeed have a hand in its composition, then there can be no doubt that he understood the genre well enough. The song opens with a classic

[86] William Cornwallis, *Essayes* (London, 1600–1), essay 15 ('Of the Observation, and Use of Things').

audience-gathering verse that can only have been penned by an expert (**Website track 13 and Appendix**).[87]

Pepys and the other collectors of ballads distanced themselves from the songs either by transcribing them or by pasting them into bound volumes that could be safely shut and shelved. In this manner, they distinguished themselves from the common consumers of balladry – who pinned up their songs until they faded – and repackaged the coarse sheets for gentle eyes and ears. Publishers evidently understood the complexities of the relationship between ballads and gentlefolk, and some of them produced distinctive 'white-letter' ballads, primarily for the privileged. White-letter script looks perfectly legible to modern eyes, but it was rather less accessible than the common black-letter form to those educated in early modern England. It therefore carried hints of a certain exclusivity, and the same characteristic was reflected in the higher prices charged for white-letter ballads. Some of these songs, moreover, seemed to cock a snook at the conventions of common balladry, thereby reassuring wealthy purchasers that they were a cut above the rest. Several of them recommended tunes chosen for the satirical import of their verbal titles alone rather than for their actual compatibility with the metre of the verses. Others dispensed with tune titles altogether, or suggested somewhat scornfully that they could be sung to any one of forty melodies. White-letter ballads were also more likely than their common cousins to contain Latin expressions and allusions to specific high-ranking individuals.[88] They thus enabled society's superior sorts to participate in balladry in a manner that minimised the fear of contamination from below.

Despite such mechanisms, commentators on matters theatrical were sometimes struck and frustrated by the evident attachment of privileged audiences to the baser forms of balladry. In 1667, Pepys spoke to Thomas Killigrew, a dramatist and theatrical entrepreneur with courtly connections, who reported that he had tried repeatedly to replace ballads with more refined music within the plays he staged at one venue, 'but he never could do it . . . , which speaks our rudenesse still'. Half a century later, one letter-writer lamented the poor taste exhibited by 'the People of Fashion'. They had, he complained, abandoned 'the Opera and the Old House' in favour of 'the Beggar's Opera which all seem to agree to be hardly fit for the delight of children. But it seems to me to be still more odd that what

[87] STAC 8/31/16, fos. 19v, 47r, NA; Sisson, *Lost Plays of Shakespeare's Age*, pp. 80–124. See also Stanley Wells, *Shakespeare and Co.* (London: Penguin, 2007), pp. 124–7.

[88] There is an enlightening discussion of this superior brand of broadside in McShane Jones, 'Rime and Reason', pp. 40, 190–2.

everybody condemns, everybody should countenance.'[89] Gay's famous work made extensive use of common broadside tunes and owed a portion of its success to the way in which it simultaneously deplored and deployed the customs of balladry, thereby enabling 'the People of Fashion' to tap their feet while shaking their heads. In doing so, they situated themselves in an alternative tradition of confused consumption that was as old as the broadside ballad itself.

Thus a cycle of attraction and repulsion operated continuously. Bigwigs and ballads were connected in a wonderfully complex relationship, something like an illicit affair between the gentleman and his low-born but irresistible maidservant (Pepys knew all about this too). Contrasting attitudes circulated among the gentry and even within the minds of its individual members, receding and recurring like the phrases of a ballad tune. It all seems to cast doubt upon models of early modern cultural transition that posit a clear and chronological withdrawal of the social elite from participation in popular culture. The ballad evidence suggests rather that love and loathing existed in a dialogic relationship, drawing energy from one another. A sense of propriety certainly did condition the relationship between gents and ballads, but it clearly did not exclude the socially pre-eminent from the audience in any straightforward sense. Gentlemen sought out and sang ballads, even if they later stacked them up beside their privies.

If status-anxiety could not drive a wedge between ballads and buyers, then perhaps religious and moral concerns could force such a separation. The rise of Protestantism during the sixteenth century had a paradoxical effect on the evolution of the ballad. On one hand, mid-century reformers stimulated balladry by specialising in religious protest songs that mocked the forces of Catholic tradition. They wrote and performed songs with titles such as 'The Hunt is Up' and 'Downe for All your Shaven Crown', though we learn of their work only when it was overheard by the wrong people.[90] On the other hand, Protestants were already developing a rhetoric within which the singing of ballads was presented as evidence of ungodliness and lazy apathy where truth was concerned. To Miles Coverdale, writing in the mid-1530s, common ballads were 'naughty', 'wanton' and 'unchristen'. They corrupted their eager consumers, entangling the young 'in the snares of unclennesse'.[91] Until the 1580s, the two

[89] *Diary of Samuel Pepys*, vol. VIII, p. 56; Henry Ellison, quoted by Edward Hughes, *North Country Life in the Eighteenth Century* (Oxford: Oxford University Press, 1952), p. 385.

[90] Simpson, *British Broadside Ballad*, p. 326; *REED Herefordshire, Worcestershire*, p. 419.

[91] Miles Coverdale, *Goostly Psalmes and Spiritual Songes* (London, *c.* 1535), preface.

strands existed together, and reformers clearly hoped that their own pure and zealous ballads (along with metrical psalms) would drive all enemies from the field. After this date, however, the first strand tended towards disintegration and the second took up the strain. Thenceforward, the most zealous of Protestants – 'puritans', for want of a better term – endeavoured to turn their backs on balladry once and for all. They abandoned their previous tactic of singing and selling suitably reformed ballads as part of the urgent but frustrating work of conversion, and they came increasingly to portray balladry as something that was by definition intolerably lascivious.[92] The rapid rise of a thoroughly commercial enterprise, within which ballads flew or floundered on the basis of their economic success rather than their spiritual qualities, was clearly an important contributory factor. According to Thomas Lovell, Satan was truly the author of all such songs, setting them cunningly to the best (or worst) tunes in his efforts to infiltrate humanity. It had become apparent that the devil could not be beaten at his own game, and a new one with stricter rules had therefore to be devised. According to Nicholas Bownde, the mass of people who preferred ballads to psalms revealed themselves to be 'voyd of Gods word, and of his spirit'.[93] Indeed, ballads were regularly portrayed as wretched rivals to the psalms, the very antithesis of Scripture. To Thomas Adams, preaching during the 1620s, broadside songs were 'the ballads of Hell'. By this time, godly critics were describing ballads and their makers as 'unclean', 'obscene', 'filthy', 'impure', 'base' and 'pestilent'. The ballad-writer, alleged H.S. in 1658, 'poysons the world' by seeking to 'tickle up the ears of people'.[94] In the estimation of such commentators, the cheap printed song was nothing less than a road-map to damnation. Its flimsy appearance and ephemeral nature belied its corrupting power, for there was nothing light and fluffy about the gates of hell.

Any straightforward association between puritanism and hostility to ballads is, however, complicated by two factors. Firstly, the pious prejudice against balladry can also be traced in the minds of those who are not normally considered puritanical. Admittedly, it here became somewhat diluted, and was expressed most commonly in the form of disquiet concerning any combination of secular tunes and sacred texts or contexts. In 1631, Bishop Laud of London joined Archbishop Abbot in rebuking

[92] Collinson, *Birthpangs of Protestant England*, pp. 108–12.

[93] Lovell, *Dialogue between Custom and Veritie*, fos. 4v–7v; Bownde, *The Doctrine of the Sabbath*, p. 243.

[94] *The Workes of Thomas Adams*, p. 151; Butler, *Principles of Musik*, pp. 130–1; H. S., *To the Musicioners*, p. 8.

a minister for daring to set the words of psalms to the tunes of ballads. In this instance, the scourge of puritanism stood shoulder to shoulder with one of its allies. Laud presumably agreed that such melodies were to some extent tainted by their association with ballads. This did not, of course, amount to an outright condemnation of balladry as a whole, but nor was it a ringing endorsement.[95] Half a century later, the organist at Gloucester Cathedral reportedly provoked scandal by playing 'upon the organ a common ballad in the hearing of 1500 or 2000 people'. Cathedral clerics were not noted for their puritanical sensibilities, but when the young gentlewomen in the congregation 'invited one another to dance' it was clear to all that the organist had gone too far. He was ordered to leave the church. George Wither, too, spoke out against those who twinned the sacred and the profane in music (he also wished to ban ballad-writers from using the name of Jesus in their songs). It seems, therefore, that the rhetoric of puritans against balladry exerted at least a measure of persuasive force over those who shared neither their ecclesiological principles nor their temperamental intensity.[96]

Secondly, not all puritans were quite as good as their word when it came to the boycott of balladry. Their spokespeople regularly distanced themselves from ballads in no uncertain terms, but there is also evidence – particularly from the middle of the seventeenth century – that people of supposedly advanced and militant godliness were sometimes unable to resist the appeal and particularly the utility of a good song. The royalist John Taylor had no doubt that cultural strategists on the parliamentarian side deployed ballads and 'scurvy songs' in their efforts to raise funds and recruit fighters. Taylor depicted a reformed Roundhead who had joined the army after finding such music as sweet 'as the fat end of a Pudding' (he had since come to his senses). During the 1640s, parliamentarian ballad-writers did indeed turn to balladry in order to enlist soldiers and scorn their enemies, publishing titles such as *The Masse Priests Lamentation* and *The Zealous Soldier*. Ironically, the latter ballad recommended that God's warriors should channel their musical energies into the singing of psalms. Only a small proportion of parliamentarian ballads has survived, and thus the impression – promoted by contemporary royalists – that the supporters of parliament eschewed balladry and other forms of merriment has been perpetuated. Zealots turned to balladry in times

95 For a fuller discussion of this case, see below, pp. 420–1.

96 Dora H. Robertson, *Sarum Close* (London: J. Cape, 1938), pp. 202–3; Wither, *A Preparation to the Psalter*, pp. 86–7.

of need. When its persuasive potential outweighed its dangers, some puritans managed to forget their qualms and augment their psalms with something rather less respectable. When the time came to put the protest back into Protestantism, ballads played their part. In this sense, there are interesting links to be made between the mid-sixteenth and mid-seventeenth centuries. Balladry was irresistible – this was part of the peril – and even Thomas Lovell had seen fit to deploy common ballad metre in his seminal Elizabethan assault on the form.[97]

Moral strictures against balladry were not, therefore, applied to the business of living in any comprehensive sense, even by those whom we might expect to have heeded them most attentively. Among the population as a whole, the shrill cries of the moralists seem to have been comprehensively drowned out by the relentless 'fa la la' of the ballad-singers. More and more songs were printed, and there is nothing to suggest that the English majority perceived the cheapest of literary forms as inevitably wicked in its influence. After all, a substantial minority of ballads dealt with religious themes throughout the period, and many that were not specifically spiritual nevertheless expressed a stern social morality and a belief in the power of God to intervene at will in the affairs of humans. In Lovell's *Dialogue*, the two characters 'Custom' and 'Veritie' clash discordantly regarding the value of popular songs on religious and moral themes. 'Veritie', true to form, rejects them just as whole-heartedly as he does more obviously ribald broadsides. 'Custom' is perplexed by such arguments, and mounts a common-sense defence of sober songs and their performers:

For some by them instructed are,
how to be godly wise,
And soe from that which minstrels sing,
a great deale more wil beare
Then [than] when of godly Preachers they
a learned sermon heare.[98]

Of course, the religion of the ballads was an eclectic blend, within which traditionalism was far more prominent than crystal-clear protestantism. This combination was, however, more than sufficient to defy the classification of balladry as necessarily ungodly. Admittedly, there was much else besides, for ballads were sung on all subjects under the sun. Many people,

[97] *Works of John Taylor not Included in the Folio Volume*, vol. IV, p. 6, 'The Generall Complaint', and vol. V, p. 9, 'The Conversion'; McShane Jones, 'Rime and Reason', pp. 177–82; Lovell, *Dialogue between Custom and Veritie.*

[98] Lovell, *Dialogue between Custom and Veritie*, D6r.

on many social levels, clearly appreciated the range of songs available. They paid their money and made their choice, in spite of the critical rhetoric.

The appeal of balladry

Ultimately, the constraints upon access to balladry were surprisingly feeble. Obstacles existed, but the evident irresistibility of this form of musical poetry meant that most of them could be clambered over or barged through without difficulty. The participating audience encompassed peers and paupers, merchants and milkmaids, bishops and bakers. Ballads were sung by and for men and women of all ages, and the pleasure they brought was shared by children too. 'There's ne'er a child in Banbury of 7 years old, but can Sing the battle of Mardyke', claimed one of Thomas D'Urfey's fictional characters in 1678.[99] Ballads were heard in theatres, milking sheds, private homes and public alehouses. In Van Heemskerck's tavern scene, several broadsides are pinned to the walls and doors, ready for customers to peruse and perform at their leisure (see jacket illustration). Ballads sounded on ships, street-corners and hillsides, and they provided music at fairs, weddings and elections. In 1679, for example, election ballads were an integral feature of the fierce contest that took place in Buckingham, and one politically partisan performer allegedly forced some local fiddlers to accompany him when he sang such a song in the George Inn. Passions had run equally high at Cripplegate on a day in July 1649. A poor woman, singing ballads to the passers-by, was confronted by a parliamentary soldier who allegedly 'assayl'd her, and tore her Ballads'. A major brawl broke out when 'many Butchers and others, came out of their shops [and] rescued her'. Balladry was so successful that it also sucked in melodies from other kinds of music. In 1586, William Webbe could scarcely think of a single English tune 'which hath not some poeticall ditties framed according to the numbers thereof, some to Rogero, some to Trenchmore, to down right Squire, to Galliardes, to Pavines, to Jygges, to Brawles, to all manner of tunes which everie Fidler knows better than my selfe'. In 1660, the diarist Thomas Rugg noted that one ballad, *The Rump Dock't*, was 'almost in eveybodys [sic] mouth', and it seems that his exaggeration may not have been unduly exuberant.[100]

[99] D'Urfey, quoted by McShane Jones, 'Rime and Reason', p. 167.

[100] Mark Knights, *Politics and Opinion in Crisis, 1678–81* (Cambridge: Cambridge University Press, 1994), p. 172; *The Moderate Messenger* 14 (23–30 July 1649), p. 93; Webbe, *Discourse of English Poetrie*, F4r; *Diurnall of Thomas Rugg*, p. 30.

Ballad-writers sometimes targeted particular groups, concentrating their penny-pulling power on virgins, young men, gallants, 'good fellows' or 'gentle wives' (typically, these were admirable categories). In more inclusive mood, however, composers packed their publications with references to dozens of different social and occupational categories, a tactic by which they simultaneously shaped and shadowed their audience. Nor did authors necessarily pull their punches in the pursuit of popularity. Some ballads presented stern moral warnings to all listeners, picking out servants, 'dainty dames', landlords, clergymen, lawyers, usurers, tradesmen, farmers, vintners, ostlers and gamesters, group by group.[101] Other songs were more idealistic, portraying a happy world in which men and women of all conditions were united by the consensual ethics of neighbourliness.[102] Alternatively, celebratory ballads might concentrate on the sheer diversity of English society. The aptly named *Roome for Companie* (to a tune that came to be known by the same title) set the record by extending a welcome to no fewer than 159 social and occupational types within its twenty-one verses. These included cobblers, broom-men, clockmakers, sow-gelders, fishermen, button-makers, clerks, scriveners and 'Whoores, Bawdes, & Beggers' (along with fiddlers, drummers, fifers and bell-founders).[103] Clearly, one of the objectives of all these ballads – whether they were thorny or rosy in tone – was to lure and acknowledge the multi-faceted audience by referring to each of its constituent parts in turn.

Many people soaked up the sound of balladry, and Shakespeare portrayed members of Autolycus's audience as utterly undiscriminating and gullible in their attachment to the form. 'I love a ballad but even too well', admits Clown, 'if it be doleful matter merrily set down; or a very pleasant thing indeed, and sung lamentably.' Mopsa agrees: 'I love a ballad in print a-life, for then we are sure they are true.' Some ballad-lovers may even have become obsessive to the point of mental disorder. This, at least, is implied by the association sometimes drawn by playwrights between the love of ballads and the losing of one's mind. Ophelia sings ballad-snatches during her mental disintegration, and dramatists of the later seventeenth century regularly deployed this form of behaviour in order to suggest madness.[104] It seems to have signified a psychological withdrawal into the distorted parallel world of the ballad, and an inability or refusal to re-emerge in the

[101] *Pepys Ballads*, vol. I, pp. 166–7, 210–11, 216–17.

[102] Ibid., vol. I, pp. 186–7. [103] Ibid., vol. I, pp. 168–9.

[104] Shakespeare, *Winter's Tale*, pp. 118, 120; Laurie, 'Music for the Stage II: From 1650', p. 311.

normal fashion. The madness of Old Merrythought in Beaumont's *The Knight of the Burning Pestle* is comparable, though it is of an altogether happier sort. He has clearly mislaid or renounced the ability to communicate except by the singing of short extracts from ballads and other sources, but his immersion in musical verse renders him permanently joyous, as if he is possessed by 'half a dozen jovial spirits'. Mistress Merrythought, understandably enough, is somewhat less content, and reports that when she criticises him 'he laughs and dances, and sings, and cries, "A merry heart lives long-a"'. Beaumont generates humour by driving the commonplace love of balladry to its logical extreme. Other characters in the play can sing ballads too, but only Old Merrythought is incapable of doing anything else. Comparable examples in the world beyond the stage are, of course, harder to find, but they do come to light from time to time. Witnesses in an ecclesiastical court case reported that the recently deceased Thomas Hopper of Medomsley (County Durham) had been 'raving' during the final days of his life. One deponent informed the court that Hopper had been 'neither of good memory, nor reason, but all distracte, singinge hey roiffe songs'.[105]

The broad social appeal of broadside ballads is also suggested by the influence they clearly wielded over the unprinted and locally composed songs with which individuals and groups habitually mocked their enemies. It appears that disgruntled inhabitants in most communities could call upon the services of at least one neighbour with the skills necessary to devise and divulge such creations. In Jacobean Thetford (Isle of Ely), Joan Gomme was said to 'exercise the makeinge of libellous and lascivious ballads' about her fellow parishioners. Thomas Chitham, a schoolmaster in Elizabethan Boreham (Essex), was more circumspect, but he too was known as a potential song-writer. When Hugh Barker, a Chelmsford barber, needed a defamatory song to be composed about the sexual behaviour of Mary Whale, he approached Chitham. The schoolmaster expressed his initial reluctance, but eventually obliged in return for a free trim and an assurance that Barker would use the song only for his own private pleasure, 'to singe to his citron [cittern] and to laughe at when he was melancholie'. The resultant song, in which Chitham replaced Barker's filthy language with more 'cleanly tearmes', pleased

[105] Beaumont, *The Knight of the Burning Pestle*, pp. 30, 53; *Depositions and Other Ecclesiastical Proceedings from the Courts of Durham*, ed. James Raine, *Surtees Society* 21 (1845), pp. 265–76.

the barber well enough, though he said he did not understand the words 'Leviathan' and 'Albion'.[106]

Surviving records from libel cases frequently present the offending verses, and the impact of broadside balladry upon local creativity is abundantly apparent. In format and style, many local songs were powerfully informed by the evolving traditions of print. In early seventeenth-century Wiltshire, one libel opened with the gathering line 'O hark a while and you shall know', while a Dorchester song was addressed more provocatively to 'Yow Puritans all wheresoever you dwell'.[107] Others adopted the two-part divisions of published ballads, or presented their material in dialogue form.[108] Many included catchy refrains like the one that brought to a close each sexually suggestive verse of an anti-puritan ballad from early seventeenth-century Wells: 'yet I doe live in quiett Rest / and hold my hoalling game the best'. In Jacobean Worcestershire, one of the songs that was allegedly concocted by John Rotton and his friends included the print-inspired appeal 'although no eloquent speeches I do use / yet the writer do not seeme to abuse' (Rotton's alleged victim, Agnes Nightingale, was hardly likely to listen sympathetically, for the song also included the lines 'but let us give over talking of her Conny / which yow say is worth such a deale of mony').[109]

Some such songs were clearly based loosely on specific publications from the London presses. In 1601, Thomas Chitham, the Essex schoolmaster, found inspiration in *A Ditty Delightful of Mother Watkin's Ale*, a huge hit in the 1590s.[110] Similarly, John Rotton obviously wrote another of his scurrilous compositions while under the influence of *A Proper New Ballad, Shewing a Merie Jest of one Jeamie of Woodicock Hill, and his wife, how he espied through a doore, one making of him cuckold, and how that for lucre of money, he was well contented therewith*, published soon after 1600. Rotton and those who assisted him were well versed in broadside balladry, and they rounded off the hand-written version of their song with the spoof notice 'Imprinted at London at the signe of the woodcocke in Paules churchyard / if you aske to the sign of the Nightingale you may

106 Fox, *Oral and Literate Culture*, p. 305; assize file 35/44/2, 18 July 1602, copy in ERO.

107 Ingram, 'Ridings, Rough Music and Mocking Rhymes', p. 179; *REED Dorset, Cornwall*, pp. 180–2 (compare with *Pepys Ballads*, vol. II, p. 11, vol. III, p. 20).

108 Fox, *Oral and Literate Culture*, p. 320; STAC 8 220/31, NA.

109 *REED Somerset*, p. 712; STAC 8/220/31, NA.

110 Queen's Bench indictments ancient, 711, pt. I, no. 118, transcript available in ERO. The song contains several clear textual references to the printed ballad.

likely find the woodcocke.' The point, of course, was not to suggest that the song had actually been published, but to deploy the conventions of print and the cultural associations of the woodcock (a feathered fool, by reputation) in order to lampoon the intended victims, Master and Mistress Nightingale.[111]

Libellous songs were allegedly sung 'in rejoycing manner', 'in scoffing manner' or 'with loude and lyfted up voyces'.[112] Information on the tunes that were used is thin, though such evidence as there is once again reveals the influence of broadside balladry.[113] Some libellers may have made up their own tunes in the broadside style. Certainly, there is no other known record of 'a new tune called Pryde and Lecherie', specified in a sexually explicit song composed at Much Brickhill (Buckinghamshire) in the summer of 1608. Alternatively, this and other untraceable titles may have been among the many common ballad tunes that have failed to reach our ears.[114]

Libellous ballads, like their more presentable broadside cousins, drew in men, women and children from a wide array of social and occupational backgrounds. In 1613, one Southwark song was allegedly composed by a group of some twenty labouring people. Around the same date, a Yorkshire landlord claimed that he had been christened 'the devil of Doncaster' by a creative confederacy consisting of two gentlemen, six musicians, a yeoman and an innkeeper. Individuals of lower-middling rank were represented particularly well, and the majority of known singers and song-writers were male. This may, in part, be a distortion created by the sources, and some women clearly did raise their voices in rude derision. In 1586, three women of West Pennard (Somerset) went to gather rushes for Whitsuntide. When Isabell Cooke broke into song, Agnes White was shocked. She later informed the bishop that her companion's ditty was 'a verie badd and lewde thinge not to be heard of any body for that it was an abhominable thinge'. Sadly, the song has not survived, though we know that it was reputedly written or commissioned by Thomas Deanes, a local man previously unknown to musicology.[115]

Servants were quite regularly involved in the production and performance of libellous ballads, but so too – a little more surprisingly – were

[111] STAC 8/220/31, NA. On perceptions of the woodcock, see Stefan Buczacki, *Fauna Britannica* (London: Hamlyn, 2002), p. 279. The Rotton ballad is recorded on the website, track 32 (see below, pp. 324–5, for further discussion).

[112] *REED Dorset, Cornwall*, pp. 501–3, 510–12; *REED Shropshire*, pp. 336–40.

[113] See below, pp. 323–5. [114] STAC 8/36/6, NA.

[115] Fox, *Oral and Literate Culture*, p. 317; STAC 8/113/3, NA; *REED Somerset*, p. 390.

clergymen. In Jacobean Pilton (Somerset), 'the vicar hath made rymes and lewd songes and deliverid them unto others to be songe to the great discontentment of the people'. His counterpart in Aberford (Yorkshire) had apparently had a hand in the composition of various songs designed to mock Thomas Shillito, the high constable of Barkston. Shillito further reported that the cleric was prone to 'tobacco takeinge and swaggering with pipers fidlers tinckards drunkards & other dessolute people'.[116] He did not merely cross the borderline between clerical and lay conduct from time to time, but actually seemed to live on the wrong side. And in Chelvey (Somerset), Hugh Davis, 'clerk', was accused of devising songs against Edward Tynte, an eminent esquire. Davis had allegedly encouraged others to perform his works, 'and did greatlie applaud & Comend his . . . sonne Benedicke for the well doinge thereof'. The clergyman claimed, in his defence, that little Benedicke had composed the songs himself, and had received just rebuke for his insolence.[117] Certainly, it was not unusual for children to participate in the dissemination of musical libels. In 1587, they were to be heard in Manchester, singing snatches from 'a noughtie songe' about one Duckworth's wife (it included the line 'I heard a beggar make her mone under a birch tree'). Twenty years later, children from Wells (Somerset) were just as happy to adopt the lascivious ballads that bounced around the streets and alleys in denigration of the unfortunately named Constable Hole.[118]

The appeal of such songs also resided in an undoubted power to humiliate their victims. In theatrical works of the seventeenth century, warring characters regularly declared their intention to have the misdeeds of their enemies turned into ballads for public broadcast. The promise 'to sing thy churlish cruelty' or 'tune ballads to thy infamy' was no empty threat, and victims sometimes expressed their anxiety at the prospect of being 'Sung up and down by minstrels'.[119] In 1613, a Norfolk gentleman claimed that the activities of a group of local libellers had made him and his relatives 'poynting stocks and Odious unto the Inhabitantes of Southcreake'. His daughter had lost her prospective marriage partner as a result of the shame, and the plaintiff warned the Court of Star Chamber that vicious songsmiths, if permitted to operate without restraint, would destroy all good order and reduce society to an anarchic state of 'hurly burly'. Hierarchical distinctions could be blown away by a little music.

[116] *REED Somerset*, p. 206; STAC 8/275/22, NA. [117] *REED Somerset*, pp. 76–7.

[118] EDC5 1587.77, ChRO; *REED Somerset*, p. 290.

[119] Various sources, reproduced in Würzbach, *The Rise of the English Street Ballad*, pp. 253–84.

In other cases, libellous songs were credited with the dismantling of livelihoods and the destruction of marriages.[120] Of course, victims will always exaggerate their plight, but it is clear that being 'balladed' was a profoundly uncomfortable experience. The damage done was reflected in the punishments available to the courts. Star Chamber judges administered heavy fines, but they also whipped, branded and, in seditious cases, cut off ears. Lesser penalties were handed out in local courts, both ecclesiastical and civil.[121] When Gabriel Raymond of Great Dunmow (Essex), yeoman, composed and performed a song that identified twelve particular Tollesbury men as cuckolds in May 1628, the quarter sessions judge ordered a composite punishment: the miscreant was to be taken to the house of correction and whipped, before being put in the stocks for two hours in Chelmsford marketplace under a notice bearing the words 'for singing of a libell'. The same punishment was later re-enacted in Tollesbury itself, perhaps before a jubilant jury of cuckolds.[122] It is impossible to say whether this little tour of torment was successful in curing one Essex yeoman of his musical habit.

The wide-ranging popularity of broadside ballads and their libellous counterparts can be explained in a number of ways. The ballad was a remarkably flexible art-form. In musical terms, the infectious tunes lent themselves to a range of differing performance styles. They were simple enough to be learned by 'Foot-boys and Link-boys' in the street, yet interesting enough to stimulate the creative energies of England's finest and most famous courtly composers. In Jacobean Nottingham, one home-made and allegedly libellous ballad was performed in three rather different forms: it was bawled in the streets to the cacophonous accompaniment of basins and tongs; it was played by pipers in local taverns; and it was 'prickt in 4 parts to the vyalls' for use in the homes of gentlemen.[123] A single ballad could thus assume a variety of guises, each shaped by the available resources and the nature of the social setting. The residents of a town might hear everything from expert performances by the civic waits of full ballads with instrumental accompaniment to bare tunes whistled by carmen in the streets or song-snippets chanted by the raucous gatherings that surrounded a punitive 'riding'.

The texts of English ballads were just as appealing and malleable. They presented a continuous set of variations on a number of stock tales

[120] STAC 8/83/1, NA; Fox, *Oral and Literate Culture*, pp. 327–8.

[121] Fox, *Oral and Literate Culture*, p. 326; Ingram, 'Ridings, Rough Music and Mocking Rhymes', p. 188.

[122] Q/SR 262/22, ERO. [123] Fox, *Oral and Literate Culture*, p. 319.

and types, stimulating simultaneously the cultural tastebuds of those who craved novelty and those who found security in similarity. Printed verses could be performed for their own sake, but they could also be applied inventively to local situations. Pepys knew how to do this, but so too did George James, the servant of a Warwickshire gentleman. In 1616, his mistress, angered by his impudent conduct, confiscated his livery coat when she found it lying about the house. James hit back with a song about an unnamed lady who was famous

For stealing of cloakes, gold Buttons or Bandes
or Cuffes for to weare to grace her false handes.
No oyster-queane putteth her down for use of her Tongue
Nor Kitchin-staff Drabb if she doe doe a wrong.

A libel charge was brought against the servant, but he claimed that his ditty had been misinterpreted. Far from being a personal libel, it was a well-known and previously published 'songe or Jygge ... which the servants to the late highe and mightie prince henry, prince of Wales, did often in the presence of his highness and manie nobles and peeres of this Reallme, act, daunce and sing'. It was thus 'a generall song without particuler nominacon or alusion to anie'.[124] This was an interesting defence, for it not only hid the accused behind a printed ballad but exploited quite deliberately the immense social reach of balladry in order to ward off his accusers. The singing servant hoped that by dropping a royal name he could protect himself against a mere country gentlewoman and her husband. Others used broadside ballads as the inspiration for newly written songs in which they recorded their feelings about everything from the Reformation to the sexual politics of the neighbourhood. The broadside ballad, with its unique combination of words, tune and pictures, had an appeal that was simultaneously visual, verbal, literary, oral and aural. In short, it struck a whole series of chords.

Meanings were flexible too, and the success of balladry across such a wide audience can also be explained in terms of the capacity of individual songs to signify different things to different people. Recent theoretical developments in the study of literature, culture and popular music have sounded a dramatic retreat from (or advance beyond) the idea that any specific text or song encapsulates a single and identifiable meaning. The object of the academic game is no longer to quarrel over the nature of that main meaning, but to explore the multiplicity of interpretative

[124] STAC 8/59/4, NA.

possibilities that jostle with one another within a single source. Nowadays, 'every word that is launched into social space implies a dialogue and therefore a contested interpretation', for the meanings of language are never clear and fixed. The reader or listener is now an active presence, absorbing and reconstituting every idea or artefact through a cultural filter. The text, once a tablet of stone, has become more like a blank page, upon which every individual inscribes meaning. Consumption emerges as a form of production, and individuals or social groups absorb and appropriate the items with which they are presented, instinctively accommodating them to their own distinctive needs. Early modern readers, in particular, are said to have interpreted texts in a highly selective and acquisitive manner, seeking out what they wished to find rather than quietly absorbing authorial ideas. In general, the song or text is now a forum for negotiation. Moral standards and social ideals are not simply purveyed: they are also contested and interrogated, both in the writing and in the reading or listening. Deals are struck between different voices within society, and the possible meanings of any single item become infinite, shifting with the range of factors that make up a specific context for contemporary interpretation.[125]

Once upon a time, ballads seemed attractive to scholars and collectors because of their simplicity and transparency. The Roxburghe collection includes an editorial note in which ballad-writers of the seventeenth century are warmly commended for their honesty: 'their words no shuffling meaning knew, / their speech was homely, but their hearts were true'.[126] Nowadays, however, it is precisely the 'shuffling meanings' contained within individual ballads that provide their interest. Indeed, the popular songs of the early modern period are well suited to the new interpretative order. Most of them were written to attract the widest possible audience, and one proven compositional tactic was to present rival viewpoints within an individual song. Ballads about gender relations, for example, are not only an enormous category in statistical terms but a veritable cacophony of contrary voices. More generally, ballads passed readily into oral and aural culture and were therefore ripe for appropriation and transformation. Texts must commonly have been selectively remembered and creatively modified as they passed around, beyond the influence of the printed text. These songs were also designed for

[125] Raman Selden and Peter Widdowson, *A Reader's Guide to Contemporary Literary Theory* (Lexington: University Press of Kentucky, 1993), p. 127; Negus, *Popular Music in Theory*, ch. 1.

[126] Roxburghe ballads, title page, BL.

performance, and the use of different tones of voice, bodily gestures and speeds of delivery opened up a world of interpretative possibilities. In most cases, it seems sensible to think of individual ballads as incorporating a primary message (that which is emphasised by the composer), around which a range of other possible meanings hum in counterpoint. Sometimes, the contrary voices are devised quite deliberately, while in other ballads they depend on some combination of inadvertent contradiction by the hasty composer and satirical will-power on the part of performers and consumers. In either circumstance, ballads could be interpreted along, against and across the grain.

Take, for example, *Rocke the Babie Joane: OR, John his petition to his loving wife Joane to suckle the babe that was none of her owne* (**Website track 15 and Appendix**). This ballad, issued in 1632 and set to the catchy tune of 'Under and over', presents the quarrels of a married couple regarding the adulterous exploits of the husband (see Figure 5.5). John opens the discussion by presenting his wife with the child of his illicit liaison and asking her to feed it. At first, Joan refuses. Twelve verses later, however, a predictable resolution is achieved when she backs down like a good wife and agrees to care for the baby 'As well as 'twere mine owne'. The message, most obviously, is that wives must obey the will of their husbands, even in such trying circumstances. This is not, however, the only message that contemporary audiences might have received from the song. Along the way, John and Joan propose a number of clashing arguments, and one can almost hear the banter of audience members: women scoffing when John declares his love for his wife and tells her, 'Thy vertue will shine clearest, / in doing this good deed'; and men bristling when Joan shouts 'Away thou false Deceiver / . . . I am resolved never / To love thee as I did'. Joan, indeed, is anything but subservient during eleven of the thirteen verses, and declares that other wives will rebuke her if she does as she is bid ('For never woman did it, / to a Bastard in this kind'). Even in her eventual obedience, she is able to set a condition: she will nurse the baby only if John promises 'to goe no more astray'. Potentially, Joan is a model both of subservience and of defiance. Her final words, quoted above, could easily have been rendered insincere by an appropriate gesture, a sarcastic tone of voice and a twinkle in the performer's eye (indeed, Joan bears comparison with Shakespeare's Katherina).

John, too, is simultaneously a role-model for would-be philanderers and a thoroughly disreputable husband whose waywardness eventually forces him to beg on his knees, thereby encouraging in his wife a dangerous display of assertiveness. There is, therefore, an ambivalence at the

Rocke the Babie *Joane:*
OR,
John his Petition to his loving Wife *Joane,*
To suckle the Babe that was none of her owne.
To the Tune of, *Under and over*

Rocke the Babie Joane

A Young man in our Parish,
His wife was somewhat currish,
For she refus'd to nourish
a child which he brought home:
He got it on an other,
And death had tane the mother,
The truth he could not smother,
all out at last did come:
Suckle tha Baby,
huggle the Baby,
Rocke the Baby Jone,
I scorne to suckle the Baby,
Unlesse it were mine owne.

His wife cry'd out on one day,
I thinke it was on Sunday.
The next day being Munday,
His Wench in sunder fell:
The Dad on't shee descried,
Which having done, she dyed,
This could not be denyed,
Alas he knew't too well.
Suckle the Baby, &c.

The Parish him inforced
To see the Infant nursed,
He being but lightly pursed,
desir'd to save the charge:
He brought it to his owne wife,
Whom he lov'd as his owne life:
To her the case was knowne rife,
he told her all at large.
Suckle the Baby, &c.

Quoth he my Jone my deerest,
Thy love to mee is nearest,
Thy virtue will shine clearest,
in doing this good deed:
This infant young is left here,
Unable to make shift here,
Twill be of life bereft heere,
Unlesse thou doe it feed.
Suckle the Baby, &c.

Away thou false Deceiver,
Quoth shee farewell for ever,
I am resolved never
To love thee as I did:
Alas quoth he my honny,
I would no for any money,
By thee my sweetest conny,
to be so shrewdly chid.
Suckle the Baby, &c.

Althouth I lov'd his mother,
Ile vow to love none other,
What needst thou keepe this pother,
since shee (poore wretch) is dead:
No more she can thee trouble,
And 'twould be charges double,
If every moneth a Noble
I pay for milke and bread.
Suckle the Baby,
Huggle the Baby,
Rocke the Babie Jone.
I scorne to suckle the Baby,
Unlesse it were mine owne.

Twould be to my discredit,
Should I both board and bed it,
For never woman did it
to a Bastard in this kind.
O Joane leave off this fashion,
Twill be thy commendation,
To take commiseration,
let not the child be pind.
Suckle the Baby, &c.

What if the brat be starved?
Experience hath observed
It should not bee preserved
by her that is thy wife.
Thy patience will appeare more,
O take it Juggie therefore,
Beare with my fault, for wherefore
should we continue strife?
Suckle the Baby, &c.

I doubt I shall be forced,
From thee to bee divorced,
Thy brood shall nere be nursed,
by me nor by my cost.
O wife be not so cruell,
Thou knowst thou art my jewell,
Be certaine if thou doe well,
thy labour is not lost.
Suckle the Baby, &c.

My neighbours will deride me,
And none that dwell beside me
Will evermore abide me
for such a President.
No Jone thou art mistaken,
Twill other wifes awaken,
Then let some course be taken
for the childs nourishment.
Suckle the Baby, &c.

Let patient Grissels storie,
Be still in thy memorie,
Who wonne a lasting glory,
throught patience in like sort:
Although it touch thee neerely,
This Barne that lookes so cheerely,
Shall binde me still more deerely,
to love thee better for't.
Suckle the Baby, &c.

Well John thy intercession
Hath chang'd my disposition,
And now upon condition
thou'lt goe no more astray:
Ile entertaine thy Baby
And love it as well as may be.
Doe so (sweet Jugge) I pray thee,
then this is a joyfull day.
Suckle tha Baby,
Huggle the Baby,
Rocke the Baby Jone:
I prethee Jugge love my Baby,
And count it to be thine owne.

I have a Girle, I bore it
But just a day before it,
Although we be but poore yet,
These two we will maintaine:
Ile suckle it, and dandle it
And very choicely handle it,
And thou shalt sope and candle get:
and thus betweene us twaine,
Weele suckle the Baby,
And huggle the Baby.
Gramerty honest Jone,
O John Ile rocke thy Baby,
As well as 'twere mine owne.
FINIS
Printed at London for H.G

Figure 5.5. Most seventeenth-century ballads came in two parts and made their impact through a combination of text, tune and pictures. This one, like many others, deals with marital discord and the tussle for control between husband and wife. The text has been re-set to improve its legibility. The Pepys Library, Magdalene College, Cambridge, Pepys Ballads, *Rocke the Babie Joane* (London, 1632).

heart of both portrayals, and it is not difficult to imagine contemporaries performing and hearing the song in a variety of different ways. Indeed, the ballad seems designed with this in mind, despite its hurried and not entirely convincing resolution. The woodcut pictures add further to the 'shuffling meaning' of the text. John is depicted, once again, in the demeaning posture of the man who must beg his wife for co-operation, but the price exacted by Joan is significantly sterner in the illustration than in the verses. Her revised words are presented beside her domineering image: 'So I may have my will, / Ile love thy Baby still.'[127] The tune too suggests the endless tussle for sovereignty between husband and wife, rather than the simplistic victory of the former over the latter that is described in the concluding verses. Its title was derived from another ballad of the previous year, with the playful and suggestive refrain,

With under and over, over and under,
under and over agen,
These two did sport together,
as women sport with men.[128]

Text, pictures, tunes and performance styles combined to create a beguiling combination of interpretative possibilities. Gender ballads, though forceful enough in presenting the conventional guidelines on the subservient responsibilities of women, also permitted some female characters a degree of operational flexibility that must have allowed listeners to take up a variety of positions.

Ballads of this sort were clearly a platform for the rehearsal of contemporary debates, and their potential as a tool of persuasion must have intensified their appeal to many people of all sorts. Broadsides helped to articulate the attitudes of those on both sides of many of the period's favourite binary divisions: not only husband/wife, but also wife/maiden, husband/bachelor, townsman/countryman, Englishman/foreigner, master/servant, rich man/poor man and so on. There is little point in seeking to categorise the ballad as either a tool of oppression or a weapon of resistance. It was both and neither. Most fruitfully, we might regard it as an instrument of negotiation. From the perspective of those in society's lower orders, for example, one element in the appeal of balladry was its capacity to call the prosperous and privileged to account. Typically, ballads about social justice rebuked the wealthy and worshipful for failing in their moral obligations to the rest of the population, though they also declared a solid attachment to the existing codes of hierarchical conduct and praised those who conducted themselves well. Such ballads called for restitution, not revolution, yet they also proposed a version of the established code of hierarchical conduct that was somewhat looser in construction than the one to which their governors adhered. Deference was promoted, but so too was the right of the

[127] *Pepys Ballads*, vol. I, pp. 396–7. There is a related discussion in Sandra Clark, 'The Broadside Ballad and the Woman's Voice', in Christina Malcolmson and Mihoko Suzuki (eds.), *Debating Gender in Early Modern England, 1500–1700* (Basingstoke: Palgrave Macmillan, 2002), pp. 103–20.

[128] *Pepys Ballads*, vol. I, pp. 264–5.

lowly to speak out in forceful and threatening terms against powerful individuals who failed in their corresponding paternalistic duties. In *The Lamenting Lady* (to the tune of 'The lady's fall'), a rich but barren woman insults a poor but fertile one when she comes begging at the door with her twin babies in her arms. Strictly speaking, the lowly victim of this verbal barrage should walk away in patient fortitude. Instead, she turns aggressor, calling upon God to perform 'wondrous works' in her defence. A more specific curse follows:

And for these children two of mine
Heaven send thee such a number
At once, as dayes be in the yeare,
to make the world to wonder.

The wealthy woman is instantly repentant, but nevertheless becomes pregnant and later gives birth to 365 tiny babies at once ('In bignesse all like new bred mice, / yet each one shap'd aright'). She is shamed by this blatant act of divine intervention, and asks all 'faire women of the world' to learn the obvious lesson:

The Lord we see his blessings sends
to many women poore
As well as to the noble sort,
that have aboundant store.

In this case, therefore, the rich lady is punished savagely for her breach of charity, but the poor woman is permitted to bend several of the supposed rules of hierarchical engagement: she begs from door to door (by *c.* 1620, when the ballad was first published, the poor laws had rendered this practice questionable); she retaliates against a social superior, admittedly under intense provocation; and she seeks to coerce God into assisting her in the confrontation (despite the fact that the final words of the ballad warn the wealthy that they must not pray for assistance in their worldly affairs).[129]

At times, ballads also came close to abandoning the convention that abusive landlords were exceptions to the rule, replacing it with an implied assumption that the gentry, almost as a class, were corrupt and cruel, while the poor were uniformly honest and hard done by. Another wronged beggar-woman, the heroine of *A Lanthorne for Landlords*, refers in passing to the country's rich men, 'Whose hearts I know are merciless / unto the

[129] Ibid., vol. I, pp. 44–5.

needy poore'. One ballad praises a wondrously charitable nobleman at great length but then switches direction radically with a killer final line: 'But such noblemen there is few to be found.'[130] Within the dominant social conservatism of the balladeer, therefore, there are numerous signs of a highly critical attitude to England's governing class and their role in upholding the great chain of being (though social climbers among the lower ranks are treated with comparable severity). The belief that words set to music allow the singer greater freedom of expression than is accorded the mere speaker was well established in early modern England, just as it is in many of the cultures studied by ethnomusicologists.[131]

On the other hand, balladry also offered the powerful a means by which they could hope to persuade and pacify their less lucky contemporaries. In 1684, Nathaniel Thompson was firmly of the opinion that royalist ballads had played a significant part in persuading the mid-century multitude to abandon rebellion. Through song, they had been 'charm'd into Obedience'. A few years later, Andrew Fletcher reported approvingly the opinion of an acquaintance that 'if a man were permitted to make all the ballads, he need not care who should make the laws of a nation'. A similar attitude may explain why the church officers of several parishes in Elizabethan London had purchased patriotic ballads, presumably for display, distribution and public performance. In 1569, the northern rising prompted the authorities at All Hallows to acquire six 'ballyts concerning rebels to be sung', while the officers at St Dunstan bought 'a dozen ballets to sing against the rebels'. Other parishes occasionally obtained ballads that were to be 'sung for the queenes majestie' or 'on the day of the queen's reign'.[132] Several of the ballads discussed in the preceding paragraphs might equally well be understood from this more authoritarian perspective. *A Lanthorne for Landlords*, for example, allowed its poor heroine to curse a cruel gentleman, but it also aimed to assure the powerless that they could trust in public opinion and the legal system to right their wrongs. If they did so, then all would be well in the end (a message reinforced by the woodcut depicting happy rural labourers at work and play under a

[130] Ibid., vol. I, pp. 146–7, vol. II, p. 56.

[131] See, for example, *Autobiography of Thomas Whythorne*, p. 40; Bonnie C. Wade, *Thinking Musically: Experiencing Music, Expressing Culture* (Oxford: Oxford University Press, 2004), p. 11.

[132] Nathaniel Thompson, *Choice Collection of 120 Loyal Songs* (London, 1684), A2r–v; 'Letter to the Marquis of Montrose', in *The Political Works of Andrew Fletcher* (Glasgow, 1749), p. 266; Fiona Kisby, 'Urban Cultures and Religious Reforms: Parochial Music in London, *c.* 1520–*c.* 1580' (I am grateful to Dr Kisby for providing me with a copy of this seminar paper).

benevolent sun). The beggar-woman eventually inherits the entire estate of her hateful landlord when he commits suicide, an act brought on by the experience of watching while various members of his family meet grisly ends after experiments with witchcraft, whoredom, treachery and bestiality. To some degree, therefore, this ballad aimed to persuade the powerless to trust in the system. It was not only a lantern for landlords, but a beacon for beggars.

Over a century later, radical and conservative commentators retained an understanding that one way into the hearts and minds of ordinary folk was through the ballad. Writing in the patronising register of the 1790s, a 'friend to Church and State' remarked 'that any thing written in voice & especially to an Old English tune ... made a more fixed Impression on the Minds of the Younger and Lower Class of People, than any written in Prose, which was often forgotten as soon as Read'. He therefore supplied twenty anti-republican ballads for printing and distribution by hawkers, and looked forward to the day when he would hear his songs 'Re-echoed by Every Little Boy in the Streets during the Christmas Holidays'.[133]

Ballads were not only malleable, but memorable. Their capacity for lodging themselves within a multitude of minds was another vital aspect of their appeal. Linguistic scholars have identified the memorability of expression as one of the defining features of oral cultures, and early modern ballads certainly scored highly in this regard, despite their status as printed literature.[134] Composers made instinctive use of familiar rhyming patterns, common proverbs, recognisable characters and recurring narratives. Ballads presented old themes in numerous variations. They were both fresh and formulaic. The battle for sovereignty between Joan and John was, for example, part of a gender war that had been familiar to Chaucer in the fourteenth century. Some of the rhymes used by this particular ballad-writer (mother/smother/other, for example) had also been deployed in previous ballads to the same tune. The frequent recycling of tunes also helped to root new texts in the brains of singers and listeners. So too did the regular appearance of a repetitive refrain at the close of each verse within an individual song. Refrains were an invitation to participation, and participation aided the memory. When Richard Hooker remarked that 'into grosser and heavier mindes whome bare words do not easily move, the sweetnes of melodie might make some

[133] Letter to John Reeves, quoted by Palmer, *Sound of History*, pp. 16–17.
[134] Ong, *Orality and Literacy*, pp. 34–6.

entrance', he was thinking of church music, but the same insight might equally well be applied to balladry.[135]

It was not only such devices that made ballads memorable, but their power to stimulate the emotions. A good, uncomplicated melody, said one eighteenth-century author, 'affects the heart and moves the passions', generating 'the most intense degree of musical pleasure'. 'Simple ballad strains', he continued, were often 'better suited to touch the feelings, than many compositions of great masters of Harmony', and he warned his readers not to dismiss them as vulgar.[136] Indeed, a pleasing ballad drew its listeners into a web of feeling, and many songs offered their singers the opportunity to become somebody else, if only for a time. Balladry was thus recreational in a literal sense and well supplied with crudely memorable characters. It allowed musical gentlemen such as Samuel Pepys to refashion themselves as lusty country labourers, itinerant beggars or even political traitors. One of Pepys's ballads, to the tune of 'Live with me and be my love', imagines the words of Ralph Banastre, who, in 1483, had followed his master, the Duke of Buckingham, into revolt against Richard III, before betraying him to the crown and bringing about his execution. The first verse is written in the words of a narrator ('Then Banister with shame may sing, / who sold his life that loved him'), but in the second the singer becomes the remorseful protagonist and maintains this identity to the end:

All you that here my wofull song,
know this, though God do suffer wrong
Yet treason foule he doth abhoare,
And traitors [?vilde] he doth not spare.[137]

Towards the other end of the social scale, lowly milkmaids could imagine life as ladies of the court, murderous midwives or serial fornicators. A common ballad character was the young and pregnant woman who could not be certain which of a dozen tradesmen and artisans was the father of her child. Men could be women and women could be men.[138] Landlubbers became sailors and cowards found their fighting spirit. In the

[135] Hooker, *Of the Lawes of Ecclesiastical Politie*, p. 76.

[136] Alexander Molleson, *Melody, the Soul of Music* (Glasgow, 1798), pp. 26–7, 30–1.

[137] *Pepys Ballads*, vol. I, p. 64. The ballad was originally issued in *c.* 1600 but must have achieved new topicality during the 1620s, following the demise of another Duke of Buckingham. The Pepys copy dates from *c.* 1630.

[138] On this point, see Bruce R. Smith, 'Female Impersonation in Early Modern Ballads', in Pamela Allen Brown and Peter Parolin (eds.), *Women Players in England 1500–1660* (Aldershot: Ashgate, 2005), pp. 281–304.

world of the ballad, all manner of transformations seemed possible, and the psychological and emotional benefits to those living in a society that was deeply and steeply hierarchical – whether they were rich or poor – may have been significant. Arguably, ballads bridged gaps and sugared pills, helping with the vital cultural tasks of releasing systemic pressure and rendering the distasteful palatable.

Just as commonly, ballad-writers aimed to connect with audience members not by offering escape, but by providing ordinary people with the means to articulate their mundane concerns in poetic and musical fashion. Courtship ballads, in particular, were often presented in ready-to-use dramatic form. *Clodds Carroll*, for example, was 'to be sung Dialogue wise, of a man and a woman that would needs be married'.[139] Other broadsides were set out as two distinct songs, the second a feminine answer to the masculine first (or vice versa). It is tempting to imagine such songs being performed in alehouses, complete with appropriate facial expressions and bodily gestures. Ballads engaged hearts and minds, but they were also an incitement to physical movement. Crowds were drawn to the sound of the ballad-singer, and the rhythmic and repetitive tunes encouraged foot-tapping, hand-clapping and head-nodding. The close relationship that existed between balladry and dance was a natural consequence of this musical stimulation.

The multi-dimensional appeal of balladry helps to explain why audiences were on occasion willing to attend performances that lasted far longer than the standard four minutes of the modern pop song. Evidence relating to the duration of such performances is extremely limited, and many must have featured extracts and snatches rather than unabridged renditions. On occasion, however, ballads were sung in their entirety. In 1590, one puritanical letter-writer expressed his disquiet at seeing 'rich men give more to a player for a song which he shall sing in one hour, than to their faithful servant for serving them a whole year'. A century later, another author reported having heard a religious radical – one of the 'Sweet-Singers of Israel' – perform a song 'of almost Half-an-Hour long, to the Tune of Jenny come tye my Bonny Cravat'. The singer, Betty Roan, augmented her performance 'with such Antick and wanton Gestures, as could not but engage us into a great Amazement'.[140] These were major

[139] Watt, *Cheap Print*, p. 32.

[140] Harris Nicolas, *Memoirs of the Life and Times of Sir Christopher Hatton* (London, 1847), appendix, p. xxx; *A Full and True Account of the Notorious Wicked Life of that Grand Imposter, John Taylor* (London, 1678), p. 6.

performances, simultaneously visual and aural. In a sense, ballads were not only the pop songs of their day, but the feature films too.

Balladry was a dynamic cultural phenomenon that developed dramatically during the sixteenth and seventeenth centuries. The breadth of its appeal was remarkable. Ballads passed backwards and forwards across the period's most notable divides, but they did as much to highlight the gaps as to close them. Through this ubiquitous form of music, men and women of all sorts explored both their common humanity and the many fractures within it. There were ballads for all occasions and moods, and the combination of text, tune and image was sufficiently complex that a single song might be used to articulate a variety of attitudes. Few people can have lived beyond the reach of balladry, and in early eighteenth-century Norfolk a proud member of the Windham household made a fascinating and unique note of the 'Tunes that Billy knew before he was 2 yrs old'. This was a musical age. Of course, we cannot know what the boy made of his melodies but he was clearly receptive. There were sixty-three titles on the list, many of them ballad tunes, and we can only assume that the older members of young Billy Windham's household sang them regularly as they went about their business. How else could a toddler have come to recognise the melodies 'Who got [the] maid with child' and 'A tidy hussy'?[141]

[141] WKC7/45, 404 X2, NRO.

6 | Balladry and the meanings of melody

Early modern balladeers of all sorts knew the importance of an ear-tickling melody. In 1637, William Collingwood, a Cambridgeshire victualler, allegedly wrote the words for a promising ditty about 'all the noted Cuckoldes in Ickleton', but he was painfully aware that a mere text would not of itself guarantee success. Collingwood was heard to say 'that he could not say his prayers for thinking of it & that it grieved him he had not a good tune for it'. In Jacobean Nottingham, a group of libellers had enjoyed better creative fortunes, and the positive impact of their endeavours was revealed in the enthusiastic reaction of a local apothecary to a performance of one of their scurrilous masterpieces. Thomas Aldred laughed heartily 'in regard of the straungeness and concyted tune sett to it'. It was the melody, as much as the words, that amused him. Aldred's response would have pleased the editor of *The Rump*, a celebrated royalist song collection of 1660. He warned potential customers, 'If thou read these ballads (and not sing them), the poor ballads are undone.' This was strong language. Lazy or ignorant consumers had to be dissuaded from the negligent practice of overlooking the tunes. A song's melody, the editor insisted, was one of its integral features, and a tuneless ballad was scarcely a ballad at all.[1]

The role of melody in shaping contemporary interpretations of ballads has often been neglected and sometimes purposefully denied by scholars. Ballad tunes, we have been told, were largely irrelevant because they bore 'no definite functional interrelation' with the all-important texts. Melody, it has been said, was 'merely a vehicle' for the words.[2] Several recent scholars, admittedly, have sounded rather more constructive, but even in their works we have not progressed far beyond a basic awareness of the musical identity of ballads and a partially developed sense of the ways in which a song's tune may have contributed to its impact.[3] This chapter will argue that texts and tunes were connected in a constantly shifting

[1] EDR K/17/94, CUL; Sisson, *Lost Plays of Shakespeare's Age*, p. 199; *The Rump, or a Collection of Songs and Ballads* (London, 1660), preface.

[2] Würzbach, *The Rise of the English Street Ballad*, pp. 9, 16; Luckett, 'The Collection', p. xv.

[3] Watt, *Cheap Print*, pp. 23, 329; Smith, *Acoustic World*, pp. 188, 191; Palmer, *Sound of History*; Dugaw, *Warrior Women*, pp. 48, 56; Collinson, *Birthpangs of Protestant England*, pp. 108–12;

relationship, and that they should properly be understood together. Of course, the words were of fundamental importance, but melodies were capable of reinforcing, altering and destabilising textual messages in a compelling manner. A flexible system of thematic associations evolved as balladry developed, and, on occasion, the reputation of a tune was strong enough to convey a message even without the presence of words. In many more cases the essential mood of a tune refined or revised the probable impact of its accompanying words. Of course, the sparsity of source materials dealing with the actual reception of specific songs means that the exercise must be somewhat conjectural, but it seems to be worth the whistle. We have, I think, been missing something: melody made meaning.[4]

The associational thought-world of early modern people is of obvious importance here. We have already encountered evidence of the role played by 'resemblance' and 'correspondence' in the construction of knowledge during the period. Of course, this is a point that has been developed in more general terms by other scholars. The perception of resemblance, it has been argued, operated in such a way that a new cultural representation might 'reanimate a former one, and juxtapose itself to it'. Two different representations might appear even as 'quasi-likenesses', brought together by 'the insistent murmur of resemblance' and 'the perpetual possibility of imaginative recall'. Written texts, it has been noted, regularly presupposed an awareness of previous material, so that reading was as much about recognition as about discovery. Intertextuality was instinctive. Correspondence was a guiding principle within the cosmological interpretation of music, and there is little doubt that the imaginative worlds of many popular writers – John Taylor, for example – were made meaningful by conspicuously connective thought processes.[5] In all these respects, we can hear clear links with balladry: in its constant recycling of tunes; in its many verbal and thematic formulae; and in the frequent interconnecting of different ballads through explicit and implicit cross-references. The role of resemblance began with the simplicity of rhyme, which, at its most basic level, has always operated by inviting listeners or readers to associate one word – and thus one object or concept – with

Fox, *Oral and Literate Culture*, pp. 318–20. See also Bertrand Harris Bronson, *The Ballad as Song* (Berkeley: University of California Press, 1969), pp. 37–8, 215.

4 Modern comparisons can be made with the role of music in film, where it often serves to stimulate emotions in the viewer-listener. Similarly, our behaviour in supermarkets can be influenced to a remarkable degree by the music that is played. On this, see North et al., 'In-store Music', 132.

5 Michel Foucault, *The Order of Things* (London: Tavistock Publications, 1970), pp. 67–71; Roger Chartier, *The Order of Books*, trans. L. G. Cochrane (Cambridge: Polity Press, 1994), p. 14.

another. Within early modern balladry, however, resemblance also performed on a grander stage, constantly connecting current tunes, themes, phrases and pictures with their previous incarnations. In this cultural environment, it seems inherently unlikely that the tune of a ballad was 'merely a vehicle' for its words. We should at least consider the possibility that there was, in the popular melodies of the period, a code of meanings and associations to which scholars have not so far devoted much attention.[6]

Of course, in seeking to explore the possibilities there is a danger of presenting them as clumsy, mechanical or implausible. Nothing sucks the humour from a joke or allusion so effectively as the effort of explaining it. On the other hand, some things come less easily to us than they did to our ancestors. We are, for one thing, saturated by musical sound, and it is arguable that this condition may tend to dull the intensity of our relationship with melody. In an age when music plays at the flick of a switch, in lifts and through telephones, people can even become consciously resistant. 'Greensleeves', hugely popular for nearly 500 years, has recently been voted the most irritating telephone 'hold tune' in England, and one listener – the editor of a website devoted to the management of stress – has reported an urge to 'smash the phone with a pick-axe' whenever he hears it.[7] Furthermore, we no longer tend to think of pop tunes as mobile creatures that migrate constantly between different texts and carry meanings with them as they go. Nowadays, most tunes stick to their original texts, even if the songs that they form together are frequently replayed or reworked as 'cover versions'. Melodic migrations are not extinct, however, for they survive in several contexts, most notably within the raucous musical culture of the football crowd. English soccer fans frequently write new words to old tunes, and they feel the humour and excitement that are generated by the potentially unstable combination.[8]

Melody and mood

If we can indeed speak of a chain of associations between melodic and verbal themes in early modern balladry, then we should probably seek its

[6] The courtly composers of the age also recycled one another's musical material with some regularity, and one wonders whether the significance of the practice has yet been fully understood. The subject is tackled in Ian Payne, 'Musical Borrowing in the Madrigals of John Ward and John Wilbye', *Consort* 64 (2008), 37–63.

[7] *The Guardian* (2 July 2001).

[8] During the 1990s, for example, Manchester City fans sang a song to the tune of an Oasis track, replacing the line 'You're my wonderwall' with the topical observation 'We've got Alan Ball' (referring to the club's new manager). Comparable examples can be heard every Saturday afternoon at all major football grounds.

origins in the ancient and enduring perception that different scale patterns (or modes) and the melodies based upon them expressed and stimulated different emotional moods. Consumers of modern mass culture in the west tend to perceive brisk tunes in major keys as cheerful, bright and lively, while slower melodies in minor keys are understood as sad or serious, though composers also enjoy plenty of scope for mixing and unsettling these perceptions through the skilful use of the various elements that make up melody: a slow song in a major key can, for example, sound to us like a poignant reminder of happiness lost. Early modern ears and brains clearly worked according to an evolving version of this essential interpretative scheme, though our understanding of past listening practices – particularly among the population at large – is complicated by several factors. In the first place, almost all early modern commentary on this subject came from the pens of highly educated and musically sophisticated authors whose opinions may not be a reliable guide to the operation of what Puttenham called 'the popular ear'.[9] Similarly, written versions of ballad tunes can be treated as only a rough (or perhaps smooth) guide to the melodies in their alehouse or marketplace forms. In particular, it is likely that courtly composers sometimes altered certain notes of the underlying scales in order to render the tunes more pleasing and flattering to aristocratic patrons (though they did not invariably do so). The early modern period witnessed a steady transition from modal music (in which tunes are organised around any one of several scale patterns) to predominantly tonal music (in which most melodies conform to one of only two scales, major and minor). This transition affected music-making on all levels, but the rate and extent of change must have varied with social status, geographical location and musical taste (in the early twentieth century, Cecil Sharp was pleased to find that modal melodic patterns survived in many of the tunes used by rural folk-singers). Unfortunately, it is impossible to be much more precise than this, but we must be aware that the altering of notes (especially the seventh of the scale) by early modern composers may have had a significant impact on both the sound and the mood of common melodies. Finally, we are limited by the extreme paucity of information concerning the tempo at which any particular tune was played. The same melody can, of course, generate subtly different moods at different speeds. This is a vital aspect of the subject, but we are almost invariably left guessing.

[9] Puttenham, *Arte of English Poesie*, p. 84.

Having sounded these notes of caution, it is nevertheless possible to deduce certain underlying principles from contemporary writings and surviving melodies. Evidence of the slow march towards modern major–minor tonality is suggested by the apparent predominance among ballad tunes of two old modes in particular: the Dorian (similar, though by no means identical, to the now familiar minor scale) and the Ionian (the originator of our major scale).[10] According to Charles Butler, 'the infinite multitude of Balads' was set to tunes in the Dorian mode, and his opinion is confirmed by the fact that the four most frequently cited melodies – 'Fortune my foe', 'Packington's pound', 'Chevy Chase' and 'O man in desperation' – all seem to have been in this mode. Butler described music in the Dorian mode as sober and slow, arguing that it moved hearers 'to sobrieti, prudence, modesti, and godlines'. The ballad-writers evidently agreed, for few of them wrote light and jocular ballads to any of the tunes listed above (though there were exceptions). And when, in 1630, William Slatyer selected a group of 'common, but solemne tunes' for his experimental metrical psalms, he included several that were unquestionably Dorian. In contrast, Butler considered the Ionian mode more appropriate for songs that were delicate, romantic and effeminate. This mode stimulated 'honest mirth and delight, chiefly in feasting and other merriments'.[11] Again, the balladeers broadly concurred, and tunes such as 'Hey boys up go we' and 'The spinning wheel' were chosen most frequently for bouncy songs involving some combination of humour, love and sex. The link was an old one, for the Ionian scale had been styled *modus lascivicus* by medieval commentators as a result of its popularity among the continental troubadours. When ballad-writers of the seventeenth century sought to boost their sales by attaching adjectives to the titles of their chosen tunes, they tended to label Ionian or major melodies as 'pleasant', 'dainty', 'delightful' or even 'lofty'. These were melodies with the capacity to induce feelings of happiness.

Musical writers also identified other melodic characteristics that could be valuable in the expression and stimulation of emotion. Of course, they were rarely thinking of balladry, though one or two sophisticated analysts did make reference to broadside tunes within their general discussions of music. Butler admired such tunes, and there is therefore a case for considering balladry in relation to what he wrote about music and

[10] On the modes, see above, p. 52 n. 51.

[11] Butler, *Principles of Musik*, pp. 1–2; William Slatyer, *Psalmes, or Songs of Sion, Turned into the Language, and Set to the Tunes of a Strange Land* (London, 1630), subtitle. See below, pp. 420–1.

emotion more broadly. Gravity and sadness, Butler advised, demanded music that was slow and plain, while harsh, short notes could be combined to suggest manliness and anger. Such qualities also required that the main notes of the chosen scale should remain unaltered, for tampering with these notes implied effeminacy and sorrow. Alexander Molleson, a later admirer of ballad music, further argued that each note of a scale was associated with a different spirit or quality: the keynote was bold and commanding (as was the fifth); the second and the sixth were plaintive; the third and the seventh were supplicative (and well known to the more musical of beggars); and the fourth was grave and solemn. Others suggested that particular combinations of notes (rising, falling, in sequence, out of sequence, chromatic and diatonic) could be useful in enhancing the sense of the words and in bringing out the appropriate emotions. Such complexities were, according to Molleson, 'easier to be felt than expressed', and simple ballad tunes, informed not by sophisticated analysis but by 'natural genius', were often far more potent in the conveyance of emotion than were the efforts of celebrated composers. He agreed with Butler that the emotional language of melody had always been understood by rich and poor alike, despite their radically different lifestyles.[12]

Not all commentators felt so inclusive, and it is therefore difficult to know how energetically we should seek evidence of this complex musical vocabulary in the fast-moving commercial world of the broadside ballad. Many tunes, after all, were used over and over again, and they were not, therefore, carefully constructed in order to suit each specific text (if anything, the relationship was often the other way round). Nevertheless, it is at least worth considering Molleson's implied argument that balladeers understood by instinct the ways in which certain melodic characteristics could be deployed in order to bring new life to their texts and to produce appropriate emotional responses. 'Welladay', for example, was the tune named in 1601 on a ballad entitled *A Lamentable Dittie Composed upon the Death of Robert Lord Devereux Late Earle of Essex, who was beheaded in the Tower of London, upon Ashwednesday in the morning* (**Website track 16 and Appendix**). The subject matter was politically controversial, and the tune – known only from a later keyboard version – played its part in expressing the popular mood of regret at the execution of Elizabeth I's former favourite. In its later written version, some of the

[12] Butler, *Principles of Musik*, pp. 96–7; Molleson, *Melody, the Soul of Music*, pp. 5, 30–1. For a stimulating discussion of Renaissance 'word-painting' (the use of various musical devices to mirror and thus to enhance the emotional effect of poetic lines), see McColley, *Poetry and Music*, pp. 16–29.

leading notes have been sharpened, thus creating a more tonal feel, but it seems likely that the tune as commonly sung was in the Mixolydian mode (like the modern major scale, but with a flattened seventh). This mode was associated variously by theorists with angelical qualities, youth and the combination of joy and sadness. According to Agrippa, it was 'meete for Tragedies, and sorrowful things, and hath force to stirre up, to drawe backe, and to put awaie forever'. The Mixolydian mode was thus perfectly suited to a song that both celebrated the exemplary attributes of a hero whose life had been cut short and bemoaned his passing.[13]

The mood of the tune suggests that it must have been performed slowly, and the running quaver motifs would certainly have been difficult to sing at pace. The most striking of these motifs falls on the second line of each verse, accompanying the double repetition of the woeful expression 'welladay' (this seems to amount to a refrain, albeit one that is set within the stanza, rather than at its close):

Sweet England's pride is gone,
welladay, welladay,
Which makes her sigh and groan,
evermore still;
He did her fame advance,
In Ireland, Spain and France,
And by a sad mischance,
is from us tane.[14]

The second 'welladay' is sung to a descending run of quavers, strongly suggestive of a mournful sigh, and the three-note downward motif that accompanies the word 'groan' is similarly expressive. In this opening verse, the celebratory fifth and sixth lines are marked by an upward octave leap and a rather more optimistic musical phrase, before the last two lines carry us downward once more to rest on the final keynote. We do not know who composed this song, but it is clear that tune and text were carefully integrated. Moreover, the evident success of the ballad suggests that the composer's efforts were appreciated by the ballad audience. This was probably the song that, according to a German visitor, was being 'sung and played on musical instruments all over the country' in 1602. The song was performed 'even at the royal court', despite the fact

[13] *Euing Collection of English Broadside Ballads*, no. 199 (a later copy); Agrippa, *Henrie Cornelius Agrippa*, fo. 28r.

[14] *Euing Collection of English Broadside Ballads*, no. 199.

that Essex's memory was officially 'condemned as that of a man having committed high treason'.[15]

'Fortune my foe' was a serious tune in the Dorian mode, and its capacity to reinforce and colour the words to which it was set can be clearly heard in *An Excellent Song wherein you shall Finde Great Consolation for a Troubled Mind* (**Website track 17 and Appendix**). This was an exceedingly successful composition, and the first four words of its opening verse swiftly became established as an alternative name for the tune:

Ayme not too hie in things above thy reach,
Be not too foolish in thine own conceit,
As thou hast wit and worldly wealth at will,
So give him thankes that shall encrease it still.

The opening line of the melody, whether by coincidence or contrivance, provides its own commentary upon the words. 'Ayme not too hie' is sung to a sombre rising motif, while the phrase 'above thy reach' is set to a step-by-step descending figure, as if the contours of the tune are part of the advice. The second musical line repeats the first, and the words of both convey a stern warning to the listener. The mood of the tune lifts somewhat in its third and fourth lines, a subtle shift that is echoed in the more optimistic (and crudely economic) words. This is a pattern that is repeated in several other verses. Overall, however, a text that continuously juxtaposes sober injunctions and reassuring promises is tilted towards its darker side by this famously sombre melody. Few listeners can have emerged from an encounter with *An Excellent Song* in cheery and light-hearted mood. Its ABC format reinforces the impression that we are here receiving a sober moral lesson.[16]

Heavy tunes in the Dorian mode did not, however, enjoy a monopoly over godly balladry, and the regular use of Ionian (or major) tunes for religious songs is equally ear-catching. Popular theology and morality were not necessarily doomful and dreary in musical mood, and the potent influence of melody over the essential character of individual songs is once again apparent. Slatyer's 'common, but solemne tunes' included several that danced along quite happily in the Ionian mode. 'The lady's fall' is a particularly interesting example. Originally known as 'In peascod time', this tune was selected in 1603 for *A Lamentable Ballad Called The Ladye's*

[15] Simpson, *British Broadside Ballad*, pp. 747–8; Fredric Gerschow, quoted by Smith, *Acoustic World*, p. 193.

[16] Roxburghe ballads, C20F7–F10, vol. I, p. 326, BL.

Fall: Declaring how a young gentlewoman, through her too much trust, came to her end; and how her lover slew himselfe. It is not a happy story. The song was nevertheless reprinted many times, and its title rapidly displaced 'In peascod time' as an identifier of the tune. The instruction 'to the tune of The lady's fall' appeared on numerous ballads, typically woeful tales in which sinners receive their comeuppance at the hands of a harsh but fair God. To our ears, tune and text often seem curiously at odds, yet this was a combination that obviously worked well during the seventeenth century.[17]

The twinning of heavy texts and light notes is an intriguing indicator of popular tastes, and it suggests the existence of considerable modal flexibility in the deployment of tunes. A typical example is the ballad entitled *Miraculous Newes from the Cittie of Holdt in Germany, where there were three dead bodyes seene to rise out of their graves upon the twentieth day of September last 1616, with other strange things that hapned* (**Website track 18 and Appendix**). Its opening words are far from cheerful: 'The dreadfull day of doome drawes neere: / oh mortal man, repent.' Hereafter, the listener is treated to a detailed account of the many woes recently visited upon the sinful people of Holdt: wondrous thunder and lightning; 'dreadfull clamours' with no obvious source; 'ghostly shapes' rising from their graves to urge repentance; and a plague far worse than any the world has ever known. And through all this, the apparently jolly tune lilts easily along.

The effect is nowadays peculiar, and it seems possible that the key to understanding the juxtaposition of terrifying text and merry melody lies in commonplace theology. Sinners will be punished but the faithful and virtuous will enjoy eternal bliss. Arguably, the less than doomful tune serves as an optimistic reminder of God's love to his chosen people. The precise theological mechanics of God's choice were rarely spelled out in ballads, yet the prospect of joy for the just helps to explain why a sizeable minority of 'solemnn tunes' were in the Ionian mode and characterised by rhythmic and melodic vitality. Such tunes suggest the hope amid the horror, and the perpetual promise of divine intervention and ultimate justice. Ballads like *Miraculous Newes*, when sounded to their tunes, were arguably more optimistic than a modern 'reading' of the bare text might reveal. Only in the closing verses of this song is the underlying tone of reassurance made more explicit:

[17] *Shirburn Ballads*, p. 208; Simpson, *British Broadside Ballad*, pp. 368–71. There are thirteen ballads to this tune in the Pepys collection.

To which most kinde and gracious god
Let us our prayers make
That all such threatning woes he may
from this our countrey take,
That we may never feele the wrath
which hee on other layes,
But still to walke, like christians true,
uprightly in his wayes.

If English people repent and live well, then they will not suffer as the Germans have done. Verbally, this message is rather tacked on at the end of the song; musically, however, it has perhaps been present throughout. If the Ionian mode was associated with lightness and lewdness, then there were also songs that hijacked it in order to make the point that morality and misery were not inseparable bedfellows.[18]

On occasion, this complicated relationship between tune and text was inverted, and melodies in minor modes were attached to seemingly light-hearted words. In the 1620s, *A Merry New Catch of All Trades* was set 'To the tune of The cleane Contrary way' (**Website track 19 and Appendix**). The very title of the melody hints at its potentially transformative influence over the words. Previous scholars – working with their eyes rather than their ears – have found in this song a somewhat perplexing list of mainly urban occupations (see Figure 6.1). It opens with the line 'All Trades are not alike in show', and proceeds to name over fifty well-known jobs and social types. *A Merry New Catch*, we have been told, was perhaps the kind of song that was designed for children to sing in the nursery.[19] This seemed a reasonable suggestion, given the apparently trite nature of the silent verse:

The Bricklayer high doth rise to flye,
The Plummer oft doth melt,
The Carpenter doth love his rule,
And the Hatmaker loves his felt.

When the tune is called into play, however, the entire song takes on a rather different aspect. 'The clean contrary way', though in a minor mode, seems to invite a brisk and lively rendition. The melody is infectiously repetitive, and its solid grounding in the minor triad suggests a darker layer of secret signification that no bright and breezy tune could have

[18] *Shirburn Ballads*, p. 76. The tunes 'Rogero' and 'Light of love' appear to have sometimes operated in a similar manner.

[19] Würzbach, *The Rise of the English Street Ballad*, pp. 207–8.

Figure 6.1. Ballad texts often contained meaningful possibilities that are difficult to detect today. In this case, the picture is perhaps a clue to the bawdy undertones that many early modern listeners would have detected. The Pepys Library, Magdalene College, Cambridge, Pepys Ballads, *A Merry New Catch of All Trades* (London, *c.* 1620), first part.

conveyed. The ballad, when sung as a round, also communicates the clamour of urban life, with its constantly competitive jostling for space and attention. It is an intensely masculine ballad, featuring only three female types (maidservants, whores and scolds). In performance, moreover, it becomes ever more clear that the song is a semi-coded assemblage of bawdy innuendo. The carpenter's rule is not what it seems, and 'felt' is suddenly a verb rather than a noun when sung in association with the hatmaker (who 'loves his felt'). Other seemingly innocuous announcements also take on new meaning: the tinker 'beats his pan'; 'The Butcher prickes'; 'The Farmer stops a gap'; 'The Cobler lives by his peece'; and 'The Taylors yard is seldome marde, / Tho it measure many a score.' The tune title now emerges as a signal to us that we are to hear the first line, as it were, backwards, in 'the clean contrary way'. Indeed, this phrase was commonly deployed by seventeenth-century speakers in order to reverse the import of a preceding statement. 'All Trades are not alike' because we all have different jobs and equipment, yet at a deeper level the chief occupation of each and every one of us, from the courtier to the collier, is sexual gratification. One tool is much like another, and fornication makes the world go round. Is this really one for the nursery? The tune, moreover, had previously been attached to a well-known bawdy song about the cuckolding of an old man by his young wife. It therefore had something of a reputation before the publication of *A Merry New Catch*, and it is to the general operation of melodic associations that we shall now turn.[20]

Meaning by association

In many cases, the moods of melodies led them to develop meaningful connections with successive texts of corresponding temper. Tunes gathered distinctive associations, thereby acquiring an enhanced capacity to amplify the messages conveyed by the words. In such cases, tunes and texts existed in mutually fulfilling relationships that frequently endured for decades. The melody, often chosen again and again for songs on similar subjects, added new momentum and depth to the meanings of a text and linked it with all the ballads for which it had previously been appointed. The human brain is particularly adept at processing music that it recognises, and we can assume that the sound of a familiar tune drifting across a seventeenth-century marketplace must have activated what modern psychologists call 'superordinate knowledge structures' among those who heard it.[21] Prior associations would have found their way uninvited into

[20] *Pepys Ballads*, vol. I, pp. 164–5; Simpson, *British Broadside Ballad*, p. 109. The tune was also used to subvert the tone of a text in a politically controversial court case of the 1620s. This is analysed in Alastair Bellany's fascinating essay 'Singing Libel in Early Stuart England: The Case of the Staines Fiddlers, 1627', *Huntingdon Library Quarterly* 69.1 (2006), 177–93.

[21] North et al., 'In-store Music', 132.

the mind, and the listener's attitude to the song would have been conditioned by his or her previous knowledge of the tune. Different listeners would thus have heard different things, depending on the nature and depth of their acquaintance with the melody in question. From the composer's perspective, the melody was also a marketing device that attracted potential customers with a preference for songs on that particular theme. Indeed, it must frequently have been the tune rather than the text that first caught the attention of potential buyers. At a distance, a well-known melody could be identified well before the precise words of a song became audible, and tunes were thus vital indicators of probable content. In some cases, however, composers seem to have worked against the associations of a chosen tune, thus setting up complex interpretative possibilities that existed beyond the text. It is generally impossible to determine whether such possibilities were generated by accident or design, and any judgements we make on this thorny issue are necessarily tentative.[22]

Ballads in which the chosen melody worked by association to identify and amplify the primary theme of a text are extremely numerous. 'Fortune my foe' (or 'Aim not too high') once again provides an impressive example. It first attracted significant attention in the Elizabethan period as the tune for a rather sober love song, but its strongest connections in the next 200 years were with weighty moralising and sensational warnings. One typical example was a ballad with the following catchy title:

A Wonderfull Wonder, being a most strange and true relation of the resolute life, and miserable death of Thomas Miles, who did forsweare himselfe, and wished that God might shew some heavie example upon him, and so it came to passe for as hee sate at his meate hee choked himselfe, and died in short space after . . . , and being ript up by the chirurgions of S. Bartholomews Hospitall, was found to have a gub of meate sticking fast in his throat, which was the cause of his death. Written to warne all rash swearers to forsake their evill wayes, which God grant we may[23]

'Fortune' also forged a particular connection with execution ballads and the 'last dying speeches' of the condemned, songs in which listeners were urged repeatedly and relentlessly to learn vital lessons from the lips of the doomed. Take, for example, *The Godly End, and Wofull Lamentation of one John Stevens* (**Website track 20 and Appendix**). In this song, the condemned

[22] There is a stimulating theoretical discussion of some of these possibilities in the introduction to Georgina Born and David Hesmondhalgh (eds.), *Western Music and its Others: Difference, Representation and Appropriation in Music* (Berkeley: University of California Press, 2000), pp. 1–46.

[23] Roxburghe ballads, C20F7–F10, vol. I, pp. 482–3, BL.

man addresses members of the audience directly, urging them all to fear God and live well (particularly in the matter of 'governing their tongues'). The message is made memorable by graphic details of this repentant traitor's judicial sentence:

My body must in quarters eke be cut,
And on the City gates they should be put,
To be a sight for others to take heed,
Where ravenous Fowles upon my flesh will feed.

The last of these memorable lines also provides the inspiration for the accompanying woodcut picture, in which four ravens peck hungrily at the displayed limbs of the departed youth.[24] When such a ballad was performed before early modern audiences, it was much more than a sensational song to a melody of sombre mood. It was also a musical link with all those who, in previous decades and centuries, had paid the price for their sins. This gave the 'dying speech' ballads a rooted and universal quality that contemporary listeners evidently found difficult to resist. Samuel Pepys collected ten execution ballads set to this hit tune of the gallows.[25]

The melody's association with hanging also added expressive force when it was recommended for ballads of more mundane moral instruction. 'Fortune' provided the tune for many such songs, typically aimed at the young. It brought to its texts a stern and threatening reminder of what became of the dissolute. Nobody dies in *The Virgins ABC*, but the rope nevertheless seems to hang ominously over the heads of the youthful women at whom the ballad is aimed. A piece of clumsy patriarchal moralising is transformed by the tune into something with dark and intimidating undertones. It opens,

All youthful Virgins,
to this song give ear,
And learn these lessons,
which are taught you here:
An Alphabet of Vertues,
here are set,
And being learn'd
will make a Maid compleat.

[24] Ibid., vol. I, pp. 490–1.

[25] *Pepys Ballads*, vol. I, pp. 124, 126, 130, vol. II, pp. 153, 154, 169, 170, 196, 200, 204. For comparison, track 7 on the website is an arrangement of the melody for lute.

There follows a weighty and uncompromising statement of the standards by which young women are expected to conduct themselves. The melody seems to hint at the dire consequences that await any maiden who allows scorn, pride, vanity, wantonness or lust to consume her (other songs to the tune described the execution of specific women who had succumbed to such vices). The tone of *The Virgins ABC* is overwhelmingly negative, and the words 'not', 'never', 'no' and 'nor' are heard on twenty-two occasions.[26]

Many other tunes accumulated strong and lasting associations in a comparable manner. Robin Hood had his own melody, specified over and over again on closely interrelated narrative ballads about his adventures (there were separate ballads with titles such as *Robin Hood and the Tanner*, pairing the hero variously with a tanner, a ranger, a stranger, a bishop, a beggar and a butcher, all to the same tune). The slow tones of 'O man in desperation' suggested the urgency of repentance and the imminence of divine punishment for those who failed to heed the call. 'Queen Dido', famously selected by Deloney for his song about the Marian exile of the Duchess of Suffolk, came to be associated during the seventeenth century with some combination of virtue, gentility and enforced travel. These connections were all called into play, for example, in a post-Restoration ballad about the escape of Charles II following the Battle of Worcester in 1651. From the 1680s, 'Russell's farewell' came to rival 'Fortune' as a tune heard at and associated with executions. Pepys collected thirty-eight ballads set to this tune, the vast majority of which reported or dramatised the public deaths of criminals and traitors. Several seventeenth-century tunes were associated particularly with politics, most frequently of the royalist or Tory variety. When listeners in the later seventeenth century heard songs set to 'When the king enjoys his own again', 'Hey boys up go we' and 'Lilliburlero' they must have known what to expect, even before they considered the words. Throughout the period, there were also numerous tunes that spoke primarily of courtship and marriage. Interestingly, individual melodies might feature with equal prominence in joyous and sorrowful love songs. Listeners needed the texts to spell out the precise details, but songs set to 'Under and over', 'Bonny sweet Robin' and

[26] *Pepys Ballads*, vol. I, pp. 500–1. The tune is here called 'The young mans ABC'. This appears to be one of several alternative names for 'Fortune' or 'Aim not too high'. A ballad entitled *The Young Mans ABC* was definitely set to 'Aim not too high' (*Pepys Ballads*, vol. I, pp. 508–9) and, as was customary, an old tune picked up a new title – but not, in this case, one that was destined to last.

'The spinning wheel' could be connected with the general subject of romance, before a single word was heard.[27]

Composers sometimes recommended two or more alternative tunes for the singing of particular songs. This tactic became more common in the later seventeenth century and presumably reflected a desire to maximise the market by ensuring that a high proportion of potential buyers could call up from their memories a suitable tune. One ballad was set

To a dainty new note, Which if you cannot hit
There's another tune which doth as well fit,
That's the Mother beguiles the Daughter.[28]

Double or multiple citations opened up the possibility that a single text might carry divergent meanings, depending on the musical choice made by the singer. In most instances, the prior associations of the recommended tunes were broadly comparable, and the subtle distinctions that may have existed between them are probably beyond our acoustic range. In other cases, however, the differences were a little more obvious, and a single song could take on a variety of identities. In 1696, for example, *The Successful Commander* was designed for singing 'To the Tune of, Let Caesar live long; or, If Love's a sweet Passion'. This ballad celebrated the action of the Earl of Athlone in burning the French magazine at Givet after hearing of Sir George Barclay's plot to assassinate King William in 1696. 'Let Caesar live long' was a bright, major melody, strongly associated with attachment to Charles II and, later, to William III. When used as the setting for *The Successful Commander*, it helps to create a mood of patriotic self-confidence, militaristic triumphalism and upbeat masculinity, while also ensuring that the king, though mentioned only sparingly in the text, nevertheless maintains a constant presence in the listener's mind (**Website track 21 and Appendix**).[29]

The second tune, 'If love's a sweet passion', sets a rather different tone (**Website track 22 and Appendix**). It was only six years old, having appeared first in Purcell's *The Fairy Queen*, but it was already a big hit on the broadside circuit. Its minor key and somewhat restless modulations combined with its origins to generate associations that were much more plaintive than those of 'Let Caesar live long'. This was primarily a romantic melody, well experienced in the task of enlisting sympathy for characters

[27] References to these tunes, too numerous to list here, can be traced via the indexes to the *Pepys Ballads* and Simpson's *British Broadside Ballad*.

[28] *Pepys Ballads*, vol. I, p. 268. [29] Ibid., vol. II, p. 340.

as they struggled with the turbulent bitter-sweet emotions of love (the opening lines in the original song asked 'If love's a sweet passion, why does it torment?'). In 1695, it had also been specified for a ballad lamenting the death of Queen Mary and expressing popular support for the grieving king.[30] When applied to *The Successful Commander* it therefore contributes to the text a mood of love and sympathy, more resonant of relief than of euphoria. To some degree, this seems to undercut the predominantly bold and celebratory tone of the words by adding more than a *frisson* of anxious concern for the constantly endangered monarch. The tune alters the balance between delight and danger, and the reference to 'that horrible thing, / Which had been contriv'd against William our King' seems to take on a new emotional prominence. In contrast, when the same words are sung to the brasher measures of 'Let Caesar live long' they hardly seem central. *The Successful Commander*, therefore, is one text but two songs.

This was by no means the only ballad in which the prior associations of a tune seemed to draw attention to one particular aspect of the text rather than to its general and predominant themes. A broadside of 1603 entitled *A New Song to the Great Comfort and Rejoycing of all True English Harts, at our most gracious King JAMES his proclamation* was set, rather remarkably, to a tune called 'Englands pride is gone'. This was another name for the well-known melody 'Welladay', most famous as the setting for the song of 1601 that lamented the execution of the Earl of Essex. In the new ballad, therefore, musical phrases that were loaded with grief were tied to joyous words of welcome for the incoming Scottish king (the tune, set to the original words, can be heard on the website, track 16). The earlier opening verse, quoted above, was replaced by something entirely different:

Sweet England Rejoyce and sing,
Lovingly: lovingly:
God hath sent us now a King,
Praised be him.
Of King HENRIES Linage is he
Princely borne by degree.
A braver Prince cannot be,
then [than] is Noble King James.

In 1603, the tune's associations with mournful eulogy were so strong that it must have been all but impossible to sing this verse without thoughts of

30 Ibid., p. 373. On the two tunes, see also Simpson, *British Broadside Ballad*, pp. 359–61, 434–7.

its predecessor. The old text haunts the new and suggests that the ballad was as much a lament for the dead monarch as a celebration of the new one. The composer's choice of tune thus reflected rather beautifully the mixed sensations of continuity and change that inevitably attended the passing of a monarch.[31]

Similarly, a white-letter ballad of 1646, *The World is Turned Upside Down*, seems a curious creation when it is read without its tune. It is full of depressed royalist commentary on recent measures taken by parliamentary authority against various forms of traditional culture, including holy days, charity and festive hospitality. Each verse, however, also features a refrain that opens with the seemingly incongruous injunction, 'Yet let's be content'. The final stanza is a representative example:

To conclude, I'le tell you news that's right,
Christmas was kil'd at Nasbie fight:
Charity was slain at that same time,
Jack Tell troth too, a friend of mine,
Likewise then did die,
Rost beef and shred pie,
Pig, Goose and Capon no quarter found.
Yet let's be content, and the times lament,
You see the world is quite turn'd round.[32]

The optimism of a single phrase in the penultimate line seems strangely isolated and inconsistent in the midst of so many regrets for a lost world. When the ballad's tune is added to the mix, however, this brief call for contentment becomes suddenly more comprehensible. The ballad was set 'To the Tune of, When the King enjoys his own again' and it is under the influence of this hit royalist melody that it must be considered. It had apparently been composed specially in the mid-1640s, probably by Martin Parker, for a ballad entitled *The King Enjoyes his Own Again* which was 'To be joyfully sung with its own proper tune'. It is a wonderful melody, and it retains the power to convey – in conjunction with its original words – a powerful sense of optimism in desperate times (**Website track 23 and Appendix**). By all accounts, it became the royalist anthem *par excellence* during the profoundly discordant decades of the mid-seventeenth century. From a war-torn perspective around 1644, the author boldly prophesied the eventual restoration of royal order to England, and each

[31] *A New Song to the Great Comfort and Rejoycing of All True English Harts* (London, 1603).
[32] *The World is Turned Upside Down* (London, 1646).

verse concluded with an uplifting refrain, 'when the King comes home in peace again'.[33] The song's instant vogue meant that by 1646 its tune conveyed to royalists a sense of optimistic anticipation, both by mood and by association. It was thus a vital component of the more verbally perplexing ballad *The World is Turned Upside Down*, and capable of conveying positive predictions and messages of reassurance, despite the predominant pessimism of the words. In association with the tune, the words 'Yet let's be content' become a crucial and central component of the song, rather than a strangely inconsistent inclusion.

A similar analysis could be applied to many other songs. In *All is Ours and Our Husbands*, a broadside of about 1672, a 'hostess' defends herself and others of her occupation against charges of cheating, over-charging and stealing. The sexual dimension of their profiteering activities is mentioned only briefly, yet the famously phallic tune – 'The carman's whistle' – ensures the centrality of bawdry in the listener's imagination. The original ballad set to this tune was Elizabethan and had been slammed by Henry Chettle in 1592 as a piece of 'odious and lascivious ribauldrie'. It had clearly retained these associations through the intervening decades, and it therefore contributed significantly to the rude mood of *All is Ours*.[34] During the 1680s, the tune to which *The Westminster Lovers* was sung had a rather gloomier impact upon its verses. At first sight, the text looks like a conventional courtship dialogue between two young lovers, Thomas and Isabella. If it had been set to a bright love tune, listeners would surely have anticipated a happy outcome, with the partners eventually settling their differences and joining together in wedlock. The melody, however, tells a different story. Unusually, the composer set this text to 'Russell's farewell', the tune associated with condemned political traitors preparing to be hanged. It thus warns us, right from the outset, that nothing good will come of this particular love affair. Sure enough, Thomas and Isabella are so tormented by their imprudent passion that they die in anguish, one after the other. This moment comes as something of a shock if the text is read alone, but with the grim associations of the tune, it becomes the inevitable outcome of a doomed passion. One of the accompanying pictures portrays Cupid flying through the clouds, his bow and arrow at the ready. In this instance, however, he brings no joy, but rather

[33] Roxburghe ballads, C20F7–F10, vol. III, p. 256, BL; Simpson, *British Broadside Ballad*, pp. 764–8. See also below, pp. 322–3.

[34] *All is Ours and Our Husbands* (London, *c.* 1672); Chettle, quoted by Simpson, *British Broadside Ballad*, p. 86.

stands in for the executioner who was a more familiar figure in ballads set to 'Russell's farewell'.[35]

In songs such as this, the existing resonances of a melody were not only called upon, but simultaneously redirected in some more or less subtle way. Elizabethan puritans went through a phase of attempting to kidnap popular melodies in their efforts to popularise Protestantism.[36] In the decades before 1580, the presses regularly issued godly ballads that 'moralised' existing songs, typically retaining the tunes but rewriting the words. The objective was clearly to overwhelm the existing associations of successful melodies by substituting more spiritual possibilities. Few of the resultant godly ballads have survived, but the Stationers' Registers bear regular witness to their existence. *O Swete Olyver* was followed swiftly by *O Sweete Olyver Altered to the Scriptures*, while *Row Well ye Mariners* generated a string of pious parodies: *Roo Well ye Marynors Moralyzed, Stande Faste ye Maryners, Row Well ye Christes Maryners, Rowe Well Godes Marynours* and the more mysterious *Rowe Well ye Marynours for those that Loke Bygge.*[37] In most cases, it seems that the prior associations of the tune were amatory, and that the godly balladeers made it their business to redefine love as primarily a bond between God and humanity rather than between man and woman. Thus the author of *The Sinner, Dispisinge the World and All Earthly Vanities* chose the tune 'Dainty, come thow to me', taking care to replace the original refrain with a new one, 'Jesu, come thow to mee'.[38] In 1567, a Scottish publication, *A Compendious Book of Godly and Spiritual Songs*, contained a number of texts apparently intended for worldly tunes. Listeners who were already familiar with the love tune 'John, come kiss me now' would probably have recognised the opening verse of one song, which seems to have been lifted wholesale from the existing secular version:

John, cum kis me now,
Johne, cum kis me now,
Johne, cum kis me by and by,
And mak no moir adow.

[35] Roxburghe ballads, C20F7–F10, vol. II, p. 510, BL.

[36] This project can be related to the use of *contrafacta* by Protestant evangelicals on the continent. See, for example, the discussion in Rebecca Wagner Oettinger, *Music as Propaganda in the German Reformation* (Aldershot: Ashgate, 2001), ch. 4.

[37] Rollins, *An Analytical Index to the Ballad-entries*, pp. 172–3, 201. See also Collinson, *Birthpangs of Protestant England*, pp. 109–10, and Simpson, *British Broadside Ballad*, pp. 269, 618.

[38] *Shirburn Ballads*, p. 84. This tune has not been traced.

The second verse, however, bore little relation to the lascivious original, and must have come as something of a surprise:

The Lord, thy God, I am,
That Johne dois the call,
Johne representit man
Be [by] grace celestiall.[39]

It was perhaps not surprising that such efforts failed to produce the desired results, and that puritans abandoned their tuneful tactic of thematic re-programming during the early 1580s. Their labours were not wholly in vain, however, for the lively tune 'Row well, ye mariners' held on to its new pious associations even after puritanism had left it behind.[40]

The technique of redirecting melodic associations did not die with the enthusiasm of the puritans. Instead, it was adopted and adapted by other ballad-writers.[41] The tune 'I'll never love thee more' was, for example, named on a ballad by Thomas Jordan entitled *[A] Dialogue betwixt Tom and Dick, the Former a Countryman, the Other a citizen. Presented to his Excellency and the Council of State, at Drapers Hall in London, March 28, 1660* (**Website track 24 and Appendix**). This unusually firm evidence of an actual rendition was confirmed by Thomas Rugg, who referred in his journal to the lavish festivities staged by various London companies in honour of General George Monck after his arrival from Scotland in January 1660. The hero of the hour was treated to 'many pretty anticks, some the cittizan and the soldier, other the country Tom and citty Dick'.[42] Monck presumably sat through at least one performance of this ballad, and one wonders what he made of the chosen tune. 'I'll never love thee more' was associated most strongly with love, courtship and marriage. Most obviously, it therefore added romantic and faintly homo-erotic undertones to a ballad in which two men, Tom and Dick, declare their adulation for the heroic general. Monck is described as a 'bonny lad', a 'gallant man' and a 'good fellow'. He has saved the nation from further civil war and economic plight. Understandably, the countryman and the citizen are united in their love for him, and each verse ends with some variation on the lines 'If GEORGE prove not a Gallant man, / Ne're trust Good-fellow more.'

[39] *A Compendious Book of Godly and Spiritual Songs*, ed. A. F. Mitchell (Edinburgh, 1897), p. 158.
[40] Simpson, *British Broadside Ballad*, p. 619.
[41] Ethnomusicologists have also encountered it in non-western cultures. See, for example, Wade, *Thinking Musically*, p. 14.
[42] *Diurnal of Thomas Rugg*, p. 71.

This tune, however, brought with it a spirit of romance that was far from simple. Earlier ballads using the melody had tended to emphasise some of the more problematic aspects of love. In one, a hen-pecked husband bitterly regrets his marriage and wishes 'Anything for a quiet life'. In several others, the tensions and suspicions that attend upon courtship are amply revealed. And in the ballad that gave the tune its title, a man threatens to imprison his sweetheart in a doorless marble cell in order to ensure that she remains faithful to him. Any sign of infidelity on her part will be matched by his hostility. 'I'll never Love thee more', he warns her at the conclusion of every verse.[43] The Restoration *Dialogue betwixt Tom and Dick* therefore carried the potential for a somewhat sharper interpretation in which the attitude of the English people towards the powerful general combined grateful adoration with a whispered suggestion of suspicion. Undeniably, Monck is praised to the skies, but the ballad's repetitive refrains also remind him of the need to fulfil his side of the bargain: 'But if GEORGE does not do the knack / Ne're trust good-fellow more'; 'And yet if GEORGE don't humme his Gigge / Ne're trust good-fellow more'; 'Yet – if GEORGE don't what we desire / Ne're trust good-fellow more'. These refrains represent a series of references – both verbal and musical – to the earlier ballad, and they suggest the possibility of an almost contractual arrangement in which Tom and Dick will love George, but only while he continues to satisfy their needs. At the date of the Drapers' performance, the political future was uncertain, but everybody recognised that Monck's military power and his role as an intermediary between parliament and the king made him a key player. Influential voices within the city of London had come to support the idea of restoring the monarchy, and they therefore sought to convince Monck of their argument. The *Dialogue betwixt Tom and Dick*, with its heavy emphasis upon recent economic hardships, can be heard as part of this effort. Thus the song, though primarily celebratory, also voiced a warning that was alluded to in words but amplified by melody. The tune's romantic associations were applied to a political relationship and deployed both to express devotion and to urge reciprocation. This was not an unconditional love.[44]

Two decades later, another composer set *The True Lovers Conquest* to the tune of 'Hark! The thundring cannons rore'. This recently composed

[43] *Pepys Ballads*, vol. I, pp. 378–9 (for a comparable example, see also vol. I, pp. 280–1), vol. III, p. 266, pt. 2; Simpson, *British Broadside Ballad*, p. 356.

[44] *Dialogue betwixt Tom and Dick* (London, 1660).

melody was strongly associated with ballads celebrating the King of Poland's heroic success in breaking the Turkish siege of Vienna in 1683. The original song mocked the Turks for their capitulation, attributing it in part to their coffee-drinking habits. In the wake of this song, other ballad-writers took up the tune, generally preserving its associations with political conflict and victory. The author of *The True Lovers Conquest* was clearly well aware of the tune's significance, and decided to appropriate it in order to bring new life and laughter to his account of a romantic tussle between a maiden and her suitor. He fashioned a musical dialogue that concluded – predictably enough – with the young woman's abject surrender:

Methinks my heart begins to yield,
I can myself no longer shield,
O youth, thou now hast won the field,
come then and use thy pleasure:
I can no longer thee withstand,
But wholly am at thy command,
Here's my heart, and here's my hand,
thou art my only treasure.[45]

It is obvious that the militaristic melody must have added depth and delight to such a verse, at least in the minds of ardent young men.

In particularly successful cases, a tune might develop a new and lasting association to rival or reinvigorate its previous attachments. This made possible a creative counterpoint between different themes that was implied by the tune rather than articulated explicitly in the text. Many melodies acquired twin-track associations in this manner. 'Dulcina' was associated, from the early seventeenth century onwards, with ballads that were either romantic or religious. It was one of Slatyer's 'solemne tunes', yet it was also chosen by Martin Parker for a ballad offering courtship advice to young men: *A Proverbe Old, yet Nere Forgot, Tis Good to Strike while the Irons Hott.* Romance was clearly the tune's dominant theme, and it seems likely that its associations with love added a certain romantic warmth to *Two Pleasant Ditties, One of the Birth, the Other of the Passion of Christ.* Indeed, the second of these songs opens with a verse that urges listeners to forsake earthly devotion and turn instead to Christ (**Website track 25 and Appendix**). Verbal messages and visual metaphors combined with the extra-textual power of melodic association to sound a persuasive call.

[45] *Pepys Ballads*, vol. III, p. 214; Simpson, *British Broadside Ballad*, pp. 287–9.

Conversely, Parker's witty courtship song, written a few years later, perhaps drew some of its humour from the tune's parallel associations with this godly ballad. *A Proverbe Old* follows its predecessor in urging members of the audience – specifically young men – to shift their gaze from something worthless to something truly valuable, but Parker's purpose is to contrast the superficial beauty of maidens with the deeper charms of widows (**Website track 26 and Appendix**). The latter, he remarks, are currently numerous, available and willing:

get one with Gold,
though nere so old,
Tis good to strike while the Irons hott.'

This amounts to a creative cross-reference in which the tune has the power to generate recollections of its previous incarnations, thereby endowing the new song with additional layers of significance, among the initiated at least.[46]

The trajectory of the lilting tune known variously as 'With a fadding', 'The pudding' and 'An Orange' is particularly intriguing. Under the first two titles, it had come to be associated in the early and mid-seventeenth century with kissing, courtship, drink, dance and innuendo. It was a good-time tune, and many of the verses to which it was set concluded with refrains in which the terms 'fadding' and 'pudding' were charged with bawdy meaning. In common parlance, one way to hint at a pregnancy was to suggest that a woman had illicitly consumed a pudding (nowadays we prefer to think of buns in ovens). These tags enabled balladeers to be smutty without being explicit, and the tune must have come to sound sexually suggestive. *The Merry Forrester* celebrated the wonders of kissing in terms that look innocent enough on paper, but the previous history of the melody must have ensured that the minds of many listeners drifted towards other types of embrace and their consequences (**Website track 27 and Appendix**). It still carried bawdy connotations during the 1680s, when the heroine of *The Passionate Damsel* explained her desperation to marry in terms of a burning desire for sexual fulfilment.[47]

During the late 1680s, the tune took an abrupt and surprising turn when it was attached to a group of ballads celebrating the coming of William III. His supporters faced the unenviable task of convincing the English that an apparently cold and suspicious Dutchman who, according

[46] *Shirburn Ballads*, p. 62; *Pepys Ballads*, vol. I, pp. 386–7. Another melody, 'Walsingham', was also associated both with spiritual and romantic devotion.

[47] Simpson, *British Broadside Ballad*, pp. 792–4; Taylor, *All the Workes*, vol. III, p. 514; *Pepys Ballads*, vol. I, pp. 224–5; *The Passionate Damsel* (London, *c.* 1686).

to Gilbert Burnet, listened to others 'with a dry silence', was in reality the loud and lusty answer to all their prayers.[48] William's balladeering friends were determined that their new hero should not go unsung and so they set to work. They could conceivably have called exclusively on tunes with patriotic associations ('Let Caesar live long', for example), but several of these were complicated by their attachment to the Stuart kings, one of whom had just been expelled. 'The pudding', in contrast, had no political past and it was hurriedly requisitioned as a Williamite tune. In 1689, one typical ballad, *The Famous Orange: or, An Excellent Antidote against Romish Poison*, opened in joyous mood (**Website track 28 and Appendix**):

There's none can express,
Your great Happiness,
The like was ne're seen since the Days of Queen Bess,
A Nation enslav'd,
And Justice outbrav'd,
To be thus redeemed, and gallantly sav'd,
By an Orange.[49]

The tune was not, however, a neutral one, and it seems possible that the ballad-writers who attempted to popularise William following the events of 1688 were instinctively using a well-known melody in order to manipulate his image in such a way that accusations concerning his defects (frostiness and sexual inadequacy, for example) were repudiated by musical association. In defiance of the Jacobite slur that William was 'not qualified for his wife', the balladeers were presenting him as hot and sexy. In response to the rumour that William had been castrated at birth by a midwife, his supporters sang loudly of his balls.[50] The fact that they did so by melodic allusion made it possible to circumvent the conventions which prevented them from proclaiming the king's sexual prowess in clear and verbal terms. These were clearly new songs, and the rhyme scheme was altered in an act of appropriation, but the tune's associations were very well established. We might also note the way in which these largely anonymous composers drew on the reputation of the citrus fruit itself as a desirable courtship gift and an instrument of celebration (see Figure 6.2). Charles II had courted his subjects by throwing oranges to them in 1661, and twenty-seven years later supporters of William III decorated their

[48] Craig Rose, *England in the 1690s: Revolution, Religion and War* (Oxford: Blackwell, 1999), p. 38.
[49] *Pepys Ballads*, vol. II, p. 260.
[50] 'Coronation Ballad', quoted by P. Kléber Monod, *Jacobitism and the English People, 1688–1788* (Cambridge: Cambridge University Press, 1989), p. 55.

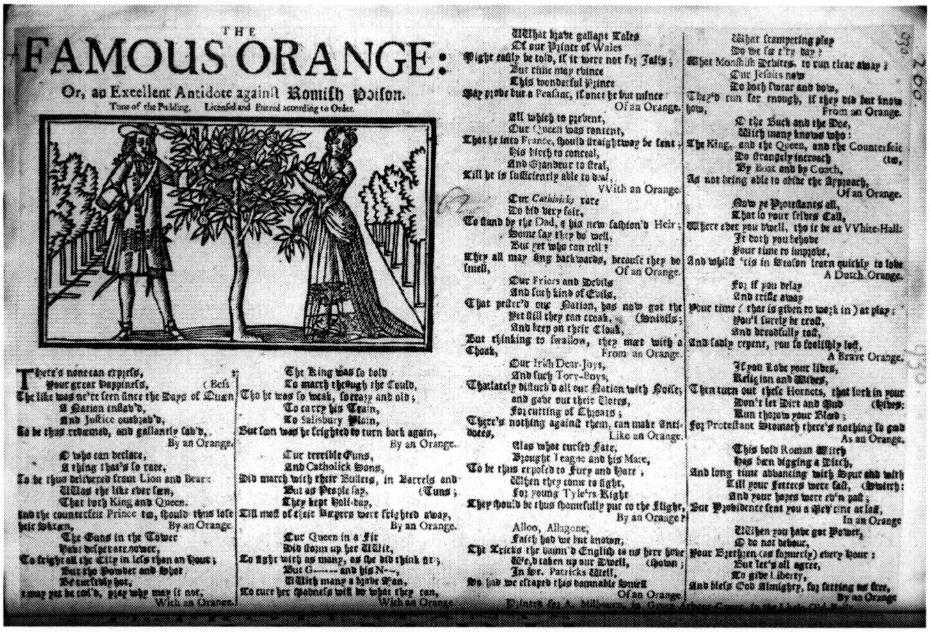

Figure 6.2. In 1689, William III's unofficial propagandists drew on the romantic symbolism of the orange and the associations of an old but sexy tune in presenting him to the English public. The Pepys Library, Magdalene College, Cambridge, Pepys Ballads, *The Famous Orange* (London, 1689).

houses with oranges in order to greet him.[51] All in all, efforts were clearly being made to portray the incoming monarch as lovable, affectionate and gallant. He was not dry but juicy. The tactic evidently caught the popular imagination, and it was not long before the old tune titles were displaced in favour of a new one, 'The Orange'.

Furthermore, the associations of this melody may just have run deeper still. The first musical phrase of 'The Orange' is virtually identical to that of another melody, 'Jog on', and this old and popular tune was itself strongly associated with songs celebrating the defeat of the Spanish Armada exactly one hundred years earlier.[52] It was also known as '88' and it retained its marketability right through into the eighteenth century. It resonated with both humour and patriotism, and it apparently held on to both associations throughout the early modern period. In the 1670s, for example, it was named in the *Oxford Drollery* for a deeply scatological song about two brothers called 'Love me' and 'Lick me', but it was also

[51] *Diurnal of Thomas Rugg*, p. 180; 'Curious Extracts from a Manuscript Diary, of the Time of James II and William and Mary', ed. Edward L. Cutts, *Essex Archaeological Transactions* 1 (1855), 124.

[52] There is an example in *Choyce Drollery* (London, 1656), pp. 38–9.

chosen by Dr Walter Pope for his satirical broadside *The Catholick Ballad: or, An Invitation to Popery.* Of course, this song was nothing of the sort: it lambasted all Catholics and 'the tune of, Eighty eight' played its part in ensuring that the central message was clear. It was well chosen, for it suggested both a spirit of mischief and a mood of patriotic Protestantism. It spoke in light-hearted vein of English nationhood, the reformed religion and a monarch of truly famous memory. The ballad was an immensely successful one, and the tune was therefore as well known in the decades before 1688 as it had been in the decades following 1588. It seems difficult to believe that the precise affinity between the unusual opening bars of the two tunes was a mere coincidence, particularly if we note the passing verbal references to Elizabeth I and the Armada itself in some of the 'Orange' songs.[53] Instead, it is at least worth arguing that one of the reasons for the selection of the 'pudding'/'Orange' tune by the political balladeers of the later seventeenth century was that it included this unusual musical reference to the Armada, thus allying 1688 with 1588, and William III by association with a great, home-grown, Protestant heroine. Having made William sexy, the balladeers were also making him English.

We should not assume, however, that this positive interpretation was the only one that contemporaries could have placed upon these ballads. In the minds of many English people, William was not a new Eliza, and his arrival was deeply controversial. The arguably flippant side of the songs and the 'pudding' tune almost invited listeners to attend to other, more satirical, possibilities. The choice of tune was a risky one, for King William could all too easily emerge as laughable rather than lovable. He was, after all, being likened to a foreign fruit. Like all fruit, the orange had the potential to turn rotten, and at least one ballad-writer was aware of the danger:

Perhaps you may think to *Peters* they Stink,
Because from our Neighbours they'r brought over Sea,
Yet sure, 'tis presum'd,
They may be perfum'd,
By th' scent of good *cloves*,
for they may be stuck in an *Orange.*[54]

[53] William Hickes, *Oxford Drollery* (London, 1679), pp. 112–13; Roxburghe ballads, C20F7–F10, vol. I, pp. 26–7, BL (*The Catholick Ballad* is also discussed in McShane Jones, 'Rime and Reason', p. 213, though she is surely mistaken in dismissing the tune title as a merely verbal joke); for references to Elizabeth and/or the Armada in the 'Orange' ballads, see above, p. 312, and also *Pepys Ballads*, vol. V, p. 132. 'Jog on' is discussed in Simpson, *British Broadside Ballad*, p. 392 (but the author makes no connection with the later tune).

[54] *Pepys Ballads*, vol. V, p. 109.

There were many ways to listen, and the receivers of ballads were just as important as the composers when it came to the construction of meaning. A great deal depended upon their prior knowledge of any specific tune and upon their prior attitudes to the subjects under discussion. Sadly, we can take this matter no further, for it is not possible to say with any certainty whether this derisory alternative interpretation of the 'Orange' ballads was popular, nor whether it contributed to the commercial success of the ballads. What proportion of the population welcomed William with a smirk?

With greater certainty, we can say that 'the tune of an Orange' reached the 1690s with the capacity to signify both Williamite patriotism and sexual humour. The dual associations came together in *The Maidens Frollicksome Undertaking to Press Twenty Taylors.* In this song, a group of ten plucky maidens disguise themselves as seamen in order to recruit twice as many reluctant tailors to the king's service. They use a combination of psychological and physical force, and the melody reinforces both the patriotism of the piece and its sexual undertones. Without the tune, this ballad might still amuse, but it would undoubtedly be a paler thing.[55]

The 'Orange' songs were not the only ones in which the associations of a melody – whether by accident or design – set up interpretative possibilities that were not explicit in the text. *A New-yeeres-gift for the Pope* was published during the mid-1620s, at a time when Prince Charles was busy courting a Spanish princess (and domestic controversy). Only half of the ballad survives, but the gist of the jest is plain enough (**Website track 30 and Appendix**). On the face of it, the text made no direct reference to the political context, concentrating instead on a contest between true and false religion in which Protestants and Catholics each try to tip the scales of justice in their favour. The Catholics load their side with all manner of trinkets, crosses, pictures and statues, but they are soundly defeated by the Protestants, who trust instead in the sheer weight of the Bible alone (see Figure 6.3). Each verse concludes with some version of a refrain that emphasises the futility of Catholic efforts: 'Yet all is in vaine, they cannot, they cannot, / Yet all is in vaine they cannot.'[56] There was nothing particularly surprising about any of this, but the lively melody – 'Thomas you cannot' – unsettles the simplicity of the text and introduces new and potentially controversial possibilities. It was associated primarily with sexual relations and, in particular, with an earlier song about the difficulties encountered by a man named Thomas as he struggles to satisfy

[55] Ibid., vol. IV, p. 276. [56] Ibid., vol. I, p. 62.

A New-yeeres-gift for the Pope.

Come see the difference plainly decided, betweene Truth and Falshood

Not all the Popes Trinkets, which heere are brought forth,
Can ballance the Bible for weight, and true worth:
Your Bells, Beads and Crosses, you see will not doo't,
Or pull downe your Scale, with the Diuell to boot.

To the Tune of, *Thomas, you cannot, &c.*

All you that desirous are to behold
the difference twixt falshood and faith,
Marke well this Emblem, one piece of pure gold,
a Cart-load of false Coyne outwayeth,
Then wisely consider and beare in your mind,
Though Sathans Instruments true faith to blind,
A thousand deuises dayly doe find;
Yet all is in vaine, they cannot, they cannot,
Yet all is in vaine they cannot.

The [illegible]erence 'twixt Papist and Protestant here,
[illegible] in a moment debated,
The [illegible] loues the Gospell that shineth still cleare,
the other is more subtile-pated,
He will not be ruld by the Scriptures large scope,
But trusts in Traditions deriu'd from the Pope,
By which to be sau'd he doth constantly hope:
Fond fooles y'are deceiued, you cannot, &c.

True Justice, 'gainst whom no falshood preuailes,
the case for both Parties decideth
[illegible] here she doth hold up her unpartiall Scales,
no actions nor lyes she abideth:
The Pope like a Martialist hardy and stout,
[illegible] marching in pompe with all his braue rout,
[illegible] by his multitude he makes no doubt:
[illegible] alas father Pope you cannot, &c.

Thus are these two opposites come to the place,
where truth must be proued by tryall,
The Pope thinks with greatnesse to carry the grace,
but Justice hath eyes to descry all:
The Scales are made euen, the Bible's in one,
Which is the true meanes of Saluation alone,
They striuing to passe it, doe striue till they grone:
Yet all is in vaine, they cannot, &c.

The Pope seeing he must be tride by the Bible,
did seeke to ouercome it by might,
He tride by all meanes that for him was possible;
but all he could bring was too light:
Their Masses and Dirges, with such superstitions,
Decrees and Decretals, with other Traditions,
The golden Legend with late new additions:
Yet all is in vaine, they cannot, &c.

Thus still the pure Gospell gainst falshood preuailes,
which when the proud Prelate did see,
A Cart-load of Trinkets he puts in the Scales,
and thrust it as full as might be,
With great wooden Crosses and many great babies,
The Pictures and Saints of a heap of Ladies,
Who dayly are worshipped by their grand Rabbies:
Yet still father [illegible] cannot, &c.
Yet still father Pe[illegible]

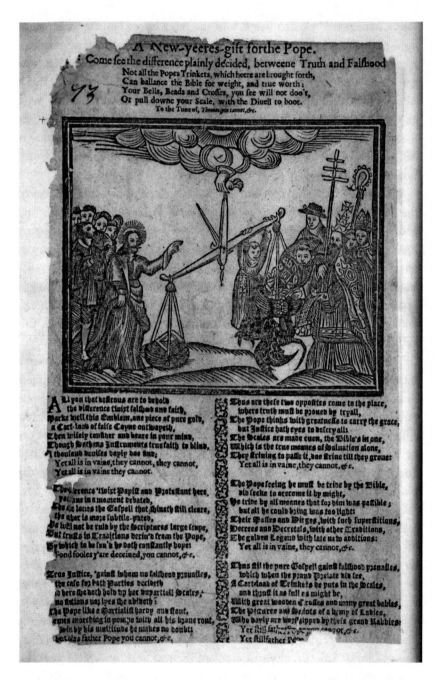

Figure 6.3. This anti-Catholic ballad of the mid-1620s combined a religious text and picture with a tune that carried bawdy associations. The Pepys Library, Magdalene College, Cambridge, Pepys Ballads, *A New-yeeres-gift for the Pope* (London, *c.* 1624).

a spirited maiden (**Website track 29 and Appendix**). At first he is eager and she undecided. Moments later, she conquers her doubts and is overtaken by desire, but now Thomas's sexual courage deserts him and the poor man fails repeatedly to perform (he perhaps manages it in the final verse, which, tragically, is lost). Throughout this tense exchange, the girl taunts the boy with cries of 'Thomas! You cannot, you cannot! / O Thomas, O Thomas, you cannot!'[57]

'Thomas you cannot' was thus a song about incompatible sexual wishes and the difficulties faced by feeble men when attached to lustful women. In the atmosphere of the mid-1620s, it is surely not stretching the bounds of credibility to suggest that, somewhere in here, there was a joke about the tortured courtship of Charles Stuart. He, like Thomas, had struggled to win a woman, and the fact that his intended spouse was a foreign Catholic princess offered a link between the divergent meanings of text and tune within *A New-yeeres-gift*. There were good reasons for burying such matter in the melody, for the governments of the day were deeply troubled by the wealth of rumour and libellous criticism that surrounded the court and the Duke of Buckingham in particular.[58] We cannot date the ballad with certainty, though it seems most plausible to argue that it belongs to the period during or immediately after the expedition to Spain by Charles and Buckingham in 1623. This mission caused extreme anxiety in England, and even loyal royalists were intensely relieved when it all came to nought. John Taylor rejoiced that a period during which Britain had suffered the pangs of 'dutifull Jealousie' was at an end, and he described the mood of near-hysteria that was stimulated by the empty-handed return of the two adventurers on 5 October. Guns fired, trumpets blasted, drums were beaten, bells rang, God was thanked and everybody got drunk. Two boatmen were so delighted that, somewhat short-sightedly, they destroyed their own boats 'in a Bonefire most merrily'. According to Taylor, 'This was a day all dedicate to Mirth'. Ballad-sellers were also in on the act, though several of the individuals who worked the streets of Portsmouth had to twiddle their thumbs in prison, where they had been placed for the offence of announcing the prince's arrival in the town before it had actually occurred. In seeking to anticipate an opportunity, they had missed one.[59]

[57] *Bishop Percy's Folio Manuscript: Loose and Humorous Songs*, ed. Frederick J. Furnivall (London, 1868), pp. 116–18.

[58] See, for example, Bellany, 'Singing Libel in Early Stuart England'.

[59] Taylor, *All the Workes*, vol. III, pp. 585–9; Fox, *Oral and Literate Culture*, p. 388.

Other commentators were more directly critical of the government, and numerous hard-hitting verses circulated in manuscript. According to convention, they aimed their darts at the royal favourite rather than at the king and the prince, but James and Charles made the justifiable assumption that many of the accusations levelled at Buckingham were also intended for them. In a world awash with rumour, the duke was associated with an interconnected litany of reprehensible failings: moral corruption, Roman Catholicism, pro-Spanish attitudes, lustful depravity (homosexual and heterosexual) and the pox. It is within this context that *A New-yeeres-gift* should be imagined, and it seems entirely possible that its infectious tune, savouring so strongly of bawdry, can be heard as a coded swipe at all three men. It may have registered with knowledgeable listeners primarily as a joke about Charles's failed courtship, but perhaps it also placed a question mark over the nature of his relationship with Buckingham. It may be no coincidence that the name reportedly adopted by the duke when he and Charles travelled incognito to Spain was 'Thomas'.[60]

A ballad of 1675 was equally dependent on a melody for its humorous impact (see Figure 6.4). It has at its head an assurance that it contains no mention of warfare, courtship, monsters, wonders and death, 'Nor any thing under the Sky, But onely of my Dog and I' (these last four words provide the ballad's title and refrain). The text opens with a man singing fondly and, for all a modern reader knows, innocently, of his beloved pet (**Website track 31 and Appendix**):

You that are of the merry Throng,
Give good attention to my Song,
Ile give you weighty reasons why,
'Tis made upon my Dog and I,
My Dog and I, my Dog and I,
'Tis made upon my Dog and I.[61]

There is, however, nothing innocent about these inseparable companions. The tune tells us immediately that this is a thoroughly bawdy ballad in which dog = penis. 'Bobbing Joan', a simple and beautiful melody that was used both for songs and dances, was associated first and foremost with lust

[60] Bellany, 'Singing Libel in Early Stuart England'; Fox, *Oral and Literate Culture*, pp. 388–9; Roger Lockyer, *Buckingham: the Life and Political Career of George Villiers* (London: Longman, 1981), p. 136; John Bowle, *Charles I: A Biography* (London: Weidenfeld and Nicolson, 1975), pp. 66, 69.

[61] *Pepys Ballads*, vol. IV, p. 229.

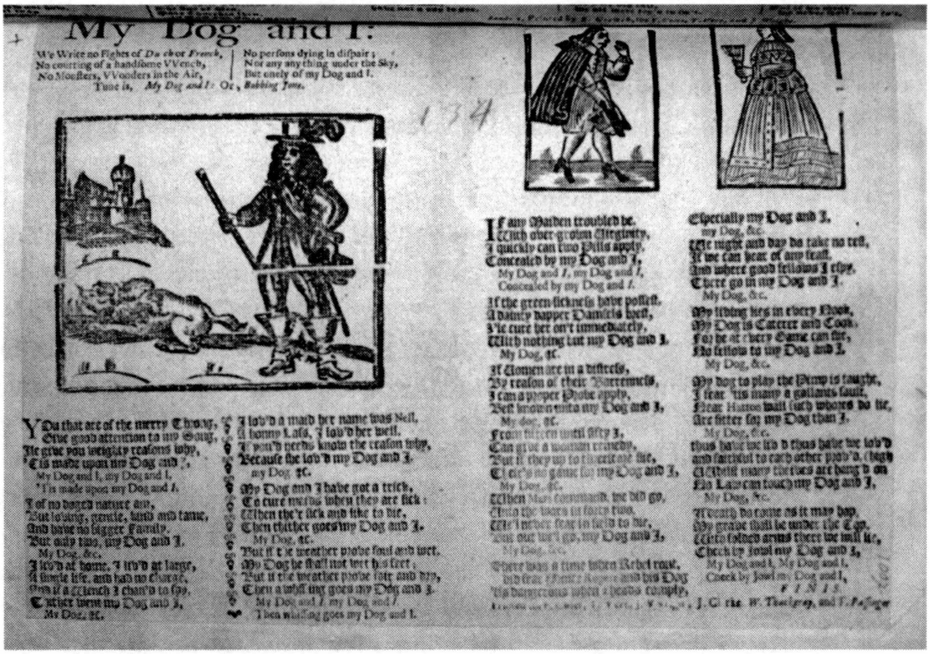

Figure 6.4. When is a dog not a dog? In this ballad, the tune's long-established association with sex told listeners that all was not as suggested by the title and introductory lines. The Pepys Library, Magdalene College, Cambridge, Pepys Ballads, *My Dog and I* (London, 1675).

and its fulfilment. It appears to have earned its name from a ballad entitled *Bobbin' Jo: or, The Longing Lass Satisfied at last*, in which the euphemistic refrain ran, 'The bobbin' jo, the bobbin jo, / And canst thou dance the bobbing jo.'[62] In *My Dog and I*, therefore, the melody helps to make the joke by calling to mind the lewdness of the more famous song.

The role of such tunes may help to explain why early modern ballads, which sometimes look rather bland to modern eyes, were regularly categorised *en masse* by moralists as dangerously licentious. Our ancestors perhaps heard more in them than we are trained or accustomed to do. Not all examples were so lascivious. Thomas Deloney, for example, wrote a ballad about the capture of a Spanish vessel in 1588 and gibingly set it to a tune that was associated with a French enemy of Philip II. In a ballad published a century later, a man declares his undying love for a Welsh woman to the tune of 'Sir John Johnson's Farewell', another name for the immensely successful execution melody 'Russell's farewell'. Surely, we are to understand that this poor lovesick man is doomed, even if the words do

[62] Simpson, *British Broadside Ballad*, pp. 46–7.

not quite tell us so (he remains hopeful). The text speaks of love, but the tune suggests that love is death.[63]

This discussion of musical allusion must end, however, with the somewhat anti-climactic admission that not all early modern melodies gathered and relied upon associations in this playful manner. The recycling of tunes was one highly effective technique, but the freshness of a previously unheard melody could pull in the punters almost as effectively. Appealing to newness was, of course, a more risky tactic than trusting to tradition, but it was nevertheless worth a try. In the Euing collection of ballads, eighty-six of 408 songs are set to tunes described as 'new' (often in association with a range of additional adjectives, including 'pleasant', 'admirable', 'delicate', 'amorous' and 'dainty'). Novelty was clearly a selling feature, and composers made the most of it in their musical instructions: 'To a pleasant new Northern Tune, Now all in fashion'; 'To a most Admirable New Tune, every where much in Request'; and 'To a Pleasant New Tune ... , Play'd and Sung at the King's Play-House'.[64] Some such tunes were one-hit wonders and failed to migrate to other songs, either because they never caught on or, in a few instances, because they were connected so strongly to their original texts that nobody deemed it appropriate to recycle them. *A Ditty Delightfull of Mother Watkins Ale* was a raunchy Elizabethan ballad with a wonderfully catchy tune ('Watkins ale' was a euphemism for semen). The song was a major hit during the 1590s, and its melody was adopted as the basis for instrumental pieces by several more courtly composers. Curiously, however, it does not appear to have been chosen as the setting for any subsequent broadside ballads.[65]

Finally, some tunes were used repeatedly by ballad-writers but never accumulated distinctive thematic associations. For some reason, they were perceived as more malleable or neutral than many of the melodies discussed so far, and they supported many different textual themes. The prime example here was 'Packington's pound', one of the early modern period's top three tunes. Its Elizabethan origins are obscure, but between the late sixteenth and early eighteenth centuries it was named on perhaps one hundred different ballads. It is a superb melody, but part of the reason for its success must lie in popular perceptions of its flexibility. This, more than any other, was a tune for all seasons. It was specified on songs about

[63] *A Joyfull New Ballad, Declaring the Happie Obtaining of the Great Galleazzo ... to the Tune of Mounseurs Almaigne* (London, 1588); *Pepys Ballads*, vol. V, p. 203. See also Simpson, *British Broadside Ballad*, pp. 495–6, 621–4.

[64] *Euing Collection of English Broadside Ballads*, nos. 49, 71 and 234.

[65] Simpson, *British Broadside Ballad*, p. 745.

tipplers, Biblical prophets, dairymaids, executed criminals, loyal lovers, exemplary aristocrats, cutpurses, Quakers, royal babies, paupers, lusty millers, Whigs and bad husbands. 'Packington's pound' does not seem to have signified anything in particular, and it shared this characteristic with melodies such as 'Greensleeves', 'Chevy Chase' and 'I am the Duke of Norfolk'.[66]

Associations in motion

Not all consumers brought the same prior knowledge to a ballad, and degrees of familiarity with the intricate web of potential melodic associations must have spanned a spectrum from the vague to the advanced. Such evidence as we have seems to suggest that relative fluency in the language of tunes was widespread. Contemporaries applied different adjectives to different categories of melody, and many must have known the difference between 'villainous tunes' (for songs about crime and execution), 'lamentable tunes' (for songs of sad love) and 'godly tunes' (for religious and moral ballads).[67] Playwrights and other authors also made reference to specific tune titles, sometimes drawing upon the associations of melodies in their efforts to stimulate audience members. In *The Two Gentlemen of Verona*, Julia and Lucetta conduct an interesting conversation about an incoming love-letter:

JULIA: Some love of yours hath writ to you in rhyme.
LUCETTA: That I might sing it, madam, to a tune.
  Give me a note. Your ladyship can set.
JULIA: As little by such toys as may be possible.
  Best sing it to the tune of 'Light o' love'.
LUCETTA: It is too heavy for so light a tune.
JULIA: Heavy? Belike it hath some burden, then?
LUCETTA: Ay, and melodious were it, would you sing it.

The exchange appears to indicate the facility with which some non-musicians could talk about tunes, texts and the relationship between them (while also punning on other familiar ballad terms, such as 'burden').[68]

There is a similarly playful moment in Aphra Behn's play *The Roundheads* (written in 1682 but set in 1660). At its conclusion, royalists gather around a bonfire to celebrate the end of the Rump Parliament and

[66] References to all these tunes are gathered and indexed in Simpson, *British Broadside Ballad*, and in *Pepys Ballads*.
[67] There is an interesting examination of the associations and use of one specific melody in Harold Love, 'That Satyrical Tune of "Amarillis"', *Early Music* 35 (2007), 39–46.
[68] *The Two Gentlemen of Verona*, in *Complete Oxford Shakespeare*, pp. 457–8.

to anticipate the return of the king. They recognise, in their midst, a former parliamentarian official, inventively disguised as a ballad-singer. The man is duly apprehended and carried triumphantly around the fire, while a leading member of the crowd calls to a nearby fiddler, 'Play Fortune my Foe, Sirrah.' To the sound of this tune, another disguised parliament-man is discovered, exposed and forced to dance. There is a sinister and wordless joke here, for the crowd's victims are being threatened with the noose by melodic association. The enormity of their error is further emphasised by the command to dance to a tune that was never designed for such a purpose. 'Fortune my foe' was a 'villainous tune', and nobody but the deranged and desperate danced to such music.[69]

This was not the only instance in which a naked tune spoke volumes. Francis Quarles's play *The Virgin Widow* contains a scene in which Quack the apothecary whistles the tune of 'As I went to Walsingham' while his wife attempts to banish him from her sight with a tirade of insults. His musical joke depended upon the ability of audience members to recognise the tune and to connect it with romantic disappointment and/or a pilgrim's life on the road.[70] During the 1660s, 'When the king enjoys his own again' was frequently played on instruments in order to express loyalty to the crown. During celebrations at Bruton (Somerset) on 29 May 1660, it sounded all day long. Around the same time, English ships sometimes greeted one another with trumpet renditions of the melody. After General Monck arrived in London in 1660, his musicians reportedly 'play'd that Tune every Morning ... till the King came himself, and then, you know, there was no more Occasion for it'.[71] In fact, the tune lived on, and it could still cause a stir when sounded in an tavern during the 1720s. In the meantime, 'When the king' had become a thoroughly controversial tune, for its attachment to the Stuart cause had survived the deposition of James II in 1688 and the accession of the Hanovers in 1714. Where once it had signified mainstream loyalism, now it carried more than a hint of Jacobite sympathy. Thus it was that William Browne, keeper of the White Hart in Barnes (Surrey), landed himself in hot water by entertaining in his alehouse 'a great Number of People in a Riotous manner who with Drums & Fidles play'd the Tune called The King shall Enjoy his own

[69] Behn, *The Roundheads, or the Good Old Cause* (London, 1682), p. 56. The tune can be heard on the website, tracks 7, 17 and 20.

[70] Francis Quarles, *The Virgin Widow a Comedie* (London, 1649), p. 32; Simpson, *British Broadside Ballad*, pp. 741–3.

[71] *Diurnal of Thomas Rugg*, p. 179; Woodfield, *English Musicians*, p. 60 n. 29; Daniel Defoe, cited by Würzbach, *The Rise of the English Street Ballad*, pp. 283–4. The original song appears on the website as track 23.

againe'. The local constable and his assistants intervened, warning the company 'to forbeare such insults upon the Government', but the musicians played on regardless.[72]

The associations of the most familiar melodies seem to have been widely known. Samuel Pepys was understandably upset when the Dutch fleet sailed up the Medway to Chatham in June 1667, capturing a famous and symbolic ship, the *Royal Charles*. He well understood the musical vocabulary that was deployed by the raiders: 'and presently a man went up and struck her flag and Jacke, and a trumpeter sounded upon her "Joan's placket is torn"'. This brilliant piece of melodic mockery can be fully understood only when the tune's associations with romantic conquest and sexual penetration are called to mind.[73] Powerful and controversial points could be made by melody alone, and in one Elizabethan play about Richard II an officious loyalist arrests a man on the grounds that he has 'whistled treason'. When the suspect refutes the charge, he receives a forthright explanation: 'Sir! Ther's a peece of treason that flyes up and downe the country in the likness of a ballad, and this be the very tune of it you whisselled.' The officer, admittedly, was presented as a figure of fun, yet the currency of the belief that a tune might enable individuals to present their opinions in disguise is also suggested by the contemporary saying 'I'll whistle instead of singing.'[74]

The authors of libellous local songs sometimes demonstrated a comparable familiarity with the vocabulary of melody. Thomas Chitham, the schoolmaster who in 1601 composed a scurrilous ballad under instruction from a Chelmsford barber, clearly drew upon the bawdy associations of the tune 'Watkins ale' in producing his masterpiece.[75] At the same date, a song-writing servant in Yorkshire was employing rather more elaborate and sophisticated tune tactics in devising a libellous jig – a set of short interconnected songs for dramatic performance – in derision of his master's enemy, Mr Michael Steel. The composer was twenty-two years old and bold enough to highlight Steel's alleged abandonment of his wife in favour of a maidservant named Frances. His use of tunes suggests a thorough knowledge of broadside balladry. In the first song, Michael bemoans the advanced age and frowning jealousy of his wife while arranging a late-night tryst with his eager employee. They sing in dialogue,

[72] QS 2/6, no. 10, SHC. For a potted history of the melody, see Simpson, *British Broadside Ballad*, pp. 764–8.

[73] *Diary of Samuel Pepys*, vol. VIII, p. 283; Simpson, *British Broadside Ballad*, pp. 388–90.

[74] '*Richard II*. Erster Teil: ein Drama aus Shakespeare's Zeit', ed. Wolfgang Keller, *Jahrbuch der Deutschen Shakespeare-Gesellschaft* 35 (1899), 87–8 (the play is often known as 'Thomas of Woodstock'); *Pepys Ballads*, vol. I, pp. 202–3.

[75] See above, pp. 272–3.

conspiring together 'To the tune of Filiday flouts mee'. This fashionable melody had been attached most recently to ballads on aspects of love and seduction, themes that were humorously reworked in the jig. The second song, set to the tune of 'Fortune', presents another dialogue, this time between Frances and her aged mistress. Here, the tune's general associations with death, tragedy and moral warnings work to exaggerate the farcicality of a situation in which an old wife, sexually neglected by her husband, unknowingly seeks comfort from the new object of his lust:

Come Frauncis Come make hast and goe with me
it is tyme to rest for suche a one as me
my bones are olde and bloude has fledd awaie
I marvell much what makes my husband staie.

More specifically, the song is also a pastiche upon the ballad that had originally produced the tune title 'Fortune my foe'. This song had presented the lamentation of a male lover, driven to desperation by the apparent indifference of his chosen woman. It is thus apparent that the young Yorkshire composer was drawing cleverly upon a range of melodic associations, and his skill was duly recognised by a troop of travelling players who took up the jig and, controversially, began performing it at the end of their productions. In all, there are six songs in the jig but, sadly, the remaining four tunes cannot be identified with confidence.[76]

Other amateur balladeers from a variety of social backgrounds showed themselves equally skilled in the libellous manipulation of melody. In Jacobean Worcestershire, John and Richard Rotton, a yeoman and a weaver respectively, clearly knew what they were about as they aimed texts and tunes at Richard Nightingale and his new wife Agnes (formerly Ballamy). According to another local weaver, Richard Rotton had been heard reading and singing songs to 'the tune called Jamey'. His choice was both well informed and amply suited for the purpose of heaping humiliation upon the newly formed marriage of his adversaries. The melody was taken from a recently printed song entitled *A Proper New Ballad, Shewing a Merrie Jest of one Jeamie of Woodicock Hill*, which opened with the lines,

One Jemie there was that dwelt in a towne,
as proper a man as proper might be:
A wife he had would scold and frowne,
and evermore call him noddie noddie,
A wife he had would scold and frowne,
and evermore call him noddie noddie.

[76] Sisson, *Lost Plays of Shakespeare's Age*, pp. 129–40; Simpson, *British Broadside Ballad*, p. 576.

When Jamey goes out to work on Woodicock Hill, another man takes his place at home 'and tickles his wives hei nonnie nonnie'. Jamey returns to witness this stimulating act, but rather than defending his honour in suitably manly fashion he accepts a compensatory payment of £5 from the interloper. In short, Jamey is a wimp and his wife is an adulteress.[77] These, then, were the associations that the tune carried as it made its way from London into Worcestershire and thus into the aggrieved mind of Richard Rotton. His malice was motivated, allegedly, by his failure to win the hand of Agnes Ballamy (also known as Nan) and by his jealousy of her husband. The text composed by or for the Rotton brothers was scurrilous and inflammatory, even without music, but 'the tune called Jamey' endowed it with additional intensity (**Website track 32 and Appendix**). It opened with the allegation that Agnes had been either seduced or raped by a local miller, some time shortly before her marriage to Richard Nightingale. Upon hearing of the matter, her sweetheart had confronted the miller, but Nightingale – like Jamey before him – failed conspicuously to defend his rights. The song described his abject retreat, and its final lines branded him a coward and a fool.[78]

The poetry of Richard Corbet was rather more refined than that of Richard Rotton, but he too knew how to draw upon the associations of common ballad tunes. In 1615, this future bishop opened an exchange of 'sharpe invectives' in which scholars from Oxford and Cambridge mocked one another in time-honoured fashion. Corbet wrote for Oxford, but his 'Grave poeme' described the entertainments famously staged at Trinity College, Cambridge, for the visit of James I in the spring of 1615. He had himself attended these festivities – including the performance of George Ruggle's controversial play *Ignoramus* – and he maintained the theatrical mood by stating that his poetic report on proceedings was 'made rather to be sung than reade to the tune of Bonny Nell'. Unfortunately, this extremely popular tune has not survived, but we do know that it carried potent sexual undertones. In 1622, Thomas Robinson referred scathingly to a community of English Catholics in Lisbon, noting that the naughty nuns liked to entertain the resident friar by playing their instruments and singing him 'ribaldrous Songs and jigs, as that of Bonny Nell, and such other obscene and scurrilous Ballads, as would make a chaste ear to glow at the hearing of them'.

77 *A Proper New Ballad, Shewing a Merrie Jest of one Jeamie of Woodicock Hill* (London, *c.* 1610). The tune is named as 'Woodicock Hill', but it picked up the new name, 'Jamey', following the publication of the ballad.

78 STAC 8/220/31, NA. The tune is printed in Simpson, *British Broadside Ballad*, p. 797.

Corbet, in setting his 'grave' words to such a tune, presumably intended to undercut his own stated purpose for humorous effect (he also pretended that his song was translated from Latin). The nomination of 'Bonny Nell' connected gravity with depravity and poured scorn upon the objects of the author's mock-praise. The text itself contained no allegations of sexual impropriety in Cambridge, but the tune hinted heavily at this unspeakable possibility. Corbet, during his visit to Cambridge, had reportedly presented himself in public as a man who wished to rise above the petty inter-varsity squabbles that were breaking out around him, but in truth he had no such intent. He was later to become famous as a pranking ecclesiastic, and this was not the only occasion upon which he deployed melody for witty effect.[79]

Corbet's song circulated widely in manuscript, and may have exerted an indirect influence over the Nottingham libellers of 1617. In that year, the town was rocked by a confrontation between puritans and their enemies. Both factions included clergymen and townsmen of high rank, and the anti-puritan group made varied and inventive use of a full range of musical weaponry. Libellous songs were penned, published and performed in numerous physical settings, and the musicians of the town were clearly drawn into the controversy as singers and instrumental accompanists. One of the songs was described, intriguingly, as 'Better to be song [sung], then [than] redd to the tune of Bonny Nell'. The instruction seemed to echo Corbet's earlier device, and it is possible that some member of the creative team in Nottingham may have been familiar with the Oxford man's song (which had singled out the puritans of Emmanuel College for particular derision). It is probably no coincidence that the Nottingham waits had in 1615–16 received payments from the steward of Trinity College, the scene of the main festivities in Cambridge.[80] This appears to be an appealing example of the way in which melodic notions could pass freely around the country, circulating among academics, musicians and provincial townsmen. The Nottingham text was, however, rather less subtle than Corbet's offering in its references to the bawdy baggage carried by 'Bonny Nell'. The composers reported on the alleged practices of the

[79] Many of the relevant documents are gathered in *REED Cambridge*, pp. 540–1, 865–88. See also Simpson, *British Broadside Ballad*, p. 58; Corbet, *Certain Elegant Poems*, pp. 58–64; John Nichols, *The Progresses, Processions, and Magnificent Festivities of King James the First*, 4 vols. (London, 1828), vol. III, p. 66; Thomas Robinson, *The Anatomy of the English Nunnery, at Lisbon in Portugall* (London, 1622), p. 13.

[80] *REED Cambridge*, p. 549.

local puritans in a tone that combined unmistakable innuendo with explicit accusation:

by night they Catichise each other
the holy sister with the brother,
and when the high preest hath well druncke
each one betakes him to his puncke.[81]

In this instance, the words inflicted the initial wound but the tune twisted the knife. All over Nottingham, the deriders of puritanism laughed and made merry with the song. On one occasion, an alderman requested a rendition in an alehouse, then rounded on the piper for playing the wrong piece: 'that's not the song, I meant the song of the Puritans of Nottingham'. The piper was duly replaced and the new one sang the right song, much to the glee of the assembled company.[82]

Listening experiences clearly varied, but for many people the chain of melodic associations was almost certainly a vital component of ballad consumption. One did not need to be conscious of such associations in order to process them during the personal act of listening. In fact, such devices are at their most effective when they are assimilated automatically. Even the composers of ballads may on occasion have been unaware of some of the associations carried by their chosen melodies. All possible associations were, nevertheless, implanted in their songs, ready to be selectively dug out or left to lie by members of the exceptionally varied audience. Melodies worked their magic in several ways. They could reinforce their texts, reiterating the primary verbal messages by calling upon a wealth of supportive musical precedent. On the other hand, tunes could undermine or subvert their verses. They could also offer listeners a number of interpretative routes along which to travel, some of which might lead in opposite directions. Something similar can perhaps be said of the many recycled woodcut pictures, which were often placed with rather more deliberation than historians have allowed. Textual echoes also connected ballads past and present, and here too we might find evidence of subtle reinforcement and meaningful revision. This was a culture within which people liked to play with cultural components, whether verbal, visual or musical, constantly reassembling them into new configurations, like children twisting a kaleidoscope. To put it in more aural terms, our ancestors thrived on riddle, rhyme and resonance.

[81] Sisson, *Lost Plays of Shakespeare's Age*, p. 202.
[82] Ibid., p. 199.

7 | 'The skipping art': dance and society

It has become difficult to imagine an age in which an array of wildly pejorative adjectives could be applied to country dancing and the clumping movements of morris men. Nowadays, these activities look and sound to many like cultural anachronisms, the laughable leftovers of 'Olde England'. In contrast, one influential strand within early modern thought considered them to be fraught with moral and social danger. According to this view, country dancing was all too often the pernicious pastime of randy young men and women with a taste for life on and beyond the border of good order. The transformation in attitudes that has occurred between then and now probably owes much to the somewhat counter-productive efforts of Cecil Sharp and all who followed him in seeking to revive (or re-invent) English folk culture during the first half of the twentieth century. Sharp and others undoubtedly performed a valuable service in tracking and recording English songs and dances, but they also began the process by which aspects of traditional culture came to appear ridiculous and archaic, except of course to their devotees. Inadvertently, dedicated collectors altered the reputation of traditional song and dance, polarising opinion between its zealous enthusiasts and those who mocked them. As a consequence, the historian must execute an ambitious leap of the imagination in order to understand the prominent and often controversial place occupied by dance within early modern culture.

There are also some terminological difficulties to be faced. What, for example, was 'country dancing'? The term looks precise enough, and we might be tempted to associate it primarily with the recreational habits of the lower orders in rural England. It was, however, a label used most frequently by privileged gentlefolk who felt some sort of affinity for those habits. Hostile moralists rarely deployed the term, and it meant little to actual dancers out in the 'country'. Paradoxically, the term 'country dance' tended to identify its users as socially superior to the rural practitioners who supposedly provided their choreographic inspiration (see Figure 7.1). Moreover, those who used it often lived in towns. It was neither a neutral nor a simple term, and an awareness of its inherent instabilities is essential. When Samuel Pepys was concerned about the developing relationship

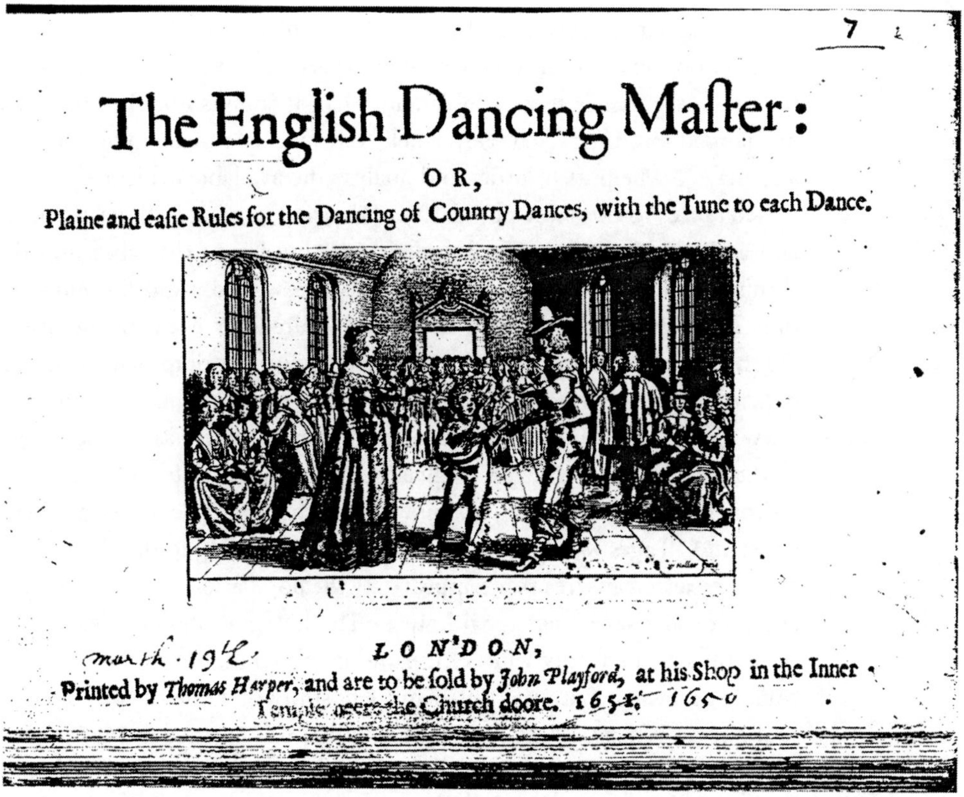

The English Dancing Maſter:

OR,

Plaine and eaſie Rules for the Dancing of Country Dances, with the Tune to each Dance.

LONDON,

Printed by *Thomas Harper*, and are to be ſold by *John Playford*, at his Shop in the Inner Temple neere the Church doore. 1651.

Figure 7.1. Playford published 'country dances' in huge numbers during the second half of the seventeenth century, but there was nothing rural about the scenes that decorated his title pages. Cleverly, he marketed a romantic brand of rusticity among society's wealthiest ranks. The British Library, John Playford, *The English Dancing Master* (London, 1651), title page.

between his wife and the man who taught her 'country dancing', one of his first thoughts was to take her out of London and into the 'country' in order to escape the danger![1] Such ironies add to the interest of the term, but they also reduce the value of 'country dancing' as a precise descriptive category. In the pages that follow, a loose distinction will instead be made between sociable dancing and performative dancing. 'Sociable' will encompass the most common and least complicated forms of dance, those that were easy to organise and were characterised primarily by the pleasures of communal participation rather than by notions of self-conscious exhibition before an audience. 'Performative' will apply more specifically to display dances that required, almost by definition, the presence of onlookers. These included dances for solo performers, but also those that

[1] *Diary of Samuel Pepys*, vol. IV, pp. 153–4.

involved larger groups, careful planning, the allocation of particular roles or functions, and an unusual degree of expertise. The distinction between the two categories is more problematic than it sounds, for they regularly overlapped and interacted. Nevertheless, it reflects a meaningful contrast and may also help us to order and analyse the available evidence.

References to the sheer popularity of dancing, among both participants and audience members, are abundant. The pulsing of the tabor and the shrilling of the pipe were enough to draw the crowds, and the numbers thus lured were said to reach into the hundreds or even, on occasion, the thousands. Also in the thousands was the number of miniature morris dancing bells imported into the country on an annual basis. Dramatists knew the pleasing power of dance, and many a play was rescued from mediocrity by the inclusion of lively choreographic interludes. Foreign visitors commented on the passion with which English people of all social ranks and all ages went about their dancing.[2] According to the chapbooks, dancing exerted an irresistible appeal over the population, and no wedding, festival or ale was complete without it. The hotter Protestants learned to contemplate this reality with a measure of suspicion, but in practice they could not always share the wet-blanket hostility of some of their literary spokesmen. When Oliver Cromwell's daughter was married in 1657, a large and mixed company of guests reportedly danced to the music provided by forty-eight violins ('a thing heretofore accounted profane'). Dancing was a national passion, though different counties evidently had their own specialities. A Jacobean author surveyed the scene: 'Westerne-men for gambouls: Middlesex-men for tricks above ground: Essex-men for the Hey: Lancashire for Horne-pypes: Worcester-shire for Bagpypes: but Hereford-shire for a Morris-daunce, puts downe, not onely all Kent, but verie neare (if one had line enough to measure it) three quarters of Christendome.'[3]

Forms and fashions

We shall begin with sociable dancing. Its development throughout the period was supported by an expanding body of musicians who were ready and able to offer instruction. On the village green, this often meant little

[2] Kemp, *Kemp's Nine Daies Wonder*, p. 4; Smith, *Acoustic World*, pp. 141–2; *REED Somerset*, p. 416; *Diary of Samuel Pepys*, vol. IV, p. 128; Pattison, *Music and Poetry*, p. 16.

[3] James A. Winn, 'Theatrical Culture 2: Theatre and Music', in Steven N. Zwiker (ed.), *The Cambridge Companion to English Literature, 1650–1740* (Cambridge: Cambridge University Press, 1969), p. 104; *Old Meg of Herefordshire.*

more than playing a tune and calling out basic directions. In common practice, the tunes were sometimes sounded by small groups of two or three musicians, but they were more often the responsibility of solo performers, particularly pipers and fiddlers. Pictorial evidence suggests that the minstrels who played for round dances positioned themselves either outside the ring or, in the absence of a maypole, right at its heart. Ordinary musicians regularly provided music and guidance, but the more specialised teachers were known by 1600 as 'dancing masters' and some of them set up schools in England's towns. London led the way, and a great increase in the number of dancing schools, attractive to 'the most lewd persons', was noted during the 1570s.[4] By the early seventeenth century, similar institutions were established in other urban centres. In 1608, a young Londoner moved to Southampton in order to open a dancing school in a rented room there (we hear of him because he was swiftly expelled from the town by the local authorities). In 1615, one of Chester's leading musicians and dance instructors petitioned the mayor in an effort to suppress the competition provided by four 'meere strangers unto the Cittie', all of whom claimed the ability to teach the locals the latest moves. There were also schools and/or dancing masters in Cambridge, Oxford, Newcastle upon Tyne and Lincoln. Documentation is patchy, but the fact that Hawkshead in the Lake District had its own resident dancing master in the eighteenth century seems to suggest that the services of such instructors were very widely available by the end of our period. They made their money by collecting fees from those who joined their schools, but also by offering more exclusive tuition to members of the gentry and aristocracy in the privacy of their own homes. During the late 1620s, for example, Judith Edwards of Fayre Crooch (Sussex) made annual payments of £3 to 'Mr Onsloe dancing master'.[5] Such men often played 'kits', highly portable pocket violins with an acoustic power far inferior to that of instruments of full size.

Sociable dancing generally involved a roughly equal number of men and women. It therefore carried a romantic and sexual charge on all social

[4] Brissenden, *Shakespeare and the Dance*, p. 10. See also Price, *Patrons and Musicians*, p. 29, and Baldwin, *Paying the Piper*, pp. 140–1.

[5] *Assembly Books of Southampton*, vol. I, p. 98; *REED Chester*, p. 290; *REED Cambridge*, p. 740; *REED Somerset*, p. 420; transcript of All Saints' parish register, City Library, Newcastle upon Tyne; *Probate Inventories of Lincoln Citizens, 1661–1714*, ed. J. A. Johnston, *Lincoln Record Society* 80 (1991), p. lviii; Spufford, *Small Books*, p. 180; *REED Sussex*, pp. 198–201. See also Jennifer Thorp, '"So great a master as Mr Isaac": An Exemplary Dancing-master of Late Stuart London', *Early Music* 35 (2007), 435–46, and Thorp, 'Dance in Late Seventeenth-century London: Priestly Muddles', *Early Music* 26 (1998), 198–210.

levels. Dance, it was said, helped city bawds to attract customers and assisted young gentlewomen in the task of luring suitors. One Londoner also warned about the dangers of life beyond the capital, where participation in rural dancing led inexorably towards sexually transmitted disease and socially transmitted disgrace.[6] Songs and ballads described dancing in terms that were often laden with sexual suggestion. Nelly would sweat herself into a jelly while the buttocks of other maidens quaked 'lyke Custards new baked'. 'Tickle her Tom with a Pipe and a Tabor', shouted one fictional dancer to another.[7] Indeed, instruments both musical and sexual were regularly set up for comparison, and dancing itself served as a euphemism for sexual intercourse. The woman who 'got a green gown' after dancing not only had collapsed onto the staining grass in exhaustion but had done so with a man on top of her.[8]

Perhaps Samuel Pepys, the collector of many such ballads, was unduly influenced by them. Certainly, he was deeply perturbed in 1663 by his wife's habit of disappearing upstairs with her private dancing master, and he could hardly conceive of an innocent explanation. He listened at the door, or in the room below, hoping thereby to establish whether the movements within were consistent with 'country' dancing. Pepys even took to checking that Elizabeth was wearing drawers before her lessons, as if the presence of such garments rendered misbehaviour impossible.[9] He knew at first hand the sexual power of dancing, and was himself regularly titillated by the sight and sound of girls, actresses and even princesses practising their moves.[10] For Pepys and others, the effect of dancing could be further enhanced by cross-dressing, an occasional pleasure that apparently knew no social bounds. Samuel and his friends tried it in 1666, almost half a century after a similar experiment had taken place in West Thorney (Sussex). Here it was reported in 1620–1 that 'certeyne maydens did daunce in mans apparrell & young men in maydes clothes uppon Sunday the 4th February at Thomas Romins & on Sunday the eleventh of February at hargoodes house'.[11] If they had chosen a different day of the week, we might never have learned of this little cell of gender-benders.

[6] Taylor, *All the Workes*, p. 258; Burton, *Anatomy of Melancholy*, p. 586; *Pepys Ballads*, vol. I, pp. 188–9.

[7] *REED Lancashire*, pp. 32–5; *Pepys Ballads*, vol. IV, p. 244.

[8] *Pepys Ballads*, vol. I, pp. 384–5, vol. III, pp. 35, 55, 72.

[9] *Diary of Samuel Pepys*, vol. IV, pp. 172–3.

[10] Ibid., vol. II, p. 212, vol. VII, p. 375, vol. IX, p. 507.

[11] Ibid., vol. VII, p. 246; *REED Sussex*, p. 180. For some more cross-dressing dancers, see Baldwin, *Paying the Piper*, p. 52.

The erotic dimension is undeniable, but at times sociable dancing also articulated single-sex solidarities, separating men and women rather than uniting them. This was particularly true among women. Maidens of all sorts were fond of dancing without male companions, though men often listened and looked eagerly from the sidelines.[12] A ballad about Hyde Park remarked on the occasional presence there of 'honest Country Girles' dancing about on the green grass. At a modest London wedding in August 1666, it was the young women who rose to dance after dinner. Decades earlier, Dudley Carlton had encountered some dancers on the road: 'a company of madd wenches ... who travayled from house to house, and to some places where they were litle knowne, still attended on with a consort of musicians'.[13] The sense of temporary release from normal constraints is palpable. Understandably, many women evidently chose not to abandon the segregated habit after marriage. 'This gallant Dame must dance: / Her Husband must say nothing', complained one fictional newly-wed about his gallivanting wife. The words could almost have been those of Samuel Pepys himself, for his spouse sometimes left him behind when she went out to pre-arranged dance meetings with her female friends.[14] One foreign visitor to London reported that fifty unaccompanied wives might gather at such a meeting. In some circumstances, the only male in attendance may have been the dancing master, and a similar sexual imbalance also characterised the dance lessons that were commonly a feature of the curriculum in socially exclusive girls' schools of the later seventeenth century.[15] The dancing master thus manned the last outpost of male authority, but he nevertheless failed to endear himself to the neglected husbands of England.

Rather less frequently, men danced without women. A Sussex fiddler played his instrument one evening in 1595 while 'Robert Haler & Robert Fast did dauns a dauns or ii'. In 1615, the churchwardens of Worthen (Shropshire) held their hands up and admitted 'that yonge men doe dance on the Saboathe day'. A few years later, in Dulcote (Somerset), one such man watched a group of women dancing at a wedding and asked his friend, a little huffily, 'will not thease townes maides give of dauncing that

[12] Forrest, *History of Morris Dancing*, p. 296; Francis Rust, *Dance in Society: An Analysis of the Relationship between the Social Dance and Society in England from the Middle Ages to the Present Day* (London: Routledge, 1969), p. 43; *Pepys Ballads*, vol. I, p. 197, vol. II, p. 212.

[13] *Pepys Ballads*, vol. I, p. 197; *Diary of Samuel Pepys*, vol. VII, pp. 262–3; SP12/275 (93), NA.

[14] *Pepys Ballads*, vol. I, p. 380; *Diary of Samuel Pepys*, vol. VII, p. 360.

[15] Magalotti, quoted in *Diary of Samuel Pepys*, vol. II, p. 212 n. 1; Brailsford, *Sport and Society*, p. 23.

wee may goe to daunce?'[16] The implication seems to be that on this occasion the men did not dance until the women had left the floor. Was social decorum being carefully preserved in the unlikely setting of a Somerset wedding, or was the behaviour of those present more probably a sign that young men sometimes felt more virile when they strutted their stuff alone?

The interplay of segregation and combination was also evident in the social composition of dancing groups. Much of the time, people practised the art primarily among those of roughly comparable age and status, but its pleasures could also bring together individuals from widely differing backgrounds. On special occasions, wealthy landowners with a taste for traditional recreations played host to their tenants and either watched them dance or even joined them out on the floor.[17] The dancing that swept through the cathedral city of Wells (Somerset) in May 1607 clearly drew in a diverse band of revellers. The man chosen as 'lord' of the company was a young gentleman, aged twenty-six, but his 'lady' was Thomasine White, the middle-aged wife of a local barber-surgeon. Thomasine also danced with other gentlemen, and was at one point hoisted aloft in order to give and receive kisses. She may therefore have been too busy to contemplate the fact that in early modern England there were few situations in which such intimate boundary-crossing encounters were possible.[18] On many occasions, dancing distinguished the young from the old, but in this case it could also serve to soften the differences. In England's dancing schools, the proceedings were probably relatively restrained, but men and women of various types came together here too. The proprietors were generally willing to take fees from anyone who could provide the necessary cash. In practice, this meant that a majority of clients came from the middling and upper ranks of society, and a number of sources reveal the eagerness of many such individuals to sign up for lessons. Students in Oxford wrote plaintively to their fathers, asking for additional funds to meet dancing school fees or to purchase appropriate ribbons and pumps. John Bruen, the future puritan, was lured into a dancing school by the sound of the music, and Thomas Whythorne, the future musician, stepped over the threshold because of his desire to 'enrich myself with some more such exercises and qualities as young folks for the most do delight in'.[19]

[16] *REED Sussex*, p. 29; *REED Shropshire*, p. 352 (see also pp. 62–3); *REED Somerset*, p. 99.

[17] Woodfill, *Musicians in English Society*, pp. 233–4; Rust, *Dance in Society*, p. 47; *Great Diurnall of Nicholas Blundell*, pp. 118, 229, 240.

[18] *REED Somerset*, pp. 313–14, 331–2.

[19] 6729/box 7, vol. 5/150, SHC; MS Eng hist c.481, fo. 54r, Bodleian Library; *REED Somerset*, p. 20; Baldwin, *Paying the Piper*, p. 181; *Autobiography of Thomas Whythorn*, p. 11.

There are no surviving membership lists, but incidental references indicate the presence of young aristocrats and gentlefolk, along with wealthy urban citizens and/or their wives.[20] The participation of poorer people is harder to discern, though we might note the example of an illiterate sailor who, in 1686, performed for his superiors on a ship in the Philippines, having previously 'learnt to dance in the Musick-houses' near Wapping.[21]

It is difficult to be precise about the actual steps, movements and formations that characterised sociable dancing, though ballads and other literary sources supply a litany of terms through which the more prominent physical manoeuvres can at least be imagined: 'taking fast by the hand', 'turning', 'half-turning', 'bussing', 'tracing', 'jetting round', 'jumping', 'vaulting', 'capering', 'footing it', doing 'a turn o' th' toe', 'hopping about', 'keeping the stroke', 'setting foot to foot', 'passing', 'winding', 'tripping', 'skipping', 'firking it' and 'dancing about, in and out', perhaps while performing 'sprauling kicks' or 'tossing tricks'. Observers, whether scornful or sympathetic, agreed that the common people danced with great vigour. One satirical piece preserved in a Hampshire notebook of the seventeenth century refers in passing to a chandler's 'greasie daughter' who 'will sweat you a pound of candles at a dauncing meeting'. In Restoration Cheshire, Sir Peter Leycester drew on various Latin sources while compiling his notes on the refreshing power of music, but then added a personal comment of his own: 'and indeed for the Countrey fellowes, experience showes how they will throwe about their Clumzie Joints at a night before the Piper when they have been labouring very sore all day before, as if their spirits were revived with it'. Dance-loving balladeers told the same story, and one well-known tune of the late seventeenth century bore the energetic (and suggestive) title 'Oh, how they did firk it, caper and jerk it, under the greenwood tree'.[22]

Until the late seventeenth century, the most common formation for sociable dancing was probably circular. According to Stephen Gosson, Elizabethan children habitually danced 'roundelays' while chanting their own accompaniment (he mentioned the plaintive lines, 'When shall we eat white bread? When the puttock is dead'). The habit evidently persisted into adult life, and when the middle-aged dancers of Wells took to the

[20] *Diary of Samuel Pepys*, vol. I, p. 253; Price, *Patrons and Musicians*, p. 29; *Memoirs of Sir John Reresby*, p. 2.

[21] Woodfield, *English Musicians*, p. 85.

[22] 44M69/M4/3, HRO; DLT/B11, fo. 25, ChRO; *Pepys Ballads*, vol. IV, p. 250.

Figure 7.2. The hay was a circular dance for a large mixed company. Here, the identity of a community is reaffirmed ('Hey for our town') but the women appear to be heavily outnumbered by men. The Pepys Library, Magdalene College, Cambridge, Pepys Penny Merriments, *The Country Garland* (London, 1687), title page.

street on Sunday 3 May 1607, a circular pattern was one of those adopted. Frequently, such groups danced around an oak tree or a maypole (particularly in the summer) and executed a series of moves through which they swapped partners repeatedly until, finally, they returned to their starting places. The 'hay', for example, was a well-known circular dance for a theoretically unlimited number of interweaving participants (see Figure 7.2). The popularity of such formations is reflected not only in woodcut pictures of the period, but in the names of dances such as 'Selenger's round', 'Cheshire rounds' and 'The new round O'. Barnabe Rich did not share the love that many of his fellow Elizabethans felt for dancing, and he described the round format as 'too giddie a dance for my diet'. The participants, he complained, were required to 'runne about with as muche speede as thei maie: yet are thei never a whit the nier to the ende of their course, unlesse with often tourning thei hap to catch a fall'.[23]

'Long' formations, in which the dancers began in two parallel lines, also formed part of the repertoire. Throughout the seventeenth century, the inhabitants of Shaftesbury (Dorset), led by their mayor, performed an annual long dance at nearby Gillingham in order to mark and sustain their right to take water from the spring that rose there. Long formations had the advantage of allowing the company to move from place to place *en masse* as they danced. In Wells, for example, the dancers of 1607 regularly travelled about the town with their musicians in itinerant attendance. On 3 May, more than thirty married couples, presumably in long formation, danced 'hand in hand towardes the Inn or taverne'. They later danced into the east of the city for further alcoholic and musical merriment, though sympathetic witnesses were careful to observe that 'the companie was desolved before the daie lighte was gon'.[24]

In other cases, the precise format of the dances was not specified, but their sociable nature was clear enough. The hornpipe, for example, was a group dance with a notable capacity to raise the spirits and animate the limbs of its many devotees. Contemporaries did not share the modern tendency to associate the dance particularly with jolly jumping sailors, preferring instead to connect it with Lancashire. One of the songs that was recorded in the Blundell 'Hodgepodge Book' described a gathering at which the young men all took female partners,

And daunc't a hornepype merilie
tripped and skipped nott wearilie
Tyr'd out the bagpype and Fidle
with dauncing the Hornepipe and didle.

The 'didle' (or diddle) is rather more mysterious, though it was clearly well known in northern England.[25]

We can say a little more about the dances that stimulated additional excitement by the deployment of various props. 'The young girls in and about Oxford', reported White Kennet in 1695, 'have a sport called Leap-candle for which they set a candle in the middle of the room in a candlestick, and then draw up their coats in the form of breeches, and

[23] Gosson, *Trumpet of Warre*, fo. 57r–v (a puttock was a red kite, a once common scavenging bird of prey); *REED Somerset*, pp. 300–2, 347; *Complete Country Dance Tunes from Playford's Dancing Master*, nos. 129, 425, 512; Barnabe Rich, *Riche his Farewell to Militarie Profession* (London, 1581), A3v. 'Selenger's round' can be heard on track 35 on the website.

[24] *REED Dorset*, p. 294; *REED Somerset*, p. 332. [25] *REED Lancashire*, p. 32.

dance over the candle back and forth.' The famous 'cushion dance' was physically safer, though its association with flirtatious interaction ensured a measure of controversy. It was evidently a form of round dance in which the participants, one by one, knelt on a central cushion in order to be kissed by those of the opposite sex. John Taylor named it as one of the 'pretty provocatory dances' that was employed by bawds in their efforts to stimulate potential clients.[26] It was also a favourite at wedding feasts, and on St Thomas's Day in 1602 Mr Wylmot, the vicar of Tortworth (Gloucestershire), made the mistake of leading the action. He was already out of favour with his ecclesiastical superiors and declared before the assembled company that he was past caring and could no longer see the point in sobriety: 'Bycause my Lord Byshopp of Gloucester will not geve me leave to preach, I will studdy noe more on my booke and nowe I will studdy knavery.' He rejected his clerical calling and behaved like a lusty layman for the evening. In the candlelit church house, the vicar laid a cushion on the floor, knelt down upon it 'and kysse[d] a woman that then daunced with him, as all the rest ... also did'. One witness recalled that Mr Wylmot had 'ledd the Cushin dawnce with a Cushin on his sholder and kneeled downe as the order of the dawnce is, and kissed one goodwife Hickes'. Not surprisingly, cushion dances could prove quite appealing to the youth of a community. When an alehouse-keeper from Catcott (Somerset) organised one in 1625 'hee gathered mutch companie to his house of younge men, and maydens'. The cushion dance, like other forms of kissing dance, encouraged a more intimate physical relationship between participants than was common in other forms of the art. Most general references in the surviving sources are to hand-to-hand interaction, but cushion dancers supplemented this with mouth-to-mouth (or at least lip-to-cheek) contact.[27]

Sociable dancing was a dynamic cultural activity, and its most fashionable forms inevitably shifted with the passing of the decades. In general, it seems that round dances may have lost ground to long dances during the latter decades of the seventeenth century, though the process is well documented only among the gentry. At this elevated social level, the change seems to have reflected the preference of the pre-eminent for dancing in long rectangular galleries rather than on the spacious greens

[26] Kennet, quoted by Fox, *Oral and Literate Culture*, p. 204; *REED Somerset*, p. 893 n. 72; Taylor, *All the Workes*, vol. II, p. 258.

[27] *REED Cumberland, Westmorland, Gloucestershire*, pp. 342–3 (see also pp. 314–15 for further evidence of Wylmot's musical antics); *REED Somerset*, p. 72.

traditionally beloved of the population at large.[28] Published dance collections reveal the transition very clearly, though the woodcut illustrations that adorned ballads continued to favour the round dance at least until 1700 (it probably remained more common at lower social levels, or perhaps it was easier to draw).[29] Sociable dance formations may also have become more complex as the simplest choreographies were to some degree supplemented by more challenging patterns. This was a process driven in part by the country's dancing masters, who could clearly hope to benefit from the progressive complication of English dance. Some dances simply passed out of fashion. One manuscript ballad of 1641, preserved in the records of the Blundell family, reports that the 'Lord Strange hornepype' had once been exceedingly popular among Lancashire dancers, 'But now they doe hould it to[o] sober / and therefore will needs give it over.' In Elizabethan England, one list of well-known dances included 'Rogero', 'Basilino', 'Turkeyloney', 'All the flowers of the broom', 'Pepper is black', 'Greensleeves' and 'Peggy Ramsay'. A comparable list, written in the late seventeenth century, mentioned 'Selenger's round', 'Bobbing Jo', 'Jingle de cut', 'Bodkin's galliard', 'The mad man's morris', 'Drunken Barnaby', 'The bed full of bones', 'Room for cuckolds' and the 'Lancashire hornpipe'.[30] The absence of common ground suggests some degree of turnover, though we should also note that each list was merely a subjective snapshot and that other evidence demonstrates the popularity of some of these dances throughout the early modern period. 'Selenger's round' and 'Bobbing Jo' (or 'Bobbing Joan') had, for example, been around for a hundred years or more.

Such long-lived dances and tunes presumably bore some relation to their namesakes in John Playford's famous collection, *The English Dancing Master* (published in 1651 and re-issued, as *The Dancing Master*, every few years thereafter until its final edition in 1728). The precise extent of the resemblances is difficult to judge, for Playford was more than just a scribe. His pen was fitted with a cultural filter, and the nature of his interventions is a complex issue to which we shall have cause to return. Even at a more rudimentary level, Playford's choreographies are notoriously difficult to

[28] Rust, *Dance in Society*, p. 56.

[29] In the 1651 edition of Playford's *Dancing Master*, 'longways' arrangements already accounted for 80 of the 106 dances, but the 14 round formations nevertheless constituted a respectable minority. By 1716, the imbalance was much more pronounced: only 5 out of 352 titles were round dances.

[30] Rust, *Dance in Society*, p. 47; *REED Lancashire*, p. 33; Nash, *Have with you to Saffron Walden*, T1r; *The Figure of Nine*, A4r. Three of these tunes can be heard on the website: 'Greensleeves' (track 34), 'Selenger's round' (track 35) and 'Bobbing Joan' (track 31).

decipher with certainty, and he seems to have left a number of minor decisions to the discretion of the dancers or their instructors. Many of the dances required very similar figures (sets of steps) for the first part of the tune before diverging into more distinctive variations for the second part. Once the basic patterns were memorised, it would therefore not have been difficult to master the subtly different forms that were applied within a range of individual dances. The most important steps were called for again and again in shifting combinations: the single (in which the dancer steps forward with one foot, then brings the other foot forward to join it); the double (logically, two singles); set and turn single (a single to one side, then to the other, followed by a turn on the spot); siding (a double-double that brings the dancer side to side with his or her partner, first on the right and then on the left); and arming (in which partners link arms, rotate through a full circle, then repeat the move in the other direction). To these were added the various manoeuvres that enabled the dancers to swap partners in an orderly fashion until their starting positions were regained.[31] On paper, Playford's instructions look fiendishly complicated, but in practice – as anyone who has participated in a modern barn dance will know – the steps and progressions are repetitive and logical, so that even those who experience profound anxiety in advance of their involvement can find the experience manageable and even surprisingly enjoyable (see Figure 7.3).

Forty-six melodies appeared in all ten editions of *The Dancing Master* that were published before 1700, and these can probably be treated as a reasonably solid sample of England's most successful dance tunes (see Table 7.1). Of these, nineteen are known to have been referred to or notated in print or manuscript in the decades between 1560 and 1650.[32] Playford did not, therefore, make them up, and the paucity of sources makes it likely that most of the remaining tunes were similarly familiar. These forty-six melodies, supplemented by seven more of undoubted popularity, amount to an impressive collection of early modern dance music.

Tunes in triple time outnumber those in duple time by two to one, and almost all are organised in two clearly delineated sections (thus allowing the musicians to repeat each part as many times as necessary, depending on the steps required of the dancers). There are long and complex tunes ('Dull Sir John': **Website track 36 and Appendix**) and shorter, simpler

[31] *Complete Country Dance Tunes from Playford's Dancing Master*; Forrest, *History of Morris Dancing*, p. 313; Brissenden, *Shakespeare and the Dance*, pp. 112–16; http://ourworld.cs.com/BAPadget/ECDHandout.htm, last accessed 1 May 2008.

[32] References are found mainly in ballads, but also in plays, chapbooks and music manuscripts (Simpson's *British Broadside Ballad* is, as ever, the best reference work available).

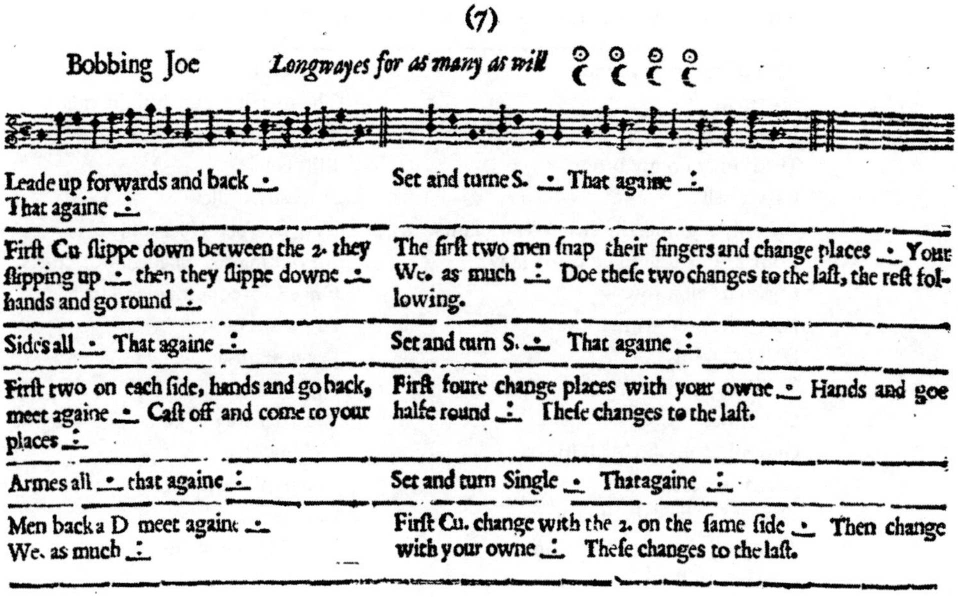

Figure 7.3. Playford provided tunes and directions for dancers and their instructors. The crescent and circle symbols (top right) represent the starting positions for men and women respectively. The tune, 'Bobbing Joe' or 'Bobbing Joan', can be heard on track 31, where it provides the setting for a ballad. The British Library, John Playford, *The English Dancing Master* (London, 1651), p. 7.

tunes ('Maiden Lane': **Website track 37 and Appendix**). Some tunes are in what we would recognise as major and minor keys, while others are clearly modal and sound rather strange to our ears ('Scotch cap': **Website track 38 and Appendix**). Many have strong and simple rhythms ('Cuckolds all a row': **Website track 40 and Appendix**), while others present interesting cross-beats ('Boatman': **Website track 39 and Appendix**). Successive editions of *The Dancing Master* also provide scholars with a fascinating source for the study of musical change. Many of the tunes underwent significant alterations across the decades, offering us an insight into the ways in which melodies evolved in common usage. Rhythms were altered, extra notes were added to fill in gaps, and some tunes passed from major to minor modes or vice versa. Playford did not include 'Selenger's round' until 1657, but his elaborate version of this established favourite seems to suggest the way in which musicians might have amused themselves by devising new variations on old tunes (**Website track 35 and Appendix**). Many of the changes that Playford made to his melodies over the years also reflect the twin transitions of the period: from medieval modality towards modern tonality, and

Table 7.1. The top fifty dance tunes (with alternative names)

All a la mode de France	Maiden Lane
Boatman	The merry merry milk maids
Bobbing Joe	The milk-maid's bob
The bonny bonny broom	Mill field
Cast a bell	My Lady Cullen
Cheerily and merrily (Mr Webb's fancy)	New Bo Peep (Piccadilly)
Confess his tune (The court lady)	An old man is a bed full of bones
Cuckolds all a row	Once I loved a maiden fair
Drive the cold winter away	Paul's steeple
Dull Sir John	Peggy Ramsay
The friar and the nun	Pepper is black
Goddesses	Petticoat wag (The tailor's daughter)
Gray's Inn mask (Mad Tom)	Picking of sticks
Greensleeves	The punk's delight
The gun (The valiant captain)	Rogero
Have at thy coat old woman	Room for cuckolds
A health to Betty	Row well ye mariners
Hit and miss	Saturday night and Sunday morn
Hockley in the hole	Scotch cap (Edinburgh Castle)
If all the world were paper	Selenger's round
Irish trot	Shepherd's holiday (Labour in vain)
Jog on	The slip (Sir Roger)
Kemp's jig	A soldier's life
The London gentlewoman (The hemp dresser; The London maid)	The Spanish gypsy
	Step stately
Lord of Carnarvan's jig	Tom Tinker
Mage on a cree (Margery Cree)	Turkeyloney

from performative discretion (under which the player was free to add certain accidentals, thus altering the notes according to taste) towards a more prescriptive attitude to rendition (as in modern classical music, where the musician is generally expected to play the notes on the page without deviation). Both of these shifts can be considered through Playford's successive versions of 'Greensleeves' (**Website track 34 and Appendix**).[33]

There was also enthusiastic cross-fertilisation between dance tunes and the music of balladry. Dancers sometimes sang their own accompaniment, either because they enjoyed doing so or because the local musicians were otherwise engaged. Later in the period, dances were invented to fit ballads,

[33] The tunes can all be found in *Complete Country Dance Tunes from Playford's Dancing Master* and Simpson, *British Broadside Ballad.*

and ballad melodies were adopted as dancing tunes. Indeed, some ballads may actually have been intended specifically for dancing. *The Beggers Intrusion*, for example, was set to the famous dancing tune of 'Selenger's round', and presented the words of a poor man as he travelled through society, addressing sharp criticisms to a series of individual social types (the serving man, the dainty dame, the lawyer's clerk and so on). It seems likely that this format deliberately mimicked that of a partner-swapping round dance, and that the song would have been well suited to use by those who skipped and tripped on the green or the alehouse floor. More obviously, ballads that told tales of exuberant dancing events were designed to animate their audiences. *The Winchester Wedding* described a dancing session that became an orgy: 'twenty great bellys were gotten / all on one Wedding night' (see Figure 7.4). The ballad also inspired the publication of an atmospheric print (see Figure 7.5), and one of our recordings is an attempt to bring both song and picture to life (**Website track 33 and Appendix**). Dancing to songs was probably a common practice, and a rare dance manuscript of the early sixteenth century demonstrates that the gentry too enjoyed the mixture: many of the dances that are contained in the source have words as well as tunes. On occasion, the crossover between song and dance may have encouraged their combination in simple dramatic performances. We cannot be sure exactly what went on in Thomas Wynter's Herefordshire alehouse on 20 December 1609, but he was accused both of allowing Sunday dancing and of 'sufferinge idel persons to play unsemely partes'.[34] This looks rather like a rustic version of the stage 'jig', a short song-and-dance drama that was often performed after the main play in London's theatres.

Sociable dancing brought people together, but it also stimulated their competitive instincts and provided a source of individualistic pride. In the upper echelons of society, it was important to be able to dance well (but not too well), and one feature of Pepys's personal anxiety concerning dance was his fear of public humiliation. Lower down, dancing for prizes was clearly a long-established custom. John Stowe recalled the sight and sound of London maidens dancing 'for garlandes hanged athwart the streets' during the mid-sixteenth century. He suggested that the habit

[34] *Pepys Ballads*, vol. I, pp. 216–17, vol. IV, p. 106; D77 box 38, pp. 51–79, DRO. See also David Fallows, 'The Gresley Dance Collection, *c.* 1500', *Royal Musical Association Research Chronicle* 29 (1996), 1–20; *REED Herefordshire, Worcestershire*, p. 73. The interplay between songs and dances is suggested by the existence of ballad tunes bearing titles such as 'Dance after my pipe', 'Caper and ferk it' and 'Frogs galliard'.

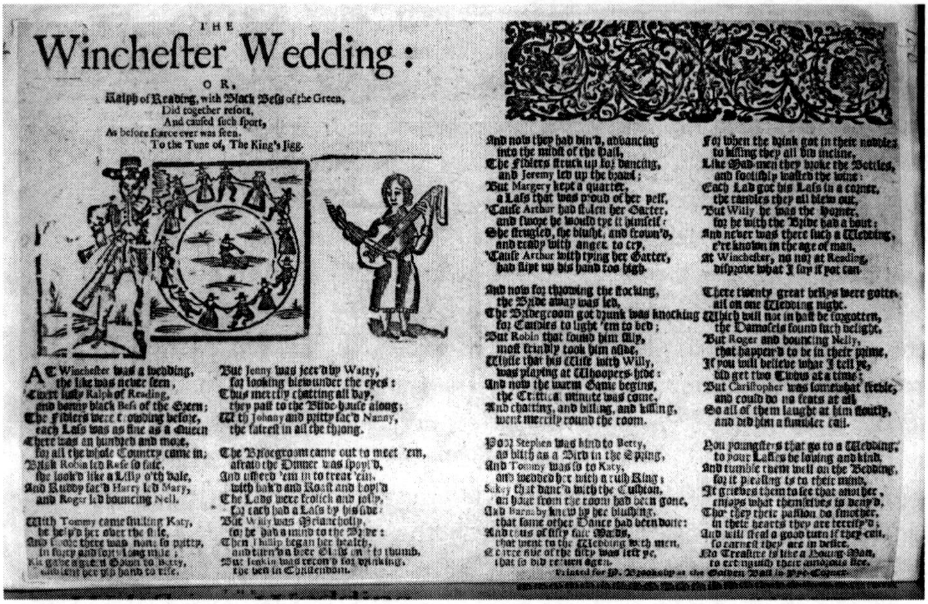
THE

Winchester Wedding:

OR,

Ralph of Reading, with Black Bess of the Green,

Did together resort,

And caused such sport,

As before scarce ever was seen.

To the Tune of, The King's Jigg.

Figure 7.4. Ballads that described specific dance sessions in intricate detail were fairly common during the seventeenth century. Here, the chosen tune was also associated with dancing and the pictures added further emphasis. The Pepys Library, Magdalene College, Cambridge, Pepys Ballads, *The Winchester Wedding* (London, *c.* 1682).

had been suppressed by the 1590s, yet there is plentiful evidence to indicate that competitive public dancing was still practised throughout the seventeenth century. In 1620, a dancing match was held at Leigh (Dorset), though we know of it only because Nicholas Perham allegedly drank too much beer, 'and did much abuse the ... daughter of Stiphen Russell'. The cheapest forms of literature referred regularly to dancing contests, and an ability to dance beautifully was a crucial piece of supporting evidence in the boldly titled ballad *Jone is as Good as my Lady.* A 'contry song', preserved only in manuscript, described a happy encounter in which three Lancashire couples 'tooke sydes' against three more, excitedly dancing for 'a wheate Cake' while shouting out encouragement to their musician ('tak't thee James Pyper of Formeby').[35]

The forms of dancing discussed so far were essentially participatory. Crowds of onlookers were a common feature, but the dancing was primarily for the dancers themselves, and it took place whether or not an

35 *Diary of Samuel Pepys*, vol. II, p. 71, vol. IV, pp. 111, 126; Stow, *A Survey of London* (London, 1598), p. 70; *REED Dorset*, p. 287; *Pepys Ballads*, vol. I, p. 236; *REED Lancashire*, pp. 32–4.

Figure 7.5. Dancing at weddings was extremely common. In this print, the guests are packed into a barn and the musicians, perched upon barrels, bring the company to life (the man who sits between the two instrumentalists may be singing, though we cannot be sure). © Trustees of the British Museum, Prints and Drawings, 1850,1109.75, Robert Robinson, *The Winchester Wedding* (London, *c.* 1683–95).

audience was present. Of course, there was always an element of show but sociable dancing was not principally defined by public display. In contrast, there also existed in this period a variety of more specialised, performative dances in which theatricality and the presence of witnesses were more crucial. Typically, these involved the injection of an element of danger as a means to the extraction of cash from witnesses. 'Dancing on ropes' was an activity that could be relied upon to draw an urban crowd. In Chester, the mayor's clerk noted an event that caught his imagination in 1606–7: 'A strange man Came to this Cittye and his wife & the[y] did daunce upon a Rope. Tyed overCrosse the streete: with other pleasante trickes: which was rare to the behoulders.' The diarist Thomas Crosfield also noted dancing on a rope as one of the 'Things to be seene for money' in Oxford during the early 1630s (there was also a dancing horse and, for those who tired of music, 'a dutch-wench all hairy and rough upon her body'). The Master of the Revels occasionally issued licences to performers such as Sisley Peadle, who headed a company of six entertainers in 1631. They were granted permission 'to use and exercise dauncing on the Roapes, Tumbling, Maulling and other such like Feates' as they travelled around the country. Perhaps it was the danger rather than the dancing that caused the crowds to gasp, though Sisley's licence also allowed her to use 'such musiccke drumme or Trumpettes' as she considered appropriate.[36]

On occasion, the perilous novelty was provided not by ropes but by swords. When Charles I visited the Scottish town of Perth in the summer of 1633, the city's company of skinners and glovers staged an elaborate sword dance, 'Which (God be praised) was acted and done without hurt or skaith to any'. On Ash Wednesday 1638, a similar dance was performed at Latham House (Lancashire) for the benefit of the attendant gentry. One of the dancers introduced the performance with a short health-and-safety announcement: 'The common proverb teacheth us to say / tis hasardus with sharp edg tooles to play.' He proceeded, however, to suspend the operation of this normal rule, asking his audience to 'be but auspitious to our platt while wee / this night shall marse preferr to mercury'.[37] Sword dances were spectacular, challenging and intensely masculine.

For obvious reasons, such performances were hardly commonplace. A far better-known dance was the morris, and it deserves detailed consideration. Morris dancing typically involved groups of between four and fifteen young men who staged displays of virile virtuosity for the stimulation of their neighbours and/or patrons. A morris dance had to be planned in advance, for it required the acquisition of specialist equipment, the recruitment of performers and the assignment of particular parts. These parts varied somewhat over time and place, but several standard favourites

[36] *REED Chester*, p. 218; *Diary of Thomas Crosfield*, p. 54; *REED Herefordshire, Worcestershire*, pp. 539–40.

[37] Helen Bennet, 'The Perth Glovers' Sword Dance of 1633', *Costume* 19 (1985), 40; *REED Lancashire*, p. 184.

can be identified. Most morrises presented a simple and loose narrative plot in which the brightly clad dancing men, their limbs decorated with ribbons and bells, competed with one another and with a free-ranging Fool for the hand of Maid Marion (often played by a man). The Fool inevitably emerged triumphant, aided no doubt by his habit of making merry with an inflated animal bladder while collecting money from onlookers in a wooden ladle. On occasion, Robin Hood, Friar Tuck or a wild and disruptive hobby-horse added further colour to proceedings. In some places, the costumes and equipment could be hired from a parish or a civic company, but this became increasingly rare after 1600 and most would-be morris men probably had to buy, beg or borrow the materials they needed. Normally, it seems, a particular individual took it upon himself to co-ordinate the proceedings. In 1617, for example, Philip Abree of Stanton Lacy (Shropshire) was reported to the courts for missing Sunday prayers. Instead, he had 'guised' himself in a suitable costume before 'leading the waie' to a morris dance.[38]

He and other morris leaders would also have taken responsibility for recruiting musicians. A range of instruments accompanied morris dancing, but it seems that often the heavy dub-a-dub of the drum was its most important aural component (along with the sound of small bells: 'we'll have brave jingling' says one of the morris dancers in a Jacobean play). When William Kemp danced the morris from London to Norwich in 1599, the attendant musician clearly played tunes on his pipe, yet the published account generally refers to him as the 'tabourer'. Morris was defined by the primal drum. Partly for this reason, there was probably no specific and separate body of morris tunes, though one or two titles imply a particular connection with this form of dance. Playford included in his collections melodies called 'Stanes morris' (**Website track 41 and Appendix**) and 'Maid's morris' (**Website track 42 and Appendix**), but the dance steps he called for were all of the 'country' variety. Beyond these examples, it seems likely that morris men and their musicians selected their melodies from the wider dance repertoire. In plays of the period, morris men use general dance tunes such as 'Trip and go' or 'The flowers in May'.[39]

If the bodily movements of country dancers were frisky, those of morris men were frenetic. The origins of the morris are obscure, but it was commonly felt to convey a sense of exoticism and otherness (or madness,

[38] Forrest, *History of Morris Dancing*, pp. 119–22, 146, 168–9, 23; Hutton, *Rise and Fall of Merry England*, pp. 117–18; *REED Dorset, Cornwall*, pp. 507–9; *REED Shropshire*, p. 324.

[39] Forrest, *History of Morris Dancing*, pp. 243, 286–7, 307–8; Kemp, *Kemp's Nine Daies Wonder*; *Complete Country Dance Tunes from Playford's Dancing Master*, nos. 97, 304, 437.

in the eyes and ears of its critics). The idea that morris dancing derived ultimately from the Moors gathered credence during the early modern period, and it was occasionally called 'morisco' dancing.[40] Early modern dancers probably expended little energy in contemplation of the roots of the morris, but they knew in their bones the manner of movement that was appropriate. In 1576–7, the treasurer of Chester paid 6s 8d to one Thomas Gillam 'for his leaping, called dancing, in the play called morris dance'. The vocabulary employed by Kemp in describing his marathon morris is equally suggestive: he 'frolics', he 'jumps' and he 'leaps'. Most of the individuals who attempted to join in Kemp's dance as he made his way along the road soon found themselves exhausted. In Shakespeare's *The Second Part of King Henry the Sixth*, the scheming Duke of York speaks admiringly of the fearless soldier who, at the end of a long battle, is still strong enough to 'caper upright like a wild Morisco', shaking the enemy's arrows out of his legs as if they were dancing bells. This image draws cleverly on the militaristic dimension of the morris: the dancers had their eyes fixed romantically upon Maid Marion, but they all knew that what she was looking for in a man was combative prowess rather than elegance and refinement. Some morris dances featured 'Musketts pistolls bills swords drawen and other unlawful weapons'. Even the hobby-horse, nowadays an increasingly out-dated children's toy, was once a symbol of warfare.[41]

The virile vibe was further enhanced by the generally processional nature of the morris. The dancers not only 'jumped' and 'jerked', but also did so while moving energetically from place to place. Kemp's hundred-mile journey carried this characteristic to an extreme, and most morris teams moved the shorter distances that separated different villages or urban streets. Morris dances were often incorporated into civic processions during the mid-sixteenth century, particularly where the event had some connection with the symbolic militarism of the urban 'watch'. On Sundays in the Jacobean countryside, however, morris men on the move might attract suspicion. In 1619–20, a group from Yazor (Herefordshire) was reported 'for dauncing the morrice betwene morninge & eveninge prayer . . . & goeinge dauncinge the morrice out of that parishe'. Two years previously, several men of Glastonbury (Somerset) had stayed in the parish

[40] Forrest, *History of Morris Dancing*, ch. 1; Smith, *Acoustic World*, pp. 143–4; Malcolmson, *Popular Recreations*, p. 32.

[41] *REED Cheshire*, p. 505; Kemp, *Kemp's Nine Daies Wonder*; Shakespeare, *2 Henry VI*, in *Complete Oxford Shakespeare*, p. 21; Forrest, *History of Morris Dancing*, p. 267; Smith, *Acoustic World*, pp. 143–5.

but had 'daunced the Morris upon the Saboath day up & downe the Towne in & rownd about the hie crosse'. It was all calculated to excite the onlookers, and in 1607 a labourer from Wells admitted that he and others had danced the morris through the streets on an evening in May before a crowd of a hundred people, 'some of them hoopinge laughing & sporting in merriment as is used to be done in such like games'.[42] Opportunities for a mere labourer to earn the public and noisy approval of a substantial section of local society were rare and therefore not to be missed. Some morris men even embarked on local tours, drumming up excitement in one village after another and thereby enhancing the reputation of their home parish.[43]

Whom were the prancing, dancing morris men seeking to impress? Presumably, members of the opposite sex were a key component of the target audience, and the small groups of women who were sometimes reported to the courts along with the offending morris men may often have been interested onlookers rather than actual participants. The male dancers who featured in stage plays of the seventeenth century were sometimes explicit on the subject of their lustful strategies. In *The Witch of Edmonton*, for example, Cuddy Banks is desperate to play the part of the hobby-horse as an aid in his courtship of the watching Katherine, and one suspects that similar priorities occupied the minds of many non-fictional practitioners.[44] On the other hand, morris dancing was perhaps just as strongly associated with the formation of bonds between young men. Arguably, when good fellows dressed up in bright tunics and little bells while carrying weapons and dancing competitively for the attention of Maid Marion, herself often a cross-dressing man, they were not performing exclusively for the benefit of the watching women. In most cases, the comparable social or occupational status of team members – typically servants, apprentices, shoemakers, tailors and so on – must also have helped to generate solid affinities, and the requirements of co-operative endeavour presumably reinforced these further. Take, for example, the two-day dance that took place during Whitsun week at Clee St Margaret (Shropshire) in 1619. A substantial group of men participated, and the various interlocking responsibilities were divided up among them: Adam Wilding beat the all-important drum (no other instrument is mentioned) and John Bottrell carried a sword; Nicholas Raynoldes played the friar and Richard Eudlicke was the hobby-horse; Walter Millichap took the role of 'the lord's vice or

[42] Forrest, *History of Morris Dancing*, pp. 94, 117; *REED Herefordshire, Worcestershire*, p. 182; *REED Somerset*, pp. 135, 281.

[43] Forrest, *History of Morris Dancing*, pp. 268–9.

[44] William Rowley, *The Witch of Edmonton* (London, 1658), p. 27.

fool' while William Poulter acted the part of 'the lord's shepherd' (mysteriously, the 'lord' himself was not identified); several others merely danced; Nicholas Millichap undertook to find a suitable flag, and opted imprudently to borrow the communion cloth from the church in Abdon; he then passed this distinctive item to Thomas Chelmick, who in turn handed it on to Edward Millichap, the man who carried it during the dance. Clearly, active participation in this choreographical communion was restricted to men.[45]

English morrises revealed many common characteristics, but the dance was nevertheless a flexible entity with no standard format. It was mainly manly, but it was not exclusively so. When Kemp danced to Norwich, he was twice challenged by individual young women, eager to join in for a time. The first, a fourteen-year-old maiden of Chelmsford (Essex), was duly provided with bells and a napkin, and she managed to match him jump for jump during an entire hour. The second, 'a lusty Country lasse' with 'thicke short legs', danced alongside him on the road for a mile, amusing the onlookers by shaking her 'fat sides' while her hips went 'swig and swag' (perhaps she asked the pipe and tabor man to play 'Maid's morris', recorded on the website, track 42). 'And to give her her due', remarked Kemp, 'she had a good eare, daunst truly, and wee parted friendly'. Clearly, she already knew the form. It seems that this was no fictional fancy, for in 1602 Rebecca Tower and Jane Conney of Tedstone Delamere (Herefordshire) were both reported to the ecclesiastical courts for 'dauncing the morrice' during time of divine service, along with eight named men. The morris was predominantly masculine but it was nevertheless a recreation in which, on occasion, men could play women and women could play men. Its adaptability was revealed in other ways too. The morris was a distinct activity, but it both drew on and contributed to the steps and music that were associated more strongly with sociable dancing. Morris dancing was predominantly a group activity but solo performance was possible. In 1561–2, a lone morris dancer was paid a small sum for performing at the house of a gentleman in Lincolnshire. Half a century later, John Myllett was apprehended in Salisbury, 'wandering as a vagrant, having bells for his legs & using a kind of dancing'.[46]

The interaction of elements customary and innovative can also be seen in the famous dance that reportedly took place in Hereford in 1609, and it

[45] Ibid., pp. 110, 126, 163; *REED Herefordshire, Worcestershire*, pp. 12–13; *REED Somerset*, p. 372; *REED Shropshire*, pp. 40–50, 523–31. See also Smith, *Acoustic World*, p. 145.

[46] Kemp, *Kemp's Nine Daies Wonder*, pp. 7, 9–10; *REED Herefordshire, Worcestershire*, pp. 169–70; Forrest, *History of Morris Dancing*, p. 279; Hutton, *Rise and Fall of Merry England*, p. 114; *Poverty in Early Stuart Salisbury*, p. 39.

is with a brief account of this remarkable event that our discussion of the morris will conclude. According to the author of *Old Meg of Herefordshire*, a morris was staged in which the traditional roles of youthful dancers and aged spectators were deliberately reversed. The two musicians, Squire and Hall, were aged 108 and 97 respectively, and the four whifflers (who cleared the way for the dancers) were all centenarians. The author, having set the scene, further stimulated the readers' expectations with a question and some advice: 'Doe you not long to see how the Morris-dancers bestir their legs . . . lift up your eyes, leape up behind their heads that stand befor you, or else get upon stalls, for I heare their bells, and behold, here they come.' The team of twelve, amazingly, had an average age of 102 years and was led by a 'foreman', James Tomkins of Llangarren (aged 106). Next in the list was John Willis, an ancient bone-setter who not only kept up with his dancing fellows but undertook to repair them should they suddenly find themselves out of joint. Dick Philips, small of stature but big of heart, was still capable of shaking his heels most neatly. John Carelesse, at 96, had begun to stoop, 'but for a bodie and a beard, he becomes any Morris in Christendome'. The retired soldier William Maio danced merrily despite the ancient wounds he had sustained in battles of the mid-sixteenth century (on one occasion, he had 'carried his liver and his lights home halfe a mile and you may still put your finger into them, but for a thin skin over them'). The hobby-horse was John Hunt, a man who could be trusted to 'forget himselfe' while in character, crying 'nothing but O, the Hobbie-horse is forgotten'. This was apparently the kind of line that might be expected to attract the attention of on-lookers and the affection of Maid Marion, a role that was played by 'Meg Goodwin, the famous wench of Erdisland', the oldest member of the party at 120. Her advanced age earned the author's comment, though he evidently did not consider it particularly unusual that the part should be played by a woman. Also battling to win Marion's heart were the remaining dancers, William Waiton, William Mosse, Thomas Winney, John Lace and John Mando.

The clothing of the company was described in unique detail:

> The Musitians, and the twelve dauncers, had long coates of the old fashion, hie sleeves gathered at the elbowes, and hanging sleeves behind: the stuffe red Buffin, stript with white, Girdles with white, stockings white, and redde Roses to their shooes: the one sixe, white Jewes cap with a Jewell, and a long red Feather: the other a scarlet Jewes cap, with a Jewell and a white Feather: So the Hobbi-horse, and so the Maide Marrion attired in colours: the wiflers had long staves, white and red.

On the big day, the musicians began to play 'and the Morris-dauncers fell to footing' while the whifflers held back the crowd in order to make room for the antics of the hobby-horse. The ancient dancers put the younger generation to shame, a fact that was attributed to their moderate lifestyles ('these white-bearded youths of Hereford-shiere, were never given to wine or to wenches'). Despite a combined age of well over 1,000 years, they still danced thunderously well. 'These, shewed in their dauncing, and mooving up and downe, as if Mawlborne hilles, in the verie depth of Winter, when all their heades are covered (in steade of white woollie cappes) with snow, had shooke and daunced at some earth-quake.' It was only at the very end of proceedings that one of the 'nimble-legd old gallants' finally collapsed onto the ground, quite unable to foot it for a moment longer.[47]

Of course, *Old Meg* must be treated with a degree of scepticism, though it is an interesting and mildly reassuring fact that several of the details are at least consistent with information gleaned from other sources. The existence of a highly regarded Hereford musician named Squire has already been noted. The author also listed the gentry who attended the festivities, and most of them were alive at the time and well-known in the county. Lastly, several of the surnames identified among the performers can be linked with independent evidence of dancing in the county during the same period. Thomas Winney of Holmer, for example, may have been related to Hugh Winney of nearby Yazor, who staged 'a great morris dance' in 1619, despite being one of the two serving churchwardens of the parish.[48]

The morris was a potent pastime, yet it was also the one major form of dancing that may have suffered something of a decline during the seventeenth century. Between 1570 and 1640, the morris had strongholds in Herefordshire and the Welsh borders, though its presence was also recorded more occasionally all over southern England. It was never prominent in northern England, despite the evidence of its role in Chester. After 1660, references to morris dancing become significantly more sporadic, though the southern midlands now emerged as an area of particular strength.[49] To some extent, this impression of the rise and fall of a recreation is created by the records: the Jacobean high point probably owed as much to escalating levels of prosecution as to any increase in the

[47] *Old Meg of Herefordshire*. See also Patrick Collinson, 'Elizabethan and Jacobean Puritanism as Forms of Popular Culture', in Christopher Durston and Jacqueline Eales (eds.), *The Culture of English Puritanism, 1570–1700* (Basingstoke: Macmillan, 1996), pp. 38–9; Hutton, *Rise and Fall of Merry England*, pp. 165–6.

[48] *REED Herefordshire*, pp. 264, 280–2.

[49] Forrest, *History of Morris Dancing*, pp. 40–1, 43–5, 194, 289, 291, 327–9.

number of dances held. On the other hand, contemporary commentary from the second half of the century tends to confirm the general pattern of a dance in retreat. While there was an upsurge in morris events during the early 1660s, it evidently did not last. The Restoration recovery was a response to the enforced austerity of the previous decade, and, just for a time, it became fashionable to mark the return of the monarchy and of all that was good about customary culture by morris dancing. Most famously, the returning Charles II was greeted, as he travelled across Blackheath, by an enthusiastic team of morris men. Commentators, however, tended to view such events as throwbacks, the modish revivals of something that had all but vanished. When Samuel Pepys witnessed morris dancing on Leadenhall Street in London on May Day in 1663, he described it as a recreation 'which I have not seen a great while'. Anthony Wood noted the Restoration resurgence in morris dancing, but also remarked upon the rapidity with which enthusiasm subsequently faded.[50]

Dancing – whether sociable or performative – required physical space and the approval of some combination of patrons and neighbours. Of course, most sociable dancing took place for pleasure rather than profit, and the participants therefore asked no more patronage than the permissive nod of a village elder or the readiness of their fellow parishioners to tolerate the recreational use of the green. Such accommodating attitudes leave little trace in the records, and we are therefore dependent on references to more formal arrangements. Here, however, some interesting shifts in the practice of patronage can be detected. During much of the sixteenth century, dancers who hoped to receive a fee for their efforts could look with reasonable optimism towards parish churches, town corporations and urban companies. In Elizabethan Chester, for example, the cordwainers and shoemakers paid four pence to the 'cheldren that dansed the hoobe horses' in June 1562, and a year later the city's treasurer rewarded one Hugh Gillom to the tune of seven shillings 'for daunsinge at midsomer'. In the same decade, the churchwardens of distant St Breock (Cornwall) made regular payments of around four shillings to dancers who visited the parish from other villages, presumably to participate in fund-raising church ales. At this date, such payments remained common all over England.[51] In the 1580s, the situation began to change, and dancers of the next century were far more likely to receive support from

[50] Forrest, *History of Morris Dancing*, p. 210; *Diary of Samuel Pepys*, vol. IV, p. 120; Anthony Wood, quoted by Forrest, *History of Morris Dancing*, p. 138.

[51] *REED Chester*, pp. 69, 70; *REED Dorset, Cornwall*, p. 506.

private patrons, whether alehouse-keepers or traditionalist gentlefolk. Representative examples, drawn from the Herefordshire records, included John Wilkes of Tedstone Delamere, who in 1613–14 was in trouble 'for keepeinge of dancinge, tipling and drinkinge in his howse', and Joyce Jeffreys, a wealthy resident of the county town, who in 1639 paid a penny to 'megge A dawncer' (presumably not Old Meg herself, who would by this date have been 150 years old). After 1660, a few official institutions were tempted to hire dancers once again. The barber-surgeons of Chester paid sixpence to some morris dancers at midsummer in 1663, and it is an intriguing fact that the Sussex parish of Warnham came to possess a copy of Playford's *Dancing Master* (the edition of 1665, though we do not know exactly when or why the book was obtained). In general, however, private forms of patronage retained their dominance into the eighteenth century.[52] Broad changes of this sort were clearly related to the cloud of controversy under which much dancing took place during the period, and it is high time that we examined the contents of this cloud rather more closely.

The dance debate

During the sixteenth century, those who praised and promoted dance were generally more interested in courtly practice than in the pastimes of the population at large. One intellectual commonplace, inherited from ancient and medieval philosophy, drew attention to the connections between sophisticated earthly dancing and the orderly movements of the stars. The universe, it was sometimes supposed, had been drawn from chaos into a state of dance, and the spheres continued forevermore in exquisitely patterned musical motion. As it was in the macrocosm, so it was in the microcosm: the sea danced on the edges of the land just as the moon danced 'in her pallid sphere', and humans, dancing in due order, could imitate the planets and touch their perfection.[53] Dance was also, therefore, a teaching aid through which people might come to know the duties required of the ideal citizen, learning – by correspondence – the moves that were appropriate to their particular earthly stations. 'Practise these dances carefully', advised one fictional teacher, 'and you will become a fit companion of the planets, which dance of

[52] *REED Herefordshire, Worcestershire*, pp. 172, 191; Z G2/1, fo. 86r–v, ChRO; Par. 203/7/40, WSRO; Forrest, *History of Morris Dancing*, pp. 30–3.

[53] *The Poems of Sir John Davies*, ed. Clare Howard (New York: Columbia University Press, 1941), p. 81.

their own nature.' Men and women could dance their way into model marriages, learning about domination and subordination as they trod their measures, and courtiers could feel through their feet the need to respect and revere their prince. John Davies's *Orchestra*, written in 1596, presents the period's fullest development of these ideas. The author was at pains to distance himself from the dancing of mere peasants, yet his vision of a commonwealth in musical movement was an inclusive one:

Concords true picture shineth in thys Art,
Where divers men and women ranked be,
And every one doth daunce a severall part,
Yet all as one, in measure do agree,
Observing perfect uniformitie.[54]

Ancient Greek philosophers had detected an affinity between dance and moral virtue, and authors of the sixteenth century sometimes explored the same theme. For Thomas Elyot, writing in 1531, no other pastime could match dancing, 'wherin may be founden both recreation and meditation of vertue', and he went on to list prudence, honour, love, reverence and industry as particular qualities that participants might aspire to acquire.[55]

Many dramatists of the Elizabethan and Jacobean periods found in dance a symbol of good order and an image of the ideal. In *A Midsummer Night's Dream*, Oberon invites Titania to dance at the moment of their reconciliation: 'Come, my queen, take hands with me, / And rock the ground whereon these sleepers be.'[56] Courtly masques drew regularly on the imagery associated with the cosmic dance: in *Pleasure Reconciled to Virtue*, performed in 1618, Prince Charles and eleven noblemen danced to the music of thirty viols in order to drive away the disorderly characters of the anti-masque. Not all writers treated the cosmic dance with quite such reverence, but the currency of the metaphor is undeniable. In Marston's *The Scourge of Villanie*, a work of 1598, one character mocks a lover of dance by mentioning John Davies's grandiose

54 Brissenden, *Shakespeare and the Dance*, p. 4; Skiles Howard, *The Politics of Courtly Dancing in Early Modern England* (Amherst: University of Massachusetts Press, 1998), pp. 47–8; *Poems of Sir John Davies*, p. 101.

55 Elyot, *The Boke Named the Governour*, fos. 79r–86r. See also John M. Major, 'The Moralization of the Dance in Elyot's *Governour*', *Studies in the Renaissance* 5 (1958), 27–36.

56 Shakespeare, *A Midsummer Night's Dream*, in *Complete Oxford Shakespeare*, p. 593; Brissenden, *Shakespeare and the Dance*. For a more complex version of the argument, see also Howard, *Politics of Courtly Dancing*, ch. 3.

poem in close proximity to the more earthly (and earthy) dances associated with William Kemp, the period's most famous comic actor:

Praise but Orchestra and the skipping Art,
You shall commaund him; faith, you have his hart
Even capring in your fist. A hall, a hall,
Roome for the spheres! The orbes celestiall
Will daunce Kempes Jigge.[57]

Given the orderly potential of dance, it is not surprising that several early modern authors discussed it in relation to the cultural accomplishments proper to members of the aristocracy and gentry. In 1570, Roger Ascham identified dancing as one of the pastimes that was 'not onelie cumlie and decent, but also verie necessarie, for a Courtlie Jentleman to use'. Several decades later, John Playford was more fulsome in his recommendation. Dance, he observed, had been approved by a litany of ancient authors from Plato onwards and practised by the noble heroes of all ages. It was an excellent recreation, a promoter of strong and graceful bodies and 'a quality very much beseeming a Gentleman'.[58] Yet there was also a certain caution in the minds of those who offered lifestyle guidance to the gentry. Ascham attached to his recommendation of dance the condition that it be done 'in open place, and on the daylight', while Henry Peacham scarcely mentioned the subject at all when he published *The Compleat Gentleman* in 1622.

One important reason for such circumspection was the rapidity with which dancing became a controversial topic as the central focus of the debate shifted in the decades after about 1570. The humanist consensus of previous years was fractured by a fierce quarrel about the dangers of dance on all social levels, but particularly among the demographic majority. This concern, while not without precedent, rapidly achieved a new intensity, driven primarily by a group of Elizabethan Protestant moralists who found in popular dance far too many traces of sin, paganism and spiritual laxity. Without doubt, they were equally unhappy about some of what reportedly went on at court, but most of them were pragmatic enough to realise that the common people were an easier target. Between 1579 and 1583, at least five separate works attacked popular dance with unprecedented vehemence. Their authors comprised two

[57] Brissenden, *Shakespeare and the Dance*, p. 4; Smith, *Acoustic World*, pp. 92–3; John Marston, *The Scourge of Villanie* (London, 1598), H3v.

[58] Roger Ascham, *The Scholemaster* (London, 1570), p. 20; John Playford, *The English Dancing Master* (London, 1651), preface.

preachers (John Northbrook and Christopher Fetherston), two men of unknown background (Thomas Lovell and the anonymous author of *A Treatise of Daunses*) and the enigmatic Philip Stubbes.[59] In theory, their fiercest words were directed at the habit of Sunday dancing, and they therefore conceded that weekday dancers might be permitted to indulge themselves, provided of course that they did so in a state of sobriety and strict sexual segregation. In practice, they clearly did not believe that much of what the English got up to on any day of the week met these requirements, and their remarks on the particular practice of Sunday dancing therefore had a habit of shading into wider attacks on the pastime as a whole. The efforts of this quintet of writers set the tone for the more sporadic anti-dance publications of the century that followed, and it is therefore important to identify the salient features of their concerted critique (they were clearly familiar with one another's work).

The Elizabethan moralists hurled a barrage of adjectives at contemporary dance, and their chosen words tended to cluster around three dominant objections. Above all, most of the dancing they witnessed or heard about was 'filthy' (also 'lewd', 'stinking', 'wanton', 'shamelesse', 'fleshly' and 'lascivious'). The potent reproductive charge that was carried by most common forms of dancing rendered them entirely reprehensible. It was disgusting to see young men and women dancing 'in mingle mangle', and their cherished pastime comprised 'nothing els but impudent, shameles, and dissolute gestures, by which the lust of the flesh is awaked, stirred up, and inflamed, as well in men as in women'.[60] For Lovell, Sunday dancing was a form of 'spirituall whoredome', and he and others warned young people against looking for potential spouses at dance meetings. The risks were different for men and women, but far too great on both sides: a wife chosen for her dancing would surely be a 'wilde wanton' rather than a 'myld matrone', while a husband would more likely prove 'a spendall than a sparer'.[61] On balance, it was far better to seek one's spouse at a sermon. The Elizabethan moralists' penchant for statistics came to the fore in Fetherston's estimate that nine out of every ten girls who went into the woods with their sweethearts after dancing on May Day returned home pregnant (contemporary

59 Northbrooke, *Spiritus est Vicarius Christi in Terra*; Fetherston, *Dialogue*; Lovell, *Dialogue between Custom and Veritie*; *A Treatise of Daunses* (London, 1581); Stubbes, *Anatomie of Abuses*. See also Mary Pennino-Baskerville, 'Terpsichore Reviled: Antidance Tracts in Elizabethan England', *Sixteenth Century Journal* 22.3 (1991), 475–93.

60 *Treatise of Daunses*, A5r, A8v–B1r.

61 Lovell, *Dialogue between Custom and Veritie*, A5r, B6v; Fetherston, *Dialogue*, C8v–D1r.

fertility rates made this unlikely). Stubbes was less pessimistic, setting the figure at one in three, but he nevertheless regarded mixed dancing as a shocking sexual free-for-all, 'For what clipping, what culling, what kissing and bussing, what smouching & slabbering one of another, what filthie groping and uncleane handling is not practised every where in these dauncings?' (The words fall into a strong and obvious duple rhythm, as if Stubbes was drawing energy from the horrible habits of his adversaries.)[62]

Common dancing practices were also 'wild', 'devillish', 'unchristian', 'wicked' and 'heathen'. All too often, dancers appeared to be out of control, as if they had resigned themselves into the hands of some lower power. According to Fetherston, dancing men 'fling themselves into the aire, as if they would leape out of themselves'. Stubbes was always alarmed to see and hear morris dancers, 'their pipers pipeing, their drummers thundring, their stumps dauncing, their bels jyngling, their handkerchefs swinging about their heds like madmen'. Lovell was similarly concerned, and speculated in verse about how a typical dance might look to somebody who could not hear the music:

For if a man remoove him self
from place where they do skip:
And stop his eares from sound of pipe,
and see them only leap,
He would suppose them to be mad,
like men not wel in wit:
To see them leap towards heaven, & eke
the ground thump with their feet.[63]

In truth, every heavenward leap was a skip towards hell, and strenuous but not altogether successful attempts were made to demonstrate from Scripture that the evil of dance heavily outweighed its goodness. Here, the problem was that a great deal of Biblical dancing was clearly praiseworthy and expressive of admirable spiritual joy. The moralists dealt with this difficulty by arguing that the style of dancing favoured by the heroes of Scripture was modest, sober and sexually segregated. It bore no relation whatsoever to the lewd thrustings of the modern age, which, explained Lovell bluntly, 'stinck before the Lord'.[64] The prophet David, insisted

[62] Fetherston, *Dialogue*, D7v; Stubbes, *Anatomie of Abuses*, M4r, M8r–v.

[63] Fetherston, *Dialogue*, D3v; Stubbes, *Anatomie of Abuses*, M2v; Lovell, *Dialogue between Custom and Veritie*, D1v.

[64] Stubbes, *Anatomie of Abuses*, O1r; Lovell, *Dialogue between Custom and Veritie*, B5r–v.

Stubbes, had danced without the presence of either women or musical instruments 'to effeminate the minde' (it is interesting that dance could both soften men by making them womanish and harden them by inflaming their lust). He and others trawled the Scriptures for evidence that dancing led to death, devilry and disaster. The star turn was provided by Salome, whose lust-provoking dance deprived Herod of his judgement and John the Baptist of his head, but beyond this the moralists struggled for solid evidence. The anonymous author of 1581 was clearly unhappy with his meagre catch and resorted to arguing that warnings about the dangers of dance were implicit in Biblical injunctions against whoredom and adultery. Fetherston pointed out that Cicero had condemned dance, and used this fact to heap shame upon his contemporaries: 'Did the heathens thinke thus evil of dauncing, and shall not Christians thinke much the worse of the same?'[65]

Lastly, English dance betrayed its practitioners as 'vayne', 'idle', 'sluggish' and 'ignorant'. People thought too much of themselves and too little of God, a basic feature of the times that had appalling consequences. Self-love and moral laxity led English men and women to concentrate their dancing on the Lord's Day, when they should have been far more profitably occupied. The nation's young, complained Lovell, worshipped the idol of pleasure on the Sabbath and did 'service unto it with their bodyes'. Dance music pulled people towards it like moths to a candle, forming an attraction with which sermons could scarcely compete. Piper and preacher did battle for the ears of the English and, all too often, the former drowned out (and out-droned) the latter. Those who should have taken the dancers to task – parents, churchwardens and magistrates – were often guilty of looking on in bogus benevolence, preferring to earn the good will of their neighbours than that of Almighty God. Fetherston had harsh words for such individuals: 'here shall they have mirth and melodie but when as they are gone hence, mone and mourning, here shall they have solace and singing, but when they have left this life, sorrow, sobbing, and sighing'.[66]

The mixing of scurrility and divinity on Sundays was a product of the same mentality that allowed the use of dancing and other worldly pastimes in parochial efforts to raise money for church repairs. Lovell despised such pragmatism, and his response was predictably stern: 'Sinne may at no time

[65] Stubbes, *Anatomie of Abuses*, N4v; *Treatise of Daunses*, A5r, B4v–5r; Fetherston, *Dialogue*, D1r.

[66] Lovell, *Dialogue between Custom and Veritie*, dedicatory epistle; Fetherston, *Dialogue*, C6v (see also A3v–4r).

well be used.' People danced with a bodily vigour that was unmatched by the mental energy they put into the critical analysis of their pernicious obsession. In any case, even the physical activity of dancers had negative social and economic effects. According to Fetherston, dancing caused 'incurable diseases' (especially 'agues and shaking') through the bodily heat it generated, and it left many lame in later life. More immediately, exhausted servants lay 'snorting in hedges' as they endeavoured to recover from their exploits, and their masters lost valuable income as a result. Fetherston had heard stories about 'those which have daunced one halfe day for pleasure, and have laide in bedde two whole dayes for payne. Cal you this a recreation?'[67]

It was an interesting question, for one of the issues at stake was the nature of recreation itself. Fetherston defined it as

> a seconde making, or a making agayne of that thing which was once made, and by a metaphore we call it a refreshing of that thing which is wearied with much laboure (if it be applied unto the bodye): but if it be applied unto the mynde, we say it is a renewing of the minde beeyng worne with much labour & studie, greate cares, and unmeasuarable sorrowe.

Dancing, needless to say, did not meet his criteria because it wearied body and mind. True recreations, in Fetherston's book, included attending church, hearing sermons and receiving the sacrament. He urged his readers to rejoice in the Lord rather than in the sound of the pipe and tabor. 'If you will daunce this daunce, not onely I but all the Godly will daunce with you.'[68]

Five authors took four years to establish an anti-dance agenda that endured in its essentials for several decades, despite the many changes and challenges of the age. In 1633, the political climate was so tense that William Prynne lost his ears for a book denouncing dancing and other pastimes. He brought fresh passion and style to the debate, yet his objections were familiar:

> The way to Heaven is too steepe, too narrow for men to dance in, and keepe revell rout: No way is large or smooth enough for capering Roisters, for jumping, skipping, dancing Dames, but that broad beaten pleasant road that leads to Hell ... Men never went as yet by multitudes, much less by Morrice-dancing troopes to Heaven: Alas there are but few who finde that narrow way; they scarce goe two together.

[67] Lovell, *Dialogue between Custom and Veritie*, C1v; Fetherston, *Dialogue*, B1r–2r.

[68] Fetherston, *Dialogue*, A8v–B4v, B8r. See also Stubbes, *Anatomie of Abuses*, M8v.

H.S. put pen to paper in the kingless England of 1658, and his tone was particularly zealous, but he summoned Salome to illustrate his central point, just as his Elizabethan predecessors had done. And in 1661, Thomas Hall set his back against the permissiveness of Restoration England by printing for the first time 'The May Poles Speech to the Traveler', a revised version of an earlier manuscript poem. The talking maypole was a novelty, but the author's remarks concerning its pagan roots and the raucous disorder of its admirers could equally well have been made in 1580. Between the 1580s and the 1660s, English dance seemed to such individuals filthy, wild and vain.[69]

The first literary figures to defend dancing against this assault were the immensely endearing fictional characters dreamt up as whipping boys by the Elizabethan moralists. The fact that they were devised by their detractors makes it all the more remarkable that they too presented arguments that were built to last. Fetherston, Lovell, Northbrook and Stubbes all conceived their works in dialogue form, hoping thereby to communicate more effectively with the 'simple folke'. In each case, a sober puritan bashes his head for hours on end against the brick wall of English popular opinion as represented by a genial but heroically unreceptive youth. Only at the eleventh hour does a dramatic and implausible transformation overtake the young man as he at last sees the error of his ways ('oh, what a suddaine change do I feele in my self', exclaims one, 'even in a moment'). This amounts to a simultaneously spiritual and cultural conversion of the thunderbolt variety, the sort of experience that all zealous Protestants were supposed to have enjoyed. In this miraculous moment, filthy dancing becomes for these individuals a pastime of times past.[70]

Nevertheless, the trenchant defences of dancing mounted in earlier pages by these spokesmen for common culture seem more memorable than their ultimate conversions. The title page of Fetherston's book announced his intention to denounce 'light, lewde, and lascivious dauncing' by refuting 'all those reasons, which the common people use to bring in defence thereof'. Such reasons, though filtered through the moralising mind of each author and expressed only in abbreviated form, constituted a serious defence of dancing. Fetherston's 'Juvenis' and Lovell's 'Custom' are well qualified to lead us through this terrain. The latter accuses his personal adversary, 'Verity', of concentrating too keenly on isolated

[69] Prynne, *Histrio-mastix*, p. 244; H.S., *To the Musicioners*, p. 4; Hall, in *REED Somerset*, p. 736. See also Bownde, *The Doctrine of the Sabbath*; William Harrison, *The Difference of Hearers* (London, 1614); Henry Burton, *A Divine Tragedy Lately Acted* (London, 1641).

[70] Lovell, *Dialogue between Custom and Veritie*, B1r, E1r; Fetherston, *Dialogue*, E3v.

instances of bad dancing practice. It would be better, he suggests, if Verity were to calm himself down and acknowledge that 'The sober, wise, and wary take, / no harme at all by daunce'. In Fetherston's dialogue, Juvenis clearly agrees, and he encourages the puritanical 'Minister' either to contemplate the goodly flowers of the field as an aid to relaxation or, failing this, to join a monastery full of similarly joyless individuals (not a suggestion that was likely to appeal to a zealous Protestant clergyman). He recognises Minister as 'one of these busibodies which cannot abide dauncing' and invites him to learn from the sensibly permissive attitudes of most churchwardens and justices of the peace. These wise men understand, as Minister does not, that people – including the prophet David himself – sometimes need to dance.[71] The opponents of dance fail to grasp the fact that the practice is good for body and mind: 'It doeth recreate both, and for that cause mens servants having labored harde all the weeke, doe use to daunce upon the Sundays.' This was personal recreation as Juvenis understood it, and he associated dancing particularly with the exuberant energies of youth. Quite simply, it was an essential part of growing up. Custom was similarly nonplussed by the case against dance, and he tried to imagine how the youth of England might respond to a ban:

Our youthful race how shall we run,
wil lusty Lads reply:
On Saboths, Feasts and holy dayes
if you lay dauncing by?
Shall we sit dumpish, dum and still,
All day like stones in street?
With tripping toyes, and footing fine,
we wil eche other meet.[72]

Indeed, the notion of dance as a practice that encouraged meeting and greeting was an important one. Just as it recreated individuals, so it recreated communities. 'I pray you sir', Juvenis asked Minister, 'where shall young men and maydens meete together, if not at the dauncing place, and playing oke?' He was deliciously oblivious to his opponent's sensibilities, declaring at one point, 'I marvel very much why you should disprayse dauncing, sithence a great many have gotten their wyves, and that rich wives also, onely by dauncing.' In Juvenis's mind, dancing made good

[71] Lovell, *Dialogue between Custom and Veritie*, B5r–v, C1r; Fetherston, *Dialogue*, A1v, A7v, B2r–v.

[72] Fetherston, *Dialogue*, A8r–v; Lovell, *Dialogue between Custom and Veritie*, B7v–8r.

marriages and good marriages made healthy communities. Custom harped on the same string, arguing that the dancers in a town or village brought merriment not only to themselves but to 'all the people in that place'.[73] As his name implied, he was also conscious of the manner in which the tradition of dancing tied members of the current community to their predecessors and, indeed, to their as yet unborn descendants. Juvenis was typically blunt in advising Minister of the irresistible power of tradition: 'dauncing hath been used in your fathers time, and in your fathers fathers time, and will be used when you are both dead and rotten'. Dancing, far from being a source of disorder, was for Juvenis and Custom an honest and healthy outlet for youthful energies, and it actually had the effect of preventing crime. England's youth desired and deserved opportunities to let off steam, and there was plenty of time for them to quieten down and sober up in later life. Juvenis was uncompromising in blaming the suppressers of dancing for the rising tide of whoredom and thieving in English society. The skipping art had, in previous times, brought all disruptive energies into the open, where they could be managed and dissipated. Now, however, these energies were being slyly concealed and permitted to fester, to the obvious detriment of all. The developing campaign against dancing therefore endangered communities, even depriving parochial churches of the vital funds that harmless communal entertainment had traditionally helped to generate.[74]

Before long, others too were speaking up in defence of dancing, and the literary battle-lines that divided traditionalists from reformers lost little of their clarity before the later decades of the seventeenth century. Interestingly, the highly educated authors who served as apologists for dancing in the century after 1580 rarely strayed far from the agenda laid down by Juvenis and Custom, preferring their down-to-earth arguments to the head-in-the-clouds speculations of Sir John Davies and others. John Stowe followed Juvenis in arguing that the suppression of public dancing was likely to prove counter-productive, warning darkly that 'worser practises within doores are to be feared'. By 1660, the same argument had taken on a more urgently political aspect: in the aftermath of two decades of devastating disruption, William Cavendish advised the restored king that dancing and other diversions 'will amuse the peoples thoughts, & keepe them In harmles action which will free your Majestie from faction & Rebellion'. Juvenis and Custom had anticipated much of this, though later

[73] Fetherston, *Dialogue*, C7r, C8r; Lovell, *Dialogue between Custom and Veritie*, B8v.
[74] Fetherston, *Dialogue*, B5v, D6r; Lovell, *Dialogue between Custom and Veritie*, C1v.

authors did manage to develop and extend one or two of their arguments. In 1618, for example, the clergyman Christopher Windle claimed that Sunday dancing was not only an admissible recreation but an activity through which honest young men and women could 'show their joy, happiness and exultation in the Lord'. Far from being antithetical to worship, dancing was its most boisterous supporter. Windle further suggested that the 'contentious puritans' and 'useless busybodies' who sought to ban such dancing actually made it all too easy for Catholics to resist conversion. Recusants were able to argue that Protestantism, a religion that 'admits no happines', could not possibly be pleasing to God.[75]

One of the most intriguing statements in defence of dancing was not literary but pictorial. Decades before William Cavendish counselled Charles II, he had painted a comparable message on his ceiling in the Heaven Room at Bolsover Castle (Derbyshire). This extraordinary work of art, completed in 1619, depicts the ascension of Christ into the firmament (see Figure 7.6). Around him, eleven cherubs dance to the exuberant music provided by thirty more who together form a remarkable outer circle. The more normal arrangement, in which the musician stands inside the ring of dancers, is thus inverted. Music and dance are here presented as the producers and proclaimers of Christian unity, both in heaven and on earth. It has been observed that the cherubs look like ordinary Derbyshire folk rather than glamorous Italians, and in each corner of the painting one of them proudly holds up a page from Thomas Ravenscroft's recent work *Melismata. Musical Phansies, Fitting the Court, Citie and Countrye Humours.* This assures us that music is for all, though the particular part-song that is thus displayed suggests the intrusion of a distinctly aristocratic ego: it concerns Robin Hood, that heroic figure who, like Cavendish himself, had interests in Sherwood Forest (see Figure 7.7). Despite this, the painting is a thoroughly inclusive creation, and the central image of a dancing, upwardly mobile Christ seems to confront head-on the puritan insistence on the impossibility of dancing one's way into heaven. Here the members of a happy, mixed company appear to be doing just that.[76]

The dance debate cooled steadily in the decades following the Restoration in 1660. The failure of godly efforts to transform popular culture by

[75] Stowe, quoted by Rust, *Dance in Society*, p. 43; Cavendish, quoted by Forrest, *History of Morris Dancing*, p. 210; Windle, in *REED Cumberland, Westmorland, Gloucestershire*, pp. 403–4, 409, 412.

[76] Lucy Worsley, *Bolsover Castle* (St Ives: English Heritage, 2000), pp. 24–5; Collinson, 'Elizabethan and Jacobean Puritanism', p. 42; Timothy Mowl, *Elizabethan-Jacobean Style* (London: Phaidon Press, 1993), pp. 117–23.

Figure 7.6. The ceiling of the Heaven Room at Bolsover Castle was both an image of the ascension of Christ and a pointed statement about the positive social value of dancing and music within Jacobean society. Bolsover Castle, Derbyshire, English Heritage, Heaven Room painting, 1619.

ordinance during the 1650s left the critics of common dancing practices with little option but to scowl in private. Angry voices were still heard occasionally – in 1667 Solomon Eccles warned dancing masters to abandon their 'filthy practice' – but this form of recreation was rarely opposed with the kind of public passion that had characterised earlier decades. It is difficult to say whether this represented a comprehensive victory for traditionalists or merely an agreement to differ, but it is clear that dancers no longer had to watch their steps in quite the same way. The diary of Samuel Pepys does not present dancing as a morally controversial topic during the 1660s (except when he suspected his wife of committing adultery with her private instructor), nor did the ballads and chapbooks that Pepys collected in later decades portray dancing as a generally problematic pastime. There are traces of the old criticism in occasional warnings about the dangers – 'dancing in Bawdy-houses' appears on one

Figure 7.7. One of the Bolsover cherubs draws our attention to a page from Ravenscroft's *Melismata*, a work that aimed to bring court, city and country together in music. Bolsover Castle, Derbyshire, English Heritage, Heaven Room painting, 1619, detail.

chapbook list of five dangerous exercises – but most of the songs are peopled by model maidens and their carefree sweethearts, who join hands in green spaces to celebrate the community of youth. If a state of consensus regarding the validity of dance had at last returned to English culture, then it was one that accepted the social benefits of participation.[77]

(Dis)orderly dancing

It remains to consider in greater detail the often messy application of these contradictory ideas to the rough-and-tumble of everyday life in the towns and villages of England. Representatives of the rival camps in the literary dance debate articulated two very different visions of the Christian community, and their respective allies in the localities went energetically about the belligerent business of winning the day. For hard-line Protestant moralists, God himself showed the way, intervening regularly in earthly affairs to draw attention to the sinfulness of Sunday dancers. In the late 1630s, Henry Burton, angered by royal policy, gathered dozens of providential anecdotes and presented them to the world with grim glee. A Gloucestershire miller had watched his house burn to the ground after he staged a Whitsun ale, complete with dancing. Meanwhile in Sussex, a man made a scoffing quip about the pleasures of Sunday dancing, and died within a week (as did two other members of his family). And in

[77] Eccles, *A Musick-lector*, p. 14; *Strange Wonders of the World* (London, 1683), p. 3.

Somerset, a gentleman, recovering from an episode of severe pain in his feet, remarked that he planned to celebrate his return to form by dancing around the maypole on the following Lord's day. 'But behold the hand of the Lord', wrote Burton, 'for before he moved out of that place, he was smitten with such a feeblenesse of heart, and dizzinesse in the head, that desiring help to carry him to an house, he died before the Lords day came, so fearfull it is to fall into the hands of the living God.'[78]

Divine efforts at the reformation of English dancing were also supported by an evolving and varied corpus of earthly legislation. Concern over the relationship between dancing, morality and worship had received periodic expression since at least the twelfth century, but levels of anxiety were unusually high during the decades between 1570 and 1660.[79] Legislators were in broad agreement regarding the need to prohibit dancing that either coincided with church services or took place in the sacred space of the church or churchyard. These were therefore fairly common stipulations in visitation articles of the period (dancing was only rarely mentioned specifically, but we can assume that it was encompassed within more general enquiries about sports, games and pastimes). An influential set was produced by Archbishop Toby Matthew for the province of York in 1607. He asked all ministers and churchwardens 'Whether are there within your saide parish or chappellry any rush bearings, bull-baitings, may-games, morrice-dances, ailes, or any such like prophane pastimes or assemblies on the sabboth to the hinderance of prayers, sermons, or other godly exercises'. Occasionally, bishops and archdeacons asked more specifically for information regarding any dancing that had taken place on church property or any ministers who had abused themselves by dancing. Particularly licentious or anti-social forms of dancing were covered implicitly by articles on immorality or disorder, but these were sometimes augmented by local, secular authorities. In 1554 and 1603, for example, attempts were made in Newcastle upon Tyne to prevent the city's apprentices from dancing publicly in the streets, particularly at night. In London, the common council attempted in 1582 to ban apprentices from attending dancing schools, which were evidently perceived in some quarters as dens of depravity.[80]

[78] Burton, *Divine Tragedy*, pp. 6–7, 10–11.

[79] For an earlier example, see *REED Herefordshire, Worcestershire*, pp. 396, 598.

[80] *Visitation Articles and Injunctions of the Early Stuart Church*, vol. I, pp. 59, 70, 181; *REED Newcastle upon Tyne*, pp. 25, 139; Common Council ruling, quoted by Winn, 'Bibliography', p. 132.

Beyond these basic priorities, however, there was continual tension between those who were happy to press no harder and those who felt the need to extend or reinforce existing prohibitions. In May 1585, Bishop Thomas Cooper of Winchester sent out a letter to the ministers, churchwardens and constables of his diocese, ordering a ban on all 'Church Ales, maygames, morish daunces, and other vaine pastimes upon the Sabath dayes'. He had clearly been reading his Lovell and Stubbes, for he denounced such pastimes as 'heathenish' and lamented the fact that people regarded communal ales as a legitimate method of raising money for church repairs.[81] He further instructed his ministers to call upon the justices of the peace in order to deal with particularly obstinate offenders. In several other regions, Protestant zealots did indeed turn to secular justice in order to bolster their efforts. In Lancashire, puritanical clergymen and magistrates expended tremendous energy between the 1580s and the 1610s in issuing orders that were designed to cleanse the Sabbath of 'Enormities'. Most of their commands concentrated on activities that directly disrupted church services, but in 1616 the justices of the county went further, ordering 'That theire be no Pippinge, dauncinge, Bowlinge, Beare, or Bull baitinge or any other prophanation upon anie sabboth daie in any parte of the daie'. Comparable instincts were at work in Somerset, Dorset and Devon, where festive dancing was permanently in the sights of those who sought to eradicate the traditional church feasts or wakes of the region by banning them via the courts of assize and quarter sessions.[82]

Not surprisingly, such efforts met with stern resistance from influential individuals who felt greater sympathy for the common and customary culture of their localities. Such people appear to have been particularly determined and resourceful during the years between 1615 and 1635. This twenty-year period began promisingly for England's dancers when the influential friends of traditional culture in Lancashire persuaded James I that orderly Sunday pastimes were a force for the common and national good. On 24 May 1618, the 'King's Declaration Concerning Lawful Sports' (commonly known as the Book of Sports) extended to the whole country a relatively permissive set of orders that had initially been applied to Lancashire alone. James took issue with the 'Puritanes & precise people' who had participated in 'the prohibiting and unlawfull punishing of Our good people for using their lawfull Recreations, and

[81] LM/COR/3/377, SHC. For comparable examples, see Collinson, 'Elizabethan and Jacobean Puritanism', p. 37.

[82] *REED Lancashire*, pp. xxiv–xxvi, 228; *REED Somerset*, pp. 432–8; *REED Devon*, pp. 293–300; *REED Dorset, Cornwall*, p. 119.

honest exercises upon Sundayes and other Holy dayes'. Henceforward, he ordered, people were not to be obstructed in their pursuit of such recreations, provided that these took place 'after the ending of all Divine Service' for the day and did not compromise public worship and due reverence in any way. Suitable pastimes included archery, leaping, vaulting, may games and 'dauncing, either men or women'.[83] In Somerset, the climactic year was 1633: Charles I intervened directly in the tense local debate, just as his father had done in Lancashire, and forced the revocation of all previous judicial orders that had banned customary church wakes and feasts, along with the dancing that was one of their central characteristics. Lord Chief Justice Richardson was severely rebuked for his part in spearheading the assault on traditional culture, and the Book of Sports was reissued for proclamation from the pulpits of the entire nation. Both editions of this famous and controversial text exerted some influence over the content of visitation articles, a few of which came to include inquiries about dancing that had taken place 'before the end of all divine Service appointed for that day' or, more simply, 'before evening prayers'.[84]

By the mid-1630s, 'Puritanes & precise people' were on the back foot in their struggle to discipline dancers. Richard Baxter would later recall a childhood during which his godly family struggled to sing psalms at home on Sunday against the head-piercing background noise of the dancers and their piper out in the street.[85] During the 1640s and 1650s, however, the puritans stepped forward once more, using parliamentary authority and the secular courts in a renewed effort to impose their will upon the population. In theory, dancing was curtailed to an unprecedented degree. In September 1641, members of the Long Parliament ordered that 'the Lord's Day should be duly observed and sanctified' and that 'all dancing or other sports either before or after divine service be forborne and restrained'. This requirement was periodically repeated and reinforced during the 1640s, and the regulations of the subsequent decade were just as demanding. In 1650, the Rump Parliament ordered all justices to take action against those whose notion of Sunday sobriety encompassed 'dancing, profanely singing, drinking or tippling'. Four years later, 'An Ordinance for Ejecting Scandalous, Ignorant and Insufficient Ministers' defined as reprehensible the habit of allowing morris dancers to perform,

[83] The declarations are reproduced in *REED Cumberland, Westmorland, Gloucestershire*, pp. 367–9, and *REED Lancashire*, pp. 229–31 (see also p. 369).

[84] *REED Somerset*, pp. 426–9, 438–47, 485; *REED Herefordshire, Worcestershire*, p. 59; *Visitation Articles and Injunctions of the Early Stuart Church*, vol. II, p. 120.

[85] Baxter, *The Divine Appointment*, pp. 116–17.

apparently on any day of the week. In 1657, 'An act for the better observation of the Lords day' imposed a hefty ten-shilling fine on 'Every person Dauncing, or prophanely Singing or Playing upon Musical Instruments' on Sundays.[86] At the Restoration, the tide turned again. In the decades that followed, neither visitation articles nor acts of parliament mentioned dancing with any regularity. The concerns of officialdom had clearly shifted decisively.

At the end of our period, therefore, dancers were relatively free to frolic, and serious disputes were rare. In earlier decades, however, discord over dancing had been a more frequent and widespread phenomenon in the localities, its rise and eventual fall mirroring the contours of concern that were visible in the varied legislation. The earliest cases arose during the 1570s, but most were concentrated in the first three decades of the seventeenth century. Confrontations of one sort or another were recorded in all regions of the country, but they were at their fiercest and most regular in the western counties (Herefordshire, Worcestershire, Shropshire, Gloucestershire, Somerset, Dorset and Devon). Herefordshire was a key battleground, and the chronology of its dance cases was mirrored elsewhere in the turbulent western region. As many as 153 such cases were recorded in Herefordshire between 1570 and 1640, with the heaviest concentrations in the 1610s (55 cases) and the 1620s (53 cases). Overall, we witness an increase in cases between 1570 and 1590, followed by a small dip during the 1590s and a rapid acceleration between 1600 and 1630. The single year that produced the highest number of cases was 1619–20, when thirty men and women were reported for dancing. In contrast, the 1630s generated a mere five cases altogether. It seems that the first Book of Sports, unlike the second, generated controversy by simultaneously encouraging the defenders of dance and leaving their opponents with little option but to enforce the letter of the new law with as much rigour as they could muster. There were particular hotspots even within regions of high tension. Such centres of controversy were probably defined by the presence of unusually militant individuals on both sides of the argument. It is certainly difficult to imagine an alternative explanation for the concentration of trouble in the widely distributed Herefordshire parishes of Ross, Tedstone Delamere, Withington, Yazor and Colwall. Ross topped the rankings with forty dance disputes, a figure that contrasts strikingly with the seventeen cases known to have arisen in the entire county of

[86] Christopher Durston, 'Puritan Rule and the Failure of Cultural Revolution', pp. 214, 226; Forrest, *History of Morris Dancing*, p. 207; *Acts and Ordinances of the Interregnum*, pp. 1163–4.

Sussex during the same period. Here, tension over dancing was by no means unknown but appears to have been uncommon, perhaps because the Sabbatarian agenda was more widely accepted by the general population in this county than it was by people further west. The peak years, as in Herefordshire, were between 1600 and 1630, though the fact that only twelve cases have been traced during this period hardly suggests acute and continual tension.[87]

Cases took a variety of forms. By far the largest category of dancing deviants comprised those who allegedly indulged themselves at the wrong time. Sometimes, this meant in the middle of the night or at other unseasonable hours. The majority, however, stood accused of dancing when they should have been in church. In about 1600, for example, a servant named Arthur was reported at visitation 'for dauncinge at tyme of divine service' in Tedstone Delamere (Herefordshire). Arthur clearly felt picked upon, and he claimed in his defence 'that mooste parte of the youth of the parishe did daunce at service tyme'. Inevitably, the judge ordered him to identify the other culprits, but Arthur, 'being demaundede who they wer . . . saide he woulde not name any [of] them'. He was loyal, if not tactically astute. Frequently, the inquisitorial spotlight fell not upon the dancers but upon their patrons (commonly alehouse-keepers) and their musicians. In May 1637, John Sprigg of Tuxford (Nottinghamshire) was in trouble 'for suffering young people to dance att his house in tyme of divyne service', while 'Tho[mas] Haggs musitians' were reported for playing the tunes.[88]

Individuals of acute moral sensitivity sometimes attempted to tighten the temporal restrictions upon Sunday dancing. In most counties, dancers and their facilitators were now and again reported for pursuing their activities on the Sabbath, even if they had dutifully avoided service time. Early in 1588, the Lancashire gentleman Adam Holte must have been surprised and affronted to hear that the local churchwardens had reported him to the court of quarter sessions for hosting a Christmas dancing session in his own house 'uppon the Saobothe daye in the Eveninge beinge eyther the Laste Sunday in december or the fyrste in Januarie'. Five years

[87] See the *REED* volumes for the following counties: Herefordshire and Worcestershire; Shropshire; Cumberland, Westmorland and Gloucestershire; Somerset; Dorset and Cornwall; Devon; and Sussex. Dance disputes were also relatively rare in the dioceses of Ely and Norwich. Lancashire produced surprisingly few cases, though it seems certain that many of the pipers who fell foul of the law had been caught playing for dancers, even if the sources did not generally record the fact.

[88] *REED Dorset, Cornwall*, p. 208; *REED Herefordshire, Worcestershire*, p. 168; AN/PB 341/4/45, HL.

later, William Wakeford of Petworth (Sussex) admitted to the church court that he had danced and played at maygames on Sundays, 'but not in service tyme'. His defence was swiftly crushed by the judge, who warned Wakeford 'to kepe holy the saboth days & not to prophane the same'. At Easter in 1618, a group of men and women received the communion in church at Huntspill (Somerset), but attracted the attention of the ecclesiastical judge for what they did immediately afterwards: 'in verie prophane manner', they allegedly 'daunced in the house of one Hooper of the same parishe to the scandall & offence of theire honest, and well disposed neighbors'.[89]

After 1618, however, it became much more difficult for precisians to bring general charges against those who 'profaned the Sabbath' by dancing. The Book of Sports set the goalposts more firmly into the ground and was clearly welcomed by England's dancers as a royal licence to operate. Admittedly, the book does not appear to have been rigorously enforced in all regions, but there is evidence to suggest that, on both sides of the conflict, it soon established itself as a significant point of reference. Reluctantly, those who brought accusations became more likely to concentrate on dancers who had failed to attend church or whose fun had begun in the supposedly quiet and reflective period between morning and evening prayer. The precisians were clearly unwilling to give up the fight, and some counties – Lancashire, Herefordshire and Shropshire, for example – witnessed small surges in carefully worded accusations against dancers. In Mathon (Worcestershire), several young men and women were reported to the consistory court in 1624 'for daunceinge uppon the Sabbath day before Eveninge prayer'. They were lucky enough to have a sympathetic curate who knew the Book of Sports just as thoroughly as his opponents. Edward Reese therefore wrote directly to the Bishop of Worcester, insisting that 'our yong people in this respect are verie orderly and carefull, takeinge noe further libertie then is by the Kings Majestie allowed for their recreations uppon the Sabbath day, being conforme in comeinge to devine service upon those daies wherein they daunce' (though he admitted that they might have erred on one solitary feast day). On the rare occasions when the scrupulous strayed beyond the book in framing their charges, they sometimes found that England's dancers were ready to set them straight. In 1624, several Wiltshire men were reported for attending 'a dancing match upon a Sunday after evening prayer'. One of

[89] *REED Lancashire*, p. 89; *REED Sussex*, p. 40; *REED Somerset*, p. 141.

them responded by telling the court that such dance meetings were perfectly admissible under the terms set out in the Book of Sports.[90]

Not everybody studied the Book of Sports quite so assiduously. In 1623, the churchwardens of Yapton (Sussex) sounded hazy and lazy when they responded to an enquiry from their archdeacon. They admitted that dancing took place in their parish every Sunday during the hours between morning and evening prayer, adding the deflective remark, 'now whether this bee lawfull or noe wee referre to the Court to Judge'. It was partly to deal with such uncertainty that Charles I reissued the book in 1633, and the recycled text once again emerged as an important touchstone in dancing disputes. In 1634–5, for example, Richard Lovell of Wells (Somerset) was reported to the church court 'for heweinge and trimmeinge of a maypole uppon a sabbath daie in the morneinge when the bell tolled to prayer'. He was not accused of failing to attend divine service, but in performing this crude carpentry at the last minute he had, as it were, been cutting it fine. The churchwardens were determined to get their man, though they also knew that activities preparatory to dancing occupied a grey area and might not be sufficient to secure a conviction. They therefore strengthened the charge by alleging 'that the May pole was sett upp before eveninge prayer contrarie to his Majesties Declaration And that there was a drumbe beate upp att the settinge upp of the maypole' (a sonic rival to the tolling church bell). Nobody actually danced before evening prayer began, but Lovell was obviously setting the scene and his musicians were warming up their instruments (they too were presented to the court). It appears that Lovell and his critics knew the rules equally well, and both parties hoped that they had done just enough to secure their goals. As it transpired, the ecclesiastical judges sided with the presenting officers, and Richard Lovell was ordered to don the customary clothes of contrition and acknowledge his fault before the entire congregation.[91] Here was a small victory for the precisians of Somerset, but such moments appear to have been rare during the 1630s. Instead, Laudian domination of high church office seems to have dissuaded the enemies of Sunday dancing from pursuing their objectives through the ecclesiastical courts, and the number of cases declined markedly in most regions. These were dark days for disciplinarians, and Richard Baxter later recalled that the Book of Sports had made it difficult for ministers to

[90] *REED Herefordshire, Worcestershire*, pp. 384–5 (see also the volumes covering Lancashire and Shropshire); Underdown, *Revel, Riot and Rebellion*, p. 84.

[91] *REED Sussex*, p. 181; *REED Somerset*, pp. 384–5.

instil godliness in their congregations. Admittedly people came to church, but they did so with their thoughts firmly fixed on the dancing that was to follow, 'And sometimes the Morrice-Dancers would come into the Church, in all their Linnen and Scarfs and Antick Dresses, with Morrice-bells jingling at their leggs. And as soon as Common Prayer was read, did haste out presently to their play again. Was this a Heavenly Conversation? Was this a help to holiness and Devotion?'[92]

Total opposition to Sunday dancing was a product of the Reformation and can be associated particularly – though not exclusively – with puritanism. The hottest Protestants were concerned primarily with the defence of holy time, though in practice they doubtless shared with many moderates an anxiety regarding the profanation of sacred space. This anxiety was much older than Protestantism, but the regular reiteration of the rules during the reigns of Elizabeth I and the first two Stuart kings altered the picture somewhat. The decades between 1570 and 1640 produced a steady trickle of cases in which men and women stood accused of dancing not at the wrong time, but in the wrong place. In 1617, for example, Lewis Thomas of Pembridge (Herefordshire) reportedly 'daunced in the church porch amongst a companie of girles of the parrishe'. A century earlier, he might just have got away with it, but in mid-Jacobean England Thomas was chancing his arm. In Somerset, the issue surfaced repeatedly, and it inevitably became entangled in wider arguments over the legitimacy of church ales and the relationship between dancing and devotion. On a Sunday evening in 1580, a man from Frome walked through the churchyard and 'found a minstrell plaing ... uppon a rebick having many youths about him daunsing'. He was not impressed and duly rebuked the company 'for daunsing in the churchyard' (further details of this interesting case are now illegible). At the same date, the churchwardens of Glastonbury were themselves reported to the ecclesiastical authorities for organising a church ale during which the morris dancers actually performed in the church. The wardens' relaxed attitude to the relationship between sociable recreation and sacred space was thoroughly traditional and was probably shared by the individuals who occasionally saw fit to store their freshly cut maypoles in the church. In 1587, John Cornishe of Pawlett 'didd sett upp the may pole in the steple or tower of the church'. He claimed to have done so 'for a meryment' and to safeguard the pole against thieves.[93] Thirteen years later, Stephen Baker

[92] Baxter, *The Divine Appointment*, p. 117.

[93] *REED Herefordshire, Worcestershire*, p. 157; *REED Somerset*, pp. 121, 129, 202.

of Catcott also used the 'merriment' defence. He was in trouble firstly 'for bringing a somer pole into the church' and secondly for using the steeple bells to ring a peal, 'naming yt to be the somer poles Knell' (this mock-ritual presumably marked the end of the season's festivities). He was dismissed with a warning after he denied any intention to cause offence and produced several witnesses who were prepared to testify that it had only been a bit of fun.[94]

The language of the investigators in this case was interesting. Baker was asked about 'the profanacion of the temple', an expression that seemed to anticipate later Laudian sensitivities over sacred space. We might compare it with the terms used in 1634 by Bishop Piers, Laud's ally in the diocese of Bath and Wells: he was disturbed to learn that a chapel in East Coker had been 'prophan'd diverse ways, and at diverse times heretofore, by weddinge dinners kept there, and by dancinge in the Chappell at those weddinges'.[95] In between the two dates, the ecclesiastical courts had also dealt with allegations of churchyard dancing in North Wootton (1611), Pitcombe (1615), Dundry (1621) and Catcott (1625).[96] Clearly, the habit had not died out completely despite the pressure under which it had been placed. In 1637 the churchwardens of Portishead were reported for their general tolerance of 'fives playeinge, dauncing, Cudgill playeinge, and fightinge in the churchyard there'.[97] Such inveterate traditionalism was, however, probably unusual by this date, for most Protestants agreed that the church and its precincts were inappropriate settings for primarily secular pastimes. In the course of fifty years, prevalent attitudes to dancing in or near the church had shifted dramatically. Where once it had seemed a more or less tolerable recreational pursuit, it now carried with it the unmistakable scent of sacrilege.

Equally conspicuous were the dancers who aggravated their offences by descending further into sin, thus demonstrating neatly the supposed link between dancing and debauchery. In Elizabethan Kent, zealous ministers and churchwardens were painfully aware that the people were 'styrred to wantonnes' by dancing, and their fears were amply justified on an evening in 1579 when a group of soldiers allegedly danced 'starke naked' on the streets of Queenborough. They were apparently enjoying a final fling before heading overseas, and the sound of their hired piper acted as a siren to Elizabeth Brett, a lustful old widow who was already well known

[94] *REED Somerset*, p. 72. [95] Ibid., p. 113.
[96] Ibid., pp. 185, 206, 100, 72 (in order cited).
[97] Ibid., p. 207.

'for keping of naughtye Rewle in her howse'. She and her daughter eagerly took to the streets and joined in the dancing, 'without all shame'.[98] Such conspicuous cases were isolated in all regions, but they can help us to understand how one puritan clergyman in Wiltshire came to hold the furious opinion 'that all women and maids that were singers and dancers were whores, and as many as did look upon them no better than they' (male dancers were evidently not quite so repulsive). He would certainly not have relished the situation that developed in a house in Dorchester (Dorset) on a spring evening in 1634. Before a mixed company, Walter Haggard promised to give a man named Buck a loaf of bread if he would dance before them and 'shew forth his privy members to the women then in the chamber'. Buck kindly obliged, though he may have experienced second thoughts when one of the women 'took a candle and lighted to the said Buckes members that they might be seene'. Before the borough court, she claimed ignorance of the injury he thereby sustained (bravely, he kept his mouth shut and did not 'complayne of any harme' until some time later).[99]

The county of Somerset, rarely outdone in such matters, generated a small but impressive number of similarly compelling cases. In Glastonbury, it was the punishment rather than the crime that must have caught the eyes and ears of passers-by on a summer's day in 1617. Some time previously, Nicholas Ruddock and Katherine Chauker had danced together on a Sunday and, when one thing led to another, she had become pregnant with his 'base childe'. The case was heard at quarter sessions, and the two judges ordered that the couple be whipped through the streets 'untill their bodies shalbe both bloody'. It was further commanded 'that there shalbe during the time of their whipping two fiddles playeing before them in regard to make it knowne their lewdnes in begetting the said base childe uppon the sabboth day coming from danceing.' Here was an attempt by two creative magistrates to reform popular culture by turning it upon itself. The link between dancing and debauchery was even more direct at Broomfield on All Saints' Day in 1633. In the evening, Thomas Cornish allegedly had sex with Joane Coale up against the village maypole, a choice of location that must have seemed exciting at the time but that ultimately proved misguided: Thomas's rhythmic movements 'made a bell hanging on topp of the pole to ring out whereby he was ... discovered & by some seene'. The phallic symbolism of the maypole can rarely have been

98 *REED Kent*, pp. 304, 819–21. For more nude dancing, see Martin Ingram, *Church Courts, Sex and Marriage in England, 1570–1640* (Cambridge: Cambridge University Press, 1987), p. 240, and Underdown, *Revel, Riot and Rebellion*, p. 95.

99 Underdown, *Revel, Riot and Rebellion*, p. 59; *REED Dorset, Cornwall*, p. 205.

more beautifully illustrated. Dancing could indeed inflame lust and reduce self-control, and no dancer revealed the risks more conspicuously than Henry Pillchorne of Bridgwater. One wild night in 1639, he reportedly 'daunced with his britches downe about his heeles in the house of one John Chute . . ., and did show his privie members unto the companie most uncivillie there being then many women present, and said he did daunce Piddecocke bolt upright, and readie to fight'. The precise meaning of the final clause is perhaps best left to the reader's imagination.[100]

Others aggravated matters not by debauchery but by defiance. When Catherine Jones of Aston Botterell (Shropshire) was rebuked by her minister for dancing on the Sabbath in 1608, she apparently made little effort to respond with due deference. 'I care not for parson Acton', she was heard to say, 'toord [turd] in his teathe; I will dance on the Saboath daie in despite of him even at his nose.' A few years later, Nicholas Vocle of Winforton (Herefordshire) was singled out by his minister as the chief upholder of Sunday dancing. Vocle, when warned to cease such dancing, declared that 'he would have it in despite of Sir Priest or Sir Parson' (old-fashioned terms of address that were probably calculated to cause offence). We have already encountered Richard Serle, the constable of Alton (Hampshire) who, in 1615, struggled to arrest an allegedly disorderly minstrel. According to Serle, the musician had come to town partly to feed the dance addiction of a raucous band of locals who gathered expectantly at the summer house. The constable's bill of complaint demonstrates the depth of feeling on both sides of the confrontation. When he politely requested that the dancers postpone their recreation until another day 'more meete for the same', John Abrey answered angrily, saying 'they would doe it that day or not at all'. Serle struggled manfully to arrest the minstrel, but the dancers stationed a lookout on top of the summer house while they proceeded to recreate themselves within. If ever the poor constable came close to success, the dancers assaulted him, throwing him into the dirt and inciting one another to tread upon him. John Farrington *alias* Verndell called him 'puritan' and mocked his habit of gadding to godly sermons in order to 'heare the devill'. A local gentleman endeavoured to calm the mob down, but they chanted 'agayne, agayne' and returned to the attack. This was a fight for the cultural heart of a community, and the dancers were also heard to shout 'the towne is ours' as they went about their business. It is striking that all the named defendants in this case were men, though we can safely assume that the

100 *REED Somerset*, pp. 133, 3, 60 (in order cited).

defenders of dancing in Alton were a mixed company.[101] The women, as so often, exerted their influence beyond our auditory field.

There is nothing in this case to suggest that the constable suspected his opponents of recusancy, though in some circumstances Protestants of all shades clearly did believe that stubborn and resourceful Catholics were deliberately dancing to wreck the Reformation. In 1660, John Barwick looked back on the years around 1617 and commented,

> It was no small policie in the leaders of the Popish party to keep the people from Church by danceing and other recreations, even in the time of divine service, especially on holy days and the Lords Day in the after noon. By which meanes they kept the people in ignorance and luke warmnesse, and so made them the more capable to be wrought upon by their emissaries.

Barwick was no puritan, but the same opinion had been held for several decades by the fiery Protestants who shouldered the distinctly unenviable task of carrying the Reformation to Lancashire. In between, it appears to have been almost a commonplace in Cheshire that shady recusancy and Sunday recreation danced hand in hand. In 1628, Anne Hughes was presented to the diocesan authorities as 'a seduceinge papist and for daunceinge upon the Saboth daie'.[102]

In a number of cases, clerics and churchwardens were themselves reported to the courts, either for failing to prosecute dancers or for irresponsibly joining in the jollity. In Elizabethan Surrey, one clergyman caused offence by dancing in his shirt at a house in Guildford, while another was reported for leading the dancing at a wedding feast. The latter's behaviour, according to his accusers, was 'a discredit to [his] calling, a sport to papistes, and a greefe to honest men' (the curate in question was also said to be a seducer of women and a connoisseur of fashionable continental clothes, hence his nickname, 'Parson Newcut').[103] In Farleigh Hungerford (Somerset), it was the churchwarden William Mathew who had allegedly disgraced his office: according to his critics, Mathew was 'a keeper of brawling & swearing companie and minstrelsye & dauncing in his house' when he and his friends should have been in church. Many more churchwardens merely turned a blind eye to dancing, but they too could find themselves in the church courts for their

[101] *REED Shropshire*, p. 11; *REED Herefordshire, Worcestershire*, p. 175; STAC 8 262/11, NA.

[102] John Barwick, *Hieronikes* (London, 1660), p. 80; *REED Lancashire*, pp. xxiv–xxvi; Baldwin, *Paying the Piper*, p. 51.

[103] LM/768, SHC. To catch a glimpse of some more dancing vicars, try Baldwin, *Paying the Piper*, p. 51, and *REED Herefordshire, Worcestershire*, p. 180.

negligence. In 1609, the officers at Costock (Nottinghamshire) were reported by their parson 'for that they would not present at the last visitacion that a piper was suffred in a barne of Tho Morri[s] to withhould all the youth for the most part at dancing in prayer tyme, in the afternone, on Aprill 25 ... being St Markes day'.[104]

Finally, there were cases in which dancing was not the central cause of trouble but instead a serviceable weapon that could be used to humiliating effect in broader interpersonal disputes. In 1608, a team of morris dancers was allegedly recruited at Strelley (Nottinghamshire) in order to inject its own militaristic brand of madness into Huntingdon Beaumont's efforts to intimidate his enemy, John Martyn. This was a financial dispute between gentlemen, but Beaumont knew the value of hiring some musical muscle from among the lower orders. According to the bill of complaint, he therefore 'contrived and plotted' with the morris dancers, inviting them to dance their way to Strelley with the sole purpose of bullying Martyn and his allies. The dancers' pithy brief was 'to quarrell with them and beat them'. Martyn recalled that one dancer had worn a vizor while the rest had all played their parts in disguise. The tactic was clearly designed to ensure that the ensemble was both menacing and anonymous (none of the dancers was named). When the visitors entered town, they gave every appearance of coming 'in sportinge daunceinge and jestinge fashion'. This, however, was just another layer of disguise, though it must have been one that was difficult to don with conviction, given that the dancers were also 'armed and arrayed in warlik Manner with Swords daggers Pickforkes pike staves and other weapons as well invasive as defensive'. In any case, they soon abandoned their dancing and proceeded to assault Mr Martyn, according to their instructions. Indeed, he might have sustained serious injury had he not been rescued by onlookers.[105]

The merits of dancing were obviously at issue in many English communities during the years between 1580 and 1660. On very rare occasions, the agents of cultural reformation hit back at trenchant traditionalism not with irate words and legal cases but with dancing – albeit somewhat satirical – of their own. In the mid-1640s, royalist opinion was outraged by reports of an incident at Peterborough Cathedral. Parliamentarian soldiers had raided the church and stolen 'a

[104] *REED Somerset*, p. 118 (see also p. 386); AN/PB 293/8/37, HL. There are comparable examples in *REED Sussex*, pp. 25–6, 39, and *REED Herefordshire, Worcestershire*, pp. 63, 69, 73, 152, 156.

[105] STAC 8 215/13, NA.

paire of organs' before 'piping with the very same about the market-place, whilst their Comrades daunced after them, some in Coapes, others with Surplices'. Of course, the account may be grossly exaggerated, but it is also possible that the soldiers were deliberately deploying the cultural vocabulary of their enemies in order to drive their point home. Organs, pipers, ecclesiastical vestments and public dancing were all symbols of royalism, Laudianism and customary culture. In Peterborough, they were purposefully ridiculed by parliamentarians who – we should also note – knew enough about the conventions of their enemies to put on a mocking show. As always, there were points of contact between opponents.[106]

By 1660, passions were at last beginning to fade. At the Restoration, the godly minister Adam Martindale faced one of the last blasts of active defiance in Cheshire. His local enemies sought to affront him 'by setting up a May-pole in my way to the church'. This symbolic erection, deliberately placed on a site that was associated by custom with Sunday music and dancing, attracted what the minister called 'a randezvouz of rake-hells'. Martindale, in his own version at least, proved more than a match for them. He allowed the dancers some time to cool off, and then he began preaching against maypoles as 'a relique of the shamefull worship of the Strumpet Flora in Rome'. He clearly hoped that this would leave the maypole with few friends in the parish. Just in case the tactic failed, however, a more direct approach was also adopted, and here we are afforded a welcome glimpse of forceful female agency: 'my wife, assisted with three young women, whipt it downe in the night with a framing-saw'. Martindale and his supporters had thus won a local battle for the puritan cause, but it was too little and too late.[107]

Of course, court cases draw our attention towards the extremes of behaviour, privileging the militant, the malicious and the maladjusted. The result can be a distillation of disputation and a misguided impression that dancing, in the fractured communities of early modern England, was almost inevitably divisive. Discord dominates the air, and centre-stage belongs to those who did active service in the battle to define dance in one of two ways: either as an orderly pursuit that benefited human society and even pleased God; or as something devilish and disorderly that

[106] John Barwick, quoted by Winn, 'Bibliography', pp. 331–2. The same event is, I think, referred to more cryptically in Henry King, *Poems, Elegies and Paradoxes* (London, 1664), p. 27.

[107] *The Life of Adam Martindale, Written by Himself*, ed. Richard Parkinson, *Remains Historical and Literary Connected with the Palatine Counties of Lancaster and Chester, Chetham Society* 4 (1845), pp. 156–7.

endangered social harmony and undermined true religion. As ever, the majority of the population probably occupied the ground between and did their best to avoid the wrath of passionate precisians and turbulent traditionalists alike. To the historian, they appear deeply reticent, for they also avoided the written record like the plague. At the time, however, they presumably played some role as brokers between those who glared angrily at one another from opposite ends of the spectrum. Members of the silent majority almost certainly continued to dance while the controversy raged around them, but they perhaps became more conscious of the need to be cautious on Sundays and to distance themselves from conduct that was purposefully provocative or obviously disgraceful. They rarely spoke loudly enough for historians to hear, but once in a while we catch a snatch or two. In 1634, Peter Gray of Compton Bishop (Somerset) was in trouble. It was rumoured that he had behaved appallingly on Shrove Sunday, stripping to his shirt in a local inn before dancing around the room making a series of 'verie unseemelie gesture'. Moreover, he had done so in the presence of his neighbours, most of whom were 'ashamed thereof'. These individuals were clearly not zealots – they were, after all, drinking in the inn on Sunday – but they were nevertheless troubled by Gray's cavorting.[108]

Dancing through society

The defining polarities of the picture may also be softened somewhat by an exploration of the ways in which dancing articulated more normal social relations. We have already encountered evidence of its important role in facilitating social contact between individuals of differing rank. To optimistic observers, this phenomenon was pleasing and positive. John Selden wrote approvingly of the scene in a model aristocratic house: 'all the Company Dance, Lord and Groom, Lady and Kitchen-Maid, no distinction'. Others, however, viewed such togetherness with deep and cynical suspicion. In Jacobean Somerset, William Walton accused the suspected Catholic Sir Edward Parham of participating actively in a disorderly local morris dance, 'the better to gette the love and affection of the common people'. A puritan satire, written in the same county, scornfully imagined how a talking maypole might boast of its capacity to stimulate dancing among all sorts of people:

[108] *REED Somerset*, pp. 79–80.

And least yow thinke my nobell sport
maytayned allone by baser sort
I have somm of a better note
that Jett it in a silkin coate.[109]

Nor did it take a puritan to perceive the dangers inherent in socially mixed dancing. In 1595, a merchant tailor in London was clearly irked when he arrived for a session at his dancing school only to find that his apprentice had also joined the institution for ten shillings, behind his back. The apprentice's assumption 'that his said Mr woulde not be offended with him yf he should in some honest sorte seeke to recreate himself' was seriously wide of the mark, and the relationship between the two men never recovered. Twenty years later, the crime allegedly committed by a man from Linton (Herefordshire) was rather more glaring. He was reportedly in the habit of 'keepinge companie and goeinge abroade with his owne maide servant dancinge', and his neighbours – not surprisingly – considered his behaviour 'unfittinge'.[110] Overall, it is clear that dancing, like other forms of musical recreation, both articulated and mitigated social distinctions. It could bring men and women or rich and poor together, but it could also separate them. To this extent, the social choreography of the art mirrored the intricate ins and outs, the comings-together and the driftings-apart, that were executed by the dancers themselves.

Privileged commentators perceived (or promoted) significant differences between the courtly dancing of the gentry and the unrefined practices of the common people. Among the social elite, there were to be no flailing limbs and no unrestrained 'whoops' of joy. Instead, bodies were to remain under control, their movements characterised by moderation, decorum and grace.[111] At the Jacobean and Caroline courts, the evolving tradition of the masque required that the subtle artistry of the aristocratic dancers be clearly distinguished from the exaggerated and exuberant gestures of those who performed in the anti-masque. In 1663, Edward Waterhouse drew a distinction based on the types of dance favoured at different social levels: 'With us we have onely French dancing and Country dancing used by the best rank of people. Morris-dancing is an exercise that the loose and vile sort onely use, and that onely in faires and meetings of lewdness.' In practice, members of the gentry also kept their distance from the vulgar by paying dancing masters to visit their houses for private lessons. The gentry and aristocracy generally preferred to dance indoors, enclosed by the walls and

109 Selden, *Table Talk*, p. 83; *REED Somerset*, pp. 167–70, 741.

110 REQ 2 284/11, NA; *REED Herefordshire, Worcestershire*, pp. 149–50.

111 See, for example, Cleland, *Hero-paideia*, pp. 224–6.

ceilings of a gallery, rather than out on the green, restrained only by the high sky. They learned not only country dances and common jigs, but courtly branles, galliards, pavans, courants and almains, all dances that were little known at the average alehouse. Playford pandered to their tastes by including in his published collection titles such as 'A la mode de France', 'Bouree la bass' and 'Lane's trumpet minuet' (both the instrument and the dance in this last number signified high status).[112] In *A Nest of Ninnies*, published in 1608, Robert Armin sought to capture the spirit of Christmas in a traditionalist gentry household. The atmosphere was one of old-fashioned hospitality with an 'open house for all commers'. Even here, however, a distinction was carefully drawn: while the aristocrats were entertained in the great chamber by a group of musicians, the tenants in the hall indulged in 'common dauncing' to the coarser tones of a Lincolnshire bagpipe. Last but not least, the socially pre-eminent wore suitably costly shoes. When, in 1612, Lord William Howard of Naworth spent four shillings on three pairs of 'red dauncing pumpes for the children' he was not only promoting their comfort but setting them apart from the ranks of the rough-shod.[113]

As usual, however, the relationship between the cultural pursuits of the gentry and those of the people was rather more complex than such evidence might indicate. There was unstoppable two-way traffic. 'Country dancing', for example, was perceived as a recreation that began in England's villages before being taken up at court and in other highly privileged settings. This was as much a subtle transformation as a simple transfer, but it nevertheless demonstrated that many aristocrats nursed a somewhat problematic admiration for the dancing of the drones. The courtly vogue for country dance gathered momentum particularly during the last third of Elizabeth I's reign, and her visit to Lord Montagu at Cowdray (Sussex) in 1591 has been identified as a crucial moment. On the evening of her sixth day there, 'the countrie people presented themselves to hir Majestie in a pleasant daunce with Taber and Pipe'. The queen responded with suitably 'gentle' applause, and during the subsequent decade country dances were practised at court with increasing frequency. Elizabeth's seventeenth-century successors all indulged in country dance, and John Selden felt that the practice had gone too far by the

[112] Walls, *Music in the English Courtly Masque*, pp. 117–20; Edward Waterhouse, *Fortescutus Illustratus* (London, 1663), p. 534; *Complete Country Dance Tunes from Playford's Dancing Master*, nos. 2, 220, 361. An elaborate almain is recorded on the website, track 3.

[113] Robert Armin, *A Nest of Ninnies* (London, 1608), B1r; *REED Cumberland, Westmorland, Gloucestershire*, p. 135.

1630s (there were limits to his celebration of cultural crossover). Elizabeth, he remarked, had maintained an appropriate degree of royal gravity by mixing country dances with more stately 'measures', 'But in King Charles' time, there has been nothing but Trench-more and the Cushion-dance, Omnium gatherum, tolly polly, hoite come toite.' Three decades later, Samuel Pepys witnessed a ball at Whitehall on the last day of 1662. Charles II led his most glittering courtiers through a series of dances, opening in refined style with a branle and a coranto. At this point, he signalled a change of mood: 'Then to Country dances; the King leading the first which he called for; which was – says he Cuckolds all a-row, the old dance of England.'[114]

A succession of rulers thus proclaimed the simple charms of supposedly rustic dance, and their example was enthusiastically followed by several generations of gentry. The appeal of country dancing to the leaders of society had several strands. Copying the king was usually a good idea, as Pepys and many others knew. Copying the people was more risky, but the act of appropriating their dances was to some degree therapeutic. It had the potential to release tension either through satire (the people could be gently mocked) or through the imposition of order and elegance (they could be tamed) or through the experience of temporary escape to an imagined world of rustic simplicity (they could be embraced). Among aristocratic traditionalists, country dancing also demonstrated a measure of solidarity with the people at large (implied in Charles II's phrase 'the old dance of England'). Most of these strands were woven together in the anti-masque, a courtly form in which cavorting commoners were simultaneously scorned for their roughness and commended for their loyalty to the crown. Lastly, country dance forms were appealing because of their inherent sociability: each participant circulated among all the others, a characteristic that contrasted with the more 'monogamous' traditions of courtly dance. 'Ladies, will you be pleased to dance a Countrey Dance or two', suggested a fictional master in 1658, 'for 'tis that which makes you truly sociable, and us truly happy; being like the Chorus of a Song, where all the parts sing together.'[115]

John Playford, the most famous figure in the history of English country dance, worked instinctively with each of these possibilities. His *Dancing Master* was aimed primarily at the gentry, yet it drew much of its appeal

[114] *REED Sussex*, p. 194 (see also Rust, *Dance in Society*, p. 47); Selden, *Table Talk*, p. 83; *Diary of Samuel Pepys*, vol. III, pp. 300–1. The tune that Charles requested can be heard on the website, track 40.

[115] Edward Phillips, *The Mysteries of Love and Eloquence* (1658; London, 1685), p. 12.

from the supposed bucolic simplicity of its dances. The collection had to combine reassuring refinement with recognisable rusticity. So it was that the elite of London danced to tunes called 'The shepherd's daughter', 'Simple Simon' and 'The merry, merry milkmaids'. For the leaders of society, the collection was attractive because it brought the idealised sociability of the village green into their grand domestic interiors, where it contrasted with the stiffer conventions of courtly dance. It was unwise, however, for a gent to take rusticity too far, and we can probably assume that Playford's choreographies, while preserving many features of country dance, also promoted a somewhat satirical spirit and a measure of decorum that may not have suited England's more exuberant villagers. Anxious aristocrats were further soothed by the inclusion of dances called, for instance, 'My Lady Cullen' and 'Lord of Carnarvan's jig'. In a variety of ways, therefore, hierarchical tensions were released and order reaffirmed. Indeed, the very act of collecting together England's dances and then assembling them for systematic presentation on the printed page suggested a desire to impose order on a phenomenon that was sometimes said to foment the opposite. We cannot be sure exactly how Playford conducted his research, nor what he did to his dances and tunes in the interval between discovery and dissemination. It seems certain, however, that the *Dancing Master* included a range of types: dances that Playford or his assistants simply lifted from common practice (his directions for the 'Cushion dance' bore a striking resemblance to the moves reportedly performed many years earlier by the company at Gloucester); dances that were gathered in the same manner, but then modified in one way or another for consumption by the gentry ('Stanes morris' may once have been a popular version of the morris, but Playford extended the tune and choreographed a genteel kissing dance in long formation); and dances that were invented in the 'country style' by Playford's men or by successful dancing masters of the period (the latter group were probably responsible for titles such as 'Mr Eaglesfield's new hornpipe' and 'Mr Staggin's jig'). Overall, the mixture was thoroughly eclectic, and it reflected the complex and continuous currents that connected the cultural worlds of the gentry and the commonalty.[116]

Even the more courtly of dances revealed the influence of the people. The gavotte originated among the French peasantry, and the galliard is said to

[116] These tunes are all indexed and transcribed in *Complete Country Dance Tunes from Playford's Dancing Master*. See also Forrest, *History of Morris Dancing*, pp. 278–9, 296–9, 307–12; Rust, *Dance in Society*, pp. 56–8.

have drawn some of its features from the common jig. 'Capering', for example, may well have been imported into the galliard from more humble forms of dance. The hornpipe was strongly associated with rustic revellers, yet Barnabe Rich included it on his list of fashionable courtly dances in 1581. 'Nor was I ever in suche a dump', admitted gentleman George Wither in 1619, 'but that a Scottish Jigge or a Horne-pipe would have insinuated a little with me.'[117] His enthusiasm was cautious, but it was also unmistakable. The lavolta, a famously sprightly dance favoured by Elizabeth I, originated among the people of Provence. Selden may have credited the queen with great gravity, but some of her contemporaries felt that she blotted her copybook in loving the lavolta so. In a famous painting, Elizabeth (or somebody very like her) is manhandled by a courtier and lifted some way above the ground in the midst of an excited company. She was probably not the only high-ranking Englishwoman to experience the base animal pleasure of a peasant dance. The orator who addressed the Tutbury minstrels at an unspecified date credited the members of his audience with inducing the temporary loss of control among those whose dances they accompanied:

> The tender & delicate Lady who often disdaines to touch the ground with the soles of her feet yet when you Minstrells strike upp she forgets her state & delicacy, treads boldly on the floore & trips & bounds like a young Fawne in the Forest of Needwood while her spirits all the while are raised by your Musick & her feet keepe time to your measures.[118]

Country dancing was a complicated business for pre-eminent individuals: it was simultaneously a courtly accomplishment and a rustic escape (it is no easy matter to forget oneself while remembering who one is).

Appropriation worked the other way too. In Elizabethan England, courtly dance tunes were sometimes taken up on the streets. The grandly named 'Quadran pavan', for example, was a favourite at the Inns of Court, but it also acquired the name 'Gregory Walker' on the grounds that 'it walketh amongst the barbars and fidlers more common then any other'.[119] The spread of dancing schools and dancing masters during the late sixteenth and seventeenth centuries also reflected the process by which the recreational habits of the gentry, though designed to signal distinction, could spread rapidly within society's middle orders. Morris dancing descended further still. Although it

[117] Rust, *Dance in Society*, pp. 50, 54; Forrest, *History of Morris Dancing*, p. 307; Rich, *Riche his Farewell*, A3v; Wither, *A Preparation to the Psalter*, p. 81.

[118] Rust, *Dance in Society*, p. 45; speech delivered at Tutbury, D4530/76/8, p. 10, DRO.

[119] Brissenden, *Shakespeare and the Dance*, p. 6; Thomas Morley, *A Plaine and Easie Introduction to Practical Music* (London, 1597), R1v.

was a marker of coarseness by the early seventeenth century, it had its English origins as a form of entertainment that was associated primarily with the early Tudor court. Elite patronage of the morris had very different meanings in the early sixteenth and early eighteenth centuries. When Henry VII paid 26s 8d to witness a morris in 1501, he was buying a distinctively courtly entertainment in which hired performers probably danced a drama involving the wooing of a lady by various knights. It was a recreation little known beyond the court, and in the minds of audience members it therefore helped to separate the best from the rest. In contrast, when Sir Thomas Cartwright of Aynho House (Northamptonshire) paid a morris team from nearby Brackley 10s 6d in 1725, he was demonstrating a paternalistic curiosity regarding the rude recreations of the multitude.[120] Now, the lady was probably Maid Marion and the knights were Robin Hood and his men. Cartwright, like Henry VII, was setting himself apart, but his paradoxical method was to feign temporary intimacy and shared interest rather than to commission an obviously exclusive art-form.

Those who received the morris at their expansive estates in the decades following its appropriation by the people may also have been aspiring to tame and tether one of the wilder recreational beasts known to roam the English countryside. A comparable objective is perhaps reflected in the famous Jacobean painting of morris dancing beside the Thames in Richmond (see Figure 7.8). Despite the tempestuous reputation of the dance, the scene is thoroughly sedate. There is no crowd, and the hobby-horse looks anything but warlike. There are only four dancers, and none of them carries a weapon. The musician looks almost apologetic, and the fool bends his knees in deferential fashion while collecting coins in his ladle from a finely dressed gentleman and his wife. Only the barking dog, pictured in the foreground, appears genuinely excited by the event (track 41 on the website is our attempt to put sound into this scene, while track 42 is a little less restrained).

The two-way transmission of dance forms and features was promoted particularly by the occupational dancing masters and musicians who traversed even the most conspicuous social divides. Take, for example, George and Robert Cally of Chester. George was well known in his home city as one who 'professed musicke and the arte and facultie of teachinge to daunce'. In a petition to the mayor, dated 1615, he explained that his occupation had enabled him to raise a family of ten children and to earn 'a good respecte and estimacion from men of the best sort & generall fashion'. He must have taught dancing in the homes of aristocrats and gentlemen on many occasions, yet he

[120] These examples can be found in Forrest, *History of Morris Dancing*, pp. 58, 70, 327–9.

Figure 7.8. Morris dancing could be wild and dangerous, but here the artist presents a more peaceful image. The hobby-horse, Maid Marion and the fool with his ladle were all common features of the dance. The Fitzwilliam Museum, University of Cambridge/Bridgeman Art Library, FIT65998, *The Thames at Richmond with the Old Royal Palace* (*c.* 1620).

had also presided at the feasts of Chester's shoemakers and beer-brewers. Beyond this, he was probably equally familiar in many less formal social contexts. His brother Robert, another musician, most certainly was. In 1613, for example, we hear by chance of a local apprentice who departed from his master's house without permission. After a recreational trip to the Wirral, he eventually fetched up on Robert's doorstep 'about 4 of the Clock in the morning and desyred him to teache him daunce & stayed dancing one hower'.[121] The Callys, and many others like them, were cultural conduits who transported tunes, terms and choreographies from one place to another, thus reducing the capacity of any particular social group – rich or poor – to claim something as its own. This was surely how the morris dance broke out from its courtly confines during the early sixteenth century, and it has been

[121] *REED Chester*, pp. 204, 265, 290; Baldwin, *Paying the Piper*, p. 70.

noted that the non-courtly morris made its first known appearance in 1507 at Kingston upon Thames. A dancer, in good physical condition, could easily have moved to and fro between this location and the royal palaces at Richmond and Hampton Court without breaking sweat.[122] Actors, too, opened and maintained channels of communication, performing dances courtly and rustic according to the requirements of their playwrights, and frequently doing so before audiences that were themselves socially and sexually mixed. The fact that the female dancers were, until the later seventeenth century, male actors in disguise must have added a further charge to the complex cross-currents that flowed through the theatre.

In conclusion, the many types of dance simultaneously revealed and concealed the major dividing lines within English culture and society. Single-sex dancing allowed men and women to articulate their differences, yet other forms brought them together in combined and concordant activity. Recreation and procreation were closely connected, and dancing certainly provided an important context for courtship and thus the continuation of society. On occasion, dancing men and women swapped clothes and imagined life, just for a moment, in the opposite camp. Dancing distinguished gents from commoners, but it suggested simultaneously the existence of certain bonds that held them together. It also enabled the members of each group to escape, again temporarily, into the somewhat mysterious world of the other. It brought wealthy townsfolk a taste of the country, but rustic dancing was tamed and transformed in the process. Dancing was often associated with youth, yet there were some occasions upon which old and young danced together, and many more upon which the aged watched benevolently from the sidelines as the next generation rehearsed its routines. In 1615, this was probably the attitude of the respectable churchwardens of Worthen (Shropshire), who acknowledged defensively that their young people danced on Sundays, 'but not in time of divine Service'. The Elizabethan curate of East Lavington (Sussex) was far less sympathetic. In 1579, he warned the authorities that on Sundays his parishioners, 'olld & young', were in the habit of walking to an unruly neighbouring parish where they indulged in 'daunsing &c [etc.]'.[123] This case reminds us that dancing also separated reformers and traditionalists. This was a particularly stark divide, though even here there were points of

[122] Ronald Hutton, *Stations of the Sun: A History of the Ritual Year in Britain* (Oxford: Oxford University Press, 1996), pp. 264–5; Smith, *Acoustic World*, p. 141.

[123] *REED Shropshire*, p. 352; *REED Sussex*, p. 26.

contact. The gulf was to some extent bridged by a largely silent and therefore uncountable section of the population whose members were willing to see both sides of the argument. Moreover, moderate puritans clearly did not refrain from dancing altogether, though their enjoyment can rarely have been wholly unrestrained. One wonders whether the guests at the Cromwell wedding in 1657 danced to any of the tunes that John Playford had so recently gathered from common (and, in godly eyes, questionable) practice.

All in all, early modern dance was characterised, despite the frequently contrary public pronouncements of its more courtly connoisseurs, by what we nowadays term crossover and fusion. This applied not only to the categories discussed above, but also to many other aspects of dance culture. Country dancing and morris dancing borrowed tunes and ideas from one another. The hobby-horse had traditionally featured in the matachin, a sword dance, but it migrated into the morris during the late sixteenth century. Dance tunes and ballad tunes were intimately interrelated, and several English dance forms had their origins in continental Europe. Dance, on all levels of society, was eclectic, a characteristic that is nicely reflected in a final selection of Playford's tune titles: 'Simple Simon', 'The Lady Banbury's hornpipe', 'Gray's Inn mask', 'From Aberdeen', 'The Devonshire lass', 'The French riguadon', 'The London gentlewoman' (also known as 'The London maid') and, most tellingly of all, 'Nobody's jig'.[124]

[124] Forrest, *History of Morris Dancing*, pp. 102, 293; *Complete Country Dance Tunes from Playford's Dancing Master.*

8 | Parish church music: the rise of 'the singing psalms'

We now move the short but significant distance from the village green to the parish church in order to consider a resounding form of music that proved, perhaps surprisingly, every bit as popular as the tunes associated with balladry or dance. Congregational psalm-singing provided one of early modern England's most distinctive sounds, though its role in persuading the English people to accept the Reformation has, until recently, been strangely neglected by scholars.[1] We have often been told that Protestantism, a religion of the intellect and the written word, faced an inevitable struggle in seeking the conversion of a partially literate and patchily educated population. Nevertheless, by 1600 an overwhelming majority of English people considered themselves to be Protestants, even if many of them allegedly remained a little hazy about what, in theological terms, this actually meant. The Reformation's success, at least in forging new personal identities, is still under investigation. Arguably, one of the most convincing explanations for the transformation will be a musical one.[2] Ordinary parishioners may not always have welcomed

[1] Psalmody received scant coverage in celebrated texts such as A. G. Dickens, *The English Reformation* (1964; London: B. T. Batsford, 1989), J. J. Scarisbrick, *The Reformation and the English People* (Oxford: Blackwell, 1984) and Eamon Duffy, *The Stripping of the Altars: Traditional Religion in England, 1400–1580* (New Haven: Yale University Press, 1992). Indeed, the main contribution made to the musical debate by Duffy's otherwise brilliant book was the wonderfully succinct but somewhat misleading index entry, 'music: silenced in 1549'. Psalm-singing has fared much better in the following works: Collinson, *Birthpangs of Protestant England*, pp. 95–7, 106–12; Watt, *Cheap Print*, pp. 55–7, 64–5; Robin A. Leaver, *'Goostly Psalmes and Spirituall Songes': English and Dutch Metrical Psalms from Coverdale to Utenhove, 1535–1566* (Oxford: Clarendon Press, 1991); Green, *Print and Protestantism*, pp. 503–53; John Craig, 'Psalms, Groans and Dog-whippers: The Soundscape of Sacred Space in the English Parish Church, 1547–1642', in Will Coster and Andrew Spicer (eds.), *Sacred Space in Early Modern Europe* (Cambridge: Cambridge University Press, 2005), pp. 104–23; Hamlin, *Psalm Culture*, especially pp. 43–50; Beth Quitslund, *The Reformation in Rhyme* (Aldershot: Ashgate, 2008). Of course, all such accounts are hugely indebted to Nicholas Temperley for his pioneering *Music of the English Parish Church*, chs. 2–6.

[2] This argument is expertly developed in Jonathan Peter Willis, 'Church Music and Protestantism in Post-Reformation England: Discourses, Sites and Identities', unpublished PhD thesis, University of Warwick (2009). The author concentrates on Elizabethan England but illuminates many of the broader issues and debates that are covered in the present chapter. His thesis will shortly appear in book form, published by Ashgate.

lengthy sermons, but they loved to sing psalms. Participation in this activity helped to bind people to the new church and to generate feelings of membership and ownership. According to Richard Hooker, good church music 'doth much edify if not the understanding because it teacheth not, yet surely the affection, because therin it worketh much. They must have hearts very dry and tough, from whom the melody of psalms doth not sometime draw that wherein a mind religiously affected delighteth.'[3]

Of course, where there was pleasure there was also controversy, and psalmody must be understood within a wider debate about the role of music in worship. England's leading Protestants all agreed on the need to leave behind forever the supposedly obscurantist musical traditions of the late medieval church, but they were permanently divided on the question of what precisely this should entail in practical terms. Commentators took up many positions along a spectrum, but it seems possible to discern three particularly important arguments. Firstly, moderate Protestants shared Luther's view that music was a vital tool of persuasion, and should be allowed to play a full part in the service of God. Music was 'the Handmaid to Divinity', and Holy Scripture provided many examples to demonstrate God's approval. It had the capacity to touch the affections and spirits of all manner of men and women, from the highest to the lowest, and a good tune could aid the essential process by which Scriptural words became permanently lodged in the memory. Music provided congregations with a pattern for life in heaven, a moment of revelation in which divine bliss became fleetingly audible. According to Thomas Wright, music 'worketh so divinely in the mind, that it elevateth the heart miraculously, and resembleth in a certaine manner the voices and harmonie of heaven'. Voices and words were the heart and soul of church music, but musical instruments – particularly organs – could also assist in rendering godly messages more intense and memorable. This argument earned support from churchmen as diverse as the Laudian Humphrey Sydenham and the presbyterian Richard Baxter (though the latter was much more cautious). These two men would have disagreed on many issues, but they both understood that music, in Sydenham's words, 'rockes the very soule'. Of course, it was always necessary to warn that the power of music should not be abused by over-elaboration or by anything else that obstructed the sense of the words, but its benefits far outweighed its

[3] Hooker, *Of the Lawes of Ecclesiastical Politie*, bk. V, ch. 38, p. 76.

dangers. To judge from the literary record, this moderate opinion was predominant (though never secure) within English Protestantism.[4]

Protestants of the hotter sort often looked to continental Calvinism for their arguments, and they consequently developed a more suspicious attitude to church music. In their ears, the lascivious resonances of merely recreational music vibrated uncomfortably, and echoes of pre-Reformation sacred polyphony caused a throbbing pain. 'Popish' music represented a violent assault on Scripture: it 'dismembered', 'prophaned', 'minced' and 'mocked' the holy words. It played to the senses and not to the soul. For William Perkins, the performance of consort music during divine services was a popish superstition, 'feeding the ears, not edifying the mind'. In contrast, the unaccompanied congregational singing of psalms was not only permissible, but essential. To this degree, the situation as it evolved in the parish churches of Elizabethan England was generally to the satisfaction of these zealous spirits, yet there was plenty to fire their ire in the retention of a much more elaborate musical regime – complete with choirs, organs and polyphonic anthems – in the country's cathedrals. In 1572, the authors of 'An Admonition to Parliament' were presumably thinking of these institutions when they complained about musicians who 'live in great idleness' and 'tosse the Psalmes ... like tennice balls'. Dudley Fenner had observed 'great numbers that tarrye while the service is songe but depart so soone as the Sermon beginneth'. 'While the Organes pipe', he continued, 'some are drawen with the sweetnes of musike to come up; but while the preacher cryeth out, continue beneath, and in laughter or brawling be louder than he oftentimes.' Overall, this critical puritan case against any but the simplest of church music waxed and waned in intensity during the early modern period, and appeared in different ecclesiological guises, but it never went away.[5]

Lastly, there were those on the more radical wing of English Protestantism who denied the validity of virtually all music in the public praise

4 John Playford, *The Whole Book of Psalms* (London, 1677), preface; Hooker, *Of the Lawes of Ecclesiastical Politie*, bk. V, ch. 38, pp. 75–6; Walton, *The Lives of Dr. John Donne* ..., p. 60; Wright, *Passions of the Minde*, bk. V, p. 164; Sydenham, *Sermons*, pp. 4–32; Richard Baxter, *A Christian Directory* (London, 1673), pp. 884–5. See also Brady, *Church-musick Vindicated*; Naish, *A Sermon*; Baxter, *The Divine Appointment* (London, 1671), p. 106.

5 Foxe on Bilney, quoted in Elizabeth Gow, 'Thomas Bilney and his Relations with Sir Thomas More', *Norfolk Archaeology* 32 (1961), 297; Thomas Becon, *Relikes of Rome* (London, 1563), fos. 116v–17v; William Daman, *The Psalmes of David in English Meter* (London, 1579), A3r (preface by Edward Hake); William Perkins, *A Golden Chaine* (London, 1591), G1v; John Field and Thomas Wilcox, 'An Admonition to the Parliament', in *Puritan Manifestoes*, ed. W. H. Frere and C. E. Douglas (London: SPCK, 1954), p. 29; Dudley Fenner, *A Briefe and Plaine Declaration* (London, 1586), pp. 67–8.

of God. The argument is associated most famously with the Quakers in the mid-seventeenth century, but it had clear and interesting antecedents. The interlocutors in Thomas Becon's *The Jewel of Joy* (1550) adopt various positions in regard to music, both sacred and profane. Theophile is the most outspoken: 'A Christen man's melodie, after S. Paules mynde consisteth in herte, whyle we recite Psalmes, himnes and spirituall songes, and syng to the Lorde in oure hertes.' 'Al other outward melodye', he continues, 'is vain and transitory.' This argument anticipates the one later proposed by Solomon Eccles and other members of the Society of Friends. For the Quaker who was portrayed in Eccles's *A Musick-lector* (1667), the only music in which God had the slightest interest was 'inward'. His partner in conversation, a rather dim-witted musician, finds himself nonplussed by this, so the Quaker invites him to come and meet his teacher, whose name is 'The Word of God'. The musician still does not follow the argument, and asks what sort of music the teacher writes: 'doth he prick Plain-Song or Intableture?' The penny begins to drop only when he is informed that the music teacher does not in fact write conventional music, but instead 'pricks at the Heart'. This was the sonic equivalent of the inner light.[6]

Organs and choirs in the English Reformation: down but not out?

Before we consider in detail the rise of psalmody we must consider the related fate of the parochial church music that preceded it. In the early sixteenth century, the music of the parish church was dominated by Latin plainsong, usually performed by small numbers of priests and parish clerks. Of course, there was considerable variety, depending on levels of parochial prosperity, and the period saw a conspicuous general tendency for the musical resources of English churches to become more elaborate. Wealthier parishes might hire additional singers, or 'conducts', who formed a male choir. In some places, such ensembles were further augmented by choirboys or lay singers, and it therefore became possible for parishioners, particularly on major feast days, to experience what one scholar has called 'the virtuosic, expansive and sonorous beauty of five-part polyphonic music sung by the voices of boys and men'. London was particularly privileged in this regard, as were parishes in cathedral cities and the small number of towns with endowed 'song schools' for choirboys (Banbury and Newark, for example).

[6] Becon, *The Jewel of Joy*, F3r–v; Eccles, *A Musick-lector*, pp. 16–17.

Prosperous parishes were also the most likely to possess organs, which complemented the sound of the choir or the chanting priests. Organs were increasingly common during the late medieval period, and scholars are coming to realise just how vibrant were the musical regimes that operated in an indeterminate minority of communities. It remains true, however, that many parishes – particularly in the countryside – had neither organs nor sizeable choirs. Instead, their inhabitants heard liturgical music that generally involved only three or four singers (the parish priest, the parish clerk and a couple of chantry priests). These performers delivered their chants in fairly simple fashion, adding an improvised harmonic line in a style known as 'faburden'. English laymen with musical inclinations could and did join choirs where choirs existed, but most parishioners – including all women – were listeners rather than singers.[7]

The official religious changes of 1547–53 and 1558–9 placed these cherished traditions under severe pressure. As early as 1562, an archetypal 'gossip', quoted unsympathetically in one of the official homilies, was heard to remark: 'what shall wee now doe at Church . . . , since wee cannot heare the like piping, singing, chaunting, and playing upon the organes that we could before[?]' The musical world was indeed changing rapidly, though the story is more subtle than we might have imagined. The official status of the organ, for example, was complex and uncertain. The legislation that enacted the English Reformation under Edward VI and Elizabeth I did not, in fact, ban the use of organs in worship (though there were those who wished that it had). There was no mention of them in the royal injunctions of 1547, nor in those of 1559. Visitation articles of the sixteenth and seventeenth centuries do not, in general, include questions about organs. Some bishops, admittedly, sought to ban their use, but for others, organs were apparently a 'thing indifferent', not one of the artefacts by which the success or failure of the Reformation was to be

[7] Temperley, *Music of the English Parish Church*, ch. 2; Stephen Bicknell, *The History of the English Organ* (Cambridge: Cambridge University Press, 1996), ch. 2; Beat Kümin, 'Masses, Morris and Metrical Psalms: Music in the English Parish, *c.* 1400–1600', in Fiona Kisby (ed.), *Music and Musicians in Renaissance Cities and Towns* (Cambridge: Cambridge University Press, 2001), pp. 70–81; Clive Burgess and Andrew Wathey, 'Mapping the Soundscape: Church Music in English Towns, 1450–1550', *Early Music History* 19 (2000), 1–46; Caroline Barron, 'Church Music in English Towns 1450–1550: An Interim Report', *Urban History* 29 (2002), 83–91; Roger Bowers, 'Polyphonic Voices in the English Parish Church, *c.* 1460–1570', seminar paper read at the 'Worship, Liturgy and Music' conference, Durham University, 10–11 September 2008. I am grateful to Professor Bowers for kindly sending me a copy of his paper (the quotation appears on the first page). Finally, it should be noted that historians and musicologists are, at present, continually and positively revising their impressions of the musical resources that were available within late medieval parish churches (with a particular concentration on urban environments).

measured.[8] Organs, therefore, came under remarkably little official pressure in England before the Civil Wars, and Laudian bishops of the 1630s were actively supportive of the instrument. Archbishop Laud himself urged the parishes of London to put any disused organs back into working order.[9] During the decades between 1558 and 1640, the leading churchmen who attempted to use their authority in order to suppress organ-playing appear to have been unusual. Puritanical hostility to the organ was undoubtedly a significant feature of religious culture in this period, but it was not, in general, promoted officially by the leaders of the church.

It is not easy to determine the number and distribution of parochial church organs during this turbulent period. Despite the lack of legislation during the mid-sixteenth century, there is little doubt that many organs ceased to sound. Between 1547 and 1580, organs suffered a variety of fates. Some, like those at Boxford in Suffolk, were actively removed at an early date (in this case 1548), often, one presumes, by zealous Protestants. Others were dismantled by pragmatic parishioners in order to prevent confiscation. At St Lawrence's, Reading, the organs in the chancel were taken down in 1558 for fear that they might otherwise fall 'into the hands of the organ takers' (the identity of these menacing individuals is unclear). The pipes were to be sold and the wood redeployed – rather pointedly – to make bigger and better seats in church for the mayor and his brethren. An anonymous Jacobean author reckoned that at least a hundred organs had been pulled down in the years following 1567, adding to the destruction that had already occurred in earlier years (though he seems to have been referring primarily to organs in cathedrals and collegiate churches). Other parochial instruments remained in place, but were allowed to fall into disuse and disrepair. In scores of parishes all over England, the churchwardens' accounts ceased to mention organs during the 1560s and 1570s.[10] In

[8] *Certaine Sermons or Homilies Appointed to be Read in Churches* (1562; London, 1623), p. 131; *Documents of the English Reformation*, ed. Gerald Bray (Cambridge: James Clarke, 1994), pp. 247–57, 335–48. Under Elizabeth, Bishop Horne of Winchester banned the use of organs in his diocese (Temperley, *Music of the English Parish Church*, p. 42) and Archbishop Grindal tried to silence them in York Minster (Griffiths, *A Musical Place of the First Quality*, p. 7). There is a wealth of evidence relating to organs in Kenneth Fincham and Nicholas Tyacke, *Altars Restored: The Changing Face of English Religious Worship, 1547–c.1700* (Oxford: Oxford University Press, 2007).

[9] Temperley, *Music of the English Parish Church*, p. 52.

[10] List of musical events in Suffolk, MANN MS 17/443, p. 43, NRO; John Man, *The History and Antiquities Ancient and Modern of the Borough of Reading* (Reading, 1816), p. 315; 'The Praise of Musicke', Royal MS 18 BX, fo. 5v, BL. A valuable collection of primary source extracts can be found in 'Parish Church Musicians in England in the Reign of Elizabeth I: An Annotated Register', ed. Alan Smith, *Royal Musical Association Research Chronicle* 4 (1964), 42–92.

London, the collapse of organ-playing seems to have been dramatic. It has been calculated that during the 1540s, seventy-eight out of ninety-six parishes possessed two or more instruments. By the 1580s, only a handful retained even a single organ.[11] Many London parishes continued to repair their instruments until 1571, but then abandoned their efforts following the death in that year of John Howe, unrivalled as a maker and repairer of organs in the capital. This narrative suggests the operation in some places of motives other than Protestant zeal. Parish leaders were evidently reluctant to abandon a trusted servant, and they therefore employed him through his later years. When Howe was no longer available, however, they chose to save themselves money by doing without organ music.[12]

The citizens of early modern England, ever practical, were willing to recycle organ parts. Our lamenting Jacobean complained that the metal from organ pipes had frequently been sold, melted and moulded into pewter tableware (this was reformation gone mad). Other organ transplants included sounding-boards, a number of which have survived in their new guises to tell a valuable technical tale to modern historians of the instrument. In 1977, a domestic door in Suffolk was found to be a long-lost board from the pre-Reformation organ at Wetheringsett. The 360 holes in its surface were related to the original organ pipes rather than to woodworm, and dendrochronological tests have dated the board to around 1520. This and other chance survivals help to confirm the view that most of the parochial organs in sixteenth-century England were small, both by modern standards and by those that prevailed in continental Europe. English organs, in contrast to those found in the Netherlands and elsewhere, had no pedals, and therefore lacked the rich, reinforced bass sound that we have come to associate with the instrument.[13]

Organs were under pressure, but the story is not one of unmitigated gloom. Although destruction tends to catch the eye, a substantial minority of parishes retained their organs at least until the last decades of Elizabeth's reign. The absence of clear governmental directives to the contrary meant that this was a perfectly permissible choice. There was clearly a scattered minority of parish churches in which organ music was still to be heard. Further work remains to be done but it seems probable that the instrument was a little more resilient than we might have imagined.[14] When, in 1700, Henry Dodwell claimed that during Elizabeth's reign organs had

[11] Price, *Patrons and Musicians*, p. 49; Temperley, *Music of the English Parish Church*, p. 44.

[12] The final phase of Howe's career can be tracked in 'Parish Church Musicians'.

[13] Bicknell, *History of the English Organ*, p. 30; Spink, 'Music and Society', p. 22.

[14] Further work is now well underway. See Willis, 'Church Music and Protestantism', ch. 3.

continued to sound 'in most Parish Churches in England, not only in the greater Towns, but in abundance of lesser ones, in some very small Parish Churches', he was undoubtedly exaggerating. On the other hand, he may have been justified in opposing the view that, under official pressure, the playing of organs in ordinary parish churches had virtually stopped during this period. The parishes that are known to have maintained their organs during the last two decades of the sixteenth century include a number in the counties of the north and west, where older religious traditions were generally at their most tenacious. There were, for example, organs in Oswestry (Shropshire), Houghton-le-Spring (Durham), Newcastle upon Tyne (Northumberland) and Hull, Kirkby Malzeard and Sheffield (Yorkshire). The remaining parishes demonstrate, however, that it was perfectly possible for organs to survive in the generally less amenable atmosphere of the south and east of England. One London parish (St Margaret Westminster) continued to repair its organs. The same was true at Shipdham (Norfolk), Shillington (Hertfordshire), Long Sutton (Lincolnshire) and two parishes in the cathedral city of Salisbury.[15]

Overall, the number of organs rose somewhat under the first two Stuarts. A few parishes abandoned their instruments, but several that are not known to have maintained organs under Elizabeth now did so (Framlingham in Suffolk, for example).[16] This modest recovery gathered momentum during the 1630s, presumably with the approval of Laudian bishops. In this decade, there were organs at Prescot (Lancashire), Romsey (Hampshire), Grantham (Lincolnshire), Bath (Somerset), Stradbroke, Walberswick, Stowmarket, Bungay, Mellis, Peasanhall and Hensted (Suffolk), Hartland (Devon) and Beaconsfield, Bishop's Woburn and Waddesdon (Buckinghamshire). New organs were installed at St Giles-in-the-Fields (Middlesex) in 1631 and at Bruton (Somerset) in 1637. In this period, organs were also repaired at Aldborough (Yorkshire), Sidbury (Devon) and St Ives and Launceston (Cornwall).[17] When Lieutenant Hammond, an enterprising soldier from Norwich, went on a sight-seeing, sound-hearing tour of England in the mid-1630s, he listened to organs not only in numerous cathedrals, but at

[15] Henry Dodwell, *A Treatise Concerning the Lawfulness of Instrumental Musick in Holy Offices* (London, 1700), p. 74. Most of the information gathered here can be found in 'Parish Church Musicians', but see also the will of Thomas Allen, Misc Dep 37/5, LA; *REED Newcastle upon Tyne*, pp. 89, 103.

[16] MANN MS 17/443, p. 100, NRO.

[17] Woodfill, *Musicians in English Society*, p. 155; Spink, 'Music and Society', p. 44; MANN MS 17/443, p. 139, NRO; *The Journal of William Dowsing*, ed. Trevor Cooper (Woodbridge: Boydell Press, 2001), pp. 288, 305, 372–3, 375–6, 378–9; Temperley, *Music of the English Parish Church*, pp. 51–2. For additional survivals, see Fincham and Tyacke, *Altars Restored*, p. 246.

Southwark (Surrey), Wigan (Lancashire) and Wimborne (Dorset). In the city of Bristol, he counted eighteen parish churches, 'and in the major part of them, are neat, rich, and melodious Organs, that are constantly play'd on'. In Salisbury, he noted that all four churches had organs. And he passed through Romsey (Hampshire) just as a new organ was being erected in the church. Hammond remarked, with uncharacteristic cynicism, that this organ had been 'given by a Old and rich snudge yet living ..., to blow and trumpett forth his Liberality'.[18] Admittedly, parishes with organs remained unusual, but most regions had at least a few.

Not surprisingly, the official status of the organ declined under parliamentary rule during the middle decades of the seventeenth century. In the tense atmosphere of 1644, a parliamentary ordinance commanded that all the organs in England's churches and chapels be 'taken away, and utterly defaced'.[19] They were hereby banned for the first time, and the surviving evidence, though often anecdotal, indicates that the pressures exerted by warfare and by ascendant puritanism brought the lives of a number of organs to a violent close. William Dowsing, on his iconoclastic journey around East Anglia, destroyed or ordered the destruction of organs in the seven Suffolk churches listed above. In 1646, several incidents were described in the royalist publication *Mercurius Rusticus: or, The countries complaint of the barbarous out-rages committed by the SECTARIES of this late flourishing kingdome.* At Corfe (Dorset), for example, parliamentary soldiers 'broke downe the Organs, and made the Pipes serve for Cases to hold their powder and shot'. For decades afterwards, royalists remembered how the larger organ in Peterborough Cathedral had been 'thrown down upon the ground, and there stamped and trampled on, and broke in pieces, with such a strange, furious, and frantick zeal, as cannot be well conceived, but by those that saw it'. In 1647, Bishop Hall described a similarly 'sacrilegious and profane procession' in Norwich. In 'a hideous triumph on the market day before all the country' the destroyers somehow tooted on the removed organ pipes while carrying the rest of their ecclesiastical loot to a bonfire in the marketplace. 'Lord, what work was here', remarked the uncomprehending bishop.[20]

18 *A Relation of a Short Survey of 26 Counties*, pp. 46, 92, and *A Relation of a Short Survey of the Western Counties*, pp. 60, 64, 69.

19 The ordinance is transcribed in *Journal of William Dowsing*, p. 343.

20 Bruno Ryves, *Mercurius Rusticus* (1646; London, 1685), p. 120; Simon Gunton, *The History of the Church at Peterborough* (London, 1686), p. 333; Barwick, quoted by Winn, 'A Bibliography', pp. 331–2; Joseph Hall, *Hard Measure*, published as *The Shaking of the Olive Tree* (London, 1660), p. 63.

In the years between 1547 and 1660, the organ therefore endured what one historian has called 'a rough ride', and the route travelled by the parochial choir was even more bumpy.[21] English Protestants of the mid-sixteenth century objected strongly to what they perceived as over-elaboration within the sacred choral music of tradition. They were not, however, bent on the destruction of all parochial choirs. Cranmer, in a famous letter of 1544, was firm but moderate in seeking to establish new principles for church music in the vernacular: 'In mine opinion, the song that shall be made thereunto would not be full of notes, but, as near as may be, for every syllable a note: so that it may be sung distinctly and devoutly.' The Edwardian Reformation, however, placed most parochial choirs in grave danger. It did so not by outlawing them, but by destroying some of the institutions that had traditionally supported them and by failing to provide them with clear directions regarding the appropriate music for the new services. The abolition of chantries in 1547 removed at a stroke the salaries of many of the conducts or singing men who had previously been the professional mainstay of most parish choirs. The suppression of confraternities removed another source of support. Where parishes managed, against the odds, to retain their choirs, the singers no longer knew what to sing. The vernacular services, set out in the Prayer Books of 1549 and 1552, included no musical settings. Many choirs tried to cope by fitting the traditional music to the new texts. A few parishes purchased copies of John Marbeck's *Booke of Common Praier Noted* following its publication in 1550. This work provided musical settings for matins, evensong, the communion, the Creed and the burial services. Shortly afterwards, the churchwardens of St Mary Magdalen, London, obtained 'three books of partes of the service in English in note in print', and it seems certain that the reference is to Marbeck's publication. A few other London parishes are known to have obtained manuscript copies of other musical settings for the new services, such as those contained in the Wanley Partbooks (which include simple homophonic music for parts of the 1549 Prayer Book services).[22]

These were valiant efforts to sustain local choral traditions, and the documents of the Elizabethan Settlement suggest official sympathy for the view that properly reformed choral music might help to harmonise the

[21] Bicknell, *History of the English Organ*, p. 26.

[22] Temperley, *Music of the English Parish Church*, pp. 12–17; Fiona Kisby, 'Urban Cultures and Religious Reforms: Parochial Music in London, *c.*1520–*c.*1580', paper delivered at Leeds Medieval Conference, July 1998. I am grateful to Dr Kisby for supplying me with a copy of this paper.

nation during a potentially discordant phase of its life. The injunctions of 1559 sometimes seemed to assume the existence of a choir in the typical church, and envisaged its role in singing the Litany. The document also presented some rather more explicit guidance on the role of music within the services established by the Prayer Book of 1559:

Item, because [in] divers collegiate and some parish churches heretofore, there hath been livings appointed for the maintenance of men and children, to use singing in the church, by means whereof the laudable science of music hath been had in estimation and preserved in knowledge, the Queen's Majesty neither meaning in any wise the decay of anything that might conveniently tend to the use and continuance of the said science, neither to have the same in any part so abused in the church, that thereby the common prayer should be the worse understanded of the hearers, willeth and commandeth that first, no alteration be made of such alignments of living, as heretofore hath been appointed to the use of singing or music in the church, but the same to remain. And that there be a modest and distinct song so used, in all parts of the common prayers in the church, that the same may be as plainly understanded as if it were read without singing. And yet nevertheless, for the comforting of such as delight in music, it may be permitted that in the beginning or in the end of common prayers, either at morning or evening, there may be sung an hymn or suchlike song, to the praise of Almighty God, in the best sort of melody and music that may be conveniently devised, having respect that the sentence of the hymn may be understanded and perceived.[23]

The Queen's Majesty may not have intended the decay of parochial choirs, but for several reasons their fate continued to hang in the balance, as it had done under Edward VI. Firstly, nothing was done to make good the loss of financial support that followed from the abolition of chantries. Many choirs were, by this date, severely depleted, and would have needed a period of intensive care if they were to survive and prosper. Secondly, the Elizabethan Settlement was no more helpful than its Edwardian counterpart in providing precise instruction on the actual music that might be used in the new services. Parishes would have to find the creative energy and the money necessary to identify and acquire suitable music. Many churchwardens, quite understandably, were less than willing to commit themselves to this enterprise in such uncertain circumstances. Thirdly, by offering vague encouragement to those who hoped to hear congregations participating for themselves in 'an hymn or suchlike song', the injunctions opened up the possibility that choirs, like organs, would in time become

[23] *Documents of the English Reformation*, pp. 344–5.

redundant. To this list, we might add the influence of more radical reformers who, in the decades that followed, expressed their hostility to the very notion of a select choir that had the effect of restricting popular participation in worship by monopolising the music and distracting congregational attention from the sense of the all-important, all-sufficient Scriptural words. One Jacobean commentator, no friend of the puritans, looked back on Elizabeth's reign and remarked: 'divers preachers being set a work by the humours of the aforesaid reformers, were bold to set out books and also in their sermons did perswade the people from the reverent use of service in song'.[24] For these reasons, parochial choirs that withered steadily away were much more representative than those that somehow sang bravely on.

In this difficult atmosphere, it is perhaps surprising that a number of parochial choirs survived as long as they did. Choirs, like organs, did not all disappear at a stroke, and a minority of parishes evidently continued to maintain choral worship in some form during the 1560s and even beyond. At Broomfield (Kent), there was a good deal of the old within the new, and the diocesan authorities investigated reports that communion was still being administered to the accompaniment of 'popish singing' during the early 1560s. At Sandwich in the same county, however, Archbishop Parker was entirely happy with choral dimension of the service as he witnessed it in 1563, and he provided William Cecil with a note to this effect: 'ther service songe in good distinct harmonie, and quiett devotion. The singinge men, beinge the Mayor and the Jurattes with the head men of the town, placed in the queere [choir] fayre and decent in so good order as I cowde wishe.' At Faversham, suggestively, several men were reported to the church courts during the early part of Elizabeth's reign because they were refusing to sing in the choir, despite having done diligent service under Mary. In this case, the culprits seem to have been motivated by religious conservatism (one of them was also said to be negligent in attending the new services, and seems to have been particularly hostile to sermons).[25] In the early years of the new church, parish choirs could find themselves caught uncomfortably between the disapproval of traditionalists and the hostility of zealous puritans. The auguries were not promising.

As the reign proceeded England's choirs fared even less well than its organs. Most of the parishes that maintained choirs during the 1560s had

[24] 'The Praise of Musicke', Royal MS 18 BX, fos. 5v–6r, BL.

[25] *Church Life in Kent*, pp. 14, 29–30; Parker, quoted by Winn, 'Bibliography', pp. 88–9.

abandoned their efforts well before 1580. The records once again convey the impression that charitable churchwardens were reluctant to impoverish their singing men by withdrawing financial support. Instead, they waited for the musicians to leave the parish or depart this life, and then chose not to replace them. In Chudleigh (Devon), the churchwardens paid threepence to 'poor Robin the singing man' in 1574, and three years later the choir was mentioned in the accounts for the very last time. In Newcastle upon Tyne, the first city chamberlains of the new reign paid annual sums of up to 40s to four boys for singing in the choir of St Nicholas' Church (quite probably, they *were* the choir), but only until 1568. A taste for tradition and a sense of benevolent responsibility motivated the seventy-nine parishioners of Christ's Church, London, who in about 1580 petitioned for the continuing maintenance of their five poor singing men, 'in respect they have bene trayned in the scyence of musick all theyr life'.[26] Ordinary parishes that kept their choirs beyond 1590 were few indeed. At Hartland in Devon, new partbooks for singers were purchased in 1598–9 but, even here, payments for choral music ceased in 1608.[27]

Very occasionally, individual parishes bucked the trend. In Kibworth Beauchamp (Leicestershire), for example, the curate established or re-established a small choir of men and boys in 1572. One of its younger members later recalled that 'diverse of the parish which had skill in songe were removed from their places where they usually sate into places nerer the ministers seate'. Here, they made use of 'half a dozen song books' that had recently been bequeathed to the parish.[28] It was, however, an unusual initiative, and we do not know how long it lasted. In most places, choirs were fading out and, by 1600, Christians with an appetite for fully choral services generally had to take themselves into one of England's cathedrals or surviving collegiate churches.

26 'Parish Church Musicians', pp. 71, 80; *REED Newcastle upon Tyne*, pp. 33, 36, 47; *CSPD 1547–80*, p. 703. On the Christ's Church singers, see also H. Gareth Owen, 'Tradition and Reform: Ecclesiastical Controversy in an Elizabethan London Parish', *Guildhall Miscellany* 2.2 (1961), 63–70, and Fincham and Tyacke, *Altars Restored*, pp. 95–9.

27 Temperley, *Music of the English Parish Church*, p. 51. As with organs, however, the current historiographical trend is towards an optimistic revision of the extent to which parochial choirs were maintained during the reign of Elizabeth. See Willis, 'Church Music and Protestantism', ch. 3.

28 Archdeaconry depositions, 1D 41/4, box ix/6, Leicestershire Record Office. This reference came to me via a relay team comprising Bernard Capp, Diarmaid MacCulloch and John Craig. I am grateful to them all.

The modest recovery of the organ during the early seventeenth century does not seem to have been shared by the parochial choir. References to the existence of such ensembles in ordinary parishes were rare in Jacobean and Caroline England. In the decades following the Restoration, however, organists and singers together experienced an improvement in fortunes, driven by the desire of influential musicians, clerics and gentlemen to reform and enhance parochial music-making. Many new organs were erected, particularly in urban parishes. On 21 April 1667, for example, Samuel Pepys attended church in Hackney, partly to ogle at young ladies from the local schools, but also to see and hear the new organ. The instrument was also 'mighty pretty, and makes me earnest to have a pair at our church' (St Olave's). In the years that followed, the rival organ-makers Bernard Smith and Renatus Harris provided new instruments for churches all over London. When John Playford published his *Whole Book of Psalms* in 1677, he had good reason to remark that 'many of our Churches are lately furnished with Organs'. One of the new instruments, built by Harris in the early eighteenth century for the church of St Botolph without Aldgate, can be heard on track 43 on the website (see Figure 8.1).[29] The same trend was observable in England's provincial towns, and the installation of an organ at Tiverton in Devon was marked, in 1696, by a special sermon.[30] Country churches, in contrast, often did without organs until the nineteenth century. Instead, they led the renaissance of the parochial choir from the 1680s onwards. Within a hundred years, nearly all rural churches had choirs again. At first, they sang to support the musical efforts of the broader congregation, but they soon began to perform more ambitious music – psalm settings in four parts, new hymns and anthems – to audiences of passive parishioners (see Figure 8.2).[31] The eighteenth century produced reams of written music, in print and manuscript, designed for the use of small country choirs. We are, however, getting ahead of ourselves. In order to understand the role of organs and choirs in these changed times, we must turn our ears towards the sound of congregational psalmody.

[29] *Diary of Samuel Pepys*, vol. VIII, p. 174; Spink, 'Music and Society', pp. 22, 49; Playford, *Whole Book of Psalms*, preface. The Aldgate organ has recently been restored to its original magnificence and is both visually and acoustically stunning.

[30] See below, pp. 451–2. Roz Southey notes, however, that the distribution of organs in urban churches of the north-east remained patchy in 1700: see her *Music-making in North-east England*, p. 107.

[31] Temperley, *Music of the English Parish Church*, pp. 97–8, 104, 116–63, 202–3. On Tiverton, see below, pp. 451–2.

Figure 8.1. Many new organs were constructed in England's urban churches during the late seventeenth and early eighteenth centuries. This one was originally built by Renatus Harris for St Botolph without Aldgate. During the last few years, the organ-makers Martin Goetze and Dominic Gwynn have painstakingly restored the instrument to the condition it enjoyed in 1744. © Martin Goetze and Dominic Gwynn Ltd.

Metrical psalmody: an overview

The English metrical psalms had their background in courtly verse of the 1540s, and the versions that came to dominate English parish church music for 200 years were originally aimed very narrowly at Edward VI and his entourage. In about 1549, a royal servant named Thomas

Figure 8.2. By the mid-eighteenth century, choirs were common in country churches once again and their efforts sometimes attracted the attention of satirical artists. In this print, the choir consists of seven men singing from a book. One of them sets the pitch by blowing a pipe, and the congregation listens but does not participate. © Trustees of the British Museum, Prints and Drawings, 1878,0713.1314, John Golder, *The Country Choristers* (London, 1773).

Sternhold dedicated *Certayne Psalmes Drawen into Englishe Metre* to the boy king, whose tender zeal found 'more delight in the holy songs of verity than in any feigned rhymes of vanity'.[32] The songs were evidently successful among their target audience, and further editions were soon published, with additional psalms added by a recent Oxford graduate named John Hopkins. Sternhold and Hopkins wrote for aristocratic circles, but others

[32] Thomas Sternhold, *Certayne Psalmes Drawen into Englishe Metre* (London, *c.* 1549), preface.

followed Luther in hoping that a body of spiritual songs could be created that would displace the profane alternatives among the population as a whole. Many reformers shared the hope of Miles Coverdale, expressed in the mid-1530s: 'Would God that our minstrels had none other thing to play upon neither our carters and ploughmen other thing to whistle upon, save psalms, hymns, and such godly songs as David is occupied withal.'[33] Coverdale's own *Goostly Psalmes* appear to have made little popular impression, but his ambition survived him and was eventually to play a critical role in popularising the Sternhold–Hopkins songs under Elizabeth I.

Another important phase in the early history of the musical psalms took place during the intervening reign of Queen Mary. In Geneva, the English Protestant exiles were influenced by Calvinist models and experimented freely with the congregational singing of psalms during acts of worship. The psalms of Sternhold and Hopkins were modified and reissued with successive editions of the Genevan service book. Such ventures laid vital foundations for what was to follow in England, though congregational psalm-singing was not written into the Elizabethan religious settlement. The royal injunctions of 1559, as we have heard, allowed the introduction of 'an hymn or suchlike song' within church services, but neither specified nor encouraged the singing of metrical psalms. The term 'hymn' referred to any song of praise, whether or not its text was based squarely on a Scriptural passage, and early modern England produced many examples. Seventeenth-century records contain occasional references to the use of such hymns in worship, but it was without doubt the metrical psalms that came to dominate congregational singing. In the years immediately following the accession of Elizabeth I, psalm-singing rapidly became established as a feature of worship, particularly in London. In September 1559, the diarist Henry Machyn described 'the new mornyng prayer at sant Antholyns in Boge-row', during which 'men and women all do syng, and boys'. In 1560, John Jewel wrote to Peter Martyr in resoundingly positive terms regarding the effectiveness of the new participatory church music:

as soon as they had once commenced singing in public, in only one little church in London, immediately not only the churches in the neighbourhood, but even the towns far distant, began to vie with each other in the same practice. You may now sometimes see at Paul's Cross, after the sermon, six thousand persons, old and young, of both sexes, all singing together and praising God. This sadly annoys the

[33] Coverdale, *Goostly Psalmes and Spirituall Songes*, preface 'Unto the Christian Reader'.

mass-Priests, and the devil. For they perceive that by these means the sacred discourses sink more deeply into the minds of men, and that their kingdom is weakened and shaken at almost every note.[34]

The first full edition of all the psalms was published in 1562 (now with contributions from several additional authors). Other editions soon followed, and from 1573 the verbal content of the Sternhold–Hopkins *Whole Book of Psalms* was stable, comprising 159 psalms, 7 other Scriptural texts, 5 liturgical pieces and 9 original hymns.[35] A total of 143 of the psalm texts used common metre (8.6.8.6), with the remaining 16 written in either short metre (6.6.8.6) or long metre (8.8.8.8). The success of the Sternhold–Hopkins psalms is beyond dispute. The *Whole Book* was a lucrative enterprise for John Day, the printer who secured the monopolistic licence. In 1582, the queen's printer, Christopher Barker, clearly wanted a piece of the action. He complained to Lord Treasurer Burghley that the psalms were 'a parcel of the Church service' and therefore 'properly belongeth to me'. The venture, he claimed, was highly profitable because the book of psalms was nowadays 'occupied of all sorts of men, women and children' and required 'not great stocke for the furnyshing thereof'. Recent historians agree: the Sternhold–Hopkins collection went through approximately 482 editions between 1562 and 1640, selling perhaps a million copies and becoming the most frequently printed book of its age. It was often bound with copies of the Bible and the Book of Common Prayer, and a swing towards smaller format editions during the early seventeenth century suggests increasing private ownership at this time.[36]

The singing psalms spread steadily during the decades that followed the Elizabethan Settlement, though the precise mechanisms of dissemination remain rather mysterious. From the 1560s, the title page of the *Whole Book* proclaimed proudly that the psalms were 'set forth and allowed to be sung in all churches of all the people together, before and after Morning and Evening prayer, as also before and after sermons'. This went some way beyond the allowance made in the injunctions, and it has never been quite clear whether John Day was deliberately stretching a point or merely

[34] *Documents of the English Reformation*, pp. 344–5; Edna D. Parks, *Early English Hymns: An Index* (Metuchen: Scarecrow Press, 1972); *Diary of Henry Machyn*, p. 212; *The Works of John Jewel*, ed. John Ayre, 4 vols. (Cambridge, 1845–50), vol. IV, pp. 1230–1.

[35] Temperley, *Music of the English Parish Church*, pp. 55–8; Hamlin, *Psalm Culture*, p. 30. In the pages below, references to the *Whole Book of Psalms* will denote the Sternhold–Hopkins version unless otherwise indicated.

[36] Barker, quoted by Winn, 'Bibliography', p. 128; Green, *Print and Protestantism*, pp. 501, 509, 512.

recording a degree of official approval that was not registered in other written sources. Either way, his statement seems to have had the desired effect, and by 1580 a typical Sunday service in an English parish church probably included the singing of a psalm both before and after the sermon or homily. Parish clerks across the land had obtained their copies of the text, and local purchases of the *Whole Book* were recorded sporadically in churchwardens' accounts (it seems that copies were generally purchased by individuals rather than by parishes). Steadily, it became customary for a psalm to be sung while the congregation received the communion, when the bodies of the dead were carried to their graves and, in some places, during the annual perambulation of the parish bounds.[37]

Official approval had been elusive during the 1560s, but when in 1576 Elizabeth's government introduced a special church service for the anniversary of her accession it included 'The xxi psalm in meter before the sermon, unto the end of the vii verse. And the c psalm after the sermon.' In 1580, another special service, intended 'to avert Gods wrath from us, threatned by the late terrible earthquake', ordered that Psalm 46 be sung 'after the sermon, or homily'. Each of these texts was carefully chosen to suit the circumstance. Such examples demonstrate that, by the middle years of the reign, Elizabeth and her leading ecclesiastical advisers had come to accept that psalm-singing was a valuable device. In 1574, the future archbishop John Whitgift commented, a little clumsily, 'The psalms beeing song [sung] may as well be understanded as being said, and better too.'[38]

By 1600, therefore, English congregations regularly sang psalms within their church services. This situation remained fundamentally unchanged until the Civil Wars, despite the efforts of those who aimed to reform congregational psalm-singing (while making a few pounds on the side). In 1621, Thomas Ravenscroft published a large collection of four-part settings in his *Whole Book of Psalms*. His method of notation influenced subsequent editions of Sternhold–Hopkins, but there is little to suggest that it had much influence on parochial performance (he probably found

[37] Temperley, *Music of the English Parish Church*, p. 48; Henry Bourne, *Antiquitates Vulgares* (Newcastle, 1725), p. 22; AN/PB 295/6/61, HL. The psalms were also sung in Cambridge chapels during this period: Jesus College purchased thirteen metrical psalters between 1566 and 1572. See Ian Payne, 'Music at Jesus College, Cambridge, *c.* 1557–1679', *Proceedings of the Cambridge Antiquarian Society* 76 (1988 for 1987), 98.

[38] *A Fourme of Praier with Thankes Giving, to be Used Every Yeere, the 17 of November* (London, 1576); *The Order of Prayer, and Other Exercises upon Wednesdayes and Frydayes* (London, 1580); John Whitgift, *The Defense of the Aunswere to the Admonition* (London, 1574), p. 741.

his main market amongst the musically educated).[39] Ravenscroft was not alone in regarding the Sternhold–Hopkins settings with elitist disdain (despite their courtly origins), and the 1620s also witnessed an attempt by George Wither to displace the dominant version. His *Hymnes and Songs of the Church* (1623) provided new translations with new music, and earned him royal approval. Wither obtained a royal patent for the sole printing of his book, transcripts of which were also to be bound with all subsequent copies of the psalms in metre. He was empowered to inspect the premises of rival printers, and the generous terms of the licence offered him the prospect of breaking the Sternhold–Hopkins stranglehold. Sadly for him, it was not to be. Wither was unable to enforce his licence in the face of opposition from the Stationers' Company, which held its own monopoly over the printing of all metrical psalters. He was beaten back, and commented bitterly, 'I wonder what divine calling HOPKINS and STERNHOLD had more then I have, that their metircall [sic] Psalmes may be allowed of rather then my hymnes.'[40] Similarly unsuccessful was Charles I's attempt to promote a rival version of the psalms, prepared in part by his father. In the 1630s, Archbishop Laud and his followers were not enthusiastic advocates of congregational psalm singing in the Sternhold–Hopkins version, but Bishop Cosin's efforts to stamp out communal participation at Durham Cathedral had perhaps taught them that aggressive reform was likely to prove inflammatory. It was one thing to order the redecoration of church interiors; it was quite another to transform the singing of psalms.[41]

Congregational psalm-singing also survived the political polarisation of the 1640s, and was practised by royalists and parliamentarians alike. Indeed, it was officially enjoined for the very first time. In 1644, parliament passed an ordinance commanding that the Book of Common Prayer be replaced by the *Directory for the Publique Worship of God.* An attempt was hereby made to establish a presbyterian form of church government, and the *Directory* was assertive on the subject of church music: 'it is the duty of Christians to praise God publikely by singing of psalms, together in the congregation, and also privately in the family. In singing of psalms

[39] Temperley, *Music of the English Parish Church*, pp. 63–4. One of Ravenscroft's psalms is recorded on the website, track 44.

[40] Wither, *The Schollers Purgatory*, pp. 16, 40; see also Hamlin, *Psalm Culture*, pp. 20–1, 41–2, 58 and 83.

[41] The psalms of James I are discussed in William Beveridge, *A Defence of the Book of Psalms* (London, 1710), pp. 115–17. See also Green, *Print and Protestantism*, pp. 531–2. On Cosin, see below, p. 449.

the voice is to be tuneably and gravely ordered; but the chief care must be to sing with understanding and with grace in the heart, making melody unto the Lord.' The *Directory* placed sermons at the centre of worship, but made space for two musical psalms (one of which was optional). Henceforth, there was to be no other form of music within church services. In 1646, the Westminster Assembly also attempted to replace the Sternhold–Hopkins psalter with a new version of the metrical psalms written by Francis Rouse, but once again the old songs proved unmovable.[42]

In 1660, negotiations to determine the shape of Charles II's restored Church of England touched on the subject of psalm-singing. At the Savoy Conference, presbyterian representatives made their pitch: 'Because singing of psalms is a considerable part of publick worship, we desire that the version set forth and allowed to be sung in churches may be amended; or that we may have leave to make use of a purer version.' They were firmly put in their place by the legalistic bishops: 'Singing of the psalms in metre is no part of the liturgy, and so no part of our commission.' Again, Sternhold and Hopkins reigned supreme, and in 1662 the Act of Uniformity brought in the revised *Book of Common Prayer* and the Psalms of David 'as they are to be sung or said in Churches'. At the end of the century, a new version of the metrical psalms by Nahum Tate and Nicholas Brady earned royal approval, and became the first alternative edition in 150 years to threaten in any significant way the market leadership of Sternhold and Hopkins.[43] Even so, the old Tudor version remained dominant over its rivals into the eighteenth century.

The psalm melodies

The tunes to which English psalms were sung tell an interesting story of their own. Those that were notated in the Sternhold–Hopkins *Whole Book* from 1562 were drawn predominantly from the earlier Genevan editions. Some were French in origin but the majority have so far proved untraceable. It has been suggested that many of the tunes were drawn from a now hidden tradition of courtly song, and that they lost musical coherence,

[42] 'An Ordinance for taking away the Book of Common Prayer', in *Acts and Ordinances of the Interregnum*, vol. I, pp. 592–607; Green, *Print and Protestantism*, p. 519; Hamlin, *Psalm Culture*, ch. 2.

[43] Edward Cardwell, *A History of Conferences* (Oxford, 1849), pp. 308, 342; *Statutes of the Realm*, vol. V, p. 364; Nahum Tate and Nicholas Brady, *A New Version of the Psalms of David* (London, 1696).

except to initiates, when they were severed from their original instrumental accompaniment as a consequence of Protestant sensibilities regarding the use of lutes in church.[44] Certainly, they were not the most memorable or accessible of melodies, yet they nevertheless appeared on the pages of the *Whole Book* during the musical lives of several generations. In the early Elizabethan publications, a certain amount of alteration and substitution took place, but there was no radical overhaul of the tunes. The edition of 1570 included sixty-seven tunes, the highest total in the entire series. There were always, therefore, many fewer tunes than texts because some melodies were recommended for more than one psalm.

Despite their literary longevity, these tunes do not appear to have caught on. There were several exceptions – the melodies set for Psalms 100 and 119 are particularly fine – but English congregations evidently found most of the Sternhold–Hopkins tunes unsuitable to their needs, capacities or tastes. The melodies were predominantly eight lines long so that one rendition of a typical tune occupies two verses of a psalm text. Many of them also seem rather featureless and lacking in a clear sense of direction. Of course, it is nowadays impossible to hear them as once they were heard, but contemporaries too sometimes grumbled about the Sternhold–Hopkins psalms because of 'the difficultie of their tunes'.[45] They were hard to remember and harder to love. Consequently, most of them failed the popularity test during the first two or three decades of Elizabeth's reign.

By the closing decades of the sixteenth century, a remarkable transformation of the psalm tunes was underway. The eight-line melodies of the Sternhold–Hopkins collection were steadily being displaced by a new generation of four-line tunes, many of them named after historic towns or cities (the 'Oxford' tune, and so on). According to various accounts, most congregations apparently came to sing their psalms to a mere handful of the new, short tunes or 'common' melodies. In 1594, Thomas East identified four tunes to which the psalms were now sung 'in most churches of this Realme'.[46] This was probably an exaggeration, for it seems unlikely that individual congregations in Kent and Cumberland would have settled on the same four tunes. Nevertheless, there clearly existed a stock of melodies that enjoyed very considerable currency. Many of the common tunes survived and thrived throughout the early modern period.

44 *The Forme of Prayers and Ministration of the Sacraments* (Geneva, 1556; 2nd edn., 1558); Temperley, *Music of the English Parish Church*, pp. 27–33; Leaver, '*Goostly Psalmes*', pp. 118–31.

45 Henry Dod, *Certaine Psalmes of David* (London, 1603), preface.

46 Thomas East, *Psalmes* (London, 1594), p. 1.

Table 8.1. The top thirty psalm melodies

I. 'Common tunes'	**II. Long-lasting 'official' tunes**
Bristol	Psalm 1
Cambridge	Psalm 51
Cambridge short/Southwell	Psalm 68
Cheshire	Psalm 81
Exeter	Psalm 100
Glastonbury	Psalm 113
Hackney	Psalm 119
Hereford	Psalm 148
Hertfordshire	
Kentish	
London/Lichfield	
London new	
Low Dutch	
Martyrs	
New	
Oxford	
St David's	
Westminster	
Winchester	
Windsor/Suffolk	
Worcester	
York	

Fortunately, they were regularly written down by musical authors and by some of the individuals who kept manuscript tune books.

The common melodies deserve careful analysis. There were a great many of them, but those listed in Table 8.1 were identified by contemporary authors as the tunes that they considered to be the most widely sung during the decades between 1590 and 1700.[47] Together, they amount to a fascinating and immensely solid body of extraordinarily successful music. Their success can be explained by comparing them with their counterparts in the Sternhold–Hopkins collection. Most importantly, the common melodies are half the length, each comprising four distinct musical phrases. They also make somewhat lighter demands upon the vocal range of the singer. Admittedly, most of the official tunes are not exactly taxing

[47] The list is based on remarks made in the following works: Daman, *The Psalmes of David in English Meter* (London, 1579); East, *Psalmes*; Richard Allison, *The Psalmes of David in Meter* (London, 1599); Henry Dod, *Al the Psalmes of David* (London, 1620); and Playford, *An Introduction*.

in this regard, but the common melodies achieve a new simplicity. All but four of them are contained within a range that is narrower than an octave, and the most limited tunes – 'Oxford' and 'Low Dutch' – require only four adjacent notes.[48] In general, the melodic movement is by step to consecutive notes, though intervals of a third are fairly common. A comparison of the two groups also suggests that the common tunes are somewhat more compact and comprehensible in structural terms. Within most of the melodies, the four phrases comprise a unified whole that makes good sense, even at first hearing. Eighteen of the melodies begin and end on the keynote (the first of the scale). All twenty-four generate a feeling of movement towards the last note of one of the two middle phrases (typically reaching the second, third or fifth of the scale) and then back towards the keynote at the end of fourth and final phrase. The highest notes touched within the melodies are also concentrated heavily in the middle two phrases, preceding the return to the starting point. In contrast, the eight-line duration of the official melodies tends to render such patterns less discernible. The common tunes, in sum, are shorter, tighter, more memorable and easier to sing.

By the seventeenth century, the common tunes were well known to rich and poor alike. When William Leighton published a book of hymns and spiritual sonnets in 1613, he reassured those who could not manage his elaborate music that they might nevertheless 'read them or sing them in the common and ordinarie tunes beseeming such a subject'. Decades later, Thomas Mace criticised the standards of parochial performance but argued that no campaign of musical improvement should dare to touch the tunes. These were, he said, well known by all the common people, and 'so excellently good, that I will be bold to say, Art cannot mend them or make better'.[49]

Three of the common tunes require special mention. In 1672, Playford included 'York', 'Martyrs' and 'St David's' on his list of the most widely used tunes, and there is no doubt that all three belonged to the popular stock by this time. In certain characteristics, however, they mark a significant departure from the other successful tunes. These three melodies stretch the singer over an unusually wide range ('St David's' covers a perfect eleventh), and they make regular and distinctive use of motifs based on the notes of the triad (the first, third and fifth of the scale).

[48] The second of these tunes is used on the website, track 45. See below, p. 440.

[49] William Leighton, *The Teares or Lamentations of a Sorrowfull Soule* (London, 1613), preface; Mace, *Musick's Monument*, p. 2.

The explanation is simple: these tunes were among those purposefully composed by Thomas Ravenscroft during the 1620s, and – unlike most of his melodies – they earned themselves a place within the congregational repertoire.[50] The success of the three melodies was probably a consequence of their unusual beauty.

Playford's list of 'The most usual Common Tunes Sung in Parish Churches' also included eight of the official tunes, each identified by the specific psalm with which it was primarily associated, rather than by a place name.[51] The success of this select group of tunes is also suggested by the fact that all but one of them featured in every single musical edition of the Sternhold–Hopkins psalter printed between 1562 and 1687.[52] And when, in 1694, a woman named Agnes Veere, perhaps from Chichester, recorded her favourite psalm tunes in a notebook, most of those listed above were among them.[53] These were, without doubt, the best known official psalm tunes of the early modern period, highly unusual in that they had managed to survive the competition from their common rivals. It is not difficult to identify some of the factors that contributed to their popularity. They are coherently structured and aesthetically satisfying. Some are bright and joyous while others are more doleful, but every one is accessible and pleasing. The melody for Psalm 119 is, for example, a creation of haunting beauty, and the famous tune set to Psalm 100 ('All people that on earth do dwell') was both joyous and memorable.[54] It also possessed an extra advantage, being constructed in an unusual metre (8.8.8.8). This could have led towards obscurity, but because the text of Psalm 100 was popular, so too was its tune. Put simply, there were few other melodies to which it could be sung. The 'Old hundredth' therefore became one of the tunes that was associated very strongly with a specific psalm.

The distinctions between the common and official tunes help to explain the success of one and the relative failure of the other. In several respects, however, the two breeds of melody are more similar. Surviving notation reveals comparable patterns of semibreves and minims, and all the tunes reach natural pausing points at the ends of their phrases. Both sets of

[50] Thomas Ravenscroft, *Whole Book of Psalms* (London, 1621). 'York' can be heard on the website, track 43.

[51] Playford, *An Introduction*, pp. 72–89.

[52] Temperley, *Music of the English Parish Church*, p. 60. See also Nicholas Temperley, *The Hymn Tune Index*, 4 vols. (Oxford: Clarendon Press, 1998), vol. I, pp. 61–2. The top five official tunes, as measured by the frequency with which they appeared in print during the early modern period, were also among those included in Playford's list.

[53] Agnes Veere's music notebook, Cap VI/1/2, WSRO.

[54] The Psalm 119 tune can be heard on the website, track 44 (in the tenor part).

Example 8.1. The 'Oxford' psalm tune (from Sternhold and Hopkins, *The Whole Booke of Psalms . . . Composed in Foure Parts*, 1592). It seems unlikely that the sharpened leading notes (F sharps in this case) would have featured in a normal congregational rendition. Rather, they reflect the efforts made repeatedly by sophisticated composers to make sense of this curious and circular tune.

tunes make use of the medieval modes, drawing particularly on the Dorian, Aeolian and Ionian scales. Individual tunes in both categories also remained remarkably stable, undergoing only minor alterations in their printed versions during periods of a century and more.

One of the most ear-catching features of official and common tunes alike is the manner in which key musical phrases recur in shifting configurations within different melodies. The common tunes, for example, are closely interrelated in a variety of ways, and the listener who hears them all at one sitting is forcibly struck by the frequent recycling of musical phrases and motifs. This feeling intensifies as the tunes become more familiar. The final phrase of 'Oxford' (see Example 8.1) also features at the close of 'Cambridge', 'Windsor', 'Westminster' and 'Worcester'. The last three of these tunes also display identical third phrases. 'Winchester' shares its middle two phrases with 'Hereford', 'Hertfordshire' and 'New' (with slight variations). The first of these phrases is also found in 'York' (and in the tune to the later hymn 'All Things Bright and Beautiful'). The final phrase of 'Hertfordshire' also appears in the 'Low Dutch' and 'New' tunes. 'Kentish' and 'Westminster' are virtually identical in their opening two phrases, and the final phrase of 'Kentish' also draws 'York' to a close. Individual tunes also present more distinctive motifs and phrases, but the unique is invariably framed by the familiar. A few of the tunes are merely variant versions of one another. 'Windsor' and 'Worcester', for instance, are very closely related, and their opening phrases, though different, fit together in perfect harmony. It seems possible that the 'Worcester' phrase emerged as a descant to the first motif in 'Windsor'. There are several such instances of harmonically compatible phrases, and it has previously been observed that the whole of the 'London' tune can be sung as a descant to

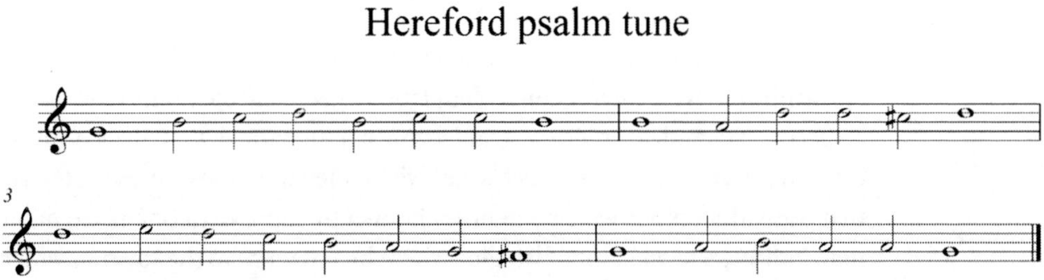

Example 8.2. The 'Hereford' psalm tune (from Playford, *An Introduction*, p. 75)

'Oxford'. Overall, these tunes are thoroughly interwoven. They touch at numerous points, and they grow into and out of one another.[55]

There is also significant evidence of movement between the official and the common tunes. This offers us some insight into the mysterious process by which the latter group evolved, suggesting that anonymous local composers or experimental congregations – somewhat frustrated with the cumbersome official tunes – constructed new, shorter melodies, drawing freely upon the more memorable phrases from the official psalter. The melody known as 'Hereford' (see Example 8.2) is the most impressive example among several: its first phrase is lifted wholesale from the middle of the tune for Psalm 3; its second phrase can be traced to the tunes for Psalms 68 and 122; its third phrase comes from the last section of Psalm 81's tune (with one note altered), while variant forms can also be heard in Psalms 41, 77 and 78; and its fourth phrase might have come from any one of five official tunes (Psalms 3, 14, 30, 141 and 145). Among the common tunes as a whole, 29 per cent of the ninety-two phrases can be traced to the official psalter.

The possibility that some at least of the common melodies were genuinely 'common' in their origins – the products of parochial creativity and evolution – has received little consideration. Improvised descants and experimental musical collage were just two of the possibilities. Some of the common tunes are perhaps just as likely to have evolved out of the medieval Latin psalm tones, well known to the parish clerks of early Elizabethan England. The circular 'Oxford' tune, for example, bears a considerable resemblance to the first of the old tones, while the 'Glastonbury' and 'Westminster' tunes are strongly reminiscent of traditional liturgical chant. It is not possible to identify precise and unmistakable genealogies, but we can certainly speak

[55] Temperley, *Music of the English Parish Church*, p. 75. See below, p. 442, for further consideration of this point.

in terms of family resemblances.[56] The habit of naming the tunes after towns is also interesting, though it is difficult to establish whether 'Worcester' and 'Westminster' were merely convenient labels or actually the home cities of the respective melodies. In 1694, Daniel Warner remarked that the common tunes were 'call'd by the Places Names where they were most in use'. The fact that individual tunes were sometimes known by more than one place name may indicate a local habit of labelling them by reference to the town in which they were thought, whether rightly or wrongly, to have originated. In the Sussex notebook of Agnes Veere, dated 1694, the tune known to Playford as 'Hackney' is entitled 'St. Mary's' (under which name it is still sung today on the Isle of Lewis). By the 1720s, the 'Worcester' tune was familiar to Richard Alderson from Cumbria, but in his notebook he called it 'Lichfield'.[57]

Different types of tune, whether common or official, were appropriate for different categories of psalm. This principle was laid out in Archbishop Parker's *Whole Psalter* (*c.* 1567), which provided eight tunes by Thomas Tallis, each with its own spiritual and emotional charge:

The first is meeke: devout to saie,
The second sad in majesty,
The third doth rage; and roughly brayth,
The fourth doth fawne; and flattrye playth.
The fyfth delighth; and laugheth the more,
The sixt bewayleth; it weepeth full sore,
The seventh tredeth stoute in froward race,
The eyghte goeth milde; in modest pace.[58]

A comparable approach seems to have prevailed in the case of the Sternhold–Hopkins tunes and, later, among their common competitors. Towards the end of our period, Playford subdivided his list of the best-known common psalm tunes into those appropriate for each of four categories of psalm texts: 'Psalms Consolatory', 'Psalms of Prayer, Confession, and Funerals', 'peculiar Psalms' and 'Psalms of Praise and Thanksgiving'. Appropriately enough, tunes in the more cheerful Ionian mode dominate the last of these categories (praise), while Dorian and Aeolian melodies feature more heavily in the first two (consolation and prayer or

[56] I am grateful to David Mateer for discussing this possibility with me, and for generously providing me with a number of valuable references.

[57] Daniel Warner, *A Collection of Some Verses out of the Psalms of David* (London, 1694), preface; Agnes Veere's music notebook, Cap VI/1/2, WSRO; Richard Alderson's notebook, WDX/219, Cumbria Record Office.

[58] Matthew Parker, *The Whole Psalter Translated into English Metre* (London, *c.* 1567), W4v.

confession).[59] Elsewhere, Playford distinguished between 'Psalms of Prayer and Confession, to solemn grave Flat Tunes' and 'Psalms of Thanksgiving and Praise, to lively chearful Sharp Tunes'.[60] Early modern writers clearly knew that different types of melodic scale produced different emotional effects in the listener.

The sound of the psalms

English congregational psalm-singing has not, in general, attracted rave reviews from musicologists. We have been told that the psalm tunes, in common practice, became 'stultified in a monotonous succession of minims', 'sung lethargically at that'. The musical psalms were 'trite verse sung to a dull tune'. Illiterate people 'hobbled' through the psalms, unaided but desperately in need of aid: 'congregations must usually have found their psalm singing almost wholly a spiritual exercise, and very little musical'. The best musicological account available adopts a more constructive attitude, but even here we are warned that most congregations were thoroughly unmusical and that the parish clerks who led the singing were no better ('As we know, very few clerks could even sing the tunes properly themselves'). There is a questionable tendency in all such accounts to equate musical ability with formal musical education. The style of psalm-singing as it evolved after 1600 has been described as 'uncouth and discordant'. It was thus 'unacceptable or laughable to educated people of the time, as it probably would be to us today'.[61] Indeed, modern commentators have tended to rely heavily and readily on contemporary criticism of psalm-singing, which was often driven by a desire on the part of its authors to sell their reforming musical literature. In 1619, for example, George Wither complained that most churchgoers sang their psalms 'with the same devotion wherewith (as the Proverbe is) Dogges goe to Church'. A few decades later, Thomas Mace was similarly dismayed to note 'what whining, toting, yelling, or screeking there is in many Country

[59] Playford, *An Introduction*, p. 72. There are, however, some interesting discrepancies. The mournful-sounding 'Martyrs' tune, in the Dorian mode, is, for example, recommended for psalms of praise.

[60] Playford, *Whole Book of Psalms*, preface. For other examples, see William Barton, *The Book of Psalms* (London, 1645), A1v, and Mace, *Musick's Monument*, p. 2.

[61] Wulstan, *Tudor Music*, pp. 24–5; Woodfill, *Musicians in English Society*, p. 156; Temperley, *Music of the English Parish Church*, pp. 146, 91, 99.

Congregations'.[62] Both men had ulterior motives. It is apparent that we should attend to privileged scorn for communal psalm-singing with a critical ear. There is no such thing as uncomplicated testimony. The challenge is to use derisive commentary as a source of insight into a lost but powerful aesthetic within English popular music.

We should begin, however, with a practical question: how did English people learn the tunes of the psalms? For the early Elizabethan decades, a conclusive answer is hard to find. The conventional wisdom holds that congregations must at first have sung their psalms to popular ballad and dance tunes that had the obvious advantage of being lively and well known.[63] The use of existing secular melodies would, it is argued, have enabled eager reformers to establish with speed and efficiency a popular habit of psalm-singing. Had they used the drearier official tunes, no such celerity would have been possible. The evidence for this view is, however, rather slim. When Henry Machyn heard a psalm after a sermon at Paul's Cross in March 1560, he reported that it was sung to 'the tune of Genevay ways' (a reference to Geneva, presumably implying that the melody sounded strange and foreign). On another occasion, 'all the pepull dyd syng the tune of Geneway' at a church service. There are no printed Elizabethan collections of metrical psalms that recommend the use of worldly tunes. By the close of the century, moreover, the mixing of holy texts and worldly tunes was widely frowned upon and occasionally disparaged. In *The Merry Wives of Windsor*, Mistress Ford alleges that Falstaff's inward disposition and his audible words 'do no more adhere and keep place together than the hundred psalms to the tune of Greensleeves'. In 1597, a Kentish vicar brought a case in the church courts against 'certain evil disposed persons' who had accused him of leading his congregation in a rendition of Psalm 25 to the tune of 'Greensleeves'.[64] The similarity of these two references suggests that the connection between psalmody and 'Greensleeves' had become a proverbial slur, useful in implying the deceitfulness or impropriety of one's opponents.

The case of William Slatyer is more fully documented. In 1630, this successful clergyman, whose *curriculum vitae* included a spell as chaplain to James I's queen, published his fourth book. Its title, *Psalmes, or Songs of*

[62] Wither, *A Preparation to the Psalter*, p. 68; Mace, *Musick's Monument*, p. 9.

[63] Temperley, *Music of the English Parish Church*, p. 66; Collinson, *Birthpangs of Protestant England*, p. 109.

[64] *Diary of Henry Machyn*, p. 228; Shakespeare, *The Merry Wives of Windsor*, in *Complete Oxford Shakespeare*, p. 639; Patrick Collinson, *From Iconoclasm to Iconophobia* (Reading: Reading University Press, 1986), p. 18 n. 70.

Sion, sounded safe enough, as did his selective translations of the sacred texts. Slatyer's innovative approach to the melodies, however, generated controversy. His title page explained that his versions of the psalms were 'Intended for Christmas Carols, and fitted to divers of the most noted and common, but solemne tunes, every where in this Land familiarly used and knowne'. He had in mind not the common psalm tunes, but a selection of melodies generally associated with broadside balladry, and his purpose was presumably to inject a little festive fun into English psalmody. A table at the end of the publication therefore listed his recommendations. Psalms 8 and 11, for example, were to be fitted to the tune 'Goe from my window', while Psalm 47 would bounce along to the strains of 'All in a garden green'. Dr Slatyer had evidently put considerable thought into his list, taking care to select tunes with pre-existing moral and spiritual associations (for example, 'The man of life upright' and 'The lady's fall'). His creative care notwithstanding, Slatyer was summoned to appear before the High Commission on 20 October 1631. He confessed before Archbishop Abbot and Bishop Laud that he had added to his *Psalmes* 'a scandalous table to the disgrace of religion and to the incouragement of the contemners thereof', and he pleaded for forgiveness. Abbot then subjected him to 'a very sharpe reproofe for being ever busy about bables'. As if this were not enough, Laud called him back as he left the court and harangued him for dressing in the vain fashions of a layman ('with ruffes up to your elbowes almost'). In more ways than one, therefore, Slatyer had allegedly crossed the line that properly separated a shepherd from his flock. The fact that the first of his errors was the consequence of an urge to reach out to members of the laity apparently cut no ice with his superiors.[65]

Such cases were controversial and exceptional. Indeed, there is little reason to suppose that ordinary English men and women ever routinely sang their psalms to secular tunes, though Protestant activists of the mid-sixteenth century possibly did so.[66] The mixing of godly texts and worldly tunes – along Lutheran lines – may in fact have been a practice that was

[65] Slatyer, *Psalmes, or Songs of Sion*; *Reports of Cases in the Courts of Star Chamber and High Commission*, ed. Samuel Rawson Gardiner, *Camden Society*, n.s. 39 (1886), p. 186. Later editions of Slatyer's book omitted the 'scandalous table', though one of the copies held in the British Library includes a handwritten copy, apparently added by a seventeenth-century owner.

[66] In *The Winter's Tale* (*Complete Oxford Shakespeare*, p. 901), Clown discusses a group of singers, with 'but one Puritan amongst them, and he sings psalms to hornpipes'. 1611 is rather late for such a reference, and Shakespeare may have been recalling an earlier period in the development of Protestantism.

associated at this early date with the more zealous of reformers. It was, of course, designed as a proselytising strategy, and in the early decades of Elizabeth's reign it typically involved not the singing of a psalm text to a worldly tune but the substitution of moralising lyrics for the supposedly debauched words of a successful ballad, without changing the melody.[67] During the closing decades of the sixteenth century, however, this strategy was abandoned. It had apparently failed to deliver the promised harvest, and a sterner and more Calvinist attitude towards musical mixing had come to prevail.[68] Furthermore, the period provides very few examples in which psalm tunes were used in popular balladry, and it seems that a sturdy cultural wall was constructed between the two genres. Arguably, English parishioners did not in general want their psalms to sound like their ballads.

It seems more probable that people did, after all, learn the official Sternhold–Hopkins tunes during the 1560s, but that, in time, these proved unsatisfactory. The shorter common tunes therefore evolved or were composed as a more viable alternative. During this early phase, the resources of the pre-Reformation church must have contributed significantly to the success of the new congregational music. When Henry Machyn heard (or heard of) the congregational singing of psalms at St Martin Ludgate, he remarked that the efforts of the people were supported by 'the base of the organes'.[69] The old organ was clearly playing its part in teaching the new tunes to the congregation. Many of the organs that were retained through the 1560s probably fulfilled this function, falling finally out of favour only when the tunes were commonly known and psalm-singing firmly established.[70]

In the minority of parishes that continued to maintain organs into the seventeenth century, it can be assumed that this remained the instrument's primary role. Historians of music have presented the use of organs to enhance psalmody as a development of the later seventeenth century. Admittedly, the new organ at Hackney seems to have been a novelty to Samuel Pepys when he heard it in 1667. He noted with admiration the manner in which the instrument 'tunes the psalm and plays with the people'. Nevertheless, the practice was clearly long established in a small number of churches. In Grantham (Lincolnshire), for example, the evidence in a dispute from 1640 reveals that the organs were customarily used

[67] See above, pp. 307–8.

[68] Collinson, *Birthpangs of Protestant England*, pp. 106–12. On Calvin's view, see Hamlin, *Psalm Culture*, p. 23.

[69] *Diary of Henry Machyn*, p. 228.

[70] On this point, see also Willis, 'Church Music and Protestantism', pp. 168–72.

in the parish 'to accompany the singing of Psalmes'. It is impossible to know exactly what they played. Towards the end of the seventeenth century, printed settings of the psalm tunes were published for the first time. In earlier decades, we can only assume that parochial organists improvised their accompaniment, probably adding simple chordal harmonies and ornamental embellishments to the basic tunes (**Website track 43 and Appendix**). The less accomplished among them perhaps picked out the tune alone, a practice that was later recommended by Thomas Mace.[71] Some organists, however, were already more ambitious. Solo interludes and voluntaries were heard in Elizabethan times, mainly in the cathedrals but perhaps elsewhere too. In 1570, William Stead, the parish clerk of Holy Trinity, Hull, was allegedly in the habit of making an extraordinary exhibition of himself during church services, 'for all his delight is in ringing and singing and organs playing'. A critical report on his conduct suggests that Stead had deliberately missed the point of the Reformation: 'when there is any sermon ... so he consumeth the time with organs playing'. He was even in the habit of 'setting forward the clock' so that 'there can be no convenient time for the word to be preached'. Interestingly, his accusers did not say that his music was poor, rather that there was just too much of it. At every service, it was said, 'he playeth for several times, and every time a long space'. George Wither later expressed his disapproval of all organists who 'runne on too fantastically in their voluntaries'.[72]

Some organists, therefore, may have over-elaborated, forgetting that their primary role was to guide the congregation in its melodic singing. In Rotherham, on the other hand, an organist named Peter Curry was accused in 1620 of under-elaborating. His alleged musical incompetence was spectacular, and the case casts valuable light on congregational expectation and customary practice. A churchwarden, Richard Barrows, alleged that Curry combined an obsessive taste for organ-playing with a woeful lack of aptitude. He put this unhappy blend on display whenever he accompanied the congregation during the singing of psalms. On one notorious occasion, Curry had commenced his accompaniment 'in such disorderly manner and with such untuneable sound as that [he] had for shame desisted to play any longer'. The congregation had been forced to sing on alone, 'which moved many to laughter and other some better affected to great grief and discontent'. It was also reported that Curry,

[71] *Diary of Samuel Pepys*, vol. VIII, p. 174; SP16 370 (83), NA; Temperley, *Music of the English Parish Church*, vol. I, p. 129, vol. II, pp. 53–5; Mace, *Musick's Monument*, p. 11.

[72] 'Parish Church Musicians', 73; Wither, *A Preparation to the Psalter*, p. 85.

> through his want of skill in musicke is not able to play above 3 or 4 tunes and that of the ordinarie Psalmes and those so untuneablie and unperfectly using but few keyes of the Organes as that it is farre from a decent and melodious harmonie neither is the sound he makes correspondent soe much as with the vulgar ordinarie tune nor doth concurre or agree with the voyces of the congregacon and in his common Psalmes tunes by [h]is disorderly playeing hee makes the noyse soe confused partly through the untuneablenes of the Organes and partly through his want of skill that the people cannot conveniently joyne with him in the singing of any Psalme at all.

Because of Curry's failings, 'the congregacon is restrained and forced to sing continually onely a few such Psalmes as hee can play the tune of which is a great hinderance to divine service and a distast and disturbance to the congregacon'. It was because of Curry, said the warden with a final flourish, that 'divine service in the said Church of Rotherham is become ridiculous and the word of god less esteemed and many of the inhabitants there occaconed to absent themselves from the same'. In his defence, Peter Curry could only claim that his instrument had been sabotaged.[73]

The Rotherham case demonstrates that not all congregations were content by the 1620s to settle down with a limited range of psalms and tunes. Here, they wanted variety, and they apparently liked to sing not only the 'vulgar ordinarie tunes' but also the longer melodies from the Sternhold–Hopkins collection. They clearly cherished their local tradition of singing psalms to organ accompaniment. The parishioners were thoroughly unaccustomed to singing without instrumental support, and they did not enjoy the experience. They also expected the organist to go beyond the bare minimum of picking out the tunes, and Curry's failure to use more than a few keys caused them upset. Overall, these were perhaps fairly typical expectations in parishes that had retained their organs, but the standards set in Rotherham were rather different from those that prevailed in the overwhelming majority of organ-free parishes. Ironically, it was probably the presence of the organ that had stimulated different musical desires. An organ, properly used, could effectively cajole a large congregation into melodic conformity and rhythmic precision. It therefore made possible the use of a wider range of tunes. Where the organist was skilful, chordal accompaniment also encouraged people to think and perhaps to sing harmonically. In such circumstances, congregational psalm-singing must have sounded rather different, and those who grew up within this subculture of English psalmody evidently preferred it to the main alternative.

[73] CP H1460, Borthwick Institute of Historical Research, York, discussed in Stephen Cooper, 'Music in Tudor Rotherham', *Ivanhoe Review* 7 (1994), 30–3. I am grateful to Celia Parker for bringing this case to my attention.

Back in the Elizabethan era, the remnants of Marian church choirs may also have played their part in attempting to disseminate the official psalm tunes. At St Michael's, Cornhill, the man who served as parish clerk between 1555 and 1590 had previously been a conduct or singing man in two other London parishes. An obvious role for such a man during such a period would have been to assist in the development of metrical psalm-singing. In Hull, similarly, two singers assisted the parish clerk with unspecified musical aspects of common prayer. At Chudleigh in Devon, the churchwardens paid ten shillings 'to Nycholas Sexson the singinge boye' in 1580, three years after the final reference to a choir. In some parishes, congregational psalmody received support from local schoolchildren. During the 1560s, the statutes of schools at Worcester, Sevenoaks (Kent), Southwark (Surrey) and Kirkby Stephen (Westmorland) all specified that the boys were to lead the singing when they attended church.[74] Lastly, a curious and fascinating presentment from Lincolnshire suggests that small numbers of local children in several parishes were receiving special musical instruction in the church towards the end of Elizabeth's reign. A recently appointed curate, accused of Catholic sympathies, accounted for his movements between 1599 and 1602 in the following terms: he had 'taught a singing school at Kirton in Holland, by the space of a yeare and d [a half], and after that taught a singing school at Frampton one yeare when he fell sick ... & after that he taught children to sing at Ruskington in the church ... and afterwardes he came to Sleford and taught the singing school there'. He may not have been telling the whole truth, but he must have judged that this mini-*curriculum vitae* would at least appear plausible to his accusers. Did some parishes organise informal schools for the rehearsal of psalmody, as they certainly did in subsequent centuries?[75] It is an intriguing possibility.

We can say with greater assurance that the part played by England's parish clerks in the promotion of psalm-singing was sustained throughout the early modern period. When the seventeenth-century Derbyshire yeoman Leonard Wheatcroft composed a witty ditty for use 'when

[74] 'Parish Church Musicians', pp. 59, 67, 73, 82; *REED Devon*, p. 58. On psalmody in schools, see Temperley, *Music of the English Parish Church*, pp. 63, 80, and Green, *Print and Protestantism*, p. 510. In Bishop's Stortford (Hertfordshire), the two sons of a local man led the 'reading and singing' of the psalms in 1684 (MANN MS 449, p. 4, NRO).

[75] The Lincolnshire case is transcribed in Edward Peacock, 'Extracts from Lincoln Episcopal Visitations in the 15th, 16th and 17th Centuries', ed. Edward Peacock, *Archaeologica: or Miscellaneous Tracts Relating to Antiquity* 48 (1885), pp. 267–8. For evidence of 'peripatetic psalm teachers' in eighteenth-century England, see Southey, *Music-making in North-east England*, p. 122.

I gather Clerk-wages' (to the tune of 'Gerard's mistress'), he included the lines 'And to you all I will be thankfull / and teach you Davids psalmes to sing.' He regarded this as one of his principal duties, and we certainly should not assume that most parish clerks were musically incompetent. The parish clerks of London were probably the best, and they had an official company of their own. Prospective clerks in the city were examined in their ability to sing psalms to the common tunes. Even in the capital, however, parish clerks occasionally made mistakes: on 5 January 1662, the clerk of St Olave's began singing Psalm 116 to the metrically incompatible tune of Psalm 25, much to the delight of Master Pepys.[76] Those who served in the remainder of the nation's parishes may, in general, have been somewhat less competent than most of their counterparts in London, but it is probably mistaken to accept John Playford's self-motivated and jaundiced argument that they were musically inept. It is notable that clerks were reported to the church courts only very occasionally for their musical shortcomings.[77]

Through most of the period, therefore, there was no serious obstacle to the learning of psalm tunes by congregations. Early modern people were thoroughly accustomed to picking up melodies by ear, and the evidence from balladry suggests that they could hold hundreds of tunes in their memories. Even George Wither came close to acknowledging the widespread distribution of musical ability: one of the obstacles in his reforming path was, he admitted, the commonly held opinion that 'every man almost, is so well exercised in the Psalmes and tunes allowable in our Church, that he can make one of the Quire'.[78] The texts are a more complicated matter, and it has never been explained how 6,000 individuals at Paul's Cross in 1560 could possibly have known what to sing. The problem was less acute in the more typical setting of a parish church, yet a problem it remained. There are two main possibilities. In some places, the singing may have been left to a combination of psalter-owners and those who had memorised the texts (the latter presumably formed a tiny minority). By the mid-seventeenth century, local custom in Grantham required the organist to perform a solo rendition of the designated

[76] D5433/1, DRO; James Christie, *Parish Clerks* (London, 1893), p. 122; *Diary of Samuel Pepys*, vol. III, p. 4.

[77] John Playford, *Psalms and Hymns in Solemne Musick of Foure Parts* (London, 1671), preface. In April 1663, the parish clerk of Sutton (Sussex) was reported by the local churchwardens because he 'can neither write read nor sing' (EP1/17/28, fo. 127v, WSRO).

[78] Wither, *A Preparation to the Psalter*, p. 9.

common psalm tune before the singing commenced, so that 'all persons that can Reade have time to turne to the Psalme'. The alternative was to devise a system by which the words of each verse might be communicated to the congregation just before they broke into song. In 1636, Bishop Wren of Norwich asked the churchwardens of his diocese whether congregational psalm-singing was 'done according to that grave manner (which first was in use) that such doe sing as can reade the psalmes, or have learned them by heart: and not after that uncouth and undecent custome of late taken up, to have every line first read, and then sung by the people'. There was a distinctive Laudian subtext here: keep the psalms decorous and the people quiet. Wren's question suggests that the second method – usually known as 'lining out' – had developed as a way of integrating the bookless majority into the music of the parish church. The notion that so obvious and useful a method had only recently evolved is peculiar, and yet this is the earliest definite reference to the practice in England. Quite possibly, it was significantly older than Wren either knew or acknowledged. Lining out was still referred to as 'new' during the later seventeenth century, which suggests that the label was sometimes a derogatory tactic rather than a chronological truth. To add insult to injury, detractors also alleged that it was 'the Scots way' of doing things.[79]

If lining out was not already practised in Elizabethan England, it seems impossible to explain how entire congregations joined together in song. A century later, one author spoke critically of lining out on aesthetic grounds, but explained its history in terms rather different from those used by Bishop Wren: 'There is a custom of reading each Line of the Psalm as it is sung, which by long use has obtain'd in all places, and which in the beginning of the Reformation in England, when none of the poorer sort were able to read, was very commendably taken up.' The technique, he argued, was out of date in an age of universal literacy (an interesting perception in itself). A manuscript held in Lambeth Palace Library goes some way towards corroborating this thesis. It contains draft instructions relating to the conduct of services among the Protestant exiles in Wesel during the mid-1550s. Psalms were to be sung by all members of the congregation, 'provided alwayes that the verse wich shalbe so sung be befoer playnly & distinctly read of the minister'. Perhaps the vestrymen of

[79] SP 16370 (83), NA; *Visitation Articles and Injunctions of the Early Stuart Church*, vol. II, pp. 148–9; Playford, *The Whole Book of Psalms*, A3r; Warner, *A Collection of Some Verses*, preface. See also John Cotton, *Singing of Psalms a Gospel-ordinance* (London, 1650), pp. 62–3.

St Michael, Cornhill, had something similar in mind when, in 1592, they launched a search for 'a skylfull man to begyne the syngynge salmes' in their church.[80]

The surviving sources are considerably richer for the seventeenth century than for the sixteenth, and a clearer idea of the sound of the psalms can be developed. There was, of course, considerable variety: some parishes may have spoken their psalms, or left the singing to the parish clerk and a select few; lining out was probably not a universal custom; a minority of congregations continued to sing to the accompaniment of an organ, or even, in at least one case, a viol. Nevertheless, as psalm-singing ceased to be a novelty and became a tradition, a more or less standard mode of unaccompanied performance came to predominate. Typically, it was the responsibility of the parish clerk to set or nominate the specific psalm that was to be sung, usually before and/or after the sermon. Between 1655 and 1661, for example, the chamberlain of Norwich made annual payments of twenty shillings to John Brown, presumably a clerk, 'for his yeares wages for setting of the Psalme at the Chappell'.[81] There were comparable payments in some other accounts, though in most parishes this aspect of the parish clerk's duty did not earn specific mention.

In setting the psalm, the clerk was expected to take account of the calendar date and of any particular local circumstances that might guide him towards psalms and tunes that were either joyous or sorrowful. Several printed works offered assistance in this matter. In 1644, William Barton took great care to specify the type of tune appropriate to each psalm (for example, a 'doleful' tune, a 'joyful' tune, or a 'solemn mixed' tune). Benjamin Payne's guidebook for parish clerks, first published in 1685, included an alphabetical list of psalms suitable for particular topics: 'Afflicted state of the godly', 'Atheists', 'Conspiracies', 'Enemies', 'Hail, frost and snow', 'Lightning, thunder and darkness', 'Plague or contagion', 'Tumults and uproars', 'Victory' and so forth.[82] In theory, the entire psalter was open to the clerk; in practice, it seems that individual parishes

80 *Singing of Psalms Vindicated from the Charge of Novelty* (London, 1698), preface, pp. vii–viii; MS 2523, fo. 3v, Lambeth Palace Library, quoted by Leaver, *'Goostly Psalmes'*, p. 214; Willis, 'Church Music and Protestantism', pp. 166–7.

81 In Herriard (Hampshire), a Jacobean incident, noted by Sir Richard Paulet, seems to imply that the psalms in this parish were read aloud, but perhaps not sung (HRO, 44M69/E4/31, note dated 19 June 1614); John Taylor, *A Three-fold Discourse between Three Neighbours* (London, 1642), A3v; NCR case 18, shelf A, fos. 129r, 169r, 189r etc., NRO.

82 Barton, *The Book of Psalms* (London, 1644), A3r–A8v; Payne, *The Parish-clerk's Vade-mecum* (London, 1694), p. 137. Some editions appeared as *The Parish Clerks Guide.*

may have developed special familiarity with a smaller number of the psalms. There was no official rota for the musical psalms, but patterns and associations nevertheless developed. Psalms 23 and 118, for example, came to be sung during the communion. In 1719, Isaac Watts remarked that wise parish clerks concentrated on two dozen of the psalms, rather than aspiring to cover them all. In some parishes, the clergy evidently did not wish to leave the important matter of psalm-selection in the hands of mere parish clerks, and they took the role upon themselves. In West Retford (Nottinghamshire), for example, it was the curate who named the psalm, at least during the late 1630s. For this piece of information, we owe thanks to the drunken man who interrupted him as he announced his choice to the throng. The intrusive words 'there is it, there's it' may not look particularly offensive, but we should note that they were allegedly delivered 'in a ridiculous manner'.[83]

The parish clerk's role as the primary singer was, however, rarely questioned. Clerks were, in Playford's words, 'the leaders of those Tunes in their Congregations', and they set both pitch and pace, calling the people to order with an announcement in the form, 'Let us sing to the praise and glory of God the 100th psalm'. Where lining out was practised, the clerk recited each line of text immediately prior to its rendition by the congregation. Some clerks merely spoke these prompting lines, but others evidently developed a mode of musical delivery that helped to maintain the flow of the psalm. Payne's printed guide advised that the lines should be 'read ... tunably, i.e. in a singing tone, and after the manner of chanting'. Lining out was also to be done, he advised, in rhythmic style and at double the tempo used by the singing congregation. In this way, 'the break betwixt the falling from one line to the taking up of the next, may be so quick, as that due harmony may be kept in some measure, notwithstanding the reading'. Payne perhaps had in mind the objection, made by critics of lining out, that it threatened the unity of each verse as a whole by dismembering it. Above all, Payne advised, lining out was to be performed 'with deliberation, that every syllable may have its proper emphasis, which is the only way to be understood by such of the congregation as may stand at a distance'.[84]

[83] Isaac Watts, *Psalms of David* (London, 1719), pp. vii–viii, quoted by Green, *Print and Protestantism*, p. 525; AN/PB 341/9/39, HL.

[84] Playford, *An Introduction*, p. 71; Benjamin Payne, *The Parish Clerks Guide* (London, 1709), pp. 29–31; the final quotation is from the edition of Payne's work published in 1685 (quoted by Christie, *Parish Clerks*, p. 196).

As each line was sung by the congregation, the clerk led the way, opening with a long 'gathering note' that enabled the parishioners to ready themselves and join in. The ubiquity of such a note is suggested by its regular appearance as a semibreve at the opening of printed versions of the common and official psalm tunes. As the melody unfolded, some parish clerks reportedly altered notes that they considered peculiar or out of place. Slight local variants therefore developed, and if they proved successful they might eventually feed back into printed versions of the tunes. This process may account for the minor differences between the same tunes as published in late sixteenth-century and mid-seventeenth-century sources. The parishioners apparently remained in their seats throughout the psalm, and they tended to sing at a remarkably slow pace. Scholars have argued that this leisurely tempo developed over several decades, and that the first generation of congregational singers performed at a far more sprightly speed. It has been suggested that the application of the derogatory term 'Geneva jigs' to the metrical psalms during the early Elizabethan years, particularly by Catholics, illustrates this phenomenon.[85] Hereafter, we are told, the circumstances of performance and the musical incompetence of those involved combined to slow the psalms, generation by generation, until they were sung at the almost unbelievably sluggish pace of one note per two or three seconds.

There is no doubting the slow speed of congregational psalm singing, but the conventional interpretation may exaggerate the inadequacy of the singers, thereby neglecting more aesthetic considerations. Nor is it clear why psalm-singing should have taken such a long time to slow down. If the practicalities of mass singing did indeed exert such a telling influence, they probably did so most markedly during the 1560s, when congregations were learning the art for the very first time. It would surely not have taken two or three generations for the problem to emerge. If 6,000 people cannot sing a bouncy song together without losing speed, the difficulty is likely to become obvious in six seconds rather than six decades. There can be no certainty on this issue, but it may well be that congregational psalms were more largo than allegro almost from the outset. Under this interpretation, terms such as 'Geneva jig' and 'Hopkins jig' may have been

[85] Temperley, *Music of the English Parish Church*, pp. 94, 63, 67, 92–3. The best seventeenth-century evidence is found in the preface to Thomas May, *The Whole Booke of Psalmes, as they are Now Sung in Churches* (London, 1688), preface. May defined a breve as equivalent to eight pulses of 'a person in good health and temper', but said that parochial performance often slipped from this standard to a rhythm of three pulses per note. Assuming a pulse rate of 70 beats per minute, this suggests that the duration of a typical note was 2.7 seconds.

ironic nicknames for congregational psalms, mocking by inversion their somewhat cumbersome delivery. This would help to explain why the labels were still used during the seventeenth century when, as all scholars agree, congregational psalms were anything but jig-like.[86]

Alternatively, 'Geneva jig' began life as a jibe at the early puritans, who may have been unusual in preferring their psalms to rattle along at a brisk pace. Arguably, they were misguided in believing that psalms sung at such a speed would appeal to the majority of English parishioners. Indeed, the slow tempo of congregational singing perhaps owed as much to popular taste as to logistical problems. One possible chronology runs thus: at first, during the early 1560s, the practicalities of mass singing dictated a slow pace that was probably not to the liking of the godly Protestants who promoted congregational psalmody; by the time congregations had learned the tunes, they had formed a habit of slow delivery that was both pleasing and deeply rooted; the rise of the common tunes brought a new singability to psalmody, but congregations saw no reason to celebrate this fact by increasing the tempo. They could have done so, but on aesthetic grounds they did not.[87] Critical commentators also alleged that parishioners sang all their psalms at the same slow pace, rather than reflecting in their performance the distinction between psalms of joy and psalms of tribulation (as Ravenscroft and others wished them to do). Such characteristics of musical psalmody deserve to be investigated as the consequences of popular preference rather than of common incompetence. It is difficult to resist the conclusion that early modern English Christians actually wanted their religious music to be slow, serious and weighty. 'Ye never hear them, or any of them, complain', remarked Bishop William Beveridge in 1710, 'that the Psalms which they sing in their Churches, are too plain, too low, or too heavy for them. But they rather love and admire them the more for it, and are more edified by the use of them.'[88] The ponderous pace of congregational psalm-singing meant that the

[86] See, for example, Cotton, *Singing of Psalms*, p. 61; *Singing of Psalms Vindicated*, p. 13. In the late seventeenth-century dispute over the legitimacy of psalm-singing, its opponents dismissed the songs as 'Geneva jigs' and scorned the performers as 'Ballad-Singers'. These terms were designed as hurtful slurs, and were clearly not intended to imply that psalms were sung at a lively pace.

[87] Modern football crowds demonstrate on a weekly basis that it *is* possible for thousands of musically untrained people to sing unaccompanied without necessarily slowing to a virtual standstill.

[88] Beveridge, *A Defence*, p. 42. Beveridge did, however, acknowledge that the logistics of performance were one of the factors that contributed to a popular preference for slow psalms: 'the heavier they go, the more easily they can keep pace with them'.

rendition of a single psalm might take an hour or more, though it seems likely that congregations often sang sections of six to twelve verses, rather than entire psalms.[89]

The slow tempo of psalm-singing may also have reduced awareness of a tune's underlying rhythmic structure, despite the best efforts of musical publishers to prevent this from happening. Across the early modern period, composers grew increasingly likely to include bar lines and clear rhythmic patterns in printed versions of the tunes, but congregations sang on obliviously. In 1752, Charles Avison complained that people everywhere sang the common psalm tunes 'without the least Regard to Time or Measure, by drawling out every Note to an unlimited Length'. To his annoyance, they appeared entirely ignorant of the fact that common and official (or 'proper') tunes alike were designed for singing in 'the Alla-Breve Time, or the regular pointing of two, three, or four Minims in a Bar'.[90] Such irritation was closely related to rising levels of musical literacy and knowledge among the gentry. In the age of music meetings, the self-consciously sophisticated leaders of society learned that the true musician always sharpened the leading note of a minor scale, as in modern tonality. An awareness that psalm-singing congregations still did not do so was just one reason for voicing criticism.[91] To ordinary parishioners, however, the flattened sevenths and the slow, undifferentiated pace of the common tunes continued to make perfect sense, for the singer who is utterly immersed in a form of music will perceive rhythmic and melodic patterns that are obscured from the hostile or ignorant listener.

Nor should we assume that slow delivery necessarily implied lethargy. The potential for musical dullness was mitigated by several additional features of English psalm-singing. The predominant style of congregational singing, for example, involved a degree of melodic ornamentation that must have reduced somewhat the sense of slowness. In what later became known as 'the old way of singing', singers tended to slide between notes, and they were said to add scoops and flourishes to the main notes of the melody.[92] The more inventive members of a congregation may also have improvised descants and simple harmonies (reminiscent of medieval 'faburden'). As Professor Temperley has skilfully demonstrated, this was sometimes how new tunes evolved out of the older ones (though he argues that the process

89 For evidence of hour-long psalms, see *Diary of Samuel Pepys*, vol. II, p. 6, and *The Second Part of the Fryer and the Boy* (London, 1680). For a shorter example, see below, p. 440.

90 Avison, *Essay on Musical Expression*, pp. 76–7.

91 See below, p. 441.

92 The best summary of the 'old style', as reconstructed from surviving musical representations, is in Temperley, *Music of the English Parish Church*, pp. 94–7.

occurred as a result of musical incompetence rather than as an expression of creativity). To listeners who presented themselves as musically advanced, this could all sound quite horrid. At the start of the eighteenth century, Elias Hall was deeply scornful of congregational psalm-singing in Lancashire:

Then out the people yawl an hundred parts,
Some roar, some whine, some creak like wheels of carts:
Such notes the gamut yet did never know,
Nor num'rous keys of harps'cals on a row
Their heights or depths could ever comprehend.
Now below double A re some descend,
'Bove E la squealing now ten notes some fly:
Streight then, as if they knew they were too high,
With headlong haste down stairs they again tumble;
Discords and concords, O how thick they jumble,
Like untam'd horses, tearing with their throats
One wretched stave into a thousand notes.[93]

Accounts of the old way of singing also suggest that congregations valued sheer volume, high pitch and a somewhat nasal tone of voice. They sang, said Thomas Mace, 'as if they were affrighted or distracted'. When the writers of the parish records of Buxted (Sussex) penned a little eulogy for their parish clerk in 1666, they noted with particular warmth that he had for forty-three years 'warbled forth as if he had been thumped on the back by a stone'.[94] Playford advised parish clerks to avoid the squeaky upper register of the human voice, but his moderate counsel does not seem to have been universally heeded. Congregational singers, furthermore, were said to invest such energy in the production of each note that they needed to draw breath after every single syllable. The basic pulse may therefore have been slow, but the congregational performance of a psalm cannot have been particularly soporific. Individual parishioners regularly fell asleep during sermons and prayers, but one searches the ecclesiastical court records long and hard before finding the man or woman who managed to nod off during the singing of a psalm.[95]

[93] Elias Hall, *The Psalm-singer's Compleat Companion* (1706; London, 1708), p. 2.

[94] Mace, *Musick's Monument*, p. 9; K. H. MacDermott, *Sussex Church Music in the Past* (Chichester: Moore and Wingham, 1922), p. 27.

[95] A comparable style of psalm-singing has survived on some of the Hebridean islands. It shares several features with early modern English practice: lining out; sliding between notes; slow delivery; and lack of instrumental accompaniment. It is an extraordinary and elemental sound, combining a feeling of community with the tone of a poignant plea.

Historians have sometimes emphasised the similarities between psalmody and balladry, but the evidence presented here suggests that this argument deserves to be flipped on its head. Admittedly, the metre and the language of the Sternhold–Hopkins psalms will be familiar to those who have read or sung ballads of the period.[96] Presumably, this reflects once again the belief of the early Elizabethan promoters of psalm-singing that the way to people's souls was through the appropriation and redeployment of familiar imagery, vocabulary and rhythmic patterns. When the psalms are considered as music rather than merely poetry, however, the comparisons are much less striking. Ballad tunes and psalm tunes may have used the same musical modes, but the dominant style of delivery constituted an extraordinary and crucial difference. Psalms begin to sound like ballads only if they are played or sung at quadruple speed and with greater rhythmic precision. We can be fairly sure that, in a congregational setting, they hardly ever were. Moreover, evidence suggesting that particular psalm tunes derived from particular ballad or dance tunes is rarely persuasive. The 'Oxford' tune, for example, has been compared to that of the lively Henrician song 'Pastime with Good Company', but the two melodies share little beyond their restricted melodic ranges.[97] The evolving common tunes of late sixteenth-century and seventeenth-century England were far more likely to derive material from one another or from the official tunes than from other categories of melody. Elizabethan puritans presented psalms and ballads as fundamentally incompatible, but during the early years of the reign some of them may have hoped that psalmody could exterminate balladry by stealing its style, verbally and perhaps melodically. It transpired, however, that the musical dimension of this synthesis did not accord with majority tastes. Across the country, parish congregations drove psalmody in a new direction, creating an unprecedented musical sound. New short melodies evolved, replacing most of the official ones. The parish clerk took upon himself a vital solo role. The pace of performance was extremely slow. Great energy went into a typical rendition, but it cannot have been expended in the excited tapping of feet. This was not balladry or anything like it. Instead, the population of England declared and developed a preference for participatory ecclesiastical music that was distinctively and unequivocally sacred. First and foremost, it was the sound of the church.

[96] Green, *Print and Protestantism*, pp. 546–7.

[97] The comparison is made in Temperley, *Music of the English Parish Church*, pp. 69–70.

Psalmody, harmony and discord

Psalm-singing became established on all levels of society. At the start of Elizabeth's reign, the feature of psalmody that most impressed itself upon Henry Machyn was its unprecedented inclusiveness: 'men and women all do syng, and boys'.[98] From the late sixteenth century onwards, a love of this form of music was sometimes associated particularly with the common people. According to John Patrick, ordinary parishioners 'show more affection for this than any other part of the service'. Daniel Warner agreed: 'This kind of devotion the common people are most intent upon.' In 1710, Bishop William Beveridge defended 'the Singing-Psalms' against their educated critics, arguing that hardly a family in the land did not possess a copy and that ordinary Christians 'have such a Value and Fondness for these Old Psalms, that they would not part with them for the World'.[99] It is difficult, of course, to find records that articulate such feelings in the unmediated words of actual commoners, but a clause in the will of Alexander Torkinton, a tanner in early seventeenth-century Stockport (Cheshire), at least offers us a clue: 'Item my mynde and will is and I doe hartely desyre, that the Clerk, John Ouldham and some boyes that can singe, doe fetche my bodye from my house, and accompanye the same unto the churche in singinge of psalmes to the prayse of God. And for their laboure I give and bequeath everie one of them sixepence.'[100]

The psalms were also sung outside church. English sailors, for example, carried the habit all around the world. On board ship, psalms were sung not only during services but also to mark the setting of the watch. In 1579, Drake and his men sang psalms to a group of native Americans in order to dissuade them from performing a sacrifice. In 1627, the merchants of the East India Company purchased '50 Psalters for every ship with Singing Psalms in them', thus demonstrating a serious commitment to this form of music. And when sailors found themselves *in extremis*, the psalms were the songs that sprang to mind. In 1593, for example, an English ship called the *Tobie* ran aground off the Barbary coast during a storm and was damaged beyond repair. As the ship began to break up, its

[98] See above, p. 407.

[99] John Patrick, *A Century of Select Psalms* (London, 1679), A1v; Warner, *A Collection of Some Verses*, preface; Beveridge, *A Defence*, pp. 103, 96. For an Elizabethan example of the same opinion, see below, p. 439.

[100] *Stockport Probate Records 1620–1650*, ed. C. B. Phillips and J. H. Smith, *Record Society for the Publication of Original Documents Relating to Lancashire and Cheshire* (1992), p. 41. Other wills in the series reveal the ownership of psalm books by an alderman, a spinster and a tailor (who bequeathed his copy to a local gentlewoman).

desperate crew scaled the rigging in order to delay the inevitable. Their thoughts turned to God, and they began 'with dolefull tune and heavy hearts' to sing Psalme 12: 'Helpe, Lord, for good and godly men / do perish and decay' (**Website track 46 and Appendix**). Before they were halfway through, however, 'the waves of the sea had stopped the breathes of most of our men'. Thirty-eight men drowned, leaving a mere twelve survivors to tell their tale.[101] This tragic episode reflects not only the mysterious workings of the divine will but the deep roots that the musical psalms had sunk into the hearts and souls of English people by this date.

Back at home, the psalms were said to be on the lips of 'the soldier... in war, the artisans at their work, wenches spinning and sewing, apprentices in their shops, and wayfaring men on their travels'. Nothing, complained the Catholic author of this list, had done more to draw the ordinary people of England towards Protestantism. Weavers, in particular, were sometimes associated with psalm-singing, and some individuals practised the habit when they were all alone at work or play.[102] In 1645, a Suffolk widow sang psalms as she milked her cows (her habit came to light only because the devil appeared before her on one occasion, insisting her godly music was futile and tempting her into a life of witchcraft). On 8 February 1663, the godly young Lancashire diarist Roger Lowe went out and about to buy 'swines grasse', 'and when I cam home I was very pensive and sad in consideracion of my povertie, and I sunge the 24th psalme, and after I was very hearty'. He even provided his own personal gloss on the psalm, helping us to understand why it cheered him so: 'God will comfort and supply the wants of his poor servants, and God at present deny [w]orldly things, yet if in the meane while God put com[fort?] into hurt, this is better.' Lowe sang psalms at happy times too. On 29 September 1663, his romantic prospects were improving, and he wrote, 'James Naylor envited me to their house. I went and found Mary alone and very pleasant. This night I sange in shopp by a candle the cheife verses of the 71 psalme with alacritie and heart chearfullnes.'[103] Interestingly, this is not one of the more joyous of the psalms, but it clearly met Roger's needs at the end of a good day.

101 Richard Hakluyt, *The Principal Navigations*, ed. James MacLehose, 12 vols. (Glasgow: James MacLehose and Sons, 1903–5), vol. VII, pp. 124–9.

102 Woodfield, *English Musicians*, pp. 43–4, 102; T. Harrap, quoted by Helen Constance White, *English Devotional Literature* (Madison: University of Wisconsin, 1931), p. 61.

103 C. L'Estrange Ewen, *Witch Hunting and Witch Trials* (London: Kegan Paul, 1929), p. 297 (I am grateful to Malcolm Gaskill for this reference); *The Diary of Roger Lowe*, ed. Sachse, pp. 15, 36 (see also pp. 28–9, 44).

The extent of domestic psalm-singing is difficult to gauge, but it was certainly a well-known practice in wealthy households characterised by religious devotion and/or musical aptitude. The godly Hobyes sang psalms, but so too did the less virtuous household headed by Samuel Pepys ('with much pleasure').[104] Numerous publications existed to stimulate and satisfy the need for psalm-settings appropriate for such gatherings, often providing three or four vocal parts and suggestions for instrumental accompaniment.[105] In such settings, we encounter once again the combination of inclusivity and exclusivity that characterised the recreations of the socially pre-eminent. Composers drew freely upon the most widely used tunes but enabled their wealthy customers to distance themselves from the general population by singing in parts from printed music, sharpening their leading notes and probably employing a rather brisker tempo (the predominance of crotchets rather than minims in some such works presumably indicates this). On Sunday 27 November 1664, for example, two musical visitors called at Pepys's house in the evening and, as the diarist noted happily, 'we sung with my boy Ravenscrofts four-part psalms, most admirable music' (**Website track 44 and Appendix**).[106]

Indeed, psalmody provides further evidence of the problematic relationship between the culture of the gentry and that of the population at large. Congregational singing had its educated admirers throughout the period, but others felt the need to distance themselves from the practice by heaping scorn upon it.[107] One hostile witness complained that psalms were sung 'by a company of rude people, cobblers and their wives, and their kitchen-maids and all, that have as much skill in singing them, as an ass to handle a harp'. Members of the gentry nevertheless joined in the singing of psalms when they attended their parish churches, and many must have owned personal copies of the *Whole Book*.[108] On Sunday

[104] *The Private Life of an Elizabethan Lady... Lady Margaret Hoby*, pp. 38, 42, 48; *Diary of Samuel Pepys*, vol. V, p. 321. According to Robert Cleaver, one of the duties of any master was to ensure that all of his servants regularly sang psalms together: *A Godlie Forme of Householde Government* (London, 1598), p. 38. For further examples, see Hamlin, *Psalm Culture*, pp. 35–6.

[105] See, for example, Daman, *The Psalmes of David in English Meter*; John Cosyn, *Musike of Six, and Five Partes* (London, 1585); Thomas Sternhold and John Hopkins, *The Whole Book of Psalms ... Composed in Foure Parts* (London, 1592).

[106] *Diary of Samuel Pepys*, vol. V, p. 332.

[107] Admirers included Richard Hooker, Jeremy Taylor, John Harington, John Cotton, Richard Baxter and William Beveridge.

[108] W. Nicholls, *A Comment on the Book of Common Prayer* (London, 1710), Fffff1r. Sir Richard Paulet's accounts for 1605 record a payment of five shillings 'for mending my wiefs bible having all the com[mon] prayer bk and singing psalmes put in & newbound' (44M69/E4/130,

13 November 1664, Samuel Pepys attended divine service, 'where mighty sport to hear our Clerke sing out of tune, though his master sits by him and keeps the tune for the parish'.[109] This gentleman, at least, knew the psalms and their tunes well enough to rescue a floundering employee. In some contexts, a simple and well-known psalm tune could even serve as a reassuring signal of unity across otherwise marked social boundaries. According to one chapbook, the mid-seventeenth-century criminal James Hind abused this possibility in cynical fashion while committing a robbery. As a gentleman approached him on horseback, Hind stood in full view, 'whistling the Tune of an Ordinary Psalm'. The gentleman, lulled into a false sense of security, asked Hind the time of day, but the only reply he received was a fierce blow with a long pole. This knocked him out of the saddle, and Hind rode off on the stolen steed. Gallantly, he paused to give his victim two shillings for his charges, 'But to this day the Gentleman loves not the Tune of a Psalm.'[110] Once more, the power of melodic association is clear.

On occasion, it is possible to hear both the positive and the negative registers in the voice of a single commentator. On Sunday 9 August 1663, Samuel Pepys attended evening prayer at St Dunstan's:

> I was amuzed at the tune set to the psalm by the clerke of the parish; and thought at first that he was out, but I find him to be a good songster, and the parish could sing it very well and was a good tune. But I wonder that there should be a tune in the psalms that I never heard of.[111]

His first reaction on hearing an unfamiliar tune was one of self-consciously superior merriment, but he soon had to concede that there was nothing much wrong with the music. Pepys could be a fierce musical critic, and the fact that he commented only very rarely on the supposedly poor quality of congregational psalm-singing should warn us to read more scathing testimony with caution. The Newcastle organist Charles Avison, writing in 1752, sent out similarly discordant signals. He displayed the scorn of an educated man for the unmusical majority in complaining about their dreary performance of psalms, and he apologised to his readers for even bothering to discuss so 'trifling' a musical form as popular

HRO). For discussion of such practice, see Green, *Print and Protestantism*, pp. 511–12, and Hamlin, *Psalm Culture*, pp. 39–40.

109 *Diary of Samuel Pepys*, vol. V, p. 320.

110 *No Jest like a True Jest: Being a Compendious Record of the Merry Life, and Mad Exploits of Capt James Hind, the Great Robber of England* (London, 1657), A2v.

111 *Diary of Samuel Pepys*, vol. IV, p. 269.

psalmody. With the next stroke of his pen, however, he remarked, 'I cannot but own, that I have been uncommonly affected with hearing some Thousands of Voices hymming the Deity in a Style of Harmony adapted to that awful Occasion.'[112] He was moved by congregational psalm-singing, but it was necessary to sound apologetic.

The musical psalms were well known throughout society, but not everyone agreed that they were permanently on the lips of all and sundry. Nicholas Bownde complained, in 1595, that the habit of extra-ecclesiastical psalm-singing was practised by pitifully few. Such singing, he insisted, was a matter of duty among the godly. The truly religious were bound to 'testifie their holy mirth, not of the flesh, but of the spirite, by singing Psalmes'. In recent years, other kinds of music, particularly ballads, had 'cleane shut out in a great many of places the singing of Psalmes'. He acknowledged that the communal singing of psalms in church was thoroughly established by this date, but insisted that this was merely the beginning of a Christian's necessary engagement with the songs of David: 'the Psalmes are sung in many places, after a plaine, distinct, and profitabel manner, and may be everywhere if men will, yet men content themselves with that, and are not mindfull to sing at home by themselves alone, or with the rest of their houshoulde'. Domestic psalmody, then, was nothing like as common a habit as he would have wished. On the other hand, the bibliographical evidence regarding the commercial success of the *Whole Book* suggests that Bownde may have been unduly pessimistic.[113]

The rapid spread and immense resilience of psalm-singing, particularly in church, is one of the more mysterious phenomena to be discussed in this book. What, then, was its appeal to men and women of many sorts? Sir John Harington, writing in about 1597, could not be sure. In his unpublished 'Treatise of Playe', he listed the singing of metrical psalms among the more worthy of pastimes available to the people of England. He had heard humble folk claim that in musical psalmody they 'have had more pleasure, and theyr mindes more lifted up to devotion, then [than] with all the sollom church musycke of organs and voyces: whether it weare the matter, or the meeter, or the maker, or the musycke, or all together that so ravysht them'.[114]

One of the main secrets of psalmody's success was the outlet it provided, in an intensely hierarchical world, for the massed ranks of ordinary

112 Avison, *Essay on Musical Expression*, pp. 76–7.

113 Nicholas Bownde, *The Doctrine of the Sabbath*, pp. 235–7, 241; Green, *Print and Protestantism*, pp. 506–25.

114 Harington, *Nugae Antiquae*, ed. Henry Harington, 3 vols. (London, 1779), vol. II, p. 159.

parishioners to express themselves and even to influence the conditions under which they lived. In 1660, the bishops at the Savoy Conference noted that the musical psalms formed the part of the service 'where the people bear as great a part as the minister'.[115] Whether one regards church services as an instrument of elite domination or a context for comprehending the sacred (or some combination of the two), it remains true that the average parishioner usually had limited control over their precise content. Where music was concerned, however, the vagueness of the Elizabethan Settlement accidentally created a wonderful opportunity for congregations to shape the church services that they would attend on a weekly basis. As psalmody developed, England's unexceptional Christians, through their parish clerk, nominated the text, chose the music and set the pace. An ordinary layman literally called the tune. The parish clerk was rarely a man of high social standing, and the influence he wielded was therefore a matter of some considerable significance.

Laypeople owned and influenced the psalms. In September 1671, the worst flood for half a century struck the parish of Dersingham in Norfolk. The tide came over the tops of the banks, and the marshes overflowed. John Chamberlain the elder, a leading layman, took the time to document the event in the parish register. At the end, he added,

> I doe desire that the Clarke of the parish of Dersingham might yearely and every yeare on the 12th daye of September or aboute that time of the yeare sing to the praise of god the nine & twentyeth psalme or some other psal: to that purpose to put the Inhabitants of the same parish in minde of the Mercies of Almighty God.

By this date, it seems most unlikely that the clerk was to sing alone. The phraseology of this request echoed the terms of the announcement that clerks commonly made when they invited their neighbours to sing, and we should probably imagine a congregational rendition of the specified psalm (**Website track 45 and Appendix**). The author proceeded to transcribe three verses of Psalm 29, each carefully chosen for its applicability ('His voice doth rule the warters all / Even as him selfe doth please').[116]

This sense of lay involvement with the psalms was rarely documented so specifically, but it may have been extremely common. The experience of singing in a crowd can be an overwhelming one, particularly when the atmosphere is charged with a sense of the sacred. The resonance of a church building extends and intensifies music's power to envelop, penetrate and unify. The psalm texts are also rich in verbal references to the

[115] Cardwell, *History of Conferences*, p. 339. [116] Dersingham parish register, PD 603/1, NRO.

power of music as an instrument of praise and supplication, a characteristic that must have contributed additional and self-reinforcing intensity to the performance. Congregational psalm-singing occupied body and mind simultaneously. It was felt as well as heard, and it drew holistically upon all the resources of the individual. 'The blessing thrills thro' all the lab'ring throng', wrote Alexander Pope, 'And Heav'n is won by violence of song.'[117]

Crucially, psalmody also set the individual within a *holy* community, encouraging earthly singers from all levels of society to lose themselves for a time. For many, the power of the musical psalms may have lain in their capacity to generate and articulate a mysterious sense of oneness under God, reinforced by the architectural setting. In 1562, the preface to the *Whole Book* spoke of the 'common place of prayer, where altogether with one voyce render thankes & prayses to God'.[118] At its best, psalmody promoted the temporary elimination of social distinctions and the calming of controversy. The Elizabethan scholar John Case quoted St Austen with joyous approval: 'A Psalme is the quietnesse of souls, the standardbearer of peace, a restrainer of the perturbations and rage of our cogitations, repressing wrath, brideling wantonnesse, inciting to sobriety, making friendship, bringing those to concord which were at variance, and a reconciler of utter enemies.'[119] For members of the gentry, collective oneness could be stressful as well as seductive, and it is not surprising that they sometimes attempted to step out of the melting pot by disparaging its other occupants. The musically educated among them may even have sung slightly different melodies, distinguishing themselves from other parishioners by sharpening their leading notes. This led sophisticated commentators to complain of the hideous clashing sounds that sometimes characterised congregational psalmody.[120] Singing 'with one voyce' was, like the priesthood of all believers, a potentially uncomfortable proposition in such a hierarchical age.

The tunes themselves were clearly considered potent and meaningful. Setting the psalms to music was, argued Jeremy Taylor, a way to 'make religion please more faculties'.[121] The most successful melodies used musical modes that were associated with the stimulation both of sobriety

[117] Pope, quoted by Green, *Print and Protestantism*, p. 550.

[118] *Whole Book of Psalms* (1562), preface. [119] Case, *Praise of Musicke*, pp. 120–1, 91–115.

[120] See, for example, May, *Whole Booke of Psalmes*, preface, and Daniel Warner, *The Singing-master's Guide to his Scholars* (London, 1719), preface.

[121] Jeremy Taylor, *Ductor Dubitantium or The Rule of Conscience*, 4 bks. (London, 1660), bk. III, pp. 329–30.

and of joy. As we have heard, they formed an intricately interconnected musical web within which individual melodies not only accumulated distinctive associations of their own – for example, with particular psalms or with particular sorts of psalm – but also alluded frequently to other psalm tunes. We can only imagine how this web contributed to the profound satisfaction that many people evidently found in the metrical psalms. Close analysis suggests that the sharing of phrases and motifs tended to occur within a group of tunes that were generally associated either with joy or with sorrow. The movement of musical phrases across the border between these basic emotional categories was much less pronounced. In practice, this meant that a recycled melodic motif occurring, for example, in a joyous psalm might subconsciously have reminded singers of other psalms of similar mood. This added depth to the text as it flowed through the mouth, the ears and ideally the mind of the performer.

The appeal of psalmody also lay partly in its potent combination of simple, singable tunes and holy, homely words. It was sometimes objected that, under the conditions of parochial performance, the one got in the way of the other. According to Charles Butler, writing in 1636, the metrical psalms, when sung in church, were often incomprehensible, 'the multitude of voices so confounding the words, that a good ear listening attentively can seldom apprehend them'.[122] We should not, however, accept such testimony at face value, and, in any case, Butler's argument was that psalm-singing should be improved by the introduction of musical instruments, rather than discontinued. The possibility that an outsider may have been unable to hear the words with clarity need not have detracted from the power of those words within the mind of individual participants. Those participants, after all, knew what they were singing, even if the outsider did not. It is obvious that the *Whole Book of Psalms* contained much that grabbed and held the attention of ordinary parishioners, though any attempt to identify its appeal more precisely must, of course, be speculative. It was often said that the psalter summarised in admirably succinct form many of the central tenets of Christian theology. The Bible itself was, of course, the ultimate guide, 'But because the whole Booke of God to idle schollers may seeme too tedious, we have the Psalms of David more compendiously teaching doctrine for us.' Thus spake the composer Richard Allison in dedicating his collection of psalm settings to his godly patroness, the Countess of Warwick, in 1599. One wonders whether his

122 Butler, *Principles of Musik*, p. 111.

perception of the psalms as a kind of 'Scripture-light' for the lax and lazy was entirely in keeping with her own.[123]

The psalms also articulated the possibilities of a personal relationship between each individual worshipper and God. They thus formed a vital teaching aid for the first generations of Protestants. Each singer addressed God directly, and sometimes did so in terms that were forceful and demanding:

O Lord, likewise when I do pray,
regard and geve an eare:
Marke well the wordes that I do say,
And all my prayers heare

(Psalm 86)[124]

When God seemed slow to respond, the singer accused Him of neglect: 'How long wilt thou forget me, Lord? / shall I never be remembered?' (Psalm 13). The *Whole Book of Psalms* also captured perfectly the interplay between self-doubt and self-confidence, anxiety and joy, mournful pleading and exuberant praise that has always characterised the life of Christians. The desperation of Psalm 13, quoted above, is balanced by the relative self-satisfaction of Psalm 17 ('Thou has well tride me in the night, / and yet couldst nothing finde') and the extravagant happiness of Psalm 96:

Sing ye with prayse unto the Lord,
new songes of joy and mirth,
Sing unto him with one accord,
All people on the earth.

Yet the psalms touched more mundane human concerns just as effectively, comforting parishioners in their battles with their foes, their dealings with neighbours and their moral lapses.

In a society characterised by an increasingly strong sense of nationhood, the psalms also presented their singers as the chosen people of God, inhabitants of a metaphorical island of virtue in a sea of vice. The singing congregation portrayed itself as God's 'faithful flock', His 'elect', His 'anointed', His 'folk', His 'chosen Israel', His 'chosen flock' and His

[123] Allison, *Psalmes of David*, dedicatory epistle. See Green, *Print and Protestantism*, p. 534, for further discussion of the book of Psalms as 'an epitome of Christian teaching'.

[124] All quotations in this section are from the 1582 edition of the *Whole Book*, unless otherwise specified.

'children'.[125] There was an obvious intersection between such representation and the tales of miraculous deliverance from tyrants and terrorists that were associated with the Armada and the Gunpowder Plot. When English adventurers sang such songs in the Americas or in the Far East, they were asserting their sense of nationality as well as their faith. Several of the psalms also commended the earth's royal rulers, as if David himself were praising Elizabeth Tudor or her successors ('God even thy God hath nointed thee / with joy above the rest').[126]

Above all, congregations must have found the psalmist's portrayal of God persuasive and compelling. The God of the psalms is mighty indeed, capable of great wrath and great mercy. He is protective of His own people, and brutal in his treatment of their enemies:

The Lord preserves all those to him
that beare a loving hart:
But he them all that wicked are,
Will utterly subvert.

(Psalm 145)

He is responsive to well-meaning prayer, and will reward those who trust in Him. The greatest treasures lie, of course, in heaven, but there are hints of earthly prizes too ('With goodly gifts will he reward / all them that fear his Name').[127] God is a tower of strength to all who follow Him, and a particular friend of the weak:

He is protector of the poore,
what time they be opprest:
He is in all adversity
Their refuge and their rest.

(Psalm 9)

He hears their prayers and sides with them in their struggles with 'men of worldly might' (Psalm 10), those 'which wallow in their worldly wealth, / so full and eke so fat' (Psalm 17):

The poore do perish by the proud,
and wicked mens desire:
Let them be taken in the craft
Which they themselves conspire.

(Psalm 10)

[125] Psalms 15, 18, 20, 25, 29, 90. [126] Psalm 45 (edn. of 1629).

[127] Psalm 61 (edn. of 1629). By 1720, the expression 'goodly gifts' had been replaced by the cruder term 'riches great'!

There may have been something profoundly cathartic in this for the ranks of ordinary parishioners who sang their psalms from the less prestigious pews within every parish church. In Psalm 4, they could sing, loudly and legitimately, that

The greater sort crave worldly goodes,
and riches do embrace:
But, Lord, graunt us thy countenaunce,
Thy favour and thy grace.

Lastly, the Sternhold–Hopkins psalter presented all this in words that were accessible and familiar. The voice of David became that of the ordinary congregation, and its members obviously relished their weekly experience of stepping into the prophet's sandals.

As these quotations suggest, psalmody was not inevitably concordant and cohesive. We conclude, therefore, with an exploration of its role within early modern conflict. The disdainful comments of educated men have rumbled away like indigestion through much of this chapter. Musical psalmody came under fire for the manner of its performance, the crudity of its verse ('that low and vicious plainness') and the very fact of its popularity.[128] There were other grounds for objection too. Some doubted that congregational psalm-singing was a legitimate form of worship at all, and they supported their instincts with arguments that were moral and religious as well as aesthetic. Negative comment issued from the lips and pens of all manner of commentators, for attitudes to this form of music were never merely or clearly the corollary of religious and political affiliations (except perhaps in the case of radical sectaries such as the Quakers). During the 1560s, the Catholic exile Thomas Harding stood out against the spread of psalmody, arguing that the people did not understand the words they sang. An anxiety that the psalm-singer's experience of 'delight' was sensual rather than properly spiritual lingered on into the eighteenth century. One or two Elizabethan bishops were suspicious of congregational singing, probably because they associated the practice with puritanism.[129] In the mid-seventeenth century, conversely, there were puritans who had come to feel that congregational psalmody was illegitimate. In 1650, John Fry asked whether most members of a typical congregation

[128] Playford, *Whole Book of Psalms*, preface; John Angier, *An Helpe to Better Hearts for Better Times* (London, 1647), pp. 69–70; Richard Goodridge, quoted by Winn, 'Bibliography', p. 440.

[129] John Jewel, *A Replie unto M. Hardinges Answeare* (London, 1565), pp. 211–13; Craig, 'Psalms, Groans and Dog-whippers', p. 107.

were 'in a fit frame of Spirit to sing as David'. He doubted the existence of a single psalm in the *Whole Book* that could 'rationally be sung by such a mixed multitude' of godly and ungodly individuals. 'How absurd, and irrational is it', he asked, 'for men of all conditions to personate David, as they do' and to do so with 'such a great cry and shew of Religion[?]' A more representative puritan position was taken up by the clergymen who attended the Savoy Conference in 1660. They did not ask the bishops to abolish congregational psalmody, but only to purify the wretched Sternhold–Hopkins translations.[130] Sterner objections came from the more radical nonconformists of the period. Some complained that the prevailing style of psalm-singing had no Scriptural precedent or justification; others classified the psalms as songs created by men, and therefore objected to their use in divine service; and the most extreme nonconformists denied the validity of all church music.[131]

Very occasionally, hostile or disrespectful attitudes towards the psalms also surfaced among the lower social orders. In early Elizabethan Canterbury, the wife of William Bell allegedly walked out of the church of Holy Cross, cursing and railing, when the congregation began to sing psalms. Her reported possession of an unlawful book of prayers probably reflects committed religious conservatism. At the other end of the reign, in 1592, Thomas Howling of Pampisford (Cambridgeshire) was reported to have said 'that davids psalmes is dronckenes and heresye'. The record does not explain precisely what he meant, but his alleged practice of acting suspiciously with the wives of other men may indicate that the moral high ground was not his normal habitat. In 1604, a group of men in Wrington (Somerset) staged a mock-service, complete with a makeshift pulpit, during which they 'began a psalm, beginning the spiritt of grace etc, & song it to the end'. Their performance was full of 'ribaldrye & knaverye' but does not seem to have constituted a theologically purposeful challenge to the practices of the established church. In fact, the group knew the psalter well enough to devise a parody, and in other respects they drew quite knowledgeably on the orthodox liturgy.[132]

130 John Fry, *The Clergy in their Colours* (London, 1650) pp. 40–2; Cardwell, *History of Conferences*, p. 308.

131 Richard Baxter approved thoroughly of psalm-singing, but took time to address the arguments of those who did not: see *The Divine Appointment*, pp. 97–8. For various radical criticisms of psalmody, see Isaac Marlow, *Some Short Observations* (London, 1691), pp. 1–16. For opposition to all church music, see above, pp. 50–1, 63–4, 393–4.

132 *Church Life in Kent*, p. 31; EDR B/2/12, fo. 137r, CUL; *REED Somerset*, pp. 398–9.

The periodic role of the psalms as the theme music of cultural combat was scarcely surprising, for the original texts were born out of Biblical conflict, and the early modern musical versions came to prominence amid the new sectarianism of the Reformation. It was therefore natural that the musical psalms should have played their part in the tense religious politics of the age. Just as the psalms could articulate the somewhat mythical unity of an entire parochial congregation or nation, so too could they express the more disruptive togetherness of a particular segment of society.[133] These two possibilities converged rather nicely in late seventeenth-century Bristol, where groups of dissenters reacted to official raids on their meetings by switching from their more controversial practices to the singing of psalms. This had the double advantage of legality and, by questionable implication, orthodoxy.[134] Throughout the early modern period, psalm-singing was sometimes associated most particularly with puritans, for whom the established church was but half reformed. The self-proclaimed godly sang psalms in their homes, at their meetings and while gadding to sermons. In 1620, a famous group of English exiles waited excitedly at their pastor's house in Leiden, shortly before departing for the New World on the mother of all gads: 'we refreshed ourselves, after tears, with singing of psalms, making joyful melody in our hearts, as well as with the voice, there being many of our congregation very expert in music'. It was, said Edward Winslow, 'the sweetest melody that ever mine ears heard'. For Josias Nichols, writing approvingly in 1602, so-called puritans were 'the people [who] do hear sermons, talk of the Scriptures, [and] sing Psalms together in private houses'.[135]

The mid-seventeenth-century drive to create a truly godly society encouraged puritans to make bold use of the singing psalms. Their enemies mocked them, alleging that the godly had plans to abolish the worldly music that typically broke up the action at London's theatres by replacing it with the songs of David. In the world beyond the walls, zealous parishioners sometimes broke up the action in a different way, by singing psalms of their own choosing in order to disrupt official church

[133] For a discussion of this theme in a French context, see Barbara B. Diefendorf, 'The Huguenot Psalter and the Faith of French Protestants in the Sixteenth Century', in Diefendorf and Carla Hesse (eds.), *Culture and Identity in Early Modern Europe* (Ann Arbor: University of Michigan Press, 1993), pp. 41–63.

[134] See Horton Davis, *Worship and Theology in England ... 1603–90* (Princeton: Princeton University Press, 1975), pp. 447–8.

[135] Edward Winslow, *Hypocrisie Unmasked* (London, 1646), pp. 90–1; Nichols, *The Plea of the Innocent* (London, 1602), p. 12.

services.[136] On 30 March 1645, afternoon prayer was proceeding peacefully at Sible Hedingham (Essex), but then 'in the singing of the psalms before the preaching of the word of God' seven labourers 'riotously entered the parish church and disturbed the congregation, and said these words in a loud voice, viz., "All that are for Jhesus Christ singe the eleven and twentieth Psalm", and thereon the said malefactors read and sang the psalm at their own setting ... to the great disturbance of the people in the church'. The curate asked the village constables to intervene, and when they did so a fight broke out, during which 'divers women in the church exclaimed in a loud voice, "Oh my husband, Oh my brother"'. In the end, the whole congregation left the church 'in great fear and terror'. The psalm was here being employed as a device of division, a tool with which the godly and the ungodly could be forced apart. Psalm 31 includes the lines

I hate such folke as will not part
from thinges that be abhord:
When they on trifles set their hart,
My trust is in the Lord.

Nor was this a unique episode in Sible Hedingham. The previous week, a slightly different group of labourers had allegedly ruined the service by chanting the psalm nominated by the curate so loudly that 'the greater part of the congregation were in great fear'. They encouraged the terrified parishioners to follow their example by shouting 'All: All; All'. The local justice, Arthur Barnardiston, attempted to bring them into line, but 'was quite unable to quiet their noise'.[137] The hierarchical unity of the congregation, traditionally expressed through the singing of psalms in unison, was under extreme strain in this parish.

The songs of David put into words and music the hopes and fears of several generations of English puritans. The political and religious environment within which such people operated, nearly always as a somewhat uncomfortable sub-society, shifted from decade to decade, but the songs remained largely unchanged. Paradoxically, the puritan love of musical psalmody was both a point of contact with wider society and a signal of distinction. John Bunyan advised his followers that Psalm 128 was ideal for singing 'even as thou art in thy calling, bed, journey, or whenever'. 'Sing out thine own blessed and happy condition', he continued, 'to thine

[136] *Certaine Propositions Offered to the Consideration of the Honourable Houses of Parliament* (London, 1642), p. 5; Green, *Print and Protestantism*, p. 530.

[137] Q/SR 342/32 and 324/110, ERO; Sternhold and Hopkins, *Whole Booke* (London, 1582).

own comfort and the comfort of thy fellows.'[138] These 'fellows' were, in all probability, members of a troubled minority (themselves divided over the legitimacy of congregational psalmody), yet the text and tune that Bunyan had in mind were drawn from the Sternhold–Hopkins psalms and from widespread parochial custom. In the main, therefore, psalm-singers of all sorts shared their tunes and their texts, but the puritans felt them differently, or believed that they did.[139] For them, the wondrous completeness of the psalms meant that there was neither need nor justification for the existence of lewd ballads and dance music. Earlier experiments in the mixing of genres for educational effect had not brought the promised riches, and by 1600 a new orthodoxy prevailed. Such musical forms, wrote Nicholas Bownde in 1595, simply could not co-exist.[140] The majority of people, in contrast, refused to accept that such a stark choice had to be made. There was a time and a place for each kind of music. For most parishioners, psalm-singing may have been associated primarily with Sunday and the church, and this left plenty of time for the appreciation of ballads and dance tunes in other social contexts. For the puritans, all times and all places called for the singing of the psalms, which was as much a domestic as an ecclesiastical obligation.

Opponents of puritanism sometimes responded to its associations with psalmody by restricting the opportunities for congregational singing. In the mid-1620s, John Cosin, prebendary of Durham Cathedral, provoked fierce controversy when, in the words of his enemies, he 'banished the singing of psalms in the vulgar tunes'. Worse still, he replaced it with elaborate choral polyphony, provoking complaints about 'the confusedness of voices of so many singers, with a multitude of melodius instruments'. As a result, 'the greatest part of the service is no better understood, than if it were in Hebrue or in Irish'.[141] It would be misguided, however, to suggest that the musical psalms took sides decisively in the conflicts that preceded and contributed towards the outbreak of civil war in 1642. While it is true that Cosin was deprived of office by the Long Parliament in that year, and that parliamentary soldiers sang psalms at the Battle of Marston Moor, it should be noted that their opponents also expressed themselves

[138] John Bunyan, *A Treatise of the Fear of God* (London, 1679), in *The Works of John Bunyan*, ed. George Offer, 3 vols. (Glasgow, 1854), vol. I, p. 473. In *The Pilgrim's Progress*, even the birds sing psalms from the Sternhold–Hopkins version.

[139] Certain puritans, however, preferred to use what they considered to be the truer translations of the psalms contained in alternative versions. See Green, *Print and Protestantism*, p. 532.

[140] Bownde, *The Doctrine of the Sabbath*, p. 242.

[141] *The Correspondence of John Cosin*, ed. G. Ornsby, *Publications of the Surtees Society* 52 (1868), p. 166.

through sacred song. On 29 January 1643, the parish clerk of Great St Mary's, Cambridge, responded to the iconoclastic activities of Cromwell's men by setting Psalm 74 for the service on that day: it implored God to save his temple from those who had come to attack it, 'As men with axes hew down trees'.[142]

The atmosphere must have been similar during the eleven-week siege of York in 1644, but here there was solace to be had. Thomas Mace heard 'the very best harmonical-music' imaginable, performed by a congregation of 1,000 royalists in the minster. The sound of the powerful organ, as it began the psalm tune, was stirring enough,

> But when that vast-conchording-unity of the whole congregational-chorus, came ... thundering in, even so, as it made the very ground shake under us: (Oh the unutterable ravishing soul's delight!) In the which I was so transplanted, and wrapt up into High Contemplations, that there was no room left in my whole Man, viz. Body, Soul and Spirit, for anything below Divine and Heavenly Raptures.

The parliamentary soldiers, gathered outside the city walls, knew the same psalms and probably the same tunes, but there was little prospect of unity across the divide. Instead, each side sang the psalms in order to articulate, among other things, their antagonistic feelings towards the other. In such circumstances, psalms could be weapons, the sonic response of the besieged to the bullets that, according to Mace, came flying in through the minster's windows during services, bouncing from pillar to pillar but, miraculously, injuring no one.[143]

Mace was ecstatic at the music of the organ but many of the parliamentarians gathered outside the city walls would probably have frowned at the muffled sounds emerging from the minster. Throughout the period, the ecclesiastical use of organs in support of psalmody carried its own controversial charge. In 1638, for example, Edward Fleetwood, the puritan vicar of Kirkham (Lancashire), was accused by the parish's leading laity, the 'Thirty Men', of deliberately obstructing them in their efforts to make use of the church's ancient organ. Fleetwood, it was alleged, had usurped the responsibility of the Thirty Men for the selection of the parish clerk. He had purposefully appointed a man who had no ability to play the organs, in direct contravention of local custom. In the ecclesiastical court record, his accusers addressed him directly: 'and rather to hinder the use of the aforesaid Organs through your discontent and dislike of them you have

[142] Diary of Dr Dillingham, quoted by Trevor Cooper in *Journal of William Dowsing*, p. 201.
[143] Mace, *Musick's Monument*, pp. 18–19.

caused the way formerly leadeinge to them to be stopped up, soe as the Organs are not used at divine service-tyme'.[144]

Elsewhere, organ warfare was more fitfully described but its traces are nevertheless discernible. On 29 December 1603, Thomas Allen of Sutton St Mary's (Lincolnshire) took the unusual step of using his will in order to express his views. This gentleman doubled as the local organist and he evidently knew that, in the latter capacity, he belonged to an endangered species. Allen's will is a model of orthodox Protestant piety, and includes the bequest of several pieces of land to the local vicar, partly for general church repairs and 'partlye towarde the maintenance of the lawdable solemnitie of Church musick and of the Instriment in that Chirche to be perfourmed according as it shalbe allowed by the lawes of the land or as it hathe beene usually heare to fore by me the said Thomas allen in my lyffe time perfourmed I meane with all Christian decencye'. Lieutenant Hammond, the musical traveller of the 1630s, shared this positive attitude. He did not refer explicitly to current tensions over organ music, but he pointedly described the various instruments he heard as 'sweet', 'deep', 'delightful', 'fair', 'rich', 'neat' and 'tunable'. John Taylor said even less on the subject, but noted with grim satisfaction the death of a Worcester man who had attempted to destroy the organs but 'fell from the top of them down upon the pavement of the Church, and brake his bones'.[145]

Much of the evidence lacks detail, but a dispute at Tiverton (Devon) – one of several to break out in the late seventeenth century – allows us to summarise the arguments on both sides of the controversy. In 1696, an organ was erected in the church and John Newte, the rector, adored it. He marked the occasion with a sermon in which he justified the new addition on various grounds. Its 'Majestick Loudness' would, he suggested, have the immediate effect of regulating the 'untunable Voices of the Multitude', rendering their psalm-singing 'more orderly and harmonious'. The organ would also stir the affections of the people, leaving them suitably serious and reverential for the exercise of their public devotions. Moreover, its music would 'compose their Thoughts, and drive away Evill Suggestions from their Minds'. It might even manage, in time, to 'melt us into Love'. Newte, despite this sentiment, had no time whatsoever for those in the locality who declared bluntly, 'They don't like it, and they shall never

[144] EDC5 1638.14, ChRO.

[145] Misc. Dep 37/5, LA; *Relation of a Short Survey of 26 Counties* and *Relation of a Short Survey of the Western Counties*; Taylor, *Works of John Taylor not Included in the Folio Volume*, vol. V, p. 5, 'The Noble Cavalier Caracterized'. See also Fincham and Tyacke, *Altars Restored*, pp. 51, 54, 96–9.

endure it.' Objections to the Tiverton organ were set out in an anonymous letter, written in direct response to Newte's sermon. It was disgraceful, argued the author, to spend such a large sum of money on a musical instrument at a time when the nation's poor were in dire need. He denied that organs had been used in the early church and insisted that the proper attitude of good English Protestants towards them was one of profound suspicion. Instrumental music, alleged the author, was a pointless vanity in church. It would undermine the power of the metrical psalms by obscuring the words. The letter also pointed out that untunable voices cannot, by definition, be tuned, and that an organ would only drown out the singing of the people.[146] Clearly, this was an argument that had not moved on significantly in 150 years. Other musical controversies may have lost some of their heat by the late seventeenth century, but this one rumbled on.

The English Reformation, in its musical aspects as much as in its other characteristics, was a complex and contrary affair. Congregational psalmody was perhaps its greatest success, and certainly its loudest. It drew people of all sorts to the church and encouraged an entirely new form of liturgical participation. It helped parishioners to think of themselves as Protestant, both individually and collectively. Some combination of the 'matter', the 'meeter', the 'maker' and the 'musyke' pulled people together during a remarkably difficult period in the nation's religious history. And yet psalmody also contributed to fierce arguments among Protestants and to friction between rich and poor. It was widely loved, but the mere popularity of psalmody was not sufficient to convince the most demanding of godly ministers that the people of England had truly sung their way onto the path of righteousness. It was as if the Reformation could not be completed, a perception that may have intensified in the late seventeenth century when choirs and organs began to multiply once more. Indeed, there was something curiously circular about what happened to parochial church music during the early modern period. A mixture of puritanism and pragmatism had driven choirs and organs to the brink of extinction during the later sixteenth century, replacing them with the unaccompanied psalmody of many voices. Eventually, however, the

[146] John Newte, *The Lawfulness and Use of Organs in the Christian Church* (London, 1696), pp. 20–1, 35, 42; *A Letter to a Friend in the Country, Concerning the Use of Instrumental Musick in the Worship of God* (London, 1698), pp. 2, 6, 16, 50, 82–3. See also Brookbank, *The Well-tuned Organ*; Gabriel Towerson, *A Sermon Concerning Vocal and Instrumental Musick in the Church* (London, 1696); Dodwell, *A Treatise Concerning the Lawfulness of Instrumental Musick*.

traditional providers of church music proved indestructible, returning to prominence on the back of a post-Restoration reform movement whose supporters argued that psalm-singing congregations were in desperate need of expert support. There was an irony here: under Elizabeth, psalm-singing had contributed to the decay of many choirs and organs, but under the later Stuarts it provided the justification for their reinstatement.

In many places, moreover, those who sang in the choir or played upon the organ were interested not only in supporting psalmody but in supplanting it. Congregational psalm-singing was popular, but because it was popular it could also seem unruly, unsophisticated and unmusical. Did not the dignity of the church require something more refined and exclusive? A wheel had indeed come full circle, and local parishioners sometimes voiced their anger at the fact. In the mid-eighteenth century, one elderly woman vented her spleen against the choir that had just been introduced in her parish. She called its members 'very opprobrious names' and said 'they had put her out of her tune that she had sung forty years'.[147] Of course, the wheel was to turn again, for it made little sense to silence the congregation after so promising a debut. The great age of English hymn-singing lay in the future, and it seems fitting to conclude with the observation that a number of the songs that are still sung in churches today have their roots, both culturally and musically, in the metrical psalms of the early modern period. The melody to which modern congregations sing the carol 'While Shepherds Watched' was, for example, known to parishioners of the early modern era as the 'Winchester' psalm tune.

[147] Temperley, *Music of the English Parish Church*, p. 171.

9 | Parish church music: bells and their ringers

The ringing of church bells was one of the most familiar and compelling sounds to be heard in early modern England. For those who did not like it there were few places to hide: 'if all the bells in England should be rung together at a certain hour', commented Bishop Latimer unhappily in 1552, 'I think there would be almost no place but some bells might be heard there'. He doubtless hoped to see most of them melted down, but during the next two centuries the bells that were destroyed by zealous reformers were heavily outnumbered by new additions. The English, reported a German visitor in 1598, were 'vastly fond of great noises that fill the air, such as the firing of cannon, drums, and the ringing of bells'. It was, according to a chapbook of the later seventeenth century, one of the 'Nine great sounds and reports' to be heard in England.[1] England truly was 'the ringing island', and bells participated in many aspects of parochial life. They summoned people to church, accompanied most rites of passage, marked the hours of the day, greeted visiting dignitaries, warned of fire and provided men (but rarely women) with a popular form of exercise. The sonic field of the church bells was one way of marking the boundary of a community, though chimes must often have carried substantially further (on the website, tracks 47 and 48 present the sound of bells heard from the churchyard and the outlying fields respectively). Early modern people were also said to recognise the distinctive characteristics of their home 'ring'.[2]

The terminology of bell-ringing had broad currency and spread readily into other walks of life (see Figure 9.1). In 1636, there were nine inns named 'The Bell' in London alone. 'Some ring the Changes of opinions',

[1] *Sermons of Hugh Latimer, Sometime Bishop of Worcester*, ed. George Elwes Corrie (Cambridge: Cambridge University Press, 1844), p. 498; Paul Hentzner, quoted by Smith, *Acoustic World*, p. 53; *The Figure of Nine*, A5r.

[2] Glyn Holdgate, *Ting Tangs, Trebles and Tenors* (Derby: Glyn Holdgate, 1999), p. 39. There are many related observations in Alain Corbin's wonderfully evocative book *Village Bells: The Culture of the Senses in the Nineteenth-century French Countryside* (1998; London: Papermak, 1999).

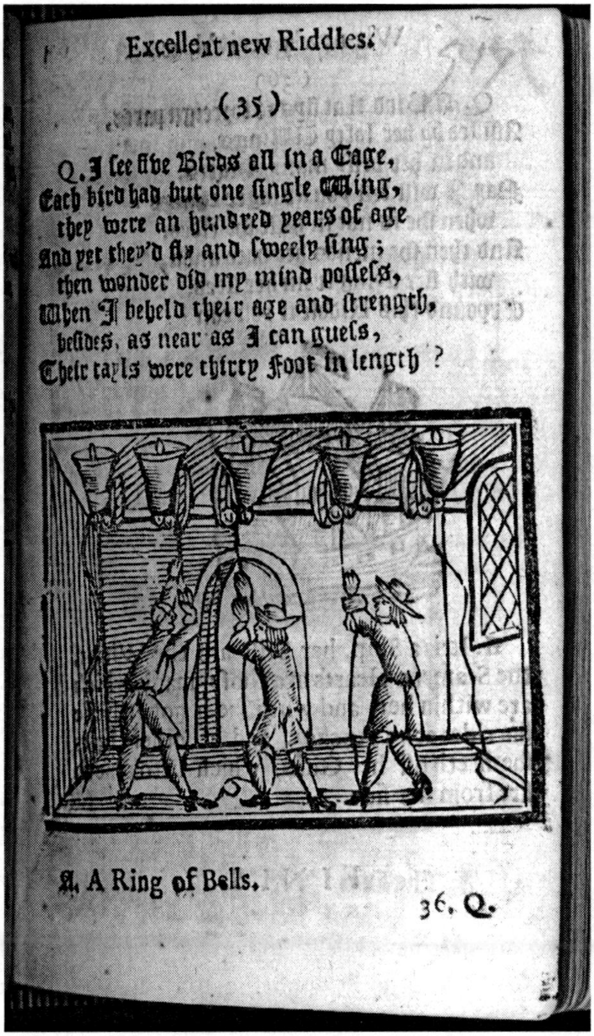
Excellent new Riddles.

(35)

Q. I see five Birds all in a Cage,
Each bird had but one single Wing,
they were an hundred years of age
And yet they'd fly and sweetly sing;
then wonder did my mind possess,
When I beheld their age and strength,
besides, as near as I can guess,
Their tayls were thirty Foot in length ?

A. A Ring of Bells.

36. Q.

Figure 9.1 Interest in bells was widespread, and the author of this riddle hoped to take advantage of the fact. Rings of five bells were common by the later seventeenth century, though in this instance full use is not being made of the available resources. The Pepys Library, Magdalene College, Cambridge, Pepys Penny Merriments, *The True Tryall of Understanding, or Wit newly reviv'd, being a book of excellent new riddles* (London, 1687), no. 35.

remarked the preacher Thomas Adams in 1614. Elsewhere, he called the human tongue 'man's clapper' and urged that its proper use was the praise of God. The expression 'ding-dong' was regularly used in literary sources, either to signify celebration or to imply frenetic and sometimes confrontational activity. Rejoicing friends and angry enemies could both be said to be 'at it ding dong'.[3] The lucky man who had cash to spare could boast of the ability to 'ring a peal in my pockets', while a rambling relative could be silenced with the exclamation, 'Oh Cousin stay the Bells'. One ballad-writer wove campanological terms into a bawdy song (to the tune of 'The Oxford bells'):

her white Thighs she does lay bare,
Whilst his Clapper does make his great Bell roar,
The first and second Peal.

Rounds and catches referred frequently to bell music, and several of the period's renowned composers imitated its sound in instrumental pieces. The great John Jenkins recorded several fine examples and was an accomplished bell-ringer himself.[4]

It is curious, then, that bell-ringing receives barely a mention in the classic musicological study of the English parish church.[5] Historians of the Reformation, similarly, are only slowly beginning to take the subject seriously. The study of ringing has been left to ringers, and the rest of us have tended to behave as if it was not properly a musical activity at all. On this last point, our early modern ancestors generally disagreed: the minister Thomas Holland told his listeners and readers in 1601, 'it is natural to the mind of man to be ravished with great joy by the notes and harmony of music, which things bells well rung commonly effect in men's hearts, first being well tuned by a skilful artisan and experimental practitioner'; three years later, Thomas Dekker listened sadly to the sounds of plague-ravished London and commented, 'No musick now is heard but bells, / And all their tunes are sick mens knells'; in happier times, James I's queen visited Bristol in 1612 and 'The Bels most joyfully did ring, with Musickes simphony'. Admittedly, bell-ringers were not the most highly respected of musicians, and they sometimes sounded defensive. 'As ringing is a branch of music', ran one eighteenth-century couplet, 'Let none

[3] Taylor, *Works of John Taylor not Included in the Folio Volume*, vol. III, p. 18, 'Taylors Travels'; Thomas Adams, quoted by John C. Eisel, 'The Development of Change Ringing in the Seventeenth Century', in Sanderson (ed.), *Change Ringing*, vol. I, p. 40; *The Workes of Thomas Adams*, p. 144; Thomas Otway, *The History and Fall of Caius Marius* (London, 1680), p. 33.

[4] Francis Beaumont, *Wit without Money* (London, 1661), F3r; Nicholas Breton, *The Court and the Country* (London, 1618), D3v; *Pepys Ballads*, vol. III, p. 77; Thomas Lant's roll of catches, MS Rowe 1, King's College, Cambridge; Wulstan, *Tudor Music*, p. 52; William T. Cook, 'The Organisation of the Exercise in the Seventeenth Century', in Sanderson (ed.), *Change Ringing*, vol. I, p. 72.

[5] Temperley, *Music of the English Parish Church*.

despise those men that use it.' We might do well to listen: in early modern England, bell-ringing was a form of music that echoed everywhere, and it matched other genres in its capacity to generate both admiration and suspicion.[6]

The care of bells

Virtually all parishes spent money on the maintenance of their rings. The number and type of bells kept by a typical parish was changing throughout the period, and a brief introductory overview may be useful. Late medieval parish churches housed a variety of bells, and an Edwardian inventory relating to Bonsall (Derbyshire) provides a fairly typical example: 'iii small bells, i sanctus bells [sic], iii bells in the stepul'. The smaller bells were strongly associated with the celebration of mass, and they fell foul of new Protestant sensibilities during the reigns of Edward VI and Elizabeth I. The larger bells in the steeple also faced criticism but in most churches they survived to ring another day.[7] By the later sixteenth century, English church bells were beginning to multiply as parishes grew more confident about investing in them. In 1584–5, for example, the parish of Lambeth increased its ring to four bells and organised a celebratory dinner for the 'churchwardens, bellfounder and other honest men of the parishe'. A few years later, a Nottinghamshire esquire made a will in which he bequeathed 'to Holme church a Bell to make up the Rynge to be three bells If I make it not in my lyfe tyme'. Some of the wealthier London parishes were ahead of the pack, and courtly composers were already quoting six- and eight-bell rings by the turn of the century.[8]

[6] Holland, quoted by David Cressy, *Bonfires and Bells* (1989; Stroud: Sutton Publishing, 2004), p. 69; Thomas Dekker, *Newes from Graves-end Sent to Nobody* (London, 1604), E3r; *REED Bristol*, pp. 175–94; Ernest Morris, *The History and Art of Change Ringing* (1931; Wakefield: E. P. Publishing, 1976), p. 98.

[7] Morris, *History and Art of Change Ringing*, p. 24. See also John C. Eisel, 'Developments in Bell Hanging', in Sanderson (ed.), *Change Ringing*, vol. I, pp. 18, 24; Cook, 'The Organisation of the Exercise', p. 70; Duffy, *Stripping of the Altars*, pp. 97, 126.

[8] *Lambeth Churchwardens' Accounts, 1504–1645, and Vestry Book, 1610*, ed. Charles Drew, *Surrey Record Society* 18 (1941), p. 156; PRSW 22/8 (Rauff Barton), Nottinghamshire Archives; *The Fitzwilliam Virginal Book*, ed. Blanche Winogron, 2 vols. (New York: Dover Publications, 1979), vol. I, p. 274.

The gradual expansion of resources continued after 1600, when the development of new change-ringing techniques added further incentives for the installation of extra bells. It has been estimated that nearly one in five of the bells that were still hanging in English steeples during the mid-nineteenth century had been cast during the first half of the seventeenth. At Great St Mary's in Cambridge, the number of bells increased in stages with successive recastings and additions: there were four in 1596, five in 1611, six in 1622, eight in 1668 and ten in 1722. In Norfolk, rings of five bells were established at the Norwich parish of St Margaret and St Swithin (1610), at Thetford (1630) and at Catfield (1630).[9] Rural parishes rarely maintained more than four bells before the later seventeenth century, but five was a common number in urban churches. Some went further still, and Samuel Pepys noted at Norton St Philip (Somerset) 'a very fine ring of six bells and chimes mighty tuneable'. Salisbury had for years been an important centre for church music of all forms, and the bells particularly impressed Lieutenant Hammond when he visited the city during 1635. In the cathedral close, there stood 'a strong and stately high Bell-Clotcher, with a merry and brave Ring, of 8 tunable Bells therein'. The ordinary parish churches of Salisbury were scarcely inferior in this regard: 'in every one of them are neat Organs, and a sweet Ring of tunable Bells, equally exceeding each other, 6, 7 and 8 a peece'.[10]

Throughout the early modern period, churchwardens kept careful records of the money they spent on the maintenance and improvement of their bells. Visitation articles sometimes reminded them of this duty, but it is obvious that parish officers perceived the importance of church bells for themselves. From time to time, they also received bequests towards bell maintenance from local testators. In 1571, a baker from Maldon (Essex) left 5s to assist with the 'wheeling and trimming' of his parish church's great bell. A few years later, Thomas Ellement, a yeoman from West Hanningfield (Essex) set 13s 4d aside for the repairing of the church's bell frame. And in 1623, a Suffolk yeoman named Robert Man was still more generous, bequeathing a total of 26s towards the maintenance of the bells in four local parishes. Some gave not of their money but of their time. In Sidlesham (Sussex), William Rumbridger told an

[9] Morris, *History and Art of Change Ringing*, p. 32; C. M. G. Ockelton, *The Tower, Bells and Ringers of Great St. Mary's Church, Cambridge* (Cambridge: Society of Cambridge Youths, 1981), pp. 5–9; PD 153/27, PD 531/1, PD 313/42, NRO.

[10] Morris, *History and Art of Change Ringing*, p. 33; *Diary of Samuel Pepys*, vol. IX, p. 232; *A Relation of a Short Survey of the Western Counties*, p. 64.

ecclesiastical court in about 1576 that he repaired the parish bell-ropes not as a matter of obligation, but 'rather of devotion' (he spoiled the effect somewhat by withdrawing his labour when the queen seized a parcel of his land, aptly named 'Bell Crofte', claiming that it was monastic in origin and therefore hers by right).[11]

A well-used ring of church bells required a good deal of attention. The corporation of Stratford-upon-Avon was responsible for the maintenance of the town's Guild Chapel, and the records kept by its officers provide a wealth of evidence. New bells were hung during the Catholic reign of Queen Mary, and were carefully maintained during the subsequent reigns of the Protestant Elizabeth and her Stuart successors. In normal years, money was spent on replacement bell-ropes, baldrics, cords, tacklings, clips, gudgeons, irons, clappers and joiners. The great bell was rung very regularly, and its rope was replaced on numerous occasions. The officers clearly had recurrent trouble with this, their main bell, and it was recast in 1591–2, 1606, 1616 and 1622. On such occasions, sums were paid out for hemp, wax, rosin, callow, metal, nails, timber (for the bell frame) and wood (burned in a furnace dug into the ground in order to melt the bell). The bell-founder received a substantial fee (£6 16s in 1606, out of a total cost of £26 17s 1d). The moving of the bell inevitably damaged the floor in the steeple, and this too was repeatedly repaired. Such frequent recasting was highly unusual, but accounts from many other parishes reveal similar evidence of the mundane, year-by-year attention that was paid to England's bells. Both before and after the Reformation, the upkeep of bells was a major component in the workload of the parochial officers. Bells were also a source of income for many parishes, but it is obvious that this was not the primary motive for their maintenance.[12]

When a congregation wished to recast its bells in order to increase their number or improve their sound, it first had to seek permission from the bishop or his chancellor. Documents surviving from Norfolk during the first third of the seventeenth century provide some rich evidence. In 1610, twenty-two parishioners from St Margaret and St Swithin, Norwich, signed or marked a petition addressed to the bishop. The existing bells, they reported, were 'in greate decaye untunable & Broken'.

[11] *Essex Wills*, vol. IX, no. 18, vol. X, no. 297; *Wills of the Archdeaconry of Suffolk, 1620–24*, ed. Marion E. Allen, *Suffolk Records Society* 31 (1989), no. 532; EP I/11/3, pt. 3, fo. 2r, WSRO.

[12] BRU 4/1, 4/2, 4/3, Shakespeare Birthplace Trust; *Minutes and Accounts of the Corporation of Stratford-upon-Avon*, vol. I, pp. 121–40, vol. II, pp. 19–114, vol. III, pp. 12–163, vol. IV, pp. 14–145, vol. V, pp. 4–78. On bells as a source of income, see below, pp. 473–4.

They continued, 'wee the inhabitans [sic] are desirous to have them in good tune'. The churchwardens had already spoken with a bell-founder, and had established that the parish's existing ring (presumably of three or four bells) could be increased to five 'by adding to the ould mettell twoo or iii hundred weight more'. The bishop duly granted a licence, urging the petitioners to complete their work within six months.[13] In more rural parishes, specialist bell-founders generally had to be summoned from urban centres some miles away, and the churchwardens were keen to bind them to contracts guaranteeing a period of on-going maintenance following the installation of the new bells. The founding and tuning of bells was a complex process requiring the involvement of experienced specialists. A bell is tuned, for example, by shaving small quantities of metal from very particular locations on its inner surface. The churchwarden who attempts such work himself is foolhardy in the extreme. In 1630, therefore, the church officers from Methwold recruited John Draper, a bell-founder from Thetford. Draper 'cast and new founded' a ring of five bells, and then signed a bond guaranteeing his work. He was to be discharged only if the bells proved 'whole sound Cleere & tewneable in a good toen & tuneable accord & note & tewneable eyther wth other' for a term of seven years. The text was not clearly written, but an emphasis on 'tunability' – referring to the melodic compatibility of the bells – was more than apparent. If, however, any of the bells were to 'decaie breake crack or prove untewneable' within this period, then Draper undertook to replace and recast them at his own charges.[14]

In the same year, comparable work was underway in Catfield, and the vicar, Anthony Harrison, wrote a remarkably full record of it in the parish register. 'Some of the parishioners were desirous to have the fower olde belles in Catfield to be cast into fyve', and they successfully persuaded all but a few of their neighbours to support the project. Voluntary contributions to the tune of £24 were raised, and the parishioners submitted a petition to the diocesan chancellor. In this document, they explained that there were currently 'fower unforceable Bells belonging to their church the greatest of which is somewhat to[o] greate for the other three & to[o] waightie for the steeple' (recently weakened by 'earthquakes'). They were particularly concerned to hear the chancellor's advice in view of the fact that three or four parishioners had refused to make contributions. He readily approved their plans, and expressed his hope that the small group of resisters 'would not persist to be untuneable in so Harmonicall a worke'.

[13] PD 153/27, NRO. [14] PD 313/42, NRO.

Following this ringing endorsement, the work began in earnest: 'the 4 olde belles were carried to the howse of William Brend the bellfounder in twoe cartes on Friday at night the 18th June'. This was a ten-mile journey to Brend's foundry in Norwich, during which the bells were accompanied by the churchwardens and four prominent parishioners. Before witnesses, Brend weighed the bells, and Harrison kept careful notes. The heaviest, Catfield's 'Great bell', weighed 'twelve hundred & a half & 27 pounds & a half every hundred containing fyve skore & twelve poundes'. In other words, it tipped the specialist scales at 1,427.5 pounds, and was more than 300 pounds heavier than the second-largest bell. The lightest weighed 491 pounds, and the total weight of all four bells was 3,385.5 pounds. For some reason, the work proceeded with an air of urgency: 'That night before day they were runn & cast into 5 bells.' On the following day, the new bells – now called base, tenor, contra tenor, mean and treble – were weighed. The heaviest now came in at 1,023.5 pounds, and was thus lighter than each of the two largest bells in the old ring. The lightest of the new bells, the treble, weighed 450 pounds. The total weight of the bells was now 3,300 pounds, and no further mention was made of the leftover metal (in another comparable case, this went to the founder). On Saturday night, the bells were transported back to Catfield, where, in the yard of Richard Postell, a churchwarden and carpenter, they were 'fitted for stocks & wheels'. This took some time, and the bells were not hung in the steeple until 10 July. Harrison appended to his notes a list of the principal charges: £13 to the bell-founder (£7 at the time of casting, and £6 to be paid six months later); £6 to Postell and another carpenter; £3 to a blacksmith for clappers and iron work; and a further 20s to Postell for five wooden baldrics.[15]

The money spent on bells in a period of economic hardship is a sure sign of their perceived importance within English parish life. Only rarely did individual parishioners refuse to contribute to the costs of maintenance. The work was indeed 'harmonicall' but churchwardens were nevertheless well aware of the need to keep the expenses under control. An early Jacobean bell in the church of St Benedict, Cambridge, therefore bears the proud and worldly inscription, 'Of all the Bells in Bennet I am the Best / And Yet for my Casting the Parish paid lest.'[16]

15 PD 531/1, NRO.

16 J. J. Raven, *The Church Bells of Cambridgeshire* (Lowestoft: Samuel Tymms, 1869), appendix 'Inscriptions', p. 7.

Ringing techniques

The rising level of parochial investment in church bells during the first half of the seventeenth century was one aspect of a broader trend towards higher expenditure on the fabric of the church. It was also related, however, to advances in bell-ringing technique which necessitated changes in the design of the accompanying machinery. Before about 1600, church bells tended to be heavier than their modern counterparts, and were swung into musical motion by ropes that were attached to half-wheels. This limited the height to which a bell could be raised and thus the variations in ringing style that were available to the ringer. The music of bells, at its simplest, involved the rhythmic clanging of a single instrument, struck by the clapper on one side of the bell only. At its most complex, it comprised the ringing of rounds in which a church's bells, tuned to some of the principal notes of a musical scale, chimed repeatedly, one after the other, in a repetitive downward sequence. Such rounds were alluded to frequently in music composed by England's highest-ranking musicians and were clearly a very familiar sound. The habit of tuning sets of church bells in tonal relationship to one another had developed during the fourteenth and fifteenth centuries, probably reflecting a desire to deploy simple two- or three-note fragments of liturgical melody in the combined ringing of the bells.[17]

The use of three-quarter-wheels and full wheels became steadily more common during the seventeenth century, and alterations were also made to the point of attachment between bell and rope. With these developments, the history of change-ringing began. The skilful ringer, with his bell newly attached to a full wheel, was now able to hold it stationary in the inverted position, thus vastly increasing his control over the timing of its chiming. Moreover, the ability to raise the bell higher also ensured that, once underway, it rang during its descent from the near-vertical position on both sides. There were risks, however, and the unskilful ringer could easily 'overthrow' his bell by pulling the cord with too much enthusiasm (though the introduction of special 'stays' in the middle of the century reduced the danger). An overthrown bell played havoc with the sequence and inflicted damage upon the supporting structure. The risk was worth it, however, for full wheels opened new possibilities in sequential ringing,

[17] Holdgate, *Ting Tangs, Trebles and Tenors*, pp. 9–11; Eisel, 'Developments in Bell Hanging', pp. 18, 24, 26; George P. Elphick, *Sussex Bells and Belfries* (Chichester: Phillimore, 1970), pp. 200–2.

and additional patterns gradually developed. Under this system, ringers ideally needed four or five bells rather than three, and they required them to be lighter and more manoeuvrable than those of the past. It was also essential that the bells were 'tunable'. For these reasons, parishes found the money to enhance and modify their rings.[18]

Of course, traditional rounds, simple tolls and basic repetitive chimes on some or all of the bells were still heard, and examples of the latter are probably preserved in nursery songs such as 'Three Blind Mice' and 'Oranges and Lemons (Say the Bells of St Clement's)'. Bells were also pealed backwards, from the lowest to the highest, in order to raise the local countryside in times of riot or rebellion. Exciting though this must have been, it was change-ringing that really caught the seventeenth-century imagination. Changes differed from rounds in that pairs of ringers periodically reversed the order in which their bells chimed, thus bringing new variety to their music. In its early stages, each change sounded repeatedly until the conductor called another one. This style of ringing gradually evolved into numerous 'methods' of growing complexity in which bells swapped their positions according to logical pre-arranged progressions rather than at the whim of the caller. Individual patterns acquired their own distinctive names: 'Churchyard bob', 'Grandsire' and so on. Numerical representations of ringing schemes were passed around between groups of ringers on pieces of paper, copied into private notebooks and even scratched into the woodwork inside belfries. At some point during the mid-seventeenth century, ringers began practising and performing 'cross peals' in which some or all of the changes were 'double' (in other word, two pairs of ringers swapped their positions at the same time). Many patterns of all sorts were gathered and presented in the two classic bell-ringing textbooks of the period, the anonymous *Tintinnalogia* (1668) and Fabian Stedman's *Campanalogia* (1677). A well-known method, later known as 'Plain bob minimus', worked its way through all the possible permutations on four bells, beginning and ending – as was the norm – with a simple descending round.[19] One of our recordings features this sequence, though it involves a set of five rather than four bells (**Website track 48 and Appendix**). It has long been customary in such circumstances to treat the tenor – the deepest bell – as the extra one, sounding it 'behind' the others without alteration:

[18] Eisel, 'Developments in Bell Hanging', p. 26; John C. Eisel, 'Tintinnalogia', in Sanderson (ed.), *Change Ringing*, vol. I, p. 57; Holdgate, *Ting Tangs, Trebles and Tenors*, pp. 9–10.

[19] Wulstan, *Tudor Music*, pp. 49–52; Eisel, 'The Development of Change Ringing', pp. 41–3; *Tintinnalogia, or The Art of Ringing* (1668; London, 1671), p. 62.

1234(5)
2143(5)
2413(5)
4231(5)
4321(5)
3412(5)
3142(5)
1324(5)
1342(5)
3124(5)
3214(5)
2341(5)
2431(5)
4213(5)
4123(5)
1432(5)
1423(5)
4132(5)
4312(5)
3421(5)
3241(5)
2314(5)
2134(5)
1243(5)
1234(5)

By the 1670s, the possibilities of change-ringing on four and five bells had been exploited almost to the full ('we can Ring Changes, Ad infinitum', wrote the author of *Tintinnalogia*) and attention shifted to the potential of six-bell variations. As the number of bells in a church's ring increased, the possible permutations available to change-ringers followed suit at an exponential rate. It was a phenomenon that appealed particularly to men of mathematical bent. In the early 1650s, Peter Mundy picked up his pen and calculated that 'the 10 bells in St Michaell's in Cornehill may be rung into 3628800 changes'. He further calculated that this performance would occupy the ringers for 2,520 days and nights. The permutations available on the twelve bells of Bow were still more astonishing. On the other hand, change-ringing evidently pleased many casual listeners too (including Elizabeth I) and cannot be dismissed as merely the recreation of number-loving eccentrics. In any case, the composition of satisfying sequences was not without its creative dimension. In mathematical terms, the patterns of changes must be clear and logical because change-ringers memorise the progressive shifts in the position of their bells rather than the mind-numbing rows of numbers (this can be explored by tracking the movements of the first bell in 'Plain bob minimus' as it 'hunts' up and then down – forwards and backwards – within the group). In musical terms, the composer was also expected to select from the total number of available permutations as high a percentage as possible of the more aesthetically pleasing ones. This combination of priorities was challenging, particularly where six or more bells were concerned, and a well-constructed method was satisfying on a number of levels.[20]

'Toll for a soul': ringing and religion

Bells were perhaps even more irresistible as a means by which humans could communicate with God. In many cultures of the world the music of bells is associated with speaking to the gods and warding off evil spirits. This characteristic is probably related to the complex and voluminous sound quality of big bells. The tone of such instruments is a strange mixture of up to one hundred partials extending over several octaves. Many of the relationships between these partials are dissonant, and we therefore experience the sound of a bell as particularly vibrant and arresting. Most of the partials decay rapidly once the bell is chimed, and we perceive one of the longer-lasting partials as the principal note. In acoustical terms, however, this note is just an overtone rather than properly the fundamental, thus distinguishing the sound of a bell from that of most other musical instruments. Arguably, therefore, the supernatural power of bells is a consequence not only of their sheer size but of their peculiar and somewhat dissonant sound. Local cultural factors – puritan disquiet in early modern England, for example – are also highly influential, but at a deeper level there resides a persistent belief in the otherworldly influence of bells.[21]

In early modern England, church bells were, first and foremost, instruments of communal piety, though their precise role in parochial religion changed significantly during the sixteenth and seventeenth centuries.

[20] *Tintinnalogia*, p. 2; Rawlinson MS A 315, fo. 215b, Bodleian Library, transcribed in H. T. Ellacombe, *The Bells of Gloucestershire* (Exeter, 1881), pp. 127–9. The shortest of web searches will reveal that mathematicians are still attracted to bell-ringing in droves.

[21] Percival Price et al., 'Bell (i)', *Grove Music Online*, *Oxford Music Online*, www.oxfordmusiconline.com/subscriber/article/grove/music/42837, last accessed 12 April 2010.

The Latin inscription on one famous medieval German bell describes in admirably succinct terms the role of such instruments in most European countries at the start of our period:

Laudo Deum verum, plebum voco, congrego clerum,
Funera plango, fulgura frango, sabbata pango,
Defuntos ploro, pestum fugo, festa decoro.

I praise the true God, call the people, assemble the clergy,
Toll for funerals, subdue the thunder flash, signal the Sabbath,
Mourn the dead, drive away plague, and beautify festivals.

In medieval England, the ringing of church bells had remarkable protective power, and considerable care was taken over the rituals of consecration. Bells were regularly baptised and given names. In a ceremony at one Reading church during the last year of the fifteenth century two godfathers and a godmother were also named. A typical prayer for such occasions ran, 'Almightie everlasting God, besprinckle this bell with thy heavenly blessing, that at the sound thereof, the fierie darts of the enemie, the striking of lightnings, the stroke of thunderbolts, and hurts of tempests may farre be put to flight.'[22]

A bell's subsequent music was reputedly capable of carrying such prayers all the way to heaven, where they might help to speed the passage of departed souls through the pains of purgatory. Many of the inscriptions placed on medieval English church bells implored named saints to pray for such souls ('Sancte Maria ora pro nobis', says one of the bells at Rampton in Cambridgeshire). In addition, the smaller bells of a parish were rung to announce mass or mark particular moments in the service. The churchwardens' accounts from Peterborough refer variously to the 'houseling' bell, the 'morrow mass' bell, 'procession' bells and the 'sacring' bell. Of these, the last was particularly important in late medieval England, sounding from its position in the nave to inform congregation members, ideally preoccupied by their own prayers, that the consecration and elevation of the host were about to occur. Handbells were also used, most notably to summon prayers for the dead at funerals. The ringers of such bells apparently toured the streets and then walked before the corpse as it was carried to church.[23]

[22] Quoted by Cressy, *Bonfires and Bells*, p. 71; Man, *History and Antiquities*, p. 315; Simon Harward, *A Discourse of Lightnings* (London, 1607), B2r.

[23] Raven, *Church Bells of Cambridgeshire*, p. 19; *Peterborough Local Administration: Parochial Government before the Reformation: Churchwardens' Accounts, 1467–1573*, ed. W. T. Mellows, *Publications of the Northamptonshire Record Society* 9 (1939), p. xli; Duffy, *Stripping of the*

Bell music gave English Protestants of all shades something of a headache. How could its deeply customary sound and associations possibly be incorporated within a new religious order? On the other hand, what could possibly replace booming bells as a means of essential ecclesiastical communication? They were popish by association but also irresistibly practical for Protestants. The more critical of the two perspectives was expressed in various sources, both official and unofficial. The Edwardian injunctions of 1547 banned the use of bells during church services, with the exception of a single bell to signify the imminence of the sermon. A parish's smaller bells were particularly vulnerable. Many were confiscated during the closing years of Edward VI's reign, while others were sold off before the royal commissioners arrived. Some were pressed into secular roles, and one sacring bell later graced a horse's harness. The larger bells fared better, despite the suspicions they aroused among Protestants. Bishop Latimer regarded the custom of tolling them against thunder as one of the 'phantasies and delusions of the devil', but it was much harder to snatch big bells than little bells. In consequence, the mighty metal instruments that hung in England's church towers generally held their position.[24]

Under Elizabeth, Henry Barrow and other radical separatists attempted to keep up the pressure on such bells by arguing that they should all be destroyed along with the tainted church buildings in which they hung. Godly Elizabethans sometimes asked to be buried without bell music, and a hostility to the sound also became one of the characteristics of the caricatured literary puritan. At Earls Colne (Essex), flesh-and-blood puritans were deeply troubled by the ghostly tolling of a medieval priory bell, long since removed, during the later 1620s. In Nottinghamshire, there were even efforts to ban the ringing of the curfew bell that was customarily sounded from the church to signal the end of the day. Indeed, numerous bishops of the late sixteenth and early seventeenth centuries used their visitation articles in order to express concern over the survival of Catholic customs.[25] The debate reached considerable intensity during the 1640s, though a parliamentary proposal 'that the Bells in all the churches of

Altars, p. 97; Peter Marshall, *Beliefs and the Dead in Reformation England* (Oxford: Oxford University Press, 2002), p. 162.

24 *Documents of the English Reformation*, p. 254; Duffy, *Stripping of the Altars*, pp. 585–6; *Sermons of Hugh Latimer*, p. 498.

25 Barrow, quoted by Keith Thomas, *Religion and the Decline of Magic* (1971; London: Penguin Books, 1973), p. 67; Marshall, *Beliefs and the Dead*, p. 164; Dolly MacKinnon, 'Hearing the English Reformation: Earls Colne, Essex', in Ros Bandt, Michelle Duffy and Dolly MacKinnon (eds.), *Hearing Places: Sound, Place, Time and Culture* (Newcastle: Cambridge Scholars Publishing,

the Kingdome may be taken down, and melted for the service of the State' apparently came to nothing. Parliamentarians nevertheless assaulted England's church bells from time to time. When the royalist John Taylor toured the west country in 1649, he noted that ringing was now impossible at St Michael's Mount because hostile soldiers had ripped out the cords: 'the Bells being ropelesse, the people are hopeless', he added sadly.[26] It was only in the 1660s and subsequent decades that the tide of tension finally receded.

It should be noted, however, that Protestants also heard bells with tolerance and, in time, affection. Even the more puritanical could be surprisingly indulgent. Clearly, there was no party line, and the Nottinghamshire squire who in 1592 left money for the enhancement of the local bells also opened the document with a long and personal preamble in which he trusted 'to be one of the Electe poore creatures of god'. William Dowsing, who toured the churches of East Anglia in 1644 with the express purpose of destroying the remaining accoutrements of Catholicism, left most of the bells untouched (though Captain Gilley, another iconoclastic tourist, defaced a number of unacceptable inscriptions). Unusually, Dowsing ordered the churchwardens of Toft (Cambridgeshire) to remove what he considered a superstitious inscription from one of the bells. The parish was associated strongly with puritanism, and he trusted the locals to execute the work after he had gone. They did no such thing, and the second bell still implores St Catherine to pray for the souls of the faithful.[27] It seems that some puritans had come to accept, presumably with some degree of disquiet, that church bells had their legitimate uses in prayer, praise and pronouncement. These are topics to which we shall return.

It has also been noted that Protestant suspicion of traditional bell beliefs was tempered by the support some of them received from early seventeenth-century science. Bells could indeed fight thunder, but not because they had been consecrated by superstitious ancestors who sought to coerce God. Instead, the explanation lay in the natural and physical forces that God had established in the world. When a storm struck Bletchingley

2007), pp. 255–67; 'Extracts from the Act Books of the Archdeacon of Nottingham', pp. 28–9; *Visitation Articles and Injunctions of the Early Stuart Church*, vols. I and II.

[26] *Mercurius Elencticus* (London, 5–12 November 1647), B3v; Taylor, *Works of John Taylor not Included in the Folio Volume*, vol. I, p. 12, 'John Taylors Wandering, to See the Wonders of the West'. See also *Journal of William Dowsing*, pp. 356, 376.

[27] PRSW 22/8, Nottinghamshire Archives; *Journal of William Dowsing*, p. 256; John Blatchly, 'In Search of Bells: Iconoclasm in Norfolk, 1644', in *Journal of William Dowsing*, pp. 107–14.

church (Surrey) in 1606, Simon Harward picked up his pen and wrote *A Discourse of Lightnings.* Locals, he reported, had watched the storm destroy the spire and 'melt into infinite fragments a goodly Ring of Bells'. He sought to advise his readers on how best to prevent such disasters in the future. The only true remedy, he admitted, was repentance and faith in Almighty God. But just in case the only true remedy failed, anxious parishioners might also 'shoot up ordinarie into the aire, or ring bels that by the stirring of the aire the cloudes may be the sooner dispersed and driven away'. Mechanical and spiritual forces were always intertwined in this period, and the combination allowed a degree of common ground to exist between traditionalists and even the more unyielding of Protestants. It is often impossible to decide exactly which beliefs lay behind particular pieces of contemporary commentary. When, for example, James Heath remarked that the bell-ringing that accompanied the Restoration of Charles II in 1660 had helped to 'purify and cleanse the air of London, dispelling those dark mists of the rebellion', we cannot know whether his insight was informed by up-to-date science or out-of-date theology.[28]

At the parochial level, religious ringing during the century after the Edwardian Reformation was similarly attended by a curious mixture of conflict, consensus, continuity and change. The steeple bells retained many of their traditional uses, albeit in modified form, and also acquired some new ones. Their sound continued to call the people to church, a sonic summons that was regularly represented in vocal catches of the period (Lant's bells said 'ding dong' but Ravenscroft's went 'bim bome'). This was not, of course, elaborate change-ringing but probably the simple tolling of one or two bells. 'Hark the first and second Bell', advised one ballad-writer, 'That every day at four and ten, Cries / Come, come, come, to Prayers.' As ever, surviving evidence from church court records identifies only the irregular episodes in which matters went awry. On Sunday 20 August 1609, three men of Cromwell (Nottinghamshire) reportedly spent the day in the alehouse, occupying themselves in 'pipinge & dauncing & other prophane exercises'. They missed the morning service, 'And when the bels were chiminge to eveninge prayers George Towell als Holmes said in derision & contempt of gods worship and service, "hold them to the belstringes, & we will hold to the piper".' He did not like the

[28] Harward, *Discourse of Lightnings*, title page and C2r; Richard Cullen Rath, *How Early America Sounded* (Ithaca: Cornell University Press, 2003), p. 50; Heath, quoted by Cressy, *Bonfires and Bells*, p. 88.

sound of bells but he at least knew what it meant.[29] Richard Ramsbotham of Holcombe (Lancashire) was even worse. One Sunday in 1616 he summoned his neighbours to church by tolling a bell, but when they arrived they were treated to a scurrilous and profane sermon, delivered by a visiting ballad-monger. In 1631, one of the churchwardens at Fledborough (Nottinghamshire) jangled the bells for a more orthodox service, but then refused to stop ringing when the curate signalled that he was ready to begin.[30]

Several references mention more specifically the role of a single bell in marking the imminence of the sermon or homily. This was a precise Protestant substitute for the moment of sacring, and it seems possible that the same bell, presumably hanging in the nave, was sometimes used. The existence of a portable 'saintes bell' in the church of St Stephen, Ipswich, in 1594 may suggest such recycling (we hear of the bell only because John Rands allegedly stole it). In the Ipswich town accounts, such a bell was referred to more properly as 'the sermon bell', and individuals regularly received payments for ringing it. The fact that it rang not only on Sundays but on weekdays too indicates that the bell took its place within a commitedly Protestant regime. The same can be said of Cratfield (Suffolk), where the sexton was paid during the mid-seventeenth century for ringing 'the lecture bell'. Other parishes had long used a bell in the same way. On a Sunday back in 1564, the parishioners of Burnham (Somerset) were already assembled in church when the vicar instructed the parish clerk 'to toll to a sermon'. He duly did so, only to find himself cursed 'for tollinge so longe' by a member of the congregation who was keen to attend a bear-baiting event.[31]

After the Reformation, church bells also held onto their role as the musical markers of various rites of passage. There is little mention of bell-ringing at baptisms, but ringing at weddings was evidently commonplace. In 'The Bridal Day', Spenser delivers the instruction, 'Ring ye the bells ye young men of the town / And leave your wonted labours for this day.' Residents of Elizabethan Loughborough were regularly married to the sound of ringing, a privilege for which they paid sixpence towards the maintenance of the bells and a further sixpence to the poor man's box.

[29] Thomas Lant's roll of catches, MS Rowe 1, nos. 1, 54, King's College, Cambridge; Ravenscroft, *Melismata*, no. 16; *The True Lovers New Academy* (London, *c.* 1695), p. 24; AN/PB 294/2/308, HL.

[30] EDC5 1626.56, ChRO; AN/PB 328/3/43, HL.

[31] *Diocese of Norwich: Bishop Redman's Visitation, 1597*, p. 158; *The Town Finances of Elizabethan Ipswich*, pp. 50, 68, 78; *Churchwardens' Accounts of Cratfield, 1640–60*, ed. L. A. Botelho, *Suffolk Records Society* 42 (1999), pp. 54, 59, 76; *REED Somerset*, pp. 66–7.

Decades later, the Derbyshire yeoman Leonard Wheatcroft recalled his wedding on 20 May 1657. At the memory, the sound of bells seemed to fill his head once more: 'Then did my chosen ringers ... with flying colours tied to the wrist of their hand, cause the merry bells to ring aloud, so that at last many came and went along with me to fetch the bride.' The music of the bells was a signal to all interested parties that the festivities were about to begin.[32] Such information was recorded only rarely, for the simple reason that the use of bells at baptisms and weddings was generally uncontroversial.

Not so the ringing that was associated with death. In late medieval England, this sound informed parishioners that one of their number was dying or dead, and reminded them to pray for the departing soul. Such prayers, properly delivered, might help to reduce the time spent by that soul in purgatory. After the Reformation, the ringing survived, but its theological justification was officially transformed. Henceforth, the acceptable purpose of the single passing bell that tolled before death was to encourage the living to recommend the departing soul into God's hands 'out of a fellow-feeling of their common mortality'. It clearly worked for John Donne ('Now, this Bell tolling softly for another, saies to me, Thou must die'). During the 1620s, the moderate puritan minister Thomas Adams also approved the tolling of this 'heavie bell'. It was, he told his parishioners, a permissible ceremony, even if it was not strictly necessary. The passing bell, he continued, was valuable for several reasons. 'It puts into the sicke man a sense of mortalitie', speaking with all the wisdom of 'an impartiall friend'. Even while attending the bedside, it ran 'like a speedie Messenger ... from house to house, from eare to eare, on thy soules errand', begging prayers from the living. The power of such prayers was not to be underestimated: 'The faithfull devotions of so many Christian neighbours sent up as Incense to Heaven for thee, are very availeable to pacifie an offended Justice.' Adams, at least, had overcome any personal reservations about the dangers of the passing bell by this date, though he still felt the need to tread a careful path between the 'old wives' who yet retained superstitious beliefs and the super-zealous who detected such beliefs wherever they looked and listened.[33]

32 Spenser, quoted by Morris, *History and Art of Change Ringing*, p. 23; 'The Autobiography of Leonard Wheatcroft of Ashover, 1627–1706', ed. Dorothy M. Riden, *Derbyshire Record Society* 20 (1993), p. 84.

33 Clare Gittings, *Death, Burial and the Individual in Early Modern England* (London: Routledge, 1984), p. 133; John Donne, *Devotions* (London, 1624), p. 410; *The Workes of Thomas Adams*, pp. 248–9.

Any bell music that sounded *after* death was potentially controversial. Officially, the function of the posthumous death knell was now to stimulate the offering of thanks to God for the deliverance of a neighbour's soul, or merely to announce a death or the commencement of the burial service. Several bishops advised that the only acceptable ringing at this time comprised three short episodes: the tolling of a single bell just before and just after the moment of death, followed by one short peal immediately before the burial service and another at its conclusion. The ringers were apparently permitted to use more than one bell at the funeral (as implied by the term 'peal'), even though this seems to have represented an elaboration of the late medieval norm. They were to ring, however, for a limited period only. By 'short', the bishops seem to have meant something in the region of thirty to sixty minutes per peal.[34] Anything more than this suggested the illegitimate survival of purgatorial beliefs and customs.

It is hardly surprising that a certain degree of confusion attended the theology of the passing bell and death knell in Reformation England. When the Duke of Stettin-Pomerania visited England in 1602, an informant fed him the godly line that bells no longer sounded for the dead, but only to spread the news of a grave illness within a parish. In all likelihood, this was wishful thinking. Belief in purgatory was difficult to eradicate, particularly in view of the fact that some of the late medieval rituals that had given it form were retained. In Oxford, the handbell that had traditionally encouraged local people to pray for a dead neighbour now merely announced the fact of death and reminded them of their own mortality. Mortuary ringing from the belfry was similarly confusing, and Bishop Hall of Lincoln endeavoured to clear up the muddle: 'we call them soul-bells for that they signify the departure of the soul, not for that they help the passage of the soul'.[35] It is impossible to know how widely and deeply this nicety was comprehended, though there is plenty of evidence to imply the survival of earlier beliefs. The catches recorded by Thomas Lant in 1580 include two in which the singers imagine themselves ringing bells to aid the souls of departed friends (an honest man and a cat respectively). Sixty years later, the appearance of the line 'Toul, Toul, gentle bell for a soule' in a ballad is similarly suggestive. Even Sir Thomas Browne sounded a little unsure of himself, or perhaps he was purposefully

[34] *Visitation Articles and Injunctions of the Early Stuart Church*, vol. I, p. 182, vol. II, p. 207; Marshall, *Beliefs and the Dead*, p. 162.

[35] 'Diary of the Journey of Philip Julius', p. 7; Marshall, *Beliefs and the Dead*, p. 166; Gittings, *Death, Burial and the Individual*, p. 133.

leaving something unsaid. In *Religio Medici*, first published in 1642, he identified prayers for the dead as one of the 'little heresies' to which he had been drawn. He confessed, 'I could scarce contain my prayers for a friend at the ringing of a Bell.' Put like this, however, the practice involved nothing that was necessarily heretical, unless we are to understand that the author's residual belief in purgatory is legible between the lines.[36]

English bishops sometimes expressed a suspicion that the rituals of the passing bell and death knell were not practised in all parishes. This anxiety featured in several sets of visitation articles from the late sixteenth century onwards, but was perhaps felt most acutely by Laudian bishops during the 1630s. In 1638, for example, Richard Montagu, Bishop of Norwich, alleged that the custom was 'in many places neglected'.[37] This reflects a perception that puritans were undermining mortuary ringing because of its associations with 'popery'. On this point, the evidence is mixed. Puritanical vicars and sextons were occasionally reported to the courts for refusing to allow mortuary ringing. Radical nonconformists sometimes denounced the passing bell, and in 1642 the puritan rector of Tarporley (Cheshire) allegedly struck one of his parishioners 'in a most inhumane manner' while he was quite legitimately tolling a bell at the death of a neighbour. In Newcastle upon Tyne, the parish of All Saints ended its tolling in the years between 1643 and 1655. On the other hand, the ringers of Newcastle were back in the belfry five years before the Restoration of Charles II.[38] Meanwhile, in puritan Dorchester, the ringing of knells before local burials continued throughout the 1650s, despite the disapproval of some leading residents. Such ringing was, after all, a significant source of income in parishes of all sorts, and could not easily be forgone. In Elizabethan and Jacobean Tewkesbury, the churchwardens charged 2s for the ringing of funeral bells. Richard Mathews, for whom the early seventeenth century was clearly not a good time, paid twice this sum in about 1607 'for the bells for his two wives'. In Stratford-upon-Avon, the chapel's great bell tolled for twenty-nine individuals in 1605, raising a grand total of 52s 8d for the corporation. In Nottingham, the town chamberlain

[36] Thomas Lant's roll of catches, MS Rowe 1, nos. 8, 41, King's College, Cambridge; *Pepys Ballads*, vol. III, p. 38; Browne, *Religio Medici*, p. 8. See Ralph Houlbrooke, *Death, Religion and the Family in England, 1480–1750* (Oxford: Clarendon Press, 1998), p. 39, for evidence suggesting the survival of purgatorial beliefs into the eighteenth century.

[37] *Visitation Articles and Injunctions of the Early Stuart Church*, vol. I, pp. 59, 104, vol. II, p. 203.

[38] Marshall, *Beliefs and the Dead*, p. 163; Judith Maltby, *Prayer Book and People* (Cambridge: Cambridge University Press, 1998), p. 57; Bourne, *Antiquitates Vulgares*, p. 6.

received 12d every time 'Passinge Peales' sounded, 'And those that are desireous to have all the Bells Runge shall have them at the rate accustomed.'[39]

Moreover, suggestions that ringing at the time of death was a custom on the wane are overwhelmed by evidence that the passing bell and death knell provided one of England's most familiar sonic signatures (indeed, in times of plague the sound could seem *too* familiar, and the authorities sometimes ordered ringing to cease because of its potentially negative effect on local morale).[40] In Elizabethan Peterborough, the man who rang the passing bell was called into action regularly enough to earn a special reward. The churchwardens, having noted the devoted service of their sexton, 'beyng a poore olde man and rysyng oft in the nyghtes to tolle the bell for sicke persons the wether being grevous', decided to make a contribution 'towardes a gowne to keepe hym warme'. Literature of all sorts contained allusions to the sound of such bells, and one of the most successful religious ballads of the period, describing the death of an exemplary parish clerk, opened with the lines

Now my painfull eyes are rowling,
And my passing Bell is towling:
Towling sweetly: I lye dying,
And my life is from me flying.

To Shakespeare, it was 'the surly sullen bell' and a rich source of imagery:

For sorrow, like a heavy-hanging bell,
Once set on ringing, with his own weight goes;
Then little strength rings out the doleful knell.[41]

The poet Henry King reminded his readers of their mortality by connecting the rhythm of ringing with that of the human body: 'The beating of thy pulse (when thou art well) / Is just the tolling of thy Passing Bell.' In lighter vein, John Taylor recited a jest about a horse that rang a knell for a dead bull (the bull died in the church porch, and the horse somehow

[39] David Underdown, *Fire from Heaven: Life in an English Town in the Seventeenth Century* (London: HarperCollins, 1992), p. 218; *Tewkesbury Churchwardens' Accounts, 1563–1624*, ed. C. J. Litzenberger, *Bristol and Gloucestershire Archaeological Society: Gloucestershire Record Series* 7 (1994), pp. 63, 103; BRU 4/1, p. 137, Shakespeare Birthplace Trust; *Records of the Borough of Nottingham*, vol. IV, p. 224, vol. V, p. 320.

[40] Cockayne, *Hubbub*, p. 113.

[41] *Peterborough Local Administration: Parochial Government before the Reformation*, pp. 174–6; *Pepys Ballads*, vol. I, pp. 48–9; William Shakespeare, *The Sonnets* (London: Leopard, 1988), no. 71; Shakespeare, *The Rape of Lucrece*, in *Complete Oxford Shakespeare*, p. 192.

found its way into the ringing chamber and ate the wads of hay that the local ringers had wrapped around the rope handles, 'which caused every Bell to toll in an untuned Diapason'). At the conclusion of the story, Taylor wisely added a concise disclaimer: 'Although there be no impossibilitie in this Tale, yet I am not guilty of the beleefe of it, nor am I bound to prove it.'[42] True or not, the jest depended for its impact on the familiarity of the passing bell's sound.

This ubiquitous bell did more than simply announce a grave illness in the parish. It also informed listeners of the age and sex of the victim. A common code deployed nine strokes of the bell for a man, six for a woman and three for a child, followed in each case by a stroke for every year of life. Systems must have varied from locality to locality, and some parishes may have used more than one bell in conveying the essential information. In one ballad, it is even implied that there was a distinctive multi-bell peal to signal the imminent hanging of an unwanted dog (evidently this was a form of entertainment). Where ailing humans were concerned, the tolling of the 'nine tailors' on a single bell was so commonly understood that it featured in a frequently recycled riddle: how was it possible that 'nine Taylors make but one man'? Typically, the tolling was gentle in the hours before death, with the ringer using one side of the bell only. When death arrived, the transformation was marked by a corresponding change in the tone of the ringing. The relatively weak pulse of the passing bell was replaced by the louder ringing of the death knell. The ringer achieved this effect by pulling more energetically so that the bell was raised higher and sounded on both sides. The new timbre, argued John Donne, 'argues a better life'. All bells, he said, compelled the ear to listen, but the passing bell was uniquely arresting.[43]

Many parishes evidently permitted their ringers to make music that went some way beyond the sober minimum specified by the bishops. Some bishops were concerned about the neglect of the passing bell, but others enquired instead whether any 'superfluous ringing' had taken place after the time of death. A tendency towards too much funeral ringing demonstrates again the popularity of bell music, but it also suggests the importance of such music within the religious rituals that recreated the social chain following the disintegration of one of its links.

[42] King, *Poems, Elegies and Paradoxes*, p. 138; Taylor, *Works of John Taylor not Included in the Folio Volume*, vol. III, pp. 22–4, 'Taylor's Travels'.

[43] Gittings, *Death, Burial and the Individual*, p. 133; *Pepys Ballads*, vol. II, p. 119; George Villiers, *The Rehearsal* (London, 1672), p. 21; Wulstan, *Tudor Music*, pp. 49–50; Donne, *Devotions*, pp. 415–16.

As Augustine Coulinge of Dean (Oxfordshire) lay sick in 1624, he decided to bequeath 'to them that shall Ringe for mee tenn shillinges'. This was a tidy sum, and the testator must certainly have anticipated funeral ringing that made an appropriate impression. William Stanshall of Nottingham died in 1632, and parishioners heard the bells ring 'all the day of his funerall'.[44] The sound of bells at such a time was comforting to the bereaved, perhaps reminding them that their loved one was now listening to the music of angels. When the rector of Solihull (Warwickshire) lost his son during the early 1690s, he paid 20s in two parishes for funeral ringing that lasted a full week. He should, of course, have known better than to put on such a show. In worldly terms, bell music made a statement about the status of the deceased and the size of the hole that their departure left in the social fabric. In 1676, the Common Council of Nottingham decided that it was time to tighten up on the excessive 'Ringeinge of Bells at Funeralls'. Henceforth, the councillors declared, the sextons of the town's parish churches 'shall forbeare to tole the Bell any Longer then one quarter of an houre in that houre that is appoynted for the meetinge of the Guests to attend the Funerall, and then noe longer untill the Corps be brought oute to be Carryed to the Church'.[45] This seems to suggest that, in the past, the bells had rung almost continuously for several hours before the funeral was due to commence.

From time to time, those who rang too much were called to account in the ecclesiastical courts. The parish clerk of Holy Trinity, Hull, was reported in 1570 because, at burials, 'he maketh such business with ringing, that the minister cannot be heard of the people'. A few years later, the parish clerk in a Chester parish was accused of ignoring warnings and continuing to ring 'mo peales at the funeralles of the dead than is decent'. In 1638, the embattled curate of Cromwell (Nottinghamshire) presented members of his flock for a number of ecclesiastical offences, including 'superstitious ringeing for the dead contrary to Canon long peales one after another for the space of 5 or 6 houres'. The culprits, to make matters worse, 'say they will doe it whether I will or no'.[46]

The church bells also sounded to mark important feast days throughout the year. Much of this attracted comment only when it went wrong. It did so in spectacular fashion in Cotgrave, Nottinghamshire, on 'the Feast of St Stephen the Proto-Martyr' (26 December) in 1604. Interestingly, it was

[44] 197/45, Oxfordshire Archives; Houlbrooke, *Death, Religion and the Family*, p. 276 n. 48.
[45] Houlbrooke, *Religion and the Family*, p. 284; *Records of the Borough of Nottingham*, vol. V, p. 320.
[46] 'Parish Church Musicians', p. 73; Marshall, *Beliefs and the Dead*, p. 163; AN/PB 328/11/42, HL.

the rector rather than the ringers who found himself presented to the archdeacon's court. He had been incensed by the refusal of four men to cease their 'excessive' ringing and by their insulting words ('be good in your office', one of them had said to him rather menacingly, 'you cannot tell howe longe you shale have yt'). In a moment of madness, the cleric therefore beat each and every one of them with a cudgel, 'and so left them'. In his defence, he pointed out that it was only a light cudgel (more of a walking stick really) and that the blows he administered had drawn no blood. The archdeacon was not impressed: an exemplary sentence of excommunication was passed, though the reckless rector was soon absolved. In Ousebridge (Yorkshire), it was the ringers themselves who earned rebuke when, on Christmas Eve in 1606, they swung their bells right through the night, 'until the middle bell-string broke next morning'.[47] Ringing at this time of year was a perfectly legitimate practice, and the peal that features on track 47 of the website eventually came to be known as 'Christmas Eve'.[48] This band of Yorkshiremen had, however, pursued custom to excess.

All Saints' Day on 1 November was a far more controversial occasion, and any attempts to mark it with the music of bells caused trouble during the years between 1558 and 1590. In Catholic tradition, church bells were rung on this day or its eve in order to stimulate prayers for the souls of dead friends and neighbours in purgatory. Visitation articles of the later sixteenth century often required local church officers to report any evidence of 'superstitious' ringing, and some of them obligingly did so. In early Elizabethan Kent, six men from Wye went into the belfry one Sunday after evening prayer on All Saints' Day and rang the bells, despite having been warned that such behaviour was no longer appropriate (meanwhile, in Benenden, the sexton was reported for knolling the great bell during a thunderstorm). Two decades later, an audible minority of Elizabethan ringers remained reluctant to relinquish the custom. In Leverington (Cambridgeshire), William Acres, William Typpinge and Nicholas Denison waited until the end of evening prayer on All Saints' Day in 1582, then called for the key to the steeple, 'intending to have ronge the bells superstitiouslye as yt can be conjectured'. When permission was denied they uttered 'many rigorouse & contumeliouse words against one of the Churchwardens'. Acres was a bewildering fellow

[47] 'Extracts from the Act Books of the Archdeacon of Nottingham', p. 30; Cressy, *Bonfires and Bells*, p. 69.

[48] I am grateful to Paul Norman for this information.

with years of what the police nowadays call 'form', and the local officers were clearly out to get him.[49] Not so the ringers of Hickling in Nottinghamshire. Here, the churchwardens showed more sympathy for the offenders, reporting to the court that 'Our parishioners did Ringe corfew upon alsayn[ts day] even but who the[y] were we do not perfectly knowe.' There was an on-going problem in this parish, and four years later a group of men 'used violence against their parson ... to maintain their ringing' on All Saints' Day. By the 1590s, however, such cases were a rarity. Conservative parishioners may still have been praying for the souls of the dead at this time of year, but they no longer did so to the booming accompaniment of the bells. As late as 1639, the Archdeacon of Northumberland included in his visitation articles a question about superstitious ringing on abrogated holy days, but by this date the question was an oddity.[50]

Despite the rumbling of controversy, most parishes managed to negotiate the transition from the old bell-ringing world to the new without audible animosity. During the seventeenth century, tensions were more likely to arise over access and ringing rights than over the spiritual significance of the bells, and several examples will be considered below. The inscriptions placed on hundreds of new bells, up and down the country, are testament to the way in which the residents of many communities were able to pick their way through the minefield. John Taylor probably spoke for the majority when he argued, without much attempt to tackle the more complex issues, that England's bells had, like most of their ringers, converted to Protestantism: 'Wee doe not Christen Bells, and give them Names / Of Simon, Peter, Andrew, John and James.' Indeed, the custom of baptising bells appears to have passed quite quickly away. The times were changing, and new bells no longer called upon the saints for intercessory prayers. After 1560, many inscriptions simply recorded the name of the bell-founder or the names of the churchwardens, but a sizeable proportion combined these details with religious messages suitable to a reformed society. Most inscriptions were pithy, uncontroversial and suggestive of a direct relationship between individual Christians and God (unless we are to suppose that church bells had become metal mediators, filling the gap left by the saints). Examples

[49] *Church Life in Kent*, pp. 32, 61; EDR B/2/10, fos. 113–14, CUL. For further information on the case against Acres, see Christopher Marsh, *Popular Religion in Sixteenth-century England* (Basingstoke: Macmillan, 1998), pp. 4–6.

[50] AN/PB 292/1, HL; 'Extracts from the Act Books of the Archdeacon of Nottingham', p. 29; *Visitation Articles and Injunctions of the Early Stuart Church*, vol. II, p. 215.

from the belfries of Sussex include 'Praise the Lord' (Bepton, 1598), 'God save the Quen [sic]' (Bury, 1625), 'Praysed be thy name o Lord' (Chichester, 1580), 'I live in hope' (Chidham, 1586) and 'Gloria Deo in excelsis' (Climping, 1636). Other inscriptions enabled churchwardens and bell-founders to indulge their taste for simple and instructive couplets (often presented with one line on each of two adjacent bells): 'The God of mercie heareth us all / When upon him that we doe call' (Shepreth, Cambridgeshire, 1623) or 'O priese the Lord thearefore I say / I sound unto the living when the sole doth part away' (Graveley, Cambridgeshire, 1624).[51]

Recent work on the bells of Nottinghamshire encourages some more systematic analysis of inscriptions over a longer period. In the decades between 1550 and 1700, pious pleas and moral warnings were entirely dominant. During the second half of the sixteenth century, for example, the most common inscriptions appealed directly to divine power: 'Jesus Be Oure Spede' and 'God Save His Church'. In the next fifty years, many bells were cast and a greater variety of inscriptions employed. The two inscriptions listed above continued to top the list, revealing that they were employed by a number of founders across several generations and that they were favoured by leading parishioners. A new patriotic variant was 'God Save the King'. Another popular form of words referred to the bell's role in calling parishioners to worship: 'I sweetly toling men do call / to taste on meats that feeds the soule'. Two other leading inscriptions reminded listeners of their mortality and of the need to contemplate their sins: 'All men that heare my mornful sound / repent before you lie in ground' and 'My roaringe sounde doth warning give / that men cannot heare always live'. Between 1650 and 1700, pithy four-word prayers ('God Save His church' and 'God Save the King') remained the most popular, but messages of pure praise ('All Glory be to God on High' and 'Soli Deo Gloria') also rose in prominence. During the eighteenth century as a whole, the traditional moral and religious inscriptions remained in favour, but there was a growing tendency to supplement these by adding the names of founders and churchwardens. In the following century, this trend intensified, and the most common inscriptions by a considerable margin were those that named the bell-founder and included no other message whatsoever. Across 300 years, the standard form of inscription had shifted from

[51] Taylor, *Works of John Taylor not Included in the Folio Volume*, vol. I, p. 8, 'Mad Fashions, Od Fashions'; Amherst Daniel-Tyssen, *The Church Bells of Sussex* (Lewes: G. P. Bacon, 1864), pp. 63–70; Raven, *Church Bells of Cambridgeshire*, appendix 'Inscriptions', pp. 1–6.

'Jesu Be Oure Spede' to something like 'J. Warner London 1891'.[52] This final transition serves to emphasise an important characteristic of earlier church bells: they lived and they spoke. Throughout the early modern era, bells were personified and given voices ('Miles Graye made me 1665').[53] Words were put into their mouths and then rung out again. Church bells existed as integrated members of their parochial communities, more like neighbours than mere objects (in popular story-telling, for example, the famous bells of Bow called Dick Whittington back when they felt that he had made a mistake). Bells may have encouraged the survival of certain 'little heresies', but arguably they also helped their flesh-and-blood friends, slowly but surely, to form a new kind of relationship with God.

'Ringing for the queen's majesty': peals and politics

Religion gave bells their *raison d'être*, but over the decades they also acquired additional uses that were either complementary or contradictory, depending on one's point of view. During the late sixteenth and seventeenth centuries, a whole new set of celebratory dates evolved, and church bells helped to make these both musical and memorable. The story has already been skilfully told by others and it is one in which some of the devotional energy that had once found expression on the days dedicated to Christian saints came to re-attach itself to dates associated with England's monarchs and their moments of remarkable deliverance.[54] One of the explanations for the eventual fading-out of bell-ringing on All Saints' Day was surely the campanological crescendo that attended another November date, this one associated with Queen Elizabeth. Her accession to the throne had occurred on 17 November 1558 and, by the end of the reign, it seems likely that most of the nation's parishes rang their bells on 'crownation day'. In 1593, for example, the chamberlain of Newcastle upon Tyne paid 2s 6d to some unnamed men 'for ringing their belles the 17 daie of november for joie of our majesties raign'. Many parishes purchased 'candles, bread and drink for the ringers'. 'Crownation day' became the primary bell-ringing occasion in the year. At St Edmund's, Salisbury, the ringers were paid in pence for their efforts at Christmas and Easter, but they earned several shillings 'for ringing for the queen's

[52] The inscriptions are gathered in George A. Dawson, *The Church Bells of Nottinghamshire*, 3 vols. (Loughborough: G. A. Dawson, 1994–5).
[53] Raven, *Church Bells of Cambridgeshire*, p. 19.
[54] See especially Cressy, *Bonfires and Bells*.

majesty'. It is tempting to perceive 'crownation day' as evidence of the crude secularisation of bell-ringing, but it is also rather simplistic. Many parishes referred to 17 November as 'the queen's holy day' and clearly experienced it as a quasi-religious occasion. In 1576, the churchwardens of Minchinhampton (Gloucestershire) set money aside 'for ringing the day of the queen's majesty's entering unto the crown, whom God long time we beseech to preserve'.[55] The bells were still tools of prayer, even if they were also instrumental in encouraging and expressing a new sense of patriotic nationhood.

Under the first two Stuart kings, the dates on which 'crownation day' was celebrated changed – first to 24 March, and then to 27 March – but the ringing went on. Other new dates were also added to the bell-ringer's diary. James I's escapes from the Gowry conspiracy and the Gunpowder Plot were celebrated on 5 August and 5 November respectively. The latter date, in particular, caught the English imagination and obviously meant a great deal to John Hills, a Suffolk bricklayer who, in 1637, made a will in which he set aside '2s yearely to be bestowed by the churchwardens of Clare upon ringers to ring upon the fifth of November in perpetual memory of that famous deliverance to be so long continued as that solemnity of ringing upon that day shall be used'. He need not have worried, for his favourite day was not about to fall out of memory. It was one of very few dates that was regularly marked by bell-ringing during the mid-century interregnum. Many parishes had continued to ring for Charles's 'crownation day' up until his execution in 1649, but hereafter the majority ceased. When his son returned to rule England in 1660, however, the royalist bells swung back into motion. Charles II's 'crownation day' on 23 April (also St George's Day) was commonly celebrated to the music of bells, and Royal Oak Day – the anniversary of the occasion upon which the king had hidden in a tree to escape his parliamentary persecutors after the Battle of Worcester – also generated a good deal of ringing on 29 May.[56]

The political use of bells did not begin and end with such fixed dates. Many other occasions, less regular but no less important, were also marked by ringing. Royal coronations, weddings and baptisms were greeted by the sound of bells across the land. When monarchs went on the move, bell music announced and celebrated the fact. In the autumn of

[55] *REED Newcastle upon Tyne*, p. 94; Cressy, *Bonfires and Bells*, pp. 50–5.

[56] Cressy, *Bonfires and Bells*, pp. 50–66; *Wills of the Archdeaconry of Sudbury, 1636–1638*, ed. Nesta Evans, *Suffolk Records Society* 35 (1993), pp. 105–6.

1588, the churchwardens of Lambeth paid for the bells to ring whenever Elizabeth travelled between Greenwich, Richmond, St James, Lambeth and Somerset House. This was the year of the Spanish Armada, and the anxiety concerning its arrival and the queen's survival clearly brought new intensity to the ringing. Decades later, when Prince Charles returned home after his journey to Spain in 1623, England's bells apparently jangled as never before. According to John Taylor, 'The Bels proclaim'd aloud in every Steeple / The joyful acclamations of the people.'[57] News of the most exciting moments in early modern politics often flew through the air on the sonic waves generated by church bells. In 1571, the bells of St Michael Cornhill (London) rang to spread word of 'the overthrow given to the Turk' at the Battle of Lepanto. Fifteen years later, St Margaret's Westminster paid a shilling 'for ringing at the beheading of the Queen of Scotts'. In 1605, the same parish 'Paid the ringers for ringing at the time when the Parliament Hous should have been blown up'. As we have already heard, this was the beginning of a lasting custom. Bells gave natural expression to popular relief whenever monarchs survived such plots against them. In 1585–6, the chamberlain of Nottingham had paid 'for ringinge for joye that the Quene scaped the daunger of her enimies the Pope and his adherents' during the Babington Plot.[58]

Bell music sometimes united Protestants but on many occasions it also rang out their differences. Although it was often presented in ballads of the seventeenth century as a royalist form of music, bell-ringing was also useful to those who opposed the government. Prickly officials can sometimes be heard complaining about the neglect of authorised dates and the subversive advancement of others. During the 1620s and 1630s, the cult of Elizabeth I gathered momentum, and a considerable number of parishes began ringing with enthusiasm on 17 November once again. This was a gesture of respect for the memory of the long-dead queen, but it carried more than a hint of disrespect for her successors. The birthdays of Queen Henrietta Maria and King Charles I fell on 16 and 19 November respectively, neatly sandwiching Eliza's 'crownation day', and there is evidence of official fears that the filling was proving more popular than the bread. On 19 November 1630, the Lord Mayor of London 'received a check [rebuke] from the lords of the council because he suffered the bells to stand so silent, and a commandment to set them all on work, both in city and

[57] *Lambeth Churchwardens' Accounts*, pp. 173–4; Taylor, *All the Workes*, vol. III, p. 586.

[58] Cressy, *Bonfires and Bells*, p. 76; Morris, *History and Art of Change Ringing*, p. 22; *Records of the Borough of Nottingham*, vol. IV, p. 213.

suburbs'. Pressure was clearly applied to the leaders of London parishes, but some responded with a provocative kind of obedience. In November 1634, the puritans of St Botolph without Bishopsgate spent 3s to hear the bells on Henrietta Maria's birthday 'by command from the Lord Mayor', but a full 10s for ringing on 'Queen Elizabeth's coronation day'. Some parishes also rang to celebrate royal acceptance of the Petition of Right (1628) and the Protestant victories of Gustavus Adolphus on the continent. In the tense political atmosphere of the late 1630s, the Laudian Bishop Matthew Wren asked the parishioners of his Ely diocese, 'Is the 27 day of Marche also well and duely observed? Are the bels usually rung in joy of those days?' He also suspected puritans of devising new bell codes that informed their brethren whether or not an imminent service was to include a sermon.[59] Most churchwardens simply ignored his enquiry on this point.

By the 1640s, puritans and parliamentarians had clearly come to realise that church bells were too powerful a force to be left to the opposition. These giant metal symbols of the 'popish' past could easily be made to swing the other way in order to confront religious traditionalism and its political adherents. The royalist John Taylor accused his enemies of using public thanksgiving during the 1640s in order to stir up the people, 'with jangling your Bells, and blazing zealous Bonefires in your streets'. A big bell was a useful tool within political discourse, and an important sonic marker of territory. It was audible several miles away, and an inscription that was regularly placed on large tenor bells in Berkshire celebrated their capacity to 'Hum all Round'. When dozens of churches rang simultaneously to celebrate, for example, a royal wedding or the coronation day of a dead queen, the sound reached the ears of all, whether great or small. In courtly music of the period, the habit of representing bell music in the form of overlapping, repetitive phrases may recall the experience of hearing several sets of church bells sounding simultaneously in an urban environment. The music of bells enveloped the population and, if all went according to plan, it integrated them by sonic force. We should not be surprised, therefore, that bells rang both when Oliver Cromwell was proclaimed Lord Protector (for the second time) in 1657 and when Charles II returned to England in 1660.[60]

[59] *Pepys Ballads*, vol. II, pp. 251–2, 256–7, 261; Cressy, *Bonfires and Bells*, pp. 60, 76, 138; *Visitation Articles and Injunctions of the Early Stuart Church*, vol. II, pp. 146–7, 153, 160.

[60] Taylor, *Works of John Taylor not Included in the Folio Volume*, vol. II, p. 7, 'Mad Verse, Sad Verse'; Frederick Sharpe, *The Church Bells of Berkshire: Their Inscriptions and Founders* (Bath: Kingsmead Reprints, 1971), p. 151; W/E1/135, HRO; Cressy, *Bonfires and Bells*, p. 88.

There can be no doubt that bell-ringing also helped to foster a consciousness of nationhood. The sound of bells on the fifth and seventeenth days of November, for example, asserted the existence not only of individual parish communities but of the greater entity to which they all belonged. It was simultaneously urban and rural, local and national. As the seventeenth century wore on, it can be assumed that an increasing proportion of this celebratory political music involved the ringing of changes rather than simple rounds, and this too had its nationalistic dimension. Change-ringing was a peculiarly English development, and it never caught on in continental Europe. Of course, we cannot tell whether most ringers were aware of this fact, nor whether it mattered to them, but it seems a possibility. Peter Mundy probably spoke for others when he wrote proudly in his notebook, 'Ringing in changes no where out of England'. One of the characteristic sounds of London, he added, was 'the sweet ringing of our tuneable bells, especially in changes' – 'Not the like nor nothing near to bee heard in the whole world'. And in mid-seventeenth-century Bedford, a local poet and bell-ringer followed the example of continental visitors by referring to England as 'the Ringing Ile'.[61]

'Pleasure peals' and the fellowship of ringers

For the ringers themselves, there was yet another aspect to the music of bells. In the century after the Reformation, ringing emerged as an important and sometimes controversial form of recreation. In 1598, a foreign visitor to London described the fondness of the natives for bells, and reported that it was common for groups of inebriated Englishmen 'to go into some belfry, and ring the bells for hours together, for the sake of exercise'. Other tourists reported that the youth of England competed with one another over who could ring loudest or longest, and they regularly placed bets on the matter. The combination of alcohol, gambling and machismo was potentially a troubling one but it did not prevent Henry Peacham from listing bell-ringing, in 1641, as an acceptable physical recreation for gentlemen, along with hunting and bowling.[62]

Recreational ringing sometimes caused trouble. It often took place after church on Sunday, but by the seventeenth century it was not restricted to

[61] Rawlinson MS A 315, fo. 215v, Bodleian Library, transcribed in Ellacombe, *The Bells of Gloucestershire*, pp. 127–9; Eisel, 'Development of Change Ringing', p. 48.

[62] Various sources quoted by Smith, *Acoustic World*, p. 53; Peacham, *The Worth of a Penny*, p. 30.

the Sabbath. The manner in which such ringing colonised weekdays and night-times may have soothed Sabbatarians but it clearly did not please everybody. In Cassington (Oxfordshire), nocturnal ringing was considered such a nuisance during the 1590s that the church was locked and somebody smeared the door-handle with dung in order to discourage entry. In 1587, 'Pleasure peals' were banned by the governors of Preston (Lancashire). In 1611, the churchwardens of Lambeth, hoping 'to kepe the people from ringing at their pleasure', ordered the construction of a partition to separate the belfry from the nave. Henry Hargreve of Normanton on Trent (Nottinghamshire) was in trouble in 1631 'for hiringe three men to Ringe at an unfitt tyme betwixte Nighte and daye after sonsettinge'. This was the 'unseasonable ringing' about which bishops sometimes enquired in their visitation articles.[63]

The enthusiasm of ringers was not always matched by their expertise, and several bells were damaged as a result. One Sunday in 1639, John Needom of Tollerton (Nottinghamshire) broke the second bell's wheel when he tried to persuade its ringer to give him a turn. The following week, he followed this up by 'overthroweinge the great Bell' with his 'disorderly ringeinge'. On 13 October 1641, William Cant of Wollaton in the same county entered the bell chamber and 'rang disorderly whereby hee cracked us a bell'. John Hudson of Kingston-on-Soar (Nottinghamshire) managed not to damage the bells, but was nevertheless reported by the churchwardens in 1625 'for ringing our bells in our church out of order and turning them over & some times leaving them on end'. When the wind later blew the bells back down, they rang out in the night, 'as though some thing were amisse by fire in the towne' (incidentally, the presentment indicates that danger was customarily signalled by the random jangling of all the bells at once).[64]

Others were more accomplished but found it impossible to heed the warnings of their church officers. Successful bell-ringing requires considerable self-discipline, and some ringers behaved as if they had none left for deployment during interaction with their ministers and churchwardens. In 1613, John Smith junior of Balsham (Cambridgeshire) was identified by

[63] Martin Ingram, 'From Reformation to Toleration: Popular Religious Cultures in England, 1540–1690', in Tim Harris (ed.), *Popular Culture in England, c. 1500–1850* (Basingstoke: Macmillan, 1995), p. 115; William T. Cock, 'The Development of Change Ringing as a Secular Sport', in Sanderson (ed.), *Change Ringing*, vol. I, p. 36; *Lambeth Churchwardens' Accounts*, p. 257; AN/PB 328/3/28, HL; *Visitation Articles and Injunctions of the Early Stuart Church*, vol. II, pp. 5, 143.

[64] AN/PB 315/16/48, 298/266, 314/5/10, HL. I am reliably informed that, in modern campanological parlance, 'firing' the bells is the act of ringing them all at once.

the wardens as 'one of the exessive & inordinat ringers ther on the Sundays'. They also reported 'that after he was willed & requested by the parson there to surceasse & leave of ringinge he would not leave of'. He was not a man who regularly found himself in trouble with the authorities. One sometimes has the impression that ringers were touched by a kind of ecstasy, and temporarily lost their moral and social bearings. When Smith had finally released the bell-rope and calmed down, he apologised to the parson and promised to mend his ways. A year later, a group of ringers at Washington (Sussex) proved exceedingly abusive when their minister attempted to end their session with the bells. One of their number asked, 'Shall we be ruled by one peeled scurvy forward wrangling priest?' He then answered his own question with the resounding declaration, 'We will ring!' At Nantwich (Cheshire) in 1625, five men, intent on 'recreatinge themselves in ringinge' one evening, anticipated the censure of the churchwardens and took the precaution of locking the church door from the inside before they began.[65]

It was presumably behaviour of this sort that motivated parliament in 1644 to ban the 'Ringing of Bells for Pleasure or Pastime' on Sundays. Perhaps this measure contributed to John Bunyan's decision to renounce bell-ringing in 1648. He was already uncomfortable with the delight he found in the recreation, and his decision was primarily a scrupulous one. The fact that it coincided with his marriage suggests that he also perceived the ringing of bells as a young man's habit, inappropriate in the cultural repertoire of a more sober and settled individual. Ringing was addictive, however, and Bunyan struggled to adhere to his decision, often visiting the church tower to watch and hear his former companions pull the ropes. He finally put the bells behind him once and for all when he began to imagine them falling on top of him in an act of providential punishment for his campanological cravings.[66]

Many of the issues at stake came together in a dispute at Rudgwick (Sussex) in 1638–9. At its heart, this dispute pitted a group of enthusiastic bell-ringing laymen against a stern and disapproving vicar. Several of the ringers made depositions in which they explained that, a couple of years previously, the parish had spent at least £40 'about the new making and trimminge of the Bells'. The bell-founder had guaranteed his work for a year, 'And therefore the parishioners did ring the same Belles the oftener to

[65] EDR D/2/32, CUL; Ingram, 'From Reformation to Toleration', p. 114; Baldwin, *Paying the Piper*, p. 176.

[66] *Acts and Ordinances of the Interregnum*, vol. I, p. 420; John Bunyan, *Grace Abounding to the Chief of Sinners*, ed. John Brown (1666; London, 1692), pp. 15–16.

trye whether they were fine & tuneable or not.' Their vicar, Mr Adams, did not take kindly to what he clearly experienced as a frenzy of ringing. On four occasions between May and July in 1638, he therefore intervened in an effort to curtail the activity. On a Saturday shortly after Whitsuntide, a group of men rang the bells during the hour of sunset. Adams entered the belfry and ordered them to stop, warning them 'that if they stayed there all the night hee would stay there too'. Grudgingly, they left the building. The tension escalated at lunchtime on Wednesday 30 May when the ringers again took to the belfry. Matthew Napper heard the bells and was drawn to the church. When he arrived, he noted that 'John Naldrett rang the Treble bell above in a gallery, and the other men rang the rest of the Bells below.' The ringers told the court that they had sought and received the permission of the churchwardens before beginning their peal. Notwithstanding, Adams came in and ordered them all to desist. They duly obeyed, though conveniently it always took time for the bells to stop swinging and ringing once the decision to cease had been taken (Mr Adams, they implied, did not understand this). The group left the church, locking the door behind them. One of the ringers asked Adams to explain why he had ordered them to stop. His reply was menacing: 'Lett me see who dares ring.' Enter Henry Thayer. This new arrival on the scene met his minister's challenge head-on: 'That would I doe if I had the key.' Ralph Naldrett pulled the key out of his pocket, and four of the men, their courage resurgent, went back into the church and began to ring another peal. The deponents admitted their brazen defiance of Mr Adams, but denied that they had rung the bells 'either profanely or unseasonably' (Adams, they said, was in any case accounted a hateful figure in the parish).

The dispute continued throughout the summer months. On a Sunday in June, the ringers set to work after morning prayer, only to be interrupted by their dogged vicar. He ordered them to stop, and they later admitted having failed to comply. One insolent deponent said it had been difficult for the ringers to hear Mr Adams, 'by reason of the noyse of the bells'. Around St James's Day (25 July) Mr Adams got physical. Ralph Naldrett claimed that the vicar 'did violently pull lugge and gripe' him by the arm while he stood ringing his bell in the church. Adams also struck off John King's hat with the back of his hand, though he had to assault the ringer 'three severall tymes' before the symbolic headgear was finally dislodged. Such episodes destroyed all prospects of fruitful negotiation between the warring parties. When Adams summoned John Naldrett to the vicarage for discussions, the ringers' representative was defiant.

'Sire', he said, 'lett us ring agayne & lett us goe all to Chichester together.' The tone of respectful communality was, however, deeply ironic, for Naldrett meant that there remained no alternative but to settle the case at ecclesiastical law. Unfortunately, the outcome of this development is not known.[67]

Similarly informative was an argument at Staunton (Nottinghamshire) during the same decade. In 1630, John Read, the vicar, presented Thomas Richardson, blacksmith, to the courts. Normally, it was the churchwardens who took responsibility for making the presentments, and their absence from proceedings may suggest a reluctance to become involved. Richardson was reported 'for entering (with diverse others) in the night-time, into Staunton church by a privy key. Where drawing together a tumultuous company of rude servants (some dwelling in, some out of the parish) they made a common practise of picking open the steeple-door locke: & of ringing night by night, neare the space of three weekes together.' There were only three bells in the steeple, so the ringers must have taken turns at the ropes. One night, the clerk, 'fearing that some inconvenience might follow', made his way to the church and 'requested them to come in the day-time, and (with reason at seasons fitt) ring at their pleasure'. The ringers' interesting answer 'was that neither Clarke nor Priest had ought to doe with the bells, which (they thought) were ordained & maintayned for recreation: & therefore poore servants that could not attend it by day, might (as they meant to doe) take it by night'. It seems that a group among the local youth believed in their virtual ownership of the bells and in their unbounded right to ring them during their free time. A happy and jovial vicar might have told himself optimistically that the bells were, at least, drawing the young people of the locality to the church and providing them with a stake in its fortunes. Mr Read, however, was not such a man. He informed the court that he had trouble finding people to ring the bells for service time, 'yet every Evening (till the wheeles went to wrack) the steeple was full of these night-ringers'. In the middle of Lent, they had 'jangled' two or three peals at midnight, 'much disquieting many of the inhabitantes'.

Then, on Easter Monday, something still more serious occurred. The ringers, reported their vicar, rang the bells from daybreak onwards 'with clamorous rudeness ill beeseeming that place'. In the afternoon, 'certaine maidens were gotten in among them: one of which being by a stander-by cast on a bell-rope, shee was daungerously plucked up by the

[67] EP 1/11/16, fos. 157r–162, WSRO.

feet, & fell uppon her neck & shoulders: & was carried out senceless, & (at this present) lyes unrecovered'. The vicar feared some further mishap, 'unlesse the place may be governed: where this licentious irreverence at all other times among rurall persons, breeds daily lesse & lesse reverence even in divine service time'.[68] He was, of course, adding his own gloomy gloss to recent events in the belfry, and unfortunately we do not know what the ringers said in their defence (they would presumably have denied all such 'licentious irreverence'). The impression conveyed by this case is of a ringing chamber dangerously packed with ringers, would-be ringers and 'standers-by'. One can well understand how the scene appeared to the vicar alarmingly dissolute and poorly governed (he clearly struggled to understand 'rurall persons'). To insiders, it may have been nothing of the sort. Exciting and deafeningly loud it most certainly was, but the relative infrequency of serious accidents in the surviving record as a whole suggests that there was discipline and management too. At Mixbury (Oxfordshire), two men quarrelled when one refused to hand over a bell-rope to the other, but such incidents were rarely serious enough to generate court records for the historian.[69] The problem was not that the ringers were ungoverned but that they were governing themselves and coming to believe that the belfry was their personal property. This was a place in which ordinary laymen experienced feelings of power and control.

Evidence drawn from disputes about bells inevitably emphasises the divisive aspects of the subject. In this period of strain, the ringers emerge as representatives of a resistant, profane and youthful sub-culture, aggressively appropriating a part of the church for their own irreligious purposes. Other sources must therefore be examined in order to assess the more positive dimensions of this form of music, particularly its incorporative potential. It may have been only a minority of ringing groups that defined themselves in opposition to rival alliances of local critics. In the cases discussed above, such alliances appear rather small, consisting typically of a hostile clergyman and a more or less supportive church officer. Phrases alleging the deep offence caused to entire congregations are much less conspicuous in bell disputes than in arguments dealing, for example, with misbehaviour in the church during service time. It seems likely that a majority of the population generally interpreted bell-ringing as an inclusive form of music that sounded on behalf of whole communities.

[68] AN/PB 328/1/34, HL.

[69] *Oxford Church Court Depositions, 1570–74*, ed. Jack Howard-Drake (Oxford: Oxfordshire County Council, 1993), no. 26.

Within the terms of this interpretation, the close fellowship that often existed among the ringers themselves was not antithetical to wider solidarities, but was rather one of the intermediate affiliations that formed the bridge between the individual and society.

Bell-fellowship found its way into the written record in various ways. The Elizabethan catches recorded by Thomas Lant include several in which bell-ringing and close male fellowship are allied:

Lets have a peale for John Cookes soule
for he was an honest man
with belles all in an order
the crase with blacke boole
the tankerd lykewise with the can.
And I myne owne selfe will ring the treble bell
& drinke to you every one.
Stand faste notes my mates,
Ring merilye & well
Till all the goode ale is gone.[70]

The best of the recreational ringers were probably those who performed for the parish on special occasions. At such times, they were usually paid as a group, and it can be assumed that they often retired to the alehouse following the final peal and drank their earnings around a table together. With some regularity, they were rewarded not in cash but in consumables. In 1615, the churchwardens of Bere Regis (Dorset) spent 2s 4d 'in beer for the ringers when the king came through our town'. The wardens of Cratfield (Suffolk) were more generous than this when they paid 4s 10d 'to the Widow Brodbanke for beere and bread and meate for the ringers the 5th of November 1646'.[71] After ringing, they presumably assembled at her house in order to devour their edible wages.

Not all interested parties could ring at such special moments, and we should probably think in terms of an elite core of experts in each parish, around which there circulated a larger group of hopeful hangers-on. The intricacies of such parochial politics are largely beyond us, though once in a while the existence of a ringers' hierarchy provoked audible tension. On 26 April 1633, Roger Welsh of Bolton (Lancashire) explained to the judge at quarter sessions why he was such a frightened man. As parish clerk, Welsh was responsible for appointing the men who would

[70] Thomas Lant's roll of catches, MS Rowe 1, no. 41, King's College, Cambridge.

[71] Cressy, *Bonfires and Bells*, p. 72; *Churchwardens' Accounts of Cratfield*, p. 74.

ring for the town on Sundays, feast days, coronation days and so on. On Michaelmas Day in the previous year, he reported, a man called Thomas Draper had come to the church and, in Welsh's absence, rung one of the bells with others in the elite group. This opportunistic self-promotion had given Draper a taste of glory, and he subsequently grew increasingly assertive. He claimed a share of the Michaelmas Day money, and tried at other times to muscle his way into the belfry when the established ringers were making their music. On one such occasion, he 'gott hould on the second bell rope and sayd hee would ringe'. Welsh ordered him to relinquish it, but he refused. More disturbingly, Draper also took to stalking the parish clerk as he went about his business in the town. Then, on Saturday 20 April 1633, he followed the ringers into Widow Horrock's house (probably a tavern) after their session ended, and confronted the increasingly anxious parish clerk. Welsh bravely reiterated his decision that Draper could not be one of the select ringers, at which the latter 'swore a greate oath sayinge thou banckrupt Roge is this the worst thou canst doe'. He also raised his hand and said 'he could find in his hart to beate him backe and side'. Fortunately, a female witness intervened at this point and prevented bodily violence. This brought only a temporary respite, and the clerk reported that on several subsequent occasions he had observed the disgruntled Draper 'walkinge about the Church early and late'. This conduct so alarmed Roger Welsh that he hired somebody else to ring the eight o'clock bell in his place.[72]

Thomas Draper clearly felt that he was missing something by not belonging to the group of leading ringers, and a remarkable notebook kept by the Derbyshire yeoman Leonard Wheatcroft can help us to establish what that something might have been. Wheatcroft was one of the leading lights of the parish of Ashover during the second half of the seventeenth century, and served the church devotedly as parish clerk, singer and ringer. He composed many songs and poems, a number of which deal explicitly with named local ringers. The bell-ringing community was at its most intense within the parish but was clearly not exclusively parochial in nature. Instead, each local group was part of a wider web of ringers and enjoyed regular contact with those from other parishes. Indeed, most of Wheatcroft's verses were written to honour visiting ringers rather than those of Ashover itself. After the ringers of Shirland came to Ashover on Lady Day in 1689, Wheatcroft composed a song with which to commemorate their visit. It opened,

[72] QSB/1/119/74, Lancashire Record Office.

You Gentellmen of Derby shire
that minding are to here me sing
I ernestly do you desire
That to my church you'l come and Ring
Then your names and fames shall florish
Up and downe the Cunteree
And the clerke of Asher-parish
Will thanke you for your Companee.

The visitors sought the parish clerk's permission before approaching the bells and, later in the day, they expressed their gratitude:

There was five young men came unto me
desiring mee to let them ring
the[y] afterwards did kindnes sho me
when they had handled each a string.

Evidently there was a second group of visiting ringers present on the day, and Wheatcroft drew comparisons between them and the men of Shirland:

Winfield men did Ring most Bravly
And did behave themselves right well
But Shire-land men did far excell them
As you that heard can justly tell.

Wheatcroft proceeds to describe each of the Shirland ringers in turn. 'The first was Wright by name and nature', who rang the treble bell. Harry Lees, the second ringer, was young and pretty but he nevertheless rang 'bravely like a strong man' and 'did not freeze' during two long hours of music-making. 'Little Farmery' was similarly proficient, 'Scorning to o'erthrow his bell'. The next ringer was an unnamed 'Heir' (perhaps a young gentleman), and the tenor was rung by Mr Miles. 'I'le advance him very hey [high]', commented Wheatcroft. The song concludes with a verse in which Wheatcroft toasts all who practise the honourable art:

Now hear's a glas to all true ringers,
That live in Citty or in towne,
With all my hart I'le drink two [sic] swingers,
If it cost me halfe a croune,
For I doe love all merry Ringers,
Let them com from sea or shore,
And he that loves not merrey singers,
I pray you put him out of doore.

In this and other verses by Wheatcroft, several points stand out. The bell-ringers of Ashover and surrounding parishes enjoyed a sense of fellowship that was warm, masculine and competitive. Their bond involved the interweaving of individualistic talent and co-operative endeavour. Ringers worked together, but they also pulled against one another. Inevitably, there must have been occasional confrontations, but internal tensions were to be dissolved in alcohol. Another verse explained,

And when we drink a merry pot,
We non of us may quarrel:
But all agree to pay the shot,
And broach the other barrel.

The cultural context within which the group met was obviously musical, and involved voices as well as bells. 'These five ringers are brave singers', declared another verse, 'Or they their changes could not tell.' It is probably safe to assume that the singing followed the ringing as the group migrated from belfry to tavern towards the end of the day. It was also a loyalist, royalist context, and several of Wheatcroft's verses include exuberantly supportive references to King William:

And now you see my bretheren all,
How well we do agree,
To ring, and sing, and glass our King,
And make us to agree.[73]

The recreational dimension of ringing has contributed to the received opinion that the activity was becoming fundamentally secular during the early modern period. It has also been suggested that godly suspicion of bells reinforced the same process by effectively abandoning the belfry to the worldly.[74] These arguments seem to embody an assumption – perhaps inherited from Bunyan – that those who are practising a pleasurable pastime must necessarily be untouched by more spiritual concerns, even when their hobby involves bells that carry religious inscriptions and hang inside the steeple of a church. We might note that parochial investment in bells was a phenomenon driven not only by secular ringers but also by an urge to beautify the church for the praise of God. Most of the time,

[73] Wheatcroft's verses are all contained in his notebook, D5433/1, DRO.

[74] See, for example, Cock, 'The Development of Change Ringing', pp. 28, 38–9, and Wilfrid G. Wilson and Steve Coleman, 'Change Ringing', *Grove Music Online, Oxford Music Online*, www.oxfordmusiconline.com/subscriber/article/grove/music/05399, last accessed 12 April 2010.

we cannot tell what ringing meant to the ringers, and it should certainly be admitted that not all of them had God in the forefront of their minds. Nevertheless, the notion that ringing was purely and simply secular appears rather simplistic. Of course, it was in the interests of the opponents of 'pleasure peals' to present recreational ringers as anti-religious: such people were not only 'rude' but 'profane', 'irreverent' and disrespectful of sacred space (this was why they sometimes kept their hats on). From the ringers' perspective, however, these confrontations probably did not pit their own profanity against the godliness of the vicar or parish clerk. Instead, conflict may have been experienced as a clash between two very different forms of reverence: the first honest, open-hearted and sincere (if a little boisterous); the other cold, hard and suspicious of all pleasure.

After 1660, such clashes were in any case rare, and in Ashover the parish clerk was actually one of the recreational ringers himself. Within Wheatcroft's bell-ringing fraternity, there was beer and banter aplenty but there was also a whiff of sobriety in the air. There was an etiquette to be observed. Visiting ringers were expected to seek permission, express gratitude and 'behave themselves right well'. One of the poems in Wheatcroft's book sets out the rules that applied to the ringers of his own parish. Those who aspired to belong to the elite bell-ringing team were required, on 5 November each year, to present themselves and to read the clerk's orders. 'If here you enter, and intend to ring', Wheatcroft warned, 'Be sure you do observe here everything.' Numerous instructions were laid out, and fines assigned for each failure to obey. Every ringer was to remove his gloves, spurs and hat before beginning, or pay a twopenny forfeit. If he overthrew his bell or made a mistake during change-ringing, he owed a farthing. There were also fines for damaging the bells and their carriages, for leaving the ropes dangling on the floor after ringing, and for smoking tobacco in the belfry. 'And if he will by force enter my steeple / He shall be lashed in sight of all the people.' Any money earned by the ringers was to be carefully shared out. 'Be all agreed', urged the author, warning the potential trouble-maker that 'the rest will call him knave'. The final couplet reminded readers of the benefits and dangers of ringing: 'And to conclude – I wish you strength – And hope / A store of money: but beware the rope.'[75] None of this was explicitly religious but nor were these the sentiments of a mere pleasure-seeker. Similar rules and regulations survive

[75] D5433/1, poem beginning 'You noble ringers that at Random run', DRO.

from a number of other locations and it is obvious that morality and order were pillars of this pastime.

Some of these documents suggest, moreover, that at least a measure of piety was expected from those who rang the bells. 'If in this place you soeare or curse; sixpence to pay, pull out our purse', said the rules from Tong (Shropshire). In St Stephen's, Bristol, the twenty-second rule imposed punishments on any ringer who was 'so rude as to run into the Belfrey before he do kneel down to pray as every Christian ought to do'. Not all ringers were therefore unconscious of the godly overtones that added colour and meaning to their recreation. The ringers of St Paul's, Bedford, noted proudly that bells were 'of a diviner Birth' than other musical instruments. The painted panels that were placed on the belfry walls at St Nicholas, Gloucester, during the late seventeenth century included a verse commending the changes,

Which may be rung on Bells and thereby raise
Your thoughts to Admiration and to praise
Such Musicke, and the Author of such skill,
Jehovah, who makes Changes as he will,
Within this Ringing I'land, and else-where,
Throug'ht the Universe, that men might feare
Him who hath Soverigne power, and in him trust
Who changeth not but turneth man to Dust.

There were nine verse-filled panels, all praising ringing to the skies. On two of them, the poems were embellished with suitably resounding quotations: 'Psalme 150. Praise ye the Lorde' and 'Praise ye him upon the loude Cymbals'.[76] The ringers of Gloucester clearly would not have recognised the historiographical orthodoxy that change-ringing existed 'quite independently of the church'.[77]

Indeed, the poetic outpourings of Leonard Wheatcroft and others are strongly reminiscent of the founding charters of many medieval confraternities, those remarkable alliances of laypeople that supported and supplemented the work of the pre-Reformation church. The two forms of fraternity shared ground in their spirited communality, their voluntary attachment to the church and their blending of sociability and sobriety. Some bell-ringers of the seventeenth century went so far as to

[76] Cook, 'The Organization of the Exercise', pp. 69, 75; Eisel, 'The Development of Change Ringing', p. 48. The Gloucester verses are transcribed in Ellacombe, *The Bells of Gloucestershire*, pp. 26–8.

[77] Cock, 'The Development of Change Ringing', p. 39.

bind themselves into formal fellowships, complete with written rules and records. By 1700 there were numerous examples in locations spread all over the country.[78] The first ringers' club, however, was in London. The British Library holds a delightful little manuscript book, first begun on 2 February 1603/4 and entitled 'Orders Conceived and agreed upon by the Company exerciseing the Arte of Ringing knowne and called by the name of the Schollers of Cheapeside'. This volume covers the years between 1603 and 1661, and contains detailed notes about the company's operations. According to its rules, laid out in 1610, the Scholars of Cheapside elected annually four 'wardens' and a chief officer known as 'The Generall'. All former generals automatically became 'Assistants' for the remainder of their lives. The election took place upon the Feast of St Michael the Archangel (29 September) and was followed by a supper for all members of the company.

The responsibilities of the general and wardens included the organisation and direction of 'certeyn sett Peales' at various dates throughout the year. At meetings of the company, the general was to 'appoint every man his place to Ringe in' during forthcoming peels. All members paid an admission fee of 2s 6d and a yearly rate thereafter. The financial year ended, significantly, on 5 November. A treasurer was appointed to collect all fines. These were levied for a variety of offences, including non-attendance, refusal to accept the ringing place allotted by the general and failure to accept other decisions. No member was to 'talke or make any noyce to the disturbance of the Company in the tyme of Ringing'. The scholars rang competitively against other similar fraternities, but members had to seek the general's permission before offering or accepting challenges. The spirit of the medieval guilds was particularly striking in two further orders: disputes between the scholars themselves were to be settled by small committees of arbitration, and when any member died, 'The Company . . . shall accompany the deceased to his Grave And for a further token of their love shall Ringe one knell Peale'. The scholars committed themselves to 'honnest recreation', and agreed that any man who persistently broke the rules should be 'expulst the Society as unfitting to use his recreation in honest Company'.[79]

'Honest company' was a deceptively straightforward description. The social composition of recreational ringing groups, whether formal or informal in nature, suggests the simultaneous proclamation and complication of various contemporary hierarchies. It will be obvious from much

[78] See Cook, 'The Organization of the Exercise'. [79] Sloane MS 3463, BL.

of what has been said that active participation was a manly matter. Bell-ringing tested the strength and co-ordination of the male body and fed the male ego. All bells rang for the glory of God, but they also sounded to the praise of the ringers. Bell-ringing was body-building work, an early modern equivalent of pumping iron ('And ev'ry manly muscle looks robust', commented an eighteenth-century poet).[80] Women listened and sometimes looked but they did not pull the strings (nowadays, there are many female bell-ringers, three of whom can be heard on the website, tracks 47 and 48). The situation was, however, more complex than it seems. In Sussex, for example, medieval bells were more likely to carry inscriptions calling upon female saints than upon their male counterparts. Were women the primary carers, in heaven as on earth? In contrast, the actual names with which bells were christened suggest a reverse imbalance. In this county, at least, pre-Reformation bells were slightly more likely to be named after famously devout male figures (John, Gabriel, James, Simon and so forth) than after female saints (Catherine, Margaret and Mary). The evidence, admittedly, is slim, yet what little we have suggests that English people tended to imagine their bells as masculine.[81] They still did so in Singleton (Sussex) in 1586. At this date, one of the church bells 'burst' and had to be carried away for recasting. In its absence, the locals grew restless and told the churchwardens of their wish to 'have hym home againe'.[82]

During the eighteenth and nineteenth centuries, however, bells apparently became disproportionately female. In 1771, the new treble bell at Ticehurst (Sussex) was inscribed with the declaration, 'I am she that leads the van / Then follow me now if you can' (here was a woman on top). During the 1930s, one of Dorothy L. Sayers's fictional characters noted the curious fact that church bells, though still given masculine nicknames, were nevertheless spoken of by affectionate ringers as if they were female. This is all rather perplexing. We can perhaps conclude that church bells have for centuries served both to articulate the differences between the sexes and to play games with the distinctions. At times, bells have been seen and heard as men among men, participants in masculine fellowship. At others, they have been women among men, perhaps requiring discipline from the strong hands of their male operators (rather like the cars and boats of modern playboys).[83]

[80] Quoted by Ellacombe, *Bells of Gloucestershire*, p. 169.

[81] Based on the inscriptions transcribed in Daniel-Tyssen, *Church Bells of Sussex*.

[82] EP 1/11/5, Chichester archdeaconry, 1582–88, WSRO.

[83] Daniel-Tyssen, *Church Bells of Sussex*, p. 90; Dorothy L. Sayers, *The Nine Tailors* (1934; London: Hodder and Stoughton, 2003), p. 19.

Recreational ringers spanned the social spectrum. Those who lined up against the vicar in Rudgwick (Sussex) during the 1630s included a miller, two husbandmen and three yeomen. Two of them were sufficiently literate to sign their depositions, and the others made marks. At Staunton (Nottinghanshire), the provocative night-ringers were mainly servants but their apparent leader was an established blacksmith. In Derbyshire, Wheatcroft's men were a mixture of young gents and persons of more humble social origins. His habit of addressing them all as 'Gentlemen', regardless of their rank, suggests the unifying energy and the heightened sense of status that could flow from such togetherness. The ringers who joined more formal societies were likely to be relatively prosperous, though it is noticeable that the office-holders among the Scholars of Cheapside were not all fully literate. Other examples suggest that some ringing fellowships were socially exclusive while others were more open. One group, the Esquire Youths, admitted only gentlemen of high rank. In contrast, the society founded at Lincoln Cathedral in 1612 included a solitary gentleman alongside an assortment of local shoemakers, tailors, butchers, gardeners and carpenters. Most of these men registered their commitment with marks rather than signatures. Ringing clubs thus provided a setting in which social distinctions could be both displayed and disguised.[84]

Something similar can be said of the link between such institutions and the age hierarchy. The prominence of societies named 'Youths' or 'Scholars' suggests that bell-ringing was a recreation associated particularly with the young and single. The evidence of less formal fellowships generally points in the same direction. Servants and sons appear with such frequency in the court records that their disproportionate involvement is clear. At Rudgwick in 1638, the ringers who came before the court were all aged between twenty and twenty-five. Older men were not, however, excluded completely. Several of the standers-by were more senior, and one had reached the grand old age of forty-three. In Ashover, Leonard Wheatcroft set practice times according to age and experience: 'Each Monday night, I'd have th'old ringers ring, / And every Thursday, the young ones have their swing.'[85] Wheatcroft himself was in his sixties, and perhaps he was not ringing as regularly as once he had done.

[84] EP 1/11/16, fos. 157r–162, WSRO; AN/PB 328/1/34, HL; D5433/1, DRO; Sloane MS 3463, BL; John R. Ketteringham, *Lincoln Cathedral: A History of its Bells, Bellringers and Bellringing* (Lincoln: J. R. Ketteringham, 1987), p. 55.

[85] EP1/11/16, fos. 157r–162, WSRO; D5433/1, DRO.

Nevertheless, he was no mere onlooker. On the contrary, he clearly exerted a form of benevolent control over his younger companions. Wheatcroft was capable both of joining in their jubilance and of reprimanding his juniors when they misbehaved. He was by early modern standards an elderly man, yet one senses that the jangling bells helped to keep this long-serving parish clerk young in head and heart.

The durability of bells

Church bells revealed a remarkable capacity to survive during the difficult decades of the never-ending English Reformation. To some, they were potent and unwelcome reminders of the popish past, and they consequently fell under suspicion, particularly during the mid-sixteenth and mid-seventeenth centuries. Yet bells held their nerve, earned the renewed respect of their neighbours and even began to multiply. There were moments of meltdown, but most of these were merely preparatory to the founding and sounding of additional and more 'tunable' bells. Even in difficult economic times, parishes gathered the funds to improve their ringing facilities. By the later seventeenth century, church bells existed in greater numbers than ever before, and their concerted voices had all but silenced the ecclesiastical and economic opposition. How do we account for this extraordinary resilience?

Church bells survived because they met many needs and they did so with unmistakable loudness. Versatility and volume were thus their greatest strengths. In a pre-electronic and only partially literate society there was no more effective mechanism for communicating instantly with a large number of people. 'By speaking they'l make all the Town to hear', as Bunyan put it.[86] Bells could also say many different things and they played important roles in several contrasting walks of life: they fought fire and thunder; they expressed joy and grief; they spoke to God on behalf of humans and to humans on behalf of God; they asserted the identity of individual parishes but also helped to build a nation; and they connected the present to the past, thus helping to ensure the continuity of community during a period of dramatic change. Bell-ringing contributed both to cohesion and to division. It gathered people together but it also articulated their many differences. The bells were heard by all but, at times, they also

[86] Bunyan, *A Book for Boys and Girls: or, Country Rhimes for Children* (London, 1686), p. 36.

separated Catholics from Protestants, puritans from moderates, royalists from parliamentarians, men from women and the living from the dead. Their sound was familiar in country and town, but the larger numbers and denser concentrations of bells and ringers in closely packed urban parishes meant that this form of music sounded richer, louder and longer there. Bells spoke of community but also of hierarchy. 'When Bells Ring round, and in their Order be', said the author of *Tintinnalogia*, 'They do denote how Neighbours should agree.' Neighbourliness was a comparatively egalitarian set of principles, yet the same writer also reminded his readers that, in bell-ringing, 'the Treble to the Tenor doth give place'.[87] All would be well in the commonwealth, mused Thomas Jordan in the momentous year of 1649, if people could only be more like bells in managing the tensions between individuality and community: 'a discord in the bells arise, / And yet they disagreeing, sympathise'.[88] Bells spoke of unity, yet they also provided the prosperous with yet another instrument for the proclamation of their pre-eminence. At weddings and funerals, the more a family paid the longer the bells rang. And while God still figured prominently in the inscriptions placed on bells, the individuals who supervised, financed or executed the work were not above indulging in some fairly crude self-promotion: 'Sir Henry Palavicini did us bring / God's name and fame abroad to sing' (Babraham, Cambridgeshire, 1614); 'Feare the Lord and on him call / William Hausley made us all' (Fen Ditton, Cambridgeshire, 1623); 'In true desier for to do well / the Lady Litcot gave this bell' (Basildon, Berkshire, 1662).[89]

To some, bell music seemed to set disorderly male youth dangerously apart from mainstream society. It was like rock'n'roll. Yet it was equally possible to believe, as Wheatcroft clearly did, that bell-ringing gave young male 'swingers' an outlet for their energies that was comparatively benign. It was loud and potentially dangerous, but it also required self-discipline and co-operation. It even took place in church and thus perhaps offered the youth of the parish a sacred connection that they might otherwise have resisted. It also provided one possible channel of control for use by the elders of the parish. Admittedly, it was not ideal that young men sometimes preferred ringing for fun on Wednesday night to ringing for divine service on Sunday morning, but there were worse ways in which to seek recreation. Bells, finally, were symbols both of change and of continuity.

87 *Tintinnalogia*, A3r–v. 88 Thomas Jordan, *Divine Raptures* (London, 1649), F1r–v.

89 Raven, *Church Bells of Cambridgeshire*, appendix 'Inscriptions', pp. 1–30; Sharpe, *Church Bells of Berkshire*, p. 29.

Their constantly evolving music helped English society through a period in which order often felt perilously vulnerable.

It was the genius of church bells that their messages could be received and interpreted in different ways. Older beliefs in the power of bells were in practice permitted to co-exist with more rigorous reformist attitudes (rather like the combination of discordant partials that characterised the sound itself). According to Robert Burton, 'He that hears bells will make them sound what he list. As the soule thinketh, so the bell clinketh.'[90] It seems that conformist Protestants of many complexions were, by 1600, content to agree on the value and validity of bell-ringing, even if the underlying foundations of their attitudes covered an extensive spectrum. At one end stood those puritans who steadily overcame their reservations and accepted bells as functional communicators and, to some degree, instruments of supplication; at the other were found the people who considered themselves Protestant, but who nevertheless retained certain vestiges of pre-Reformation beliefs concerning the supernatural power of ringing. Sir Thomas Browne was probably not the only individual in whom bells induced thoughts of a strange Protestant purgatory. There were many intermediate positions, and a minority of individuals placed themselves beyond the spectrum at one end or the other, but a working consensus seems to have prevailed, growing notably stronger in the second half of the seventeenth century. At the end of our period, Whigs and Tories were swinging their bells for different reasons, but they agreed on the validity and value of the exercise.

The bells of St Bartholomew the Great in Smithfield (London) present a wonderful encapsulation of the many complex cross-currents. They began life around 1510, at which date they adorned the local priory. The five fine bells must have been the pride and joy of the monks, and their individual inscriptions called for intercessory prayers from Saints Bartholomew, Katherine, Anne, John the Baptist and Peter respectively. As ailing residents of the priory approached death, they could listen to the tolling of the bells and take comfort from the messages that were being carried heavenward. In 1539, however, the priory was dissolved and its buildings sold to a wealthy layman. Though the nave of the chapel was largely destroyed, parts of the building remained in use as the parish church. Somehow, the bells survived not only this assault upon tradition but all subsequent periods of danger (including the Great Fire of London in

[90] Burton, quoted by Ellacombe, *Bells of Gloucestershire*, front page.

1666). Considerable care was taken of the bells, and a solitary set of Elizabethan churchwardens' accounts, dated 1574–8, details the money spent on new ropes, replacement wheels and repairs to the irons and baldrics. The bells also brought money into the parish coffers, particularly from the grieving families of well-to-do parishioners, who regularly paid 4s 4d to hear 'all the bells' when they made their farewells. Poorer people presumably made do with the tolling of a single bell, a sound for which they evidently did not pay. What sort of prayers, one wonders, did these sounds stimulate among the parishioners, some of whom were old enough to recall the distant day upon which the same blessed bells had first sounded in order to call upon that formidable quintet of saints? Most of the accounts are missing, but we can assume that, by 1600, the bells were also sounding in commemoration of Elizabeth I's 'crownation day'. They were certainly doing so in 1697, and a document from that year also reveals that the ancient and once Catholic bells now rang to celebrate the successes of the Protestant William III in Europe. The bells, though fixed firmly in place, had come a long way, adding politics to their piety and alluding to the interconnections between the two categories. They must also have participated in the new art of recreational change-ringing, though the sparse sources are silent on this point. Over two centuries, these majestic instruments had helped to guide the community through a mass of disconcerting changes, and the note added to the parish accounts by the churchwarden of 1697 could almost have been rung out by one of the five bells on behalf of them all: 'Gentlemen I have served you to the utmost of my power. God bless the parish of St. Bartholomew the Great.'[91]

One of our recordings presents the early seventeenth-century peal known as 'The twenty all over', rung on these very bells (see Figure 9.2). It serves as a concluding metaphor for the troubled pursuit of hierarchical order in England between the early sixteenth and late seventeenth centuries. The peal starts smoothly enough (12345) with each bell securely in its allotted position. The music then passes through a period of perpetual change in which order is shaken and the component parts of

[91] *The Records of St. Bartholomew's Priory [and] St. Bartholomew the Great, West Smithfield*, ed. E. A. Webb, 2 vols. (Oxford: Oxford University Press, 1921), vol. II, pp. 106–28, 510–31. See also http://london.lovesguide.com/bartholomew_great.htm, last accessed 6 september 2009. The endless adaptability of these bells is further demonstrated by the fact that, in the summer of 2008, they rang to celebrate a somewhat controversial civil partnership between two gay parishioners.

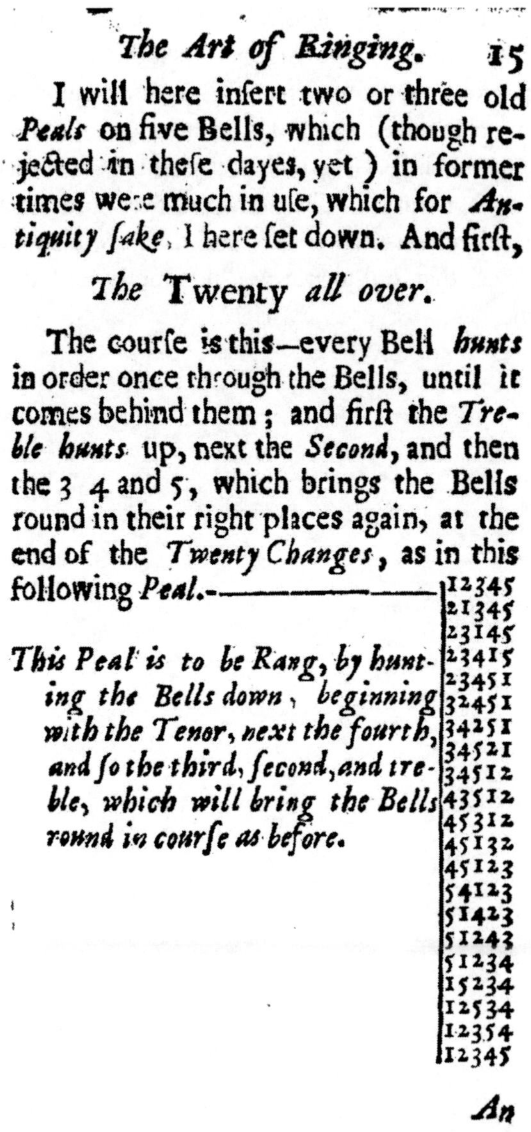

The Art of Ringing. 15

I will here inſert two or three old *Peals* on five Bells, which (though rejected in theſe dayes, yet) in former times were much in uſe, which for *Antiquity ſake*, I here ſet down. And firſt,

The Twenty *all over.*

The courſe is this—every Bell *hunts* in order once through the Bells, until it comes behind them; and firſt the *Treble hunts* up, next the *Second*, and then the 3 4 and 5, which brings the Bells round in their right places again, at the end of the *Twenty Changes*, as in this following *Peal.*

12345
21345
23145
23415
23451
32451
34251
34521
34512
43512
45312
45132
45123
54123
51423
51243
51234
15234
12534
12354
12345

This Peal is to be Rang, by hunting the Bells down, beginning with the Tenor, next the fourth, and ſo the third, ſecond, and treble, which will bring the Bells round in courſe as before.

An

Figure 9.2. *Tintinnalogia* (1668) and *Campanalogia* (1677) presented a wealth of information on all aspects of bell-ringing and both texts are still in use today. 'The twenty all over' is very rarely performed nowadays and it therefore presented an interesting challenge to the ringers who recorded track 47. The Bodleian Library, Oxford, *Tintinnalogia* (1668; London, 1671), p. 15.

the whole swap their positions repeatedly. The sequence 51243 is a long and disconcerting distance from the orderly opening rounds, though the logical nature of the progressions suggests the urge to find and preserve a sense of pattern amid the musical mayhem. Eventually, we experience a satisfying return to the original melodic hierarchy (**website track 47 and Appendix**). Of course, real life was never quite like this and the comparatively stable societies of 1500 and 1700 were different in more ways than could be listed here. Nevertheless, it seems possible that one reason for the evident popularity of 'The twenty all over' and other similar sequences was that they reassured ringers and listeners, at some deep and subconscious level, that turbulence was temporary and that order would return in time.

Conclusion: the musical milieux of Machyn and Pepys

On 29 October 1553, Henry Machyn, a merchant tailor in London, looked and listened as the Lord Mayor's annual procession moved through the city streets. The sights and sounds impressed him equally, and he decided to record the event in his manuscript chronicle. Machyn's prose is generally concise and unemotional, and some of his words have long been illegible, but we can nevertheless sense the impact that the musical dimensions of the parade made upon him:

> ... toward Westmynster ... craftes of London in their best leveray ... with trumpets blohyng and the whets [waits] playng ... then cam on [with a] drume and a flutt playng, and a-nodur with a great f[ife?], all they in blue sylke ... and then cam xvi trumpeters blohyng; and then cam the pagant of sant John Baptyst gorgyusly, with goodly speeches; and then cam all the kynges trumpeters blowhyng, and evere trumpeter havyng skarlet capes, and the wetes capes and godly banars ... and after dener to Powlles ... with all the trumpets and wettes blowhyng thrugh Powlles, thrugh rondabowt the qwer [choir] and the body of the chyrche blowhyng, and so home to my lord mere howsse.[1]

Machyn had evidently enjoyed a great day out. There is a certain breathlessness in his report, and the active verb 'blowing' is particularly effective in conveying the energy of the occasion.

One hundred and ten years later to the day, a rather more familiar observer attended the same procession. Samuel Pepys was not so favourably impressed and clearly did not approach the proceedings with the wide eyes and open ears of his Elizabethan predecessor. On 29 October 1663, Pepys's comment on the aural component of the show was short and sharp: 'I expected Musique, but there was none; but only trumpets and drums, which displeased me.'[2]

A contemplation of the contrasts between these two sources seems a fitting device with which to bring this book to a close. We have ranged widely in time and space, meeting hundreds of individuals along the way. There is therefore a case for settling down, finally, for a conversation with

[1] *Diary of Henry Machyn*, pp. 47–8. [2] *Diary of Samuel Pepys*, vol. IV, pp. 355–6.

two Londoners, separated from one another by a short mile on the streets but a long century in England's musical history. The records kept by Machyn and Pepys are of course very different in tone and content. The earlier writer was influenced by the tradition of impersonal city chronicles, and his manuscript is a 'diary' only in embryo.[3] Pepys, on the other hand, was driven by profound self-awareness and an obsession with confession. Thus we recognise his creation as a personal diary in the modern sense. Despite the differences, both sources have much to tell us about the place of music in society, and we shall begin with what they reveal of the balance between change and continuity during the early modern period. The contrasting reactions of the two men to the music of the mayor are informative. The superficial impression – of one writer who adored music and another who felt indifferent – is, of course, misleading, for both men were lovers of the art. Their divergent responses can be explained in two ways. Firstly, their tastes differed. Machyn was drawn to and thrilled by public processions, partly as a consequence of his professional interest in funerals, while Pepys generally preferred the music of intimate indoor settings. Of course, this also speaks of deeper contrasts between the social identities of the two men, a point to which we shall return. The second explanation is connected: the tastes of Machyn and Pepys were different partly because music-making had changed significantly during the turbulent century that stood between them. This was perhaps particularly true in London, though the situation was echoed all over the country. In short, Pepys's musical world was richer and more varied than Machyn's. To him, the music of trumpets hardly counted as music at all. It retained its aristocratic aura, but by a strange paradox it had also become 'dull, vulgar music'.[4] In the socially ambitious mind of Master Pepys, trumpet calls were far inferior to the many available forms of sophisticated domestic music with which the diarist so often busied himself. Machyn, as far as we can tell, knew little of these forms because their heyday lay in the future. He, therefore, was rather taken with the brazen bluster of the mayor's trumpets.

Machyn's chronicle covers the years between 1551 and 1563. Although it does not originate in the earliest decades of our period, it is in many

[3] On the nature of the source, see Ian Mortimer, 'Tudor Chronicler or Sixteenth-century Diarist? Henry Machyn and the Nature of his Manuscript', *Sixteenth Century Journal*, 33:4 (2002), 981–98; and Gary G. Gibbs, 'Marking the Days: Henry Machyn's Manuscript and the Mid-Tudor Era', in Eamon Duffy and David Loades (eds.), *The Church of Mary Tudor* (Aldershot: Ashgate, 2006), pp. 281–308.

[4] *Diary of Samuel Pepys*, vol. II, p. 29.

ways a late medieval document. The writer, resident in the parish of Trinity the Little, provides us with a largely impersonal account of public life in the capital. He speaks of himself only rarely and nearly always in the third person. There is much of tradition in the music he hears. Machyn is entirely comfortable with the old term 'minstrel' and there are few signs of music as the controversial stimulant of vice and disorder. During the reign of Mary, he also refers regularly to the customary music of the late medieval church, something in which he had an active interest as a serving parish clerk. At funeral masses, he notes the singing of priests and the 'goodly ryngyng' of church bells. He also mentions the music of organs and the traditional singing that accompanies religious processions on saints' days. The non-liturgical music that Machyn documented was similarly rooted in the past. On the streets, the bellman rings his handbell to warn of fire and to stimulate prayers for the dead. Trumpets fulfil their traditional function as the sonic signifiers of aristocratic status and public celebration. Their music catches Henry's attention on many occasions and trumpets outnumber all other instruments in the pages of his manuscript. He also hears drums, flutes, shawms and the occasional regal (a small, portable reed organ). Their combined sounds amount, in Henry's estimation, to 'all the mysyke [music] that cold be'. Having said this, he is also drawn to music of the 'rough' variety. Punitive ridings, aimed at miscreants of several sorts, therefore find their place in Henry's text. A bawd is paraded on horseback 'with a basen ryngyng', and a stand-in for a man whose wife has beaten him is carried through the streets at Charing Cross with 'a bagpype playng, a shame [shawm] and a drum playhyng'.[5]

Henry Machyn, however, also stood on the cusp of a new age, and his chronicle presents several signposts to the future. Although the sound of trumpets fills the air, he also notes the presence of viols at the annual feast of London's grocers in June 1561. The viol was, at this point, much closer to the beginning of its journey through English society than to the end. Machyn's remarks on the celebratory ringing of church bells do not in general suggest controversy, yet on 19 June 1563 he noted official attempts to fine all the parishes that 'did not ryng when that the quen whent to Grenwyche'.[6] As we have heard, such political sensitivities were to become a regular feature of English bell culture during the early seventeenth century. Most notably, Machyn was struck by London's first experiments in congregational singing during the early years of Elizabeth's reign. He

[5] *Diary of Henry Machyn*, pp. 206, 220, 301. [6] Ibid., pp. 260, 310.

was not given to indulgent elaboration, but in the repeated references he made to the practice there is no mistaking his sense of surprise. Machyn, like many others, pricked up his ears when 'all the pepull did syng the tune of Geneway'.[7]

One hundred years later, Samuel Pepys lived a short distance to the east in the parish of St Olave, Hart Street, and he moved through many of the same neighbourhoods. Of course, there were also numerous continuities in the music that he heard. The bellman still walked the streets during the early hours of the day, announcing the time and warning sleepy citizens of the weather that awaited them in the world beyond their windows. Pepys, like Machyn, understood without thinking the many musical signals that carried news through the city air: church bells ringing to celebrate various royal occasions or to announce the deaths of parishioners; the drums of the trained bands when warfare seemed imminent; and the sound of trumpets to publicise the movements of the great (and, increasingly, the not quite so great). They both heard organs playing in church, though the later diarist was witnessing a recovery rather than a simple continuity. Samuel was a child of the destructive civil war years, and during the 1660s he experienced this traditional musical sound as an arresting novelty.[8] Noisy ridings, in contrast, enjoyed an unbroken history. On 10 June 1667, Pepys witnessed one at Greenwich, where the local constable had, like Machyn's unfortunate contemporary, been soundly beaten by his wife.[9]

The cosmological resonances of music were implicit in such events, even if neither writer spelled them out. Pepys, of course, was of a more scientific bent than Machyn, and he might well have scoffed to hear how sixteenth-century Londoners had dropped to their knees in their hundreds upon hearing the rumble of thunder – a divine drumbeat – that accompanied the execution of the Duke of Somerset in 1552.[10] On the other hand, Pepys read books that proclaimed the mysteries of music's power, and he does not seem to have been particularly intent upon analysing the phenomenon in terms of the developing discipline of acoustics. Indeed, when the celebrated Robert Hooke told him about sonic frequency with reference to the buzzing of a fly's wings, Pepys considered the explanation ingenious but 'a little too much raffined'.[11] Perhaps he preferred to preserve some sense of wonder. He certainly seems to have experienced music with a vague but potent awareness of its place within the grand

[7] Ibid., p. 228. [8] *Diary of Samuel Pepys*, vol. I, pp. 195, 283, vol. VIII, pp. 150, 174.
[9] Ibid., vol. VIII, p. 257. [10] *Diary of Henry Machyn*, p. 14.
[11] *Diary of Samuel Pepys*, vol. VII, p. 239.

created order. Pepys particularly liked to play and sing outdoors, often in the garden or the park and ideally under 'moonshine'. On 28 May 1667, he found great pleasure in a walk in the 'spring garden' at Vauxhall: 'to hear the nightingale and other birds, and here fiddles and there a harp, and here a jew's trump, and here laughing, and there fine people walking, is mighty divertising'.[12] Moreover, Pepys – like other wealthy citizens – also tried to recreate the musical sounds of nature within his own home. During the years covered by the diary, he sought solace in the singing of three feathered pets: a blackbird, a canary and a starling.[13]

The differences between the musical milieux of Machyn and Pepys are, however, just as compelling, and they point to the many changes that had occurred in England between the 1560s and the 1660s. Although the bellman remained active, he had long since abandoned his practice of inviting citizens to pray for the dead. Church bells continued to sound, but in Pepys's London there were many more of them and they probably rang with greater frequency. Indeed, background noise levels must have grown significantly louder in a century that saw London's population rise from approximately 85,000 to something like 500,000. In this bustling metropolis, Pepys was personally acquainted with many musical practitioners but he rarely if ever attached to them the tainted label 'minstrel'. He was also familiar with a far wider range of musical instruments than Machyn had been. Pepys played the viol, the lute, the violin, the flageolet and the recorder, and he at least owned a spinet. He also heard others playing these instruments, along with organs (domestic and ecclesiastical), harps, dulcimers, bagpipes, whistles, guitars, drums and trumpets. Admittedly, Pepys was unusually committed to music but his practical interest in the subject clearly did not mark him as a maverick. As we have heard, he estimated that one in three city households possessed virginals (though his sample was probably a wealthy one).[14] In Pepys's London, recreational music-making was highly fashionable, and many of those who took part could read music. Mere literacy was not enough to impress Pepys, and he reserved his compliments for those who could play or sing a piece perfectly at first sight. The efforts of recreational musicians were sometimes thoroughly impressive. On 27 July 1663, Pepys overheard some singers while riding towards Epsom. The sound was so fine that he and others, listening from a distance of approximately 450 yards, 'took them for the waytes'. When he rode closer, however, he realised that the open-air

[12] Ibid., vol. V, p. 215, vol. VII, p. 206, vol. VIII, p. 240.

[13] Ibid., vol. IV, pp. 150, 152, vol. VI, p. 8, vol. IX, p. 209.

[14] See above, p. 179.

musicians were merely 'some Citizens, met by chance, that sing four or five parts excellently'. Samuel concluded his report with a thoroughly characteristic expression of delight: 'I have not been more pleased with a snapp of Musique, considering the circumstances of the time and place, in all my life anything so pleasant.'[15]

The recreational scene also generated plenty of work for those who made their livings principally from music: they could teach singing, dancing or instrumental skills; they could bolster domestic resources by joining in at musical sessions; and they could tune instruments or supply music, either in print or in manuscript. The more enterprising of them composed and distributed their own music, or published instruction manuals. Pepys made regular visits to London's top music shop, and on 22 March 1667 managed to walk all the way from Greenwich to Woolwich while engrossed in Playford's *Introduction to the Skill of Musick* ('wherein are some things very pretty').[16] Machyn's private world may well have been a musical one, but during the 1550s and 1560s many of the facilities that would later be so familiar to Pepys were only just beginning their development. The earlier writer, sadly, lacked Samuel's instinct for the documentation of domesticity.

There were other differences too. Congregational psalmody, so new to Machyn, was generally taken for granted by Pepys. He attended church regularly, but referred to the singing of psalms only when it lasted a full hour or on the rare occasions when the parish clerk amused him by making a mess of things. Samuel was far more likely to mention the psalms that he and his musical friends sang at home, often on Sundays, from one of the various books of four-part settings that were available by the 1660s.[17] This was a form of domestic harmony that Machyn is unlikely to have experienced. Ballads, in contrast, must have been familiar to both men, but in the century that separated them the business had boomed. Pepys, therefore, heard and saw broadside songs far more frequently than his predecessor. He mentions them only occasionally in his journal, but we know that he later became an avid collector. Pepys's diary dwells more devotedly on the rich variety of music that its author heard at the theatre, and this too was an interest that distinguished him from Machyn. In Henry's day, there were no purpose-built public theatres in London, and the complex early modern narrative of construction, controversy, abolition and recovery lay ahead. He therefore never shared Pepys's memorable

[15] *Diary of Samuel Pepys*, vol. IV, pp. 248–9. [16] Ibid., vol. VIII, p. 124.
[17] Ibid., vol. II, p. 6, vol. III, p. 2, vol. V, p. 332.

experience of the ravishing effects of invisible recorders, though he made up for it by immersing himself in the street drama of religious processions and royal or civic ceremony.

One final contrast is more complicated. Pepys, a child of the 1630s, can scarcely have shared Machyn's apparent innocence regarding the moral and social dangers of musical excess. As a boy, Samuel had supported parliament against the king and must therefore have conversed with individuals who harboured grave suspicions where secular music was concerned. By 1660, he had of course changed sides and most of his qualms were successfully suppressed. Nevertheless, the puritanism of his past occasionally protruded in rare moments of moral anxiety over the disorderly potential of music. On 11 November 1661, he watched 'a company of pretty girls' practising at a dancing school and commented that he did not like to see such youngsters 'exposed to so much vanity'.[18] He occasionally felt guilty when he played non-religious music on Sundays, and his regular self-improving vows sometimes led to a marked but temporary reduction in all forms of musical activity. On 9 March 1666, he sang with one of his favourite female companions and later rebuked himself in his diary: 'God forgive me, I do still see that my nature is not to be quite conquered, but will esteem pleasure above all things.' His resolutions were normally aimed primarily at drinking and theatre-going, but on this occasion other demons loomed larger: 'music and women I cannot give way to, whatever my business is'. Pepys's hedonism was thus complicated by a nagging awareness of the bad press that musical pastimes had received from moralists during the previous one hundred years. 'My love of pleasure is such', he wrote in the summer of 1666, 'that my very soul is angry with itself for my vanity in so doing.'[19]

The monarchy could be welcomed back but the simple musical pleasures of Henry Machyn could never quite be restored. It was impossible for an intelligent man of the 1660s to live as if the moralising message of the past century – Lovell's legacy – had never been sounded, but Samuel Pepys did his best. By 1668, he seems to have been making headway. On 26 March, he and his friends indulged themselves in a long evening of song and dance. Samuel's review of proceedings revealed none of the angst of the entries quoted above. As the relaxed musical culture of the Restoration began to establish itself, he described his 'mighty great content' and added, 'I did, as I love to do, enjoy myself in my pleasure, as being the heighth of what we take pains for and can hope for in this world – and

[18] Ibid., vol. II, p. 212. [19] Ibid., vol. VII, pp. 69–70, 151.

therefore to be enjoyed while we are young and capable of these joys.'[20] Was the puritan within finally vanquished? Perhaps not entirely, but we should certainly note that Pepys, like Machyn, was living and listening during the closing of one phase and the opening of another. The two transitions had political, religious and economic dimensions, and they may provide one of the explanations for the decision of both men – sensing something significant – to reach for pen and paper. In musical terms, the 1660s appear to have been particularly important as a decade in which long-lasting anxieties over the value and status of music within society finally began to ease. Solomon Eccles, the musician-turned-Quaker, was not alone in campaigning against musical disorder after the Restoration, but angry voices were no longer to be heard so frequently from within the Church of England, and their power to influence the conforming majority was consequently reduced. The notion that music was a seriously dangerous pastime had not been eradicated but it had been discredited and pushed towards the cultural margins.

The dawning of a new phase had other aspects too, some of which have remained a feature of England's musical culture ever since. In Pepys's diary, there is evidence of a deepening distinction between what we nowadays call amateurs and professionals. Most of the time, admittedly, Pepys mixed freely and easily with recreational and occupational musicians alike. From time to time, however, he revealed explicitly that he did not quite regard them as members of one happy and harmonious household. On 29 July 1664, for example, Pepys made his way home during the afternoon, 'and there came Mr. Hill, Andrews and Seignor Pedro, and great store of Musique we had, but I begin to be weary of having a master with us, for it spoils methinks the ingenuity of our practice'. In other words, the presence of the professional – in this case an Italian – cramped the style of the amateurs (it probably did not help that 'Seignor Pedro' was, according to Pepys, a 'slovenly and ugly fellow').[21] Here, we seem to be witnessing the evolution of a now familiar relationship in which amateurs play among themselves while professionals perform publicly for the admiration of all. As the two categories began to emerge more clearly, so the era of the celebrity musician was inaugurated. Again, Pepys was witnessing only the early days in a new age, but he did consider 'the famous singer' Captain Henry Cooke to be without doubt the best in the world, and on another occasion he heard 'the famous Mr. Stefkins play admirably well' on his viol. In this instance, he also experienced a

[20] Ibid., vol. IX, p. 134. [21] Ibid., vol. V, pp. 217, 226.

sensation that will be familiar to all who have found themselves disappointed upon hearing a much-vaunted superstar perform live: 'and yet I find it as it is always, I over-expected'.[22]

It is also wise to consult our two Londoners as we draw some conclusions regarding the many roles that music played within early modern English society. In this age of change and challenge, both individuals understood by instinct that music was a vital tool in the construction and presentation of identity. Music, as we noted at the outset, was a complex and vital means of communication, assisting people of all conditions in the tricky business of social negotiation. In conclusion, we must therefore pick up our metaphorical lute once more and consider the significance of music within the social relationships that were documented by Machyn and Pepys. Music, for example, helped both men to situate themselves on the all-important string that connected gentry and commoners. Machyn was a man of middling rank, comfortable in his station. On the streets, the sound of trumpets told him that he was not an aristocrat, and he seems to have received the message without complaint. According to Machyn's report, the Company of Barber-surgeons also knew what was appropriate to them, and at their feast in June 1562 there were no trumpets but six drums and a heavily outnumbered flute.[23] The chronicler was also alive to the music of mortuary bells, particularly when the high status of the deceased was signified by 'goodly ryngyng' or 'grett ryngyng as ever was hard [heard]'.[24] The more monotonous music of the itinerant bellman urged Henry to pray at such moments, but at other times it also reminded him to provide for the poor.[25] Bell music of one sort or another thus reassured him that there were people far beneath him in the social hierarchy just as there were people far above.

Pepys's condition was more complicated. He was the son of a tailor and a serving woman but by the 1660s, through the careful nurturing of his talents and connections, he could with justification consider himself a gentleman. Through music, Samuel sought to consolidate and proclaim his new status. He played fashionable instruments such as the lute and the violin (itself on the rise) and he paid professionals to visit him and provide lessons. In his house, he endeavoured to set aside and decorate a 'music room'.[26] He also knew the social value of employing live-in musical servants and he devoted considerable energy to locating, auditioning

[22] Ibid., vol. I, p. 223, vol. II, p. 142, vol. IV, p. 233. [23] *Diary of Henry Machyn*, p. 286.
[24] Ibid., pp. 44, 291. [25] Ibid., p. 187.
[26] *Diary of Samuel Pepys*, vol. V, p. 233, vol. VII, p. 243.

and appointing such individuals. When he visited a neighbour in June 1667 and overheard the sounds of his own servants 'singing at my house', he felt 'the joy of my heart that I should be the maister of it'.[27] Music brought pleasure, but so did the ability to control it. For his musical soirées, Pepys was happiest when he managed to secure the services of the finest musicians in town (though sometimes a little troubled when he came to pay the bill). On special occasions, he even hired the royal trumpeters to wake him up in the morning with loud aristocratic blasts from the street outside.[28] Did Samuel imagine himself a monarch in the precious seconds before reaching full consciousness? He and other privileged persons also projected their identities downwards, reinforcing their high status by self-consciously imitating the music of the lower orders. On 5 June 1660, Pepys was on board a ship at Deal, killing time before returning to London. He spent the first part of the evening learning one of Henry Lawes's celebrated songs by heart, but the music changed when he later got together with his patron, Edward Mountagu, and others: 'After supper my Lord called for the Lieutenant's Gitterne, and with two Candlesticks with money in them for Symballs we made some barber's Musique, with which my Lord was much pleased.'[29]

Many gentlemen-musicians must have played with the dominant distinctions in this manner, but one senses that in Samuel's case this behaviour sometimes came a little too naturally. An uncontrollable love of music provides one explanation for his habit of practising and performing, sometimes in public, not only with 'music masters' but also with butchers and bargemen. Samuel did not only imitate musical barbers but knew and admired some of them too. His lowly social origins may provide another explanation. Pepys travelled between court and alehouse with remarkable regularity, trying always to focus his ambitions upon the former but sometimes, arguably, forgetting (or perhaps remembering) himself by falling into the latter. He mixed with musicians of all sorts – occupational and recreational – and he once embarrassed himself terribly by mistaking the familiar face of a passing gentleman for that of a mere theatre musician.[30] The role of music as both a marker of boundaries and a pathway across them was confusing at the best of times, but for Pepys the anxiety could be acute. On 24 March 1668, he and his superior Lord Brouncker were at Whitehall with Sir Francis Hollis, who led them into a 'handsome room' and called for his bagpiper. This musician, evidently

[27] Ibid., vol. VIII, p. 283. [28] Ibid., vol. VII, p. 422, vol. IX, p. 403.
[29] Ibid., vol. I, p. 169. [30] Ibid., vol. III, p. 36.

connected with the royal guards, played on an instrument 'with pipes of ebony tipped with silver' and provoked in Pepys a contradictory reaction. At first the diarist sounded thoroughly impressed: 'he did play beyond anything of that kind that ever I heard in my life'. The next sentence also began well, but Samuel changed direction rather abruptly after the first clause: 'And with great pains he must have obtained it, but with pains that the instrument doth not deserve at all; for at the best, it is mighty barbarous music.'[31] These sound like the words of a man who remained a little unsure of himself, both musically and socially.

Music was just as intricately involved in the management of gender relations. In Machyn's world, the rough music of basins and other instruments served to reflect and correct breaches in the interactive order that properly existed between men and women. In the episode at Charing Cross, the masculine music of bagpipe, shawm and drum was an integral component of the stern rebuke that was being forced upon the beaten husband. Within his marriage, the miscreant had sung a submissive song, thereby inviting his wife to add her own discordant descant. The heavy thumping of the drum reminded him and all who heard it of a man's essential duty. In a related deployment of masculine music, the militaristic sounds of drums and trumpets that attended Queens Mary and Elizabeth wherever they went had the effect of reminding all hearers that both women were, by virtue of their office, effectively men (like admirable versions of the Charing Cross wife). Machyn made the point with impressive economy when he described the sounds at a courtly feast in March 1559: 'ther was all maner of artlere [artillery], as drumes, flutes, trumpets, gones [guns], mores pykes, halbardes . . .' Elizabeth I was evidently determined to make her mark during the first months of her reign, and on 25 April she 'rowed up and down the Temes [Thames] . . . with trumpettes and drumes and flutes and gones' (of course, she was also famed for her abilities on the gentle and feminine virginals). Music could thus send messages across the gender divide, but it could also eradicate that divide, for a few moments at least. The first time that Henry mentioned congregational psalmody, he commented, 'men and women all do syng'.[32] In an ecclesiastic setting, this was an extraordinary development.

Once again, Pepys's diary is an even richer source. It is obvious that some instruments were primarily female (virginals, in particular) while others were almost exclusively masculine (drums, trumpets and bagpipes, for example). On the other hand, there were no written rules, and Samuel

[31] Ibid., vol. IX, pp. 130–1. [32] *Diary of Henry Machyn*, pp. 191, 196, 212.

provided plenty of evidence to suggest that men and women regularly crossed into one another's territory. Most amateur players of viols and violins were male, but Pepys also encountered gentlewomen who were proficient on these instruments (one senses that they had a certain novelty value).[33] Conversely, he heard a 'Harpsicon' played by 'a perfect good Musician' with the reassuringly manly name of Captain Allen.[34] Pepys's own wife played the flageolet, thereby suggesting that the old prohibition against women learning wind instruments was losing its force. Indeed, Samuel was keen that Elizabeth develop her musical competence, clearly believing that this was a compulsory accomplishment in a gentleman's wife. His efforts to encourage her were often clumsy, and they were as likely to drive the couple apart as to bring them together. When it went well, Samuel experienced 'content', 'pleasure', 'comfort' and 'delight'. Elizabeth's progress on the flageolet was particularly encouraging, and on 18 May 1667 he noted that her 'growth in music' had begun to please him 'mightily'. He sometimes used the language of command in recording the more successful aspects of his musical interaction with her. On 13 August 1668, Pepys returned home at night 'and made my wife sing and play on the flagelette to me till I slept with great pleasure in bed'.[35] When matters went awry, however, he found it very difficult to tolerate his wife's shortcomings and he sometimes reduced her to tears. In more general terms, music was a vital tool in his authority over her, though he did not always employ it to his advantage. Samuel wanted Elizabeth to learn singing, but the impetus for dancing came very much from her. From the outset, Pepys was uneasy, and when his wife took to shutting herself away with Pembleton, the dancing master, for hours at a time, he rapidly found himself losing his personal battle with the green-eyed monster. Jealousy threatened to consume him, and he poured his anxieties onto the pages of his diary: 'I fear, without great discretion, I shall go near to lose too my command over her; and nothing doth it more then giving her this occasion of dancing and other pleasure, whereby her mind is taken up from her business and finds other sweets besides pleaseing of me.'[36] Music was both a tool of rule and an instrument of rebellion.

In his extra-marital activities too, Pepys's desires were inflamed by and pursued through music. The woman who combined comely looks with an ability to sing or play was irresistible to him, and he groped the musical

[33] *Diary of Samuel Pepys*, vol. II, pp. 116, 286, vol. IV, p. 48, vol. V, p. 54.
[34] Ibid., vol. II, p. 71. [35] Ibid., vol. I, pp. 233, 239, vol. VIII, pp. 171, 204, 221, vol. IX, p. 279.
[36] Ibid., vol. IV, p. 150.

maidservants almost as a matter of daily routine. When Pepys attended musical evenings elsewhere, singing and sex were intimately intertwined. On 2 January 1666, Pepys found 'perfect pleasure' in the rendition of a song by the actress Elizabeth Knepp. Later, he travelled home in a coach with her, 'and got her upon my knee (the coach being full) and played with her breasts and sung'. Seven months later, he took a fancy to a pretty widow named Mrs Estwood while visiting a friend's house. With amusement, he noted that the singing of a particular jig by another member of the company plunged the widow into despair, it having been one of her late husband's favourites. 'But by and by', continued Pepys, 'I made her as merry as is possible, and tossed and tumbled her as I pleased.'[37] Most of the individuals whom he treated thus had attracted his attention through some combination of feminine qualities, but Pepys was equally aroused by the sight and sound of musical women pretending to be men. At the theatre, in particular, he liked to see girls dancing in boys' apparel or prancing around the stage dressed as shepherds. On occasion, such stunts were the only feature of a play that earned his approval. He was surely not alone in enjoying both the enforcement and the transgression of the established but endlessly debatable rules of sexual engagement.

Music also articulated the relationship between old and young. In Machyn's manuscript, this was once again most apparent in his reaction to congregational psalm-singing. On 17 March 1560, he described a godly gathering at Paul's Cross: 'and after the sermon done they songe all, old and yong, a salme in myter [metre]'.[38] Here, the generations were unified, but a century later Pepys also described several exchanges in which the divisions between age and youth were expressed through music. In his early thirties, Samuel clearly considered that music-and-dance marathons, stretching into the small hours of the morning, were appropriate primarily to young and vigorous individuals like himself. This was partly a matter of physical strength, and Pepys occasionally passed unfavourable comment upon the efforts of ageing singers whose voices, though once pleasing, were now in rapid decline. In his relationships with his musical servants, however, Samuel was cast as the more mature party. He hired them, watched over them and enjoyed his command over them. 'So home and to supper and to bed', he wrote on 11 November 1664, 'after prayers and having my boy and Mercer give me some, each of them some, music.'[39] Sometimes, however, a forceful rebuke was necessary. Tom Edwards, who

[37] Ibid., vol. VII, pp. 2–3, 232. [38] *Diary of Henry Machyn*, p. 228.
[39] *Diary of Samuel Pepys*, vol. V, p. 320.

joined Pepys's household in 1664 after several years as a boy singer in the Chapel Royal, was a talented musician. Pepys loved to listen to him, but Tom's 'clownish' ways meant that he also needed watching. He came to be a great favourite of the family, but in the early years his neglect of duty sometimes aroused his master's anger. 'Up, and very angry with my boy for lying long a-bed and forgetting his Lute', wrote the diarist on 11 January 1665.[40] Pepys did not strike the boy for such musical offences, but others were less restrained. In March 1661, for example, the diarist attended a play that was performed 'with so much disorder ... that in the Musique-room, the boy that was to sing a song not singing it right, his master fell about his eares and beat him so, that put the whole house in an uprore'.[41] Music, when working well, could produce harmony across the ages, but the effect was not easy to achieve and errors on all sides sometimes marred the performance of the social miracle.

Machyn had little to say on the distinctions between urban and rural music. Nevertheless, much of what he heard was more or less distinctively the sound of the town. The penetrating music of shawms, played so frequently by London's waits, would have been far less familiar to him had he lived in the countryside. In other cases, major towns and cities were distinguished from the surrounding landscape not by the precise nature of the music but by the sheer concentration of resources. Bells, instruments and musicians gathered in urban centres as nowhere else. They competed with one another, but also with the comparatively high level of background noise that characterised England's towns. All in all, the urban musical environment felt different, though the contrasts were of course constantly undermined by the passage of musicians and others from town to country and back again. Machyn may not have been particularly conscious of the urban–rural relationship, but Samuel Pepys certainly was. As ever, there was nothing simple about the distinction. Pepys, a man of the town, was both soothed and unsettled by country music. Most positively, he and the favoured members of his household sometimes took trips by river or road in order to take the air and escape from London. These ventures were in part musical. The participants not only walked in the fields and gathered dew but also listened to the birds and made their own music in the refreshing acoustic of the countryside.[42] Samuel does not tell us what they played and sang, though the 'country rounds' that were readily available in print may well have been on the musical menu. It was, above all, the supposed innocence of the countryside that impressed

[40] Ibid., vol. VI, p. 7. [41] Ibid., vol. II, p. 58. [42] Ibid., vol. VIII, p. 240, vol. IX, p. 221.

England's greatest diarist. On 13 October 1662, he and his father watched milkmaids at work in rural Cambridgeshire and were both pleased 'to see with what mirth they come all home together in pomp with their milk, and sometimes they have musique to go before them'.[43] In the city, 'country dancing' was imagined both as a preparation for rural life – Elizabeth took lessons 'against her going next year into the country' – and as a means of virtual escape from the stresses of urbanity.[44] In this sense, it was like taking the air without taking to the road.

In Pepys's mind, however, country music could also be depressing. Even the Cambridgeshire milkmaids did not produce in him an uncomplicated sensation of pleasure: Samuel described his rustic promenade as 'a melancholy walk'. Perhaps the rural simplicity that he imagined in their music contrasted a little too sharply with the complexities of his own urban existence. Alternatively it may have reminded him of his own lowly roots and thus of the fragility of his sophisticated lifestyle among lutes, viols and virginals. Certainly, Samuel was sometimes troubled by the contacts that he maintained with the less privileged of his rural relatives in Cambridgeshire. He was uneasy when, in May 1661, Frank Perkin, a cousin whose mill had blown down in a storm, begged him for an old fiddle with which to entertain the 'country girles' and thus make some money. Two years later, Pepys visited the Perkins in their 'sad poor thatched cottage'. He took them to the 'miserable Inne' in which he was staying, and cousin Frank thanked him by playing upon 'his Treble (as he calls it), with which he makes part of his living'. Perhaps this was the very instrument that Pepys had supplied. If so, the man from town was unimpressed. He endured his cousin's rendition of 'a country bawdy song' and then settled down to supper with 'the whole Crew and Frankes wife and children (a sad company, of which I was ashamed)'.[45] Back in the city, Pepys was sometimes impressed by the 'country' music that accompanied dancing, but on occasion he also used the word pejoratively. On 24 July 1663, he visited Mr Bland and friends for a good dinner, but was typically scathing in describing the postprandial entertainment: 'They have a kinswoman they call daughter in the house, a short, ugly, red-haired slut that plays upon the virginalls and sings, but after such a country manner, I was weary of it but yet could not but commend it.'[46]

[43] Ibid., vol. III, p. 221. [44] Ibid., pp. 213–14. [45] Ibid., vol. II, p. 96, vol. IV, p. 310.

[46] Ibid., vol. IV, p. 242. Similarly, Thomas Whythorne applied the adjective 'rural' to musicians who lacked sophistication and skill, regardless of their geographical origins (*Autobiography of Thomas Whythorne*, p. 92).

This was tiresome, but 'country' music could also be downright dangerous. In ballads of the period, many of which Pepys later collected, the dancing of rural youths was strongly associated with a measure of sexual freedom. Naturally, Samuel was more than happy to read and sing about musical orgies in the countryside, and he doubtless found the experience arousing. He was less contented, however, when it seemed that his wife planned to recreate the rural atmosphere within his own house, aided and abetted by Pembleton, the dreaded dancing master. In Pepys's mind, therefore, 'country' music was thus not only pure but perilous. It was a shifting and contested category, and could both comfort and enrage. It brought urban and rural culture together, but it also divided them. Pepys crossed from one world to the other and was evidently unsure where authenticity was to be located.

Neither writer dealt explicitly with the role of music in relations between the clergy and the laity. We have already encountered a number of clerics who lost their bearings under the influence of music and began to sing, play and dance as if they were mere laymen, and unruly ones at that.[47] Machyn and Pepys, however, do not add to the list, a fact that may suggest the relative infrequency of such conspicuous misconduct. The boundary-crossing cleric was, however, a common enough figure in popular literature of the period, and Pepys later collected several chapbooks and ballads in which members of the clergy – usually anachronistic 'friars' – display an inappropriate taste for dancing and sex. Characteristically, they are outwitted and humiliated, sometimes to the sound of music, by laypeople who themselves exhibit the kind of probity that ought properly to characterise their priestly opponents. The idea that music could both define and undermine the distinctions between clergy and laity was therefore a familiar one.

Machyn and Pepys generally observed England's priests and vicars from a distance, but their writings nevertheless reveal the crucial role of music within the early modern reconfiguration of lay–clerical relations. Machyn, as a parish clerk, was ideally placed to mediate between the two categories and to document the shifts but, as usual, he kept his views to himself. He did at least keep records of the music he heard. During the reign of Mary, Machyn's chronicle contained numerous references to the liturgical singing of priests (and perhaps choirs) at funerals and other celebrations of the mass. He was living through the last decade of official Catholicism in England, and it was a religious culture characterised by chanting clerks – of

[47] See above, pp. 275, 338.

whom he was one – and listening laypeople (though a small number of male parishioners sometimes helped to form the choir). All this changed after 1558, and we have already noted the curious deadpan astonishment with which Machyn described the first months of the new era. In several of London's parish churches, the singing was no longer performed by clerks from the chancel but by 'all the people' in the nave. It was, as we have heard, a practice that would spread steadily throughout the nation. Of all the changes that the Reformation brought to pass, this was one of the most remarkable. In England's churches, the combined forces of all parishioners now raised their voices to God, addressing him directly through music, without the musical mediation of the priesthood. From the perspective of many Christians, there was a great deal to regret in the changes associated with the Reformation, but this, it seems, was a winning development. To Machyn, it constituted a revolution; to Pepys, one hundred years on, it was an established practice. The post-Reformation clergy continued, of course, to play many important roles within the lives of the laity, but they no longer called the tune. Within the new musical relationship, it was not the minister but the parish clerk – himself selected from among the parishioners – who led the way, bridging the gap between clergy and laity as he had done for centuries. As so often, we find a stubborn survivor among the casualties.

Lastly, music helped Machyn and Pepys to think of themselves as Englishmen, though at times it also formed a channel of positive communication between people of different nations. During the 1550s, the music of Spaniards was heard regularly in London because of Mary's marriage to Philip. On 8 December 1554, it was the difference between one country's music and another's that caught Henry Machyn's attention. The Spaniards staged 'a goodly prossessyon' to mark the Feast of the Conception of the Blessed Virgin Mary. There were trumpets and sackbuts, but the chronicler reserved special mention for the man who 'cared [carried] ii drumes on ys backe', both of which were struck by the next participant in line. This perhaps seemed to him a distinctly continental custom.[48] Two months earlier, however, Machyn reported on the funeral in Westminster Abbey of a renowned Spaniard. Amid great ceremony, the deceased was laid to rest, 'with syngyng boyth Englys and Spaneards'.[49] Here, it was the symbolic coming-together of the two groups that occupied Machyn's mind. We cannot tell what impact these subtly contrasting experiences had upon his sense of nationality, but Henry clearly greeted the accession of Elizabeth I

[48] *Diary of Henry Machyn*, p. 78. [49] Ibid., p. 71.

in 1558 with considerable happiness. He felt a surge of patriotic pride when, on 5 December 1558, the new queen travelled by river to Somerset Place, 'with trumpetes playng, and melody and joye and comfortt to all truw Englys-men and women, and to all pepulle'.[50] For the cautious Machyn, this amounted to a spontaneous outburst of approval, and the warmth of his royalism overwhelmed the coolness with which he seems to have regarded the new religion.

A century later, Samuel Pepys experienced a similar mixture of emotions as he contrasted English music with that of other nations. There were still Spaniards in London, and on 8 July 1667 Samuel and his wife made their way home by boat 'in the cool of the evening ... , and sang with pleasure upon the water and were mightily pleased in hearing a boat full of spaniards sing'.[51] The two groups might have been like ships passing in the night, but music brought them momentarily together. In other instances too, Pepys found in music a means of exploring cultural differences that did not cause him to sound a note of nationalistic superiority. He sang French psalms with pleasure and, on one occasion, he befriended a German musician who played and praised his theorbo. Pepys hereby overcame or at least suspended the prejudice that had caused him, just a few days earlier, to describe the wife of another musician as 'a Germane lady but a very great beauty'.[52] Moreover, many of the ballad and dance tunes with which Pepys was familiar crossed backwards and forwards over the North Sea, sometimes acquiring new titles as they went. Thus it was that a trumpeter in the Dutch navy was able to taunt his English enemies with what they considered to be one of their own tunes.[53] At other times, music confronted Pepys with the differences in taste and style between the English and their neighbours. In May 1660, for example, he visited the Netherlands with the party that had been sent to collect Charles II and return him home. The trip occurred during a period of peace between the two nations, but even at such a time there was peculiar pleasure to be found in making English music abroad. One Thursday, Samuel and two compatriots met at a place called 'the Echo' in order to sing. It was all exceedingly pleasant, reported Pepys, 'the more because in a haven of pleasure and in a strange country'. By way of reinforcement, he added, 'I never was taken up more with a sense of pleasure in my life.' Back in London, Scottish music could also remind him forcefully of his Englishness. On 27 July 1666, he found himself eating supper in the house of

[50] Ibid., p. 180. [51] *Diary of Samuel Pepys*, vol. VIII, p. 325.
[52] Ibid., vol. III, pp. 99, 218, 228. [53] See above, p. 323.

Lord Lauderdale among a 'pretty odd company' of visiting Scots. One of them pulled out a violin and proceeded to play what the rest regarded as their nation's finest tunes. 'But Lord', commented Pepys, 'the strangest ayre that ever I heard in my life, and all of one cast.'[54]

Most striking of all was the diarist's reaction to the rampant fashion for French and Italian music that gripped the English court during the first decade of Charles II's reign. We might have expected that Pepys, a recent convert to royalism, would have jumped enthusiastically onto the bandwagon, but his response was a mixed one. At times, admittedly, he declared himself impressed by what he heard. His first encounter with the king's French-style band of twenty-four violinists was a positive one, and towards the end of the decade he was rather taken with the singing of a French eunuch.[55] More often, however, he expressed his doubts. Courtly French performers, visiting violinists and Italian singers at the Queen's Chapel all received lukewarm reviews (though the latter group was not, said Pepys, as bad as some of 'our people' maintained).[56] In an interesting series of entries, he felt his way towards the conclusion that English men and women were far better off with their own music than with that of aliens. 'I am convinced more and more', wrote Pepys on Easter Day in 1667,

> that as every nation hath a perticular accent and tone in discourse, so as the tone of one not to agree with or please the other, no more can the fashion of singing to words; for that the better the words are set, the more they take in of the ordinary tone of the country whose language the song speaks; so that a song well composed by an Englishman must be better to an Englishman then [than] it can be to a stranger.[57]

Interestingly, the argument was not that English music was superior, merely that it was better suited to the English. It was surely his unflagging interest in hearing music of all sorts that enabled him to hold this subtle opinion, and one suspects that many of 'our people' were rather more forthright in their reactions. Music, as ever, was both a barrier and a bridge.

To the people of early modern England, music was a rich source of recreation (the potent concept defined by one of Fetherston's characters as 'a making agayne of that thing which was once made' and 'a refreshing

[54] *Diary of Samuel Pepys*, vol. I, pp. 144–5, vol. VII, pp. 224–5.
[55] Ibid., vol. II, p. 86, vol. IX, pp. 327, 329. [56] Ibid., vol. VII, p. 99.
[57] Ibid., vol. VIII, p. 154 (see also pp. 55, 65, 384).

of that thing which is wearied with much laboure').[58] Musical sound contributed to an evolving sense of national identity but it also helped to recreate the many categories of community that lay like stepping stones between society and the self. Amid all the divisions associated with rank, gender, age, location and occupation, music played its paradoxical part both in the expression of distinction and in preventing the social disintegration that such expression sometimes threatened to cause. It helped to define cities, towns, villages, parishes and social groups based on occupation, temperamental affinity and family relationship. In all such cases, it bound insiders together and pushed outsiders away.

Different types of music recreated different sorts of community, though such collectivities overlapped and intersected at numerous points. In a typical parish, congregational psalmody linked the singers to their maker and drew them all together, excepting only those who absented themselves from divine service. Domestic psalmody, on the other hand, united households and in some circumstances served to distinguish committedly godly or musically literate families from the rest. The young men who rang the church bells formed another sub-set of the whole, united by their own distinctive music and by their rituals of belonging. Beyond the church, those who danced on the green or in the alehouse were again predominantly youthful, though in this case women were at least as prominent as men. Sometimes they claimed to represent the entire parish ('hey for our town'), but other residents might resist such incorporation. If the dancers indulged themselves when they should have been in church, then the group's relationship with the larger community of psalm-singers was potentially problematical. If they practised their art at other times, however, then the two communities might complement one another. Within the parish, those who could play instruments or sing with distinctive skill formed another group, tied together by a shared aptitude but also potentially stressed by the pressures of internal competition. Pepys referred to 'my musical friends', but they were bound as much by a kind of underlying creative tension as by their harmonious affinity.[59] Moreover, some instruments were courtly by repute while others were merely common. The borderline was regularly crossed, but it remains true that few bagpipers possessed viols. The culture of song was wider and more varied. Balladry had the potential to draw in men and women of all ages and ranks, though street composers also specialised in probing and satirising the many distinctions that set people apart. Home-made musical libels articulated

[58] See above, p. 360. [59] *Diary of Samuel Pepys*, vol. V, p. 349.

these distinctions even more crudely and sought to turn local society against some of its more controversial members. Only the zealously puritanical stood outside the culture of balladry during the seventeenth century, and even they were not entirely repulsed by the dishonour of the genre. Finally, the moral majority within any town or village could attempt to impose its will upon those who failed conspicuously in their duties by treating them with a dose of rough music. Inclusivity bred ostracism.

And beneath it all, individuals of all sorts made their way in the world to the accompaniment of music. The anxious practitioner Thomas Whythorne thought of his lute, virginals and voice as instruments 'whereby I might tell my tale ... as well as by word or writing'.[60] Music could bring solace in solitude but it also helped people with the complex task of setting themselves into society. Samuel Pepys was distinctive in providing us with such a wealth of information, but he was by no means alone in developing and articulating his social identity partly through the musical choices that he made. This was true both of those who adored music and of those who abhorred it. To Pepys, writing in 1666, music was 'the thing of the world that I love most, and all the pleasure almost that I now take'. By this date Solomon Eccles, another star of this book, had chosen a different path, rejecting virtually all outward melody, rhythm and harmony as wicked by definition. Both men, however, defined and expressed themselves with reference to music, and on one memorable occasion they momentarily shared the same physical space. Pepys watched on 29 July 1667 as Eccles walked through Westminster Hall, almost naked, 'with a chafing-dish of fire and brimstone burning upon his head'. It was an 'extraordinary' spectacle. Little did the diarist know that the man crying 'Repent! Repent!' was a former master of music.[61] And even if he had known, it is unlikely that Samuel would have followed Solomon's lead and laid down his instruments forever (Pepys was never in any serious danger of succumbing to scruple). Eccles, in contrast, had loved music but now professed to loathe it. He, like John Bunyan, had struggled to leave it behind once and for all because, as he later remarked with an almost Pepysian rush of feeling, 'my life was in it'.[62]

[60] *Autobiography of Thomas Whythorne*, p. 40.

[61] *Diary of Samuel Pepys*, vol. VII, p. 228, vol. VIII, p. 360.

[62] See above, p. 166.

Appendix: notes on the recordings

The website that accompanies this book (www.cambridge.org/musicandsociety) features new recordings by the Dufay Collective and invited guests:

Singers: John Potter, Simon Grant, Vivien Ellis and Clara Sanabras (all choruses and refrains were also sung by these performers and by other members of the Dufay Collective).

Instrumentalists: William Lyons (bagpipes, curtal, jew's harp, pipe and tabor); Peter Skuce (virginals, organ, percussion); Jacob Heringman (lute, cittern); Clare Salaman (violin); Nicholas Perry (shawm, cornett).

Bell-ringers: Romee Day, Christine Stratford, Pauline Dingley, Paul Norman, James Ingham.

Dancers: Pilar Subirà, Peter Skuce.

All arrangements are by William Lyons.

Recording and pronunciation supervisors: William Lyons, Peter Skuce.

Recording technician: Glenn Keiles.

Additional recording: Peter Skuce, William Lyons, Fernando Rosende.

Editing: Peter Skuce.

Additional editing: Fernando Rosende.

Mixing and mastering: Peter Skuce.

Produced by Peter Skuce and William Lyons.

Recorded at High View Studios, Pinner, Middlesex (March 2008), and on location.

Track 1: 'Rough music' in Burton-upon-Trent, 1618

See above, p. 47, and Figure 1.2. One of the early modern period's most distinctive forms of punishment. In this case, it was aimed at a young man and woman who were accused of sexual immorality. Drum, basins, candlesticks, spoons, voices.

Track 2: Town waits playing 'Kemp's jig', 1599

See above, p. 119, and Figure 3.1. The sound of the Norwich waits, playing in honour of the actor William Kemp after he danced all the way from London to their city. The tune can be found in *Complete*

Country Dance Tunes from Playford's Dancing Master, no. 49. Shawms, cornett.

Track 3: 'Almain' by Thomas Strengthfield (from Elizabeth Rogers's virginal book, *c.* 1656)

See above, p. 210. A courtly dance, composed for a wealthy young woman by a little-known virginalist, who may also have been her teacher. A full transcript can be found in *Elizabeth Rogers hir Virginall Booke*, no. 17. Solo virginals.

Track 4: 'Yes, I could Love' by Thomas Brewer (from the same source)

See above, p. 210. In this song, the female pupil imagines herself as a man and then muses on the characteristics of the perfect woman. See *Elizabeth Rogers hir Virginall Booke*, no. 104. Voice and virginals.

Yes, I could love; could I but find
a mistress fitting to my mind.
Whom neither pride nor gold could move,
to buy her beauty, sell her love;
were neat, yet cared not to be fine
and love me for myself, not mine.
Not lady proud nor 'quettey coy
but full of freedom, full of joy.

Not wise enough to rule a state,
Nor fool enough to be laughed at;
Not childish young nor beldame old;
Not fiery hot nor icy cold;
Not richly proud nor basely poor;
Not chaste, yet no reputed whore:
If such a one I chance to find,
I have a mistress for my mind.

Track 5: 'Troule the Bowle to me' (catch from Thomas Lant's roll, 1580)

See above, pp. 194–5, and Example A.1. A typical Elizabethan catch, guaranteed to stimulate musical and alcoholic camaraderie among any small group of men (references to women singing catches are rare). Unaccompanied voices.

Troule the bowle to me

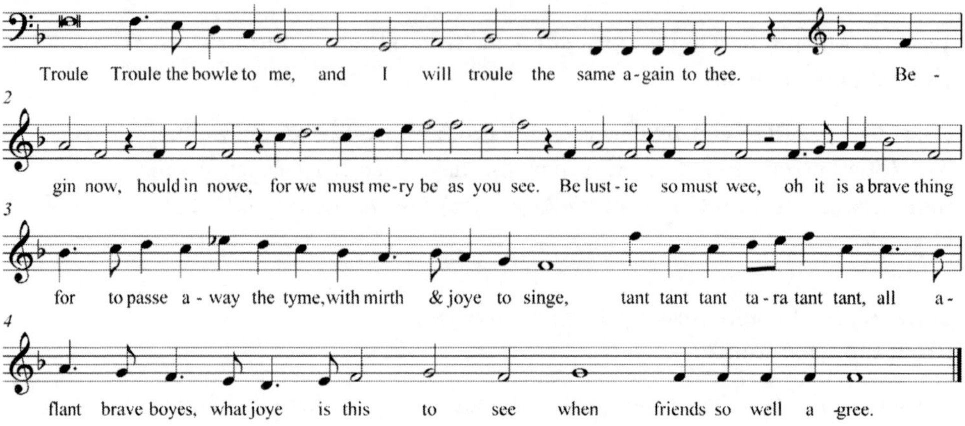
Troule Troule the bowle to me, and I will troule the same a-gain to thee. Be -
2
gin now, hould in nowe, for we must me-ry be as you see. Be lust-ie so must wee, oh it is a brave thing
3
for to passe a - way the tyme, with mirth & joye to singe, tant tant tant ta - ra tant tant, all a -
4
flant brave boyes, what joye is this to see when friends so well a -gree.

Example A.1. 'Troule the Bowle to me' (from Thomas Lant's roll of catches, 1580)

Track 6: 'Spanish pavan' in a setting by Francis Pilkington (from Richard Mynshall's lute book, late sixteenth century)

See above, pp. 209–10. Mynshall, the son of a Cheshire mercer, learned the lute by playing arrangements of well-known tunes. The music can be found in *The Mynshall Lute Book*, ed. Spencer, fo. 5r. Solo lute.

Track 7: 'Fortune' in a setting by John Dowland (from the same source)

See above, pp. 209–10. One of the period's most famous tunes as arranged by one of its most famous musicians. For the music, see *The Mynshall Lute Book*, fo. 9v. Solo lute.

Track 8: 'Let Mary live long' (from Henry Atkinson's violin book, 1695)

See above, p. 213. A royalist ballad tune that may also have had personal significance for the Newcastle coal merchant who wrote it out in his notebook (see above, p. 54). From 'Henry Atkinson his Book', pp. 6–7. Solo violin.

Track 9: 'Farinells ground' (from the same source)

See above, p. 213. A set of divisions upon a famous ground bass, almost certainly transcribed from a printed source. From 'Henry Atkinson his Book', pp. 42–5. Solo violin.

The farther be in the welcomer

Example A.2. 'The farther be in the welcomer' (from Henry Atkinson's violin book, 1695)

Track 10: 'The farther be in the welcomer' (from the same source)

See above, p. 213, and Example A.2. One of Atkinson's more rustic melodies, probably of Northumbrian or Scottish origins. From 'Henry Atkinson his book', pp. 77–8 (we have adjusted some of the note values in an attempt to correct Henry's errors). Solo violin.

Track 11: Excerpt from 'A Carol for Innocents Day' to the tune of 'As at noon Dulcina rested' (from *Good and True, Fresh and New*, London, 1642)

See above, p. 196, and Example A.3. Carols of this type may have been 'new', but most of them were highly traditional in subject matter and tone. Our version of the tune is taken from Simpson, *British Broadside Ballad*, p. 202. Unaccompanied voices.

This was the day when cruell Herod
heard that Jesus Christ was borne
(A King, a Saviour and a Prophet)
in his land did thinke it scorne;
Command did give
He shuld not live,

Dulcina

Example A.3. 'Dulcina' or 'As at noon Dulcina rested' (from Simpson, *British Broadside Ballad*, p. 202)

And more his malice to unfold,
Streight charge did give,
No male should live
The which were under two yeares old.

Now what great terrour 'twas to Mothers
Children sucking at their brest
Bloody villaines with their Poniards,
From their Mothers nipple wrest,
In peeces there
They did them teare,
And with their Swords they did them hew
As 'tis exprest,
Among the rest,
King Herods young son had his due.

Track 12: Excerpt from 'A merry caroll for the same day' to the tune of 'The Spanish pavan' (from the same source)

See above, p. 196. This song, in contrast to the previous one, celebrates the social dimensions of the festive season. For the tune, see Simpson, *British Broadside Ballad*, p. 679 (we have modified it slightly in order to accommodate the words). Unaccompanied voices.

Cast care away, tis Holyday,
This is no time to worke, but play,
With this good cheere I'll make a fray,
and meane to fill my belly;

And quickly for to end the strife,
I with my spoone and with my knife,
Doe meane to keepe a heavy life;
I tell ye [I tell ye].

And now my Friends and Neighbours all,
Your cheere and beere it is not small,
And boldly to your victuals fall,
by leave I give you warning;
I now will drinke a full carouse
Unto the Owners of this house,
And for our foes care not a Louse
nor farthing [nor farthing].

Track 13: *Kepe the Widow Waking* to the tune of 'The blazing torch' (transcribed in Star Chamber records, 1624–5)

See above, p. 265, and Example A.4. A libellous ballad of the early 1620s, allegedly sung in the street to humiliate a wealthy widow who had been drugged and tricked into marriage. Our tune is a simplified version of the one that appears in *Anne Cromwell's Virginal Book, 1638*, ed. Howard Ferguson (Oxford: Oxford University Press, 1974), p. 36. Unaccompanied voices.

Yow yong men whoe would marrye well,
but are through want restrain'd,
Come list to that which I shall tell,
of one who wealth obtayn'd,
by wedding of a widow rich
all poore yong girles forsakeing,
he got this prize his hap was such,
to keepe the widow wakeing.

This yong man who thus lived by fame,
when he heard all this doeing,
A gallant state he did assume
And to her went a wooing.
Thought he, 'if I can gett this prize,
Twill suerly be my making'
Then he this Crochet did devise,
to keepe the widow wakeing.

The blazing torch

Example A.4. 'The blazing torch' (from *Anne Cromwell's Virginal Book*, p. 36)

Nowe they that rightlie would conceive,
the meaning of this phrase,
Marke what ensues, & then perceive,
The sequell all bewrayes,
The widow being plyed with wyne,
Untill her braynes were akeing,
She married was in such a vaine,
Twas hard to keepe her wakeing.

Thus sometimes that haps in an houre,
that comes not in seaven yeare,
therefore lett yong men that are poore,
come take example here,
And you whoe faine would heare the full
discourse of this match-making,
The play will teach you at the Bull,
to keepe the widdow wakeing.

Track 14: 'Weep, Weep' (a Catholic lament, 1594)

See above, p. 261, and Example A.5. An anti-Protestant song that exists only in manuscript. The composer re-worked a popular tune ('Sick, sick') in order to express his distaste for the Reformation. The tune can be found in Simpson, *British Broadside Ballad*, p. 661. Voice and cittern.

Weep, weepe, and still I weepe,
For who can chuse but weepe,
to thinke howe England styll in synne,
and heresy doth sleepe.

Sick, sick

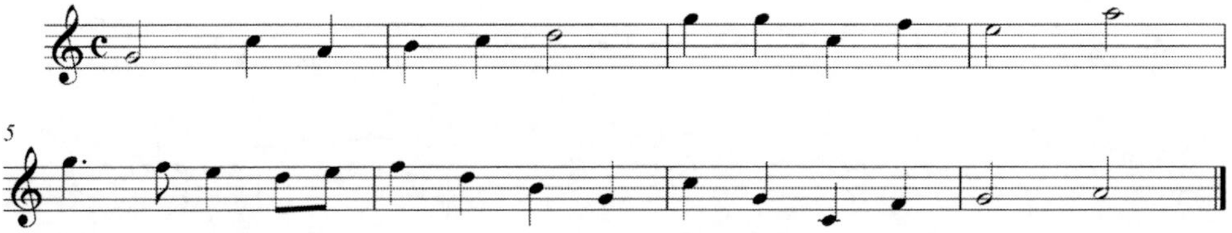

Example A.5. 'Sick, sick' (from Simpson, *British Broadside Ballad*, p. 661)

The Christian faythe and Catholick,
is every where detested,
the holy service, and such like,
of all degrees neglected.

The Churches gaye defaced be,
our altars are throwne downe,
the walls lefte bare, a greefe to see,
that once coste maney a Crowne.

The monuments and lefe of saints,
are brent and torn by violence,
some shed the holy sacraments,
O Christe thy wondrous pacyence.

Track 15: Excerpt from *Rocke the Babie Joane* to the tune of 'Under and over' (1632)

See above, pp. 279–81, Example A.6 and Figure 5.5. An infectious ballad in which John and Joan attempt to resolve their marital difficulties (we have situated the performers in a crowded alehouse). Our tune is based on the version in *Complete Country Dance Tunes from Playford's Dancing Master*, no. 112. Voices and cittern.

A Young man in our Parish,
His wife was somewhat currish,
For she refus'd to nourish
a child which he brought home:
He got it on an other,
And death had tane the mother,
The truth he could not smother,
all out at last did come:

Under and over

Example A.6. 'Under and over' (from *Complete Country Dance Tunes from Playford's Dancing Master*, no. 112)

'[O] Suckle the Baby,
huggle the baby,
Rocke the Baby Jone.'
'I scorne to suckle the Baby,
Unlesse it were mine owne.'

Quoth he, 'My Joan, my dearest,
Thy love to me is neerest,
Thy vertue will shine clearest,
in doing this good deed:
This infant young is left here,
Unable to make shift here,
Twill be of life bereft heere,
Unless thou doe it feed.
[O] Suckle the Baby,
huggle the baby,
Rocke the Baby Jone.'
'I scorne to suckle the Baby,
Unlesse it were mine owne.'

'Away thou false Deceiver',
Quoth she, 'Farewell for ever,

I am resolved never
To love thee as I did'.
'Alas', quoth he, 'my honey,
I would not for any money,
By thee my sweetest conny,
to be so shrewdly chid.
[O] Suckle the Baby,
huggle the baby,
Rocke the Baby Jone.'
'I scorne to suckle the Baby,
Unlesse it were mine owne.'

Let patient Grissels storie,
Be still in thy memorie,
Who wonne a lasting glory,
through patience in like sort:
Although it touch thee neerely,
This Barne that lookes so cheerely,
Shall binde me still more deerely,
to love thee better for't.
[O] Suckle the Baby,
huggle the baby,
Rocke the Baby Jone.'
'I scorne to suckle the Baby,
Unlesse it were mine owne.'

'Well John thy intercession,
Hath chang'd my disposition,
And now upon condition
thou'lt goe no more astray:
I'll entertaine thy Baby,
And love it as well as may be.'
'Doe so (sweet Jugge) I pray thee,
Then this is a joyfull day.'
'We'll suckle the Baby,
And huggle the Baby.'
'Gramercy honest Joan.'
'O John I'll rocke thy Baby,
As well as 'twere mine owne.'

Welladay

Example A.7. 'Welladay' (based on Simpson, *British Broadside Ballad*, p. 747)

Track 16: Excerpt from *A Lamentable Dittie Composed upon the Death of Robert Lord Devereux* to the tune of 'Welladay' (1601)

The text is quoted and discussed above, on pp. 293–5. For the tune see Example A.7. A controversial song that expressed profound sadness at the execution of the Earl of Essex in 1601. On this recording, we have imagined a poor ballad-singer who uses a thoroughly modal version of the tune (based on Simpson, *British Broadside Ballad*, p. 747). Unaccompanied voice.

Sweet England's pride is gone,
welladay, welladay,
Which makes her sigh and groan,
evermore still;
He did her fame advance,
In Ireland, Spain and France,
And by a sad misschance,
is from us tane.

Track 17: Excerpt from *An Excellent Song wherein you shall Finde Great Consolation for a Troubled Mind* to the tune of 'Fortune my foe' (1656)

See above, p. 295. An influential piece of musical moralising, sung by a ballad-seller in a marketplace. Our version of the famously sober tune is based on the one that appears in Simpson, *British Broadside Ballad*, p. 227 (see above, Example 5.2, p. 237). Unaccompanied voice.

Ayme not too hie in things above thy reach,
Be not too foolish in thine own conceit,

As thou hast wit and worldly wealth at will,
So give him thankes that shall encrease it still.

Beware of pride, the Mother of mishap,
Whose sugred snares shall seek thee to intrap,
Be meek in Heart, and lowly minded still,
So shalt thou Gods Comandements fulfill.

Cast all thy care upon the Lord, and he,
In thy distress will send to succour thee,
Cease not therefore to serve him every day,
Who with his blood thy ransom once did pay.

Track 18: Excerpt from *Miraculous Newes from the Cittie of Holdt in Germany* to the tune of 'The lady's fall' (1616 or later)

See above, pp. 296–7. A dismal text sung to a surprisingly cheerful melody by a ballad-seller in the street. For the tune, see Simpson, *British Broadside Ballad*, p. 368. Voice and cittern.

The dreadfull day of doome drawes neere:
oh mortal man, repent;
For all the world is full of sinne,
and unto mischiefe bent.
The lord hath shewed his anger late
by lightning and in Thunder,
With many other fearfull threats
of terror and great wonder.

As late, at Holdt in Germany,
the heavens all burning bright
Appeared, full five houres and more,
there in a fiery light.
At length the people unto Church
did generally repaire,
Intending there unto the lord
to sacrifice in prayer.

But in the churchyard, as they went,
the graves did open wide,
From whence rose up three ghostly shapes
Which long before had dyed.

Whereof the first was seene to be
from flesh consumed quite,
Yet of a humane shape to see,
most semly cleere and white:

Quoth he, 'Repent, with speede,
you Nations on the earth;
For God intends to plague you all
with pestilence and death.'
[And], in that cittye, at this day,
so great a plague is seene,
That like not in the world (I thinke)
Before hath ever beene.

To which most kinde and gracious god
Let us our prayers make
That all such threatning woes he may
from this our countrey take,
That we may never feele the wrath
which hee on other layes,
But still to walke, like christians true,
uprightly in his wayes.

Track 19: Excerpt from *A Merry New Catch of All Trades* to the tune of 'The cleane contrary way' (*c.* 1620)

See above, pp. 297–9. At one level, this distinctive round merely presents a pithy list of occupations, but is there rude humour between the lines? Our tune is a slightly modified version of the melody in Simpson, *British Broadside Ballad*, p. 109. Unaccompanied voices.

All Trades are not alike in show,
All Arts do not agree:
All Occupations gaines are small,
As heer they all shall see.
The Bricklayer high doth rise to flye,
The Plummer oft doth melt,
The Carpenter doth love his rule,
And the Hatmaker loves his felt.

The weaver thumps, his olde wife mumps,
The Barber goes snip snap,

The Butcher prickes, the Tapster nickes,
The Farmer stops a gap.
The Grosers pates 'bout thinges of weight,
Is often troubled sore,
The Taylor's yard is seldome marde,
Tho it measure many a score.

Dissentions seede, the Parators neede,
And Scoulds him money give:
And if there were no swaggering Whore,
The Pander could not live.
Thus all arise by contraries,
Heaven send them crosses ten:
Unlesse they all both great and small,
Doe live and dye honest men.'

Track 20: Excerpt from *The Godly End, and Wofull Lamentation of one John Stevens* to the tune of 'Fortune' (1632 or later)

See above, pp. 300–1. One of the many 'dying speech' ballads that were issued in the period. On this recording, we have imagined our singer in a crowded marketplace, competing for attention with a variety of hawkers (street traders were famous for their musical advertising cries). For the tune, see above, track 17, and Example 5.2, p. 237. Unaccompanied voices.

Give ear, give ear! Come buy a new ballad! 'Twill cost a penny alone! Proper to be stuck up in all righteous households! 'Tis The godly end, and wofull lamentation of one John Stevens, a youth, that was hang'd, drawne, and quartered for High Treason at Salisbury in Wiltshire, upon Thursday being the seventh day of March last 1632.

Now like the Swan before my death I sing,
And like the Raven heavy newes I bring,
Oh dismall fate, and cruell destiny,
Which brought me here in this same sort to die.

To God above I doe for mercy crie,
Tis for High-Treason that I here must die,
Drawne, hang'd & quarterd, this is now my doome,
My body must have neither grave nor tombe.

My members, and my Bowels forth be cut,
And in a flaming fire they should be put,

There to consume and unto ashes turne,
As wicked members there they then must burne.

My body must in quarters eke be cut,
And on the City gates they should be put,
To be a sight for others to take heed,
Where ravenous Fowles upon my flesh will feed.

But now, O Lord, for mercy I intreat,
Thou canst forgive although my sinnes are greate,
Lord make me cleane, & make me cleare as glasse,
And then the Snow I shall in whitenes passe.

Vaine world farewell, I am prepar'd to die,
My Soule I hope, shall straight ascend the skie,
I come, Lord Jesus, now I come to thee,
To thee one God, yet holy Trinitie.

Track 21: Excerpt from *The Successful Commander* to the tune of 'Let Caesar live long' (1696)

See above, p. 303. Ballad-writers sometimes specified a choice of tunes for their songs. In this case, the first possibility was a highly patriotic melody (see Simpson, *British Broadside Ballad*, p. 435). Unaccompanied voice.

You true-hearted Protestants pray now attend,
Here's joyful good tydings from Flanders we send,
The Earl of Athlone a brave project hath plaid,
By which the poor French-men are clearly dismay'd,
For joy that the Plot was discover'd and crost,
We made a Burn-fire, Boys, at their own cost.

So soon as we heard of that horrible thing,
Which had been contriv'd against William our King;
The noble Commanders was all in a rage,
And strait they resolved Monsieur to engage;
For joy that the Plot was discover'd and crost,
We made a Burn-fire, Boys, at the French cost.

Track 22: Excerpt from *The Successful Commander* to the tune of 'If love's a sweet passion' (1696)

See above, pp. 303–4. Here, the same text is set to a tune with sad and romantic associations (Simpson, *British Broadside Ballad*, p. 360). Unaccompanied voice.

Track 23: Excerpt from *The King Enjoyes his Own Again ... To be joyfully sung to its own proper tune* (*c.* 1644)

See above, pp. 305–6. Perhaps the most famous political song of the early modern period: an anthem by Martin Parker that is said to have accompanied the Restoration of Charles II in 1660. For the tune, see Simpson, *British Broadside Ballad*, p. 766. Voice and virginals.

What Booker can Prognosticat,
or speak of our Kingdoms present state;
I think my self to be as wise,
as he that most looks in the skies:
My skill goes beyond the depths of the Pond,
Or River in the greatest Rain:
By the which I can tell, that all things will be well,
when the King comes home in peace again.

There is no Astrologer, then I say,
can search more deep in this then [than] I,
To give you a reason from the Stars,
what causeth peace, or civil Wars:
The man in the Moon, may wear out his shoone,
In running after Charles his Wain,
But all to no end, for the times they will mend
when the King comes home in peace again.

Till then upon Ararats hill,
my hope shal cast her Anchor still,
Until I see some peaceful Dove,
bring home the branch which I do love;
Still will I wait till the waters abate,
which most disturbs my troubled brain,
For Ile never rejoyce, till I hear that voice,
that the King comes home in peace again.

Church Government shall setled be,
and then I hope we shal agree,
Without their help whose high-brain zeal
have long disturbd our Common-well:
Greed out of date, and Coblers that do prate,
of Wars that still disturb'd their brain,
The which you shall see when the time it shalbe
that the King comes home in peace again.

When all these things to pass shall come,
then farewell Musket, Pick and drum,
The Lamb shal with the Lyon feed,
which were a happy time indeed;
O let us all pray, we may see the day,
that peace may govern in his name,
For then I can tell all things will be well,
when the King comes home in peace again.

Track 24: Excerpt from *[A] Dialogue betwixt Tom and Dick* to the tune of 'I'll never love thee more' (performed at the Drapers' Hall, London, 1660)

See above, pp. 308–9. Another song of the Restoration, but in this case the romantic associations of the tune contribute an added layer of meaning. This piece was performed before General Monck and the Council of State on a formal occasion in 1660, and it therefore seems fitting to imagine a more elaborate instrumental accompaniment than was normal for a ballad performance. For the tune, see *Complete Country Dance Tunes from Playford's Dancing Master*, no. 251. Voices, virginals, violins, curtals.

TOM: Now would I give my life to see,
  This wondrous Man of might,
DICK: Dost see that Jolly Lad? That's he,
  I'le warrant him he's right,
  There's a true Trojan in his Face:
  Observe him o're and o're.
CHORUS: Come Tom, If ever GEORGE be base,
  Ne're trust Good-fellow more.
DICK: Shall's ask him what he means to do?
TOM: Good faith, with all my heart;
  Thou mak'st the better Leg o'th'Two:

Take thou the better part.
I'll follow, if thou't lead the Van.
DICK: Content – I'll march before.
BOTH: If GEORGE prove not a Gallant man,
Ne're trust Good-fellow more.
DICK: My Lord:- in us the Nation craves
But what you're bound to do.
TOM: We have liv'd Drudges: RIC: And we Slaves
BOTH: We would not die so too.
Restore us but our Laws agen;
Th'unborn shall thee adore:
If GEORGE denies us his Amen,
CHORUS: Ne're trust Good-fellow more.

Track 25: Excerpt from *Two Pleasant Ditties, One of . . . the Passion of Christ* to the tune of 'Dulcina' (*c.* 1585–1616)

See above, p. 310. An individual tune might be pulled in different directions by successive texts. Here, 'Dulcina' is full of righteous purpose (for the tune, see above, track 11, and Example A.3). Voice and cittern.

Turne your eyes, that are affixed
on this world's deceavinge things;
And, with joy and sorrow mixed,
Looke upon the kinge of kings,
Who left his throne, with joyes unknowne;
Tooke flesh like ours; like as [us?] drew breath,
For us to dy: heere fixe your eye,
And thinke upon his precious death!

Track 26: Excerpt from *A Proverbe Old, yet Nere Forgot* to the tune of 'Dulcina' (*c.* 1625)

See above, p. 311, and Example A.3. This ballad, by Martin Parker, may well have been written with the previous example in mind. In this case, however, the melody is hijacked and forced into the alehouse and a new world of scurrility. Voice and cittern.

Doe not dote on Maydens features,
Widows are the only ware,
It is many Young-mens natures
To love Maydens young and fayre,

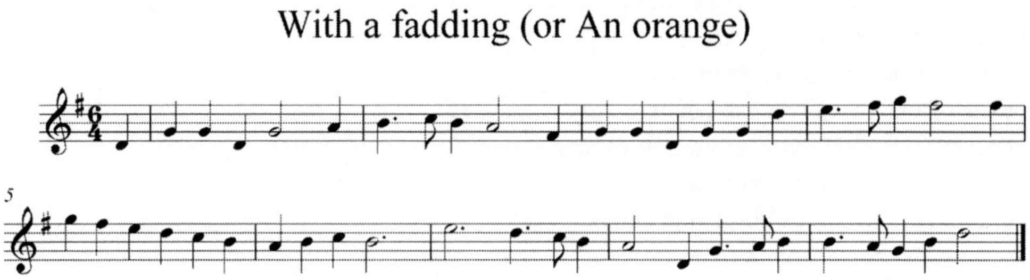

Example A.8. 'With a fadding' (from Simpson, *British Broadside Ballad*, p. 793)

tis Cupids wile
thus to beguile
Young Lovers, therefore trust him not,
get one with Gold,
though nere so old,
Tis good to strike while the Irons hott.

Track 27: Excerpt from *The Merry Forrester* to the tune of 'With a fadding' (*c.* 1635)

See above, p. 311, and Example A.8. Ballad-singers sometimes worked with uninspiring texts, but luckily the tune in this case carried an additional weight of bawdiness through its associations (it was to have an interesting career in subsequent decades). We have used a modified version of the melody in Simpson, *British Broadside Ballad*, p. 793. Unaccompanied voice.

The neat and handsome Servingman
a clownish mind he scornes to carry,
His master dead, his mistris then,
gives her consent with him to marry
for kissing.

I know no Country Gentleman,
that hath but any fashion or breeding,
But he will endeavour or doe what he can,
to have a smug Lasse thats of his own feeding,
for kissing.

The aged man of three score yeeres,
oft takes to wife a girle of twenty,

The cause whereof you may suppose,
which makes him take this girle so dainty,
is kissing.

Track 28: Excerpt from *The Famous Orange* to the tune of 'The pudding' (1689)

See above, p. 312, and Figure 6.2. One of a number of ballads in which the tune heard on the previous track (see Example A.8) came to play an active part in the street politics of the late 1680s. Unaccompanied voice.

There's none can express,
Your great Happiness,
The like was ne're seen since the Days of Queen Bess,
A Nation enslav'd,
And Justice outbrav'd,
To be thus redeemed, and gallantly sav'd,
By an Orange.

When you have got Power,
O do not devour,
Your Brethren (as formerly) every hour:
But let's all agree,
To give liberty,
And bless God Almighty, for setting us free,
By an Orange.

Track 29: Excerpt from 'Thomas you Cannot' to a new tune (early seventeenth century)

See above, pp. 316–17. This ribald ballad is known only because of its partial preservation in the Percy Folio MS in the British Library. We have placed it in an alehouse. For the tune, see Simpson, *British Broadside Ballad*, p. 704. Unaccompanied voice.

Thomas untied his points apace,
& kindly he beseeches,
that shee wold give him time & space,
for to untye his breeches.
'Content, Content, Content!' shee cryes.
He down with his breeches imedyatlye,
& over her belly he cast his thye,

But then shee cryes 'Thomas! You cannot, you cannot!
O Thomas, O Thomas, you cannot!'

This maid was discontented in mind,
& angry with Thomas,
that he the time soe long had space,
& cold nott performe his promise.
he promised her a thing, 2 handfull att least,
which made this maid glad of such a Feast:
but shee Cold not gett an Inch for a tast,
which made her cry [Thomas, you cannot, you cannot,
O Thomas, O Thomas, you Cannott!]

Track 30: Excerpt from *A New-yeeres-gift for the Pope* to the tune of 'Thomas you cannot' (*c.* 1624)

See above, p. 315, and Figure 6.3. In this song of the mid-1620s, the tune heard on track 29 was applied to a very different text but its prior associations surely remained potent. Unaccompanied voice.

All you that desirous are to behold
the difference twixt falshood and faith,
Marke well this Emblem, one piece of pure gold,
a Cart-load of false Coyne outwayeth,
Then wisely consider and beare in your mind,
Though Sathans Instruments true faith to blind,
A thousand devises dayly doe find:
Yet all is in vaine, they cannot, they cannot,
Yet all is in vaine they cannot.

The difference 'twixt Papist and Protestant here,
[you'll hear] in a moment debated,
The one loves the Gospell that shineth still cleare,
the other is more subtile-pated,
He will not be ruled by the Scripture's large scope,
But trusts in Traditions deriv'd from the Pope,
By which to be sav'd he doth constantly hope:
Fond fooles y'are deceived, you cannot, [you cannot,
Fond fooles y'are deceived, you cannot].

Track 31: Excerpt from *My Dog and I* to the tune of 'Bobbing Joan' (1675)

See above, pp. 318–19, and Figure 6.4. Once again, the chosen tune brings its own crucial associations to bear on the text (an alehouse seems the natural location). Our version comes from *Complete Country Dance Tunes from Playford's Dancing Master*, no. 10. Unaccompanied voices.

You that are of the merry Throng,
Give good attention to my Song,
Ile give you weighty reasons why,
'Tis made upon my Dog and I,
My Dog and I, my Dog and I,
'Tis made upon my Dog and I.

I lov'd a maid her name was Nell,
A bonny Lass, I lov'd her well,
If you'd needs know the reason why,
Because she lov'd my Dog and I.
[my Dog and I, my Dog and I,
'Tis made upon my Dog and I].

If Women are in a distress,
By reason of their Barrenness,
I can a proper Probe apply,
Best known unto my Dog and I
[My Dog and I, my Dog and I,
'Tis made upon my Dog and I].

Thus have we liv'd thus have we lov'd
and faithful to each other prov'd,
Whilst many thieves are hang'd on high,
No Law can touch my Dog and I,
[My Dog and I, my Dog and I,
'Tis made upon my Dog and I].

If death do come as it may hap,
My grave shall be under the Tap,
With folded arms there we will lie,
Cheek by Jowl my Dog and I
[My Dog and I, my Dog and I,
'Tis made upon my Dog and I].

Track 32: Verses to the tune of 'Jamey' (transcribed in a Star Chamber court case, 1607)

See above, p. 325. This mocking song was sung in public by Richard Rotton, a Worcestershire weaver whose supposed sweetheart Nan had just married Richard Nightingale, much to his annoyance. Our version of the tune is based on no. 105 in *Complete Country Dance Tunes from Playford's Dancing Master* (where it is called 'Woodycock'). Voice and fiddle.

There is a maid of Moseley towne
her leggs be short she will soone be downe
for she went on a time to Hoselwall
that there she chauncte [chanced] to catch a fall.
Yf you will know who this same maide should be
forsooth it is Nan Ballamie
Her busines was to the mill as I did heare
with a batch for to make her woers [wooer's] good cheare.

But marke you well what I shall say
before this mayden came away
the miller gott her a topp of the baggs
but his breeches fell down about his legges,
though how it fell out I cannot tell,
but the miller sayd he used her well.
But sure I thinke he dealt unkind
For she with him great faulte did finde.

There was a woer that came from Tole Inn
Which the milner cared not for a pinne
Did seeme to be grieved in his mind
& told the milner he dealt unkind.
'Oh I pray', said the milner, 'be content,
for no harme unto the[e] was meant.'
'But if thou seemed to be grieved in mind
Thou mayest turn the buckell of thy girdell behind.

An[d] in good faith I for myself
would scorne to be beaten by such an elf,
and I think the worst that was here in place,
would be ashamed to looke your worship in the face.'
Nightingale seeing the milner cared not for him
thought good to lett him alone & not beate him

The Winchester wedding

Example A.9. 'The king's jig' (from *Complete Country Dance Tunes from Playford's Dancing Master*, no. 229)

saying milner to beate thee I am very lothe
bycause thou tellest me the very troth.

Track 33: Excerpt from *The Winchester Wedding* to the tune of 'The king's jig' (*c.* 1682)

See above, p. 343, Figures 7.4 and 7.5 and Example A.9. A typical example of a seventeenth-century dance ballad. On this recording, the vocalist delivers the lines in a style that is 'betwixt speaking and singing' while the fiddle plays a more precise version of the tune. Together, they animate the dancers. For the melody, see *Complete Country Dance Tunes from Playford's Dancing Master*, no. 229. Voice and fiddle.

At Winchester was a wedding,
the like was never seen,
'Twixt lusty Ralph of Reading,
and bonny black Bess of the Green;
The Fidlers were crowding before,
each Lass was as fine as a Queen
There was an hundred and more,
for all the whole Countrey came in;
Brisk Robin led Rose so fair,
she look'd like a Lilly o'th vale,
And Ruddy fac'd Harry led Mary,
and Roger led bouncing Nell.

And now they had din'd, advancing
into the midst of the Hall,
The Fidlers struck up for dancing,
and Jeremy led up the brawl;

But Margery kept a quarter,
a Lass that was proud of her pelf,
'Cause Arthur had stolen her Garter,
and swore he would tye it himself:
She strugled, she blusht, and frown'd,
and ready with anger to cry,
'Cause Arthur with tying her Garter,
had slipt up his hand too high.

Poor Stephen was kind to Betty,
as blith as a Bird in the Spring,
And Tommy was so to Katy,
and wedded her with a rush Ring;
Sukey that danc'd with the Cushion,
An hour from the room had been gone,
And Barnaby knew by her blushing,
that some other Dance had been done:
And thus of fifty fair Maids,
that went to the Wedding with men,
Scarce five of the fifty was left ye,
That so did return agen.

There twenty great bellys were gotten
all on one Wedding night,
Which will not in hast be forgotten,
the Damosels found such delight,
But Roger and bouncing Nelly,
that happen'd to be in their prime,
If you will believe what I tell ye,
did get two Twins at a time:
But Christopher was somewhat feeble,
and could do no feats at all,
So all of them laught at him stoutly,
and did him a fumbler call.

You youngsters that go to a Wedding,
to your Lasses be loving and kind,
And tumble them well on the Bedding,
for it is pleasing to their mind,
It grieves them to see that another,
enjoys what themselves is deny'd,

Tho' they their passion do smother,
in their hearts they are terrify'd;
And will steal a good turn if they can,
so earnest they are in desire,
No Treasure is like a Young Man,
to extinguish their amorous fire.

Tracks 34–40: medley of dance tunes

See above, pp. 340–2. Seven of the period's most successful dance melodies, performed as a set. The tunes can all be found in *Complete Country Dance Tunes from Playford's Dancing Master*, unless otherwise indicated.

34: 'Greensleeves' (fiddles, cittern)
35: 'Selenger's round' (fiddles, jew's harp, cittern, pipe and tabor; the Playford tune is here preceded by a simpler, earlier version transcribed in Simpson, *British Broadside Ballad*, p. 644)
36: 'Dull Sir John' (fiddles, cittern)
37: 'Maiden Lane' (bagpipe, cittern, jew's harp)
38: 'Scotch cap' (fiddles, cittern)
39: 'Boatman' (fiddles, cittern)
40: 'Cuckolds all a row' (pipe and tabor, fiddles, cittern, jew's harp; on this tune, see also above, p. 384)

Track 41: 'Stanes morris' (from Playford's *Dancing Master*)

See above, p. 347 (also p. 387). Playford chose the tune for a country dance but the title implies a possible connection with the morris. Our arrangement draws inspiration from the famous painting *The Thames at Richmond* (see Figure 7.8). The melody can be found in *Complete Country Dance Tunes from Playford's Dancing Master*, no. 97. Pipe and tabor, morris bells.

Track 42: 'Maid's morris' (from Playford's *Dancing master*)

See above, p. 347 (also p. 387). Morris dancing was a predominantly masculine pursuit, but the active involvement of women was not unknown. The tune is in *Complete Country Dance Tunes from Playford's Dancing Master*, no. 304. Bagpipe, drum, morris bells.

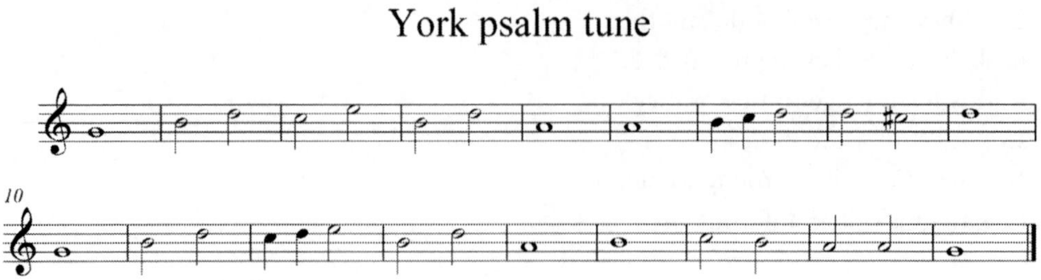

Example A.10. 'York' psalm tune (from *Anne Cromwell's Virginal Book*, p. 2)

Track 43: 'York' psalm tune (played on the organ in the church of St Botolph without Aldgate, London)

See above, p. 423 (also p. 404), Example A.10 and Figure 8.1. This rendition of the melody is based on the keyboard arrangement in *Anne Cromwell's Virginal Book*, p. 2. Solo organ.

Track 44: Four-part setting of Psalm 119 (from Ravenscroft, *Whole Book of Psalms*, 1621)

See above, p. 437, and Example A.11. Here, we imagine Samuel Pepys and friends singing from Ravenscroft's book on 27 November 1664. The Sternhold–Hopkins tune for Psalm 119 was one of the most successful of the official tunes. In this setting by Giles Farnaby, it can be heard in the tenor part. For the full score, see Ravenscroft, *Whole Book of Psalms*, pp. 206–7. Unaccompanied voices.

Blessed are they that perfect are
And pure in minde and heart
Whose lives and conversation
From God's laws never start.
Blessed are they that give themselves,
His statutes to observe:
Seeing the Lord with all their heart,
And never from him swerve.

Oh would to God it might thee please
My wayes so to addresse:
That I might both in heart and voyce,
Thy lawes keepe and confesse.
So should no shame my life attaine,
Whil'st I thus set mine eies:
And bend my minde alwayes to muse
On thy sacred decrees.

Tune for Psalm 119

Example A.11. The tune for Psalm 119 (tenor part, from Ravenscroft, *Whole Book of Psalms*, pp. 206–7)

Low Dutch psalm tune

Example A.12. The 'Low Dutch' psalm tune (based on Playford, *An Introduction*, p. 78)

Track 45: Congregational rendition of Psalm 29 to the 'Low Dutch' tune

See above, p. 440, and Example A.12. This psalm was sung once a year at Dersingham (Norfolk) during the late seventeenth century to mark the anniversary of a terrible flood. The 'Low Dutch' tune was recommended for this text by Richard Allison in 1599. Our version is based on the one that appears in Playford, *An Introduction*, p. 78, though we have rendered all the note values equal in accordance with congregational practice. We have also employed the 'lining out' technique by which the parish clerk informed the congregation of the words that they were about to sing (see above, pp. 427–30). Unaccompanied voices.

Parish clerk: 'Let us sing to the praise and glory of God the twenty-ninth psalm'

Example A.13. The 'Cambridge' psalm tune (based on Playford, *An Introduction*, p. 76)

His voice doth rule the warters all
Even as him selfe doth please
He doth prepare the thunder claps
And governe all the seas.

The lord was set above the floud
Ruling the rageing sea
So shall he raigne as lord & kinge
For ever and for aye.

The lord will give his people pouer
In vertue to increase
The lord will blesse his chosen flocke
With everlasting peace.

Track 46: Psalm 12 as sung by sailors in peril, 1593, to the 'Cambridge' tune

See above, p. 436, and Example A.13. The 'Cambridge' tune was recommended for the singing of this psalm in Playford, *An Introduction*, p. 76. Our version is based on the tune that appears at the same location. We have chosen not to sharpen the leading notes, though it is impossible to know whether this reflects common practice or not. We have also assumed that adrenalin would have quickened the pace of performance! Unaccompanied voices.

Helpe, Lord, for good and godly men
do perish and decay:
And fayth and trueth from worldly men
Is parted cleane away.

Who so doth with his neighbours talk,
His talke is all but vaine:
For every man bethinketh how
to flatter, lye and fain.

Track 47: 'The twenty all over' (from *Tintinnalogia*)

See above, pp. 502–4, and Figure 9.2. Our recording features the ringers and the sixteenth-century bells of St Bartholomew the Great, Smithfield.

Track 48: 'Plain bob minimus' (from *Tintinnalogia*)

See above, pp. 463–4. On this recording, the ringers of St Bartholomew the Great, heard from a distance, perform one of the early modern period's best-known peals.

Select bibliography

In compiling this bibliography, it has been necessary to concentrate almost exclusively upon items that have been cited in the pages above. Regrettably, this has led to the omission of a great deal of interesting material from both the primary sources and the secondary literature.

Manuscript Sources

Bodleian Library, Oxford

MS Ashmole 48, book of songs, mid-sixteenth century.

MS Eng hist c.474, c.481, Heyricke papers, late sixteenth and early seventeenth centuries.

MS Rawl. D. 1114, Chelmsford diary, late seventeenth century.

British Library, London

Add. MS 10337, 'Elizabeth Rogers hir Virginall Booke', 1656.

Add. MS 37999, fo. 66, satirical music lecture delivered at Oxford, *c.* 1642.

Add. MS CH 42681, 'Orders for Regulating the Minstrels' Court at Tutbury', 1629.

C20F7–F10, Roxburghe ballads.

C40M9–M11, Bagford ballads.

Royal MS 18 B XIX, 'The Praise of Musicke', early seventeenth century.

Royal MS 18 BX, fos. 63r–67r, 'The Trew Maner, Use and Forme of the Kinges Majesties Court of Musicke Holden at Tutburie', ?early 1620s.

Sloane MS 3463, 'Orders Conceived and Agreed upon by the Company Exerciseing the Arte of Ringing Knowne and Called by the Name of the Schollers of Cheapeside', 1603–61.

Sloane MS 3992, music book of Charles Cavendish, seventeenth century.

Cambridgeshire Record Office, Cambridge

P27/14/1/3, apprenticeship indenture, 1619.

Cambridge University Library

EDR B/2/10, Ely diocesan records, book of acts upon presentments, 1581–2.
EDR B/2/12, Ely diocesan records, book of comperta and proceedings, 1592–3.
EDR B/2/18, Ely diocesan records, various proceedings, 1601–3.
EDR D/2/32, Ely diocesan records, office act book, 1613.
EDR K/17/94, Ely diocesan records, court papers, 1637.

Cheshire Record Office, Chester

DLT/B11, Sir Peter Leycester's music book, mid-seventeenth century.
EDC5 1587.77, 1614.7, 1626.56, 1638.14, ecclesiastical court cases (Chester).
MA/B/V/9, musician's licence, 1750.
QSE/9/69, quarter sessions, 1610.
ZA/B/2, Chester city assembly book, 1660s and 1670s.
Z G2/1, account book of the Chester barber-surgeons, 1660s.
Z QSE/3/84, Z QSE/5/46, Z QSE/9/2, Z QSE/9/8, quarter sessions, late sixteenth and early seventeenth centuries.

City Library, Newcastle upon Tyne

Newcastle Courant (17 February 1759).
Transcript of All Saints' parish register.

College of Arms, London

John Anstis, 'Officers of Arms', vol. III.
'The Observations and Collections of Tho: Lant Portcullis, Concerning the Office and the Officers of Armes', *c.* 1590.

Cumbria Record Office, Kendal

WD Ry box 119, account book of Sir Daniel Fleming, 1660s.
WDX/219, Richard Alderson's notebook, 1720s.

Derbyshire Record Office, Matlock

D37 M/RE2, Revell household accounts, early seventeenth century.
D77 box 38, pp. 51–79, Gresley dance manuscript, early sixteenth century.
D4530/76/8, speech delivered at the Tutbury minstrels' court, ?late seventeenth century.
D5433/1, Leonard Wheatcroft's poems, late seventeenth century.

Durham University, Archives and Special Collections

DPR Henry Atkinson (will), 1759.

Essex Record Office, Chelmsford

Ass 35/50/1/39, assize case, 1608.

Assize files 35/36/2, 35/44/2, transcripts of court records, late sixteenth and early seventeenth centuries.

D/B 3/1/33, apprenticeship indenture, 1597.

D/B 3/3/397/18, information against Thomas Spickernell of Maldon, 1594.

D/DBa A5, A8 and A9, Barrington household accounts, mid-seventeenth century.

D/DW Z5, untitled play, *c.* 1642.

Q/SR 42/18, quarter sessions petition, 1572; Q/SR 43/23, list of moonlighting musicians, 1573; Q/SR 189/81, calendar of quarter session, early seventeenth century; Q/SR 262/22, case against Gabriel Raymond, 1628; Q/SR 342/32 and 324/110, dispute at Sible Hedingham, 1645.

Queen's Bench indictments ancient, 711, pt. 1, no. 118, transcript of case against Thomas Chitham, 1601.

Fitzwilliam Museum, Cambridge

MS Mu 688, Christopher Lowther's music book, 1637.

Hallward Library, University of Nottingham

AN/PB 292/1, 292/9/27, 293/8/37, 294/2/308, 295/6/61, 298/266, 314/5/10, 315/16/48, 328/1/34, 328/3/28, 328/3/43, 328/11/42, 339/2/56, 341/4/45, 341/9/39, presentment bills (archdeaconry of Nottingham), late sixteenth and early seventeenth centuries.

Portland Literary Collection, Pw V 25, notebook of Sir William Cavendish, seventeenth century.

Portland Literary Collection, Pw V 41, manuscript ballads, seventeenth century.

Hampshire Record Office, Winchester

44M69/E4/28, 31 and 130, Paulet household accounts, early seventeenth century.

44M69/M4/3 Jervoise papers, seventeenth century.

1577 B 70/1–2, will and inventory of Thomas Saunders *alias* Wheler.

1620 B 27/2, inventory of Thomas Monday.

1628 AD 98, inventory of Thomas Smithe.

1646 A 25/1 and 2, inventory of Nicholas Fishborne.
1667 B 16/1–2, will and inventory of Richard Colley.
W/E1/135, Winchester city accounts, seventeenth century.
W/K5/8, p. 8, investigation of three musicians, 1599.

King's College, Cambridge

MS Rowe 1, Thomas Lant's roll of catches, 1580.

Lancashire Record Office, Preston

DDBL 24/22, estreat roll of fines relating to the Cheshire minstrels' court, 1703.
QSB/1/119/74, QSB/1/199/7, quarter sessions cases, seventeenth century.

Lincolnshire Archives, Lincoln

3 DIXON/5/17, diary of Thomas Haynes Bayley, nineteenth century.
Anc VII/A/2, Bertie household accounts, 1560s.
INV 134/49, probate inventory of Richard Bell, 1628.
Misc. Dep 37/5, will of Thomas Allen, 1603.

National Archives, London

Prerogative Court of Canterbury wills, 94 Cope (Henry Walker) and 18 Meade (Robert Bateman).
REQ2 181/11, 235/17, 284/11, court of requests cases, late sixteenth and early seventeenth centuries.
SP11/7 (46), deposition of [William] Hunnis, 1556.
SP12/175 (109), petition of Simon Brewer, *c.* 1584; SP12/275 (93), letter of Dudley Carlton, 1600.
SP16/370 (83), organ dispute in Grantham, 1640.
SP18 153 (123), musicians' petition, 1656.
STAC 5 H16/2, H22/21, H50/4, and STAC 8 31/16, 36/6, 59/4, 83/1, 104/20, 113/3, 215/3, 215/13, 220/31, 262/11, 275/22, 281/13, Star Chamber cases, late sixteenth and early seventeenth centuries.

Norfolk Record Office, Norwich

DN/INV2A/5, probate inventory of Robert Munde, 1584; DN/INV44/168, probate inventory of Thomas Quashe, 1638; DN/INV45/129, probate inventory of Robert Strowger, 1633.

LEST/P5, P6, P7 and P10, Le Strange household accounts, seventeenth century.
MANN MS 17/443, list of musical events in Suffolk; MANN MS 449, List of musical events in Hertfordshire.
NCR 16a/24, fo. 359r, petitions of the waits, 1676.
NCR case 18, shelf A and shelf B, Norwich chamberlain's accounts, seventeenth century.
PD 153/27, PD 313/42, PD 531/1, PD 603/1, various parish documents, seventeenth century.
WKC7/45, 404 X2, Windham papers, early eighteenth century.

Northumberland Record Office, Gosforth

MS MU 207, 'Henry Atkinson his Book', 1695.
ZGRx, Atkinson ledgers.

Nottinghamshire Archives, Nottingham

DC/NW/3/1/1, fo. 103v, inventory of items in the possession of the Newark song school, 1595.
DP 123/26 and 125/4, letter describing conduct of John Mace, 1624.
PRSW 22/8, Rauff Barton's will, 1592; PRSW 65/26, inventory of Mathias Johnson, 1638; PRSW 70/24, Francis Parker's will, 1645; PRNW Solomon Sebastian's will, 1667.

Oxfordshire Archives, Oxford

Original wills/inventories, 12/3/29 (Thomas Charles), 77/1/12 (Thomas Burte), 141/1/39 (John Michell), 197/45 (Augustine Coulinge).

Shakespeare Birthplace Trust, Stratford-upon-Avon

BRU 4/1, 4/2, 4/3, Borough of Stratford chamberlain's accounts, 1585–1678.

Surrey History Centre, Woking

6729/box 7, vol. 5/150, letter of Robert More, 1622.
LM/COR/3/106, letter by Thomas Coppeley, 1569.
LM/COR/3/377, letter by Bishop Thomas Cooper, 1585.
LM/768, charges against Martin Lory, late sixteenth century.
LM/1800, Molineux family papers, late seventeenth century.
QS 2/6, no. 10, quarter sessions case against William Brown, 1723.

West Sussex Record Office, Chichester

Cap VI/1/2, Agnes Veere's music notebook, 1694.
EP1/11/3, depositions, Chichester archdeaconry, 1576–9.
EP1/11/5, depositions, Chichester archdeaconry, 1580s.
EP1/11/16, depositions, Chichester archdeaconry, 1630s.
EP1/17/28, detection book, Chichester archdeaconry, 1641–67.
EP1/88/41, calendar of detection book, Chichester archdeaconry, 1601–3.
Par. 203/7/40, copy of Playford's *Dancing Master* (1665 edn.) owned by the parish of Warnham.

Printed primary sources

A., H. [Henry Hawkins?], *Parthenia Sacra* (London, 1633).
The Actors Remonstrance, or Complaint: For the Silencing of their Profession (London, 1643).
Acts and Ordinances of the Interregnum, 1642–60, ed. C. H. Firth and R. S. Rait, 3 vols. (London: His Majesty's Stationery Office, 1911).
Adams, Thomas, *The Workes of Thomas Adams* (London, 1629).
Agrippa, Henry Cornelius, *Henrie Cornelius Agrippa, of the Vanitie and Uncertaintie of Artes and Sciences*, trans. James Sanford (London, 1569).
Allison, Richard, *The Psalmes of David in Meter* (London, 1599).
All is Ours and Our Husbands (London, *c.* 1672).
An Apology for the Service of Love (London, 1656).
Angier, John, *An Helpe to Better Hearts for Better Times* (London, 1647).
Armin, Robert, *Foole upon Foole* (London, 1600).
A Nest of Ninnies (London, 1608).
Ascham, Roger, *The Scholemaster* (London, 1570).
Toxophilus, the Schole of Shooting (London, 1545).
The Assembly Books of Southampton ... 1602–08, ed. J. W. Horrocks (Southampton: Southampton Record Society, 1917).
Aubrey, John, *Brief Lives*, ed. R. Barber (Woodbridge: Boydell Press, 1982).
Avison, Charles, *An Essay on Musical Expression* (London, 1752).
Bacon, Francis, *Sylva Sylvarum* (London, 1627).
Bacon, Nathaniel, *Papers of Nathaniel Bacon of Stiffkey ... 1556–77*, ed. A. Hassell Smith, G. M. Baker and R. W. Penny, *Norfolk Record Society* 46 (1979).
Baldwin, William, *A Marvelous Hystory Intitulede Beware the Cat* (London, 1584).
Barrough, Philip, *The Methode of Phisicke* (London, 1583).
Barton, William, *The Book of Psalms* (London, 1644 and 1645).
Barwick, John, *Hieronikes* (London, 1660).
Batman, Stephen, *Batman upon Bartholome, his Booke De Proprietatibus Rerum* (London, 1582).

Baxter, Richard, *A Christian Directory* (London, 1673).

The Divine Appointment of the Lords Day Proved (London, 1671).

Beaumont, Francis, *The Knight of the Burning Pestle*, ed. Michael Hattaway (London: Ernest Benn, 1969).

Wit without Money (London, 1661).

Becon, Thomas, *The Jewel of Joy* (London, 1550).

Relikes of Rome (London, 1563).

Behn, Aphra, *The Roundheads, or the Good Old Cause* (London, 1682).

Beveridge, William, *A Defence of the Book of Psalms* (London, 1710).

Beverley Borough Records, 1575–1821, ed. J. Dennett, *Yorkshire Archaeological Society Record Series* 84 (1933).

Bicknell, John, *alias* Collier, Joel, *Musical Travels through England* (London, 1774).

Blundell, Nicholas, *The Great Diurnall of Nicholas Blundell of Little Crosby, Lancashire*, ed. Frank Tyrer, *Record Society of Lancashire and Cheshire* 110 (1968).

The Book of Examinations and Depositions ... 1627–34, ed. R. C. Anderson, *Publications of the Southampton Record Society* (1931).

Books in Cambridge Inventories, ed. E. S. Leedham-Green, 2 vols. (Cambridge: Cambridge University Press, 1986).

Borough Sessions Papers, 1653–88, ed. A. J. Willis and Margaret Jean Hoad, *Portsmouth Record Series* 1 (1971).

The Boston Assembly Minutes, 1545–75, ed. Peter and Jennifer Clark, *Lincoln Record Society* 77 (1987).

Bourne, Henry, *Antiquitates Vulgares* (Newcastle, 1725).

The History of Newcastle upon Tyne (Newcastle upon Tyne, 1736).

Bownde, Nicholas, *The Doctrine of the Sabbath* (London, 1595).

Brady, Nicholas, *Church-musick Vindicated* (London, 1697).

Brathwaite, Richard, *The English Gentleman* (London, 1630).

Whimzies: or, A New Cast of Characters (London, 1631).

Breton, Nicholas, *The Court and the Country* (London, 1618).

Brocklesby, Richard, *Reflections on Ancient and Modern Musick, with the Application to the Cure of Diseases* (London, 1749).

Brookbank, Joseph, *The Well-tuned Organ* (London, 1660).

Brown, William, *Britannia's Pastorals. The Second Book* (London, 1616).

Browne, Thomas, *Religio Medici and Other Works*, ed. L. C. Martin (Oxford: Clarendon Press, 1964).

Bunyan, John, *A Book for Boys and Girls: or, Country Rhimes for Children* (London, 1686).

Grace Abounding to the Chief of Sinners, ed. John Brown (1666; London, 1692).

The Works of John Bunyan, ed. George Offer, 3 vols. (Glasgow, 1854).

Burton, Henry, *A Divine Tragedy Lately Acted* (London, 1641).

Burton, Robert, *The Anatomy of Melancholy* (Oxford, 1621).

Burton, Thomas, *Diary of Thomas Burton*, ed. John Towill Rutt, 4 vols. (London, 1828).

Burwell, Mary, 'Miss Mary Burwell's Instruction Book for the Lute', ed. Thurston Dart, *Galpin Society Journal* 11 (May 1958), 3–63.

Butler, Charles, *The Principles of Musik, in Singing and Setting* (London, 1636).

Butler, Samuel, *Sidneiana, Being a Collection of Fragments Relative to Sir Philip Sidney* (London: Roxburghe Club, 1837).

Calendar of Assize Records: Kent Indictments, 1649–59, ed. J. S. Cockburn (London: Her Majesty's Stationery Office, 1989).

Calendar of Assize Records: Surrey Indictments, Elizabeth I, ed. J. S. Cockburn (London: Her Majesty's Stationery Office, 1980).

Calendar of Assize Records: Surrey Indictments, James I, ed. J. S. Cockburn (London: Her Majesty's Stationery Office, 1982).

Calendar of Letters, Despatches, and State Papers, Relating to the Negotiations between England and Spain, 13 vols. (London: His Majesty's Stationery Office, 1862–1954).

'A Calendar of References to Music in Newspapers Published in London and the Provinces, 1660–1719', ed. Michael Tilmouth, *Royal Musical Asssociation Research Chronicle* 1 (1961), 3–107.

A Calendar of Southampton Apprenticeship Registers, 1609–1740, ed. A. L. Merson, *Publications of the Southampton Record Society* 12 (1968).

Calendar of State Papers: Domestic Series, 1547–1625 (London: Longman, 1856–72).

Calendar of State Papers: Domestic Series, 1625–49 (London: Longman, 1858–97).

Calendar of State Papers: Domestic Series, Mary I, 1553–58 (London: Public Record Office, 1998).

Case, John, *The Praise of Musicke* (Oxford, 1586; facsimile edn., New York, 1980).

Cavendish, Margaret, *CCXI Sociable Letters* (London, 1664).

Cavendish, William, *The Triumphant Widow* (London, 1677).

Certaine Propositions Offered to the Consideration of the Honourable Houses of Parliament (London, 1642).

Certaine Sermons or Homilies Appointed to be Read in Churches (1562; London, 1623).

Chamber Accounts of the Sixteenth Century, ed. Betty R. Masters, *London Record Society Publications* 20 (1984).

Chamberlayne, Edward, *Angliae Notitia* (London, 1669).

Chesterfield Parish Register, 1558–1600, ed. Mary Walton, *Derbyshire Record Society* 12 (1986).

Chesterfield Wills and Inventories, 1521–1603, ed. J. M. Bestall and D. V. Fowkes, *Derbyshire Record Society* 1 (1977).

Chettle, Henry, *Kind-Hart's Dreame* (London, 1593).

Choyce Drollery (London, 1656).

Christmas Carolls (London, 1674).

Church Life in Kent being Church Court Records of the Canterbury Diocese, 1559–1565, ed. Arthur J. Willis (London: Philimore, 1975).

Churchwardens' Accounts of Cratfield, 1640–60, ed. L. A. Botelho, *Suffolk Records Society* 42 (1999).

Cleaver, Robert, *A Godlie Forme of Householde Government* (London, 1598).
Cleland, James, *Hero-paideia, or The Institution of a Young Noble Man* (London, 1607).
Clement, Francis, *The Petie Schole* (London, 1587).
Cleveland, John, *The Character of a Country Committee-man* (London, 1647).
Clifford, Lady Anne, *The Diaries of Lady Anne Clifford*, ed. D. J. H. Clifford (Stroud: Alan Sutton, 1990).
Collier, Jeremy, *Essays upon Several Moral Subjects* (London, 1697).
A Commpendious Book of Godly and Spirtual Songs, ed. A. F. Mitchell (Edinburgh, 1897).
Coperario, John, *The Maske of Flowers* (London, 1614).
Corbet, Richard, *Certain Elegant Poems* (London, 1647).
Cornwallis, William, *Essayes* (London, 1600–1).
Cosin, John, *The Correspondence of John Cosin*, ed. G. Ornsby, *Publications of the Surtees Society* 52 (1868).
Cosyn, John, *Musike of Six, and Five Partes* (London, 1585).
Cotgrave, Randle, *A Dictionarie of the French and English Tongues* (London, 1611).
Cotton, John, *Singing of Psalms a Gospel-ordinance* (London, 1650).
Coverdale, Miles, *Goostly Psalmes and Spirituall Songes* (London, *c.* 1535).
Cromwell, Anne, *Anne Cromwell's Virginal Book, 1638*, ed. Howard Ferguson (Oxford: Oxford University Press, 1974).
Crosfield, Thomas, *The Diary of Thomas Crosfield*, ed. Frederick S. Boas (London: Oxford University Press, 1935).
Culmer, Richard, *Cathedrall Newes from Canterbury* (London, 1644).
'Curious Extracts from a Manuscript Diary, of the Time of James II and William and Mary', ed. Edward L. Cutts, *Essex Archaeological Transactions* 1 (1885), 117–27.
Daman, William, *The Psalmes of David in English Meter* (London, 1579).
Davies, John, *The Poems of Sir John Davies*, ed. Clare Howard (New York: Columbia University Press, 1941).
Davies, John, *A Scourge for Paper-prosecutors* (London, 1625).
Dekker, Thomas, *The Guls Horn-booke* (London, 1609).
Newes from Graves-end Sent to Nobody (London, 1604).
The Raven's Almanacke (London, 1609).
The Delectable History of Poor Robin the Merry Sadler of Walden (London, *c.* 1680).
Deloney, Thomas, *The Gentle Craft* (1598; London, 1637).
A Joyfull New Ballad, Declaring the Happie Obtaining of the Great Galleazzo (London, 1588).
The Pleasant History of John Winchcomb, in his Younger Years Called Jack of Newbury, in Paul Salzman, ed., *An Anthology of Elizabethan Prose Fiction* (Oxford: Oxford University Press, 1987), pp. 311–92.
Depositions and Other Ecclesiastical Proceedings from the Courts of Durham, ed. James Raine, *Surtees Society* 21 (1845).

Desainliens, Claude, *The French Schoolemaister* (London, 1573).
Dialogue betwixt Tom and Dick (London, 1660).
Diocese of Norwich: Bishop Redman's Visitation, 1597, ed. J. F. Williams, *Norfolk Record Society* 14 (1941).
Documents of the English Reformation, ed. Gerald Bray (Cambridge: James Clarke, 1994).
Dod, Henry, *Al the Psalmes of David* (London, 1620).
Certaine Psalmes of David (London, 1603).
Dodwell, Henry, *A Treatise Concerning the Lawfulness of Instrumental Musick in Holy Offices* (London, 1700).
Donne, John, *Devotions* (London, 1624).
Dorne, John, *The Day-book of John Dorne, Bookseller in Oxford, A.D. 1520*, ed. F. Madan, *Oxford Historical Society*, 1st series (1885).
Dowland, John, *A Pilgrimes Solace* (London, 1612).
The Downfall of Temporising Poets (London, 1641).
Dowsing, William, *The Journal of William Dowsing*, ed. Trevor Cooper (Woodbridge: Boydell Press, 2001).
Dryden, John, *Albion and Albanius* (1685; London, 1691).
A Song for St. Cecilia's Day (London, 1687).
Earle, John, *Micro-cosmographie or A Piece of the World Discovered*, 6th edn. (London, 1633).
East, Thomas, *Psalmes* (London, 1594).
Eccles, Solomon, *A Musick-lector* (London, 1667).
Elyot, Thomas, *The Boke Named the Governour* (London, 1531).
Erondell, Peter, *The French Garden* (London, 1605).
Essex Wills, on-going project with multiple vols. (Chelmsford: Essex Record Office, 1982–).
The Euing Collection of English Broadside Ballads in the Library of the University of Glasgow (Glasgow: University of Glasgow Publications, 1971).
Evelyn, John, *The Diary of John Evelyn*, ed. E. S. De Beer (London: Oxford University Press, 1959).
'Extracts from Lincoln Episcopal Visitations in the 15th, 16th and 17th Centuries', ed. Edward Peacock, *Archaeologia: Or Miscellaneous Tracts Relating to Antiquity* 48 (1885), 249–69.
'Extracts from the Act Books of the Archdeacon of Nottingham', ed. R. B. F. Hodgkinson, *Transactions of the Thoroton Society* 30 (1926–7), 28–57.
Extracts from the Records of the Company of Hostmen of Newcastle upon Tyne, ed. F. W. Dendy, *Surtees Society* 105 (1901).
The Famous History of Friar Bacon (London, 1679).
Farmer, J., *First Set of English Madrigals* (London, 1599).
Felltham, Owen, *Resolves, Divine, Moral, and Political* (1623; London: Temple Classics, 1904).
Fenner, Dudley, *A Briefe and Plaine Declaration* (London, 1586).

Ferne, John, *Blazon of Gentrie* (London, 1586).

Fetherston, Christopher, *A Dialogue against Light, Lewde, and Lascivious Dauncing* (London, 1582).

Fiennes, Celia, *The Journeys of Celia Fiennes*, ed. Christopher Morris (London: Cresset Press, 1947).

The Figure of Nine (London, 1662).

The Fitzwilliam Virginal Book, ed. Blanche Winogron, 2 vols. (New York: Dover Publications, 1979).

Flecknoe, Richard, *Enigmatical Characters* (London, 1658).

Fletcher, Andrew, *The Political Works of Andrew Fletcher* (Glasgow, 1749).

The Forme of Prayers and Ministration of the Sacraments (Geneva, 1556; 2nd edn., 1558).

Fotherby, Martin, *Atheomastic: Clearing Foure Truthes, against Atheists and Infidels* (London, 1622).

The Foundation of Peterborough Cathedral AD 1541, ed. W. T. Mellows, *Publications of the Northamptonshire Record Society* 13 (1941).

A Fourme of Praier with Thankes Giving, to be Used Every Yeere, the 17 of November (London, 1576).

Fox, George, *The Journal of George Fox*, ed. Norman Penney (London: J. M. Dent and Sons, 1924).

Freeman, Francis, *Light Vanquishing Darkness* (London, 1650).

Fry, John, *The Clergy in their Colours* (London, 1650).

The Fryar and the Boy (London, 1680).

A Full and True Account of the Notorious Wicked Life of that Grand Imposter, John Taylor (London, 1678).

Fuller, Thomas, *Joseph's Partie-colored Coat* (London, 1640).

Gamble, John, *Ayres and Dialogues* (London, 1657).

The Garland of Good-will (London, 1688).

Good and True, Fresh and New, Christmas Carols (London, 1642).

Gosson, Stephen, *The Ephemerides of Phialo* (London, 1579).

Playes Confuted in Five Actions (London, 1582).

The Schoole of Abuse (London, 1579).

The Trumpet of Warre (London, 1598).

Grantham During the Interregnum: The Hallbook of Grantham, 1641–49, ed. Bill Couth, *Lincoln Record Society* 83 (1995).

Greene, Robert, *A Disputation between a Hee Conny-catcher, and a Shee Conny-catcher* (London, 1592).

The Third and Last Part of Conny-catching (London, 1592).

Greville, Fulke, *The Life of the Renowned Sir Philip Sidney* (London, 1651).

Gunton, Simon, *The History of the Church at Peterborough* (London, 1686).

Hakluyt, Richard, *The Principal Navigations*, ed. James MacLehose, 12 vols. (Glasgow: James MacLehose and Sons, 1903–5).

Hall, Elias, *The Psalm-singer's Compleat Companion* (1706; London, 1708).

Hall, Joseph, *The Shaking of the Olive Tree* (London, 1660).
Harington, John, *Nugae Antiquae*, ed. Henry Harington, 3 vols. (London, 1779).
Harrison, William, *The Difference of Hearers* (London, 1614).
Harsnett, Samuel, *A Declaration of Egregious Popish Impostures* (London, 1603).
Harward, Simon, *A Discourse of Lightnings* (London, 1607).
Henslowe, Philip, *Henslowe Papers: Being Documents Supplementary to Henslowe's Diary*, ed. W. W. Greg (London: A. H. Bullen, 1907).
Herbert, Henry, *The Dramatic Records of Sir Henry Herbert, Master of the Revels, 1623–73*, ed. Joseph Quincy Adams (New Haven: Yale University Press, 1917).
Hickes, William, *Oxford Drollery* (London, 1679).
Higford, William, *Institution of a Gentleman* (London, 1660).
Hilton, John, *Ayres* (London, 1627).
Catch that Catch Can (London, 1652).
The History of the Birth, Travels, Strange Adventures, and Death of Fortunatas (London, 1682).
Hoby, Margaret, *The Private Life of an Elizabethan Lady: The Diary of Lady Margaret Hoby, 1599–1605*, ed. Joanna Moody (Stroud: Sutton Publishing, 1998).
Holder, William, *A Treatise of the Natural Grounds and Principles of Harmony* (London, 1694).
Hooker, Richard, *Of the Lawes of Ecclesiastical Politie* (1594–7; Menston: Scolar Press, 1969).
The House and Farm Accounts of the Shuttleworths, ed. John Harland, *Remains Historical and Literary Connected to the Palatine Counties of Lancaster and Chester, Chetham Society* 46 (1858).
Ingpen, William, *The Secrets of Numbers* (London, 1624).
Isham, Thomas, *The Diary of Thomas Isham*, ed. Gyles Isham (Peterborough: Gregg International Publishers, 1971).
Jewel, John, *A Replie unto M. Hardinges Answeare* (London, 1565).
The Works of John Jewel, ed. John Ayre, 4 vols. (Cambridge, 1845–50).
Jones, Robert, *The First Booke of Songes and Ayres* (London, 1600).
Jonson, Ben, *Bartholomew Fair*, ed. E. A. Horsman (Manchester: Manchester University Press, 1960).
Jordan, Thomas, *Divine Raptures* (London, 1649).
London Triumphant (London, 1672).
Julius, Philip, 'Diary of the Journey of Philip Julius, Duke of Stettin-Pomerania, through England in the Year 1602', ed. Gottfried von Bülow, *Transactions of the Royal Historical Society*, n.s. 6 (1892), 1–67.
Kemp, William, *Kemp's Nine Daies Wonder: Performed in a Dance from London to Norwich*, ed. Alexander Dyce (London: Camden Society, 1840).
King, Henry, *Poems, Elegies and Paradoxes* (London, 1664).
The King's Musick: A Transcript of Records Relating to Music and Musicians, ed. Henry Cart de Lafontaine (London: Novello and Company, 1909).

Kirkwood, James, *The True Interest of Families* (London, 1693).

Lambeth Churchwardens' Accounts, 1504–1645, and Vestry Book, 1610, ed. Charles Drew, *Surrey Record Society* 18 (1941).

Laneham, Robert, *Captain Cox, his Ballads and Books; or, Robert Laneham's Letter*, ed. Frederick J. Furnivall (London: Ballad Society, 1871).

A Letter whearin Part of the Entertainment unto the Queenz Majesty at Killingworth Castle . . . is Signified (London, 1575).

Lant, Thomas, *Daily Exercises of a Christian, Gathered and Collected out of the Holy Scripture* (London, 1590).

Sequitur celebritas and Pompa funeris (London, 1587).

Latimer, Hugh, *Sermons of Hugh Latimer, Sometime Bishop of Worcester*, ed. George Elwes Corrie (Cambridge: Cambridge University Press, 1844).

Leigh, Edward, *A Treatise of Religion* (London, 1656).

Leighton, William, *The Teares or Lamentations of a Sorrowfull Soule* (London, 1613).

Le Strange, Nicholas, 'Merry Passages and Jeasts: A Manuscript Jestbook of Sir Nicholas Le Strange', ed. H. F. Lippincott, *Elizabethan and Renaissance Studies* 29 (1974), 1–258.

L'Estrange, Roger, *Truth and Loyalty Vindicated* (London, 1662).

A Letter to a Friend in the Country, Concerning the Use of Instrumental Musick in the Worship of God (London, 1698).

Lichfield, H., *First Set of Madrigals of 5 Parts* (London, 1613).

Lodge, Thomas, *A Reply to Stephen Gosson's Schoole of Abuse, in Defence of Poetry, Musick, and Stage Plays* (*c.* 1580; London: Shakespeare Society, 1853).

Lovell, Thomas, *Dialogue between Custom and Veritie Concerning the Use and Abuse of Dauncing and Minstrelsie* (London, 1581).

Lowe, Roger, *The Diary of Roger Lowe*, ed. Ian Winstanley (Wigan: Picks Publishing, 1994).

The Diary of Roger Lowe of Ashton-in-Makerfield, Lancashire, 1663–73, ed. William L. Sachse (London: Longmans, 1938).

M., R., *Micrologia. Characters* (London, 1629).

Mace, Thomas, *Musick's Monument; or, A Remembrancer of the Best Practical Musick* (London, 1676).

Machyn, Henry, *The Diary of Henry Machyn*, ed. John Gough Nichols (London: Camden Society, 1848).

Macky, John, *A Journey through England* (London, 1714).

Malcolm, Alexander, *A Treatise of Musick, Speculative, Practical and Historical* (Edinburgh, 1721).

Marlow, Isaac, *Some Short Observations* (London, 1691).

Marston, John, *The Scourge of Villanie* (London, 1598).

Martindale, Adam, *The Life of Adam Martindale, Written by Himself*, ed. Richard Parkinson, *Remains Historical and Literary Connected with the Palatine Counties of Lancaster and Chester, Chetham Society* 4 (1845).

Martine Mar-Sixtus (London, 1591).

Matchett, Clement, *Clement Matchett's Virginal Book*, ed. Thurston Dart (London: Stainer and Bell, 1963).

May, Thomas, *The Whole Booke of Psalmes, as they are Now Sung in Churches* (London, 1688).

Medieval Carols, ed. John Stevens, *Musica Britannica* 4 (1958).

Memoirs of the Royal Society; or A New Abridgement of the Philosophical Transactions ... [from] 1665 to 1740, 2nd edn., 10 vols. (London, 1745).

Mercurius Elencticus (London, 5–12 November 1647).

A Merry Dialogue between Andrew and his Sweet Heart Joan (London, *c.* 1682).

Middleton, Thomas, *The World Tost at Tennis* (London, 1620).

Milton, John, *Areopagitica* (London, 1644).

Minutes and Accounts of the Corporation of Stratford-upon-Avon and Other Records, 1553–1620, 5 vols., *Publications of the Dugdale Society* 1, 3, 5, 10, 35 (1921–90).

The Moderate Messenger 14 (23–30 July 1649).

Molleson, Alexander, *Melody, the Soul of Music* (Glasgow, 1798).

Morley, Thomas, *The First Book of Consort Lessons. Collected by Thomas Morley, 1599 and 1611*, ed. Sydney Beck (New York: C. F. Peters Corp., 1959).

A Plaine and Easie Introduction to Practical Music (London, 1597).

Mulcaster, Richard, *Positions wherin those Primitive Circumstances be Examined, which are Necessarie for the Training Up of Children* (London, 1581).

Munday, Anthony, *A Banquet of Daintie Conceits* (London, 1588).

Mynshall, Richard, *The Mynshall Lute Book*, ed. Robert Spencer (Leeds: Boethius Press, 1975).

Naish, Thomas, *A Sermon Preach'd at the Cathedral Church of Sarum, Novemb. 22. 1700* (London, 1701).

Nash, Thomas, *The Anatomie of Absurditie* (London, 1589).

Have with You to Saffron Walden, or Gabriell Harvey's Hunt is Up (London, 1596).

Nash, Thomas, *Quaternio or a Fourefuld Way to a Happie Life* (London, 1633).

The New Balow: or A Wenches Lamentation for the Loss of her Sweetheart (London, 1670).

New Carolls for this Merry Time of Christmas (London, 1661).

A New Song to the Great Comfort and Rejoycing of All True English Harts (London, 1603).

Newte, John, *The Lawfulness and Use of Organs in the Christian Church* (London, 1696).

Nicholls, W., *A Comment on the Book of Common Prayer* (London, 1710).

Nichols, Josias, *The Plea of the Innocent* (London, 1602).

No Jest like a True Jest: Being a Compendious Record of the Merry Life, and Mad Exploits of Capt James Hind, the Great Robber of England (London, 1657).

North, Roger, *Roger North on Music*, ed. John Wilson (London: Novello, 1959).

Northbrook, John, *Spiritus est Vicarius Christi in Terra* (London, 1579).

Old Meg of Herefordshire (London, 1609).

Oldmixon, John, *The False Steps of the Ministry after the Revolution* (London, 1714).

The Order of Prayer, and Other Exercises upon Wednesdayes and Fridayes (London, 1580).

Osborne, Francis, *Advice to a Son* (London, 1656).

Otway, Thomas, *The History and Fall of Caius Marius* (London, 1680).

Oxford Church Court Depositions, 1570–74, ed. Jack Howard-Drake (Oxford: Oxfordshire County Council, 1993).

'Parish Church Musicians in England in the Reign of Elizabeth I: An Annotated Register', ed. Alan Smith, *Royal Musical Association Research Chronicle* 4 (1964), 42–92.

Parker, Matthew, *The Whole Psalter Translated into English Metre* (London, *c.* 1567).

Parrot, Henry, *Cures for the Itch* (London, 1626).

The Passionate Damsel (London, *c.* 1686).

Patrick, John, *A Century of Select Psalms* (London, 1679).

Payne, Benjamin, *The Parish Clerks Guide* (London, 1709).

The Parish-clerks Vade-mecum (London, 1694).

Peacham, Henry, *The Compleat Gentleman* (London, 1622).

The Worth of a Peny (London, 1641).

Pepys, Samuel, *The Diary of Samuel Pepys*, ed. R. C. Latham and W. Mathews, 11 vols. (London: HarperCollins, 1995).

The Pepys Ballads, ed. W. G. Day, 5 vols. (Woodbridge: D. S. Brewer, 1987).

Percy, Henry, *Advice to a Son by Henry Percy*, ed. G. B. Harrison (London: Ernst Benn, 1930).

Percy, Thomas, *Bishop Percy's Folio Manuscript: Loose and Humorous Songs*, ed. Frederick J. Furnivall (London, 1868).

Perkins, William, *A Golden Chaine* (London, 1591).

Person, Samuel, *An Anatomical Lecture of Man* (London, 1664).

Peterborough Local Administration: Elizabethan Peterborough: The Dean and Chapter as Lords of the City, ed. D. H. Gifford, *Publications of the Northamptonshire Record Society* 18 (1956).

Peterborough Local Administration: Parochial Government before the Reformation: Churchwardens' Accounts, 1467–1573, ed. W. T. Mellows, *Publications of the Northamptonshire Record Society* 9 (1939).

Phillips, Edward, *The Mysteries of Love and Eloquence* (1658; London, 1685).

Playford, John, *Booke of Newe Lessons* (London, 1652).

Choice Ayres and Songs to Sing to the Theorbo Lute and Bass-viol. The Fourth Book (London, 1683).

The Complete Country Dance Tunes from Playford's Dancing Master, ed. Jeremy Barlow (London: Faber Music, 1985).

An Introduction to the Skill of Musick, 6th edn. (London, 1672).

A Musicall Banquet (London, 1651).

Musick's Delight on the Cithren (London, 1666).

Psalms and Hymns in Solemne Musick of Foure Parts (London, 1671).

The English Dancing Master, or, Plaine and Easie Rules for the Dancing of Country Dances (London, 1651).
The Whole Book of Psalms (London, 1677).
The Pleasant and Delightful History of King Henry the 8th and a Cobbler (London, c. 1670).
A Pleasant Dialogue betwixt Honest John and Loving Kate (London, 1685).
Poverty in Early Stuart Salisbury, ed. Paul Slack, *Wiltshire Record Society* 31 (1975).
Prescott, Henry, *The Diary of Henry Prescott*, ed. John Addy, John Harrop and Peter McNiven, *Record Society of Lancashire and Cheshire* 133 (1997).
Price, Laurence, *Make Room for Christmas All You that Do Love Him* (London, c. 1686).
Probate Inventories of Lichfield and Diocese, 1568–1680, ed. D. G. Vaisey, *Collections for a History of Staffordshire*, 4th series 5 (1969).
Probate Inventories of Lincoln Citizens, 1661–1714, ed. J. A. Johnston, *Lincoln Record Society* 80 (1991).
A Proper New Ballad, Shewing a Merrie Jest of one Jeamie of Woodicock Hill (London, c. 1610).
Prynne, William, *Histrio-mastix* (London, 1633).
Puritan Manifestoes, ed. W. H. Frere and C. E. Douglas (London: SPCK, 1954).
Puttenham, George, *The Arte of English Poesie*, ed. Gladys Doidge Willcock and Alice Walker (Cambridge: Cambridge University Press, 1936).
Pygge, O., *Meditations Concerning Praiers to Almighty God, for the Safety of England, when the Spaniards were Come into the Narrow Seas* (London, 1589).
Quarles, Francis, *The Virgin Widow a Comedie* (London, 1649).
Ravenscroft, Thomas, *Deuteromelia, or The Second Part of Musicks Melodie* (London, 1609).
Melismata. Musical Phansies (London, 1611).
Pammelia. Musicks Miscellanie (London, 1609).
Whole Book of Psalms (London, 1621).
The Records of a Church of Christ in Bristol, 1640–1687, ed. Roger Hayden, *Bristol Record Society Publications* 27 (1974).
Records of Early English Drama: Bristol, ed. Mark C. Pilkinton (Toronto: University of Toronto Press, 1997).
Records of Early English Drama: Cambridge, ed. Alan H. Nelson, 2 vols. (Toronto: University of Toronto Press, 1989).
Records of Early English Drama: Chester, ed. Lawrence M. Clopper (Toronto: University of Toronto Press, 1979).
Records of Early English Drama: Coventry, ed. R. W. Ingram, (Toronto: University of Toronto Press, 1981).
Records of Early English Drama: Cumberland, Westmorland, Gloucestershire, ed. Audrey Douglas and Peter Greenfield (Toronto: University of Toronto Press, 1986).
Records of Early English Drama: Devon, ed. John M. Wasson (Toronto: University of Toronto Press, 1986).

Records of Early English Drama: Dorset, Cornwall, ed. Rosalind Conklin Hays, C. E. McGee, Sally L. Joyce and Evelyn S. Newlyn (Toronto: University of Toronto Press, 1999).

Records of Early English Drama: Ecclesiastical London, ed. Mary C. Erler (Toronto: University of Toronto Press, 2008).

Records of Early English Drama: Herefordshire, Worcestershire, ed. David N. Klausner (Toronto: University of Toronto Press, 1990).

Records of Early English Drama: Kent, ed. James M. Gibson, 3 vols. (Toronto: University of Toronto Press, 2002).

Records of Early English Drama: Lancashire, ed. David George (Toronto: University of Toronto Press, 1991).

Records of Early English Drama: Newcastle upon Tyne, ed. J. J. Anderson (Toronto: University of Toronto Press, 1982).

Records of Early English Drama: Norwich, ed. David Galloway (Toronto: University of Toronto Press, 1984).

Records of Early English Drama: Shropshire, ed. J. Alan B. Somerset, 2 vols. (Toronto: University of Toronto Press, 1994).

Records of Early English Drama: Somerset, ed. James Stokes and Robert J. Alexander, 2 vols. (Toronto: University of Toronto Press, 1996).

Records of Early English Drama: Sussex, ed. Cameron Louis (Toronto: University of Toronto Press, 2000).

The Records of St. Bartholomew's Priory [and] St. Bartholomew the Great, West Smithfield, ed. E. A. Webb, 2 vols. (Oxford: Oxford University Press, 1921).

Records of the Borough of Nottingham: Being a Series of Extracts from the Archives of the Corporation of Nottingham, 9 vols. (Nottingham: Thomas Forman, 1882–1956).

A Relation of a Short Survey of 26 Counties, Observed in a Seven Weeks Journey Begun on August 11, 1634, ed. L. G. Wickham Legg (London: Robinson and Company, 1904).

A Relation of a Short Survey of the Western Counties: Made by a Lieutenant of the Military Company in Norwich in 1635, ed. L. G. Wickham Legg, *Camden Miscellany* 16 (1936).

Reports of Cases in the Courts of Star Chamber and High Commission, ed. Samuel Rawson Gardiner, *Camden Society*, n.s. 39 (1886).

Reresby, John, *Memoirs of Sir John Reresby*, ed. Andrew Browning et al. (London: Royal Historical Society, 1991).

Rhodes, John, *Countrie Mans Comfort, or Religious Recreations* (1588; London, 1637).

Rich, Barnabe, *Riche his Farewell to Militarie Profession* (London, 1581).

'*Richard II*. Erster Teil: Ein Drama aus Shakespeare's Zeit', ed. Wolfgang Keller, *Jahrbuch der Deutschen Shakespeare-Gesellschaft* 35 (1899), 3–121 [this play is more commonly known as 'Thomas of Woodstock'].

The Robin-Red-Breast Famous for Singing Every Day on the Top of Queen Mary's Mausoleum (London, 1695).

Robinson, Thomas, *The Anatomy of the English Nunnery, at Lisbon in Portugall* (London, 1622).

Schoole of Musick (London, 1603).

Rogers, Elizabeth, *Elizabeth Rogers hir Virginall Booke*, ed. Charles J. F. Cofone (1975; New York: Dover Publications, 1982)

Rogers, Thomas, *A Golden Chaine* (London, 1587).

Rous, John, *The Diary of John Rous*, ed. Mary Anne Everett Green (London: Camden Society, 1856).

Rowley, William, *The Witch of Edmonton* (London, 1658).

Rugg, Thomas, *The Diurnal of Thomas Rugg, 1659–1661*, ed. William L. Sachse *Camden 3rd Series* 91 (1961).

The Rump, or a Collection of Songs and Ballads (London, 1660).

Rutland, Duke of, *The Manuscripts of His Grace the Duke of Rutland*, 4 vols. (London: Historical Manuscripts Commission, 1888–1905).

Ryves, Bruno, *Mercurius Rusticus* (1646; London, 1685).

S., H., *To the Musicioners, the Harpers, the Minstrels, the Singers, the Dancers, the Persecutors* (London, 1658).

The Sack-ful of News (London, 1685).

Salisbury, Marquis of, *Calendar of the Manuscripts of the Most Honourable the Marquis of Salisbury*, 24 vols. (London: Historical Manuscripts Commission, 1883–1976).

Saltonstall, Wye, *Picturae Loquentes* (1631; London, 1635).

S[andys], G[eorge], *Ovid's Metamorphoses Englished* (London, 1632).

The Second Part of the Fryer and the Boy (London, 1680).

Selden, John, *Table Talk* (London, 1689 and 1696).

Shakespeare, William, *The Complete Oxford Shakespeare*, ed. Stanley Wells and Gary Taylor, 3 vols. (Oxford: Oxford University Press, 1987).

The Merchant of Venice, ed. Jay L. Halio, *The Oxford Shakespeare* (Oxford: Oxford University Press, 1993).

Much Ado about Nothing, ed. A. R. Humphreys, *Arden Shakespeare* (London: Thomson Learning, 2003).

The Sonnets (London: Leopard, 1988).

The Taming of the Shrew, ed. Brian Morris (London: Routledge, 1981).

The Winter's Tale, ed. Ernest Schanzer (London: Penguin Books, 1996).

The Shepherds Garland of Love, Loyalty and Delight (London, 1682).

The Shirburn Ballads, ed. Andrew Clark (Oxford: Clarendon Press, 1907).

Sidney, Philip, *An Apologie for Poetrie* (London, 1595).

Simpson, Christopher, *The Division-violist* (London, 1659).

Singing of Psalms Vindicated from the Charge of Novelty (London, 1698).

Slatyer, William, *Psalmes, or Songs of Sion, Turned into the Language, and Set to the Tunes of a Strange Land* (London, 1630).

Songs and Ballads, with Other Short Poems, Chiefly of the Reign of Philip and Mary, ed. Thomas Wright (London: J. B. Nichols and Sons, 1860).

The Statutes of the Realm: Printed by Command of His Majesty King George the Third, 12 vols. (1810–28; London: Dawsons, 1963).

Stedman, Fabian, *Campanalogia, or The Art of Ringing* (London, 1677).

Sternhold, Thomas, *Certayne Psalmes Drawen into Englishe Metre* (London, *c.* 1549).

Sternhold, Thomas, and Hopkins, John, *The Whole Book of Psalms* (London, 1562, 1582 and 1629).

The Whole Book of Psalms ... Composed in Foure Parts (London, 1592).

Stockport Probate Records, 1620–1650, ed. C. B. Phillips and J. H. Smith, *Record Society for the Publication of Original Documents Relating to Lancashire and Cheshire* (1992).

Stow, John, *A Survey of London* (London, 1598).

Strange Wonders of the World (London, 1683).

Stubbes, Philip, *The Anatomie of Abuses* (London, 1583).

Sydenham, Humphrey, *Sermons upon Solemne Occasions* (London, 1637).

Tate, Nahum, and Brady, Nicholas, *A New Version of the Psalms of David* (London, 1696).

Taylor, Jeremy, *Ductor Dubitantium or The Rule of Conscience*, 4 bks. (London, 1660).

Taylor, John, *All the Workes of John Taylor the Water Poet*, 3 vols. (London: Spenser Society, 1869).

A Three-fold Discourse between Three Neighbours (London, 1642).

Works of John Taylor not Included in the Folio Volume of 1630, 5 vols. (Manchester: Spenser Society, 1870).

Tewkesbury Churchwardens' Accounts, 1563–1624, ed. Caroline Litzenberger, *Bristol and Gloucestershire Archaeological Society: Gloucestershire Record Series* 7 (1994).

'"This little commonwealth": Layston Parish Memorandum Book', ed. Heather Falvey and Steve Hindle, *Hertfordshire Record Publications* 19 (2003), appendix 6.

Thompson, Nathaniel, *Choice Collections of 120 Loyal Songs* (London, 1684).

Tintinnalogia, or The Art of Ringing (1668; London, 1671).

Tomkins, Thomas, *Songs of 3, 4, 5 and 6 Parts* (London, 1622).

Towerson, Gabriel, *A Sermon Concerning Vocal and Instrumental Musick in the Church* (London, 1696).

The Town Finances of Elizabethan Ipswich, ed. John Webb, *Suffolk Records Society* 38 (1996).

A Treatise of Daunses (London, 1581).

The True Lovers New Academy (London, *c.* 1695).

Two East Anglian Diaries, ed. Matthew Storey (Woodbridge: Boydell Press, 1994).

Villiers, George, *The Rehearsal* (London, 1672).

Visitation Articles and Injunctions of the Early Stuart Church, ed. Kenneth Fincham, 2 vols. (Woodbridge: Boydell Press for the Church of England Record Society, 1994 and 1998).

W., R., *Mount Tabor, or Private Exercises of a Penitent Sinner* (London, 1639).
Waldstein, Baron, *Diary of Baron Waldstein*, trans. G. W. Groos (London: Thames and Hudson, 1981).
Walsall, John, *A Sermon Preached at Pauls Crosse* (London, 1578).
Walton, Izaak, *The Compleat Angler* (London, 1653).
The Lives of Dr John Donne, Sir Henry Wotton, Mr Richard Hooker, Mr George Herbert (London, 1670).
Ward, Edward, *The London Spy: Ned Ward's Classic Account of Underworld Life in Eighteenth-century London*, ed. Paul Hyland (East Lansing: Colleagues, 1993).
The Secret History of Clubs (London, 1709).
Warner, Daniel, *A Collection of Some Verses out of the Psalms of David* (London, 1694).
The Singing-master's Guide to his Scholars (London, 1719).
Waterhouse, Edward, *Fortescutus Illustratus* (London, 1663).
Webbe, William, *A Discourse of English Poetrie* (London, 1586).
Weldon, Anthony, *The Court and Character of King James* (London, 1651).
The Westminster Wonder (London, 1695).
Wheatcroft, Leonard, 'The Autobiography of Leonard Wheatcroft of Ashover, 1627–1706', ed. Dorothy M. Riden, *Derbyshire Record Society* 20 (1993), 74–97.
The Courtship Narrative of Leonard Wheatcroft, ed. George Parfitt and Ralph Houlbrooke (Reading: Whiteknights Press, 1986).
Wheeler, Adam, 'Iter Bellicosum, or A Perfect Relation of the Heroick March of his Majesties Truly Loyall Subject and Magnanimous Souldier Colonell John Windham', ed. Henry Eliot Malden, *Camden Miscellany* 12, *Camden 3rd Series* 18 (1910), 155–68.
Whitgift, John, *The Defense of the Aunswere to the Admonition* (London, 1574).
The Works of John Whitgift, ed. J. Ayre, 3 vols. (Cambridge: Cambridge University Press, Parker Society, 1851–3).
Whitlocke, Bulstrode, *Memorials of English Affairs*, 4 vols. (1682; London, 1853).
Whythorne, Thomas, *The Autobiography of Thomas Whythorne: Modern Spelling Edition*, ed. James M. Osborn (London: Oxford University Press, 1962).
Wilbye, John, *The Second Set of Madrigales* (London, 1609).
Wills of the Archdeaconry of Sudbury, 1636–1638, ed. Nesta Evans, *Suffolk Records Society* 35 (1993).
Wills of the Archdeaconry of Suffolk, 1620–24, ed. Marion E. Allen, *Suffolk Records Society* 31 (1989).
Winslow, Edward, *Hypocrisie Unmasked* (London, 1646).
Wither, George, *A Preparation to the Psalter* (London, 1619).
The Schollers Purgatory (London, 1624).
Wood, Anthony, *The Life and Times of Anthony Wood*, ed. Andrew Clark, 5 vols. (Oxford: Oxford Historical Society, 1891–1900).

The World is Turned Upside Down (London, 1646).

Wright, Thomas, *The Passions of the Minde in Generall* (1601; London, 1604).

Yonge, Nicholas, *Musica Transalpina* (London, 1588).

Secondary works

Alexander, Gavin, 'The Elizabethan Lyric as Contrafactum: Robert Sidney's "French Tune" Identified', *Music and Letters* 84 (2003), 378–42.

Ashbee, Andrew, '"My fiddle is a bass viol": Music in the Life of Roger L'Estrange', in Anne Dunan-Page and Beth Lynch, eds., *Roger L'Estrange and the Making of Restoration Culture* (Aldershot: Ashgate, 2008), pp. 149–66.

Ashbee, Andrew, and Holman, Peter, eds., *John Jenkins and his Time* (Oxford: Clarendon Press, 1996).

Ashbee, Andrew, and Lasocki, David, *A Biographical Dictionary of English Court Musicians, 1485–1714* (Aldershot: Ashgate, 1998).

Austern, Linda Phyllis, 'Musical Parody in the Jacobean City Comedy', *Music and Letters* 66 (1985), 355–67.

'Nature, Culture, Myth and the Musician in Early Modern England', *Journal of the American Musicological Association* 51 (1998), 1–48.

'"My mother musicke": Music and Early Modern Fantasies of Embodiment', in Naomi J. Miller and Naomi Yavneh, eds., *Maternal Measures: Figuring Caregiving in the Early Modern Period* (Ashgate: Aldershot, 2000), 239–81.

Bailey, Candace, 'Blurring the Lines: "Elizabeth Rogers hir Virginall Booke" in Context', *Music and Letters* 89 (2008), 510–46.

Baldwin, Elizabeth, *Paying the Piper: Music in Pre-1642 Cheshire, Early Drama, Art and Music Monograph Series* 29 (Kalamazoo: Medieval Institute Publications, Western Michigan University, 2002).

Ballantine, Christopher, *Music and its Social Meanings* (New York: Gordon and Breach Science Publishers, 1984).

Barron, Caroline, 'Church Music in English Towns, 1450–1550: An Interim Report', *Urban History* 29 (2002), 83–91.

Beardsley, Monroe C., 'Understanding Music', in Kingsley Price, ed., *On Criticizing Music: Five Philosophical Perspectives* (Baltimore: Johns Hopkins University Press, 1981).

Bellany, Alastair, 'Singing Libel in Early Stuart England: The Case of the Staines Fiddlers, 1627', *Huntingdon Library Quarterly* 69.1 (2006), 177–93.

Bennet, Helen, 'The Perth Glovers' Sword Dance of 1633', *Costume* 19 (1985), 40–57.

Betcher, Gloria J., 'Minstrels, Morris dancers and Players: Tracing the Routes of Travelling Performers in Early Modern Cornwall', *Early Theatre* 6.2 (2003), 33–56.

Bicknell, Stephen, *The History of the English Organ* (Cambridge: Cambridge University Press, 1996).

Binns, J. W., 'John Case and "The Praise of Musicke"', *Music and Letters* 55 (1974), 444–53.
Blacking, John, *How Musical is Man?* (Seattle: University of Washington Press, 1974).
Blatchly, John, 'In Search of Bells: Iconclasm in Norfolk, 1644', in *The Journal of William Dowsing*, ed. Trevor Cooper (Woodbridge: Boydell Press, 2001), pp. 107–14.
Born, Georgina, and Hesmondhalgh, David, eds., *Western Music and its Others: Difference, Representation and Appropriation in Music* (Berkeley: University of California Press, 2000).
Borsay, Peter, *The English Urban Renaissance: Culture and Society in the Provincial Town, 1660–1770* (Oxford: Clarendon Press, 1989).
'Sounding the Town', *Urban History* 21 (2002), 92–103.
Bowle, John, *Charles I: A Biography* (London: Weidenfeld and Nicolson, 1975).
Bowyers, Roger, 'Polyphonic Voices in the English Parish Church, *c.* 1460–1570', seminar paper (2008).
Boyes, Georgina, *The Imagined Village: Culture, Ideology and the English Folk Revival* (Manchester: Manchester University Press, 1993).
Brailsford, Dennis, *Sport and Society: Elizabeth to Anne* (London: Routledge, 1969).
Brayshay, Mark, 'Waits, Musicians, Bearwards and Players: The Inter-urban Road Travel and Performances of Itinerant Entertainers in Sixteenth- and Seventeenth-century England', *Journal of Historical Geography* 31 (2005), 430–58.
Brissenden, Alan, *Shakespeare and the Dance* (London: Macmillan, 1981).
Bronson, Bertrand Harris, *The Ballad as Song* (Berkeley: University of California Press, 1969).
Brydson, J. C., 'The Minstrels and Waits of Leicester', *Musical Times* 89 (1948), 142–4.
Buczacki, Stefan, *Fauna Britannica* (London: Hamlyn, 2002).
Burch, C. E. C., 'Minstrels and Players in Southampton, 1428–1635', *Southampton Papers* 7 (1969), 8–48.
Burden, Michael, '"For the lustre of the subject": Music for the Lord Mayor's Day in the Restoration', *Early Music* 23 (1995), 585–602.
Burgess, Clive, and Wathey, Andrew, 'Mapping the Soundscape: Church Music in English Towns, 1450–1550', *Early Music History* 19 (2000), 1–46.
Burke, Peter, *Popular Culture in Early Modern Europe* (Aldershot: Wildwood House, 1978).
'Popular Culture in Seventeenth-century London', in Barry Reay, ed., *Popular Culture in Seventeenth-century England* (London: Routledge, 1985), pp. 31–58.
Burstyn, Shai, 'In Quest of the Period Ear', *Early Music* 25 (1997), 692–702.
Campbell, Don, *The Mozart Effect* (London: HarperCollins, 2001).

Cardwell, Edward, *A History of Conferences* (Oxford, 1849).

Carpenter, Nan Cooke, *Music in the Medieval and Renaissance Universities* (Norman: University of Oklahoma Press, 1958).

Carter, Tim, 'The Sound of Silence: Models for an Urban Musicology', *Urban History* 21 (2002), 8–18.

Cazeaux, Isabelle, *French Music in the Fifteenth and Sixteenth Centuries* (Oxford: Blackwell, 1975).

Chappell, William, *Popular Music of the Olden Time*, 2 vols. (London: Cramer, Beale & Chappell, 1859).

Chartier, Roger, *The Order of Books*, trans. L. G. Cochrane (Cambridge: Polity Press, 1994).

Christie, James, *Parish Clerks* (London, 1893).

Clark, Sandra, 'The Broadside Ballad and the Woman's Voice', in Christina Malcolmson and Mihoko Suzuke, eds., *Debating Gender in Early Modern England, 1500–1700* (Basingstoke: Palgrave Macmillan, 2002).

Cock, William T., 'The Development of Change Ringing as a Secular Sport', in J. S. Sanderson, ed., *Change Ringing: The History of an English Art*, 3 vols. (Cambridge: Central Council of Church Bell Ringers, 1987), vol. I, pp. 28–39.

Cockayne, Emily, 'Cacophony, or Vile Scrapers on Vile Instruments: Bad Music in Early Modern English Towns', *Urban History* 21 (2002), 35–47.

'Experiences of the Deaf in Early Modern England', *Historical Journal* 46.3 (2003), 493–510.

Hubbub: Filth, Noise and Stench in England (New Haven: Yale University Press, 2007).

Collinson, Patrick, *The Birthpangs of Protestant England: Religious and Cultural Change in the Sixteenth and Seventeenth Centuries* (Basingstoke: Macmillan, 1988).

'Elizabethan and Jacobean Puritanism as Forms of Popular Culture', in Christopher Durston and Jacqueline Eales, eds., *The Culture of English Puritanism, 1560–1700* (Basingstoke: Macmillan, 1996), pp. 32–57.

From Iconoclasm to Iconophobia (Reading: Reading University Press, 1986).

Cook, William T., 'The Organisation of the Exercise in the Seventeenth Century', in J. S. Sanderson, ed., *Change Ringing: The History of an English Art*, 3 vols. (Cambridge: Central Council of Church Bell Ringers, 1987), vol. I, pp. 68–81.

Cooper, Stephen, 'Music in Tudor Rotherham', *Ivanhoe Review* 7 (1994), 30–3.

Corbin, Alain, *Village Bells: The Culture of the Senses in the Nineteenth-century French Countryside* (1998: London: Papermak, 1999).

Cowgill, Rachel, and Holman, Peter, eds., *Music in the British Provinces, 1690–1914* (Aldershot: Ashgate, 2007).

Craig, John, 'Psalms, Groans and Dog-whippers: The Soundscape of Sacred Space in the English Parish Church, 1547–1642', in Will Coster and Andrew Spicer (eds.), *Sacred Space in Early Modern Europe* (Cambridge: Cambridge University Press, 2005), pp. 104–23.

Cressy, David, *Bonfires and Bells* (1989; Stroud: Sutton Publishing, 2004).
Literacy and the Social Order: Reading and Writing in Tudor and Stuart England (Cambridge: Cambridge University Press, 1980).
Crewdson, Richard, *Apollo's Swan and Lyre: Five Hundred Years of the Musicians' Company* (Woodbridge: Boydell Press, 2000).
Cuddy, Lola L., 'Melody Comprehension and Tonal Structure', in Thomas J. Tighe and W. Jay Dowling, eds., *Psychology and Music: The Understanding of Melody and Rhythm* (Hillsdale, NJ: Erlbaum, 1993), pp. 19–39.
Daniel-Tyssen, Amherst, *The Church Bells of Sussex* (Lewes: G. P. Bacon, 1864).
Daniels, Bruce C., *Puritans at Play: Leisure and Recreation in Colonial New England* (Basingstoke: Macmillan, 1995).
Dart, Thurston, 'The Cittern and its English Music', *Galpin Society Journal* 1 (1948), 46–63.
Davis, Horton, *Worship and Theology in England ... 1603–90* (Princeton: Princeton University Press, 1975).
Dawson, George A., *The Church Bells of Nottinghamshire*, 3 vols. (Loughborough: G. A. Dawson, 1994–5).
Diack Johnstone, H., 'Claver Morris: An Early Eighteenth-century English Physician and Amateur Musician *Extraordinaire*', *Journal of the Royal Musical Association* 133 (2008), 93–127.
Dickens, A. G., *The English Reformation* (1964; London: B. T. Batsford, 1989).
Diefendorf, Barbara B., 'The Huguenot Psalter and the Faith of French Protestants in the Sixteenth Century', in Diefendorf and Carla Hesse, eds., *Culture and Identity in Early Modern Europe* (Ann Arbor: University of Michigan Press, 1993), pp. 41–63.
Dowling, W. Jay, 'Procedural and Declarative Knowledge in Music Cognition and Education', in T. J. Tighe and W. Jay Dowling, eds., *Psychology and Music: The Understanding of Melody and Rhythm* (Hillsdale, NJ: Erlbaum, 1993), pp. 5–18.
Duffin, Ross W., 'To Entertain a King: Music for James and Henry at the Merchant Taylors Feast of 1607', *Music and Letters* 83 (2002), 525–42.
Duffy, Eamon, *The Stripping of the Altars: Traditional Religion in England, 1400–1580* (New Haven: Yale University Press, 1992).
Dugaw, Dianne, *Warrior Women and Popular Balladry* (1989; Chicago: University of Chicago Press, 1996).
Durston, Christopher, 'Puritan Rule and the Failure of Cultural Revolution, 1645–1660', in Christopher Durston and Jacqueline Eales, eds., *The Culture of English Puritanism, 1560–1700* (Basingstoke: Macmillan, 1996), pp. 210–33.
Eisel, John C., 'Developments in Bell Hanging', in J. S. Sanderson, ed., *Change Ringing: The History of an English Art*, 3 vols. (Cambridge: Central Council of Church Bell Ringers, 1987), vol. I, pp. 18–28.
'The Development of Change Ringing in the Seventeenth Century', in J. S. Sanderson, ed., *Change Ringing: The History of an English Art*,

3 vols. (Cambridge: Central Council of Church Bell Ringers, 1987), vol. I, pp. 40–9.

'Tintinnalogia', in J. S. Sanderson, ed., *Change Ringing: The History of an English Art*, 3 vols. (Cambridge: Central Council of Church Bell Ringers, 1987), pp. 50–8.

Ellacombe, H. T., *The Bells of Gloucestershire* (Exeter, 1881).

Elphick, George P., *Sussex Bells and Belfries* (Chichester: Phillimore, 1970).

Elson, Louis C., *Shakespeare in Music* (1901: New York: AMS Press, 1971)

Emmison, F. G., *Elizabethan Life: Home, Work and Land* (Chelmsford: Essex County Council, 1976).

Fallows, David, 'The Gresley Dance Collection, *c.* 1500', *Royal Musical Association Research Chronicle* 29 (1996), pp. 1–20.

Fernandez, Maria P., and Fernandez, Pedro C., 'Davis Mell, Musician and Clockmaker', *Antiquarian Horology* 16.6 (1987), 602–17.

Fincham, Kenneth, and Tyacke, Nicholas, *Altars Restored: The Changing Face of English Religious Worship, 1547–c.1700* (Oxford: Oxford University Press, 2007).

Finney, Gretchen Ludke, 'Ecstasy and Music in Seventeenth-century England', *Journal of the History of Ideas* 8 (1947), 153–87.

'Music: A Book of Knowledge in Renaissance England', *Studies in the Renaissance* 6 (1959), 36–63.

'Music, Mirth and Galenic Tradition in England', in J. A. Mazzeo, ed., *Reason and Imagination: Studies in the History of Ideas, 1699–1800* (New York: Columbia University Press, 1962), pp. 143–54.

'"Organical Musick" and Ecstasy', *Journal of the History of Ideas* 8 (1947), 273–93.

Fitzmaurice, James, '"When an old ballad is plainly sung": Musical Lyrics in the Plays of Margaret and William Cavendish', in Mary Ellen Lamb and Karen Bamford, eds., *Oral Traditions and Gender in Early Modern Literary Texts* (Aldershot: Ashgate, 2008), pp. 153–68.

Fletcher, Peter, *World Musics in Context* (Oxford: Oxford University Press, 2001).

Flynn, Jane, 'The Education of Choristers in England during the Sixteenth Century', in John Morehen (ed.), *English Choral Practice 1400–1650* (Cambridge: Cambridge University Press, 1995), pp. 180–99.

Forrest, John, *The History of Morris Dancing, 1458–1750* (Cambridge: James Clarke, 1999).

Forscher Weiss, Susan, 'Didactic Sources of Musical Learning in Early Modern England', in Natasha Glaisyer and Sara Pennell, eds., *Didactic Literature in England, 1500–1800: Expertise Constructed* (Aldershot: Ashgate, 2003), pp. 40–62.

Forshaw, Chas F., 'The Minstrel Court of Cheshire', *Notes and Queries* 4 (1899), 178–9.

Foucault, Michel, *The Order of Things* (London: Tavistock Publications, 1970).

Fox, Adam, *Oral and Literate Culture in England, 1500–1700* (Oxford: Clarendon Press, 2000).

Gadd, I., 'Toy, Humphrey (*b.* in or before 1537, *d.* 1577)', *Oxford Dictionary of National Biography* (Oxford: Oxford University Press, 2004; online edn., 2008), http://oxforddnb.com/view/article/27643, last accessed 2 April 2010.

Gasper, Julia, 'Brewer, Thomas (1611–*c.*1660)', *Oxford Dictionary of National Biography* (Oxford: Oxford University Press, 2004), www.oxforddnb.com/view/article/3368, last accessed 1 April 2010.

Gibbs, Gary G., 'Marking the Days: Henry Machyn's Manuscript and the Mid-Tudor Era', in Eamon Duffy and David Loades, eds., *The Church of Mary Tudor* (Aldershot: Ashgate, 2006), pp. 281–308.

Gittings, Clare, *Death, Burial and the Individual in Early Modern England* (London: Routledge, 1984).

Gómez, Maricarmen, 'Minstrel Schools in the Later Middle Ages', *Early Music* 18 (1989), 213–18.

Gouk, Penelope, *Music, Science and Natural Magic in Seventeenth-century England* (New Haven: Yale University Press, 1999).

Gow, Elizabeth, 'Thomas Bilney and his Relations with Sir Thomas More', *Norfolk Archaeology* 32 (1961), 292–310.

Green, Andrew, 'Middle Sea', *Early Music Today* 9.3 (June–July 2001), 8–9.

Green, Ian, *Print and Protestantism in Early Modern England* (Oxford: Oxford University Press, 2000).

Griffiths, David, *A Musical Place of the First Quality: A History of Institutional Music-making in York, c. 1550–1990* (York: York Settlement Trust, 1994).

Gurney, John, *Brave Community: The Digger Movement in the English Revolution* (Manchester: Manchester University Press, 2007).

Halpern, Andrea R., Bartlett, James C., and Dowling, W. Jay, 'Perception of Mode, Rhythm, and Contour in Unfamiliar Melodies: Effects of Age and Experience', *Music Perception* 15 (1998), 335–55.

Hamlin, Hannibal, *Psalm Culture and Early Modern English Literature* (Cambridge: Cambridge University Press, 2004).

Harley, John, *Orlando Gibbons and the Gibbons Family of Musicians* (Aldershot: Ashgate, 1999).

Harris, Tim, ed., *Popular Culture in England, c. 1500–1850* (Basingstoke: Macmillan, 1995).

Hart, Eric Ford, 'The Restoration Catch', *Music and Letters* 34 (1953), 288–305.

Harvey, Brian W., *The Violin Family and its Makers in the British Isles* (Oxford: Clarendon Press, 1995).

Healey, Tim, 'The Story of the Oxford Waits', *The Consort* 59 (2003), 76–85.

Herissone, Rebecca, *Music Theory in Seventeenth-century England* (Oxford: Oxford University Press, 2000).

Hippel, Paul von, 'Questioning a Melodic Archetype: Do Listeners Use Gap-fill to Classify Melodies?', *Music Perception* 18 (2000), 139–53.

Holdgate, Glyn, *Ting Tangs, Trebles and Tenors* (Derby: Glyn Holdgate, 1999).

Hollander, John, *The Untuning of the Sky: Ideas of Music in English Poetry, 1500–1700* (Princeton: Princeton University Press, 1961).

Holman, Peter, *Four and Twenty Fiddlers: The Violin at the English Court, 1540–1690* (Oxford: Clarendon Press, 1993).

'Music for the Stage I: Before the Civil War', in Ian Spink, ed., *Music in Britain: The Seventeenth Century* (Oxford: Blackwell, 1992), pp. 282–305.

Houlbrooke, Ralph, *Death, Religion and the Family in England, 1480–1750* (Oxford: Clarendon Press, 1998).

Howard, Skiles, *The Politics of Courtly Dancing in Early Modern England* (Amherst: University of Massachusetts Press, 1998).

Hughes, Edward, *North Country Life in the Eighteenth Century* (Oxford: Oxford University Press, 1952).

Hulse, Lynn, 'Musical Apprenticeship in Noble Households', in Andrew Ashbee and Peter Holman, eds., *John Jenkins and his Time* (Oxford: Clarendon Press, 1996), pp. 75–88.

Hutton, Ronald, *The Rise and Fall of Merry England* (Oxford: Oxford University Press, 1994).

Stations of the Sun: A History of the Ritual Year in Britain (Oxford: Oxford University Press, 1996).

Ingram, Martin, *Church Courts, Sex and Marriage in England, 1570–1640* (Cambridge: Cambridge University Press, 1987).

'From Reformation to Toleration: Popular Religious Cultures in England, 1540–1690', in Tim Harris, ed., *Popular Culture in England, c. 1500–1850* (Basingstoke: Macmillan, 1995), pp. 95–123.

'Ridings, Rough Music and Mocking Rhymes in Early Modern England', in Barry Reay, ed., *Popular Culture in Seventeenth-century England* (London: Routledge, 1988), pp. 166–97.

Ingram, William, 'Minstrels in Elizabethan London: Who were they and What did they do?', *English Literary Renaissance* 14.1 (Winter 1984), 29–54.

James, Jamie, *The Music of the Spheres* (London: Abacus, 1995).

Jewell, Helen M., *Education in Early Modern England* (Basingstoke: Macmillan, 1998).

Jocoy, Stacey, 'The Role of the Catch in England's Civil Wars', in Barbara Haggh, ed., *Essays on Music and Culture in Honour of Herbert Kellman* (Minerve: Centre d'Études Supérieures de la Renaissance, 2001), pp. 325–34.

Johnson, D. A., '"Johnson is beaten!" A Case of "Rough Music" at West Bromwich in 1611', *Transactions, Lichfield and South Staffordshire Archaeological and Historical Society* 25 (1985 for 1983–4), 31–4.

Ketteringham, John R., *Lincoln Cathedral: A History of its Bells, Bellringers and Bellringing* (Lincoln: J. R. Ketteringham, 1987).

Kisby, Fiona, 'Courtiers in the Community: The Musicians of the Royal Household Chapel in Early Tudor Westminster', in Benjamin Thompson, ed.,

The Reign of Henry VIII: Proceedings of the 1993 Harlaxton Symposium, Harlaxton Medieval Studies 5 (1995), pp. 229–60.

'Music in European Cities and Towns to *c.* 1650', *Urban History* 21 (2002), 74–83.

Kivy, Peter, *An Introduction to the Philosophy of Music* (Oxford: Clarendon Press, 2002).

Knights, Mark, *Politics and Opinion in Crisis, 1678–81* (Cambridge: Cambridge University Press, 1994).

Kümin, Beat, 'Masses, Morris and Metrical Psalms: Music in the English Parish, *c.* 1400–1600', in Fiona Kisby, ed., *Music and Musicians in Renaissance Cities and Towns* (Cambridge: Cambridge University Press, 2001), pp. 70–81.

LaMay, Thomasin, ed., *Musical Voices of Early Modern Women: Many-headed Melodies* (Aldershot: Ashgate, 2005), pp. 1–13.

Langer, Susanne K., *Feeling and Form: A Theory of Art* (New York: Charles Schribner's Sons, 1953).

Laurie, Margaret, 'Music for the Stage II: From 1650', in Ian Spink, ed., *Music in Britain: The Seventeenth Century* (Oxford: Blackwell, 1992), pp. 306–40.

Leaver, Robin A., *'Goostly Psalmes and Spirituall Songes': English and Dutch Metrical Psalms from Coverdale to Utenhove, 1535–1566* (Oxford: Clarendon Press, 1991).

Lehmberg, Stanford E., *The Reformation of the Cathedrals* (Princeton: Princeton University Press, 1988).

Le Huray, Peter, *Music and the Reformation in England* (Cambridge: Cambridge University Press, 1978).

Leppert, Richard, *Music and Image: Domesticity, Ideology and Socio-Cultural Formation in Eighteenth-century England* (Cambridge: Cambridge University Press, 1988).

The Sight of Sound: Music, Representation and the History of the Body (Berkeley: University of California Press, 1995).

L'Estrange Ewen, C., *Witch Hunting and Witch Trials* (London: Kegan Paul, 1929).

Levitin, Daniel, *This is Your Brain on Music: Understanding a Human Obsession* (London: Atlantic Books, 2007).

Lockyer, Roger, *Buckingham: The Life and Political Career of George Villiers* (London: Longman, 1981).

Lord, Suzanne, *Music from the Age of Shakespeare: A Cultural History* (Westport: Greenwood Press, 2003).

Love, Harold, 'That Satirical Tune of "Amarillis"', *Early Music* 35 (2007), 39–46.

Luckett, Richard, 'The Collection: Origins and History', in R. Latham, ed., *Catalogue of the Pepys Library at Magdalene College, Cambridge*, 7 vols. (Woodbridge: D. S. Brewer, 1978–84), vol. II, pt. 2, pp. xi–xxi.

McColley, Diane Kelsey, *Poetry and Music in Seventeenth-century England* (Cambridge: Cambridge University Press, 1997).

MacDermott, K. H., *Sussex Church Music in the Past* (Chichester: Moore and Wingham, 1922).

McGuinness, Rosamond, 'Writings about Music', in Ian Spink, ed., *Music in Britain: The Seventeenth Century* (Oxford: Blackwell, 1992), pp. 406–20.

MacKinnon, Dolly, 'Hearing the English Reformation: Earls Colne, Essex', in Ros Bandt, Michelle Duffy and Dolly MacKinnon, eds., *Hearing Places: Sound, Place, Time and Culture* (Newcastle: Cambridge Scholars Publishing, 2007), pp. 255–67.

'"Poor senseless Bess, clothed in her rags and folly": Early Modern Women, Madness and Song in Seventeenth-century England', *Parergon: Journal of the Australian and New Zealand Association for Medieval and Early Modern Studies*, n.s. 18.3 (July 2001), 119–51.

Major, John, 'The Moralization of the Dance in Elyot's *Governour*', *Studies in the Renaissance* 5 (1958), 27–36.

Malcolmson, Robert W., *Popular Recreations in English Society, 1700–1850* (Cambridge: Cambridge University Press, 1973).

Maltby, Judith, *Prayer Book and People* (Cambridge: Cambridge University Press, 1998).

Man, John, *The History and Antiquities Ancient and Modern of the Borough of Reading* (Reading, 1816).

Manuel, Peter, *Popular Musics of the Non-western world* (Oxford: Oxford University Press, 1988).

Marsh, Christopher, *Popular Religion in Sixteenth-century England* (Basingstoke: Macmillan, 1998).

Marshall, Peter, *Beliefs and the Dead in Reformation England* (Oxford: Oxford University Press, 2002).

Mateer, David, 'Hugh Davies' Commonplace Book: A New Source of Seventeenth-century Song', *Royal Musical Association Research Chronicle* 32 (1999), 63–88.

'William Byrd's Middlesex Recusancy', *Music and Letters* 78 (1997), 1–15.

Merriam, Alan P., *The Anthropology of Music* (Evanston: Northwestern University Press, 1964).

Meyer, Leonard B., *Emotion and Meaning in Music* (Chicago: University of Chicago Press, 1956).

Milsom, John, 'Music, Politics and Society', in Robert Tittler and Norman L. Jones, eds., *A Companion to Tudor Britain* (Oxford: Blackwell, 2004), pp. 492–508.

'Songs and Society in Early Tudor London', *Early Music History* 16 (1997), 235–93.

Monod, P. Kléber, *Jacobitism and the English People, 1688–1788* (Cambridge: Cambridge University Press, 1989).

Morehen, John, ed., *English Choral Practice 1400–1650* (Cambridge: Cambridge University Press, 1995).

Morris, Ernest, *The History and Art of Change Ringing* (1931: Wakefield: E. P. Publishing, 1976).

Mortimer, Ian, 'Tudor Chronicler or Sixteenth-century Diarist? Henry Machyn and the Nature of his Manuscript', *Sixteenth Century Journal* 33.4 (2002), 981–98.

Mowl, Timothy, *Elizabethan-Jacobean Style* (London: Phaidon Press, 1993).

Munrow, David, *Instruments of the Middle Ages and Renaissance* (Oxford: Oxford University Press, 1976).

Mursell, James L., *Education for Musical Growth* (Boston: Ginn and Company, 1948).

Narmour, E., 'Music Expectation by Cognitive Rule-mapping', *Music Perception* 17 (2000), 329–98.

Negus, Keith, *Popular Music in Theory* (Cambridge: Polity Press, 1996).

Nichols, John, *The Progresses, Processions, and Magnificent Festivities of King James the First*, 4 vols. (London, 1828).

Nicolas, Harris, *Memoirs of the Life and Times of Sir Christopher Hatton* (London, 1847).

North, A. C., et al., 'In-store Music Affects Product Choice', *Nature* 390.6656 (1997), p. 132.

Ockleton, C. M. G., *The Tower, Bells and Ringers of Great St. Mary's Church, Cambridge* (Cambridge: Society of Cambridge Youths, 1981).

Oettinger, Rebecca Wagner, *Music as Propaganda in the German Reformation* (Aldershot: Ashgate, 2001).

Ong, Walter, *Orality and Literacy: The Technologizing of the Word* (1982; London: Routledge, 1990).

O'Regan, Noel, 'Histories of Renaissance Music for a New Century', *Music and Letters* 82 (2001), 280–1.

Owen, H. Gareth, 'Tradition and Reform: Ecclesiastical Controversy in an Elizabethan London Parish', *Guildhall Miscellany* 2.2 (1961), 63–70.

Owens, Jessie Ann, *'Noyses, sounds, and sweet aires': Music in Early Modern England* (Washington DC: Folger Shakespeare Library, 2006).

Palmer, Roy, *The Sound of History: Songs and Social Comment* (London: Pimlico, 1988).

Parks, Edna D., *Early English Hymns: An Index* (Metuchen: Scarecrow Press, 1972).

Pask, Brenda M., *Newark Parish Church of St. Mary Magdalene* (Newark: District Church Council, 2000).

Pattison, Bruce, *Music and Poetry of the English Renaissance* (London: Methuen, 1948).

Payne, Ian, 'Musical Borrowing in the Madrigals of John Ward and John Wilbye', *Consort* 64 (2008), 37–63.

'Music at Jesus College, Cambridge, *c.* 1557–1679', *Proceedings of the Cambridge Antiquarian Society* 76 (1988 for 1987), 97–104.

Pearce, E. H., *Annals of Christ's Hospital* (London: Methuen, 1901).

Pelling, Margaret, *The Common Lot: Sickness, Medical Occupations and the Urban Poor in Early Modern England* (London: Longman, 1998).

Pennino-Baskerville, 'Terpsichore Reviled: Antidance Tracts in Elizabethan England', *Sixteenth Century Journal* 22.3 (1991), 475–93.

Pickering, Michael, and Green, Tony, eds., *Everyday Culture: Popular Song and the Vernacular Milieu* (Milton Keynes: Open University Press, 1987).

Pierce, John R., *The Science of Musical Sound* (New York: W. H. Freeman, 1983).

Price, David, *Patrons and Musicians of the English Renaissance* (Cambridge: Cambridge University Press, 1981).

Quitslund, Beth, *The Reformation in Rhyme* (Aldershot: Ashgate, 2008).

Rath, Richard Cullen, *How Early America Sounded* (Ithaca: Cornell University Press, 2003).

Raven, J. J., *The Church Bells of Cambridgeshire* (Lowestoft: Samuel Tymms, 1869).

Reay, Barry, *Popular Cultures in England, 1550–1750* (London: Longman, 1998).

Reimer, Bennet, and Wright, Jeffrey E., eds., *On the Nature of Musical Experience* (Evanston: University Press of Colorado, 1992).

Robertson, Dora H., *Sarum Close* (London: J. Cape, 1938).

Rollins, Hyder E., *An Analytical Index to the Ballad-entries (1557–1709) in the Registers of the Company of Stationers of London* (Chapel Hill: University of North Carolina Press, 1924).

'The Black-letter Broadside Ballad', *Publications of the Modern Language Association of America* 34 (1919), 258–339.

Rose, Craig, *England in the 1690s: Revolution, Religion and War* (Oxford: Blackwell, 1999).

Russell, Dave, *Popular Music in England, 1840–1914* (Manchester: Manchester University Press, 1987; 2nd edn., 1997).

Rust, Francis, *Dance in Society: An Analysis of the Relationship between the Social Dance and Society in England from the Middle Ages to the Present Day* (London: Routledge, 1969).

Sanderson, J. S., ed., *Change Ringing: The History of an English Art*, 3 vols. (Cambridge: Central Council of Church Bell Ringers, 1987).

Saunders, James, 'Music and Moonlighting: The Cathedral Choirmen of Early Modern England, 1558–1649', in Fiona Kisby, ed., *Music and Musicians in Renaissance Cities and Towns* (Cambridge: Cambridge University Press, 2001), pp. 157–66.

Sayers, Dorothy L., *The Nine Tailors* (1934; London: Hodder and Stoughton, 2003).

Scarisbrick, J. J., *The Reformation and the English People* (Oxford: Blackwell, 1984).

Schellenberg, E. Glenn, 'Perceiving Emotion in Melody: Interactive Effects of Pitch and Rhythm', *Music Perception* 18 (2000), 155–71.

Scholes, Percy, *The Puritans and Music in England and New England* (London: Oxford University Press, 1934).

Seay, Albert, *Music in the Medieval World* (Englewood Cliffs: Prentice-Hall, 1965).

Selden, Raman, and Widdowson, Peter, *A Reader's Guide to Contemporary Literary Theory* (Lexington: University Press of Kentucky, 1993).

Seligman, Raphael, 'With a Sword by her Side and a Lute in her Lap: Moll Cutpurse at the Fortune', in Thomasin LaMay, ed., *Musical Voices of Early Modern Women: Many-headed Melodies* (Aldershot: Ashgate, 2005), pp. 187–210.

Sessions, Roger, *The Musical Experience of Composer, Performer, Listener* (Princeton: Princeton University Press, 1950).

Sharpe, Frederick, *The Church Bells of Berkshire: Their Inscriptions and Founders* (Bath: Kingsmead Reprints, 1971).

Sharpe, J. A., *Early Modern England: A Social History, 1550–1760* (London: Edward Arnold, 1987).

Simpson, Claude M., *The British Broadside Ballad and its Music* (New Brunswick: Rutgers University Press, 1966).

Sisson, C. J., *Lost Plays of Shakespeare's Age* (Cambridge: Cambridge University Press, 1936).

Smith, Bruce R., *The Acoustic World of Early Modern England: Attending to the O-factor* (Chicago: University of Chicago Press, 1999).

'Female Impersonation in Early Modern Ballads', in Pamela Allen Brown and Peter Parolin, eds., *Women Players in England, 1500–1660* (Aldershot: Ashgate, 2005), pp. 281–304.

Smith, J. David, 'What Child is This? What Interval was That? Familiar Tunes and Music Perception in Novice Listeners', *Cognition* 52 (1994), 23–54.

Southey, Roz, *Music-making in North-east England during the Eighteenth Century* (Aldershot: Ashgate, 2006).

Southworth, John, *The English Medieval Minstrel* (Woodbridge: Boydell, 1989).

Spink, Ian, 'Music and Society', in Ian Spink, ed., *Music in Britain: The Seventeenth Century* (Oxford: Blackwell, 1992), pp. 1–65.

'The Old Jewry "Musick-Society": A Seventeenth-century Catch Club', *Musicology* 2 (1967), 35–41.

Restoration Cathedral Music, 1660–1714 (Oxford: Clarendon Press, 1995).

Spink, Ian, ed., *Music in Britain: The Seventeenth Century* (Oxford: Blackwell, 1992).

Spring, Mathew, *The Lute in Britain* (Oxford: Oxford University Press, 2001).

Spufford, Margaret, 'First Steps in Literacy: the Reading and Writing Experiences of the Humblest Seventeenth-century Spiritual Autobiographers', *Social History* 4 (1979), 407–36.

The Great Reclothing of Rural England (London: Hambledon Press, 1984).

Small Books and Pleasant Histories: Popular Fiction and its Readership in Seventeenth-century England (Cambridge: Cambridge University Press, 1981).

Stephen, George A., 'The Waits of the City of Norwich through Four Centuries to 1790', *Norfolk Archaeology* 25 (1935), 1–70.

Strahle, Graham, *An Early Music Dictionary: Musical Terms from British Sources, 1500–1700* (Cambridge: Cambridge University Press, 1995).

Strohm, Reinhard, *Music in Late Medieval Bruges* (Oxford: Clarendon Press, 1990).

Temperley, Nicholas, *The Hymn Tune Index*, 4 vols. (Oxford: Clarendon Press, 1998).

The Music of the English Parish Church, 2 vols. (Cambridge: Cambridge University Press, 1979).

Thirsk, Joan, *Economic Policy and Projects* (Oxford: Clarendon Press, 1978).

Thomas, Keith, *Religion and the Decline of Magic* (1971; London, Penguin Books, 1973).

Thompson, E. P., *Customs in Common* (Harmondsworth: Penguin, 1991).

Thorp, Jennifer, 'Dance in Late Seventeenth-century London: Priestly Muddles', *Early Music* 26 (1998), 198–210.

'"So great a master as Mr Isaac": An Exemplary Dancing-master of Late Stuart London', *Early Music* 35 (2007), 435–46.

Tighe, Thomas J., and Dowling, W. Jay, eds., *Psychology and Music: The Understanding of Melody and Rhythm* (Hillsdale, NJ: Erlbaum, 1993).

Tilmouth, Michael, 'Some Early London Concerts and Music Clubs', *Proceedings of the Royal Musical Association* 84 (1958 for 1957–8), 13–26.

Travitsky, Betty S., 'Egerton, Elizabeth, Countess of Bridgewater (1626–1663)', *Oxford Dictionary of National Biography* (Oxford: Oxford University Press, 2004), www.oxforddnb.com/view/article/68253, last accessed 1 April 2010.

Underdown, David, *Fire from Heaven: Life in an English Town in the Seventeenth Century* (London: HarperCollins, 1992).

Revel, Riot and Rebellion (Oxford: Oxford University Press, 1985).

Vos, Piel G., and Verkaart, Paul P., 'Inference of Mode in Melodies', *Music Perception* 17 (1999), 223–39.

Wade, Bonnie C., *Thinking Musically: Experiencing Music, Expressing Culture* (Oxford: Oxford University Press, 2004).

Walls, Peter, *Music in the English Courtly Masque* (Oxford: Clarendon Press, 1996).

Watt, Tessa, *Cheap Print and Popular Piety, 1550–1640* (Cambridge: Cambridge University Press, 1991).

Weatherill, Lorna, *Consumer Behaviour and Material Culture in Britain, 1660–1760*, 2nd edn. (London: Routledge, 1996).

Wegman, Robert C., *The Crisis of Music in Early Modern Europe 1470–1530* (New York: Routledge, 2005).

'"Musical understanding" in the Fifteenth Century', *Early Music* 30 (2002), 47–60.
Wells, Stanley, *Shakespeare and Co.* (London: Penguin, 2007).
White, Bryan, '"A pretty knot of musical friends": The Ferrar Brothers and a Stamford Music Club in the 1690s', in Rachel Cowgill and Peter Holman, eds., *Music in the British Provinces, 1690–1914* (Aldershot: Ashgate, 2007), pp. 9–44.
White, Helen Constance, *English Devotional Literature* (Madison: University of Wisconsin, 1931).
Winn, James A., 'Theatrical Culture 2: Theatre and Music', in Steven N. Zwiker, ed., *The Cambridge Companion to English Literature, 1650–1740* (Cambridge: Cambridge University Press, 1969).
Wollenberg, Susan, and McVeigh, Simon, eds., *Concert Life in Eighteenth-century Britain* (Aldershot: Ashgate, 2004).
Wood, Julia K., '"A flowing harmony": Music on the Thames in Restoration London', *Early Music* 23 (1995), 553–85.
Woodfield, Ian, *The Early History of the Viol* (Oxford: Oxford University Press, 1984).
English Musicians in the Age of Exploration (Stuyvesant, NY: Pendragon Press, 1995).
Woodfill, Walter W., *Musicians in English Society from Elizabeth to Charles I* (Princeton: Princeton University Press, 1953).
Woolgar, C. M., *The Senses in Late Medieval England* (New Haven: Yale University Press, 2006).
Worsley, Lucy, *Bolsover Castle* (St Ives: English Heritage, 2000).
Wrightson, Keith, *Earthly Necessities: Economic Lives in Early Modern Britain, 1470–1750* (2000; London: Penguin Books, 2002).
English Society, 1580–1680 (London: Hutchinson, 1982).
Wulstan, David, *Tudor Music* (London: J. M. Dent, 1985).
Würzbach, Natascha, *The Rise of the English Street Ballad, 1550–1650* (Cambridge: Cambridge University Press, 1990).

Unpublished dissertations

Fleming, Michael, 'Viol-making in England, c. 1580–1660', PhD thesis, Open University (2001).
Frearson, Michael, 'The English Corantos of the 1620s', PhD thesis, University of Cambridge (1993).
McShane Jones, Angela, '"Rime and Reason": The Political World of the English Broadside Ballad, 1640–1689', PhD thesis, University of Warwick (2004).
Mepham, W. A., 'History of the Drama in Essex from the Fifteenth Century to the Present Time', PhD thesis, University of London (1937).

Thomson, Robert S., 'The Development of the Broadside Ballad Trade and its Influence upon the Transmission of English Folksongs', PhD thesis, University of Cambridge (1974).

Willis, Jonathan Peter, 'Church Music and Protestantism in Post-Reformation England: Discourses, Sites and Identities', PhD thesis, University of Warwick (2009).

Winn, V. A., 'A Bibliography of Contemporary Source Works for the Social History of English Music, 1543–1728', thesis submitted for fellowship of the Library Association (1965).

Index

Lightning Source UK Ltd.
Milton Keynes UK
UKOW03f0050030715

254478UK00003B/141/P

9 781107 61024